The American Critical Archives is a series of reference books that provide representative selections of contemporary reviews of the main works of major American authors. Specifically each volume contains both full reviews and excerpts from reviews that appeared in newspapers and weekly and monthly periodicals generally within a few months of the publication of the work concerned. There is an introductory historical overview by the volume editor, as well as checklists of additional reviews located but not quoted.

This book represents the first comprehensive collection of contemporary reviews of the writings of Ralph Waldo Emerson and Henry David Thoreau. Many of the reviews are reprinted from hard-to-locate contemporary newspapers and periodicals.

AMERICAN CRITICAL ARCHIVES 1
Emerson and Thoreau: The Contemporary Reviews

Emerson and Thoreau

The Contemporary Reviews

Edited by
Joel Myerson

University of South Carolina, Columbia

CAMBRIDGE
UNIVERSITY PRESS

Published by the Press Syndicate of the University of Cambridge
The Pitt Building, Trumpington Street, Cambridge CB2 1RP
40 West 20th Street, New York, NY 10011–4211, USA
10 Stamford Road, Oakleigh, Victoria 3166, Australia

First published 1992

Printed in the United States of America

Library of Congress Cataloging-in-Publication Data
Emerson and Thoreau: the contemporary reviews/edited by Joel Myerson.
p.   cm. — (American critical archives series)
Includes index.
ISBN 0–521–38336–6 (hardback)
1. Emerson, Ralph Waldo, 1803–1882—Criticism and interpretation.
2. Thoreau, Henry David, 1817–1862—Criticism and interpretation.
3. American literature—19th century—Book reviews.   I. Myerson,
Joel.   II. Series.
PS1638.E414   1992
810.9'003—dc20   91–26261
                                        CIP

A catalog record for this book is available from the British Library

ISBN 0–521–38336–6   hardback

Contents

RETROSPECTIVE ESSAYS BY CONTEMPORARIES

Series Editor's Preface

The American Critical Archives series documents a part of a writer's career that is usually difficult to examine, that is, the immediate response to each work as it was made public on the part of reviewers in contemporary newspapers and journals. Although it would not be feasible to reprint every review, each volume in the series reprints a selection of reviews designed to provide the reader with a proportionate sense of the critical response, whether it was positive, negative, or mixed. Checklists of other known reviews are also included to complete the documentary record and allow access for those who wish to do further reading and research.

The editor of each volume has provided an introduction that surveys the career of the author in the context of the contemporary critical response. Ideally, the introduction will inform the reader in brief of what is to be learned by a reading of the full volume. The reader then can go as deeply as necessary in terms of the kind of information desired—be it about a single work, a period in the author's life, or the author's entire career. The intent is to provide quick and easy access to the material for students, scholars, librarians, and general readers.

When completed, the American Critical Archives should constitute a comprehensive history of critical practice in America, and in some cases England, as the writers' careers were in progress. The volumes open a window on the patterns and forces that have shaped the history of American writing and the reputations of the writers. These are primary documents in the literary and cultural life of the nation.

M. THOMAS INGE
Randolph-Macon College

Introduction

A book that reprints contemporary reviews of the writings of Ralph Waldo Emerson and Henry David Thoreau must be weighted in favor of the former. Emerson published an address celebrating Concord's centennial in 1835 and followed it with his first major work, *Nature*, the next year. Before his death in 1882, he published eight books of essays, two original volumes of poetry, and five major addresses. His books were published and widely reviewed in England, where a number of original collections of his essays and addresses were put together. In addition, by the mid-1840s, he had become known as the leading spokesman for the Transcendentalist movement in America. On the other hand, Thoreau published two books during his lifetime, neither of which had an English edition until two decades after his death in 1862. The beginnings of his reputation as a major American writer did not come until nearly half a century after Emerson had been firmly established in his role as a writer of importance.

The present volume, therefore, devotes nearly four times as much space to reviews of Emerson's writings as it does to reviews of Thoreau's works. This disparity in the number of words allotted to each writer reflects both their relative importance as seen by their contemporaries and the length of their careers. Reviews of sixteen Emerson titles are represented in this book, as compared to only two by Thoreau (*A Week on the Concord and Merrimack Rivers* and *Walden*, both published while he was alive). Because of this, I have approached my discussion of the reviews of each man's works differently in this introduction. The reviews of Emerson's works, spanning a forty-year period, are discussed separately in sections dealing with each work. In Thoreau's case, I have focused my discussions of the reviews around general themes that reviewers, usually writing only six years apart, saw in them.

The reviews of *Nature* (1836), published anonymously but widely known as written by Emerson, set the basic tenor of the discussions of nearly all of Emerson's works. Reviewers found *Nature*'s style lacking in both originality and clarity, and its ideas dangerous, but its author was praised personally. Ironically, one theme that runs through nearly all reviews of Emerson's works— both positive and negative ones—is a sense of disappointment in what he has produced because he gives scattered evidence of knowing how to write well but does not. As Francis Bowen put it: "The author knows better than to offend so openly against good taste, and, in many passages of great force and beauty of expression, has shown that he can do better."[1]

Responses to Emerson's style in *Nature* generally reflected the philosophical outlooks of the reviewers. Emerson was proposing a Transcendental or intuitive form of knowledge to replace the Lockean concept of sensory experience then favored by the establishment. The conservative Bowen complained of the "darkness of language" that forced readers to "busy themselves in hunting after meaning, and investigating the significancy of terms," instead of "comparing truths and testing propositions." The resulting effect was "injured by occasional vagueness of expression, and by a vein of mysticism, that pervades the writer's whole course of thought."[2] An approving Orestes Brownson could not "analyze" the book ("whoever would form an idea of it must read it"), reflecting the experiential basis of the book itself.[3] An even more favorable Elizabeth Peabody decided that the failure to understand *Nature* was a result of the inadequacies of readers, not of the author's incomplete expression: "In other words, *to people with open eyes there are colors; to people with shut eyes, at least, to those born blind, there are no colors*," she wrote.[4] And Samuel Osgood saw *Nature* as having the potential to open up the lives of those who approached it with an open mind: "No one, we are sure, can read it, without feeling himself more wide awake to the beauty and meaning of Creation."[5]

The debate over Emerson's ideas and philosophy was from the start both religiously and nationalistically based. Because Emerson's Transcendentalist philosophy was at least partially rooted in the works of German writers, an attack on him—and them—was seen by some as a defense of America and Americans. Brownson, who wanted Continental philosophy to be introduced to America, defended *Nature* in this fashion: "We prophesy that it is the forerunner of a new class of books, the harbinger of a new Literature as much superior to whatever has been, as our political institutions are superior to those of the Old World."[6] But Bowen, attempting to stave off the invasion, complained about the foreigners to whom Emerson was indebted:

> The writers of whom we speak, openly avow their preference of such indistinct modes of reflection, and justify loose and rambling speculations, mystical forms of expression, and the utterance of truths that are but half perceived, on the same principle, it would seem, that influences the gambler, who expects by a number of random casts, to obtain at last the desired combination.[7]

In a similar fashion, the reviews of the addresses on "The American Scholar" (1837) and "The Method of Nature" (1841) followed these lines. An approving William Henry Channing, while regretting "thoughts which may not be simply expressed," nevertheless decided to "tolerate" the "quaint trappings," and pitied the "purists, who cannot see a manly spirit through a mantle not wholly courtly." And concerning Emerson's style, Channing noted, "His conclusions are hinted, without the progressive reasonings through which he was led to them. Perhaps he does not come at them by any consecutive processes."[8] But the *Knickerbocker*, in reviewing the later address, was frightened that other writers would copy Emerson's style: "We beg him to pause and reflect how much crude third-rate American transcendentalism he will be compelled to stand sponsor for, should he continue to perpetuate his peculiar style."[9]

The "Divinity School Address" (1838) created a stir unlike the response to any other of Emerson's works. It came at a crucial time in the controversy between the conservative Unitarians and the Transcendentalist Unitarians over the character of Christ and the miracles of the Bible,[10] and, therefore, it was reviewed not so much for itself as for its representative position as what some saw as a statement of Transcendentalism. Andrews Norton, often characterized as the "Unitarian Pope" in recognition of his importance among the conservative Unitarians, fired the opening salvo in the Boston *Daily Advertiser*. By writing to a daily newspaper rather than waiting for the religious quarterlies to appear, Norton underscored the seriousness with which he took Emerson's work. But his review, which scarcely mentioned Emerson by name, was really an attack on what he termed Emerson's "school," whose origin was owed "in part to ill-understood notions, obtained by blundering through the crabbed and disgusting obscurity of some of the worst German speculatists, which notions, however, have been received by most of its disciples at second-hand, through an interpreter," and its "characteristics" were "the most extraordinary assumption, united with great ignorance, and incapacity for reasoning." Norton continued:

> The rejection of reasoning is accompanied with an equal contempt for good taste. All modesty is laid aside. The writer of an article for an obscure periodical, or a religious newspaper, assumes a tone as if he were one of the chosen enlighteners of a dark age.—He continually obtrudes himself upon his reader, and announces his own convictions, as if from their having that character, they were necessarily indisputable.— He floats about magnificently on bladders, which he would have it believed are swelling with ideas.

But even after all this, Norton dismisses Emerson ("What *his* opinions may be is a matter of minor concern") to concentrate on the "main question": "how it has happened, that religion has been insulted by the delivery of these opinions in the Chapel of the Divinity College at Cambridge."[11] Samuel Gilman chose to dismiss Emerson in a similar fashion in the *Southern Rose*:

On the whole, we cannot help concluding, that a writer, who seems to entertain no clear and definite principles,—who bewilders his hearers amidst labyrinths of beautiful contradictions; who floats about among vague and impalpable abstractions, and who is but the second or third hand receiver of ideas and visions, that have already been more than once exploded in the course of human progress, and could never get a foothold in this matter-of-fact world—is destined to make no very deep or permanent impression on the minds of his generation.[12]

Often, while disagreeing about the quality of Emerson's style, reviewers did agree about the dangers of his ideas. Writing as "S.X.," Theophilus Parsons praised Emerson's "extraordinary brilliance of language, his frequent beauty of imagery, and the originality of his style," but he objected that he "preaches a doctrine which leads man to worship his own nature and himself."[13] Brownson praised the address for "its life and freshness, its freedom and independence, its richness and beauty," but he did not like "its mistiness, its vagueness, and its perpetual use of old words in new senses." He regarded its "tone as somewhat arrogant, its philosophy as undigested, and its reasoning as inconclusive." And consistently with Parsons's objection, Brownson asked, "How shall we determine which are our higher instincts and which are our lower instincts?"—a comment echoed by Richard Monckton Milnes in the *Westminster Review* ("What a battle field for enthusiasms, would the world become, did men once believe that they are not speaking, but spoken from!").[14]

The favorable responses to the "Divinity School Address" praised Emerson's noble picture of humanity and its potential. G. T. Davis gave this reason for Emerson's success: "The state of mind here described, and which we may term a craving after freedom, exists in our own community to a very great extent. To this craving Mr. Emerson has spoken; this craving he has done something to satisfy; therefore, his popularity."[15] And James Freeman Clarke somewhat sarcastically commented, "As critics, we confess our fault. We should have been more on the watch, more ready to suspect our author when he left the broad road-way of common-place, and instantly snap him up when he stated any idea new to us, and differing from our pre-conceived opinions."[16]

Milnes's long review of Emerson's works in 1840 helped set the tone for the debate over the latter's next book, the first series of *Essays* (1841). Paralleling Norton's arguments about literary influences, Milnes felt that "we would say that there is little in such of his works as have reached us . . . which would be new to the competent student of European philosophy." Specifically, Emerson's is a mind "cognate" to Thomas Carlyle's, "however inferior in energies and influences."[17] The comparison to Carlyle was hard for reviewers to avoid, not just because of similar stylistic elements but also because Carlyle wrote the preface to the English edition of *Essays*. A comment by the *Literary Gazette* was typical: "Mr. Carlyle approves of this book; and no wonder, for it out-

Carlyles Carlyle himself, exaggerates all his peculiarities and faults, and possesses very slight glimpses of his excellences."[18] Other reviewers complained of Emerson's style without invoking Carlyle's name. C. C. Felton warned against "the super-sublimated transcendentalism of the Neo-Platonistic style"; the *Monthly Review* found "in Emerson's quaint and strange modes of speech, in his queer phrases, and aphoristic enigmas, old and common-place ideas, feebly or only half-conceived"; and the *Athenæum* barked that never was "diction so rough, so distorted, so inharmonious; never was expression so opaque, so ponderous, so laboured."[19]

Brownson asked people to keep an open mind in reading the essays: To "do them justice, they should be read with reverence, with a yielding spirit, an open heart, ready to receive with thankfulness whatever meets its wants or can be appropriated to its use."[20] Others continued to see Emerson's ideas as dangerous. Felton warned that "the new opinions, if such they may be called, are ancient errors and sophistries, mistaken for new truths, and disguised in the drapery of a misty rhetoric, which sorely puzzles the eye of the judgment," and the *New York Review* dismissed it as a "godless book."[21] To the *Athenæum*, "Mr. Emerson seems to have 'gone to a feast' of Philosophy, and 'brought away the scraps.'"[22] The fact that most of the British reviewers (like the *Athenæum*'s) were so negative was discussed by John Heraud, an early friend of the Transcendentalists' in England, who gave this as the reason:

> The English are with difficulty induced to sympathize with the struggles of a man, to reach the height of contemplation and wisdom; the result of his toil, pictured in some system or logical dissertation, is their sole care. Emerson just gives us the materials of thought, and then leaves us to work out a further road by ourselves; but an English reader takes up a book to avoid the trouble of thinking.[23]

Essays: Second Series (1844) evoked similar responses. The *Southern Quarterly Review* called Emerson "the copyist of a copyist of a bad model."[24] Even otherwise favorable reviews found fault with Emerson's style. "A Disciple" complained in the *United States Magazine, and Democratic Review* that while Emerson's "mind betrays a quick apprehension of logical sequence, yet he renders no account of the actual process by which he arrives at results," and Margaret Fuller wrote that the essays "tire like a string of mosaics or a house built of medals."[25] Some reviewers found this volume of essays better than the first: To the *Spectator*, the subjects were "better chosen" and "come more home to the experience of the mass of mankind, and are consequently more interesting," and to the *Athenæum*, "the flag of conciliation is displayed; much account is made of all manner of conventions."[26] And there were again complaints about Emerson's religious ideas—such as that of Frederic Henry Hedge, who warned that Emerson "regards Christ as a mere teacher of moral and religious truths" and the Christian Church as "a school or sect, founded by Jesus, in the same sense in which any other school is founded by any other philosopher."[27]

With the publication of *Poems* (1847), Emerson changed genres but not the general nature of reviewers' responses. The New York *Daily Tribune* was alone in proclaiming "Ralph Waldo Emerson ... one of America's greatest Poets if not absolutely her greatest Poet."[28] More typical was the comment in the *Critic* that the poems contained "a repetition of the vagueness mistaken for grandeur, and mysticism for profundity," and the comparison in the *Athenæum* of Emerson's poems to Keats's "Endymion," a "production full of fine poetic material, but wanting the decision of outline and form necessary to a finished work."[29] To Francis Bowen, the poems had "some mystical nonsense, some silly pedantry, an intolerable hitch in rhythm or grammar, or an incredible flatness and meanness of expression."[30] Still, the *Critic* did say that if Emerson is "obscure, it is because he soars so high that he loses sight of his landmarks; but how can there be discovery without daring—how explore without sometimes erring?"—a thought put more pithily by C. A. Bartol's "He has, we think, more height than breadth."[31] And there were the old complaints about Emerson's religious ideas, with Bartol questioning how they could be those of the true poet ("Yet we hardly know how he could have the kind of human sympathy which we most value for the inspiration of such an undertaking, with his present views of religion") and Brownson calling the verses "hymns to the devil."[32]

One reason Emerson's poetry was never highly appreciated by his contemporaries lay in its departure from the more traditional forms of a Longfellow or a Holmes. Bowen complained about Emerson's "fragments in verse—if *verse* it can be called, which puts at defiance all the laws of rhythm, metre, grammar, and common sense."[33] The *Critic* felt that perhaps Emerson had "a meaning in many of these lyrics, but certainly it is unintelligible to his readers," an unforgivable trait, since a "poet has no right so to tax his reader's brain."[34] In a similar statement of contemporary poetic theory, the *American Review* chided Emerson because we "require that a certain propriety and regularity shall inspire the form and the measure of verses; that the line be full, sounding, and of a free construction, not feeble, harsh, or cramped. The accents and pauses must fall agreeably, and the sense follow easily along the line, rather helped than impeded by it."[35] In an indirect answer to such a statement, the *Literary World* commented that to "be free of faults has been a safer passport to the welcome of reviews and drawing rooms rather than to be fertile of excellences," and to this "we attribute in a great degree the comparatively cold reception of Mr. Emerson among his countrymen."[36] Ironically, Bowen felt that "it is only in his prose that Mr. Emerson is a poet," since quaint and pithy apothegms, dry and humorous satire, studied oddities of expression, which made an old thought appear almost as good as a new one, and frequent felicities of poetical and picturesque diction, were the redeeming qualities that compensated the reader for toiling through many pages filled with a mere hubbub and jumble of words.[37]

The reviews of *Nature; Addresses, and Lectures* (1849), a collection of *Nature* and earlier addresses, was met with "mingled delight and disgust" by the *Literary World* and other reviewers.[38] The former quality is best characterized by George E. Ellis:

> We apprehend that the highest, the most enduring, and the most just encomium which Emerson will receive will not be from the coterie who regard him as an inspired seer, but from the larger, the more discriminating, and the really more intelligent body of his readers, who find on every page of his proofs of a most pure spirit and a loving heart, without one breathing of an unholy or rancorous feeling.[39]

The latter quality was exemplified by the *Knickerbocker*, which attacked Emerson's "philosophy which would reduce all outward appearances to the mind's mode of conceiving them" as "a cold and unsympathizing philosophy"; as a result, Emerson would "make each human being an isolated, independent demi-god, instead of a weeping, laughing man, with a heart clinging in countless sympathies to every heart around him."[40]

When *Representative Men* (1850) was published, the jury was still out on the question, as the *Athenæum* phrased it, "Is this inspiration or folly?"[41] The *Spectator* felt that it was the latter ("Paradox, which formerly was confined to particular ideas, now extends to whole sections of the book; the views, if not the arguments, are often vague and unsatisfactory"), as did the *Critic*, which believed that Emerson was still "indulging in the strange sort of mysticism that he probably imagines to be philosophy, but which, to others, appears very much like nonsense—words substituted for thoughts, and the unintelligible mistaken for the profound."[42] Bartol felt that in "the midst of his discussions, masterly and original in their single points, we look back, at a loss, like a man with a vague clew in the centre of a labyrinth."[43] But the *Literary World* thought this Emerson's "best work . . . because in it he is most *objective*," and the *Yale Literary Magazine* praised the "grace and fitness of his metaphors, the freshness of his expressions, the poetic and truthful originality of his descriptions."[44] Old objections resurfaced: C. C. Felton warned of Emerson's "apparent indifference to positive religious belief, as shown by his manner of classing all beliefs together," and *Graham's Magazine* simply stated, "In matters of religious faith it may be confidently asserted that mankind is right and Mr. Emerson wrong."[45]

Representative Men was one of the works featured in a long review of Emerson's writings by Theodore Parker, who, although he often differed with Emerson, had earlier been caught up with him in attacks by conservative Unitarian writers. His review is arguably the most incisive one written about Emerson while the latter was still alive. Parker is from the start a supporter: "Mr. Emerson has won by his writings a more desirable reputation, than any other man of letters in America has yet attained." His put-down of critics who fail to appreciate Emerson is scathing:

> "What of this new book?" said Mr. Public to the reviewer, who was not "seized up and tied down to judge," but of his own free will stood up and answered: "Oh! 't is out of all plumb, my lord—quite an irregular thing! not one of the angles at the four corners is a right angle. I had my rule and compasses, my Lord, in my pocket. And for the poem, your lordship bid me look at it—upon taking the length, breadth, height, and depth of it, and trying them at home, upon an exact scale of Bossu's— they are out, my lord, in every one of their dimensions."

Like the Reverend William Ellery Channing, Emerson "offended the sectarian and party spirit, the personal prejudices of the men about him; his life was a reproach to them, his words an offence, or his doctrines alarmed their sectarian, their party, or their personal pride, and they accordingly condemned the man." Parker recognized Emerson's strength in small units of literary construction ("He never fires by companies, not even by platoons, only man by man"); his "idea of personal freedom, of the dignity and value of human nature"; and the "profoundly religious" effect of his writings ("They stimulate to piety, the love of God, to goodness as the love of man"). At the same time, Parker lamented "the want of logic in his method" and a good bit of his poetry, saying, "Good Homer sometimes nodded, they say; but when he went fast asleep he did not write lines or print them."[46]

The reviews of *English Traits* (1856) naturally fell out along nationalistic lines. Most of the American press liked the book. Its "solid realities" were praised in *Harper's*, and *Putnam's* called it "exquisitely rich."[47] Andrew Peabody felt that it "revives our early pride in our mother-land, and makes us feel anew the unparalleled queenliness of her position and belongings."[48] *Putnam's* commented that whether "you begin at the last chapter or the first—at the bottom of the page or the top, it is almost equally intelligible and equally interesting."[49]

The response from England was not as positive. The *Critic* warned that *English Traits* was unfortunately typical of books by American travelers:

Ignorance is partly concealed behind prejudice; presumption takes the place of a well-grounded confidence; everything is dwarfed to suit a preconceived and not very lofty standard; and the general result tends only to inspire us with contempt for the author, and wonder at the laudatory notices of his production that come to us from the American press.[50]

The *Athenæum* wrote that "the book, as a book, will be remembered—if remembered at all—as a work wanting in substance and genuineness," and the *New Quarterly Review* described it as consisting of "a series of diatribes upon England and Englishmen, seasoned and served up so as to pique national self-complacency, and swell local conceit in Boston."[51] The *Spectator* noted that the "volume is a cheap edition, published by Messrs. Routledge 'by arrangement with the author'; though what he can get out of it seems difficult to imagine."[52] And the *New Quarterly Review* "tersely" conveyed "the national English feeling—'If you don't like the country—d——n you—you can leave it!'"[53]

By the publication of *The Conduct of Life* (1860), reviewers realized that Emerson was not going to change, and their comments about his good and bad points settled into a familiar litany. The *Westminster Review* called the book a collection of "desultory musings" that have "been called suggestive, but this is only true in the sense that all incompleteness is suggestive."[54] The *Knickerbocker* warned its author, "THOU HAST NO CHRISTIANITY!"; and Noah Porter, Jr., decided that "Mr. Emerson is incompetent to judge of what the world thinks, by the utter shallowness and flippancy of the judgments which he expresses concerning Christianity itself."[55] William Maccall found the philosophy "far too vague," and the New York *Daily Tribune* said that "the reader who expects any fresh accessions of knowledge, or more intelligent perceptions of truth, or a clearer insight into the 'conduct of life' from its oracular 'utterances' will doubtless rise from its perusal with a sense of disappointment."[56] The *Athenæum*'s reviewer felt he knew the reason for the latter response, saying that Emerson had "come to the end of all he has to say, and is repeating himself, but with a colder and more feeble utterance."[57] James Russell Lowell gave the book its most favorable review, but even he would "only say that we have found grandeur and consolation in a starlit night without caring to ask what it meant, save grandeur and consolation."[58]

Emerson's second volume of original verse, *May-Day and Other Pieces* (1867), was treated more seriously than his first one had been. Charles Eliot Norton praised the inspirational qualities of the poems ("more fitted to invigorate the moral sense, than to delight the artistic") but said that Emerson was "still careless about the shape in which his thought embodies itself, and fails to guard his poetry against the attacks of time by casting his poems in perfect and imperishable forms."[59] William Dean Howells, too, praised the poems for giving "the notion of inspiration."[60] And David Wasson made an interesting comparison of the poems with Emerson's prose: "In prose we find of late years less color, and a more determinate form, less imagination and more reason, less of gleaming suggestion, more of steady light.... [O]n the contrary, [we see in the poetry] a richness of color and a fine flow of movement which he has never elsewhere attained."[61]

The last two volumes Emerson published in his lifetime were collections of previously published works and later lectures, often compiled and edited by family and friends as Emerson's memory and creative powers declined. The reviewers, for the most part, lamented the loss of the Emerson that had been as much as they reviewed the works before them.

Society and Solitude (1870) seemed "like stray sheets caught up at random" to Thomas Wentworth Higginson, and lacking in "*purpose*" to *Putnam's Magazine*'s reviewer.[62] To Bret Harte, Emerson's "results no longer astonish us, although we are always entertained with his processes," but the *Academy* decried Emerson as "the hierophant" of the "mischievous school of American makebelieve."[63] Even a supportive John Burroughs noted: "No one knows better than Emerson himself that he has long ago had his say, and that he has nothing essentially new to add." He also complained that the lectures had been poorly revised for book publication, having "too much point, and not enough drift.... An audience must be pleased every moment, but a good reader can afford to wait, and holds by the general result."[64]

In a review of *Letters and Social Aims* (1876), the *Athenæum* dismissed Emerson by noting that he "begins to stand, accordingly, among the men of today, a figure of the past, not yet remote enough to be venerable, but unserviceable for present needs."[65] *Scribner's* felt that "there is still enough left of the old method, or non-method, to bring back something of the old exasperation—both at the excess of choice quotation, confusing the main thread,—if thread there be,—and also in the fact that in re-arranging the loose sheets, some of the best things may have fallen out and disappeared."[66] And George Parsons Lathrop found the book "extremely fatigued reading, especially to those who wish for the elixir of Emerson's earlier volumes."[67]

Contemporary reviews of Thoreau's books, *A Week on the Concord and Merrimack Rivers* (1849) and *Walden* (1854), concentrated on a number of major points: physical versus spiritual values, philosophy versus practicality, individualism versus social responsibility, physical isolation versus social involvement, and the religious or personal hypocrisy of the author.

In general, the response of reviewers to both books was very positive. Although most of the reviews were short, general, or both, they did contain a number of effusions. *A Week* was called "a fresh, original, thoughtful work," a match for Emerson and Carlyle "in felicitous conceits and amusing quaintnesses," and "as cool and pure as the fall of dew in summer nights."[68] About

Walden, reviewers commented that it was full of "many and rich suggestions"; "a prose poem [with] classical elegance, and New England homeliness with a sprinkle of Oriental magnificence in it"; "Sometimes strikingly original, sometimes merely eccentric and odd, it is always racy and stimulating"; and that "we do not get such a book every day, or often in a century."[69]

The argument over physical versus spiritual values in *A Week* was perhaps best recognized by Horace Greeley, who said it seemed the "main purpose" in Thoreau's life "to demonstrate how slender an impediment is poverty to a man who pampers no superfluous wants, and how truly independent and self-sufficing is he who is in no manner the slave of his own appetites."[70] In a similar fashion, the Oneida community's *Circular* called *Walden* "a picturesque and unique continuation of the old battle between the flesh and the spirit."[71] In "Higher Laws," Thoreau himself explicitly stated that this subject was of interest to him: "I found in myself, and still find, an instinct toward a higher, or, as it is named, spiritual life, as do most men, and another toward a primitive rank and savage one, and I reverence them both."[72] But the Boston *Atlas* found that Thoreau's pursuit of higher laws had resulted in a loss of humanity on his part: Although it praised the "strong, vigorous, nervous truth" of the spiritual passages in *Walden*, the *Atlas* complained that "there is not a page, a paragraph giving one sign of liberality, charitableness, kind feeling, generosity, in a word—HEART." In *Walden*, body had been subordinated to spirit, and there was a "total absence of human affection."[73] In comparing the two books, the *National Anti-slavery Standard* wrote that

life exhibited in them teaches us, much more impressively than any number of sermons could, that this Western activity of which we are so proud, these material improvements, this commercial enterprise, this rapid accumulation of wealth, even our external, associated philanthropic action, are very easily overrated.[74]

Another dichotomy present in both books—that of philosophy versus practicality—was discussed by reviewers. A number of them attacked Thoreau's Transcendentalism, as did W. R. Alger in his review of *A Week*, which he found

interspersed with inexcusable crudities, with proofs of carelessness and lack of healthy moral discrimination, with contempt for things commonly esteemed holy, with reflections that must shock every pious Christian, with the transcendental doctrines of the new-light school, with obscurities of incomprehensible mysticism, with ridiculous speculations, moon-struck reveries and flat nonsense,—without moral purpose in the writing, and without practical results in the reading.[75]

The New York *Morning Express* believed that the "tendencies of his mind are at times too speculative," and the New York *Churchman* did not "expect many people to follow his example; comically, his experience is published as a curiosity, a piece of quaintness, an affectation for the simple amusement of a wicked world."[76] And the New York *Times*, referring obliquely to "The Bean-Field" chapter, noted: "Ascetics who have a taste for beans will find comfort in this volume."[77] Although Thoreau gave plenty of evidence in *Walden* that good ideas must be built upon solid bases ("If you have built castles in the air, your work need not be lost; that is where they should be. Now put the foundations under them" [p. 324]), not all reviewers noticed this. Some, like that of the Boston *Daily Evening Traveller*, simply pointed out the combination of "many shrewd and sensible suggestions" and "a fair share of nonsense" in the book.[78] *The National Anti-slavery Standard* was more positive about the philosophical parts of *Walden*: "The striking peculiarity of Mr. Thoreau's attitude is ... that the loftiest dreams of the imagination are the solidest realities, and so the only foundation for us to build upon, while the affairs in which men are everywhere busying themselves so intensely are comparatively the merest froth and foam."[79] In its odd comparison of *Walden* and P. T. Barnum's *Autobiography*, the *Knickerbocker* argued that the only similarity between the two authors was their rejection of practicality (both would not labor "very hard with their hands for a living") for a type of philosophy (both were "determined to support themselves principally by their wits").[80] In the *Westminster Review*, George Eliot called attention to "that practical as well as theoretical independence of formulae, which is peculiar to some of the finer American minds."[81] A few readers saw in *Walden*'s philosophical passages vestiges of Transcendentalism. Elizabeth Stoddard, writing in the *Daily Alta California*, called *Walden* "the latest effervescence of the peculiar school, at the head of which stands Ralph Waldo Emerson," and the *Yankee Blade* thought the "Conclusion," in which Thoreau "tries to Emersonize," the "poorest" chapter of the book.[82] But John Sullivan Dwight, himself previously aligned with the Transcendentalists, defended Thoreau as "one of those men who has put such a determined trust in the simple dictates of common sense, as to earn the vulgar title of 'Transcendentalist' from his sophisticated neighbors."[83] In a later review of *A Week*, the *Saturday Review* compared it to *Walden* by claiming that in "none of his later volumes did Henry Thoreau express his peculiar philosophy with so much geniality and so little straining after exaggerated effect" as he did in his first book.[84]

Most reviewers touched on the theme of individual versus social responsibility in both books. To the New York *Churchman*, *A Week*'s "excessive love of individuality and those constant Fourth-of-July declarations of independence, look very well on paper, but they will not bear the test of a practical examination."[85] In their discussions of this topic, few reviewers understood the genuinely antisocial basis of Thoreau's individualistic philosophy, which warned that "public opinion is a weak tyrant compared with our own private opinion" (p. 7) and that "not until we are lost, in other words, not till we have lost the world, do we begin to find ourselves, and realize where we are and the infinite extent of our relations" (p. 171). That this theme is a major one in *Walden* can be seen in the famous line "If a man does not keep pace with his companions, perhaps it is because he hears a different drummer" (p. 326). Typical of the reactions to this theme is the comment in the *Albion* that readers can "admire [Thoreau], without wishing to imitate him."[86] On the other hand, the Boston *Atlas* recognized that, unlike his "brother moralizers" who "think and speak of mankind as being themselves" units of it, Thoreau "fondly deems himself emancipated from this thraldom, and looks down upon them as an inferior tribe."[87] *The National Anti-slavery Standard* presented succinctly recognition of Thoreau's belief that individuals need to emancipate themselves before attempting to emancipate society:

> In a deeper sense than we commonly think, charity begins at home. The man who, with any fidelity, obeys his own genius, serves men infinitely more by so doing, becoming an encouragement, a strengthener, a fountain of inspiration to them, than if he were to turn aside from his path and exhaust his energies in striving to meet their superficial needs.[88]

Related to this theme is that of physical isolation versus social involvement. Most reviewers of *A Week* found that solitude did not improve the tone or attitude of the book's narrator. The *Saturday Review* commented that "Thoreau's intellectual self-absorption is apt to resemble, in its wearying capacity, the faculty of a bore"; the *Morning Courier and New-York Enquirer* found the book "at times repulsively selfish in its tone"; and James Russell Lowell asserted that "Mr. Thoreau, like most solitary men, exaggerates the importance of his own thoughts. The 'I' occasionally stretches up tall as Pompey's pillar over a somewhat flat and sandy expanse."[89] Thoreau had made it clear in *Walden* that he preferred physical isolation to social involvement: "I had this advantage, at least, in my mode of life, over those who were obliged to look abroad for amusement, to society and the theatre, that my life itself was become my amusement and never ceased to be novel" (p. 112). He made this point over and over in *Walden*, sometimes by using paradox ("We are for the most part more lonely when we go abroad among men than when we stay in our chambers" [p. 135]) and sometimes by using humor ("I would rather sit on a pumpkin and have it all to myself, than to be crowded on a velvet cushion" [p. 37]). Again, most reviewers missed the antisocial implications of the book, choosing instead to harp on what the Boston *Atlas* called "the one great, fatal error, which completely vitiates the experiment," that Thoreau was "no true hermit. . . . He only played savage on the borders of civilization."[90] In other words, while Thoreau denounced society in print, in life he crept back into town whenever he wanted meals and companionship.

Finally, many reviewers complained of Thoreau's hypocrisy. In *A Week*, the hypocrisy was seen in his professing to be religious while maintaining a negative attitude toward Christian religion. Sophia Collet found Thoreau's comments on Christianity "sometimes rather random, a defect unworthy of one who usually displays such keen justness of thought," and the Oneida community's *Circular* could not "sympathize with his glorification of Hindoo philosophy; we cannot agree with his estimate of Christ."[91] The *Literary World* made this observation about Thoreau's comments on religion: "Yet, when this writer, so just, observant, and considerate, approaches what civilized men are accustomed to hold the most sacred of all, he can express himself in a flippant style which he would disdain to employ towards a muscle [i.e., mussel] or a tadpole."[92] The perceived attitude of personal hypocrisy was probably the most complained-about aspect of *Walden*. As the *National Era* described *Walden*, it contained "many acute observations on the follies of mankind, but enough of such follies to show that its author has his full share of the infirmities of human nature, without being conscious of it."[93] A corollary to this was the argument made by Charles Frederick Briggs in his review of the book: "Although he paints his shanty-life in rose-colored tints, we do not believe he liked it, else why not stick to it?"[94] Obviously, these reviewers missed the many occasions in the book in which Thoreau said he was making a case for all people, not just himself ("If I seem to boast more than is becoming, my excuse is that I brag for humanity rather than for myself" [p. 49]); asserted that he wanted his readers to rethink their own lives and not merely imitate his ("I would not have any one adopt *my* mode of living on any account" [p. 71]); and explained that "I left the woods for as good a reason as I went there. Perhaps it seemed to me that I had several more lives to live, and could not spare any more time for that one" (p. 323). Indeed, Thoreau clearly stated that his purpose in *Walden* was not to foster clones of himself but to free people to think; he proposed—in a line that appeared on the title page of the first edition—"to brag as lustily as chanticleer in the morning, standing on his roost, if only to wake my neighbors up" (p. 84).

Three posthumous reviews of Thoreau's writings show markedly different attitudes toward his works. The review by an unknown "Parish Priest" is a surprisingly complimentary one, given the problems of earlier reviewers with Thoreau's religious ideas.[95] James Russell Lowell's review of *Letters to Various Persons* retarded Thoreau's public recognition for years with its portrayal of a dry and humorless man.[96] And Emerson's comments, ostensibly an expansion of his eulogy at Thoreau's funeral, did little to provide a picture of a man whose books the average American would wish to read. His portrait of a stoical and aloof idealist was probably more responsible for the delay of Thoreau's acceptance by the reading public than any other essay written on Thoreau during or after his life.[97]

NOTE: Most nineteenth-century reviewers give copious extracts from the works under consideration to illustrate their points; in some cases, the extracted material exceeds in length the reviewer's own comments. For reasons of space, I have omitted these extracts from the selections for this volume, except in those instances where they are necessary to understand the comments made in the review itself. Because first editions of works by Emerson and Thoreau are not readily available, I have indicated the locations of material deleted by reference to standard editions of the authors' works. References to Emerson's *Nature*, "American Scholar Address," "Divinity School Address," "Literary Ethics," and "The Method of Nature" are to the Harvard University Press edition (in *The Collected Works of Ralph Waldo Emerson*) of *Nature, Addresses, and Lectures* (ed. Alfred R. Ferguson, 1971); this edition is also used for references to *Essays [First Series]* (ed. Ferguson and Jean Ferguson Carr, 1979), *Essays: Second Series* (ed. Ferguson and Carr, 1983), and *Representative Men* (ed. Douglas Emory Wilson, 1987). References to "Michael Angelo" (in *Natural History of Intellect*), *Poems, English Traits, The Conduct of Life, May-Day and Other Pieces* (in the *Poems* volume), *Society and Solitude*, and *Letters and Social Aims* are to the Centenary Edition of *The Complete Works of Ralph Waldo Emerson*, edited by Edward Waldo Emerson (Houghton, Mifflin, 1903–4). The Princeton University Press edition of *The Writings of Henry D. Thoreau* is used for *A Week on the Concord and Merrimack Rivers* (ed. Carl F. Hovde et al., 1980), *Walden* (ed. J. Lyndon Shanley, 1971), and "Resistance to Civil Government" (the corrected title of "Civil Disobedience") in *Reform Papers* (ed. Wendell Glick, 1973). Citations of these texts in this volume give page and line ("11.25" would be page 11, line 25) and, where applicable, poem or chapter title for easy reference to other editions. Readers should be aware that the first-edition texts quoted in contemporary reviews often differ from the texts used for citation.

Readers interested in pursuing the contemporary reception of Emerson and Thoreau will find a number of works of value. A full list of contemporary comments on Emerson is in Robert E. Burkholder and Joel Myerson's *Emerson: An Annotated Secondary Bibliography*, and a number are reprinted in *Critical Essays on Ralph Waldo Emerson*, ed. Burkholder and Myerson.[98] Myerson's *Ralph Waldo Emerson: A Descriptive Bibliography* lists all of Emerson's writings.[99] Raymond R. Borst's *Henry David Thoreau: A Reference Guide, 1835–1899* and *Henry David Thoreau: A Descriptive Bibliography* list writings by and about Thoreau.[100] All the known reviews of *Walden* are reprinted in *Critical Essays on Henry David Thoreau's "Walden,"* ed. Myerson, and Bradley P. Dean and Gary Scharnhorst, "The Contemporary Reception of *Walden*"; both of these also include selections from general critical commentaries on Thoreau and his works.[101] At this writing, Scharnhorst was preparing a comprehensive bibliography of writings about Thoreau. For a good survey of scholarship on the Transcendentalist movement as a whole, see *The Transcendentalists: A Review of Research and Criticism*, ed. Myerson, and *Critical Essays on American Transcendentalism*, ed. Philip F. Gura and Myerson.[102]

All scholarship builds on the work of other scholars. I am grateful to Robert E. Burkholder for allowing me to use freely the Emerson reviews he discovered, and to Bradley P. Dean and Gary Scharnhorst for sharing their Thoreau researches with me in a similar fashion. Kenneth Walter Cameron did groundbreaking work on both Emerson and Thoreau; Walter Harding and Thomas Blanding have extended our knowledge of Thoreau and his times in their scholarship. All three men have made my job easier. I thank M. Thomas Inge for establishing this series and for his work on this book as series editor. The University of South Carolina has supported my work, and I am especially grateful to Carol McGinnis Kay, Dean of the College of Humanities and Social Sciences, and Bert Dillon and Trevor Howard-Hill, who chair the English Department. Maxine James and Alfred G. Litton provided valuable assistance in preparing the texts for this book. And, of course, my gratitude goes to Greta for her love and especially for her patience.

JOEL MYERSON
Edisto Beach, South Carolina

Notes

1 F[rancis]. B[owen]., "Transcendentalism," *Christian Examiner*, 21 (January 1837), 371–85.
2 Bowen, "Transcendentalism."
3 [Orestes A. Brownson], Boston *Reformer*, 10 September 1836, p. 2.
4 [Elizabeth Palmer Peabody], "Nature—A Prose Poem," *United States Magazine, and Democratic Review*, 1 (February 1838), 319–21.
5. [Samuel] O[sgood]., "Nature," *Western Messenger*, 2 (January 1837), 385–93.
6 Brownson, Boston *Reformer*.
7 Bowen, "Transcendentalism."
8 [William Henry Channing], "Emerson's *Phi Beta Kappa Oration*," *Boston Quarterly Review*, 1 (January 1838), 106–20.
9 "The Method of Nature," *Knickerbocker*, 18 (December 1841), 559.
10 See William R. Hutchison, *The Transcendentalist Ministers* (New Haven: Yale University Press, 1959).
11 [Andrews Norton], "The New School in Literature and Religion," Boston *Daily Advertiser*, 27 August 1838, p. 2.
12 S[amuel]. G[ilman]., "Ralph Waldo Emerson," *Southern Rose*, 7 (24 November 1838), 100–6.
13 "S.X." [Theophilus Parsons], "The New School and Its Opponents," Boston *Daily Advertiser*, 30 August 1838, p. 2.
14 [Orestes A. Brownson], "Mr. Emerson's Address," *Boston Quarterly Review*, 1 (October 1838), 500–14; R[ichard]. M[onckton].

M[ilnes]., "American Philosophy.—Emerson's Works," *London and Westminster Review*, 33 (March 1840), 345–72.

15 [G. T. Davis], Boston *Morning Post*, 31 August 1838, p. 1.

16 [James Freeman Clarke], "R. W. Emerson and the New School," *Western Messenger*, 6 (November 1838), 37–47.

17 Milnes, "American Philosophy.—Emerson's Works."

18 *Literary Gazette*, 1288 (25 September 1841), 620–1.

19 C. C. F[elton]., "Emerson's Essays," *Christian Examiner*, 30 (May 1841), 253–62; *Monthly Review*, 3 (October 1841), 274–9; *Athenæum*, no. 730 (23 October 1841), 803–4.

20 [Orestes A. Brownson], "Emerson's Essays," *Boston Quarterly Review*, 4 (July 1841), 291–308.

21 Felton, "Emerson's Essays"; *New York Review*, 8 (April 1841), 509–12.

22 *Athenæum*, 23 October 1841.

23 [John A. Heraud], "Emerson's Essays," *Monthly Magazine*, 3rd ser., 6 (November 1841), 484–505.

24 *Southern Quarterly Review*, 9 (April 1846), 538–9.

25 "A Disciple," "Emerson's Essays," *United States Magazine, and Democratic Review*, 16 (June 1845), 589–602; [Margaret Fuller], "Emerson's Essays," New York *Daily Tribune*, 7 December 1844, p. 1.

26 *Spectator*, 17 (24 November 1844), 1122–3; *Athenæum*, 896 (28 December 1844), 1197.

27 F[rederic]. H[enry]. H[edge]., "Writings of R. W. Emerson," *Christian Examiner*, 38 (January 1845), 87–106.

28 "Emerson's Poems," New York *Daily Tribune*, 9 January 1847, p. 1.

29 *Critic*, n.s. 5 (2 January 1847), 9–11; *Athenæum*, 1006 (6 February 1847), 144–6.

30 [Francis Bowen], "Nine New Poets," *North American Review*, 64 (April 1847), 402–34.

31 *Critic*, n.s. 6 (18 December 1847), 386–7; C[yrus]. A. B[artol]., "Poetry and Imagination," *Christian Examiner*, 42 (March 1847), 250–70.

32 Bartol, "Poetry and Imagination"; [Orestes A. Brownson], "Emerson's Poems," *Brownson's Quarterly Review*, 4 (April 1847), 262–76.

33 Bowen, "Nine New Poets."

34 *Critic*, 2 January 1847.

35 "Emerson's Poems," *American Review: A Whig Journal*, 6 (August 1847), 197–207.

36 *Literary World*, 1 (3 April 1847), 197–9.

37 Bowen, "Nine New Poets."

38 "Emerson's Addresses," *Literary World*, 5 (3 November 1849), 374–6.

39 [George E. Ellis], *Christian Examiner*, 49 (November 1849), 461.

40 *Knickerbocker*, 35 (March 1850), 254–63.

41 *Athenæum*, 1160 (19 January 1850), 68–9.

42 "Emerson's Representative Men," *Spectator*, 23 (12 January 1850), 42; *Critic*, n.s. 9 (1 February 1850), 59–61.

43 C[yrus]. A. B[artol]., "Representative Men," *Christian Examiner*, 48 (March 1850), 314–18.

44 *Literary World*, 6 (9 February 1850), 123–4; L.W.B., "Ralph Waldo Emerson," *Yale Literary Magazine*, 5 (March 1850), 203–6.

45 [C. C. Felton], *North American Review*, 70 (April 1850), 520–4; *Graham's Magazine*, 36 (March 1850), 221–2.

46 [Theodore Parker], "The Writings of Ralph Waldo Emerson," *Massachusetts Quarterly Review*, 3 (March 1850), 200–55.

47 *Harper's New Monthly Magazine*, 13 (October 1856), 694–6; [Parke Godwin?], "Emerson on England," *Putnam's Monthly Magazine*, 8 (October 1856), 407–15.

48 [Andrew P. Peabody], "Recent Books on England," *North American Review*, 83 (October 1856), 503–10.

49 Godwin, "Emerson on England."

50 *Critic*, n.s. 15 (15 September 1856), 446–7.

51 *Athenæum*, 1506 (6 September 1856), 1109–11; *New Quarterly Review*, 5 (4th Quarter 1856), 449–55.

52 "Emerson's English Traits," *Spectator*, 29 (13 September 1856), 981.

53 *New Quarterly Review*, 4th Quarter 1856.

54 *Westminster Review*, 75 (April 1861), 588–90.

55 *Knickerbocker*, 57 (February 1861), 217–18; [Noah Porter, Jr.], "Ralph Waldo Emerson on the Conduct of Life," *New Englander*, 19 (April 1861), 496–508.

56 "Atticus" [William Maccall], "The Conduct of Life," *Critic*, n.s. 21 (22 December 1860), 778–9; "Emerson's Conduct of Life," New York *Daily Tribune*, 15 December 1860, p. 4.

57 *Athenæum*, 1929 (15 December 1860), 824–6.

58 [James Russell Lowell], *Atlantic Monthly Magazine*, 7 (February 1861), 254–5.

59 [Charles Eliot Norton], *North American Review*, 105 (July 1867), 325–7; [Charles Eliot Norton], "Mr. Emerson's Poems," *Nation*, 4 (30 May 1867), 430–1.

60 [William Dean Howells], *Atlantic Monthly Magazine*, 20 (September 1867), 376–8.

61 D[avid]. A. W[asson]., *Radical*, 2 (August 1867), 760–2.

62 [Thomas Wentworth Higginson], *Atlantic Monthly Magazine*, 26 (July 1870), 119–20; *Putnam's Magazine*, n.s. 5 (May 1870), 617–18.

63 [Bret Harte], *Overland Monthly*, 5 (October 1870), 386–7; G. A. Simcox, *Academy*, 1 (9 April 1870), 172.

64 [John Burroughs], "Emerson's New Volume," *Appleton's Journal*, 3 (28 May 1870), 609–11.

65 *Athenæum*, 2516 (15 January 1876), 81.

66 "Emerson's 'Letters and Social Aims,'" *Scribner's Monthly Magazine*, 11 (April 1876), 896–7.

67 [George Parsons Lathrop], *Atlantic Monthly Magazine*, 38 (August 1876), 240–1.

68 [Horace Greeley], "H. D. Thoreau's Book," New York *Daily Tribune*, 13 June 1849, p. 1; "A Week on the Concord and Merrimack Rivers," *Liberator*, 15 June 1849, p. 96; unidentified newspaper clipping.

69 [Thomas Starr King], *Christian Register*, 26 August 1854, p. 135; *Worcester Palladium*, 16 August 1854, p. 3; *Graham's Magazine*, 45 (September 1854), 298–300; *Critic*, 1 May 1856, pp. 223–4.

70 Greeley, "H. D. Thoreau's Book."

71 [Oneida Community] *Circular*, 28 March 1864.

72 Henry David Thoreau, *Walden*, ed. J. Lyndon Shanely (Princeton: Princeton University Press, 1971), p. 210; page numbers hereafter cited in parentheses in the text.

73 "D'A," Boston *Atlas*, 21 October 1854, p. 1.

74 [Lydia Maria Child?], *National Anti-slavery Standard*, 16 December 1854, p. 3.

75 "A ——— R" [William Rounseville Alger], *Universalist Quarterly*, 6 (October 1849), 422–3. Alger said, however, that once these parts were purged, of those parts "of the work which would remain . . . we find it difficult to speak in terms of sufficient praise . . . . The unexaggerated simplicity of description, the uncolored fidelity to fact, the perfect freedom from cant, the childlike earnestness of sympathy for outward things, the poetic eye for interior meaning, pathetic analogy and external beauty, the felicitious phraseology which calmly paints the exact objects themselves,—these traits are beyond commendation."

76 New York *Morning Express*, 24 August 1854, p. 2; New York *Churchman*, 2 September 1854, p. 4.

77 New York *Times*, 22 September 1854, p. 3.

78 Boston *Daily Evening Traveller*, 9 August 1854, p. 1.

79 Child, *National Anti-slavery Standard*.

80 "Town and Rural Humbugs," *Knickerbocker*, 45 (March 1855), 235–41.

81 [George Eliot], *Westminster Review*, 65 (January 1856), 302–3.

82 [Elizabeth Barstow Stoddard], *Daily Alta California*, 5 (8 October 1854), 279; *Yankee Blade*, 28 October 1854, p. 3.

83 [John Sullivan Dwight], "Editorial Correspondence," *Dwight's Journal of Music*, 5 (12 August 1854), 149–50.

84 "A Week on the Concord," *Saturday Review*, 68 (17 August 1889), 195–6.

85 New York *Churchman*, 2 September 1854.

86 *Albion*, n.s. 13 (9 September 1854), 429.

87 "D'A," Boston *Atlas*.

88 Child, *National Anti-slavery Standard*.

89 "A Week on the Concord," *Saturday Review; Morning Courier and New-York Enquirer*, 9 September 1854, p. 2; [James Russell Lowell], "A Week on the Concord and Merrimack Rivers," *Massachusetts Quarterly Review*, 3 (December 1849), 40–51.

90 "D'A," Boston *Atlas*.

91 [Sophia Dobson Collet], "Literature of American Individuality," *People's Journal*, 7 (April 1850), 121–5; "Another Book by Thoreau," [Oneida Community], *Circular*, 25 April 1864.

92 "Thoreau's Travels," *Literary World*, 5 (22 September 1849), 245–7.

93 [Gamaliel Bailey?], *National Era*, 8 (28 September 1854), 155.

94 [Charles Frederick Briggs], "A Yankee Diogenes," *Putnam's Monthly Magazine*, 4 (October 1854), 443–8.

95 "A Parish Priest," "Henry D. Thoreau," *Church Monthly*, 7 (October 1864), 228–37.

96 [James Russell Lowell], "Thoreau's Letters," *North American Review*, 101 (October 1865), 597–608.

97 Ralph Waldo Emerson, "Thoreau," *Atlantic Monthly Magazine*, 10 (August 1862), 239–49.

98 Robert E. Burkholder and Joel Myerson, *Emerson: An Annotated Secondary Bibliography* (Pittsburgh: University of Pittsburgh Press, 1985); *Critical Essays on Ralph Waldo Emerson*, ed. Burkholder and Myerson (Boston: G. K. Hall, 1983).

99 Joel Myerson, *Ralph Waldo Emerson: A Descriptive Bibliography* (Pittsburgh: University of Pittsburgh Press, 1982).

100 Raymond R. Borst, *Henry David Thoreau: A Reference Guide*, 1835–1899 (Boston: G. K. Hall, 1987); Borst, *Henry David Thoreau: A Descriptive Bibliography* (Pittsburgh: University of Pittsburgh Press, 1982).

101 *Critical Essays on Henry David Thoreau's "Walden,"* ed. Joel Myerson (Boston: G. K. Hall, 1988); Bradley P. Dean and Gary Scharnhorst, "The Contemporary Reception of *Walden*," in *Studies in the American Renaissance 1990*, ed. Myerson (Charlottesville: University Press of Virginia, 1990), pp. 293–328.

102 *The Transcendentalists: A Review of Research and Criticism*, ed. Joel Myerson (New York: Modern Language Association, 1984); *Critical Essays on American Transcendentalism*, ed. Philip F. Gura and Myerson (Boston: G. K. Hall, 1982).

RALPH WALDO EMERSON

Nature

[Orestes A. Brownson],
Review of *Nature*,
Boston *Reformer*,
10 September 1836, p. 2

This is a singular book. It is the creation of a mind that lives and moves in the Beautiful, and has the power of assimilating to itself whatever it sees, hears or touches. We cannot analyze it; whoever would form an idea of it must read it.

We welcome it however as an index to the spirit which is silently at work among us, as a proof that mind is about to receive a new and a more glorious manifestation; that higher problems and holier speculations than those which have hitherto engrossed us, are to engage our attention; and that the inquiries, what is perfect in Art, and what is true in Philosophy, are to surpass in interest those which concern the best place to locate a city, construct a railroad, or become suddenly rich. We prophesy that it is the forerunner of a new class of books, the harbinger of a new Literature as much superior to whatever has been, as our political institutions are superior to those of the Old World.

This book is aesthetical rather than philosophical. It inquires what is the Beautiful rather than what is the True. Yet it touches some of the gravest problems in metaphysical science, and may perhaps be called philosophy in its poetical aspect. It uniformly subordinates nature to spirit, the understanding to the reason, and mere hand-actions to ideas, and believes that ideas are one day to disenthrall the world from the dominion of semi-shadows, and make it the abode of peace and love, a meet Temple in which to enshrine the Spirit of universal and everlasting Beauty.

The author is a genuine lover of nature, and in a few instances he carries his regard for woods and fields so far as to be in danger of forgetting his socialities, and that all nature combined is infinitely inferior to the mind that contemplates it, and invests it with all its charms. And what seems singular to us is, that with all this love for nature, with this passion for solitary woods and varied landscapes, he seems seriously to doubt the existence of the external world except as a picture which God stamps on the mind. He all but worships what his senses seem to present him, and yet is not certain that all that which his senses place out of him, is not after all the mere subjective laws of his own being, existing only to the eye, not of a necessary, but of an irresistible Faith.

Some great minds have, we know had this doubt. This was the case with the acute and amiable Bishop Berkeley, the audacious Fichte and several others we could mention. Taking their stand-point in the creative power of the human soul, and observing the landscape to change in

3

its coloring as the hues of their own souls change, they have thought the landscape was nothing but themselves projected, and made an object of contemplation. The notion is easily accounted for, but we confess that we should think so acute a philosopher as our author would easily discover its fallacy.

The Reason is undoubtedly our only light, our only criterion of certainty; but we think the Reason vouches for the truth of the senses as decidedly and as immediately as it does for its own conceptions. He who denies the testimony of his senses, seems to us to have no ground for believing the apperceptions of consciousness; and to deny those is to set oneself afloat upon the ocean of universal scepticism. The whole difficulty seems to us to be in not duly understanding the report of the senses. The senses are the windows of the soul through which it looks out upon a world existing as really and as substantially as itself; but what the external world is, or what it is the senses report it to be, we do not at first understand. The result of all culture, we think will not be as our author thinks, to lead to Idealism, but to make us understand what it is we say, when we say, there is an external world.

The author calls the external world phenomenal, that is, an Appearance; but he needs not to be told that the appearance really exists, though it exists as an appearance, as that which appears, as the Absolute. Man is phenomenal in the same sense as is the universe, but man exists. The author calls him "the apparition of God." The apparition exists as certainly as God exists, though it exists as an apparition, not as absolute being. God is absolute being.—Whatever is absolute is God; but God is not the universe, God is not man; man and the universe exist as manifestations of God. His existence is absolute, theirs is relative, but real.

But we are plunging too deeply into metaphysics for our readers and perhaps for ourselves.—In conclusion, we are happy to say that however the author may deviate from what we call sound philosophy, on his road, he always comes to the truth at last. In this little book he has done an important service to his fellow men.—He has clothed nature with a poetic garb, and interpenetrated her with the living spirit of Beauty and Goodness, showed us how we ought to look upon the world round and about us, set us an example of a calm, morally independent, and devout spirit discoursing on the highest and holiest topics which can occupy the human soul, and produced a book which must ever be admired as a perfect specimen of Art. We thank him for what he has done and commend his book—his poem we might say—to every lover of the True, the Beautiful and the Good.

4

F[rancis]. B[owen].,
"Transcendentalism,"
Christian Examiner,
21 (January 1837),
371–85

We find beautiful writing and sound philosophy in this little work; but the effect is injured by occasional vagueness of expression, and by a vein of mysticism, that pervades the writer's whole course of thought. The highest praise that can be accorded to it, is, that it is a *suggestive* book, for no one can read it without tasking his faculties to the utmost, and relapsing into fits of severe meditation. But the effort of perusal is often painful, the thoughts excited are frequently bewildering, and the results to which they lead us, uncertain and obscure. The reader feels as in a disturbed dream, in which shows of surpassing beauty are around him, and he is conversant with disembodied spirits, yet all the time he is harassed by an uneasy sort of consciousness, that the whole combination of phenomena is fantastic and unreal.

In point of taste in composition, some defects proceed from over anxiety to avoid common errors. The writer aims at simplicity and directness, as the ancient philosopher aimed at humility, and showed his pride through the tatters of his cloak. He is in love with the Old Saxon idiom, yet there is a spice of affectation in his mode of using it. He is sometimes coarse and blunt, that he may avoid the imputation of sickly refinement, and writes bathos with malice prepense, because he abhors forced dignity and unnatural elevation.

These are grave charges, but we make them advisedly, for the author knows better than to offend so openly against good taste, and, in many passages of great force and beauty of expression, has shown that he can do better. The following sentences, taken almost at random, will show the nature of the defects alluded to.

"Now many are thought not only unexplained but inexplicable, as language, sleep, dreams, beasts, sex."—p. 7.

"Standing on the bare ground, my head bathed by the blithe air,—and uplifted into infinite space,—all egotism vanishes. I become a transparent eyeball."—p. 13.

"Whilst we use this grand cipher to expedite the affairs of our pot and kettle, we feel that we have not put it to its use, neither are able."

"Therefore is Space, and therefore Time, that men may know that things are not huddled and lumped, but sundered and individual."—p. 48.

"I expand and live in the warm day, like corn and melons."—p. 73.

The purpose of the book, so far as it may be said to have a purpose, is, to invite us to the observation of nature, and to point out manifestations of spirit in material existences and external events. The uses to which the outward world is subservient are divided into four classes,—Commodity, Beauty, Language, and Discipline. These ends the writer considers as the final cause of everything that exists, except the soul. To the consideration of each he allots a chapter, and displays, often with eloquence and a copious fund of illustration, the importance of the end, and the aptitude of the means provided for its attainment. In the latter part of the work, he seems disposed to neutralize the effect of the former, by adopting the Berkeleyan system, and denying the outward and real existence of that Nature, which he had just declared to be so subservient to man's spiritual wants. Of the chapters on "Spirit" and "Prospects," with which the work concludes, we prefer not to attempt giving an account, until we can understand their meaning.

From this sketch of the author's plan, it would seem, that he had hardly aimed at originality. What novelty there is in the work, arises not from the choice or distribution of the subject, but from the manner of treatment. The author is not satisfied with that cautious philosophy which traces the indirect influences of outward phenomena and physical laws on the individual mind, and contemplates the benevolence of the Deity in particular instances of the adaptation and subserviency of matter to spirit. He contemplates the Universe from a higher point of view. Where others see only an analogy, he discerns a final cause. The fall of waters, the germination of seeds, the alternate growth and decay of organized forms, were not originally designed to answer the wants of our physical constitution, but to acquaint us with the laws of mind, and to serve our intellectual and moral advancement. The powers of Nature have been forced into the service of man. The pressure of the atmosphere, the expansive force of steam, the gravity of falling bodies, are our ministers, and do our bidding in levelling the earth, in changing a wilderness into a habitable city, and in fashioning raw materials into products available for the gratification of sense and the protection of body. Yet these ends are only of secondary importance to the great purpose for which these forces were created and made subject to human power. Spiritual laws are typified in these natural facts, and are made evident in the whole material constitution of things. Man must study matter, that he may become acquainted with his own soul.

["Language," 19.11–30]

Thus far, whatever we may think of the truth and soberness of the writer's views, he is at least intelligible. But his imagination now takes a higher flight, and the bewildered reader strives in vain through the cloud-capt phraseology to catch a glimpse of more awful truths. Who will be the Œdipus to solve the following enigmas?

["Language," 22.15–23.4]

In the chapter on "Discipline," the lessons of Nature are enforced with great energy and directness. Man is not so constitutionally active, but that he must receive repeated monitions to labor, or the powers of body and mind will rust and decay. Wants and cravings are imposed upon him, some of which his very physical constitution imperatively requires to be satisfied, and immediate stinging pain is the punishment of neglect. Once gratified, they recur, and provision must again be made. To the knowledge of higher wants he arrives by more extended observation and by every advance in knowledge. Thus, the thirst for truth is insatiable, and increases from gratification. Nature entices us to toil, by offering to gratify the lust for power, and subjecting herself to our dominion. She assumes the harness, and allows us to guide the reins, that she may carry us onward. An exact correspondence exists between the constitution of the soul and of the universe. The love of beauty, of dominion, of comfort, find their appropriate food in the various relations of things, that first called these passions into being, or at least first made us conscious of their existence. Variegated colors, brilliant appearances, curious forms, call us away from the chamber and the couch, that we may walk abroad and admire. The desire of fame and the social instinct are adapted to each other. Either principle alone would be inefficient and useless. United, they are continually pressing us to action. Industry is the great lesson of life, and the universe is the teacher.

But man is not only an active, but a moral being. The constitution of society, the relations which connect him with his fellows, are his instructers in virtue. A hermitage is no school of morals, and were man a hermit from his birth, the terms *right* and *wrong* with him would have but an imperfect and narrow application. The moral teachings of *nature*, understanding by the term all that is distinct from spirit, are auxiliary, but insufficient. Mind must act upon mind. Man must stand in need of his fellow, before he can learn to love him. The mother, indeed, may love her child, before the infant is able to pay the first instalment of its debt to her, "risu cognoscere matrem." But the feeling is instinctive, and as such, is not a subject of moral approbation, any more than when it exists in the brute. With this limitation, we accept the following remarks from the book before us.

["Discipline," 26.22–27.7]

Having thus considered the uses of the material world, its adaptation to man's physical wants, to his love of beauty, and his moral sense, the author turns and aims a back blow at the universe, which he has been leading us to admire and love. The heavens are rolled together like a scroll, the solid earth cracks beneath our feet,

"Wide wilderness and mountain, rock and
     sea, Peopled with busy transitory
     groups,"

are shadows, and exist only in mind. Matter is nothing, spirit is all. Man is alone in the vast inane with his God.

We have no quarrel with Idealism. Philosophers may form what dreams they choose, provided their speculations affect favorably their own faith and practice, and can never, from their very nature, command the belief, or bewilder the understanding of the mass of mankind. But we do protest against the implied assertion of the idealist, that the vulgar entertain opinions less philosophically just than his own. In the pride of opinion, he has overrated his own success, which at the utmost amounts only to this, that he has shown the inconclusiveness of the arguments commonly adduced to prove the outward and independent existence of matter. But he has brought no positive arguments to disprove the existence of any thing exterior to mind. He has not shown, that the common opinion involves any repugnancy or inconsistency in itself. The bridge on which we relied for support may be broken down, but we are not whelmed in the waters beneath. The belief still exists, and its universality is a fact for which the idealist cannot account. This fact puts the burden of proof upon him, and it is a load which he cannot support. The infant forms this belief before it quits its mother's arms. It has existed in every age, as a postulate for the exercise of many affections and emotions, that form a part of the primitive constitution of mind. Nay, the philosopher himself, "when he mingles with the crowd, must be content to comply with common opinions, to speak as custom dictates, and to forget, as well as he can, the doubts and the doctrines which reason perhaps permits, which speculation loves, and which solitude encourages."

On reviewing what we have already said of this singular work, the criticism appears to be couched in contradictory terms; we can only allege in excuse the fact, that the book is a contradiction in itself. A fair notice of it would be in the vein of honest Touchstone's commentary on a shepherd's life. "Truly, shepherd, in respect of itself, it is a good life; but in respect that it is a shepherd's life, it is naught. In respect that it is solitary, I like it very well; but in respect that it is private, it is a very vile life. As it is a spare life, look you, it fits my humor well; but as there is no more plenty in it, it goes much against my stomach. Hast any philosophy in thee, shepherd?"

But enough of the work itself; it belongs to a class, and may be considered as the latest representative of that class.

Within a short period, a new school of philosophy has appeared, the adherents of which have dignified it with the title of Transcendentalism. In its essential features, it is a revival of the Old Platonic school. It rejects the aid of observation, and will not trust to experiment. The Baconian mode of discovery is regarded as obsolete; induction is a slow and tedious process, and the results are uncertain and imperfect. General truths are to be attained without the previous examination of particulars, and by the aid of a higher power than the understanding. "The hand-lamp of logic" is to be broken, for the truths which are *felt* are more satisfactory and certain than those which are *proved*. The sphere of intuition is enlarged, and made to comprehend not only mathematical axioms, but the most abstruse and elevated propositions respecting the being and destiny of man. Pure intelligence usurps the place of humble research. Hidden meanings, glimpses of spiritual and everlasting truth are found, where former observers sought only for natural facts. The observation of sensible phenomena can lead only to the discovery of insulated, partial, and relative laws; but the consideration of the same phenomena, in a typical point of view, may lead us to infinite and absolute truth,—to a knowledge of the reality of things.

As the object and method of philosophizing are thus altered, it is obvious that language also must be modified, and made to subserve other purposes than those for which it was originally designed. Transcendental philosophy took its rise in Germany, and the language of that country, from the unbounded power which it affords of composition and derivation from native roots, is well adapted to express results that are at once novel and vague. Hence the mysticism and over refinement, which characterize the German school of philosophy, art, and criticism. Our own tongue is more limited and inflexible. It must be enriched by copious importations from the German and Greek, before it can answer the ends of the modern school. And this has been done to such an extent, that could one of the worthies of old English literature rise from his grave, he would hardly be able to recognise his native tongue.

Among other innovations in speech made by writers of the Transcendental school, we may instance the formation of a large class of abstract nouns from adjectives,—a peculiarity as consonant with the genius of the German language, as it is foreign to the nature of our own. Thus we now speak of the *Infinite*, the *Beautiful*, the *Unconscious*, the *Just*, and the *True*. A new class of verbs also has been formed from the same or similar roots, such as *individualize, materialize, externize*, &c. For instances of new and awkward compounds, take the following; *instreaming, adolescent, symbolism, unconditioned, theosophists, internecive*.

We deprecate the introduction of a new class of philosophical terms, as it encourages tyros to prate foolishly and flippantly about matters, which they can neither master nor comprehend. Once let a peculiar diction gain footing in philosophy, as it has already done in poetry, and we shall have as great a cloud of pretenders and sciolists in the former, as already exercise our patience in the latter. Nonsense cannot be concealed in plain and sober prose. It stands conspicuous in its jejuneness and sterility. But by ringing the changes on the poetical vocabulary, a *mirage* of meaning is produced, and the mass of readers are cheated into the belief that the author says something. So is there reason to fear that a great portion of modern metaphysics and what is termed *æsthetic* criticism, is made up of "words, words," and very awkward and affected words too. Translate a passage of such writing into English, and it will be found to transcend both reason and common sense.

We speak generally. To many writers of

the New School we confess our obligation for new and valuable hints, expressed in energetic though affected language. But their influence is most pernicious. Writers, who cannot fathom their depth of thought, will imitate their darkness of language; and instead of comparing truths and testing propositions, readers must busy themselves in hunting after meaning, and investigating the significancy of terms.

It would avail but little, perhaps, with some Transcendentalists to assert, that the deepest minds have ever been the clearest, and to quote the example of Locke and Bacon, as of men who could treat the most abstruse subjects in the most familiar and intelligible terms. If in their modesty they did not rank themselves above such names as these, they would probably allege the different nature of their tasks, and attribute the difficulty of communication to daring originality in the choice of ends and means. But it is evident that novelty both of plan and execution, though it may retard progress, ought not to vitiate results. We do not complain of the New School for doing little, but for doing nothing in a satisfactory manner; for boasting of progress, when they cannot show clear evidence of having advanced a step. We cannot believe, that there is a large class of truths, which in their very nature are incomprehensible to the greater part of mankind. Of course, we speak not of the multitude, whose incapacity results from ignorance and the want of experience in thinking. But the Transcendentalists more than insinuate, that the majority of educated and reflecting men are possessed of minds so unlike their own, that they doubt their power of constructing a bridge which may serve for the transmission of ideas to persons so little fitted to receive them. What a frivolous excuse for being unintelligible is this! There is an essential unity in Truth, in the means of research, and in the vehicle of communication. There is but one philosophy, though

there are many theories; and but one mode of expressing thought, (namely, by symbols,) though there are many languages. Philosophy is the love of wisdom, and wisdom is the knowledge of things and their relations. To perceive them at all is to perceive them clearly, and the perception cannot fail of being conveyed to others, except through a very school-boy's ignorance of the force of terms.

The alleged analogy between the new philosophy and the higher branches of mathematics, as respects the preparatory labor required for the study of either, rests upon forgetfulness of the essential difference between moral and demonstrative reasoning. One cannot read the "Mecanique Celeste" without a knowledge of geometry and the calculus. But the difficulty relates to the mode of proof, and results from the technical nature of the reasoning process. The several propositions, which are proved by La Place, admit of being enunciated in terms intelligible to the lowest capacity. A child may understand them, though he knows nothing of the means by which they have been attained and shown to be true. But in moral reasoning, where there are few technicalities, and the conclusion is but a step from the premises, the obstructions to our progress arise from the mutability and ambiguity of terms. Obscurity of language is not a defect merely in the mode of communication, but betrays a want of the power of reasoning. Words are not only the exponents, they are the substratum and essence of abstract thought. Mathematical propositions are like the rounds of a ladder placed against the side of a building; we must pass over each in succession, before attaining the summit. But in treating of moral subjects, the several steps are like the rounds of the same ladder placed flat upon the earth; we can tread on any one, provided the foothold be sure, without touching the others.

We are ashamed to labor this point. The analogy alluded to is so forced, that it can have deceived no one. If the partisans of the New School still insist upon it, let them manufacture a treatise on the rudiments of Transcendentalism, that tyros may begin with the alphabet of the science, and toil slowly but surely up its cloud-capt heights. In this connexion a few homely remarks from the writings of a philosopher, who enjoyed some repute in his day, may not appear inappropriate. "Nevertheless, this artificial ignorance and learned gibberish prevailed mightily in these last ages, by the interest and artifice of those who found no easier way to that pitch of authority and dominion they have attained, than by amusing the men of business and ignorant with hard words, or employing the ingenious in intricate disputes about unintelligible terms, and holding them perpetually entangled in that endless labyrinth. Besides, there is no such way to gain admittance, or give defence to strange and absurd doctrines, as to guard them round about with legions of obscure and undefined words; which make these retreats more like the dens of robbers, or the holes of foxes, than the fortresses of fair warriors; which if it be hard to get them out of, it is not for the strength that is in them, but the briers and thorns, and the obscurity of the thickets they are beset with. For untruth being unacceptable to the mind of man, there is no other defence left for absurdity but obscurity."[1]

But we are not left to infer vagueness and incompleteness of thought from obscurity of language. The writers of whom we speak, openly avow their preference of such indistinct modes of reflection, and justify loose and rambling speculations, mystical forms of expression, and the utterance of truths that are but half perceived, on the same principle, it would seem, that influences the gambler, who expects by a number of random casts to obtain at last the desired combination. In this respect, the philosophy of the New School is well summed up by the writer before us in the following assertions; "that a guess is often more fruitful than an indisputable affirmation, and that a dream may let us deeper into the secret of nature than a hundred concerted experiments." "Poetry comes nearer to vital truth than history." Why not follow the principle of the gambler entirely, by shaking a number of words in a hat, and then throwing them upon a table, in the hope that, after a number of trials, they may so arrange themselves as to express some novel and important truth?

"Insanam vatem adspicies, quæ, rupe sub imâ,
Fata canit, foliisque notas et nomina mandat."

If it be urged, that vagueness is not inconsistent with reality and truth, we reply, that this assertion does not meet the point, nor resolve the difficulty. In the imperfect conceptions of man, mystery may envelope truth, but it does not constitute that truth, any more than the veil of the temple is in itself the "Holy of Holies." Still less is there any *necessary* connexion between dimness and reality; for truth, considered as the object of Divine contemplation, is light itself, and glimpses of the spiritual world are blinding to man, only because they dazzle with excessive brightness. We live in the twilight of knowledge, and though ignorant of the points of the compass, it argues nothing but blind perverseness, to turn to the darkest part of the horizon for the expected rising of the sun.

We have a graver complaint to make of the spirit in which the disciples of the modern school have conducted their inquiries and answered their opponents. "It might seem incredible," says Mackintosh, "if it were not established by the experience of all ages, that those who differ most from the opinions of their fellow men, are most confident of the truth of their own." Dog-

10

matism and the spirit of innovation go hand in hand. And the reason is obvious, for there is no common ground on which the opponents can stand, and cultivate mutual good will in the partial unity of their interests and pursuits. Both the means and the ends, which other philosophers have proposed to themselves, are rejected by the new sect of hierophants. They are among men, but not of men. From the heights of mystical speculation, they look down with a ludicrous self-complacency and pity on the mass of mankind, on the ignorant and the educated, the learners and the teachers, and should any question the grounds on which such feelings rest, they are forthwith branded with the most opprobrious epithets, which the English or the Transcendental language can supply. It is not going too far to say, that to the bitterness and scorn, with which Coleridge and some of his English adherents have replied to modest doubts and fair arguments, no parallel can be found, save in the scholastic controversies of the Middle Ages.

But the world has grown too old and too proud to be sent to school again by any sect. It boasts of having accomplished something by the labor of ages, of having settled some principles and ascertained some facts; and though it will thankfully accept any addition to its treasury, it will not regard as useless all its former stores, and begin the career of discovery anew. The Transcendentalists have been unwise, therefore, in adopting an offensive tone in the outset, and promulgating new views of things in an overbearing and dictatorial manner. Dogmatists may be sincere, but they are not often successful. Their manner creates a disgust, which no acknowledged ardor in the pursuit of truth, no disinterestedness of purpose, no acuteness of inquiry can ever remove. A sneer is unanswerable, but it is no argument, and repels rather than persuades the modest inquirer. To cavil at the understandings of those who complain of obscurity, is a poor mode of rebutting the charge, since the ignorant, the foolish, and the vain may on every occasion use the same plea with equal effect. The weapon is too common, and has been too much abused, to be any longer effective. The affectation of distinguishing between *esoteric* and *exoteric* doctrines became obsolete centuries ago, and it is preposterous to attempt to revive it at the present day.

We cannot better illustrate our meaning, than by quoting a passage written in a spirit directly opposite to that alluded to. It is taken from the writings of a man, whose name will never cease to be respected, till the maxim shall come to be generally received, that strong common sense is incompatible with philosophical genius. "To Mr. Coleridge, who doubts his own power of building a bridge by which his ideas may pass into a mind so differently trained as mine, I venture to suggest, with that sense of his genius which no circumstance has hindered me from seizing every fit occasion to manifest, that more of my early years were employed in contemplations of an abstract nature, than those of a majority of his readers; that there are not, even now, many of them less likely to be repelled from doctrines by singularity or uncouthness; more willing to allow that every system had caught an advantageous glimpse of some side or corner of the truth; more desirous of exhibiting this dispersion of the fragments of wisdom by attempts to translate the doctrines of one school into the language of another; who, when he cannot discover a reason for an opinion, considers it as important to discover the causes of its adoption by the philosopher; believing, in the most unfavorable cases, that one of the most arduous and useful researches of mental philosophy is to explore the subtile illusions, which enable great minds to satisfy themselves by mere words, before they deceive others by payment in the same counterfeit coin. These habits, together with the natural influence of my age and avocations, lead me to suspect that in speculative philosophy I am nearer to indifference than an exclusive spirit. I hope, that it can neither be thought presumptuous nor offensive in me to doubt, whether the circumstance of its being found difficult to convey a metaphysical doctrine to a person, who, at one part of his life made such studies his chief pursuit, may not imply either error in the opinion, or defect in the mode of communication."[2]

The distinguishing trait of the Transcendental philosophy, is the appeal which it makes from the authority of reason and argument to that of passion and feeling. We are aware, that the miserable sophistries of skepticism can in no way be so effectually exposed, as by a reference to the original, simple, and unadulterated impressions of mind. In one sense, the heart is wiser than the head; the child is the teacher of the man. A process of reasoning, which leads to a false result, is a mere logical puzzle, and so far from establishing that result, it only demonstrates the weakness of the reasoning faculty, that cannot discover the mistake, which, through the medium of a higher power, we know must exist. The foundations of moral and religious truth are like the axioms on which the mathematician grounds his argument; if, either directly or by necessary inference, conclusions are found to be at variance with these first principles, they are at once rejected as being demonstrably absurd.

But some bounds must be set to the application of views like these. Postulates must not be confounded with axioms. He who mingles controverted propositions with essential truths, in a vain attempt to obtain the evidence of consciousness for each, corrupts, so far as in him lies, the fountain head of argument, and introduces confusion into the very elements of knowledge. The distinction, so much insisted on by the New School, between the Reason and the Understanding, if it mean any thing, must be coincident with that which exists between the mind's active and creating power on the one side, and its passive and recipient faculty on the other. If not so,—if the two faculties agree in being each perceptive of truth,—we ask, what difference in kind can there be between two classes of truths, that separate powers are necessary for their reception? In *kind*, we say; for that a variety in degree should require the exercise of different faculties, is as absurd to suppose, as that a man must have one eye to see a mountain, and another for a molehill. We know that we shall be asked, whether moral truth is recognised by the same exertion of mind that admits the demonstrations of the geometer; and we reply, that the question is not a pertinent one. Our assertion is, that the argument for the existence of a God, or the immateriality of the soul, is tested by the same power of mind that discovered and proved any proposition in Euclid. The motive for supposing the existence of a mental faculty distinct from the Understanding, and which is denominated *par excellence* the Reason, seems to have been, to obtain evidence in favor of intuitive truths, equal or superior to that which is afforded to another class of propositions by demonstration. It is a needless supposition; for demonstration itself proceeds by intuition, the several steps being linked together by the immediate and necessary perception of their agreement with each other.

The aim of the Transcendentalists is high. They profess to look not only beyond facts, but without the aid of facts, to principles. What is this but Plato's doctrine of innate, eternal, and immutable ideas, on the consideration of which all science is founded? Truly, the human mind advances but too often in a circle. The New School has abandoned Bacon, only to go back and wander in the groves of the Academy, and to bewilder themselves with the dreams

12

which first arose in the fervid imagination of the Greeks. Without questioning the desirableness of this end, of considering general truths without any previous examination of particulars, we may well doubt the power of modern philosophers to attain it. Again, they are busy in the inquiry (to adopt their own phraseology,) after the Real and the Absolute, as distinguished from the Apparent. Not to repeat the same doubt as to their success, we may at least request them to beware lest they strip Truth of its relation to Humanity, and thus deprive it of its usefulness. Granted that we are imprisoned in matter, why beat against the bars in a fruitless attempt to escape, when a little labor might convert the prison to a palace, or at least render the confinement more endurable. The frame of mind which longs after the forbidden fruit of knowledge in subjects placed beyond the reach of the human faculties, as it is surely indicative of a noble temperament, may also, under peculiar circumstances, conduce to the happiness of the individual. But if too much indulged, there is danger lest it waste its energies in mystic and unprofitable dreams, and despondency result from frequent failures, till at last, disappointment darkens into despair.

In offering these suggestions, we trust not to have appeared as arguing against a generous confidence in the power of the human intellect, and in the progress and efficacy of truth. There is a wide field still open for the exertion of mind, though we cease to agitate questions which have baffled the acuteness, ingenuity, and skill of the philosophers of all time. But arrogance and self-sufficiency are no less absurd in philosophy, than criminal in morals; and we cannot but think, that these qualities are displayed by men who censure indiscriminately the objects which the wise and good have endeavoured to attain, and the means which they have employed in the pursuit. A fair and catholic spirit will ever incline to eclecticism in its inquiries and systems; while it is the mark of a narrow mind to consider novelty as a mark of truth, or to look upon the difficulties of a question as evincing the importance of its solution. To regard Franklin as a greater name than that of Plato, might be unjust, were not the comparison itself fanciful and improper; but we may safely assert, that there are few, very few, who would not do better to look at the American rather than the Grecian sage, as their model of the philosophical character.

Notes

1 "Locke on the Understanding, Book iii, chap. 10, sect. 9."
2 "Mackintosh, Progress of Eth. Phil., p. 302. Amer. Ed."

[Samuel] O[sgood]., "Nature," *Western Messenger*, 2 (January 1837), 385–93

————For I have learned
To look on Nature, not as in the hour
Of thoughtless youth; but hearing
    oftentimes
The still, sad music of humanity,
Not harsh, nor grating, though of ample
    power
To chasten and subdue. And I have felt
A presence, that disturbs me with the joy
Of elevated thoughts: a sense sublime,
Of something far more deeply interfused,
Whose dwelling is the light of setting suns,
And the round ocean and the living air,
And the blue sky, and in the mind of
    man.
A motion and a spirit, that impels
All thinking things, all objects of all
    thoughts,
And rolls through all things.
                    —Wordsworth's *Tintern Abbey*.

It would be interesting to study the Poetry, Philosophy and Religion of Mankind, in the different stages of its progress, in order to learn the various views and sentiments with which Nature has been regarded. Such a study would lead us to consider all periods of our race:—the infant period when the heart of man had the freshness of childhood, and in childish wonder, he saw Nature clad with the freshness of its new born beauty:—the savage period, when man looked upon Nature, only as a means of supplying his physical wants, or drew from it a language for his passions; it would lead us to consider the mystic period in human progress, when as in the central oriental world,

Nature was regarded as a dreamy shadow, and the indolent soul, absorbed in its own fond visions, scorned the world of matter as being unreal, or shrunk from it as contaminating: then would come before our view, the period in which the material universe engrossed the mind, and the soul was too intent on the finite to rise to the infinite and that Grecian taste for beauty prevailed, which admired the beautiful in form, without recognising the spiritual beauty, of which all that is divine in form, is but the faint emblem: then comes the period in which Nature is prized, mainly for her physical uses—the age of natural science and material utility. In this latter period, we find our own lot to be cast, and should rejoice to find ourselves emerging from it. We should rejoice at those signs, that are appearing, which promise that Nature shall ere long have her due, and be looked on with the right spirit—that a day is coming, when the world around us shall be regarded, not only for its material uses, but shall be loved as the emblem of the Divine Beauty, and reverenced as being instinct with the Divine Spirit, and an expression of the Divine Wisdom, Love and Power. When this day comes, man will look on Nature with the same eye, as when in the Eden of primitive innocence and joy, and at the same time, with all the lights which science and varied experience afford.

Christianity teaching the immortality of the soul, and revealing to us God in all things, has been the cause of this happy change. It puts a spiritual aspect on all things—on all Providence and all creation. It forbids our being engrossed with finite things. It also forbids our being lost in the mazes of the Infinite. It reaches us to ascend to the Infinite from the Finite. It does not take us away from Nature, but in Nature shows to us our God.

Now certainly all those books, which throw a religious light on Nature, should

14

be encouraged by all, who wish to redeem the souls of men from the thraldom of the senses: not only those books which exhibit the argument for religion, drawn from a view of those final causes which a scientific view of Nature gives, but those which shew the correspondence of the material world, with our own higher nature, and teach us to look on Nature with the spiritual eye—with something of that same spirit in which God made his creation.

The strong hold, which Coleridge and Wordsworth have taken, of so many minds, while it confers a high honor on their sublime genius, also shews, that they have but given expression to thoughts and feelings, which before existed and were growing in the minds of their readers. We rejoice at the influence of such poets. We rejoice that a poetry of Nature, truly Christian, is springing up among us. We rejoice, that those to whom it is given to pass within the veil, and to see in Nature a Beauty, that is hid to common eyes, have so made the Beautiful minister to the Good and True. We hail with joy every inspiration of genius, which connects sentiment with religion. Sentiment, we well know, is not the whole of religion. But it is a rightful minister of religion. The Beautiful is the rightful priest of the True— none the less so, because the priest sometimes deserts his proper altar, and beauty of sentiment is made to throw its garlands around the altar of vice and sensuality.

In our own bustling country, where banks, steam boats and rail roads seem to engross the nation's attention, we are happy to find some spirits, who keep aloof from the vulgar melee, and in calm of soul, live for Nature and for God. No greater exception to the common spirit of our nation, could be pointed out, than the author of a little work, recently published at the East.[1] "Nature" is its title. We can illustrate the ideas, which we have vaguely hinted at above, by the aid of this author, far better, than by any essay of our own.

The work is a remarkable one, and it certainly will be called remarkable by those, who consider it "mere moonshine," as well as those, who look upon it with reverence, as the effusion of a prophet-like mind. Whatever may be thought of the merits, or of the extravagances of the book, no one, we are sure, can read it, without feeling himself more wide awake to the beauty and meaning of Creation.

Like the page of revelation, so the page of Nature is too apt to become old to our minds. As revelation too often becomes a mere tradition, and is read as a by-gone thing without any of the spirit and life, in which it was originally proclaimed, and needs to be awoke to newness of life in the soul, so nature has become an old story, and is not regarded in its living meaning, and the spirit must be roused from its slumber, before it can look on Creation with understanding eye. Truly says our author in his preface:—

["Introduction," 7.9–21]

The face of creation is as fair, as on the dawn of the first day. Truly says the bard of Weimar:

"The world's unwithered countenance
Is bright as on creation's day."

But it has not its primeval brightness in the eye of degenerate man. Our dim vision does not see its divine glory:

["Nature," 9.24–10.22]

The author first speaks of the uses of the natural world, under the following classes: Commodity; Beauty; Language and Discipline. He closes the work with some thoughts on the spiritual world, as shadowed forth by Nature. He does this under the three heads: Idealism; Spirit; Prospects.

The author is not such a dreamer on the beauties of the universe, as to forget

15

its material uses. In the chapter on Commodity, he gives a view of the advantages, which our senses owe to Nature, as broad as if he were looking down on our earth with a mighty telescope, from some distant orb.

Is not the author right in considering Beauty one of the uses—one of the true final causes of Nature? Is not Beauty in itself merely considered one form of utility? Is there not a high utility, even in Beauty of outward form? Surely this simplest aspect of Beauty gives delight, and what gives inmost delight is truly useful:

["Beauty," 13.11–34]

But a higher element than beauty of form, must be recognized, before we can see the full loveliness of Nature's beauty:

["Beauty," 15.1–9, 16.2–15]

We will not make any extracts from the remarks on the third aspect of natural beauty, namely, as it becomes an object of the intellect, or as it is shown in the creations of Art. We quote the closing passage of the chapter, for the edification of those people, who seem to think beauty a mere vanity, and to whom it is an enigma, that God has made creation so wondrous fair:—

["Beauty," 17.18–26]

In the chapter on Language, Nature is considered the vehicle of thought. As Coleridge says,

"Symbolical is all that meets the sense, One mighty alphabet for infant minds."

["Language," 19.31–20.6]

In this chapter on Language, the great law of correspondence, which runs through creation, is pointed out, that great law of analogy, which he, who shall understand truly, will know more of the universe, and be a wiser seer into the regions of undiscovered truth, than eternity spent in groping round the world, endeavoring, without such light, to classify its scattered phenomena, could make him. We can make but one more extract from this chapter:—

["Language," 21.30–22.4]

In the last chapter on the uses of Nature—that on Discipline, the world around us is considered as disciplining our understanding and conscience. Speaking of sensible objects, as disciplining the conscience, the author says:—

{"Discipline," 25.34–26.8]

Coming to the chapter on Idealism, many will be tempted to shut the book in disgust, and lament, that so sensible a man as the writer has before shewn himself to be, should shew such folly. And we ourselves doubt much the wisdom of the speculation in this chapter, although we would not call him insane, who thinks the material world only ideal, believing as we do, that as Turgot has said, "He, who has never doubted the existence of matter, may be assured, he has no aptitude for metaphysical inquiries." We do not think, that Idealism leads to such dangerous conclusions, as are sometimes apprehended, since it implies no distrust in natural laws. The idealist, who believes matter to be only phenomenal, will conduct in exactly the same way, as the most thorough going materialist. The idealist will be just as cautious about cutting his finger, as the materialist will: for both will believe, that the pain is really felt, whatever they may think as to the finger or the knife being real or only apparent.

We are unable to perceive the bearing of the writer's argument, in proof of Idealism, or to allow the advantage, which he claims for this theory. All his arguments,

16

it seems to us, go to prove merely the superiority of mind over matter. And all the advantage, which he claims for Idealism, is owned by that common spiritual philosophy, which subordinates matter to mind. We own there is much fine thought and good writing in this chapter, little as the sentiments agree with our Eclecticism. Take a specimen:—

["Idealism," 35.31–36.91]

In the chapter on Spirit, the lessons, which Nature teaches, are summed up in a single one:—

["Spirit," 37.3–11]

There are some things in this book, which we do not understand. The Orphic sentences at the end, "which a certain poet sang to the author," are especially dark to our misty vision. But probably the fault lies in ourselves. We will not make fun even of such sayings, as the following, although we verily marvel at them:—

["Prospects," 42.20–24]

The many will call this book dreamy, and perhaps it is so. It may indeed naturally seem, that the author's mind is somewhat onesided, that he has not mingled enough with common humanity, to avoid running into eccentricity, that he has been so careful to keep his own individuality, that he has confounded his idiosyncrasies, with universal truth. All this may be. But it is not for the vulgar many to call such a man a dreamer. If he does dream, the many are more deluded dreamers. His dreams are visions of the eternal realities of the spiritual world: their's are of the fleeting phantoms of earth. Indeed the real visionary is not to be found, in the mystic's cell, or the philosopher's study, but in the haunts of busy life. The sensualist is a wretched visionary: he sees but a part, and that but a mean part of the reality of things, and sees all in a false light. The man of ambition is a dreamer. Those men, who pride themselves most on their practical turn of mind, are often far more visionary, than their more romantic neighbors, whom they are accustomed to deride. The veriest votary of Mammon, who makes himself an entire drudge to money getting, and boasts, that while other men are chasing shadows, such shadows, as beauty in nature and art, or truth in science or religion, he alone is grasping the substance; this man is constantly pursuing a phantom—he is chasing a joy, that never comes to him: from the toils of the present hour, he is ever looking forward to the future, and dreaming of some distant good, as the reward of his labors, and the enjoyment of his wealth. He dreams and toils, and heaps up his treasures, and forms visions of bliss, which are never realised; never finding the time, in which he may enjoy his wealth, he lives in a realm of illusion, until death, the stern teacher of reality, comes and touches him with his cold hand, and heaped treasures and fond visions at once disappear.

Not so with him, who puts his thoughts on things eternal. He sees the world as it really is. He looks on the temporal in the light of the Eternal. "So he comes to look on the world with new eyes." So he learns the high truths which nature teaches. Let us therefore hear the Orphic poet's saying:

["Prospects," 45.6–21]

Note

1 "NATURE.—Nature is but an image or imitation of wisdom, the last thing of the soul; Nature being a thing, which doth only do, but not know.
—PLOTINUS."

17

[Elizabeth Palmer Peabody], "Nature—A Prose Poem," *United States Magazine, and Democratic Review*, 1 (February 1838), 319–21

Minds of the highest order of genius draw their thoughts most immediately from the Supreme Mind, which is the fountain of all finite natures. And hence they clothe the truths they see and feel, in those forms of nature which are generally intelligible to all ages of the world. With this poetic instinct, they have a natural tendency to withdraw from the *conventions* of their own day; and strive to forget, as much as possible, the arbitrary associations created by temporary institutions and local peculiarities. Since the higher laws of suggestion operate in proportion as the lower laws are made subordinate, suggestions of thought by mere proximity of time and place must be subtracted from the habits of the mind that would cultivate the principle of analogy; and this principle of suggestion, in its turn, must be made to give place to the higher law of cause and effect; and at times even this must be set aside, and Reason, from the top of the being, look into the higher nature of original truth, by Intuition,—no unreal function of our nature:

> Nor less I deem that there are powers,
>   Which, of themselves, our minds
>   impress;
> That we can feed these minds of ours,
>   In a wise passiveness.

But if it is precisely because the most creative minds take the symbols of their thoughts and feelings from the venerable imagery of external nature, or from that condition of society which is most transparent in its simplicity, that, when they utter themselves, they speak to all ages, it is also no less true, that this is the reason why the greatest men, those of the highest order of intellect, often do not appear very great to their contemporaries. Their most precious sayings are naked, if not invisible, to the eyes of the conventional, precisely because they are free of the thousand circumstances and fashions which interest the acting and unthinking many. The greatest minds take no cognizance of the local interests, the party spirit, and the pet subjects of the literary coteries of particular times and places. Their phraseology is pure from the ornament which is the passing fashion of the day. As, however, they do not think and speak for their own order only, as they desire to address and receive a response from the great majority of minds—even from those that doubt their own power of going into the holy of holies of thought for themselves—there is needed the office of an intermediate class of minds, which are the natural critics of the human race. For criticism, in its worthiest meaning, is not, as is too often supposed, fault-finding, but interpretation of the oracles of genius. Critics are the priests of literature. How often, like other priests, they abuse their place and privilege, is but too obvious. They receive into their ranks the self-interested, the partisan, the lover of power, besides the stupid and frivolous; and thus the periodical literature of the day is in the rear, rather than in advance of the public mind.

After this preamble, which we trust has suitably impressed the minds of our readers with the dignity of the critical office, we would call those together who have feared that the spirit of poetry was dead, to rejoice that such a *poem* as "Nature" is

18

written. It grows upon us as we reperuse it. It proves to us, that the only true and perfect mind is the poetic. Other minds are not to be despised, indeed; they are germs of humanity; but the poet alone is the man—meaning by the poet, not the versifier, nor the painter of outward nature merely, but the total soul, grasping truth, and expressing it melodiously, equally to the eye and heart.

The want of apprehension with which this *poem* has been received, speaks ill for the taste of our literary priesthood. Its title seems to have suggested to many persons the notion of some elementary treatise on physics, as physics; and when it has been found that it treats of the *metaphysics* of nature—in other words, of the highest designs of God, in forming nature and man in relations with each other—it seems to have been laid down with a kind of disgust, as if it were a cheat; and some reviewers have spoken of it with a stupidity that is disgraceful alike to their sense, taste, and feeling.

It has, however, found its readers and lovers, and those not a few; the highest intellectual culture and the simplest instinctive innocence have alike received it, and felt it to be a divine Thought, borne on a stream of 'English undefiled,' such as we had almost despaired could flow in this our world of grist and saw mills, whose utilitarian din has all but drowned the melodies of nature. The time will come, when it will be more universally seen to be "a gem of purest ray serene," and be dived after, into the dark unfathomed caves of that ocean of frivolity, which the literary productions of the present age spread out to the eyes of despair.

We have said that "Nature" is a poem; but it is written in prose. The author, though "wanting the accomplishment of verse," is a devoted child of the great Mother; and comes forward bravely in the midst of the dust of business and the din of machinery, and naming her venerable name, believes that there is a reverence for it left, in the bottom of every heart, of power to check the innumerable wheels for a short Sabbath, that all may listen to her praises.

In his introduction, he expresses his purpose. He tells us, that we concede too much to the sceptic, when we allow every thing venerable in religion to belong to history. He tells us that were there no past, yet nature would tell us great truths; and, rightly read, would prove the prophecies of revelation to be "a very present God"; and also, that the past itself involving its prophets, divine lawgivers, and the human life of Him of Nazareth, is comparatively a dead letter to us, if we do not freshen these traditions in our souls, by opening our ears to the living nature which forevermore prepares for, and re-echoes, their sublime teachings.

"The foregoing generations," he says, "beheld God face to face: we, through their eyes. Why should not *we* also enjoy an original relation to the Universe?"

Why should we not indeed? for *we* not only have the Universe, which the foregoing generations had, but *themselves* also. Why are we less wise than they? Why has our wisdom less of the certainty of intuition than theirs? Is it because we have more channels of truth? It may be so. The garden of Eden, before the fall of man, and when God walked in its midst, was found to be a less effective school of virtue, than the workshop of a carpenter, in a miserable town of Judea, of which 'an Israelite without guile' could ask. "*Can any good come out of Nazareth?*" And is not this, by the way, a grave warning to the happily circumstanced of all time to tremble—lest they grow morally passive, just in proportion to their means of an effective activity? With the religion of history must always be combined the religion of experience, in order to a true apprehension of God. The poet of "Nature" is a preacher of the latter. Let us "hear him gladly," for such are rare.

The first Canto of this song respects the outward form of Nature. He sketches it in bold strokes. The stars of Heaven above—the landscape below—the breathing atmosphere around—and the living forms and sounds—are brought up to us, by the loving spirit of the singer; who recognizes in this drapery of the world without, the same Disposer that arranged the elements of his own conscious soul. Thus, in his first recognition of Nature's superficies, he brings us to Theism. There is a God. Our Father is the author of Nature. The brotherly "nod" of companionship assures us of it.

But wherefore is Nature? The next Canto of our Poem answers this question in the most obvious relation. It is an answer that "all men apprehend." Nature's superficies is for the well-being of man's body, and the advantage of his material interests. This part of the book requires no interpretation from the critic. Men are active enough concerning commodity, to understand whatever is addressed to them on this head. At least there is no exception but in the case of the savage of the tropics. *His* mind has not explored his wants even to the extent of his body. He does not comprehend the necessities of the narrowest civilization. But whoever reads Reviews, whoever can understand our diluted English, can understand still better this concentrated and severely correct expression of what every child of civilization experiences every day. There is but one sentence here, that the veriest materialist can mistake. He may not measure all that the poet means when he says, man is thus conveniently waited upon in order "that he may work." He may

possibly think that "work" relates to the physical operations of manufacture or agriculture. But what is really meant is no less than this; "man is fed that he may work" with his mind; add to the treasures of thought; elaborate the substantial life of the spiritual world. This is a beautiful doctrine, and worthy to be sung to the harp, with a song of thanksgiving. Undoubtedly Nature, by working for man with all her elements, is adequate to supply him with so much "commodity" that the time may be anticipated when all men will have leisure to be artists, poets, philosophers,—in short, to live through life in the exercise of their proper humanity. God speed to the machinery and application of science to the arts which is to bring this about!

The third Song is of Nature's Beauty, and we only wonder why it was not sung first; for surely the singer found out that Nature was beautiful, before he discovered that it was convenient. Some children, we know, have asked what was the use of flowers, and, like little monkeys, endeavouring to imitate the grown-up, the bearings of whose movements they could not appreciate, have planted their gardens with potatoes and beans, instead of sweetbriar and cupid's delights. But the poet never made this mistake. In the fullness of his first love for his "beautiful mother," and his "gentle nest," he did not even find out those wants which the commodity of Nature supplies.

The second passage on Beauty, is one of those which recalls the critic to the office of interpreter, for it is one which the world has called mystical. To say the same thing in worse English, the oracle here tells us, that if we look on Nature with pleasurable emotions only, and without, at the same time, exerting our moral powers, the mind grows effeminate, and thus becomes incapable of perceiving the highest beauty of whose original type the

20

external forms are but the varied reflections or shadows. When man's moral power is in action, the mind spontaneously traces relations between itself and surrounding things, and there forms with Nature one whole, combining the moral delight which human excellence inspires, with that suggested by Nature's forms.

The next passage rises a step higher in the praise of Beauty. It recognizes the cherishing influence of Nature's forms upon the faculties. Nature not only calls out taste, not only glorifies virtue, and is in its turn by virtue glorified, but it awakens the creative impulse—God's image in man. Hence Art, or "Nature in miniature." And the works of Art lead back to Nature again. Thus Beauty circulates, and becomes an aspect of Eternity.

The next chapter, showing that Language is founded on material Nature, is quite didactic. But even here one critic[1] quotes a sentence, of which he says, he cannot understand "what it means."

This relation between the mind and matter is not fancied by some poet, but stands in the will of God, and so is free to be known by all men. It appears to men, or it does not appear.

Where lies the obscurity? We have heard some men say that they did not believe that the forms of Nature bore any relation to the being of God, which his children could appreciate; but even these men could not understand the simple proposition of the opposite theory. Men may think that all nations, whose language has yet been discovered, have called youth *the morning of life*, by accident; but it is inconceivable that they should not understand the simple words in which other men say that there is *no accident in the world*, but all things relate to the spirit of God to which man also has relation and

access. Perhaps, however, it is the second sentence which is unintelligible, "it appears to mean, or it does not appear." In other words, *to people with open eyes there are colors; to people with shut eyes, at least, to those born blind, there are no colors.*

But having come to this fact, viz: that "the relation between mind and matter stands in the will of God," our poet grows silent with wonder and worship. The nature of this relation he acknowledges to be the yet unsolved problem. He names some of the principal men who have attempted a solution. Many readers of his book would have been glad, had he paused to tell us, in his brief comprehensive way, what was the solution of Pythagoras, and Plato, Bacon, Leibnitz, and Swedenborg, with remarks of his own upon each.

And to his own solution, some say he is unintelligible, talks darkly. They do not seem to have observed that he says nothing in the way of solution, so that nothing can be darkly said. This is what has disappointed the best lovers of his book. But if he does not give his own solution of the enigma, he does what is next best, he tells us the condition of solving it ourselves.

A life in harmony with nature, the love of truth and virtue, will purge the eyes to understand her text. By degrees we may come to know the primitive sense of the permanent objects of Nature, so that the world shall be to us an open book, and every form significant of the hidden life and final cause.

The chapter on Discipline is still more didactic than the one on Language. The first portion treats of the formation of the Understanding by the ministry of Nature to the senses, and faculty of deduction. The second section is in a higher strain. It treats of the developement of the Reason

21

and Conscience, by means of that relation between matter and mind, which "appears" so clearly to some men, and to all in a degree.

In the last part of this chapter on Discipline, the author makes a bold sally at the cause of the analogy between the external world and the moral nature. He implies that causes (the spiritual seeds of external things) are identical with the principles that constitute our being; and that *virtues* (the creations of our own heaven-aided wills) correspond to God's creations in matter; the former being the natural growth in the moral world, the latter the natural growth in the material world; or to vary the expression once more, Goodness being the projection inward—Beauty the projection outward—of the same all-pervading Spirit.

Our author here leaves the didactic, and "the solemn harp's harmonious sound" comes full upon the ear and the heart from the next Canto of his poem—Idealism. No part of the book has been so mistaken as this. Some readers affect to doubt his Practical Reason, because he acknowledges, that we have no evidence of there being essential outlying beings, to that which we certainly see, by consciousness, by looking inward, *except 'a constant faith' which God gives us of this truth*. But why should 'the noble doubt,' which marks the limit of the understanding, be so alarming, when it is found to be but an introduction of the mind to the *superior certainty* residing in that 'constant faith?' Do we not advance in truth, when we learn to change the childish feeling by which we ascribe reality to the 'shows of things,' for a feeling involving a sense of GOD, as the only real—immutable—the All in All?

The theory of Idealism has doubtless been carried to absurdity by individuals who but half understood it; and has still more often been represented in a way which was not only useless but injurious to minds entirely dependent on what others say: for, to borrow two good compounds from Coleridge, the *half-Ideas* of many would-be Idealist writers, have passed, perforce, into the *no-Ideas* of many would-be Idealist readers. But Mr. Emerson has sufficiently guarded his Idealism by rigorous and careful expression, to leave little excuse for cavilling at his words or thoughts, except, indeed, by professed materialists and atheists, to whom he gives no ground.

["Idealism," 29.29–30.4]

He proceeds to give the progressive appearances of Nature, as the mind advances, through the ministry of the senses, to "the best and the happiest moments of life, those delicious awakenings of the higher powers,—the withdrawing of Nature before its God." The means by which Nature herself, Poetic genius, Philosophy, both natural and intellectual—and, above all, Religion and Ethics, work, to idealize our thought and being, are then minutely pointed out. No careful thinker can dispute a step of the process.

Many philosophers have stopped at Idealism. But, as Mr. Emerson says, this hypothesis, if it only deny, or question the existence of matter "does not satisfy the demands of the Spirit. It leaves God out of me. It leaves me in the splendid labyrinth of my perceptions, to wander without end. Then the heart resists it, because it baulks the affections, in denying substantive being to men and women."

Mr. Emerson then proceeds to his chapter on Spirit, by which he means to suggest to us the substantial essence of which Idealism is the intellectual form. But this chapter is not full enough, for the purposes of instruction. One passage is indeed of great significance:

["Spirit," 38.8–31]

This is not only of refreshing moral *aura*, but it is a passage of the highest imaginative power, (taking the word *imaginative* in that true signification which farthest removes it from *fanciful*,) the mind must become purified indeed which can take this point of view, to look at "the great shadow pointing to the sun behind us." Sitting thus at the footstool of God, it may realise that all that we see is created by the light that shines through ourselves. Not until thus purified, can it realise that those through whose being more light flows, see more than we do; and that others, who admit less light, see less. What assistance in human culture would the application of this test give us! How would our classifications of men and women be changed, did the positive pure enjoyment of Nature become the standard of judgment! But who may apply the standard? Not every mawkish raver about the moon, surely, but only a comprehender of Nature. And has there yet been any one in human form, who could be called a comprehender of Nature, save Him who had its secret, and in whose hands it was plastic, even to the raising of the dead?

Mr. Emerson must not accuse us of ingratitude, in that after he had led his readers to this high point of view, they crave more, and accuse him of stopping short, where the world most desires and needs farther guidance. We want him to write another book, in which he will give us the philosophy of his "orphic strains," whose meaning is felt, but can only be understood by glimpses.

He does, indeed, tell us that "the problem of restoring to the world original and eternal beauty," (in other words, of seeing Nature and Life in their wholeness), "is solved by the redemption of the soul." It is not unnecessary for the philosopher thus to bring his disciples round, through the highest flights of speculation, to the primitive faith of the humblest disciple, who sits, in the spirit of a child, at the feet of Jesus. But we should like to hear Mr. Emerson's philosophy of Redemption. It is very plain that it consists of broad and comprehensive views of human culture; worthy to employ the whole mind of one who seeks reproduction of Christ within himself, by such meditations as the following, which must be our last extract:

["Prospects," 44.4–10]

Note

1 "Christian Examiner."

Checklist of Additional Reviews

[Lewis Gaylord Clark], "Nature," *Knickerbocker*, 10 (July 1837), 96.

[John A. Heraud], "A Response from America," *Monthly Magazine*, 3rd ser., 2 (September 1839), 344–52. (Also reviews "Divinity School Address.")

J[onathan]. B[ayley]., *Intellectual Repository and New Jerusalem Magazine*, n.s. 1 (April 1840), 188–91.

[John Westall], *New Jerusalem Magazine*, 15 (October 1841), 48–52.

The American Scholar

[William Henry Channing],
"Emerson's *Phi Beta Kappa Oration*,"
Boston Quarterly Review,
1 (January 1838), 106–20

We have been not a little amused and somewhat edified by the various criticisms on this address, which we have seen and heard of all kinds, from kindling admiration to gaping wonder, shrewd caviling, sneering doubt, and even offended dignity. We wish for ourselves, to express our hearty thanks to the author, to disburden our minds of a small load of censure, and utter some thoughts on the subject-matter of the address.

There are writers whom we should designate as in the twilight state, walking ever in an opposite direction to the motion of the earth—following with longing admiration the descending glory of the past—delighting in each tall peak, each floating cloud, which reflects the lustre of a fading day. To them the present is weary and worn, and the darkness and vapors steam up from the sunken vales of common life. There is a second class, in the midnight season of thought, lone and abstracted—watching the truths of eternity as they smile through far space on a darkened world. To them the present is the gleaming lights, the snatches of music, the distasteful clamor of foolish revelry, breaking harshly in upon their hour of rapt and solemn meditation. There is a third class, in morning wakefulness. Their gaze is on the brightening orient. They stand as *muezzins* on the mosques, as watchmen on the towers, summoning to prayer and work;—for the streaks of the dawning, and the golden flushes, are heralding the sun. The present is bright to them with hope; and the dewy incense promises fruitfulness, and the rising race are going forth to husband the garden of life. There is a fourth class, in the noonday and sunny cheerfulness, and clear light, of God's providence in the present time, on whose useful the *spirit of the age* shines down to ripen and to bless.

When we read a former production by the author of this address, we feared from its tone of somewhat exclusive and unsympathising contemplativeness, that he was of the second class. But we hail him now as one of the youthful expectants of a coming brighter hour of social life. Shall we not indeed say, that in his industry, and the unreserved communication of his best nature, as a preacher and lecturer, we gratefully recognize him as one of the working men of this generation? And yet would we see him more fully warmed with the great social idea of our era,—the great idea, which he has hinted at in this very address—of human brotherhood, of sonship to God. We have full faith that in this land is this ideal to be manifested in individual character, in social life, in art, in literature, as for the last eighteen hundred years it has been in religion. We echo with joy the language of the orator.

[52.22–25, 69.11–12, 70.5–7]

Why did Providence veil our land till the fulness of time, and then gather upon it an elect people from all nations of the earth, under institutions the most favorable to individual development, if not, that in a recovered Eden of freedom, love and peace, the products of all by-gone civilization, might blossom together? And shall not such a social state of Humanity utter itself, and is not that utterance a Literature?

We see, in Mr. Emerson, many traits befitting an American, that is, a Christian, free writer. He has deep faith in a heavenly Father of souls, reverence for each brother as a child of God,—respect for his own reason as a divine inspiration,—too much love for men to fear them,—a conscientious hungering and thirsting for truth,—and a serene trust in the triumph of good. He seems to us true, reverent, free, and loving. We cheerfully tolerate therefore any quaint trappings in which a peculiar taste may lead him to deck his thoughts; and we pity the purists, who cannot see a manly spirit through a mantle not wholly courtly. At the same time we will freely express our regret that Mr. Emerson's style is so little a transparent one. There are no thoughts which may not be simply expressed. Raphael's pictures with their profound beauty are simple as a family group in a peasant's cottage, or a crowd in a market place.

The author of this address, we feel assured, does not willingly hide his thoughts from the poor vanity of being understood only by the initiated; and we have no doubt endeavors to be intelligible. He loves truth and respects man too well for such folly. His faith that man's very holy of holies enshrines no ideas too pure for popular worship, is thus beautifully expressed:

[63.27–34]

Why then should he not open himself freely, simply? We think he means to do so. He cordially welcomes us to his high summits of speculation, and to the prospect they command, in full faith that our sight is keen as his. But he forgets that he has not pointed out the way by which he climbed. His conclusions are hinted, without the progressive reasonings through which he was led to them. Perhaps he does not come at them by any consecutive processes. They rather come to him unasked. To use his own language,

[60.6–9]

There are no developments of thought, there is no continuous flow in his writings. We gaze as through crevices on a stream of subterranean course, which sparkles here and there in the light, and then is lost. The style is in the extreme aphoristic. But again, another cause of his obscurity is a fondness for various illustration. He has a quick eye for analogies, and finds in all nature symbols of spiritual facts. His figures are occasionally so exquisitely felicitous, that we have hardly the heart to complain of this habit of mind, though, we confess, that not seldom we are attracted from the feature of his thoughts to the splendid jewelry of their attire, and yet oftener annoyed by the masquerade of rural or civic plainness, in which they see fit to march.

The subject of this Address is "The American Scholar," his training, duties, and prospects; and we cannot but wish that there had been more unity and order observed in treating it. The division is good—and the thoughts are apparently cast in a form. But the truth is, there is no progress, no onward stream. The best thoughts are not the leading but the incidental ones, and their arrangement might be varied without much altering the effect of the whole. But then these thoughts are fine ones, and there is a mass of them. And they might easily be run into shape, or rather built into a beautiful composition; or yet again grow naturally forth from the root of his central idea. This idea is variously expressed:

"There is One Man—present to all particular men only partially; you must take the whole of society to find the whole man." "Man is one." "It is one soul which animates all men." "In a century—in a millennium one or two men; that is to say, one or two approximations to the right state of every man. All the rest behold in the hero or the poet their own green and crude being ripened." "A man rightly viewed comprehendeth the particular natures of all men. Each philosopher, each bard, each actor, has only done for me as by a delegate what I can one day do for myself." "The one thing of value in the world is the active soul,—the soul free, sovereign, active." "A nation of men, because each believes himself inspired, by the Divine Soul which also inspires all men."

This fundamental truth, which Jesus felt, uttered, and lived as no disciple has ever faintly dreamed of, our author has apprehended with awe. It is a thought to open the fountains of the soul. As the orator says,

[Omitted is a long summary of the address.]

Now to our thinking this is high doctrine—timely, and well put. We trust all who have heard or read will lay it to heart, and go forth in the brightening day of a Christian, free literature with solemn purpose, patient resolve, cheerful hope, and forgiving tolerance; filled with the thought that, "God is working in them to will and do of his good pleasure"; and greeting each brother heir of immortality with a reverence and a benediction.

We have endeavored to give a skeleton of this, to us deeply interesting address, and now would proceed to remark upon the subject-matter itself. The theme proposed by the orator is the "American Scholar." Why did he not say Author? Every man is or should be a "student," "man thinking." On every mind Nature, the Past, and Action, pour their influences. Some of the most active souls—the freest, bravest thinkers of our time and country, communicate their observations, make their instincts prevalent, embody their highest spiritual vision; but it is only in their lives—their manners—their public acts—their social talk. They fill up the idea of the orator's "scholar." But they are not authors; they do not utter the spirit that is in them. They are the seers, but not the poets—the teachers, but not the artists of the time. Their influence is falling on the mountains and in the vales, instilling through the mass of the universal mind the waters of life, which one day shall well forth in crystal gleams and musical trillings to swell the stream of a truly American literature, and pour along a fertilizing stream of thought. When and how shall our *Authors* be formed? They are forming. When the idea of human brotherhood, of sonship to God—of

27

eternal reason in each human soul—of respect for man—shall be assimilated and organized in our social frame, then shall American Literature go forth in vigor, symmetry, and graceful action. Men will utter when they are filled with the spirit. Our manners, our tone of life, our habits of thought, our social garniture, are a worn out casing, and the new robes of nature's handiwork to clothe a higher form of life as yet but imperfectly grown. Many a poet is walking now our green hill sides, toiling in our mechanic shops, ay, bartering in the bustling mart, even jostling in the caucus and voting at the polls, living a poem in the round of professional duties and the ever fresh romance of quiet homes. And wherever they are, the forms—the castes—the trappings—the badges—the fashion and parade of life, are seen by them as thin disguises, and the purity and vigor of the soul in each brother, the true spiritual experiences of man beneath God's sky upon God's earth, are the only things of worth. When shall they utter the music which swells sweetly in the chambers of their own spirits? When the standard of man's measure is changed, and persons are prized for what they *are*, not for what they *have*. And whenever and however any one is filled to overflowing with this grand idea of God in the soul of man, he will utter it—he must utter it. He will be an American Author. He may prophesy from the pulpit, at the Lyceum, in the schoolhouse, in the daily press, in books, in public addresses. But the burden of the prophecy will be the same: "Man measures man the world over:" Man's spirit is from God: We are brethren.

In speaking therefore of the training of American authors—we should place first, second, and third, action, or rather *Life*. A man to utter the American spirit, which is now in embryo, and will sooner or later be born into life, should walk in the noonday brightness of the great Idea of our era

and land, till he is quickened by its beams. The great author is he who embodies in language the spirit of his time. The great American author will be he who lives out the American idea—the Christian—the Divine idea of *Brotherhood*.

He must study "Nature." Yes! open his inmost soul to this beautiful smile of God's perfections, that the spirit of God may abide in him as a temple. But nowhere does nature respond to the call within, nowhere do the floods of being answer to the floods of will, as in the form and presence, the ways and deeds and will of man; nowhere, as in the mighty social movement, which ever sweeps along through a silent eternity the ever new present age. The nature of man, and the cycle of that nature, which even now is revolving, is God's voice to us—a new-born creation which angels hymn.

The author must study the "Past." Yes! For every genius, every martyr, every hero, every living soul, has been a hue of promise, which Humanity has caught from the day-spring from on high. And silently through the tide of roving hordes and the storms of desolating revolutions—in calm hours of bright prosperity—and the wide hush of peaceful eras—in the uprising of down trodden millions—and the fervent hopings and prayers of philanthropy, has the present time been slowly preparing— the aloes sometime to bloom.

And the Author must "act." Yes! but chiefly, not "subordinately." He must throw himself heartily into the moving army of the time, and serve an unnoticed private or a followed leader, as his strength may be—willing to be trampled down, so the powers of good triumph. And he must go out into life too, not to build up himself and complete his being only; not to gain wisdom, to gather raw material only—not to stock a vocabulary, not to recreate only—but from a deep insight into the sublimity of daily, hourly, common

28

life, from awe of the force of Providence stirring in the deep springs of the present generation. Not as a scholar, not with a view to literary labor, not as an artist, must he go out among men—but as a brother man, all unconscious that he has uttered any thing, all purposeless of future utterance till it is given. We rejoiced with sympathetic joy when we read that sentence in this address, "I ask not for the great, the remote, the romantic, what is doing in Italy or Arabia; what is Greek Art or Provençal Minstrelsy; I embrace the common, I explore and sit at the feet of the familiar, the low." A distinguished sculptor was asked, "where when the gods had returned to Olympus, and the iconoclastic spirit of the time had overturned the Madonnas and the martyrs, he would look for subjects for his chisel?" "To the grace and poetry of the simple acts of life," was his answer. The greatest painter of the age has breathed his purest ideal beauty through the unpicturesque attire, the easy attitude, the homely plainness, of peasant girlhood. And perfectly true is it, as our orator says, that this idea has inspired the genius of the finest authors of our day. A man must live the life of Jesus, according to his power, would he be a truly American author; yes! he must live a self-forgetting minister to men, in the charities of home and acquaintance—in thankless and unnoticed sympathy,—in painful toil amid great enterprises,—among interests of the day—sacrificing notoriety, relinquishing unfavorite tastes, penetrated through his habitual thoughts with the prayer, that the kingdom of God may come—the kingdom of truth, love, beauty, and happiness—of fresh minds and warm hearts and clear consciences, the kingdom of brother souls in their Father's mansion. And he must do this because he feels the worth of man as man—because he sees the infinite in the finite—the spiritual in the material—the eternal in the present—the divine in man. When his heart is tuned to unison with every chord that vibrates through the moral universe, and responds to the music of love through his whole being, let him pour out the joy of a spirit communing with the All Holy, of an Immoral stepping onward hand in hand with growing spirits on a brightening pathway to heaven.

All this may seem extravagant and enthusiastic. We say it with the calmest conviction. We look for a high-toned literature in this Christian, free land, where the vine of truth is not overgrown with the weeds of past civilization. We fully expect to see *American* authors. And yet more, we feel sure they will form a most numerous class, or rather be *so numerous as not to form a class*. The benefits of the existence of a literary caste have been vaunted. We have no faith in them. The change which has for years been going on, by which more and more minds have been incited to produce their store for the public good—in reviews, miscellanies, essays, fictions, lectures, is we believe auspicious. Literature has become less monkish, more manly. The days of astrology and alchemy in the world of books is over; and those of its astronomy and chemistry have come; and our bark of life will ride the safer, and our comforts be multiplied by the change. Literature should be the reflection of an age upon itself, the self-converse of the race, and the more expressions of its consciousness, the better; or again literature should be the challenge and answer of "all's well," as each generation takes its stand in time. The more minds that light up their tapers, the better. All men have genius, if they will be true to the inward voice. Let them serve God and not men, and bear what testimony they can. We cannot spare them. Literature will thus assume a more conversational, a heartier tone; and no man will be ashamed, afraid, or vain, or proud, to be an author. The age is superficial, it is said—the attention is dissipated by variety—there is a slip-shod style in vogue—thinkers are rare. We doubt much the justice of all this. The energy of the time, perhaps the genius of the time, is chiefly turned to the business of life. But never, we believe, was there a period of healthier intellectual action. The people—the public, crave thought. They passionately follow a strong man who utters his deepest self healthily, naturally; the higher, the purer his message, the better prized by them. And compare the thoughts and style of expression too of our reviews, yes even of light novels, and of newspaper pieces, dashed off as they are by ordinary minds, with what was written by the select few of earlier time, and do they not prove really a wonderful development of the thinking faculties? All writers are to some degree thinkers, if not thinking men. For their own sakes, composition is salutary; it reveals to themselves what force they have in them. The next stage will be the casting off of authority; yes, even that public opinion which now enslaves, and the rising up of an immense class of independent thinkers, to declare what they too have seen of heavenly light through the telescopes in high observatories, or with the naked eye on the bare hills. We sometimes think that the profusion, with which the knowledge of the most interesting facts, laws, and phenomena of nature, of the great miracles of art and invention, of the mighty events of history, of the original characters who have made history,—that the profusion, we say with which a knowledge of these has been diffused to readers and hearers—though done merely to amuse, will produce a fine result. Men seek novelties, something to animate and awake; where will they find them, if not in the infinity of their own spiritual natures and experiences,—in the marvels and wonders of the quite familiar and common? The crowd of authors even now has broken down the aristocracy of literature. Men are no longer notorious for being writers. Poor vanity no longer, or in a less degree, impels fools to ape sages. But yet the instinct of utterance remains. And we need not fear, that minds, which through the deep caverns of their own spirit have passed to Elysian fields, will be hindered from declaring their bright visions, because the air is full of the murmur of voices. Literature must become what it ought to be, the *best* thoughts of *all*, given out in the grand school room, debating hall, and conversazione of the world, rather let us say in the grand family group of God's children. Inspired prophets and apostles of truth will easily be recognised, —and listened to all the more eagerly by those, to whom all past utterances are familiar, and who seek something new. No Paul will be neglected at Athens. And the temptation lessens every day for a man to desert the field which heaven appointed him to till, by running into the mart to speculate in buying up popular applause. The public are tired of parrots. They want men. We feel convinced that our best minds and all minds, instead of being frittered away and dissipated by chasing the butterflies, and hunting the bright shells, and gathering the choice flowers of thoughts, to amuse or be amused with, will confine themselves more and more to laborious working in their own peculiar mines; that our public lectures will lose their desultory and take a systematic character; that private teachers will appear of higher and higher branches of knowledge. And this will prepare the way for independent, thorough, original action of the American mind. And we long to see what will be produced in that democratic age of literature, where no clan of Authors are tolerated longer as the dictators of fashion and the judges of caste in the world of books, but where appeal is only to the spirit of truth; where the court garment is always sincerity's work-day dress.

But we must bring these remarks to a close. We look, we say, for an American literature. We feel as if the old strata of thought, in the old world, had been broken up, with the old manners which clothed them and grew out from them; and as if the fused and melted mass had settled here to form a new world of higher beauty. And the rock basis of a new era will be a philosophy, which recognises the divinity of reason in every soul; which sees the identity of reason and faith, and honors common sense as the voice of truth; which feels the mystery of moral freedom in every man of that perfect liberty of the entire obedience to right, and which bows with awe before the conviction that God is in each human soul, that never is the individual so entirely himself as when at one with the indwelling Spirit. And the life, which will pervade this new world of thought, will be a poetry of love and sympathy for the commonest familiar feel-ing, as well as the higher and holier, and for every human tie and relation. Science is always liberal, for nature is no respecter of persons or of forms. She will speak to the humblest or highest of her children through the light which covers the heavens, as with a canopy for angels, through the swift flashes which rend the mountain, or the unseen influence which follows down the string of the paper kite. And shall not it be, is the world never to see a system of social manners too, growing out from this Christian idea of brotherhood, which shall embody the principles of this philosophy—the spirit of this poetry? Our manners will ever be the leaves to clothe with beauty the trunk and branches of our faith; but through them it must imbibe from the sun of God's love, and the atmosphere of human kindness, a purifying, a vital influence. We shall never have a healthy American Literature, unless we have an American Spirit, an American Manner of Life.

Checklist of Additional Reviews

"Phi Beta Kappa," *Christian Register*, 16 (9 September 1837), 67–72.

C[hristopher]. P[earse]. C[ranch]., "Mr. Emerson's Oration," *Western Messenger*, 4 (November 1837), 184–8.

Christian Register, 17 (10 March 1838), 39.

Divinity School Address

[Andrews Norton],
"The New School in
Literature and Religion,"
Boston *Daily Advertiser*,
27 August 1838, p. 2

There is a strange state of things existing about us in the literary and religious world, of which none of our larger periodicals has yet taken notice. It is the result of this restless craving for notoriety and excitement, which, in one way or another, is keeping our community in a perpetual stir. It has shown itself, we think, particularly since that foolish woman, Miss Martineau, was among us, and stimulated the vanity of her flatterers by loading them in return with the copper coin of her praise, which they easily believed was as good as gold. She was accustomed to talk about her mission, as if she were a special dispensation of Providence, and they too thought that they must all have their missions, and began to "vaticinate," as one of their number has expressed it. But though her genial warmth may have caused the new school to bud and bloom, it was not planted by her.—It owes its origin in part to ill-understood notions, obtained by blundering through the crabbed and dis-gusting obscurity of some of the worst German speculatists, which notions, however, have been received by most of its disciples at second hand, through an interpreter. The atheist Shelley has been quoted and commended in a professedly religious work, called the Western Messenger, but he is not, we conceive, to be reckoned among the patriarchs of the sect. But this honor is due to that hasher up of German metaphysics, the Frenchman, Cousin; and, of late, that hyper-Germanized Englishman, Carlyle, has been the great object of admiration and model of style. Cousin and Carlyle indeed seem to have been transformed into idols to be publicly worshipped; the former for his philosophy, and the latter both for his philosophy and his fine writing; while the veiled image of the German pantheist, Schleiermacher, is kept in the sanctuary.

The characteristics of this school are the most extraordinary assumption, united with great ignorance, and incapacity for reasoning. There is indeed a general tendency among its disciples to disavow learning and reasoning as sources of their higher knowledge.—The mind must be its own unassisted teacher. It discerns transcendental truths by immediate vision, and these truths can no more be communicated to another by addressing his understanding, than the power of *clairvoyance* can be given to one not magnetized. They announce themselves as the prophets and

33

priests of a new future, in which all is to be changed, all old opinions done away, and all present forms of society abolished. But by what process this joyful revolution is to be effected [we] are not told; nor how human happiness and virtue is to be saved from the universal wreck, and regenerated in their Medea's caldron. There are great truths with which they are laboring, but they are unutterable in words to be understood by common minds. To such minds they seem nonsense, oracles as obscure as those of Delphi.

The rejection of reasoning is accompanied with an equal contempt for good taste. All modesty is laid aside. The writer of an article for an obscure periodical, or a religious newspaper, assumes a tone as if he were one of the chosen enlighteners of a dark age.—He continually obtrudes himself upon his reader, and announces his own convictions, as if from their having that character, they were necessarily indisputable.—He floats about magnificently on bladders, which he would have it believed are swelling with ideas.—Common thoughts, sometimes true, oftener false, and "Neutral nonsense, neither false nor true," are exaggerated and twisted out of shape, and forced into strange connexions, to make them look like some grand and new conception. To produce a more striking effect, our common language is abused; antic tricks are played with it; inversions, exclamations, anomalous combinations of words, unmeaning, but coarse and violent, metaphors abound, and withal a strong infusion of German barbarians. Such is the style of Carlyle, a writer of some talent; for his great deficiency is not in this respect, it is in good sense, good taste and soundness of principle; but a writer, who, through his talents, such as they are, through that sort of buffoonery and affectation of manner which throws the reader off his guard, through the indisputable

novelty of his way of writing, and through a somewhat too prevalent taste among us for an over-excited and *convulsionary* style, which we mistake for eloquence, has obtained a degree of fame in this country, very disproportioned to what he enjoys at home, out of the *Westminster Review*. Carlyle, however, as an original, might be tolerated, if one could forget his admirers and imitators.

The state of things described might seem a matter of no great concern, a mere insurrection of folly, a sort of Jack Cade rebellion; which in the nature of things must soon be put down, if those engaged in it were not gathering confidence from neglect, and had not proceeded to attack principles which are the foundation of human society and human happiness. "Silly women," it has been said, and silly young men, it is to be feared, have been drawn away from their christian faith, if not divorced from all that can properly be called religion. The evil is becoming, for the time, disastrous and alarming; and of this fact there could hardly be a more extraordinary and ill boding evidence, than is afforded by a publication, which has just appeared, entitled an "Address, delivered before the Senior class in Divinity College, Cambridge," upon the occasion of that class taking leave of the Institution. "By Ralph Waldo Emerson."

It is not necessary to remark particularly on this composition. It will be sufficient to state generally, that the author professes to reject all belief in Christianity as a revelation, that he makes a general attack upon the Clergy, on the ground that they preach what he calls "Historical Christianity," and that if he believe in God in the proper sense of the term, which one passage might have led his hearers to suppose, his language elsewhere is very ill-judged and indecorous. But what *his* opinions may be is a matter of minor concern; the main question is how it has happened, that religion has been insulted by the delivery of these opinions in the Chapel of the Divinity College at Cambridge, as the last instruction which those were to receive, who were going forth from it, bearing the name of christian preachers. This is a question in which the community is deeply interested. No one can doubt for a moment of the disgust and strong disapprobation with which it must have been heard by the highly respectable officers of that Institution. They must have felt it not only as an insult to religion, but as personal insult to themselves. But this renders the fact of its having been so delivered only the more remarkable. We can proceed but a step in accounting for it. The preacher was invited to occupy the place he did, not by the officers of the Divinity College, but by the members of the graduating class. These gentlemen, therefore, have become accessories, perhaps innocent accessories, to the commission of a great offence; and the public must be desirous of learning what exculpation or excuse they can offer.

It is difficult to believe that they thought this incoherent rhapsody a specimen of fine writing, that they listened with admiration, for instance, when they were told that the religious sentiment "is myrrh, and storax and chlorine and rosemary;" or that they wondered at the profound views of their present Teacher, when he announced to them that "the new Teacher," for whom he is looking, would "see the identity of the law of gravitation with purity of heart;" or that they had not some suspicion of inconsistency, when a new Teacher was talked of, after it had been declared to them, that religious truth "is an intuition," and "cannot be received at second hand."

But the subject is to be viewed under a far more serious aspect. The words God, Religion, Christianity, have a definite meaning, well understood. They express conceptions and truths of unutterable moment to the present and future happiness of man. We well know how shamefully they have been abused in modern times by infidels and pantheists; but their meaning remains the same; the truths which they express are unchanged and unchangeable. The community know what they require when they ask for a Christian Teacher; and should any one approving the doctrines of this discourse assume that character, he would deceive his hearers; he would be guilty of a practical falsehood for the most paltry of temptations; he would consent to live a lie for the sake of being maintained by those whom he had cheated. It is not, however, to be supposed that his vanity would suffer him long to keep his philosophy wholly to himself. This would break out in obscure intimations, ambiguous words, and false and mischievous speculations. But should such preachers abound, and grow confident in their folly, we can hardly overestimate the disastrous effects upon the religious and moral state of the community.

S.X. [Theophilus Parsons], "The New School and Its Opponents," Boston *Daily Advertiser*, 30 August 1838, p. 2

In your paper of Monday you published an article on "The new School in Literature and Religion." The writer speaks strongly of Mr. Emerson's defects and errors; but many who agree with him in thinking these defects great and these errors dangerous, lament that they should be spoken of thus. The tone of this article is so harsh, that in many passages it seems but the outbreak of indignant contempt. It charges the objects of its rebuke with arrogance, and makes the charge with very little manifestation of humility. And while it accuses *them* of ignorance, it speaks of distinguished Europeans in a way which makes us ask with wonder, how the writer could have formed such opinions.

If it was his purpose to give to an uncomfortable feeling the relief of expression, to gratify those who were already disgusted with these "novelties," and to confirm the denial and hatred of those who already deny and hate as he does, he has written as he should. But if he wished to arrest the evil he deplores, to help the "silly women" and "silly young men" about whom the fascinations of the charmer are gathering, if he wrote in kindness and not in anger, then, and it is said with all deference, he has not written wisely.

In the fervor of his reproaches he pays Mr. Emerson and his compeers the unmerited compliment, of placing them in the same class with Cousin and Schleier-macher. But one favorable sentiment occurs in his article; and this is where he speaks of Carlyle as "an original." And this must be accidental—for that writer cannot but know, that while Carlyle *was* original, (now, long since) he was universally acknowledged as one of the most delightful writers of England; but that his admiration of Jean Paul Richter led him soon into imitation, which, in his last and largest works, he carries perhaps beyond any precedent upon the records of literature.

But there is an objection to this article which goes far deeper. The writer seems to identify the school which he attacks with all inquiry—all progress; when he objects to it that it is rhapsodical, incoherent, ignorant and presuming,—he seems to feel as if all this were expressed by calling it *new*. This is to be regretted; not merely because it is a mistake, but because it is precisely *the* mistake which the favorers of Mr. Emerson beg their opponents to make. They know and feel,—and where can he have lived who does not know,—that when the argument against them rests mainly on the supposition that they differ from the old and the past, they are placed in a position of all others the most favorable to their success. Then, all who would hope in the future, all who believe that the fountains of truth are neither sealed nor exhausted, are in fact directed to this new school as to friends who would favor their progress, while others refuse to admit its possibility.

The writer speaks of Mr. Emerson as if he were the head of this school in this country; perhaps this may be just; for his published writings, by which alone I know him, have made a stronger impression than any others of this class. In despite of peculiarities of manner, which sometime appear to go so far beyond affectation as to indicate a mind from which all discipline and order are absent,—his extraordinary brilliancy of language, his frequent beauty of imagery, and the originality of his style, which is admitted even by those who deny that this originality extends to his thoughts,—all these things have won for him decided success. But, be his faults or his mistakes what may—if they are to be encountered, by no other argument, than that they have no written precedent and were not found till the beaten pathways of thought had been deserted, they must be victorious. Nor will this argument be greatly helped, by any form or quantity of contempt or opprobrium. If you say to the young students of this country, that only clouds and misty meteors will fill their field of vision, whenever they dare to look beyond the limits which satisfied the past, you tell them what is not true; and the just and prudent things you may say in connection with this untruth, will profit them the less for it.

There have been ages, and there are lands, where the human mind seeks nothing but repose. Antiquity is there the only standard of truth; and nothing is asked of the future but that it may repeat the present and the past. But not so do we live; not so can we live. The bands of all authority are relaxed; no one seeks the shelter or acknowledges the power of precedent; and if one may speak of it in figures, it might be said that the human mind is abroad upon a pathless sea, and the waves are high, the sky is dark and the winds are loud and angry. But for all this, beyond the clouds the sun still shines; and even the pathless ocean is bounded by the steadfast land; and who can fear the triumph or perpetuity of error. And yet Error would triumph, would permanently reign, if there were nothing to resist her, but anger, derision, intolerance, and blind and fierce denunciation. He who uses only these weapons may call himself the enemy of error, but others will not call him the friend of truth. Why speak of this "School,"—which if it be a "School," embraces men among us, who, whatever be their errors, are not generally despised, and must embrace, if the words of the writer of that article have any significance whatever, some of the most distinguished men of Europe,—why speak of that "School," as if "assumption," "ignorance," "incapacity of reasoning" and whatever else is meant by "neutral nonsense,"—were their common characteristics. The reader of such an article cannot but pause, and ask, where sits the judge who passes such a sentence!

No reader can feel when a writer talks of a "Jack Cade rebellion" that he is as wise as he might be were he more temperate. Nor will it be admitted that there is any one among us authorized by his position in the world of letters, to speak of Victor Cousin as "the hasher up of German metaphysics," or of Carlyle, as a man of "some" talent. Can the writer of that article be ignorant that while Cousin is a man of remarkable originality, the views which he derives from others are drawn far more from the old philosophies than from those of any modern nation. Let his faults be pointed out, let young men be aided and protected in their study of him;—but he that can be turned from his works by this writer's contemptuous sneer at "the Frenchman," may probably employ himself to more advantage than in the study of Philosophy.

The writer calls Schleiermacher a Pantheist. This may be right, but if the subject were not too weighty for the columns of a newspaper, it would be interesting to consider the grounds of this accusation, and to inquire whether it might not be brought, on very similar grounds, and with at least equal justice, against the systems of belief of some, who speak very bitterly of German metaphysics.

Let it not be supposed that we have come forward to defend Mr. Emerson; we hope that his writings will be examined and discussed. Indeed they must be so; but in this controversy we have no part to take; and if we engaged in it, certainly it would not be in their defence.

We object to his works, not because of his "antic tricks with language;" not because he talks of "myrrh and storax and chlorine and rosemary," in a way that offends our taste,—not because he is fragmentary and inconclusive and seldom communicates to the mind of the reader a clear view of any distinct and valuable principle; not even because he sometimes degrades solemn and beautiful truths by so perverting and distorting them, that they may minister to self-admiration;— but because he can find it in his heart to speak of the Bible as in the last paragraph of this Address; because he says such things as that, "if a man is at heart just, so far he is God," and thus preaches a doctrine which leads man to worship his own nature and himself;—and because I can see nowhere in his system those emotions of obedient, trustful, humble love of our Father in Heaven which lie at the root and in the heart of all religion, unless I find them laid as a sacrifice upon the altars of self-love and self-pride. But this subject is too manifestly unfit for the columns of a newspaper, to be pursued farther. And I have touched upon it only to show that I have noticed the article in your paper, not because I am unwilling to have the faults of this "New School" exposed and dealt with, but because I would have them so dealt with as to do good, and not harm.

[G. T. Davis], Review of Divinity School Address, Boston *Morning Post*, 31 August 1838, p. 1

We notice this address, not on account of its intrinsic merits, nor because we sympathize with the peculiar views of the author; but because it has created some little excitement in certain circles, and called forth censures, which, without a word or two of explanation, may affect the characters of some who are very far from entertaining views similar to those which Mr. Emerson is in the habit of putting forth.

We are not likely to be thought peculiarly partial to Mr. Emerson. We shall not soon forget his ill-advised letter to Mr. Van Buren concerning the Cherokees. Nevertheless, we respect Mr. Emerson, as an accomplished scholar—an agreeable and entertaining lecturer—a high minded and honorable man—of a free and independent spirit, willing to utter himself and be himself, and not another. We reverence his honesty—his independence, his boldness. In this respect, we shall always be ready to enroll ourselves among his friends, and to the best of our ability defend his character.

But when it concerns Mr. Emerson's peculiar religious and philosophical views, it is quite another affair. We are not always sure that we understand him, and when we feel confident that we do catch his meaning, we do not always, by any means, approve it. But his views are his own; he has a right to entertain them, and to do his best to propagate them. All we have to do with them, is to examine them if we deem them worth examining, and to reject them, so far as they seem to us to be false or unsound. For ourselves, we have no fears that the cause of truth can be essentially injured, or retarded, by the promulgation of error. Error has always a tendency to destroy itself.

There is one thing, however, we wish to notice, and concerning which we think it desirable the public should be set in the right. There has been for sometime manifested, in certain quarters, a disposition to throw into the same category, men who have very little in common, and who entertain opinions, in philosophical and religious matters, widely different. This disposition was strikingly displayed by a writer in the Daily Advertiser of Monday last. That writer speaks of a "New School in Literature and Religion," as having lately sprung up amongst us; and he gives it, for its chiefs, the distinguished French philosopher, Victor Cousin; and the somewhat distinguished, but eccentric, Germanized-English scholar, Thomas Carlyle. He also adroitly seizes upon this address of Mr. Emerson, as a sort of exposition of the doctrines of the New School. Now in all this there is much misconception, or great disingenuousness.

There are undoubtedly, certain movements, tendencies, amongst us, which may in time, lead to the creation of a New School in Literature. A new school is certainly needed, from which may come forth a literature in perfect harmony with the higher nature of man and the democratic spirit of the institutions of this country. There are many warm hearts here craving such a school, and many noble spirits at work in earnest to create it. Nevertheless, it is hardly true to say that a New School has as yet been created.

As it concerns the movements, the tendencies, to which the writer in question alludes, it is certain that they have been much influenced by the publications of Cousin and Carlyle. But there is manifest injustice in classing the friends and admirers of one with the other. It is impossible to conceive two men more unlike than Victor Cousin and Thomas Carlyle. Cousin is a philosopher—a metaphysician—remarkable for his good taste—good sense—uncommon logical powers, and the clearness and elegance of his style. He is a rigorous logician—one of the severest reasoners that can be found. With him no proposition can be admitted till it has given an account of itself, and fully verified its claims to understanding. Carlyle, on the other hand, is no philosopher—no metaphysician. He laughs at metaphysics—at all attempts to account ourselves for ourselves—to account any phenomena of man or of nature, or to form any system of philosophy, politics, theology, or ethics. He is a poet, a seer, who has frequent and glorious glimpses of truth, and of sublime and far reaching truth, too; but one who never verifies what he sets forth as truth—who never asks how he knows what he sees is truth, or shows us how we may know that it is truth. He has genius; in many respects he is a remarkable man; and not withstanding his eccentric, and very objectionable style, he may be read with pleasure, and with profit.

Now the difference there is between these two men is still more striking between their friends in this country. The admirers of Mr. Carlyle, at the head of whom may be placed the author of the address before us, are termed, properly or improperly, Transcendentalists, and are, perhaps, in the main, correctly enough described by the correspondent of the Advertiser. But the friends of M. Cousin, ranked by the same correspondent with them, choose to be eclectics. They are a very different class of men—men of very different literary tendencies and philosophical views. The Transcendentalists, so called, are by no means philosophers; they are either dreamers, or mere speculatists, contemning logic, and holding the understanding in light esteem. The Eclectics aim to be very sober, and a very rational sort of people. They are not materialists—they do not believe John Locke finished philosophy; nevertheless, they profess to follow an experimental method of philosophizing. They differ from the Scotch school of Reid and Stewart, only in going a little further in the same route. They do not believe, indeed, that all our ideas originate in the senses; they believe that the reason furnishes from its own stores certain elements of every fact of consciousness; but at the same time they believe, with the German philosopher, Kant— "that all our knowledge begins with experience," and that the ideas or elements furnished by the reason, are developed only on occasion of experience. As philosophers, their aim is, by analysis, to separate, in the case of all the facts of consciousness, the rational elements from the sensible elements, and, by training each to their source, to determine the origin and validity of our ideas, to fix the criterion of truth, and to account for, and legitimate the universal beliefs of mankind. With the Transcendentalists, they admit Spontaneity or Instinct, the fact of primitive Intuition; but they differ from the Transcendentalists in this important particular, that whereas the Transcendentalists tell us that Instinct is to be taken as our guide without any effort to legitimate it, thereby rejecting reflection, reasoning, all philosophic thought properly so called; the Eclectics summon Instinct, Intuition itself to the bar of reason and refuse to obey it, till it has legitimated to the understanding its right to command.

To all who are competent to judge of the matter, here is surely a wide difference, and one which no man can be pardoned for overlooking. They whom we have designated as Transcendentalists, are not in the habit of speaking respectfully of Cousin. They do not study him, and we may venture to assert, that they are ignorant of both the method and spirit of his philosophy. It is wrong, altogether wrong, therefore, to represent them as the followers of Cousin. It is a wrong to them; and a still greater wrong to those individuals among us who do really study and take an interest in Cousin's system of philosophy. Honor to whom honor is due, is a good maxim; and give to every one his due, is a precept that no advocate for religion and morality has any right, on any occasion whatever, to neglect.

We have made these remarks for the sole purpose of pointing out, and requiring the public to notice an obvious, and as we regard it, a very essential difference between the two classes ranked in the same category by the correspondent of the Advertiser. For ourselves, we are not disposed to make war on either class. We say, let all opinions, all doctrines, have an "open field and fair play." We cannot, however, believe that the peculiar views set forth with so much confidence and fascination by Mr. Emerson, are likely to take a very deep root in the American heart. They are too dreamy, too misty, too vague, to have much effect except on young misses just from boarding school, or young lads, who begin to fancy themselves in love. The Americans are a sturdy race; they are reasoning people, and they will not long follow any one who cannot give to the understanding a reason for the hope that is in him.

The popularity Mr. Emerson has acquired for the moment, and which seems to have alarmed some of the grave Doctors at Cambridge, is easily accounted for, without supposing any especial regard for his peculiar notions. Something is due to his personal manners, much to the peculiar characteristics of his style as a writer and as a lecturer; but still more to his independence, to the homage he pays to the spirit of freedom. Our young men have grown weary of leading strings. They are dissatisfied with the tyranny which custom, conventionalism has exercised over them. They have felt the old formulas too straitened for them, and the air of their prison-houses too compressed, and too oppressive, and they have wished to break away, to roam at large over green fields, and to breathe the fresh air of heaven. The state of mind here described, and which we may term a craving after freedom, exists in our community to a very great extent. To this craving Mr. Emerson has spoken; this craving he has done something to satisfy; therefore, his popularity. It is as the advocate of the rights of the mind, as the defender of personal independence in the spiritual world, not as the Idealist, the Pantheist, or the Atheist, that he is run after, and all but worshipped by many young, ardent and yet noble minds. In this we see an omen of good and not of evil. It is a proof that the spirit of liberty is yet living and active in our community; that the American institutions are doing their work, and embodying their sublime Idea in literature, art, and religion. For this we are thankful, and in it we rejoice.

The Cambridge Professors who denounce Mr. Emerson, are very unwise, and seem to be verifying the old maxim, "who the Gods will to destroy they first deprive of reason." Their own sensibility to the free spirit of the age and country is the cause which leads the young men, committed to their care, to seek inspiration and instruction elsewhere. And elsewhere they will be sure to continue to go, unless their regular Professors prove themselves capable of meeting the wants of their souls. They want freedom and life, and they will go where freedom and life are to be found. Let the Professors be assured of this, and govern themselves accordingly. They must show that freedom and life can be found elsewhere than in connection with the speculations of Ralph Waldo Emerson, or to Ralph Waldo Emerson they may rest assured their pupils will resort.

[Orestes A. Brownson], "Mr. Emerson's Address," *Boston Quarterly Review*, 1 (October 1838), 500–14

This is in some respects a remarkable address,—remarkable for its own character and for the place where and the occasion on which it was delivered. It is not often, we fancy, that such an address is delivered by a clergyman in a Divinity College to a class of young men just ready to go forth into the churches as preachers of the Gospel of Jesus Christ. Indeed it is not often that a discourse teaching doctrines like the leading doctrines of this, is delivered by a professedly religious man, anywhere or on any occasion.

We are not surprised that this address should have produced some excitement and called forth some severe censures upon its author; for we have long known that there are comparatively few who can hear with calmness the utterance of opinions to which they do not subscribe. Yet we regret to see the abuse which has been heaped upon Mr. Emerson. We ought to learn to tolerate all opinions, to respect every man's right to form and to utter his own opinions whatever they may be. If we regard the opinions as unsound, false, or dangerous, we should meet them calmly, refute them if we can; but be careful to respect, and to treat with all Christian meekness and love, him who entertains them.

There are many things in this address we heartily approve; there is much that we admire and thank the author for having uttered. We like its life and freshness, its freedom and independence, its richness and beauty. But we cannot help regarding its tone as somewhat arrogant, its spirit is quite too censorious and desponding, its philosophy as indigested, and its reasoning as inconclusive. We do not like its mistiness, its vagueness, and its perpetual use of old words in new senses. Its meaning too often escapes us; and we find it next to impossible to seize its dominant doctrine and determine what it is or what it is not. Moreover, it does not appear to us to be all of the same piece. It is made up of parts borrowed from different and hostile systems, which "baulk and baffle" the author's power to form into a consistent and harmonious whole.

In a moral point of view the leading doctrine of this address, if we have seized it, is not a little objectionable. It is not easy to say what that moral doctrine is; but so far as we can collect it, it is, that the soul possesses certain laws or instincts, obedience to which constitutes its perfection. "The sentiment of virtue is a reverence and delight in the presence of certain divine laws." "The intuition of the moral sentiment is an insight of the perfection of the laws of the soul." These "divine laws" are the "laws of the soul." The moral sentiment results from the perception of these laws, and moral character results from conformity to them. Now this is not, we apprehend, psychologically true. If any man will analyze the moral sentiment as a fact of consciousness, he will find it something more than "an insight of the perfection of the laws of the soul." He will find that it is a sense of obligation. Man feels himself under obligation to obey a law; not the law of his own soul, a law emanating from his soul as lawgiver; but a law above his soul, imposed upon him by a supreme lawgiver, who has a right to command his obedience. He does never feel that he is moral in obeying merely the laws of his own nature, but in obeying the command of a power out of him, above him, and independent on him.

By the laws of the soul, we presume, Mr. Emerson means our instincts. In his Phi Beta Kappa Address, reviewed in this journal for January, he speaks much of the instincts, and bids us "plant ourselves on our instincts, and the huge world will come round to us." The ethical rule he lays down is then, "follow thy instincts," or as he expresses it in the address before us, "obey thyself." Now if we render this rule into the language it will assume in practice, we must say, obey thyself,—follow thy instincts,—follow thy inclinations,—live as thou listest. Strike out the idea of something above man to which he is accountable, make him accountable only to himself, and why shall he not live as he listeth? We see not what restraint can legitimately be imposed upon any of his instincts or propensities. There may then be some doubts whether the command, "obey thyself," be an improvement on the Christian command, "deny thyself."

We presume that when Mr. Emerson tells us to obey ourselves, to obey the laws of our soul, to follow our instincts, he means that we shall be true to our higher nature, that we are to obey our higher instincts, and not our baser propensities. He is himself a pure minded man, and would by no means encourage sensuality. But how shall we determine which are our higher instincts and which are our lower instincts? We do not perceive that he gives us any instructions on this point. Men like him may take the higher instincts to be those which lead us to seek truth and beauty; but men in whom the sensual nature overlays the spiritual, may think differently; and what rule has he for determining which is in the right? He commands us to be ourselves, and sneers at the idea of having "models." We must take none of the wise or good, not even Jesus Christ as a model of what we should be. We are to act out ourselves. Now why is not the sensualist as moral as the spiritualist, providing he acts out himself? Mr. Emerson is a great admirer of Carlyle; and according to Carlyle, the moral man, the true man, is he who acts out himself. A Mirabeau, or a Danton is, under a moral point of view, the equal of a Howard or a Washington, because equally true to himself. Does not this rule confound all moral distinctions, and render moral judgments a "formula," all wise men must "swallow and make away with"?

But suppose we get over this difficulty and determine which are the higher instincts of our nature, those which we must follow in order to perfect our souls, and become,—as Mr. Emerson has it,—God; still we ask, why are we under obligation to obey these instincts? Because obedience to them will perfect our souls? But why are we bound to perfect our souls? Where there is no sense of obligation, there is no moral sense. We are moral only on the condition that we feel there is something which we *ought* to do. Why ought we to labor for our own perfection? Because it will promote our happiness? But why are we morally bound to seek our own happiness? It may be very desirable to promote our happiness, but it does not follow from that we are morally bound to do it, and we know there are occasions when we should not do it.

Put the rule, Mr. Emerson lays down, in the best light possible, it proposes nothing higher than our own individual good as the end to be sought. He would tell us to reduce all the jarring elements of our nature to harmony, and produce and maintain perfect order in the soul. Now is this the highest good the reason can conceive? Are all things in the universe to be held subordinate to the individual soul? Shall a man take himself as the centre of the universe, and say all things are for his use, and count them of value only as they contribute something to his growth or well-being? This were a deification of the soul with a vengeance. It were nothing but a system of transcendental selfishness. It were pure egotism. According to this, I am everything; all else is nothing, at least nothing except what it derives from the fact that it is something to me.

Now this system of pure egotism, seems to us to run through all Mr. Emerson's writings. We meet it everywhere in his masters, Carlyle and Goethe. He and they may not be quite so grossly selfish as were some of the old sensualist philosophers; they may admit a higher good than the mere gratification of the senses, than mere wealth or fame; but the highest good they recognise is an individual good, the realization of order in their own individual souls. Everything by them is estimated according to its power to contribute to this end. If they mingle with men it is to use them; if they are generous and humane, if they labor to do good to others, it is always as a means, never as an end. Always is the *doing*, whatever it be, to terminate in self. Self, the higher self, it is true, is always the centre of gravitation. Now is the man who adopts this moral rule, really a moral man? Does not morality always propose to us an end separate from our own, above our own, and to which our own good is subordinate?

No doubt it is desirable to perfect the individual soul, to realize order in the individual; but the reason, the moment it is developed, discloses a good altogether superior to this. Above the good of the individual, and paramount to it, is the good of the universe, the realization of the good of creation, absolute good. No man can deny that the realization of the good of all beings is something superior to the realization of the good of the individual. Morality always requires us to labor for the highest good we can conceive. The moral law then requires us to seek another good than that of our own

souls. The individual lives not for himself alone. His good is but an element, a fragment of the universal good, and is to be sought never as an end, but always as a means of realizing absolute good, or universal order. This rule requires the man to forget himself, to go out of himself, and under certain circumstances to deny himself, to sacrifice himself, for a good which does not centre in himself. He who forgets himself, who is disinterested and heroic, who sacrifices himself for others, is in the eyes of reason, infinitely superior to the man who merely uses others as the means of promoting his own intellectual and spiritual growth. Mr. Emerson's rule then is defective, inasmuch as it proposes the subordinate as the paramount, and places obligation where we feel it is not. For the present, then, instead of adopting his formula, "obey thyself," or Carlyle's formula, "act out thyself," we must continue to approve the Christian formula, "deny thyself, and love thy neighbor as thyself."

But passing over this, we cannot understand how it is possible for a man to become virtuous by yielding to his instincts. Virtue is voluntary obedience to a moral law, felt to be obligatory. We are aware of the existence of the law, and we act in reference to it, and intend to obey it. We of course are not passive, but active in the case of virtue. Virtue is always personal. It is our own act. We are in the strictest sense of the word the cause or creator of it. Therefore it is, that we judge ourselves worthy of praise when we are virtuous, and of condemnation when we are not virtuous. But in following instinct, we are not active but passive. The causative force at work in our instincts, is not our personality, our wills, but an impersonal force, a force *we* are not. Now in yielding to our instincts, as Mr. Emerson advises us, we abdicate our own personality, and from persons become things, as incapable of virtue as the trees of the forest or the stones of the field.

Mr. Emerson, moreover, seems to us to mutilate man, and in his zeal for the instincts to entirely overlook reflection. The instincts are all very well. They give us the force of character we need, but they do not make up the whole man. We have understanding as well as instinct, reflection as well as spontaneity. Now to be true to our nature, to the whole man, the understanding should have its appropriate exercise. Does Mr. Emerson give it this exercise? Does he not rather hold the understanding in light esteem, and labor almost entirely to fix our minds on the fact of primitive intuition as all-sufficient of itself? We do not ask him to reject the instincts, but we ask him to compel them to give an account of themselves. We are willing to follow them; but we must do it designedly, intentionally, after we have proved our moral right to do it, not before. Here is an error in Mr. Emerson's system of no small magnitude. He does not account for the instincts nor legitimate them. He does not prove them to be divine forces or safe guides. In practice, therefore, he is merely reviving the old sentimental systems of morality, systems which may do for the young, the dreamy, or the passionate, but never for a sturdy race of men and women who demand a reason for all they do, for what they approve or disapprove.

Nor are we better satisfied with the theology of this discourse. We cannot agree with Mr. Emerson in his account of the religious sentiment. He confounds the religious sentiment with the moral; but the two sentiments are psychologically distinct. The religious sentiment is a craving to adore, resulting from the soul's intuition of the Holy; the moral sentiment is a sense of obligation resulting from the soul's intuition of a moral law. The moral sentiment leads us up merely to universal order; the religious sentiment leads us up to God, the Father of universal order. Religious ideas always carry us into a region far above that of moral ideas. Religion gives the law to ethics, not ethics to religion. Religion is the communion of the soul with God, morality is merely the *cultus exterior*, the outward worship of God, the expression of the life of God in the soul: as James has it, "pure religion,— external worship, for so should we understand the original,—and undefiled before God and the Father is this, To visit the fatherless and widows in their affliction, and to keep himself unspotted from the world."

But even admitting the two sentiments are not two but one, identical, we are still dissatisfied with Mr. Emerson's account of the matter. The religious sentiment, according to him, grows out of the soul's insight of the perfection of its own laws. These laws are in fact the soul itself. They are not something distinct from the soul, but its essence. In neglecting them the soul is not itself, in finding them it finds itself, and in living them it is God. This is his doctrine. The soul then in case of the religious sentiment has merely an intuition of itself. Its craving to adore is not a craving to adore something superior to itself. In worshipping then, the soul does not worship God, a being above man and independent on him, but it worships itself. We must not then speak of worshipping God, but merely of worshipping the soul. Now is this a correct account of the religious sentiment? The religious sentiment is in the bottom of the soul, and it is always a craving of the soul to go out of itself, and fasten itself on an object above itself, free from its own weakness, mutability, and impurity, on a being all-sufficient, all-sufficing, omnipotent, immutable, and all-holy. It results from the fact that we are conscious of not being sufficient for ourselves, that the ground of our being is not in ourselves, and from the need we feel of an Almighty arm on which to lean, a strength foreign to our own, from which we may derive support. Let us be God, let us feel that we need go out of ourselves for nothing, and we are no longer in the condition to be religious; the religious sentiment can no longer find a place in our souls, and we can no more feel a craving to adore than God himself. Nothing is more evident to us, than that the religious sentiment springs, on the one hand, solely from a sense of dependence, and on the other hand, from an intuition of an invisible Power, Father, God, on whom we may depend, to whom we may go in our weakness, to whom we may appeal when oppressed, and who is able and willing to succor us. Take away the idea of such a God, declare the soul sufficient for itself, forbid it ever to go out of itself, to look up to a power above it, and religion is out of the question.

If we rightly comprehend Mr. Emerson's views of God, he admits no God but the laws of the soul's perfection. God is in man, not out of him. He is in the soul as the oak is in the acorn. When man fully developes the laws of his nature, realizes the ideal of his nature, he is not, as the Christian would say, godlike, but he is God. The ideal of man's nature is not merely similar in all men, but identical. When all men realize the ideal of their nature, that is, attain to the highest perfection admitted by the laws of their being, then do they all become swallowed up in the One Man. There will then no longer be men; all diversity will be lost in unity, and there will be only One Man, and that one man will be God. But what and where is God now? Before all men have realized the ideal of their nature, and become swallowed up in the One Man, is there really and actually a God? Is there any God but the God Osiris, torn into pieces and scattered up and down through all

the earth, which pieces, scattered parts, the weeping Isis must go forth seeking everywhere, and find not without labor and difficulty? Can we be said to have at present anything more than the disjected members of a God, the mere embryo fragments of a God, one day to come forth into the light, to be gathered up that nothing be lost, and finally moulded into one complete and rounded God? So it seems to us, and we confess, therefore, that we can affix no definite meaning to the religious language which Mr. Emerson uses so freely.

Furthermore, we cannot join Mr. Emerson in his worship to the soul. We are disposed to go far in our estimate of the soul's divine capacities; we believe it was created in the image of God, and may bear his moral likeness; but we cannot so exalt it as to call it God. Nor can we take its ideal of its own perfection as God. The soul's conception of God is not God, and if there be no God out of the soul, out of the *me*, to answer to the soul's conception, then is there no God. God as we conceive him is independent on us, and is in no sense affected by our conceptions of him. He is in us, but not us. He dwells in the hearts of the humble and contrite ones, and yet the heaven of heavens cannot contain him. He is the same yesterday, to-day, and forever. He is above all, the cause and sustainer of all that is, in whom we live and move and have our being. Him we worship, and only him. We dare not worship merely our own soul. Alas, we know our weakness; we feel our sinfulness; we are oppressed with a sense of our unworthiness, and we cannot so sport with the solemnities of religious worship, as to direct them to ourselves, or to anything which does not transcend our own being.

Yet this worship of the soul is part and parcel of the transcendental egotism of which we spoke in commenting on Mr. Emerson's moral doctrines. He and his masters, Carlyle and Goethe, make the individual soul everything, the centre of the universe, for whom all exists that does exist; and why then should it not be the supreme object of their affections? Soul-worship, which is only another name for self-worship, or the worship of self, is the necessary consequence of their system, a system well described by Pope in his Essay on Man:

"Ask for what end the heavenly bodies shine,
Earth for whose use? Pride answers, "T is for mine:
For me, kind nature wakes her genial power,
Suckles each herb, and spreads out every flower;
Annual for me, the grape, the rose, renew
The juice nectareous, and the balmy dew;
For me, the mine a thousand treasures brings;
For me, health gushes from a thousand springs:
Seas roll to waft me, suns to light me rise;
My footstool earth, my canopy the skies.'"

To which we may add,

"While man exclaims, 'See all things for my use!'
'See man for mine!' replies a pampered goose:
And just as short of reason he must fall
Who thinks all made for one, not one for all."

Mr. Emerson has much to say against preaching a traditional Christ, against preaching what he calls historical Christianity. So far as his object in this is to draw men's minds off from an exclusive attention to the "letter," and to fix them on the "spirit," to prevent them from relying for the matter and evidence of their faith on merely historical documents, and to induce them to reproduce the gospel histories in their own souls, he is not only not censurable but praiseworthy. He is doing a service to the Christian cause. Christianity may be found in the human soul, and reproduced in human experience now, as well as in the days of Jesus. It is in the soul too that we must find the key to the meaning of the Gospels, and in the soul's experience that we must seek the principal evidences of their truth.

But if Mr. Emerson means to sever us from the past, and to intimate that the Christianity of the past has ceased to have any interest for the present generation, and that the knowledge and belief of it are no longer needed for the soul's growth, for its redemption and union with God, we must own we cannot go with him. Christianity results from the development of the laws of the human soul, but from a supernatural, not a natural, development; that is, by the aid of a power above the soul. God has been to the human race both a father and an educator. By a supernatural,—not an *un*natural—influence, he has, as it has seemed proper to him, called forth our powers, and enables us to see and comprehend the truths essential to our moral progress. The records of the aid he has at different ages furnished us, and of the truths seen and comprehended at the period when the faculties of the soul were supernaturally exalted, cannot in our judgment be unessential, far less improper, to be dwelt upon by the Christian preacher.

Then again, we cannot dispense with Jesus Christ. As much as some may wish to get rid of him, or to change or improve his character, the world needs him, and needs him in precisely the character in which the Gospels present him. His is the only name whereby men can be saved. He is the father of the modern world, and his is the life we now live, so far as we live any life at all. Shall we then crowd him away with the old bards and seers, and regard him and them merely as we do the authors of some old ballads which charmed our forefathers, but which may not be sung in a modern drawing-room? Has his example lost its power, his life its quickening influence, his doctrine its truth? Have we outgrown him as a teacher?

In the Gospels we find the solution of the great problem of man's destiny; and, what is more to our purpose, we find there the middle term by which the creature is connected with the Creator. Man is at an infinite distance from God; and he cannot by his own strength approach God, and become one with him. We cannot see God; we cannot know him; no man hath seen the Father at any time, and no man knoweth the Father, save the Son, and he to whom the Son reveals him. We approach God only through a mediator; we see and know only the Word, which is the mediator between God and men. Does Mr. Emerson mean that the record we have of this Word in the Bible, of this Word, which was made flesh, incarnated in the man Jesus and dwelt among men and disclosed the grace and truth with which it overflowed, is of no use now in the church, nay, that it is a let and a hindrance? We want that record, which is to us as the testimony of the race, to corroborate the witness within us. One witness is not enough. We have one witness within us, an important witness, too seldom examined; but as important as he is, he is not alone sufficient. We must back up his individual testimony with that of the race. In the Gospel records we have the testimony borne by the race to the great truths it most concerns us to know. That testimony, the testimony of history, in conjunction with our own individual experience, gives us all the certainty we ask, and

furnishes us a solid ground for an unwavering and active faith. As in philosophy, we demand history as well as psychology, so in theology we ask the historical Christ as well as the psychological Christ. The church in general has erred by giving us only the historical Christ; but let us not now err, by preaching only a psychological Christ.

In dismissing this address, we can only say that we have spoken of it freely, but with no improper feeling to its author. We love bold speculation; we are pleased to find a man who dares tell us what and precisely what he thinks, however unpopular his views may be. We have no disposition to check his utterance, by giving his views a bad name, although we deem them unsound. We love progress, and progress cannot be effected without freedom. Still we wish to see a certain sobriety, a certain reserve in all speculations, something like timidity about rushing off into an unknown universe, and some little regret in departing from the faith of our fathers.

Nevertheless, let not the tenor of our remarks be mistaken. Mr. Emerson is the last man in the world we should suspect of conscious hostility to religion and morality. No one can know him or read his productions without feeling a profound respect for the singular purity and uprightness of his character and motives. The great object he is laboring to accomplish is one in which he should receive the hearty cooperation of every American scholar, of every friend of truth, freedom, piety, and virtue. Whatever may be the character of his speculations, whatever may be the moral, philosophical, or theological system which forms the basis of his speculations, his real object is not the inculcation of any new theory on man, nature, or God; but to induce men to think for themselves on all subjects, and to speak from their own full hearts and earnest convictions. His object is to make men scorn to be slaves to routine, to custom, to established creeds, to public opinion, to the great names of this age, of this country, or of any other. He cannot bear the idea that a man comes into the world to-day with the field of truth monopolized and foreclosed. To every man lies open the whole field of truth, in morals, in politics, in science, in theology, in philosophy. The labors of past ages, the revelations of prophets and bards, the discoveries of the scientific and the philosophic, are not to be regarded as superseding our own exertions and inquiries, as impediments to the free action of our own minds, but merely as helps, as provocations to the freest and fullest spiritual action of which God has made us capable.

This is the real end he has in view, and it is a good end. To call forth the free spirit, to produce the conviction here implied, to provoke men to be men, self-moving, self-subsisting men, not mere puppets, moving but as moved by the reigning mode, the reigning dogma, the reigning school, is a grand and praiseworthy work, and we should reverence and aid, not abuse and hinder him who gives himself up soul and body to its accomplishment. So far as the author of the address before us is true to this object, earnest in executing this work, he has our hearty sympathy, and all the aid we, in our humble sphere, can give him. In laboring for this object, he proves himself worthy of his age and his country, true to religion and to morals. In calling, as he does, upon the literary men of our community, in the silver tones of his rich and eloquent voice, and above all by the quickening influence of his example, to assert and maintain their independence throughout the whole domain of thought, against every species of tyranny that would encroach upon it, he is doing his duty; he is doing a work the effects of which will be felt for good far and wide, long after men shall have forgotten the puerility of his conceits, the affectations of his style, and the unphilosophical character of his speculations. The doctrines he puts forth, the positive instructions, for which he is now censured, will soon be classed where they belong: but the influence of his free spirit, and free utterance, the literature of this country will long feel and hold in grateful remembrance.

[James Freeman Clarke], "R. W. Emerson and the New School," *Western Messenger*, 6 (November 1838), 37–47

We perceive that our friends in Boston, and its vicinity, have been a good deal roused and excited by an address, delivered by the gentleman whose name stands above. Mr. Emerson has been long known as a man of pure and noble mind, of original genius and independent thought. Formerly settled as a Unitarian Preacher over the Second Church, in Boston, he left his charge, with feelings of mutual regret, on account of his having adopted the Quaker opinion in relation to the ordinance of the Lord's Supper. Since that time he has published a small volume called "Nature," and delivered various addresses and lectures on subjects of Literature, Philosophy, and Morals. All these productions have shown a mind of extreme beauty and originality. Their style, however, has been so different from the usual one, so completely Emersonian, as to confound and puzzle some, and disgust others. Many thought too, that they detected in his thoughts and doctrines the germs of dangerous errors. On the other hand, he has been surrounded by a band of enthusiastic admirers, whom the genius, life and manliness of his thoughts attracted, and his beautiful delivery as a public speaker charmed.

Matters stood thus, when he was invited to make an address to the parting class at the Cambridge Theological School. He readily accepted their offer and the result was that they heard an address quite different, we judge, from what ever fell into the ears of a Theological class before. He told them "that the faith of Christ was not now preached," that "the Priest's Sabbath has lost the splendor of nature; it is un-holy; we are glad when it is done; we can make, we do make, even sitting in our pews, a far better, holier, sweeter for ourselves." This was not polite to the preachers, of whom we suppose many were present, and must have been rather disagreeable to bear—especially as no exception seemed to be made in behalf of his own sect. Instead of inculcating the importance of church-going, and shewing how they ought to persuade every body to go to church, he seemed to think it better to stay at home than to listen to a formal lifeless preacher. Instead of exhorting them to be always doing the duties of a pastor, he tells them not to be too anxious, to visit periodically, each family in their parish connection. Such things as these he told them, and moreover introduced them by some general remarks, which we cannot agree with him in thinking, that "while they are general, none will contest them." Notwithstanding their generality, they seemed to excite quite as much opposition as the other part of this harrangue.

Immediately after the delivery of this address, a lively discussion and controversy sprung up with respect to its doctrines, of which the end is not yet. First, there appears an article in the Boston Daily Advertiser,[1] in which Mr. Emerson is accused of rejecting all belief in Christianity as a revelation, and as probably disbelieving in the existence of a God. The graduating class are rebuked as having become accessories to the commission of a great offence, in asking him to address them, and are called upon, in a tone of great authority, to make their exculpation or excuse before the public.

Some remarks are prefixed concerning a New School in Literature and Philosophy which we shall notice again by and by. In the same paper, there shortly appears a reply to this first attack on Mr. Emerson. This reply is well written, only a little too poetical for controversy, as his opponent observed. Its author does not, however, defend Mr. Emerson, on the whole he agrees with his opponent respecting him, but does not like the *manner* of the attack. He thinks it altogether too harsh and severe to do any good.

Then comes a good democratic article in the Morning Post, censuring Mr. Emerson for some things, and praising him for others—then follow various communications in the Courier, and in the Register, with editorials appended, lamenting that Mr. Emerson should turn out an Atheist, or enquiring whether all Unitarians think as he does? which the Editor very promptly denies. Then comes a very thorough discussion of the doctrines of the Address in the Boston Review, in which, while Mr. Emerson is treated with courtesy and respect, his supposed opinions are very sharply examined. Again, we hear that Dr. Henry Ware, Jr. has published two sermons upon the subject of this Address. We are sure that his name will never be appended to any productions not written with clear thought and in a Christian Spirit.[2]

On the whole, we think that the results of this controversy will be excellent. It will show that our Unitarian plan of church union works better in a case of real or supposed heresy, than any other. How is it in those churches where they are bound together by a minute creed? A man publishes a sermon, containing some point supposed to be objectionable; he is tried by his Presbytery, condemned, appeals to his Synod, acquitted; referred to the Assembly, and deposed. He goes on preaching, his party increases, and a rent takes place in a great church, when the entering wedge was a thin pair of vol-

umes. In our church, on the other hand, we have no creed but the Christian Scriptures. A man proclaims some strange sounding doctrine. Whoever feels most keenly that this is an Anti-Christian one, comes out against it with severity. This brings out other opinions, already formed, of various characters. This excites the attention of others. The discussion follows, for the bitterness all dies away—but men who seriously set themselves to *thinking* are not apt to get angry. But when the business is not to think it down, but to vote it down, to get together a party, and bind them together and heat them up by party conventions—there, it seems to us, things are likely to go a little warmly, and we shall hear more denunciation than argument.

For ourselves, we are convinced that if Mr. Emerson has taught any thing very wrong, it will be found out, and then he will quietly drop out of the Unitarian church, or the Unitarian church will fall off from him. No *excommunication* is necessary. Where people are held together by no outward bond, if the inward attraction ceases, they will soon drop apart.

The question, however, is, *has* he taught any thing wrong? Is he opposed to historical Christianity? Has he given any ground for supposing that he does not believe in the God of Christianity?

To give our opinion at length, on these points is out of the question—we have neither ability nor will to do it. To confess the truth, when we received and read the Address, we did not discover anything in it objectionable at all. We were quite delighted with it. We read it, to be sure, looking for good and not evil, and we found enough that was good to satisfy us. Parts seemed somewhat obscure, and for that we were sorry—in places we felt hurt by the phraseology, but we bounded carelessly over these rocks of offence and pitfalls, enjoying the beauty, sincerity and magnanimity of the general current of the Address. As critics, we confess our fault. We should have been more on the watch, more ready to suspect our author when he left the broad road-way of common-place, and instantly snap him up when he stated any idea new to us, or differing from our pre-conceived opinions.

But we must be serious—we have already, perhaps, treated his subject too long ironically. The most serious charges that can be brought against a Christian man, have been laid against our author, founded on the contents of this discourse. He has been accused of Infidelity, disbelief in historical Christianity—and of probable Atheism or Pantheism. That charity which thinketh no evil, rejoiceth not in iniquity and hopeth all things, should induce every man most carefully to pause before he brings such charges against a brother. If Mr. Emerson maintains these sentiments, we can no longer hold any fellowship with him, for a wide chasm yawns between our sympathies. But not for an obscure passage in an address, would we believe this of a man whose course of life has been always open—whose opinions never lay hid, and who, being such an one, has preached and still preaches as a Christian Minister.

He is accused of opposing Historical Christianity, that is, we suppose, of disbelief in the historical account of the life of Jesus. Now he speaks very strongly against those whose faith is only an historical one—who believe in Jesus Christ, not feeling him in their own souls as a Savior and Friend, but only acquiescing in the fact of his past existence. He speaks very strongly—without perhaps sufficient care against misconstruction. But does he speak more strongly or unguardedly than Paul did, when he said that the *letter* of the New Testament KILLED, while the spirit gave life? (2 Cor. iii. 6) Does not this sound like doing away entirely with the letter of the New Testament? But Paul only meant, as Mr. Emerson we suppose means, that the letter is a dead weight in the mind, if the spirit does not animate it. How many things are there in the New Testament to show that a bare historical faith in Jesus Christ is not a saving faith—that we must have the witness in our own hearts—that our faith must stand, not in the will of men but the power of God—that our Father in Heaven must reveal it to us. The true doctrine undoubtedly is, that both witnesses are necessary to believe in Christ's divinity—an outward witness, coming down through history, and an inward witness of the spirit in our heart. This is beautifully shown in John xi. 26, 27. "But when the Comforter is come, which I will send unto you from the Father, even the spirit of truth, which proceedeth from the Father, *he shall testify of me; and ye also shall bear witness* because ye have been with me from the beginning."

Now if Mr. Emerson means to deny the value of this second testimony, we think him quite wrong, but we believe he only wishes to have it, as Christ put it, *second*. The common error is to be satisfied with the historical faith, and it is this error which he thought it necessary to oppose.

If Mr. Emerson disbelieves in all our present historical Christianity, how happens it that instead of opposing it, he opposes its *defects*? "The first *defect*" says he "of historical Christianity"—"the second *defect*." And how happened it that in this very Address he used the strongest expression we ever met with, to show the *historical influence* of Jesus Christ? "whose name is not so much written as *ploughed into the history of the world*."

We have been taking the view of the matter, which seems to us at the same time, the most correct, and the most charitable. At the same time we freely admit that there are many expressions which we would gladly have seen altered, or not seen at all; because though not so meant, they sound like irreverence or impiety to the common ear. Thus, where he says in the passage for which he was accused of Pantheism, "If a man is at heart just, then in so far, is he God; the safety of God, the immortality of God, the majesty of God, do enter into that man with justice." Why not be satisfied with the strong language of Jesus and John, and say that if he love, God dwells *in* him, and he in God? or that he *partakes* of the divine nature, as Peter declares. Why go further, and seem to destroy the personality either of God or man by saying that he *is* God? The privilege of being called the *sons of God* seemed to astonish John. "Behold! what manner of love" said he "the Father has shown us, that we should be called the sons of God!" Is it not enough to dwell *in* God, and have God dwell *in us*, but that we must also aspire to *be God*?

We might go on, and find more fault with Mr. Emerson's opinions, and his expressions. But if we prefer, if possible, to stand now as mediators, if it may be, to soften down a little the harshness of the attacks he has already experienced. The Unitarians have already fully vindicated themselves from the charge of agreeing with him in opinion. He has certainly been very soundly rated by them, in some instances we think with too much harshness and dogmatism. For it is too late in the day to put a man down by shouting Atheist, Infidel, Heretic. Formerly you could thus excite a prejudice against him that would prevent men from examining the truth of the charge. Not so now. Men cannot be in this day put down by denunciation. The whole religious pulpit and religious press has united for thirty or forty years in calling Unitarians, Deists. What is the result? That their principles are rapidly spreading. In view of this fact, let us lay aside prejudice and candidly examine every new thing.

Notes

1 "We cannot say that we like this plan of bringing Theological disputes before the world through Political and Commercial prints. There is never space for discussion, and only room to excite prejudices in the minds of those who may be supposed to be previously ignorant of the facts of the case. We do not find that Jesus Christ commands us to tell our brother's fault to the *world*, even after telling it to himself in private. He says 'tell it to the Church.' He does not say 'tell it to the world.'"

2 "And lastly we perceive that some college lad, writing a class-poem, wishing to lash existing abuses, and taking his direction, like the weather-cocks, from the winds, stands up 'severe in youthful wisdom,' tells Mr. Emerson it is very wrong to be an Infidel, and compares him to 'Gibbon and Voltaire!' Ah! unfortunate Mr. Emerson! well may you say with the sad old king

The little dogs and all,
Tray, Blanch, and Sweetheart, see they
   bark at me."

Checklist of Additional Reviews

"Z." [Horace Seaver], "Rev. Mr. Emerson," Boston *Investigator*, 27 September 1838, p. 3.

Christian Watchman, ca. mid October 1838.

Christian Examiner, 25 (November 1838), 266–7.

Quarterly Christian Spectator, 10 (November 1838), 670–4.

[J. W. Alexander, Albert Dod, and Charles Hodge], *Biblical Repertory and Princeton Review*, 11 (January 1839), 95–9.

Literary Ethics

S[amuel]. G[ilman].,
"Ralph Waldo Emerson,"
Southern Rose,
7 (24 November 1838),
100–6

A new comet, or rather meteor, is shooting athwart the literary sky of old Massachusetts, in the person of Ralph Waldo Emerson. He is the son of a distinguished clergyman of Boston, some time since deceased, and is now of middle age. He is attracting much public attention, and is an object of the severest reproaches from some, and the most profound admiration from others. He has delivered two or three courses of lectures in Boston, on moral and literary subjects, which have been attended by crowds. Many enthusiastic talented young people are represented to be perfectly fascinated by him. His reputation has, of late, extended so widely, that he was invited last July to deliver the Annual Addresses before the Literary Societies of Dartmouth College, and the Senior Class in the Divinity College of Harvard University. He appears to be a profound admirer, student, and imitator of Thomas Carlyle, several of whose works he has caused to be republished in this country. The character of his mind is poetic and imaginative, and he is strongly inclined to certain mystical and visionary habits of thought and discussion. His talents are unquestionably of a respectable order, though, as it appears to us, much inferior to the scale assigned them by his fervent admirers. The qualities, however, just mentioned, united with an irreproachable, lovely, and elevated moral character, and the graces of a commanding person and impressive elocution, go a good way to explain the effect which he has produced on a highly educated, refined, and excitable community. He delivered last winter a course of lectures on Human Culture, in which he began with Prudence, and gradually ascended to Holiness. Whatever was thought of the speculative truth, all parties allowed that the spirit was noble, and the style and manner beautiful.

From the specimens we have seen, there appears to be very little originality in his speculations,—though a youthful and miscellaneous audience might be apt to imagine quite the contrary. All his leading ideas he seems to have caught from Carlyle, who again was indebted for *his* chief resources to the modern German philosophers.[1] These ideas Mr. Emerson adorns, expands, and presents anew in a great variety of shapes, mingling them up, certainly, with much that is peculiar to himself, and occasionally yielding a profound and precious glimpse into the truth of things. At the same time, there is a good deal of mere common place in his writings, redeemed only by a quaint, fantastic, imaginative style, which deceives the young reader or hearer into the belief that it is original and valuable. Thus, instead of using the ordinary word *completed*, he talks of a thing *coming full circle*, a phrase, by the way, which seems to be a favorite one with him. He sprinkles his writings now and then with the old solemn style, as *worketh, loveth, hath*, &c. *Works, loves*, and *has*, would not so well answer his purpose. The word *forever* is too tame for him, and he employs in its stead the more sounding and poetical *forever-more*. He affects much the Saxon phraseology, as *behooted* and *behowled, skulks* and *sneaks*, &c. We do not find particular fault with all this. If it belongs to the man's original or acquired nature, let it come out. We only instance it, as partly explaining the cause which dazzles Mr. Emerson's admirers.

We learn that much bitterness has been expressed in the newspapers and private circles of the vicinity, in consequence of some of Mr. Emerson's recent utterances. Exposed to storms of obloquy and reproach, he stands calm and unmoved—replies to no criticisms—but meekly announces a new course of lectures in Boston, for the coming winter, and will probably have a crowded lecture-room, although we learn that the extravagances of his Cambridge Address have partially worked their own cure, and that his influence has begun to wane.

Some of his offensive doctrines, as far as we can comprehend them from his very involved and cloudy paragraphs, appear to be the following. He reduces all revelation to the level of our natural reason, maintaining, in fact, that there is a perpetual revelation going on in the soul of man, of equal authority with the Jewish or Christian. He denies the authority of miracles, or rather seems to claim them as in perpetual and present operation. He seems to represent the objects of true re-

ligious love and worship to be not any divine *person* or *persons*, but only certain abstract *qualities*, such as absolute *goodness, truth* and *wisdom*. He declares that *evil* is not *positive*, but only *negative*, there being nothing positive, but *good*. From which we conclude, that *murder* is not a *positive*, but only a *negative act*. And we are still further puzzled by turning over the page, and finding the author warn us against *"absolute badness."* His language respecting the human soul, appears to elevate it to an equality with the Supreme Being. "Man," he says, "is made a Providence to himself."—His views savour, at times, of the pantheistic doctrines of Spinoza, who is a favorite with modern German philosophers and has been charged with confounding creation with the Creator, making them both one. Others of his expressions are offensive, not from conveying any definite meaning at all, but only from apparently denying or contravening certain long-established opinions. But what is particularly remarkable, all this tissue of novel and unpopular opinions is strangely mixed in with expressions and sentiments, which imply directly the contrary, and are perfectly consistent with our old-fashioned doctrines and belief. Thus, almost the same page tells us that "God is well pleased," whenever a human spirit devotes itself to virtue, and that "if a man is at heart just, then in so far is *he* God! !" Having asserted, that "all things proceed out of the same spirit, and all things *conspire with* it," he soon after declares that sometimes men *seek* good ends, and sometimes *rove* from good ends, until they arrive at "absolute badness and absolute death."

Again, he says, it is a capital mistake in the infant man to hope to derive advantages *from another*—yet, in the next page, he allows that we can receive beneficial *provocation* from another soul, though not instruction; and further on, he acknowledges that there is a good ear, in some men, *that draws supplies to virtue out of every indifferent nutriment.* He tells us also that he loves the divine bards, because they *admonish* him—notwithstanding it is a capital mistake to hope to derive advantages from another! He also affirms that the office of a minister of religion is the first in the world, notwithstanding it is such a capital mistake for one man to hope to derive advantage from another.

Again, Mr. Emerson finds fault with preachers of modern times, because you cannot discover from any hint, or surmise in their sermons, whether they *personally* have ever "laughed or wept, were married or in love, have been commended, or cheated, or chagrined—ploughed, or planted, talked, bought and sold, read books; eaten and drunken; had the head-ache or heart-ache; smiled or suffered;"— and yet two public, solemn addresses of his own are before us, which we have studied and pondered with the utmost diligence, and we cannot for the life of us discover from them whether Mr. Emerson himself is a great laugher or weeper, or was ever married, or in love, or has ever been commended, or cheated, or chagrined, or has ever ploughed, planted, talked, bought, sold, or had the head-ache. Of the bad preacher, he declares that "it could not be told from his sermon, what age of the world he fell in; whether he had a father or a child; whether he was a freeholder or a pauper; whether he was a citizen or a countryman; or any other fact of his biography." Yet all this information respecting himself he perversely withholds from his hearers, and so far as we may dare to take *him* for authority, he is consequently a sorry teacher.

A single instance more of such unfortunate inconsistency shall complete this disagreeable portion of our task. Mr. Emerson tells us, p. 31, that "the Hebrew and Greek Scriptures contain immortal sentences, that have been bread of life to millions." Yet he has before said to us, p. 26—"Once leave *your* own knowledge of God, *your own* sentiment, and take *secondary* knowledge, as *St. Paul's*, or George Fox's, or Swedenborg's, and you *get wide from God* with every year this secondary form lasts."

We submit a few of Mr. Emerson's (*absurdities* is too harsh a word for the lips of the gentle *Rose*)—but *incomprehensibilities*, let us more reverently say. Speaking of the religious sentiment, he says, "wonderful is its power to charm and to command. It is a mountain air. It is the embalmer of the world. It is myrrh and storax, and chlorine and rosemary. It makes the sky and the hills sublime, and the silent song of the stars is it. By it, is the universe made safe and habitable, not by science or power."

"The very word Miracle, as pronounced by Christian churches, gives a false impression; it is Monster. It is not one with the blowing clover and the falling rain."

"A true conversion, a true Christ, is now, as always, to be made, by the reception of beautiful sentiments."

"The time is coming when all men will see, that the gift of God to the soul is not a vaunting, overpowering, excluding sanctity, but a sweet, natural goodness, a goodness like thine and mine, and that so invites thine and mine to be and to grow."

"In how many churches, by how many prophets, tell me, is man made sensible that he is an infinite Soul; that the earth and heavens are passing into his mind; that he is drinking forever the soul of God?"

"In one soul, in your soul, there are resources for the world. Wherever a man comes, there comes revolution. The old is for slaves. When a man comes, all books are legible, all things transparent, all religions are forms. He is religious. Man is the wonderworker. He is seen amid miracles. All men bless and curse. He saith yea and nay, only."

But the climax of the whole is the concluding sentence of the Cambridge Address:—

"I look for the new Teacher, that shall follow so far those shining laws, that he shall see them come full circle; shall see their rounding complete grace; shall see the world to be the mirror of the soul; *shall see the identity of the law of gravitation with purity of hearts*; and shall show that the Ought, that Duty, is one thing with Science, with Beauty, and with Joy."

The above sentence in italics, if it have any meaning, must signify that both the law of gravitation and sincerity of heart are immediate and simultaneous manifestations of one and the same divine being. But here, the author's philosophy is more shallow and dogmatic than either he or his German masters imagine it to be. For it remains yet to be shown, that the action of gravitation *is* the immediate act of the Deity. For aught we know, it may be but the consequence of numerous other laws, of which man is perfectly ignorant. The writer might, with equal propriety, have asserted that the law of evaporation, or crystallization, or congealment, or vision, or sound, or any other of the common processes of nature, is identical with purity of heart. Or, perhaps Mr. Emerson intended boldly and undesignedly to express his belief in the identity of matter and mind. But even in that case, how the *quality* of purity of heart is identical with a *law*, surpasses our utmost powers of conjecture. If we use language at all, let us use it intelligibly.

In his Dartmouth address, Mr. E. urges on his youthful hearers the duty of assuming and maintaining forever an attitude of *inquiry*. We regret that we see little of this in his own productions. We look in vain for a truly *humble* spirit. All is dogmatism, assumption, dictation. The writer, we are sorry to say, appears to consider himself the *infallible instructer* of his age, and the idea of incurring error seems not to have entered his mind.[2] How different from this is the spirit of Channing! Channing, in the loftiest flights of speculation, and while pouring in streams of light, or stirring up torrents of feeling within the souls of his readers or hearers, rarely if ever lays aside the genuine humility of the philosophic inquirer, never assuming to be the oracle of his fellow-men, even at the moment when he most becomes so.

Mr. Emerson imagines that Christendom has degenerated from its former condition, because men have lost the spirit and the views of religion which *he* and his school entertain. But can he exhibit a single proof that the Christian Church ever approximated to such a standard?

On the whole, we cannot help concluding, that a writer, who seems to entertain no clear and definite principles,—who bewilders his hearers amidst labyrinths of beautiful contradictions; who floats about among vague and impalpable abstractions, and who is but the second or third hand reviver of ideas and visions, that have already been more than once exploded in the course of human progress, and could never get a foothold in this matter-of-fact world—is destined to make no very deep or permanent impression on the minds of his generation. The young may be dazzled and delighted for a while—the old may tremble at seeing all they have ever held sacred, unceremoniously handled and rudely set at nought—but society will at length rigidly demand some solid and tangible platform for its belief—some practical and mighty remedy for its corruptions—and some available instrument for the development of its moral resources. Society, too, will ever instinctively feel, that all the disadvantages of the old order of things are preferable to the utter lawlessness and mistaken independence recommended in the Dartmouth Address. Say what Mr. Emerson pleases, men were made to *learn* from each other, and a certain degree of deference and dependence is necessary to the best interests of the species. Had Mr. Emerson the right control of his own powers,—did he know where to pause in the career of daring speculation,—had he the happy tact to perceive the exact needs and capabilities of our imperfect world—and especially, if instead of attempting to keep his eyes forever fixed on the too dazzling and burning luminary of abstract truth, he were contended with exploring the milder sunlight and the varying shades which rest upon the landscape of human destiny, he might be hailed as one of the benefactors of his kind. A reformer ought, indeed, to go ahead of those whom he wishes to improve. But if he rushes at one start so far in advance as altogether to lose the sight and sympathy of his fellow-men, his energies must be wasted. The most generous steed on earth could not move an ounce-weight, if his traces were ambitiously lengthened out at an immense distance from his burden, and he aspired to struggle full circle in the vague and far-off horizon. Mr. Emerson, at times, seems to be conscious of these truths. He acknowledges himself incapable of suggesting, and hopeless of seeing new forms of worship for the Christian world, and even advises that the existing ones be retained, and a new breath be breathed into them by spirits of his own stamp. One of his characteristic contradictions! For who has done more to shake men's confidence in these existing forms, though he coolly acknowledges that he has nothing to replace in their stead?

Ralph Waldo Emerson is like unto a man, who saith unto all the children and dear mid-aged people of his neighborhood, "Oh, come, let us go yonder and dance a beautiful dance at the foot of the rainbow. There, will be treasures beneath our feet, and drops of all colours over our heads, and we shall be in the very presence of the mysteries of nature, and we and the rainbow shall be one, and the drops shall be beauty, and the drops shall be usefulness, and the drops shall be righteousness and purity of heart; and mortality and immortality shall be identical; and sin and holiness, and labour and rest, and vulgarity and gentility, and study and idleness, and solitude and society, and black and white, shall all become one great commingled, homogeneous and heterogeneous spot of pure glorification, forevermore." Then all the children, and dear mid-aged people, exclaim, "Beautiful, beautiful; let us go yonder and dance beneath the foot of the rainbow." And they all go forth with Emerson at their head, and Carlyle in advance of him, and Richter and Spinoza several rods in advance of Carlyle, and they seek the foot of the rainbow, but it recedes forever from them as they proceed. But at length wearied and shattered, they will return to the humble village, and will be contended with admiring the rainbow at a distance, and will be grateful for the dark, colorless drops that come down to refresh their heads, and will permit both rainbow and drops to carry up their thought to the mysterious Being who created the whole together with themselves, and so continue to walk piously and practically to their graves.

Notes

1 "Mr. Emerson ought to have studied the resources and habits of his own mind, before venturing on the following authoritative admonition. 'The man who aims to speak as *books enable*, as synods use, as the fashion guides, and as interest commands,

babbles. Let him hush.' It is almost ludicrous to hear our amiable author perpetually declaiming about 'independence,' 'standing alone,' 'consulting only one's soul,' when, if the truth were known, there is scarcely a writer now on the stage, who has been more indebted for his lights and impulses to the inspiration of others. The only difference between him and more commonplace geniuses, is, that *he* has looked for inspiration chiefly to one or two channels of thought, while other men have chosen to avoid singularity, and have endeavored to drink in the *whole spirit* of the past and present, in order that they might transmit it to the future, as much improved as their own plastic powers might permit. *Such* men, however, are regarded by Mr. Emerson as 'second-hand and slavish.' Is it not equally second-hand and slavish to be the quaint disciple of a quaint and narrow school?"

2 "We may except a sentence in the beginning of the Dartmouth Address."

R[ichard]. M[onckton]. M[ilnes].
"American Philosophy.— Emerson's Works," *London and Westminster Review*, 33 (March 1840), 345–72[1]

The writings of Mr Carlyle have already received our criticism and commendation, and it may not be unpleasing to our readers to receive some supplementary notice of a mind cognate indeed to his, however inferior in energies and influences, and to us especially significant as the eldest palpable and perspicuous birth of American Philosophy. The utterances of Mr Carlyle are in the streets and schools of experienced and studious Europe, but this voice has come to us over the broad Atlantic, full of the same tender complaint, the same indignant exhortation, the same trust and distrust, faith and incredulity, yet all sufficiently modified by circumstances of personality and place to show that the plant is assimilated to the climate and the soil, although the seed may have been brought from elsewhere.

It is with no disrespect to Mr Emerson that we would say that there is little in such of his works as have reached us (and we have read all that we could find), which would be new to the competent student of European Philosophy; for we must couple this with the assertion that to the general English reader there is much that would appear extravagantly, absurdly original; and we believe that no one, however well read, would feel anything but gratification at reading thoughts already familiar to him, arrayed in language so freshly vigorous, so eloquently true.

Nor is it a matter unworthy of consideration that the Transcendental Philosophy should have been more cordially received and more generally understood in America than in Great Britain. It is certain that among the Anglo-American people, a taste for the higher speculation is large and growing, and that much is there finding its way into the popular heart which for us remains totally extraneous and unperceived. We remembering hearing Coleridge, in his latter days, remark, "I am a poor Poet in England, but I am a great Philosopher over the Atlantic. His 'Aids to' went through many editions there before the first was exhausted at home. The loftier and more suggestive poetry of Wordsworth was there working out its purposes of living good, while it encumbered the shelves of the London bookseller. Mr Carlyle received a liberal share of the profits of the American edition of the 'French Revolution' before the English one had paid its expenses; and the volumes of his collected Essays now in circulation are a portion of the large American impression, commercially transferred to this country.

In these facts, too, imagination would trace a confirmation of the analogy commonly drawn between the present state of the American nation and the childhood of the life of man; for not only do we there recognise the untiring activity, the curiosity, the imitativeness, the wilfulness, the susceptibility that characterize the early stages of sensuous existence, but there are not wanting

"those obstinate questionings
Of sense and outward things,
Fallings from us, vanishings,
Blank misgivings of a creature
Moving about in worlds not realized."

And perhaps the deeper that we look below the surface of things the more natural may we find this inclination of the Idealist Philosophy in the thoughtful inhabitants of the United States. In ancient and ordered Europe it is no easy matter for a reflective mind so to adjust the outer and the inner life that the whole machine may go on harmoniously without grittiness or stoppage. In England, indeed, the existence of a large class, born independent, and (at least in the theory of the society) set apart for intellectual pursuits, together with the habit of the majority of the men engaged in the active business of life to retire after a certain period of struggle and labour into comparative repose, shades off and softens the lines of distinction between the worlds of action and of thought; while in Germany a whole army of scholars find ample employment and emolument in the genial occupations of public instruction; and statesmen, and ambassadors, and military commanders have had time and inclination to illustrate their names as Poets, Archæologists, Historians, or Philosophers. But, in the present position of America, the task of reconciling the exercise of the daily duties of social existence with that of the higher faculties and the nobler aspirations is painfully difficult. The work of the present moment there demands the entire man; he must be of the world or out of it: the sole tenure of respectability and regard among his fellow men is his ability to do the thing that is before him; and this condition of itself operates as an exclusion from all search of truth for truth's sake, and, indeed, from all provinces of speculation whatever, except those which happen to be on the banks of some full and rapid tide of theological controversy. Therefore will the American, who, with outraged sensibilities, blasted hopes, and thwarted affections, turns from the external world, accept with earnest gratitude a theory which shall reduce all this self-important pomp and tumult to a poor unreality, which shall turn into mere phantasmagoria all those confusions and conflicts of passions and of interests, and shall invest with the one everlasting kingliness him, the thinker, alone. Nor in this consideration is the peculiar relation of man to nature in that hemisphere, to be forgotten. The growth of things, from the den of the wild beast to the hut of the savage, from the howlings of the hungry animals to the cries of the hungry hunters, does not there naturally and equally advance; but in one sharp transition the primeval forest becomes the village of skilful artizans; the silence of ages is invaded by the machinery elaborated from the ripest intellects of the west; the book latest born of the mature mind of man is read on the fresh-fallen trunk of the eldest child of vegetative nature; the red man and the newspaper have come together. And between these two regions of phenomena stands the American philosopher, resting on each a meditative eye, and rejoicing in a theory which brings them both under his spiritual control, and at once delivers him from the contest of feelings and principles in which he might else have been involved.

Thus, then, as a just reaction from the subjective life of the American acting, we find the objective speculation of the American thinking; thus, out of the difficulty of harmonizing nature and man, comes the desire of the Absolute, into which they both shall merge and be no more separately seen. And when we come to speak personally of Mr Emerson, we shall discover in his mind and its workings many slight indications of these things, many involuntary expressions all tending thitherward, many undesigned proofs that, however original and surprising he may appear, he is nevertheless such a man as this age of the American mind should naturally and healthfully engender.

Mr Emerson is the son of a country clergyman, and having distinguished himself at Cambridge, the oldest and best University of the Union, was *settled* (to use the native phrase) as pastor of an Unitarian congregation in Boston. Whether from dogmatical differences with his co-religionists, or from distaste on his part to perform some ministerial functions, we know not, but some seven years ago he resigned his pulpit, and has since remained without any charge, though generally regarded as a Christian minister. Unitarianism in America seems to have its orthodoxy like any other profession, and probably Dr Channing there exercises the same kind of Popedom as Dr Chalmers occupies in Calvinistic Scotland. Although it would seem that if Unitarianism is destined to so important a mission as to be the sole ultimate antagonist of Romanism in America, (a position asserted for her by many within, and some without her communion), she must open an ample embrace to philosophical scepticism, and not be too critical of the especial belief and disbelief of those who seek her as a great home and refuge of Christian liberty. It is only under this form that Unitarianism can have any *religious* pretensions whatever. An Unitarian should be capable, without in any degree compromising his profession, of seeing more Godhead in the lowest forms of nature and humanity, than many a Trinitarian can perceive in the person of Christ. And above all things he should be tolerant of the faiths of others, whatever they are; for without this he has only the pains of doubt, and not the good that accompanies its action on the better mind. The value of faith and its operations may perhaps be most truly estimated by those who believe no longer, and while the votary of one superstition is almost necessarily impatient of and unjust to the votary of another, the wise sceptic may look up to all belief from the level of reason, with an earnest yet tearful eye, scanning the proportions and conditions of each in a large spirit of reverential compassion, which contains at once both himself and them. The Unitarians of Boston ought not to have parted with Mr Emerson.

After this separation he retired to a little country-house at Concord, within sight of the spot, where the first soldier fell in the War of Independence: and there he has remained, reading, thinking, and writing, in evident observance of the principle enacted by Jean Paul, "never to write on a subject till you have first read yourself full on it, and never to read on a subject till you have thought yourself hungry on it."

During the winter months he generally delivers lectures in Boston, which are said to be not unlike Mr Carlyle's in general character. A series of Biographies have formed one of his courses, and we conjecture the articles which he has contributed to the 'North American Review' to be a portion of it; if so, it is only surprising that these exhibitions have not excited still more interest than they seem to have done, especially as his manner is said to be at once original and simple, and his voice to fall in the most varied and musical cadences. He has also treated of the true nature and uses of history, and of the way in which it should be written; and we should be glad to have his views on this important subject more clearly developed than we can gather from chance passages in the discourses we have undertaken to notice.

Two of these are dedicated to the illustration of the character of the American scholar (for which word our European phrase would in these writings frequently substitute Philosopher,) and the third to the development of the idea of the Christian minister, such as American institutions permit him, and such as the spiritual state of America requires him, to be. We find much text for reflection in both these objects, and the manner of their execution.

The most prominent feature of the addresses is the author's sorrowful consciousness of the want of originality in American literature and thought. He is palpably taunted with the feeling that the American mind is at best an agglomerate of ingenious and laborious imitations. It is a very shame and plague to him that Washington Irving should have been but a successful follower of the Addisonian grace, that Prescott should but claim to be a rival of Robertson, that Bryant and his compeers should in some rare passages be supposed to have attained the level of Wordsworth or Byron, that national vanity itself should have devised no higher comparison for Cooper than Walter Scott. These personal applications are not his, but the following sentences would be sufficient to indicate the state of mind:—

["Literary Ethics," 100.8–12,
105.28–30]

["American Scholar Address," 69.13–15,
52.16–22]

We have perhaps no right to take in an argumentative contest to which genius is the subject, except with arms of the same divine temper, yet we may perhaps suggest that there are certain circumstances in the present historical state of America which appear to stand in the way of vigour of speculation and originality of thought. One of these is the difficulty to which the Americas are subject in determining what is original or derived. In Europe there is a large under-current of literary criticism which soon tests the colour and taste of the streams that are ever flowing into it, but this is of necessity wanting in America: even in England it would not be difficult for any man who set himself

63

ingeniously and sedulously about weaving a crown for his own head with laurels filched from the wide evergreen forest of German literature, to deceive for a time the literary public into a belief of his originality; and how much more easy must this be in America; for not only is it impossible but that many a writer in those local circumstances must be a triton among minnows, but it is also certain that many an English minnow has grown into a lusty triton by merely swimming across the Atlantic, and that English travellers have been astonished to hear names resounding in the Great Western blast of fame, which in this country were hardly made audible to the most attentive ear through the penny-trumpet of a literary coterie. Mr Emerson himself is evidently no exception to this rule: much, nay most, of what his countrymen would probably claim exclusively for his own, has been thought of, spoken of, and written of, by Fichte, or Goethe, or Novalis, or Coleridge, or Carlyle: many propositions which his hearers would accept *ex cathedra*, have racked the intelligence, and faded the heart, and wasted the frame of the European thinker, whose last hour on earth has found him despairing and them unresolved. Let us remember how in our own bright youth we trembled with supernatural joy as some new thought arose within us, how we feared to give it utterance for its very greatness, and how, when we had done so, the strong and terrible fact fell upon us, that this thought had been born and delivered to the world some thousand times before, and left both those who gave and those who received it, to all appearance, just where they were. But in applying this reflection to the American mind, let us not forget that it is by the generation and dispersion of these phantoms, by this spiritual gymnastic, that we and the world are in truth all that we are, have won all that we have won, and that this process is the clearest of all means ordained by Providence for the progressive culture of men and nations.

Again, if we perceive in the social state of America some practical discouragements to free development of mental energies, this must imply no distrust in or disregard of the principles on which that state reposes; or indeed anything more than the existence of some counter balancing disadvantages in the very freedom of thought which the Americans believe themselves to have asserted: even as the subsistence of slavery in the United States may seem divinely permitted to check the vanity they might otherwise have felt in having done so much to determine the great problem of social equality. It is undeniable that human nature (at least as trained and habituated in the usages of modern life) is fertile in men who require something stable without themselves as the condition of their own free and happy movement. Within the walls of fixed institutions there is for them a playground where their intellects can disport themselves at pleasure, without vague dread or discomfortable reflection. They can permit themselves with an easy conscience to inquire about anything else, as long as there is something in the world taken for granted, something established beyond the control of their own judgments and imaginations; witness the large licence of dogmatical reasoning in the Roman Church up to the time of the open divisions of the Reformation, compared with the rigid assent demanded afterwards. Witness in our own day the greater tolerance of opinion among high than among low churchmen; witness the boundless heights and flights of German speculation, amid a people still contained within the rude bonds of irresponsible authority. To many minds, then, this fear of ultimate abandonment to their own conceits, this deficiency of something beyond and above

64

their own works, to rest upon in hours of weakness, confusion, and defeat, would no doubt act as an impediment to the ready development of moral influence. Nor does the substitute which the necessities of the heart of man for some one or other external power have generated in America, at all better, the case. Public opinion, the sustainer and protector, is also and often the depressor and destroyer:—if she has her Sinai-mounts and cities of refuge, she has too her Inquisitions and Star-chamber, no whit less rigorous in punishment, and thus no less effective for terror. The very existence of a topic of essential interest and largest moral and political bearings, which must not and cannot be discussed in public, and hardly may be alluded to in private,—a topic on which the conscientious opinion of an individual running counter to that of the public will probably subject him to injury, certainly to insult, probably to personal danger, and certainly to personal discomfort; and all this standing out in shameless self-contradiction to the most solemn national enunciations of universal liberty and equality; must inevitably extend its evil effect far beyond what is apparent at first sight. The infection of servility will spread wide. All original speculation, all original discovery, is in opposition to the public opinion of its own time; genius has to create the very atmosphere in which it has to live; the books and ideas that energize the brute material universe, and lead it onward to spiritual destinies, are of their very nature in a certain sense unpopular, although it is equally true that they are the satisfaction of existing wants, and the resolution of existing difficulties. Christianity, and the Copernican system, were folly to their contemporary wisdom; and public opinion rejoiced in the death of Him that divinely suffered, and the humiliation of him that humanly retracted. As civilization advances on the wheels of education, public opinion must become more tolerant and wise; but every new truth, as long as it is new, will have its martyrs; and in the new republic, as in those of old, Socrates will find his cup and Dante his exile. It has often struck us that this dread of affronting general estimation, this superfluous estimation of the respect and regard of persons who are the mere indices of common opinion, is frequently the one disadvantageous point of contrast between well-informed Americans and good European society. Hence that susceptibility which does not only feel a stain as a wound, but sees an intended blot in the falling of a drop of most limpid water,—hence that reluctance to speak freely and boldly and naturally on all subjects, at once innocent and unsuspicious of offence,—hence the difficulty of preserving that graceful balance between self-trust and self-assumption, by which it is possible to reconcile all that is most delightful in the ancient courtesy with all that is worthy of these more honest and more hopeful times.

Mr Emerson's complaint that "men here, as elsewhere, are *indisposed to innovation*, and prefer any *antiquity*, any usage, any livery productive of ease and profit, to the unproductive service of thought," is not exactly what most people, on either side of the question, expected of republican America. Not, indeed, that the latter part of the sentence contains anything surprising; for, as long as money, not money's worth—gain as a process, not gain as an end—is the sum and substance of American life, the issue cannot be otherwise. It is only where leisure cannot be innocently enjoyed, that idleness is the mother of every vice. "Ce n'est pas la victoire qui fait le bonheur des nobles cœurs, c'est le combat," says a French orator, and American existence is but a parody of this thought. Business and busyness ought to be very different things.

Labour loses its highest, its purest function, when it becomes mere employment of those who else would have nothing to do, or mere excitement to impel an otherwise stagnant existence; in the one case it is no better than selfish pleasure, in the other it is as bad as gambling or intoxication. Why must this be so? Why should America continue to authorise the assertion of the monarchists of the Old World, that there is something in the shape and character of those social institutions, which is inconsistent with the pursuit of nobler objects than lie in the street or the mart, or even the Hall of Congress? Why is industry there to be so sterile of intellectual elevation, and governed by laws "à-la-monde, et à la mediocrité?" Why is the man who is contented with the little that lies within his grasp, and prefers to limit his desires to his means, rather than extend his means even beyond his decent desires, an isolated phenomenon in the United States? Why is it disreputable to be poor, and retired, and thoughtful, and tranquil? Why is the whole country a home for genius of hand, and a desert for genius of head? These and such unanswered questions are a burden on Mr Emerson's patriotic heart, and the discourses we are noticing are the expression of this conviction, in every varied tone of exhortation, expostulation, reproof, condolence, encouragement, and hope. The very apophthegmatical style which they assume must clearly have been far more effective in oral delivery than it shows on paper, so that the reader must imagine the passages we are about to cite upon this topic of the duties and deficiencies of the American scholar, i.e., thinker (or often what we should call literary man), as addressed to youthful and sympathetic audiences, through the heads and hearts of many of whom these thoughts and feelings, in one form or other, must have frequently passed, and rejoiced to welcome them into energetic utterance:—

["American Scholar Address," 63.5–18, 63.5–65.2]

It has been frequently remarked how painfully the difficulty of a somewhat independent daily life, the continual pressure of man on man (though there at least one would suppose there must be room enough) weighs upon the European resident, or even traveller, in America. "To an English person," writes Mrs Butler in her Journal, "the mere circumstance of being the whole day in a crowd is a nuisance. As to privacy at any time, or under any circumstances, it is a thing that enters not into the imagination of an American. They do not seem to comprehend that to be, from sunrise to sunset, one of 150 people confined in a steam-boat, is in itself a great misery, or that to be left by oneself, and to oneself, can ever be desirable. They live all the days of their lives in a throng, take pleasure in droves, and travel in swarms." These national habits (so directly opposed to those of their old fatherland) must place many a practical impediment in the way of such practice as Mr Emerson inculcates in the following passage. In England and Germany, indeed, the tendency, especially among literary men, is too strongly in the other direction: *our* pride of individuality gives every man a hermitage in his own house, if he likes to take it, and he generally does so: there is, in truth, a tradition that the driver of the Highgate coach charged double fare whenever Mr Coleridge was inside, and railroads are now shaking together the separate classes of our society;[2] but hitherto the English scholar has had solitude enough at his disposal, and he has assumed it as his natural atmosphere.[3]

["Literary Ethics," 109.8–111.24]

We might here have remarked on some peculiarities of phraseology, had not so much nonsense been already written on the bad English of American writers, that it is best to be silent, except in commendation. The language of American literature cannot be yet fully matured; it is too much to expect that the development of *their* mind should exactly square itself with *our* form of expression; but this is what, in fact, the common complaint amounts to. The materials, besides, which they have at hand, are not the same as ours; many words and phrases "of great Eliza's golden time" are current with them and obsolete with us; an American poet would use the tear

"That silently doth *progress* down my
    cheek,"

as readily as Lear did, without the fear of reviewers before his eyes, and many a sentence that has to us a strange slang look in an American periodical would read without notice in the comedies of that time. The worst part of the associations we form is this, that many of these words and phrases, being now confined to certain provinces and districts, have acquired a local character, and their use cannot without an effort seem otherwise than vulgar; but we should remember that the Yorkshireism of this moment, as it flowed perhaps from the pure well of Saxon English, is there not local but national, not colonial but imperial, and may do its work in the expression of English thought,—

"When coral reefs, where none but sea-
    birds throng,
Learn Bacon's sense and echo Milton's
    song."

We should, in fine, read every American book as if it were the produce of another age of English literature than our own, without any thought of worse or better.

In the passage we have quoted, and in the very heart of the philosophy of Mr Emerson, are to be found the two principles, of which perhaps it is no vanity to call the time in which we live the mother and fosterer, and the development of which will probably be the occupation of the wisdom and activity of mankind for ages to come,—the Poetry of daily life, and the dignity of Labour. "Not Arms and the Man—Tools and the Man, that were now our epic," writes Carlyle, and

["Literary Ethics," 112.2–4, 113.13–22]

Elsewhere, too, he says—

"I hear with joy whatever is beginning to be said of the dignity and necessity of labour to every citizen. There is virtue yet in the hoe and the spade, for learned as well as for unlearned hands; and labour is everywhere welcome, always we are invited to work; only be this limitation observed, that a man shall not, for the sake of wider activity, sacrifice any opinion to the popular judgments and modes of action."

We must not imagine that this principle of the Worth of Labour has merely a democratic significance—that it refers solely to the claims and rights of those who are commonly called the *body* of the people, or the *labouring* classes (though it is thus of the highest import to humanity; and its assertion a stringent political duty); for its entire meaning is only to be discovered by penetrating into the wants and purposes of the times in which it has grown up and is every day making itself clearer to the understanding of men. The distinction of *conscious* and *unconscious* has only found so ready a welcome in the language of this generation, because the thing was there already, yearning for utterance,—because in it lay the greatest ethical question with which we have to do. There was *something* in which we knew that we differed from "the men of old," something which discriminated their wisdom from our wisdom, their folly from our folly, their happiness and sorrow from our happiness and sorrow,—and this knowledge we did not arrive at by any logical process, but by an imperative instinct that the thing was so. Therefore all examination and criticism of this distinction was grateful, and the simplest formula it could assume the most acceptable. It appeared, then, that among other characteristics of this *consciousness* was a tendency to regard everything about us from a subjective point of view; to refer all events and phenomena to their effects on ourselves; to tear to pieces our pleasures before we enjoyed them, and to suffer as much by the analysis of possible pains as we could by their actual infliction. That there was much evil in this condition could not be denied; but as this tendency was seen to be a part of our moral organization, it could only be remedied by the cultivation of some other principle, which should counteract the injury without requiring any such abnegations of consciousness as should force a man out of the just relations of independent manhood into the swaddling-clothes of a factitious infancy. It was useless, then, to exhort the mind to think about itself, but you could bid it think about other things; you could not tell the inner eye to close itself in darkness, but you could conjure it to look out upon external nature in the light of the sun; you could not make the monk of his own heart disbelieve the awfulness and glory of his sanctuary, but you could show him the wants of his fellow men which his work might supply, the good that his Labour could accomplish; you could not say to him, it is wrong to reflect, but you could say, it is right to work also: and thus would the chief burthen of the soul

be removed, thus alone could man be again brought into harmony with nature. And this, indeed, seems the only valid argument against the patronage of monastic establishments in these our days. There is enough, and more than enough, of desire for them,—more than enough of weary hearts and aching heads to take refuge in them; but, in truth, *they* would be no refuge; there the heads and hearts would wear themselves out, as fast or faster than they ever did amid the antagonisms of the outer world. It can be no peace now-a-days for a man to sit contemplating his navel like an ascetic of Mount Athos; his thoughts are not easy and smooth enough for that. To say nothing of what the world itself would come to, if all the sensitiveness and tenderness and gentleness in it were permitted to retire into the distance, and leave the whole game in the hands of hard, selfish ambition, and low, prurient activity.

Collateral with the progress of this principle was the recognition of the elements of Poetry in the circumstances of the most humble and usual life. When it once became felt that life, like land, would not remain idle, but that weeds would spring where corn was unsown—that man must toil for good or he shall toil for ill—the working classes, as such, became rather the objects of envy than of contempt, and their habits and feelings matters of interest and inquiry. Then was it seen that there was other poetry than the fanciful Idyllic in the cottage and the field; then the "huts where poor men be" were found to be as full of lessons of beauty and wisdom as

"The silence that is in the starry sky,
The sleep that is among the lonely hills;"

then was it felt that the best nature for the poet to study and enjoy was the common heart of man: while the victory of

Wordsworth over an army of prejudices proclaimed the destruction of the old monopoly of stilted sentiment and lofty circumstance, and the poetical enfranchisement of humanity. American literature had none of those artificial impediments to get over; and thus the truth, which "to the Greeks was foolishness," went straight home to all that was good in the hearts of the New World. And the practice of America has been a noble compliment to the theory of Wordsworth. For, all that he has done for poetry, the same has Washington done for history. Since the reign of Washington in the respect and admiration of mankind, the standard of heroic greatness has been changed,—real action has taken the place of theatrical; public life is no longer a stage to strut and mouth on, but a true life, animated with the same true impulses, regulated by the same true moralities, amenable to the same true judgments, as that of the simplest citizen, open to the winds of heaven, to the sun and to the falling rain.

The Philosophy of Mr Emerson is an idealistic Pantheism. It would hardly be fair to pronounce it superficial on merely negative proof, for these writings are in nowise of a controversial character; and the exposition and illustration of his system, as far as it is given, is as earnest and sincere as if the soul of the very man were laid bare before us. But, at the same time, we cannot but regard the confidence with which he proffers his doctrine, the axiomatic character with which he invests his conclusions, and the solemnity with which he urges his hearers to act them out fully and immediately, as evidence that he has not probed the depth of the ground on which he is standing, but that, knowing it to be strong enough to bear himself at that moment, he has believed it capable of supporting the world. All religious philosophy has perhaps a basis of pantheism, but here there is little or no super-structure. The identity of man with nature, the primary duty of "a wise passiveness" to the superincumbent spirit, the "occult relation between man and the vegetable," the creed "I am nothing—see all—the currents of the Universal Being circulate through me—I am part of particle of God" (*Nature*,—p. 13), have been uttered often before, and in many senses; but here they are all-in-all, and they are propounded as if they lay on the surface of truth and within the grasp of all men, and contained not problems, or parts of problems, in the solution of which the lives of thoughtful men have gone by, leaving the giant contradictions of our moral being just as they were, standing face to face, irreconcilable.

The first look of such a system as Mr Emerson's has assuredly much that is attractive for assertors of the democratic principle in general, and for a people so circumstanced as the Americans in particular. The "vox populi vox Dei," assumes a very special import when the "vox populi" does not merely mean an historical utterance, but an expression of the universal Spirit, which is at once the Thought of God and the Instinct of Man: the sense of the majority is no longer a sum of separate wills and passions, but an absolute and transcending power, only not supernatural because it is the most perfect development of nature. The question of the truth or falsehood of these conclusions lies far too deep for our present employment, but it is plain that such conclusions might be drawn. Nor can it fail to be agreeable to an American to persuade himself of the validity of such propositions as the following:

["Literary Ethics," 101.28–102.12, 102.25–27, 103.16–22, 105.30–106.1, 107.16–18, 108.9–18]

["American Scholar Address," 57.20–24, 69.3–12]

69

If this be the whole truth, then is the New World new indeed; the ocean lies between her and the nations of the East as the air between her and Saturn: in vain for her have been the successive generations of mankind,—in vain the conquests of warriors, the visions of poets, the voices of prophets, and the researches of philosophers,—in vain the labour, the endeavor, the self-sacrifice, the martyrdom,—in vain the acted inspirations, the realized ideals of other men: she has no more to do with them than the primrose on the English river's brim with the lotus on the banks of the Nile, both organs of one prolific Nature, and nothing more; she is bound to them, and to all the mighty past, by no bond or interest or tie of obligation,—so far from it, their influences on her are for nearly unmixed evil, hiding her from herself, and smothering the growth of her own magnificent nature. Yet, if these things be so, is it not strange that the greatness and virtue of young America have come about by as distinct and simple a progression of moral causes as the history of the world can show? Why was not the Republic of the United States created by the original children of American nature, the free possessors of the forest and the hunting-ground, rather than by the alien blood, and vigour, and culture, and religion of that little island of the distant seas? Can any one, looking History in the face, declare that America owes nothing, in the highest possible sense of *debt*, of inherited and communicated intelligence, to the European world? Does Mr Emerson himself owe nothing to Goethe and Carlyle? Surely many of the words we have quoted are those of a God-drunken man, as Novalis named Spinoza. It is true that Mr Emerson does occasionally attempt to qualify them by counter-positions of the comparative and relative uses of the things he has been upbraiding, but still these expressions have all the au-

thority and solemnity of a creed. And thus we cannot let them go by without registering our belief of the error which is in them, and our conviction that the wings of the spirit of human wisdom rest upon the past as upon the future, and that a reverential study of what has gone before us is the only vantage-ground from which safely and hopefully to contemplate the cloud-capt heights of human perfectibility. Honourable is the world that shall come before us "as a virgin to-day," but yet more honourable as a mother of many children, with all whose toils and works and struggles and attainments we have a brother's sympathy, and in whose recognition we rejoice with a brother's love.

We would ask Mr Emerson just to bring before his fancy what, in all probability, would be the result, if this indiscriminate self-reliance was generally adopted as the sole regulating principle of life. We find no barrier that shall prevent its falling into that moral state of imperfect sympathies which especially distinguishes the lower animals from man. The habitual dependence on instinct, which is the characteristic of their organization, seems of itself to exclude any interest in the pleasures and pains, hopes and fears, of others of their kind, except in reference to their own perceptions; and it is only in exceptions to this rule, in rare cases of affection and sympathy (and these, singularly enough, far more frequently manifested in relation to man, the higher creature, than to individuals of their own species or level in nature), that we perceive any presence of a purer intelligence. If man, then, were to be all in all to himself, if he did not feel himself (and why should not his first impulse so to do be also a higher instinct?) a link in that mystical chain of interdependence, which, in the plain Homeric image, hangs from the very throne of Jove, how are we secure that any subtlety of distinction will keep the working of his self-trust from practical arrogance, of his self-possession from simple selfishness? But, however this might be (and it is not fair to mix up too finely philosophical speculations and moral results, even though Mr Emerson does call his system one of literary ethics), the intellectual consequences might form a picture at once terrible and ludicrous. What a battle field for enthusiasms would the world become, did men once believe that they are not speaking, but spoken from! What a range for every fancy-fuddled and passion-puzzled man to wander through, proclaiming his own Messias-ship, and abjuring all other divinity! What a premium on the worst, because wilful, ignorance,—on the worst, because uneasy, idleness! What a discord of obstinate and irresponsible wills to drown the voice of conscience and opinion! And how to avoid the commixture of pride and contempt and everything hateful in mortal nature,—how to counteract the tendency of such exhibitions to make genius itself ridiculous in the eyes of the prudent and reflective, and even religion abominable to the peaceful and the just! Better, in truth, that Mr Emerson should sorrow over his countrymen as "men who grind and grind in the mill of a truism, and nothing comes out but what was put in," than that enthusiasm or inspiration, or any unconsciousness, should overlie the calm judgment of progressive humanity, the sense which can reverentially look before and after, leaving out of its scheme no possible knowledge, no imaginable sympathy. Let not Mr Emerson complain that we misrepresent him and his doctrines; if matters of this kind are so stated as to be easily misrepresented, the representation is of itself so far defective, whatever the theory itself may be.

It is pleasanter, however, to mention the vivid gratification we have derived from the illustrations of the principles of nature with which these little books abound. They are ever forcible, and each sufficiently valid for its own purpose, although it might not always be impossible to produce some other as accurate on the other side of the question. But we must cite two or three:—

["American Scholar Address," 65.15–27]

["Divinity School Address," 78.11–23, 91.25–35]

["Language," *Nature*, 21.5–17]

["Nature," *Nature*, 10.35–11.2]

["Discipline," *Nature*, 26.36–27.7]

["Prospects," *Nature*, 44.35–45.6]

One passage in the 'North American Review,' on the fact of Michel Angelo's having studied anatomy for twelve years, is very beautiful.

[*Natural History of Intellect*, 221.18–222.12]

As also this summary of Michel Angelo's character:—

[*Natural History of Intellect*, 242.19–243.8]

Another striking illustration we will not omit, if it be only for the sake of contrasting it with a passage in one of Mr Carlyle's essays. The two placed together are as good an example of the opposite colours of the same shield, as one often meets with. Mr Emerson bids us

"Observe the phenomenon of extempore debate: a man of cultivated mind, but reserved habits, sitting silent, admires the miracle of free, impassioned, picturesque speech, in the man addressing an assembly; a state of being and power how

71

unlike his own! Presently his own emotion rises to his lips and overflows in speech. He must also rise and say somewhat. Once embarked, once having overcome the novelty of the situation, he finds it just as easy and natural to speak, to speak with thoughts, with pictures, with rhythmical balance of sentences, as it was to sit silent: for it needs not to do but to suffer; he only adjusts himself to the free spirit which gladly utters itself through him, and motion is as easy as rest."

Turning from "this picture" let us look "on that;"—

"Was it never thy hard fortune, good reader, to attend any meeting convened for public purposes, any Bible Society, Reform, Conservative, Thatched Tavern dinner or other such meeting? Thou hast seen some full-fed long-ear, by free determination or on sweet constraint, start to his legs and give voice. Well aware wert thou that there was not, had not been, could not be, in that entire ass-cranium of his any fraction of an idea: nevertheless mark him. If at first an ominous haze flit round, and nothing, not even nonsense, dwell in his recollection, heed it not: let him but plunge desperately on, the spell is broken. Common-places enough are at hand, 'labour of love,'—'rights of suffering millions'—'throne and alter'— 'divine gift of song,' or what else it may be: the meeting, by its very *name*, has environed itself in a given element of common-place. But anon behold, how his talking organs get heated and the friction vanishes; cheers, applauses (with the previous dinner and strong drink) raise him to height of noblest temper.

"And now (as for your vociferous dullard is easiest of all) let him keep on the soft, safe parallel course (parallel to the truth or nearly so; for Heaven's sake, not in *contact* with it), no obstacle will meet him; on the favouring given element of common-place he triumphantly careers. He is as the ass whom you took and cast headlong into the water; the water at first threatens to swallow him, but he finds to his astonishment that he can *swim* therein, that it is buoyant and bears him along. One sole condition is indispensable; audacity (vulgarly called impudence). Our ass must commit himself to his watery element; in free daring, strike forth his four limbs from him; then shall he not drown and sink, but shoot gloriously forward and swim, to the admiration of bystanders. The ass, safe landed on the other bank, shakes his rough hide, wonderstruck himself at the faculty that lay in him, and waves joyfully his long ears; so too the public speaker."— *Carlyle's Essays*, vol. 1, p. 51.

Not only are these pictures of the same phenomenon, but there is an identity in them, easily discoverable; only is the one mood humorous, the other tragic, and the phraseology adapted to each. The "free spirit" of the one observer is the "audacity" of the other, and "the state of being and power" is but a finer way of expressing the exertions of the ass at once overwhelmed and sustained by the stream.

It may be seen that the two orations delivered before the Phi Beta Kappa Society at Cambridge, and the Literary Societies of Dartmouth College, have engaged more of our attention than the Address to the Divinity Students at the latter establishment: not, however, that the latter deserves it the less; for, inasmuch as it contains an application of the views we have already stated to the highest of all subjects, the interest is proportionably greater. The philosophy of Mr Emerson is so essentially religious, or, if we may use the word out of its slang sense, mystical, that such an application of his principles is perhaps the best possible exposition: but the notion having unhappily taken root among us, that religious philosophy carries a certain dreaminess and unreality along with it, we have rather taken texts for our observations from the other sources at hand. Yet it must not be altogether overlooked that such a religious application must necessarily be of more general character, and be encumbered with fewer local conditions, than a philosophical or literary one. And thus, indeed, the plaint of Mr Emerson is but as a note of the great Miserere of the faithful which is rising in many tones from many lands.

"The need was never greater of new revelation than now."—"The sad conviction which I share, I believe with numbers, of the universal decay, and now almost death of faith in society—the soul is not preached—the Church seems to totter to its fall, almost all life extinct."—"The Puritans in England and America found in the Christian Church, and in the dogmas inherited from Rome, scope for their austere piety and their longings for civil freedom. But their creed is passing away, and none arises in its room."

Such are his grounds of address, and in another sentence of sorrow the special instance is followed by a truth of general force.

["Divinity School Address," 88.20–33]

Two errors appear to Mr Emerson to be at the bottom of this state of things. 1st, The historical view of Christianity, which "is not the doctrine of the soul, but an exaggeration of the personal, the positive, and the ritual." 2nd, "The habit of considering the revelation as somewhat long ago given and done, as if God were dead." Thus "the injury to faith throttles the preacher, and the goodliest of institutions becomes an uncertain and inarticulate voice."

It is, perhaps, hardly possible to decide on the justice of this conclusion, and keep as clear as we must do of dogmatical divinity; yet we may be permitted to suggest the following questions as relevant to such a decision: Whether the portion of the American people least obnoxious to these reproaches of "wasting unbelief" be not those bodies which are held together by bonds of this historical Christianity, and constituted on its principles? Whether the remarkable accession to the numbers of the Roman Catholic Church in that country, a fact remarked and commented on by travellers of the most opposite opinions, does not suppose a certain living energy and sympathy with human wants in such an institution? Whether historical Christianity necessarily implies that "the count of mighty prophets is made up;" or rather, whether the continuing infallibility claimed by the Roman Church, and the incessant personal outpouring of the spirit on their members hypothesized by the Evangelical churches, are not assertions of the contrary principle? We cannot help thinking that Mr Emerson has here generalized too widely from his own communion, or what was such, to the religious world in America; who not only do not seem, from all accounts, to be wanting in religious energy, but appear to have used very much the means Mr Emerson himself recommends for their own purposes of religious excitement. We do not mean that strong Christian feeling is the universal and generating principle in America that Mr Emerson would wish it to be, but only that the remedy he proposes does not seem exactly to meet the disease; and this we think might be proved by the effects of revivals and similar spasmodic excitements.

["Divinity School Address," 84.19–27]

Noble thoughts nobly worded, but yet prefatory to such danger as soon follows.

["Divinity School Address," 89.29–32; 90.1–6, 11–16]

To prevent such passages as these, addressed to an audience of young men, from being most perilous and injurious tinder, certain conditions are requisite. The pupils *may* be of temperaments so unimaginative as to contain no inflammatory principle, and thus these exhortations would remain as harmless on their memories as in their pockets; they *may*, too, combine so much knowledge of human nature with appreciation of truth, as to see in these and such phrases nothing more than the injunctions of an eloquent and excited preacher not to submit their judgments in bigoted blindness to any human authority, and not to check by any unnatural means the development of their separate dispositions for good. Or they *may* interpret these and such words to mean, that every one there sitting and hearing, is not a man but a god; and this not as a philosophical deduction or a poetical abstraction, but as a plain practical truth,—that therefore all the free impulses of his nature, all the first-fruits of his imagination, all the intuitions of his intellect, are and ought to be acted out without let or hindrance whatsoever:— that He, especially He, is called upon to be that Self which shall reintegrate the broken harmonies of nature: that there is *that* in his ignorance which authorises him to despise all learning, and *that* in his passive reception of truth, which puts to scorn the toil of the world before him: that,— but why should we continue to express those terrible and palpable consequences, which have more than once been ejected from the volcano of unmodified Pantheism, and whose lava-currents, under most various names, from "Solifidianism" to the "Rights of Man," have desolated for a time many a fair tract of politics and religion? Take away the control of the conscience and the judgment, or, what is the same thing, override them by an *à priori* conviction of truth, and the Assassins of the East, and the Pazzi of Florence, and the Anabaptists of Munster, and the Fifth-Monarchy men of England, and the Thugs of India, and the "Tricoteuses de la Guillotine," are all not only possible but natural, and the best boy at the college becomes the "incorruptible Robespierre," and the honest-hearted and strong-headed Edward Irving, a worshipper of the uninterpreted vowel-sounds of a Christian Phythoness.[4]

But the best security against such disastrous effects of Mr Emerson's principles is the tone of his own utterances. It is admirable that a stream can be at once so rapid and so pure. All his earnest is good earnest, and unlike many critics, as well of philosophy as of literature, he shows no trace in himself of the evils he deprecates in others. Let him not, then, be disgusted or dismayed, if he find out (as no doubt he will) that his truth is not the whole truth, and cannot, without its own loss and injury, be propagated as such; and that exaggeration, however involuntary, and enlargement beyond reality, however well-intentioned, will always bring about the same result, namely, the weakening of arguments otherwise strong, and the darkening of views otherwise clear. The politician and the religionist may both gain by so increasing the magnitude of the point in hand, that it should fill up the whole mind of the recipient, and leave no room for contradictory or qualifying elements; but the philosopher, dealing with things perennial and absolute, can no more add to or take away from their weights and dimensions than can the astronomer from the proportions of the planets, without stultifying his own fundamental laws.

Reading and reflection will soon lead Mr Emerson to "believe the past," as far as it ought to be believed: the Present is nothing more than the convergence of the Past and Future, and unless we have experience of the one, and such imperfect vision as we can get of the other, we cannot call this Present our own.

There is one other point of view from which we would regard these little books before wishing them God speed,—as affording additional grounds of sympathy between the thought of England and America. Not alone for the ingenious artificer, or the inquiring politician, or the curious traveller, is the volume of the New World open; the silent student of the human heart, even he who, by sad and serious self-investigation, learns the language in which is written the being of all other men, shall find that the Atlantic makes no severance between him and many a brother of the sage and suffering spirit;—that there, too, the struggles of a generation, passing from the womb of unconsciousness into distinct and dazzling day, has voices fit though few; and that those nations, so strong in youth and hope, are not exempt from the woes and wants of a distempered, dispirited humanity.

It is the fortune of the period in which we are writing, that America is brought as near to us as Rome; already has this circumstance begun its influence, already has it been shown more clearly than was even before believed, that the links of national sympathy are to be found on each side of the Atlantic, and that the chain but wants to be well soldered together. We have heard Mr Webster speak of our ancient cathedrals, and Miss Sedgwick of our ivied cottages, and the veneration and affectionate interest in these things which they have taken home with them, will be fruitful seeds in the hands of such sowers. Let us only earnestly and freely reciprocate these feelings; let us visit the United States, not merely to enjoy the humours of a young civilization, or to write treatises on practical democracy, or to glorify our exclusive nationality, or to foster our political discontents, or for any other purpose under the sun, but to delight in the spectacle of that other and greater England, "England in a state of glorious magnification," and be proud of this our country's conquest of the world of brute and barren space, this our country's victory over incalculable provinces of time to come. And then, what American will refuse to acknowledge, in the fine language of Mr Southey, that "What Italy and Gréece are to the classical scholar, what Rome to the Roman Catholic, what Jerusalem to the Christian world," *that* England is to him.

Notes

1 Reviews are *Nature*, "American Scholar Address," "Divinity School Address," "Literary Ethics," and "Michael Angelo" in the January 1837 *North American Review*.

2 "It may be said that, within the last year, a countess and her daughter, the fairest of May-fair, two handcuffed convicts, a constable, and three servants of different capacities, were the contents of one carriage on the Birmingham railway."

3 "These and similar juxtapositions, *e.g.* in the same essay, 'Plato, Bacon, Cousin,' are examples of that deficiency of a canon of criticism common to the hand of each and every man, which we have already remarked in American literature."

4 "We should be curious to know whether Mr Emerson is acquainted with that beautiful compendium of idealistic ethics, Fichte's 'Vocation of Man'; a book at once of the firmest logic and a many-side perception of truth, and bringing out of the darkest doubt and most tumultuous difficulties such light as man can walk by in his daily life, and see at least some way into the infinite and eternal beyond. We are sorry that we cannot guide the English reader to any translation of this little work."

Checklist of Additional Reviews

[Orestes A. Brownson], *Boston Quarterly Review*, 2 (January 1839), 1–26.

Essays [First Series]

[Review of *Essays*],
New York Review,
8 (April 1841), 509–12

This volume contains twelve essays, which are severally entitled History; Self-reliance; Compensation; Spiritual Laws; Love; Friendship; Prudence; Heroism; The Over-Soul; Circles; Intellect; Art. The substance of some, if not of all, of them has been given to select audiences in the form of lectures in Boston and its neighborhood, and it may, we think without injustice, be considered as a cause, or certainly as the type of a somewhat novel and singular species of fanaticism now prevailing more or less in that region, under the name of transcendentalism. We call it fanaticism, as being a semi-philosophical theory strangely blended with certain elementary notions of religion, making as large demands on the conduct as on the faith of those who receive it, and leading to principles and forms of social organization which have no basis in the nature of man, and which experience has already condemned as impracticable. By what right this medley of opinion and fancies has received the *sobriquet* of transcendentalism, we are at a loss to understand. Kant, and Cousin, and Coleridge, would be puzzled to recognize in it any features of the system they have taught, and which has passed under that name, or if it be in any way a product of their system, it is by some equivocal generation, a *lusus naturæ*, feeble, and we trust short-lived. Once the attainment of the theory of man and of the universe, that was properly styled transcendental, was the result of patient meditation for many months, and years were not thought too long to prepare the mind for a competent judgment of it. Now, it seems to be a work of moments, and for youth. Now, we judge by illapses and revelations. Now, we have but to "*live,*" and we become the arbiters of all truth, masters of all science; nay, we "judge the angels."

There are certain views, more or less fully developed in these essays, on which we think it proper briefly to remark. We do not question the purity of the author's life, the sincerity of his conviction, or the honesty of the purpose or of the means which have led him to the position which he seems to occupy in them. But we think they are essentially false, and certainly mischievous; half-truths, which will distort the character that is formed on them, and excluding negations which shut out the true life of man.

We ought to say, at the outset, that the volume contains no system, nor any attempt at one. This, in a volume of essays, we could hardly claim. But we may fairly claim that all the author's thoughts shall be parts of a system, and at least intimations of what it is. We doubt, however, whether Mr. Emerson has carefully compared his views with each other; and indeed he himself expresses the hope that he has seen "the end of consistency and conformity." We doubt, moreover, whether his thoughts and sentiments are referable to any single principle, or are properly parts of any system, so various and incongruous often are they. They are rather fragments, and glimpses, often indeed of a bright and pure meaning, than a logical or even continuous discussion.

We are disposed to censure the book, both for its theology and its philosophy. In the former respect, it is a godless book. There is evidently no recognition of the God of the Bible, a moral governor and righteous judge. The highest approach that is made to it is the doctrine, everywhere through the volume insisted on or implied, of a universal soul; which means, in our best comprehension of it, only a pervading intellect out of which, by natural genesis, all particular souls are produced and grow, and of which they are merely the organs and the manifestation, sustaining to it the same relation, and no other, that the tree does to the earth which bears it. This universal man—for such is sometimes the conception—is but the expansion and impersonality of the individual; is mere unconscious intellect, yet to man the supreme beauty, to be admired perhaps, hardly to be feared or loved. There is nowhere a recognition of sin, as actual, or even possible. In this particular, the author is rigidly systematic; for where there is no moral law but the instincts of our own being, there can be no sin. What vulgarly goes under that name, is here only infirmity and cowardice, and a fall that may hinder our progress, or may help us by a new experience. On these, and kindred topics, is shown a sturdy indifference to all established opinions, and disregard of all time-honored institutions. His spirit finds in the Bible no response to its questionings. An implicit faith is a dead

faith, summarily. The Church is but a gathering of those who dare not think, to keep each other in countenance, by the bald show of knowing and seeing. Man must receive that only which his present experience affirms to him, and his own consciousness is of higher value and surer evidence than that of any and all other men.

In a work purely literary, we would not find fault with the absence of theological discussion; but in a didactic treatise, which professes to discuss problems of the highest interest to humanity, and the highest forms of human duty and attainment, we may well pause before we commend, when we find the saddest and deepest wants of our nature untouched, and the living God at once circumscribed into an universal man, and etherealised into an idea.

The philosophical aspects of the work, or the views which it presents of human life, are in like manner open to censure. It would render that life eminently unsocial. It represents every man as superior to all other men: every man as entitled to the deference of all other men; every man as utterly independent of all other men. It places each individual in a proud and selfish solitariness; ever on his guard, lest the entireness of his own being shall be in some way influenced by his fellow man; and checks kind sympathies and tender affections. But the true state of man in society is one of mutual trust, helpfulness, forbearance, patience. Isolation is not the condition of growth, whether it be a wilful separateness, or a perpetual seclusion in cell or desert; sympathy, fellowship, mutual reliance and counsel, are among the natural and appointed means of human culture. As well might an oak take root and grow in mid air, as a man attain anything truly noble by the pure doctrine of "self-reliance."

Follow nature—*naturam sequere*—as

taught by Cicero, and explained by Butler, was a valuable rule in determining human duties and their proper limits. But here, this wise precept has degenerated into a vague direction—"follow your instincts,"—and what, with many cautions and much discernment, might be useful as a guide, has become the supreme law, and solves the whole problem. The revealed law has no place here. A mere conscience is quite out of date, and useless. The common sentiments of men touching right and wrong are of no authority. We may not modestly apprehend that Socrates or Paul knew more of such matters than we do. "No law can be sacred to me but that of my own nature." To a friend who suggested that his impulses might "come from below," our author records his answer—the only one, indeed, which can be made with his premises—"They do not seem to me to be such; but if I am the devil's child, I will live then from the devil;" (pp. 41, 42.) and the answer is proof enough that the rule, alone, cannot be a safe one. It makes, too, what was but one among the grounds of our moral judgments and preferences, the only one. Doubtless, we admire in a child what we might condemn in a man, and this too because the action is natural in the one and not in the other; but the beauty of right is far different from the grace of appropriateness.

Throughout the volume are scattered numberless instances of this substitution of a partial truth for the whole, and a bold statement of it as the whole; and we regret that a work, in some respects so captivating, should be so calculated to mislead the unwary. The author writes with the earnestness of a genuine enthusiasm, and fearlessly speaks out his thought. There are everywhere tokens of a clear perception, and an ardent admiration of what is noble and beautiful in man, in nature, and in art. He deals in subtle analogies, which are often of great beauty, and pictures with rare skill. In a style, which on every page delights us by its simplicity and grace, and offends us by an affected quaintness, showing brilliant fancy and curious scholarship, he has uttered many brave truths, many gross and perilous errors, hints in which the meditative and wise man may find ambrosial food, but which will prove poison to the simple and undiscerning.

C. C. F[elton]., "Emerson's Essays," *Christian Examiner,* 30 (May 1841), 253–62

These essays, we believe, are substantially the lectures which Mr. Emerson delivered last year in the city of Boston. They were listened to with delight by some, with distrust by others, and by a few with something like horror. Many young people imagined they contained the elements of a new and sublime philosophy, which was going to regenerate the world; many middle aged gentlemen and ladies shook their heads at the preaching of the new and dangerous doctrines, which they fancied they detected under Mr. Emerson's somewhat mystical and oracular phraseology; while the old and experienced saw nothing in the weekly rhapsody but blasphemy and atheism. It was not very easy to make out from the varying reports of hearers, what these discourses really were; it was not much easier to say what they were, when you had heard them yourself; and the difficulty is not greatly diminished now they have taken the form of printed essays. One thing is very certain, that they excited no little attention among the philosophical quidnuncs of the good city of Boston, and drew around Mr. Emerson a circle of ardent admirers, not to say disciples, including many studious young men and accomplished young women; and that a great impulse has been given to speculations upon the weighty questions of man's nature and destiny. Among the observable effects of this new impulse, is a general extravagance of opinion, which accompanies all strong intellectual excitements, and an overweening self-confidence on the part of many inex-perienced people of both sexes, who have taken upon themselves to doubt and dispute everything, that the experience of the human race has seemed to establish. To a very great extent, the new opinions, if such they may be called, are ancient errors and sophistries, mistaken for new truths, and disguised in the drapery of a misty rhetoric, which sorely puzzles the eye of the judgment. It is idle to argue against these old, but ever-recurring errors. The human mind must revise its conclusions periodically, and these sophistries at all such times present themselves, and meet with some acceptance a little while, when they are again rejected and exploded. One of these periodical revisions seems to be taking place among us at the present moment; and intellects of various orders are engaged upon it, with various degrees of success. Some of them make sad work enough, it must be confessed; and utter their dark and oracular sayings with an air of the most self-sufficient folly. Others show ability, and even genius and eloquence. Unquestionably, some of the best writing of late years has proceeded from the pens of authors, whom the public call, for want of a better name, Transcendentalists. Mr. Emerson is not to be confounded with any class, though he has strong affinities with the transcendentalists. He is an extravagant, erratic genius, setting all authority at defiance, sometimes writing with the pen of an angel, (if angels ever write,) and sometimes gravely propounding the most amazing nonsense. To subject his writings to any of the common critical tests, would be absurd. He would probably laugh in the critic's face.

The Essays cannot be said to contain any system of religion, morals, or philosophy. The most that can be affirmed is, that they are full of significant hints upon all these subjects, from which the author's opinions, so far as he has any, may be inferred. But he has expressed such sovereign contempt for consistency, that we must not look for that virtue in what he may choose to say; if we do, we shall look in vain. In its place, we shall very often encounter point-blank contradictions; a thing very strongly said in one essay, and very strongly unsaid in the next. We find no fault with this, as the essayist has given us fair warning. But we would remark, that a writer, whose opinions are so variable, cannot wonder if they have but little value in the eyes of the world. We are perpetually struck, also, with a boldness, bordering close upon rashness, in dealing with matters which men do not usually approach, without a sense of awe. We doubt not, the feelings of many readers have been shocked by an appearance of irreverence, with which the most momentous themes are sometimes handled in this volume; an error of taste, at least, quite unnecessary to any of the aims of the freest discussion. The name of Jesus is repeatedly coupled with that of Socrates, and other great philosophers and thinkers, as if he had been on a level with them, and no more; a mere teacher, philanthropist, or system-maker. Possibly such may be Mr. Emerson's opinion; but it almost seems as if he studied this collocation of names for the purpose of startling the common sentiment of reverence for the sacred person of the founder of our religion. With many of Mr. Emerson's leading views we differ entirely, if we understand them; if we do not, the fault lies in the author's obscurity. His general doctrine, for example, with regard to the instincts, and the influence which they ought to have upon our daily conduct, is one, which, if acted upon, would overturn society, and resolve the world into chaos. The view of human nature, on which such a doctrine alone can rest, is countenanced neither by reason nor revelation, neither by individual nor national experience. It reminds us of a theory maintained by a great Hindoo philosopher, that the human eye possesses a power which the most savage beast cannot resist; which tames the ferocity of the lion and the tiger. The sage undertook to test the truth of his theory in his own person, by quelling a wild bull with the lightnings of his eye. The bull was no theorist, but a straightforward, practical bull; like the country bumpkin in Aristophanes, he most "unphilosophically kicked;" he pawed the ground with his hoofs, lashed the air with his tail, and rushed bellowing upon the sage, and upset him and his theory into the ditch together. We fancy Mr. Emerson's doctrine of instincts would meet with a similar fate, if pitted face to face with those unphilosophical things, which he somewhere calls "refractory facts."

Mr. Emerson writes in a very uncommon style. His associations are curious and subtle, and his words are often chosen with singular felicity. Some of his sentences breathe the most exquisite music, of which language is capable. His illustrations are in most cases highly poetical. An intense love of nature, and a keen perception of the beauties of the external world, are manifested on every page of his writings. but the effect of his powers of style is not a little diminished by a studied quaintness of language, acquired apparently by imitating the turns of expression in the old English authors, more frequently than becomes a man of original genius. This quaintness of expression is one of the forms which literary affectation, at the present day, most frequently takes. If used sparingly, antique phraseology gives to style a noble and imposing aspect. The Greek tragedians sometimes interweave in the Attic of their day a Homeric or Doric word or phrase, which breathes a grand and solemn air over their stately verse. Spenser's language is enriched by many forms of expression, which wore an antiquated look in Queen

81

Elizabeth's age; and Milton's mighty genius delights to clothe its majestic conceptions in venerable language, which the frivolous wits of Charles the Second would have shrunk from aghast. In our times, the zealous study of the old English ballads, and of the elder English dramatic literature, has given a strong tincture and a racy flavor to English style. It is on the whole an improvement upon the tame correctness of the last century. The English language has been enlarged and enriched. Treasures of poetical expression have been brought to light, and put into circulation, which writers of the preceding age never dreamed of. The native Saxon words,—the most graphic and affecting in our language,—have gone far towards banishing the many-syllabled pomposity of Dr. Johnson's Latin periods. All this is well, and places the writers of our day upon a vantage ground, which they ought highly to appreciate. But it requires taste and discretion on their part, to demean themselves with moderation in the midst of these literary riches; and taste and discretion are what many of them have not enough of to spare. Much as we admire the manifold beauties of Mr. Emerson's style, we must say that he oversteps the limits of propriety, and the modesty of nature in this regard. He is often quaint where there is no peculiar solemnity or gravity or originality of thought, to which the quaintness is a suitable accompaniment. He sometimes picks up a phrase that has not been used since Shakspeare, and is quite unintelligible without a glossary. His writings are thickly studded with oddities, gathered from the most unfrequented by-paths of English literature; and when we add to this the super-sublimated transcendentalism of the Neo-Platonistic style, which he now and then affects, we must not wonder if Mr. Emerson's phraseology frequently passes the comprehension of the vulgar. More-over, he plays certain tricks with words, which disfigure his pages not a little. It may be, that these whimsies are considered beauties by some; if we judge from the frequency with which they are imitated, they are so. This only makes the matter so much the worse. They are tolerable in the inventor, but detestable in the imitator. To illustrate our meaning, we will give but one example. It is a trick very easily performed by any second-rate juggler, being nothing more than a collocation of words slightly differing from the natural one. "Always the thought is prior to the fact;" "always the soul hears an admonition;" and so on, fifty times or more. This is caught up by the smaller writers. Always Mr. Emerson writes so, and always the admiring chorus do the same. Sometimes the idiomatic proprieties of the language are set at defiance. For example, in verbs compounded with *out*; the difference between the meanings, when *out* is placed before and when it is placed after the verb, is neglected. *To write out* is one thing, and to *outwrite* is quite another; just as to *run out* means one thing, and to *outrun* another. But we have seen *to outwrite*, which can only mean to beat in writing, *to write* better or faster than another, used in the sense of *to write out*; and so of that whole class of words. These are only specimens of the absurdities committed every day, in point of style merely, by a somewhat numerous body of writers. Faults of sentiment, into which they are misled by vanity and a foolish trick of imitation, are much more striking and censurable. And when they have utterly confounded their not over-robusteous intellects by following jack-o'-lanthorn guides through the fogs of sentimental philosophy and metaphysico-romantic poetry, they seem to think they are the shining ones set apart from the common herd, breathing a different intellectual atmosphere, and enjoying a sublime elevation above the rest of their fellow-beings. But alas! these high-flying pretensions, set up by young ladies of both sexes, meet with nothing but ridicule from a wicked world, and all the airs and affectations these fantastic euphuists put on only make them look like awkward children, dressed up in the brocade gowns and high-heeled shoes of their great grandmothers.

There is great refinement of feeling often shown in Mr. Emerson's essays, and occasionally a noble appreciation of the dignity of the human soul, and of the high relations of man to man. But even his views upon these he carries to an impracticable length. He underrates the value of all positive institutions, and indulges in a very unbecoming and undeserved tone of sarcasm against them. Charles Lamb, we remember, did the same, but it was not creditable to the intelligence of that gentle-hearted author. The institutions, which philanthropic men have built up to relieve the woes of suffering humanity, to spread the blessings of knowledge among the ignorant, and to raise the fallen from their low estate, are among the brightest proofs, that the spirit of Christianity is better understood now than it has been at any former time; and, though they may be made now and then the theatre for pompous fools to display their ostentatious charities upon; yet they are, on the whole, noble expressions of the universal brotherhood of man, and far too good to be set aside for the claims of individual dignity and an imaginary independence, so extravagantly urged by Mr. Emerson.

Mr. Emerson's whimsical associations often lead him out of the regions of thought, into the realm of vague, shadowy impressions. We read paragraph after paragraph, and upon closing the book can no more recall our author's meaning, than the cloudy images of a dream. We may be told, the fault is ours; and Dr. Johnson's famous piece of boorishness may be

significantly hinted at, as it has been a great many times; "Sir, I am bound to furnish you with reasons, but not with brains." We do not admit the force of the reply. The greatest writers, of all languages, are the most distinguished for their simplicity and intelligibleness; but third and fourth-rate men love to separate themselves from the mass, and to shroud their meaning, if they have any, in a sacred and awful mysticism. Homer is intelligible enough to a person of sound common sense; but Lycophron is a hard nut to crack, and when cracked there is nothing in him. Plato's style is almost always clear as crystal; but Plotinus and Iamblicus turn Plato's light into Egyptian darkness; and Schleiermacher's Introductions show the most admirable skill in hiding his own and his author's meaning, beyond all possibility of discovery. Shakespeare is perfectly easy to understand, except where his text is corrupted, or where he alludes to some forgotten opinion or custom of his age; but Coleridge is fond of piling up big-sounding words, which pass with many people for sublimity; truly a very different sublimity from that of Homer and Shakespeare. Something like this we confess we find at times in Mr. Emerson's writings. It may arise from an effort to express what no human speech can express. Undoubtedly, there are refinements of thought and feeling, which the individual soul, in certain transient moods, apprehends, but which words fail utterly to convey to others. Such refinements make up the reveries of a summer evening; such are the moods of the mind in that agreeable semi-somnambulic state, between sleeping and waking, rather nearer the former, however, than the latter. But it requires a mighty effort of the waking man to attach any definite thought to them, when the dreamy crisis is past. And so it requires an equal effort for a person of plain understanding to make out clearly the sense of many of Mr. Emerson's musical paragraphs. If he tries hard enough, he may work some meaning into them. They are like the beverage which the Marchioness told Mr. Swiveller, she made by putting pieces of orange peel into cold water, and then made believe it was wine. "If you make believe very much it's quite nice," said the small servant; "but if you don't, you know, it seems as if it would bear a little more seasoning, certainly."

We offer a few extracts. From the first Essay, that on History, we take the following short passages;

["History," 3.24–5.12]

From the essay on Compensation, which, by-the-by, contains some extravagances about the savage state, almost equal to Rousseau's famous paradoxes, we give the following striking passage;

["Compensation," 55.3–56.24]

Nothing can be more unsound than the philosophy of the Essay on Spiritual Laws. If it is true, we must believe, that man should be left to grow up like the oak or the wild-horse, instead of being carefully trained, and taught that he is a moral agent, endowed with the mighty powers of will, and bound to obey the voice of conscience. But there are many amusing things ingeniously said in this essay; amusing from their very extravagance.

Take the following, as a specimen of Mr. Emerson's whimsical mannerism;

["Spiritual Laws," 95.35–96.7]

The Essay under the affected title of the Over-Soul is the most objectionable of all of them, both with regard to sentiment and style. Not that it can do any great harm; such speculations are too vague, too unreal for that.

We think Mr. Emerson's readers will be entertained, if not instructed, by his volume. Some, no doubt, will imagine, that it is going to turn the world upside down. We have no such apprehensions. It has not the force and fervor, the passionate appeals and popular tact, to work thus upon men's minds; but it contains many single thoughts of dazzling brilliancy; much exquisite writing, and a copious vein of poetical illustration; and shows many indications of manly character and independent thinking; but from the praises, which the author's genius would otherwise deserve, large deductions must be made, on the score of oddity, whim, and affectation; and particularly on the score of great levity of opinion, and rashness of speculation on the gravest subjects.

[Orestes A. Brownson], "Emerson's Essays," *Boston Quarterly Review*, 4 (July 1841), 291–308

In this Journal for April last, we called attention to these Essays, and promised that we would take an early opportunity to speak of them more at large. The promise we then made, we proceed now to redeem. And yet we hardly know how to do it. The Essays are good and significant, but exceedingly troublesome to reviewers, for whose especial ease and convenience they seem by no means to have been written. They contain no doctrine or system of doctrines, logically drawn out, and presented to the understanding of the reader. They consist of detached observations, independent propositions, distinct, enigmatical, oracular sayings, each of which is to be taken by itself, and judged of by its own merits. Consequently, it is impossible to reduce their teachings to a few general propositions, and to sum up their worth in a single sentence.

To most persons, who read these Essays, they will seem to be wanting in unity and coherence. They will always strike as beautiful, often as just, and sometimes as profound; but the reader will be puzzled to round their teachings into a whole, or to discover their practical bearing on life or thought. Yet they have unity and coherence, but of the transcendental sort. The author seems to us to have taken, as far as possible, his stand in the Eternal, above time and space, and tried to present things as they appear from that point of vision,—not in their relation to each other as seen in the world of the senses, but in their relation to the spectator, who views them from above the world of the senses.

This fact should be borne in mind. Mr. Emerson, to speak scientifically, is no philosopher. He is a philosopher neither in the order of his mind, nor in his method of investigation. He explains nothing, accounts for nothing, solves no intellectual problem, and affords no practical instruction. He proposes nothing of all this, and, therefore, is not to be censured for not doing it. He is to be regarded as a Seer, who rises into the regions of the Transcendental, and reports what he sees, and in the order in which he sees it. His worth can be determined, that is, the accuracy of his reports can be properly judged of, by none except those who rise to the same regions, and behold the universe from the same point of view.

Writers like Mr. Emerson are seldom to be consulted for clear, logical, systematic expositions of any subject or doctrine, never for the purpose of taking them as teachers or guides in the formation of opinions; but for the suggestions, the incentives to thought they furnish, and the life they kindle up within us. They are thought by some to be writers without any practical value for mankind; but they have, in fact, a very high practical value; only not of the every day sort, only not that of dogmatic teachers or scientific expositors. They present new aspects of things, or at least old familiar objects in new dresses, the various subjects of thought and inquiry in new relations, break up old associations, and excite to greater and fresher mental activity. After having read them, we cannot say that we are wiser or more learned than we were before; we cannot say that we have become acquainted with any new facts in the history of man or of the universe, or that we have any new ideas in regard to the human soul or its Creator; but we feel, that somehow or other new virtue has been imparted to us, that a change has come over us, and that we are no longer what we were, but greater and better.

These are not the only writers we need; but they have their place, and one of high trust, and of no slight influence. Their influence is not sudden, noisy, obvious to all senses, but slow, silent, subtle, permanent, entering into and becoming an integrant part of the life of the age, sometimes of the ages. They live and exert a power over the souls of men, long after their names are forgotten, and their works have ceased to be read. They are never in vogue with the multitude, but they are admired in select circles, who inhale their spirit, and breathe it into other and larger circles, who in their turn breathe it into the souls of all men. Though they may seem to have no practical aim, and no reference to every-day life, they have in the end a most important practical bearing, and exert a controlling influence over even the business concerns of the world. Let no one, then, regard them as mere idle dreamers, as mere literary toys, with whose glitter we may amuse ourselves, but without significance for the world of reality. They appear always for good or evil, and their appearance usually marks an epoch.

Mr. Emerson's book is a sincere production. It could have been produced only in this community at the present moment, and only by a man who had been placed in the relations he has to society and the Church. Such a book could never have emanated from a man, who had not been bred a clergyman, nor from one, who, having been bred a clergyman, had not ceased to be one. We may also say, that it could have been produced by no man, who had not been bred in a creed, which he had found insufficient to meet the wants of his intellect and heart, and who had not, in some measure, deserted it, without having found another in all respects satis-factory. We may say again, he must have been bred a unitarian, and having found unitarianism defective in consequence of its materialism, have felt and yielded to the reaction of spiritualism, and yet not sufficiently to return to any of the standard forms of orthodoxy.

We would speak respectfully of unitarianism, as we would always of the dead. It had its mission, and it has, in the providence of God, done great good in our community. But unitarianism was not, strictly speaking, a religion, could not become a religion; and it is well known, that almost always persons brought up under its influence, desert it as soon as they become seriously impressed, and desirous of leading religious lives. Men never embraced unitarianism because they were pious, but because they would dispense with being pious. Unitarianism never spoke to the heart, to the soul; never waked any real enthusiasm, or called forth any religious energy of character. It is in its nature *un*spiritual, merely intellectual and material, a sort of baptized atheism. The same causes, at bottom, which produced deism and atheism in France, produced unitarianism in New England. If the American mind had been as consequent as the French, as bold to push a doctrine to its last results, and had the Church here been organized as it was in France, and been as oppressive, our unitarians would have been avowed deists or atheists. We can find no more to feed our piety in the "*Statement of Reasons,*" than in the "*Système de la Nature.*" Indeed, the author of the latter seems the more pious worshipper of the two, and betrays altogether more of peculiar religious emotion; and reverence is more readily yielded to d'Holbach's Nature than to Norton's Divinity. The one is living, plastic, active; the other is a stern, old mechanic, placed on the outside of nature, and troubling himself rarely with its operations; wrapping himself in night and silence, neither seen nor needed by men, and would be unconceived of, did he not charitably send us now and then a messenger to inform us that he really is, and no fiction,—a piece of information altogether gratuitous, as it serves no useful purpose in either the economy of nature or of salvation. With this "Statement of Reasons," unitarianism died, and there are few mourners to go about the streets, albeit there is for it no resurrection.

The old forms of faith had ceased to satisfy the minds of the generation preceding us. Calvinism could not be explained on the principles of Locke's philosophy, and the asceticism which puritanism had enjoined could not but be distasteful and offensive to the growing aristocracy of a prosperous country. Men politely educated, sumptuously clad, fond of good eating and drinking, full of hilarity and mirth, feeling in themselves an exuberance of life, and finding the world very well adapted to their tastes, and being, therefore, in no hurry to exchange it for another, were ill prepared to embrace the ascetic doctrines and practices of their stern old fathers, who never suffered their rigid features to relax with a smile, who thought to please God only by marring the beauty of his works, and by trampling under foot the choicest of his blessings. We do not blame them much. These old puritans are a very unpoetic race of beings, and neither so pious nor so ascetic, so ungiven to the flesh withal, as their admirers would fain have us believe, as may be learned by whomsoever will take the trouble to consult our old church records. They were a strong race, and able to do much; but they attempted altogether more than they could do. They undertook to demolish both the flesh and the devil, and to live on earth as they expected to live in heaven; that is, in surly communion with their own thoughts, and in singing psalms,

with no better accompaniment than a jews-harp. Peace to their ashes. They were not without their mission, and have left their track on the ages. Perhaps, with less sourness, surliness, less rigidity, and with more of the amiable, the gentle, the attractive, they could not have done their work.

But the asceticism, which our puritan fathers insisted on, can be really practised by a people only while in the wilderness; while poor, exposed to a thousand hardships, and finding earth no resting place, but a weary land, from which any deliverance may be accounted a blessing. In proportion as the wilderness is peopled, the barren waste converted into the fruitful garden, as grow the ornamental shrubs, and blossoms the rose, and delights are multiplied around us, we take more cheerful views of the world, and of life, and seek not to mortify ourselves, but to enjoy. Asceticism must, then, give way in practice, if not in theory. It did give way in practice, and for years all New England presented the spectacle of a people professing one faith, and living according to another. Some saw this, and being honest, were shocked at it. These became unitarians. Unitarianism was with us a protest against asceticism, even more than against the absurdity of Calvinism, as contemplated from the point of view of the Lockian philosophy. It was an effort of those who could not live in a perpetual lie, to reconcile their theology and their religion to their philosophy and their mode of living.

For a time it could do very well; and as long as controversy could be maintained with opposing sects, it could apparently sustain some degree of intellectual life; but no longer. As soon as the orthodox ceased to controvert, threw it back on itself, left it to its own resources, it ceased to live.

Inasmuch as it was a dissent from the popular faith, unitarianism appealed to freedom of thought and inquiry. It asserted the rights of the individual reason. They who became unitarians, then, were not bound to continue such. They had a right to examine unitarianism, as well as the doctrines opposed to it. Such, again, was its own intrinsic deficiency, its utter inadequacy, as a religion, that the moment its own friends began to investigate it, they found they had outgrown it. They found elements in their nature it did not and could not accept, wants it did not and could not meet. They revolted against its materialism, its dryness, coldness, deadness. They fell back on the religious element of their natures, and sought refuge in a more spiritual philosophy. In this state of transition from materialism to spiritualism, from unitarianism to a modified orthodoxy, if we may be allowed the expression, our unitarian community now is. This transition is represented, in certain of its phases, in the book before us. It marks a movement of the unitarian mind towards a higher, a broader, a more truly religious faith and life. In this consists its significance, and if our orthodox friends were aware of this, they would read it with avidity and profit by it.

This revolt against materialism, and this return towards spiritualism, we regard as among the chief glories of our epoch, as a proof that the reign of infidelity is well nigh over, and that we are preparing a religious future. In this point of view, the men among us who represent this movement, and are for the present condemned, in no measured terms, as was to be expected, by both unitarians and the representatives of the old trinitarian asceticism, the old Calvinistic spiritualism, are the real benefactors of their age and country; the men, who, instead of abuse and discouragement, deserve honor and coöperation. But we never recognise our redeemers till we have crucified them. We cannot say of a truth, that they are sons of God, till we perceive the darkness which comes over the earth as they leave it.

These Essays mark among us the reaction of spiritualism. This constitutes their historical value. How far they represent truly the spiritualism that should become dominant, is another question, and one which can be answered only by determining their positive value. This last can be done only by entering into a critical examination of their merits, a thing which it seems to us almost sacrilegious to attempt. They do not seem to us legitimate subjects of criticism. There is a sacredness about them, a mystic divinity, a voice issuing from them, saying to critics, "Procul, O procul, este, profani." To do them justice, they should be read with reverence, with a yielding spirit, an open heart, ready to receive with thankfulness whatever meets its wants or can be appropriated to its use. The rest, what is not congenial, should be left with pious respect; perhaps there are souls which will find it wholesome food. Why should we deprive others of appropriate nutriment, because it is no nutriment to us?

But Mr. Emerson sometimes descends from the Seer, and assumes the Reasoner. He sometimes touches on dogmas and systems, and if he adopts rarely a philosophical form, a system of philosophy lies back of his poetic utterances, and constitutes even for him the ground on which they are to be legitimated. This system we may examine without profanity. It will, moreover, be ultimately drawn out and formally taught by his disciples. His book will give it currency, and be appealed to as its authority. There can, then, be no impropriety in asking if it be true or false, complete or incomplete.

This system, we say distinctly, is not scientifically taught in the book before us. We are not sure that Mr. Emerson himself is always conscious of it. We are inclined to believe, that he thinks that he

88

eschews all systems, and entangles himself in the meshes of no theory. But every man who speaks at all implies a theory, and in general the greatest theorizers are those who profess to abjure all theory. Every man has his own point of view, from which he contemplates the universe, and whence all his reports are drawn. The question may, then, always come up, is this the true point of view, the point from which the universe may be seen as it really is, and represented in all its unity and diversity? The moment this question is asked, and we undertake to answer it, we plunge into metaphysics, and avail ourselves of system, of theory.

Mr. Emerson's point of view is, we have said, the transcendental. Can the universe, seen from this point of view alone, be truly represented? The answer to this question will enable us to determine the philosophic value of his Essays.

In the philosophy against which there is, in our times, a decided movement, there is no recognition of a transcendental world, of aught that transcends time and space. Immensity is merely space that cannot be measured; eternity is merely time without end. God, as well as man, exists in time and space, and differs from man only in the fact that he fills all space, and continues through all time. Eternal life is a life in time, but merely time endlessly continued. This philosophy never, therefore, carries us out of time and space. To all persons embracing this philosophy, transcendentalists must appear mere dreamers, endeavoring to give to airy nothing, a local habitation and a name.

Now, transcendentalism recognises a world lying back of and above the world of time and space. Time and space belong merely to the world of the senses; but the reason,—not as the principle of logic, but as the principle of intelligence,—rises immediately into a region where there is no time, no space. Immensity is not space

infinitely extended, but the negation of all space; eternity is not time endlessly continued, but the negation of all time. God does not exist in space. We cannot say that he is here, there, somewhere, but that he is everywhere, which is only saying again, in other words, that he is NOwhere. He exists not in, but out of time. We cannot say God was, God will be, but simply that he *is*, as the Hebrew name of God, *I* AM, plainly implies. To him there is no time. He has no past, no future. He inhabiteth eternity, dwells not in time, but in NO-time, as Watts implies, when he says, with God "all is one eternal NOW."

All our ideas of truth, justice, love, beauty, goodness, are transcendental. Truth is truth, independent of time and place. The just is the just at one epoch, in one country, as much as in another. The beautiful never varies; its laws, we all say, are eternal. Goodness is ever the same. The great principles of the Christian religion inhabit eternity. Hence Jesus says, "before Abraham was I am," and hence he is called "the Lamb slain from the foundations of the world," meaning thereby, that the principles of truth and duty he represented, and by which alone man can come into harmony with his Maker, were no principles of modern creation, but principles existing in the very Principle of things,—principles that have no dependence on time and space, but were in the beginning with God, and were God.

These remarks will help us to understand what is meant by transcendentalism. Transcendentalism, in its good sense, as used in our community, means the recognition of an order of existences, which transcend time and space, and are in no sense dependent on them, or affected by them. Transcendental means very nearly what our old writers, in Shakespeare's time, meant by the word *metaphysical*, from μετα, *beyond*, and φυσιχο, *physical*, natural, belonging to the outward, visible, material world. Transcendentalists recognise a world lying beyond or above the world of the senses, and in man the power of seeing or knowing this transcendental world immediately, by direct cognition, or intuition.

All persons, who believe in God, in the reality of a spiritual world, and contend that their belief has any legitimate basis, are transcendentalists. Whoever is not a transcendentalist, must, if consequent, needs be a skeptic, or a materialist and an atheist. The early Christian fathers were transcendentalists, so were the distinguished English writers of the seventeenth century; so were Descartes, Malebranche, George Fox, William Penn, and our own Edwards; so were Price, and to a feeble extent, the Scottish School; so are nearly all the Germans, and the French Eclectics. Locke and his followers were not, nor were Condillac and the old French school. In fact, all real faith implies the Transcendental, and religion is an idle dream unless we admit the reality of an order of existences, a spiritual world transcending this outward, material, sensible world; and also unless we admit in man the means of attaining legitimately to faith in that reality.

Mr. Emerson, by taking his stand in this transcendental region, evidently asserts its existence, and our power to take cognizance of it. So far his philosophy is eminently religious, and as we have demonstrated over and over again in the pages of this Journal, as well as elsewhere, is sound, and worthy of all acceptation. In this consists his chief philosophical merit. In this too consists his departure from Locke and the unitarian school proper, and his approach to orthodoxy. Thus far we go with him heart and hand, and recognise him as a fellow-laborer in that school of which we profess to be a disciple, though it may be an unworthy one.

But the transcendental, or, if you please, metaphysical, or spiritual world, exists not for the senses, nor can it be inferred from data furnished by the senses. It exists only for the reason. It is ideal, as opposed to sensible, spiritual as opposed to material, but real and substantial. Its existence is indeed involved in all the perceptions of the senses, and asserted in every thought and affirmation; but we rise to the cognition of it only by means of reason, taken, as we have said, not as the principle of logic, but as the principle of intelligence.

Now, by taking our stand on the reason as the principle of intelligence, which is partly analogous to what Mr. Emerson calls the "Over-Soul," and attending exclusively to what it reveals, we are in danger of losing sight of the world of the senses, and therefore of suffering one aspect of the universe to escape us. The moment we rise into the world of reason, we find it altogether richer, sublimer, more beautiful, than this outward visible world. This outward visible world gradually loses its charms for us, disappears from the horizon of our vision, and is therefore very naturally denied to have any existence. We thus fall into Idealism.

Again; the world of the senses is manifold and diverse, while the world of the reason is one and identical. In the transcendental world we rise to the principles of things. The principle of a thing is after all, in a certain sense, the thing itself. All principles proceed from and centre in one common principle, the principle of all things,—God. The diversity noted by the senses is then no real diversity, but merely phenomenal and illusory, and deserving no account from him who has risen to the perception of absolute unity, into which all is resolved at last. Diversity is therefore rejected, denied. The distinction between cause and effect ceases then to be intelligible; all difference between God and the universe to be perceptible. The universe is identical with God. God and the universe are one and the same; this is Pantheism.

Whoever then takes his stand exclusively in the Transcendental must fall into ideal Pantheism. From the transcendental point of view alone, a correct report of the universe cannot be made out, any more than from the point of view of the senses alone.

Now Mr. Emerson seems to us to verify in his own case the truth of this deduction. He falls in his philosophy, so far as philosophy he has, into ideal Pantheism. He is so charmed with the world of ideas, that he contemns the sensible, so struck with the unity and identity revealed by the reason, that he is led to overlook and occasionally to deny the manifold and the diverse, revealed by the senses. We cannot read a page of these Essays without perceiving that the tendency of his mind is to seek unity and identity. He brings together in the same sentence perpetually persons and things, events and transactions, apparently the most diverse, by a law of association which most readers are unable to discover, and the point of resemblance between which very few are able to perceive. Yet is he in general just. The resemblance, the identity he asserts is there. His power of detecting the identical in the diverse, the analogous in the dissimilar, the uniform in the manifold, the permanent in the transitory, is remarkable, and unsurpassed in any writer of our acquaintance. He is ever surprising us by unexpected resemblances. To him all things are the same. In all this he is right. He uttered a great truth when he declared the identity of the power by which Lazarus was raised from the dead, and that by which falls the rain or blows the clover; also when he so shocked some of our pious people by declaring the identity of

gravitation and purity of heart. This identity does run through all nature, and he has not true insight into the universe who cannot detect it.

But diversity, dissimilarity, multiplicity, are no less obvious and real in the universe than unity and identity. They have their origin too in the same source. God, the cause and principle of the universe, is not a mere unity, but a unity that has in itself the principle of multiplicity,—not pure identity, but at once identity and diversity,—a fact shadowed forth in the doctrine of a Triune God, which runs through all religious philosophies ever promulgated. Whoever overlooks this fact must fall into Pantheism. Mr. Emerson has a tendency to overlook it; and his disciples, for disciples always exaggerate the tendencies of their masters, will most assuredly overlook it. Some of them even now avow themselves Pantheists, and most of the young men and maidens who listened with so much delight to these Essays when they were delivered as lectures, virtually run into Pantheism, whether they know it or not.

The outward visible world is not the only world into which we are admitted, but it is a real world; that is, it really exists, and is no more an illusion than the world of reason; and the idealist is as exclusive and as erroneous as the materialist. The one denies the Transcendental, the other the Sensible. Both are wrong in what they deny, both are right in what they assert; and this fact, it strikes us, does not lie at the basis of Mr. Emerson's philosophy. Hence the wrong tendency of his speculations.

We are not prone to be frightened or shocked at mere words. Thank Heaven, we have strong nerves, and can bear much; but we regard Pantheism as an error of no less magnitude than Atheism itself, and consequently must earnestly protest against every tendency to it. God and the universe are in the most intimate relation, but that relation is one of cause and effect, not of identity; and while we admit that there is this identity running through all nature, to which Mr. Emerson points us, we also contend that there is a corresponding diversity to which he does not point us. We complain not of him for not doing this, but we note the fact in order to warn our readers against taking his utterances as complete expositions of the universe. He brings us one pole of truth, the one which has been too much depressed; but in bringing up that he is not sufficiently heedful not to depress equally the other. We have revolted against exclusive materialism; let us be careful not to fall now into exclusive spiritualism; we have protested against Atheism and irreligion, or the forms of religion which were in fact no religion, and we should look to it that we do not now swallow up all diversity in unity, and man and the universe in God. The latter error would turn out to be as fatal to piety and morals as the former.

But after all, we have no serious apprehensions on this score. Ideal Pantheism, though a fatal error, is not one into which our countrymen are likely to fall, at least to any great extent. Only a few of the cultivated, the refined, the speculative, the idle, and contemplative, are exposed to it. Men in active business, taking their part in the rough and tumble of life, coming in daily contact with one another in the market, the husting, the legislative halls, scrambling for power or place, wealth or distinction, have little leisure, less inclination, and still less aptitude for that order of thought which ends in the denial of matter, and of the universe as distinguished from its Creator. The cast of their minds is too practical, and they are of too sturdy, too robust a make to find anything satisfactory in so refined a spiritualism. Their

daily habits and pursuits demand a solid earth on which to work, a providence to protect them, a sovereign to rule over them, a real God to curb their headstrong violence, and to reduce them to order and peace, to chastise them for their errors, and to solace them in their afflictions. The practical tendencies of our countrymen will save them from all danger they would be likely to incur from speculative refinements like those we have pointed out; and we are not sure but Mr. Emerson's strong statements are needed to rectify their over-attachment to the material order.

As it concerns the ethical doctrines implied rather than set forth in these Essays, we have nothing to add to the remarks we have heretofore made on the same subject. Mr. Emerson's moral philosophy, reduced to its systematic element, belongs to the egoistical school; but we presume, after all, that he means little more by those expressions which imply it, and which have given so much offence, than that just self-reliance, that fidelity to one's own nature and conscience, without which it is impossible to reach or maintain a true manly worth. In this view of the case, his Essay on Self-Reliance is a noble and unexceptionable performance, and inculcates a lesson, which it were well for us all to learn and practise,—a lesson which is perhaps more appropriate to the American people than to any other Christian nation, for no other Christian nation is so timid in its speculations, so afraid of solving for itself, independently, the problem of the destiny of man and society. We regard it as decidedly one of the best Essays in the collection.

We did intend to quote from the book itself, in order to justify our criticisms, but it is not a book from which quotations can be made with much satisfaction. We could not select a paragraph that would not at once confirm and refute our general criticisms. We content ourselves, therefore, with speaking merely of its dominant tendency, as it appears to us. The book cannot be judged of without being read, and the best way to read it will be to forget its metaphysics, and to take it up as we would a collection of poems, or of proverbs.

Of the Essays we cannot speak particularly. The one on Heroism is inferior to what we expected from its author, and falls far below the general average of the book. Those on Love and Friendship are beautiful and often true, but their truth and beauty proceed from the intellect and imagination rather than the heart and soul. They read not like the confessions of a lover or a friend. There are depths in the affections, into which the author does not descend, deeper experiences than any he discloses. The Essays we have liked the best are those on the Over-Soul, Self-Reliance, and History.

These Essays are, to a certain extent, democratic, they condemn all ordinary aristocracies, and breathe much respect for labor and the laborer; but it is evident, at a single glance, that the author is at best only an amateur workingman, one who has never himself wielded spade or mattock to any great extent, and who has viewed labor with the eye of a poet, rather than with the feelings of an actual laborer. His book, though apparently radical, contains nothing more likely to give offence to the capitalist than to the proletary.

One of the most serious objections, we have to urge against these Essays, is the little importance they assign to the state, and the low rank they allow to patriotism as a virtue. This is an error of our transcendental school generally, and results, we suppose, chiefly from the fact, that its principal masters are or have been churchmen, and, therefore, not over and above acquainted with practical life. Their studies lead them to rely on preaching, persuasion, advice, appeals to the reason and conscience. Their habits and position remove them from the actual world, and its necessities, and keep them ignorant of no small part of the actual developments of human nature. Clergymen are usually able to give wholesome advice, at least, advice which will generally be regarded as canonical; but they are rarely gifted with much practical skill or sagacity. A deliberative assembly, composed entirely of clergymen, is usually a very disorderly body, and ill adapted to the speedy despatch of business. The members are all so enlightened, so wise, so good, so meek, and so conscientious, that ordinary parliamentary rules are rarely thought to be necessary; and the result is not seldom confusion, angry, disorderly debate, and no little ill feeling and ill speaking. This anti-political tendency of our transcendentalists, is, therefore, easily accounted for. Nevertheless, it is a false tendency. Man, as we have endeavored to prove in a foregoing article, is to be perfected in society, and society is to be perfected by government. More, than even politicians themselves usually imagine, depends on the right organization of the commonwealth. The science of politics, when rightly viewed, is a grand and an essential science, and needs always to be held in honor. Much is lost by not making it a subject of more serious study. Everybody talks about politics, and yet there is scarcely a man among us acquainted with the simplest principles of politics, regarded as a science. The proper organization of the state, the true exposition of the constitution, and the proper administration, so as to secure the true end of government, are matters with which we, as people, rarely trouble ourselves; and scarcely a man can be found, who can speak on them five minutes in succession, without betraying gross ignorance, both theoretical and practical. In this state of political science, our scholars are doing us great disservice by sneering at politics and the state.

As mere literary productions, these Essays must take rank with the best in the language. There is now and then an affectation of quaintness, a puerile conceit, not precisely to our taste, but it detracts not much from their general beauty. In compactness of style, in the felicitous choice of words, in variety, aptness, and wealth of illustration, they are unrivalled. They have a freshness, a vigor, a freedom from old hacknied forms of speech, and from the conventionalisms of the schools, worthy of the highest praise, and which cannot fail to exert a salutary influence on our growing literature. They often remind us of Montaigne, especially in the little personal allusions, which the author introduces with inimitable grace, delicacy, and effect.

In conclusion, we will simply add, that not withstanding the metaphysical errors to which we have referred, the Essays make up a volume unique in its character, and which all competent judges will agree in regarding as among the most creditable productions of the American press. It must secure to the author a distinguished rank among the more distinguished writers of the age. We feel ourselves deeply indebted for his present. We receive his utterances with thankfulness and reverence, and shall wait impatiently till he permits us to hear from him again. It is not often, that in our profession as a critic, we meet with a work of fewer faults, nor one that can better bear to have its faults pointed out; for it is rare that we meet with one with its positive excellencies. It is no ephemeral production; it will survive the day; for it is full of sincerity, truth, beauty. Whoso pores over its pages will find his soul quickened, his vision enlarged, his heart warmed, and his life made better.

Review of *Essays*, *Literary Gazette* [England], 1288 (25 September 1841), 620–1

Mr. Carlyle approves of this book; and no wonder, for it out-Carlyles Carlyle himself, exaggerates all his peculiarities and faults, and possesses very slight glimpses of his excellences. It imitates his inflations, his verbiage, his Germanico-Kantian abstractions, his metaphysics and mysticism; but wants the originality, the soul, the high and searching intellect, which, in spite of these "pribbles and prabbles, look ye," ever and anon burst out with something to fill the reader with admiration, and set the mind to work upon noble expressions and striking and grand ideas. Not even is the editor's follower and *protégé*, Ralph Waldo Emerson, though he does describe him and his volume, in his queer phraseology, to be "a kind of articulate human voice, speaking words" "from the heart of him," "no matter in what fashion;" and not "another of the thousand thousand ventriloquisms, mimetic echoes, hysteric shrieks, hollow laughters, and mere *in*articulate mechanical babblements, the soul-confusing din of which already fills all places."

The enigmatic style of this school is generally too prominent; and even of his own Transatlantic compeer, Mr. Carlyle is obliged to acknowledge, that "flickering like bright bodiless Northern Streamers, notions and half-notions of a metaphysic, theosophic, theologic kind are seldom long wanting in these *Essays*. I do not advise the British Public to trouble itself much with all that; still less to take offence at it. Whether this Emerson be 'a Pantheist,' or what kind of Theist or *ist* he may be, can perhaps as well remain undecided. If he prove a devout-minded, veritable, original man, this for the present will suffice. *Ists* and *Isms* are rather growing a weariness. Such a man does not readily range himself under *Isms*." And, to recommend him still farther, he adds:—"In a word, while so many Benthamisms, Socialisms, Fourierisms, *professing* to have no soul, go staggering and lowing like monstrous mooncalves, the product of a heavy-laden moonstruck age; and, in this same baleful 'twelfth hour of the night,' even galvanic Puseyisms, as we say, are visible, and dancing of the sheeted dead,—shall not any voice of a living man be welcome to us, even because it is alive? For the rest, what degree of mere literary talent lies in these utterances, is but a secondary question; which every reader may gradually answer for himself. What Emerson's talent is, we will not altogether estimate by this Book. The utterance is abrupt, fitful; the great idea not yet embodied struggles towards an embodiment. Yet everywhere there is the true heart of a man; which is the parent of all talent; which without much talent cannot exist. A breath as of the green country,—all the welcomer that it is *New*-England country, not the second-hand but first-hand country,—meets us wholesomely everywhere in these *Essays*: the authentic green Earth is there, with her mountains, rivers, with her mills and farms. Sharp gleams of insight arrest us by their pure intellectuality; here and there, in heroic rusticism, a tone of modest manfulness, of mid invincibility, low-voiced, but lion-strong, makes us too thrill with a noble pride. Talent? Such ideas as dwell in this man, how can they ever speak themselves with *enough* of talent? The talent is not the chief question here. The idea, that is the chief question. Of the living acorn you do not ask first, How *large* an acorn art thou? The smallest living acorn is fit to be the parent of oaktrees without end,—could clothe all New England with oaktrees by and by. You ask it, first of all: Art thou a living acorn? Certain, now, that thou art not a dead mushroom, as the most are?—But, on the whole, our Book is short; the Preface should not grow too long. Closing these questionable parables and intimations, let me in plain English recommend this little Book as the Book of an original veridical man, worthy the acquaintance of those who delight in such; and so: Welcome to it whom it may concern!"

As the master, so the pupil; as the recommender, so the recommended,—only that the latter is often more quaint, more stilted, and more unintelligible; for we are not understanders of "half notions," and, to say the truth, hardly of many which seem to be meant for whole ones. We select an example of the best order:—

["Compensation," 65.33–66.25]

Were we to analyse this quotation, with its axiomatic vagueness, we should have to dissect a mass of contradictions involved in words with import. We can scarcely tell what the writer would be at; but we perceive that he is wrong, and only that the principle he would establish is good.

But we proceed to a still more untractable jumble of words, which affect our common sense as phantasmagoria affect our sight. Perhaps more acute readers may make more of them:—

["Love," 99.3–15]

The illustration is more homely and intelligible; here is a piece of it:—

["Love," 101.5–28]

Not to be too prolix with a work of this sort, of which any two or three pages afford a fair criterion by which to judge of the whole, we conclude with one other sample of Massachusetts Carlylery.

["Circles," 184.11–185.15]

In short, our Ralph Waldo E. is a circular philosopher.

"Emerson's Essays," *Monthly Review* [England], 3 (October 1841), 274–9

This volume is a curiosity: it may almost class with Mr. Haughton's Essay on Sex in the World to Come, in any cabinet of unique books. At any rate it ought to occupy a shelf in the *case* assigned especially to Thomas Carlyle, although Mr. Ralph Waldo Emerson will have no right to complain should he be shoved into the darkest or least inviting corner of the mahogany. The mere act of godfathership, by reprinting the work in this country, and heralding it by a laudatory preface, proves that it is a book after Carlyle's own heart. Some portions of that preface itself must not be passed over; for it tells us something which the Essays themselves cannot be expected to do of the author; while it furnishes a striking and not unamusing or unsuggestive specimen of Carlylisms.

Thomas thus inquires and speaks,— "While so many Benthamisms, Socialisms, Fourierisms, *professing* to have no soul, go staggering and lowing like monstrous moon-calves, the product of a heavy moonstruck age; and in this same baleful 'twelfth hour of night,' even galvanic Puseyisms, as we say, are visible, and dancings of the sheeted dead,—shall not any voice of a living man be welcome to us, even because it is alive?" Mr. C. has just before told "the British public" not to trouble itself about whether this Emerson be "a Pantheist, or what kind of Theist or *Ist* he may be." The only thing is, "if he prove a devout-minded, veritable, original man, this for the present will suffice;" for that "*Ists* and *Isms* are

rather growing a weariness." Well then, "and for the rest, what degree of mere literary talent lies in these utterances, is but a secondary question; which every reader may gradually answer for himself." Even, "What Emerson's talent is, we will not altogether estimate by this book. The utterance is abrupt, fitful; the great idea not yet embodied struggles towards an embodiment. Yet everywhere there is the true heart of a man; which is the parent of all talent; which without much talent cannot exist. A breath as of the green country—all the welcomer that it is, *New*-England country, not second-hand but first-hand country—meets us wholesomely everywhere in these Essays; the authentic green earth is there, with her mountains, rivers, with her mills and farms. Sharp gleams of insight arrest us by their pure intellectuality; here and there, in heroic rusticism, a tone of modest manfulness, of mild invincibility, low-voiced, but lion-strong, makes us to thrill with a noble pride. Talent? Such ideas as dwell in this man, how can they ever speak themselves with *enough* of talent? The talent is not the chief question here. The idea, that is the chief question. Of the living acorn you do not ask first, How *large* an acorn art thou? The smallest living acorn is fit to be the parent of oak trees without end,—could clothe all New England with oak trees by and by. You ask it first of all, Art thou a living acorn? Certain, now, that thou art not a dead mushroom as most are?" "Closing these questionable parables and insinuations, let me in plain English recommend this little book as the book of an original viridical man, worthy the acquaintance of those who delight in such; and so, Welcome to it, whom it may concern!"

This is high praise from a high quarter; but praise, we suspect, which has been considerably influenced by Emerson's mannerism of thought and diction, partaking as it does of Carlyle's own; but by no means so independent, so original, so suggestive, so full of lofty or of deep and far-reaching thought, as are the "utterances" of Thomas. We much oftener find in Emerson's quaint and strange modes of speech, in his queer phrases, and aphoristic enigmas, old and common-place ideas, feebly or only half-conceived; so that the Prefacer appears to us to hit the mark pretty closely, when he describes the "notions and half-notions of a metaphysic, theosophic, theologic kind," which occur in these Essays as resembling "flickering bright bodiless northern streamers."

Mr. C. talks of his *protégé* as being a self-dependent man, and not one of your "thousand thousand ventriloquists, mimetic echoes, hysteric shrieks, hollow laughters, and mere *in*articulate mechanical babblements, the soul-confusing din of which already fills all places." Now, it appears to us that "mimetic echoes" will very frequently be detected in these Essays; and as to "hysteric shrieks," if not more abundant than in the oracular enunciations of the god-father, they are at least more harsh and less powerful—struggling half-notes—thoughts caught by the heels, but never fully grasped—often abstractions, loosely connected, and thrown out as if by random around some true principle indistinctly comprehended. One does not readily perceive evidences of plan, nor of skill in subordinating ideas according to their non-importance, nor of rejecting what helps not to develop the contemplated lesson or doctrine. In short he seems to labour under the vanity of affectation, so far as to spoil many good thoughts, rather than that he should utter them as other men of sound minds would do; and also to be so far an imitator as to have preferred Carlyle as a model to any other single writer. And yet Mr. Emerson is no servile slave, no ordinary thinker, no ev-

ery day sort of teacher. What we learn of his history from the editor might convince any one of his singularity and independence. It appears that he has relinquished the paths of business; and, even when having before him the omens of success, has withdrawn into retired walks, to "sit down to spend his life not in Mammon worship, or the hunt for reputation, influence, place, or any outward advantage whatsoever." But besides this evidence of resolution, single-mindedness, and self-dependence, his very rejection of the conventionalities of style, and a determination to utter what he believes to be truth, testify that he is a man of mark, and one that will leave a stamp upon the minds of others. He often handles great truths in a bold suggestive manner, almost worthy of his model; and his earnestness is healthy and strong.

The Essays are twelve in number; but it would yield little satisfaction were we to give the titles of each, since there seldom follows anything according to what will be expected, or to the views which most people entertain. A variety of specimens will best indicate and exhibit the Essayist's sort of mysticism, dogmatic axioms, vague metaphysics, as well as sterling and original thoughts, admirably though quaintly framed. Take a passage from the Essay on "Compensation;" a hackneyed clerical doctrine is the theme:—

["Compensation," 55.22–56.17]

Many excellent "utterances" may be found in the Essay on "Self-Reliance," and not a few paradoxes; at least the profusion of words at times is bewildering. But our readers look for examples from a writer who will not permit them to yawn over his pages. Hear him on conforming to dead usages, and also relative to the magnanimity required from the non-conformist:—

["Self-Reliance," 31.37–32.22,
32.36–33.15]

Here is a characteristic preachment.

["Compensation," 65.33–66.25]

We said that Mr. Haughton and the Massachusetts philosopher might fitly be classed together in a cabinet of unique specimens. There is also at times a considerable degree of harmony in their sentiments. An example is before us:—

["Spiritual Laws," 77.3–13]

The following is a more striking instance:—

["Love," 99.3–15]

Let us wind up with an illustration of one of Mr. Emerson's dogmas, that "all mankind love a lover:"—

["Love," 101. 6–28]

Review of *Essays, Athenæum*, 730 (23 October 1841), 803–4

A good Introduction is a great advantage, not less in the intellectual than in the fashionable or mercantile world. Mr. Emerson has been fortunate in this particular; he is brought before the English reading public by one of the "observed" of the day, and may thus gain a degree of notice, which, we will venture to affirm, he would not else have attracted: not because his 'Essays' are altogether destitute of merit, but rather because of the peculiar vein of thought which runs through them, and, above all, of the very uncouth—the very un-English—garb in which they are clothed.

Were we to look at his book in a merely literary point of view, we should pronounce it—or, rather, denounce it—at once, as absolutely below criticism. Never was diction so rough, so distorted, so inharmonious: never was expression so opaque, so ponderous, so laboured. We positively doubt, while we read, whether we are not labouring at low Saxon or high Dutch. We protest, as heretofore, against these unnatural innovations in the tongue of Milton and of Shakspeare. These defilers of the pure "well of English" ought to know that every language possesses an idiosyncracy of its own—and this wholly independent of mere grammatical rules. When this idiosyncracy is neglected—when a language is tortured into shapes contrary to the tendencies of its nature—it becomes harsh, crude, dissonant, and obscure. If the folly be countenanced, and become general, the language itself suffers; its elegance disappears,—words, which before were explicit, gradually become misty and undefined; this re-acts upon ideas, and it is very difficult to say where that reaction stops. An attention to style is one of the "social duties" of literary life,—more especially with those who deal in principles, who profess to instruct and to elevate by their writings. The style of a book is, as it were, the outward and material envelope of the inner thoughts, and, as such, ought to be in harmony with the ideas; and where this harmony is wanting, it is fair to assume that the writer has not that clear perception which is so essential to the appreciation of the Beautiful both in Nature and Art.

The subjects treated of in these 'Essays' are, History, Self-Reliance, Spiritual Laws, Love, Friendship, Heroism, Intellect, Art. Mr. Emerson is not content to skim over the surface of these vast questions; on the contrary, he is ever struggling to pierce through the relative and the phenomenal, and to grasp the absolute and the eternal—to dive beyond the ever-revolving circumference, and reach that centre where all is fixed and immutable.

It is evident that a work of this nature cannot be duly appreciated by superficial criticism. The question is, here, not of picturesque descriptions, skilful delineations of character, &c.; it is a question of pure ideas, of abstract theories, and of the applications of those theories. We shall not, therefore, attempt any detailed analysis of these 'Essays'; it would be out of place and out of character. Our duty is to disengage, if possible, from the rough and broken mass of thought before us, the fundamental ideas of the writer; to determine, in short, his method—his *system*.

This word "system" brings us back, perforce, to the Preface; for the Preface (which, by the bye, is a very choice and perfect specimen of its author's style), after telling us that all "*Ists* and *Isms*" are

"growing a weariness," adds, that "one of the merits" of the book is, that "it has no system, and points or stretches far beyond all systems." This judgment is very much after the fashion of the day, which just now delights to cry down systems— to use the word as a synonym for exclusiveness, as expressive of one-sided views and narrow theories: whereas a system, properly defined, is nothing more than a chain of deductions logically attached to some primary principle or principles; which deductions are made according to certain fixed laws; and if these laws are untrue, then is Truth beyond human attainment. It is not, therefore, the system which errs; it is the principles on which it is based. These principles being fallacious—or, which is much more probable, incomplete—the system will partake of precisely the same amount of fallacy, or incompleteness. It is mere babble, therefore, to talk of a man being "above," or "beyond" systems; every man who thinks and reasons *must* have a system, from the mere fact of his reasoning. This is not the place to determine whether Mr. Carlyle himself has a system or not; but we cannot help expressing a hope that the following observation is not logically allied to any of the principles he professes! Characterizing the work before us, he remarks of it"—"Everywhere there is the true heart of man, which is the parent of all talent; *which, without much talent, cannot exist*"! This is either pure unadulterate nonsense, or an extreme of intellectual exclusiveness which is equally pitiable and presumptuous.

With reference, however, to Mr. Emerson, although his 'Essays' do not present any connected exposition of a Philosophical Theory, yet are they all so rigorously attached to a few first principles—and this, too, by *à priori* reasoning—that we feel warranted in affirming that, so far from being "above" such control, he seems, to us, to be absolutely the slave of a system! His reason is completely bound by the chains of a logic which it has forged for its own captivity.

There are two distinct aspects under which all circumstances may be considered, and most reasoners adopt either the one or the other. They either confine their attention to *details*, and see nothing above or beneath but the actual—nothing but facts, and the relations between facts; or they contemplate *causes* alone, and see nothing but the abstract and the ideal: and these methods seem to divide pretty equally between them the past history of Philosophy. Yet both give erroneous, because incomplete, notions on all subjects they attempt to explain; both, when carried out, with rigorous logic, to their extreme consequences, lead to results equally untenable.

It is to the latter class of reasoners that Mr. Emerson belongs, and his work is replete with the errors of his method. Moreover, it is desultory to a painful degree: first principles and ultimate conclusions are stuck side by side, leaving gaps of reasoning to be filled up by the reader, wide enough to startle a German Professor. Inconsistencies and contradictions, too, abound: in short, Mr. Emerson seems to have "gone to a feast" of Philosophy, and "brought away the scraps."

The first page of his book offers a remarkable illustration of what we have here urged against him. He thus commences the Essay on History—which, we may observe, developes, without the slightest acknowledgment, the idea propounded by Hegel on the same question.

"There is one mind common to all individual men. Every man is an inlet to the same, and to all of the same. He that is once admitted to the right of reason, is made a freeman of the whole estate.* * Who hath access to this universal mind, is a party to all that is, or can be done, for this mind is the only and sovereign agent."

Now this mystical idea of "one mind common to all individual men," strikes the half-thinker as a sublime philosophic discovery; and he has often so much reverence for its enunciator as not to dare to ask him how he found it out! Yet sublime as it appears, it has a very humble origin. There is an expression universally received—"the human mind"—which is what is called an "abstract idea." An abstract idea is a pure creation of the intellect, and in all processes of reasoning such ideas are indispensable. The individual objects around us present certain obvious resemblances and differences; we seize the one and reject the other; and, including all the former under a single name, we form classes, species, &c. The nature of an abstract idea is, therefore, wholly dependent on certain mental laws, or, technically speaking, wholly *subjective*. But Mr. Emerson, disregarding this elementary truth, has given to the dependent abstract idea, "the human mind," a veritable and independent existence, and, by this simple process has arrived at his mystical theory of "one mind common to all individual men." With just the same truth might a Naturalist tell us of one tail common to all individual cats, or one odour common to all individual roses! This is a very prevalent mistake in certain systems of modern philosophy. The mind which can raise itself to the consideration of abstractions, proud of the apparent increase of its vision, and rejoicing in the despotism which it can so easily exercise over a world filled with its own creations, is very apt to neglect—nay, to deny—the whole universe of realities; forgetting that it is these alone which have enabled it to attain the ideal sphere in which it revels.

101

After creating his "universal mind," Mr. Emerson is easily led to his philosophy of History. "Of the works of this mind, History is the record." But, of course, this mind, like individual minds, must be developed in time—must be subject to various passions—must give place to ever-changing ideas; and so thinks Mr. Emerson:—

"Without hurry, without rest, the human spirit goes forth from the beginning to embody every faculty, every thought, every emotion which belongs to it, in appropriate events.*
* Epoch after epoch, camp, kingdom, empire, republic, democracy, are merely the application of this manifold spirit to the manifold world."

By way of illustration, Mr. Emerson informs us that ancient Greece represents the youth of man, and that "our reverence for the Greeks is our reverence for childhood." If this thought had been left in its vague form, it might have passed as a pretty conceit, possessing some dim, cloudlike resemblance to reality. But Mr. Emerson does not shrink from putting it to a severer test, and boldly assures us that "a great boy, or a great girl, with good sense, *is a Greek*!" Now this ludicrous idea is a direct result of Mr. Emerson's *system*. Recognizing nothing but abstractions—regarding man as pure intellectuality—he is logically led to such conclusions. If the hypothesis which he sets out with were true—if man were really a being of pure intellect, instead of one compounded of intellect and sensibility—a very close analogy might exist between the terms selected. But, as man is actually constituted, the comparison can never be received in any other than a metaphorical sense: for the character of the Greek was not dependent merely on the state of his intellect; it was dependent, as national character must be, on a thousand external influences—influences wholly contingent and temporal; influences of religion, of politics, of society, of climate: all of them long since changed, ever changing, and not, therefore, acting upon the "great boys" and "great girls" of Mr. Emerson's world. It is, indeed, almost bewildering to think over all the elements of individuality which must be annihilated before this doctrine can become truth.

A speculative philosopher, who dispenses with experience, has no limits to his range. After dogmatizing on man, Mr. Emerson makes a grasp at Nature also. Here again, he propounds his *à priori* theory, and proceeds to build upon it the whole system of creation. All physical laws, he tells us, may be summed up in a dualism—action and re-action. Behold the animating idea of the Creator when the universe grew beneath his hands! This law—

"We meet with in every part of nature,—in darkness and light, in heat and cold, in the ebb and flow of waters, in male and female, &c. * * An inevitable dualism bisects nature, so that each thing is a half, and suggests another thing to make it a whole: as spirit, matter, man, woman; subjective, objective; *in, out; upper, under:* motion, rest; *yea, nay.*"

Here, be it observed, Mr. Emerson goes a step further. Not content with *objectiving* abstract ideas, as before shown, he objectives the mere relative terms,—in, out; upper, under; yea, nay! Dualism is transported from the material into the intellectual world! of course; for with Mr. Emerson matter and intellect are identical—are both forms of the eternal unity.

"The supreme critic is that great nature in which we rest, as the earth lies in the soft arms of the atmosphere,—that unity, that *over-soul* within which every man's particular being is contained, and made one with all other.* * And that deep power in which we exist, and whose beatitude is all accessible to us, is not only self-sufficing and perfect in every hour, but the act of seeing, and the thing seen—the seer and the spectacle—the subject and the object, *are one*! We see the world piece by piece, as the sun, the moon, the animal, the tree; but the whole, of which these are only the shining parts, *is the soul*."

Before this system of Pantheism, man's freedom of volition must of course vanish. "I am constrained every moment," observes this slave of logic, "to acknowledge a higher origin for events than the will *I call mine*." Now this *will* is evidently a thorn in Mr. Emerson's path. Ever falsifying his theories, can we wonder that he loses no opportunity of decrying it!

"Our moral nature," he declares, "is vitiated by any interference of our will. People represent virtue as a struggle, and take to themselves great airs upon their attainments; and the question is everywhere vexed when a noble nature is commended,—Whether the man is not better who strives with temptation? But *there is no merit in the matter*: either God is there, or he is not there."

This "Quietism" is the legitimate offspring of the Pantheism in the preceding paragraph. It is also a result of Mr. Emerson's *system*! Denying the relative and the contingent, he is forced to deny man's individuality; to save humanity, he absorbs it into one "universal mind." This universal mind must either be coequal or

identical with the Deity: to make it coequal would lead to a thousand absurdities, and the only alternative is to absorb it.

These 'Essays,' however, are not without their value, for they afford striking illustrations of the current fallacies of the school to which Mr. Emerson belongs. An enthusiast and a recluse, he is so shut out from all external influences, that he is wholly unconscious of the startling contradictions which daily experience offers to his abstractions. He shrinks not, therefore, from their application to the realities around him, and, thus exposes their insufficiency and their weakness to the light of common sense. So far from being "above" a system, Mr. Emerson, we repeat, is the veritable slave of the theories he has adopted.

We have bestowed five minutes' attention on this book, because, from its intellectual tendencies, it may be viewed as the representative of a class of works (chiefly foreign importations) which have met with some success in "Young England." But let it not be supposed that we are contending against all abstractions; on the contrary, no philosophy is complete which does not recognize their value—which does not combine, in its method, the abstract with the concrete. It is the undue preponderance given to either one over the other, which is the basis of all the erroneous systems which have so long made a battlefield of intellectual Europe. What England especially wants at this moment, is, a philosophy which shall accept both as of authority, and draw its conclusions accordingly. When this is worthily given us, we shall hear no more of our indifference to Metaphysics, and our contempt for Psychology.

In conclusion, and in justice to Mr. Emerson, we will observe, that notwithstanding his crabbed jargon—his un-English English—the ludicrous *bathos* of

103

many of his would-be climaxes,—there are, scattered about these Essays, bright with passages of a certain obscure beauty, fine ideas and elevating sentiments. He is evidently a man accustomed to reflection; a man imbued with reverence for Truth, Beauty, and Virtue: but *originality* we cannot allow him. His first principles are all borrowed from Schelling, or, more frequently, from Hegel. We must doubt, therefore, whether Mr. Emerson has yet found the "true heart," which his Prefacer claims for him; for we cannot consider that man as "speaking from the *heart* of him" who has made himself not merely the slave of a system, but the slave of the system of another.

[John A. Heraud] "Emerson's Essays," *Monthly Magazine* [England], 3rd ser., 6 (November 1841), 484–505

The American is proud of any man, whose genius tends to give his country an apparent superiority in any pursuit; be that pursuit what it may. As is the general case with young nations, America pants with the ambition (glorious, however vain,) of accomplishing in months, what other states have found to be the labour of centuries. Jealous to an excess of its national character, almost before it has had time to attain one—burning to distinguish itself in all things that can possibly lend notoriety, from the founding a new school of metaphysics, to the new-fashioning of a hair-comb—we need not wonder that America quickly endowed Emerson with name and place. Whether the Americans understood his outpourings or not, they recognized a soul of greatness in the man; and their policy will not permit them to hide their lights under a bushel. Accordingly, travellers began to set him down among the lions; and thus tidings, that in New England, some "spiritual notability, called Emerson," was to be found, gradually made their way into Britain.

It was lucky for Emerson that he was born in America. In England, a dozen years would have supplied him with about as many admirers. Carlyle's reputation for a long time laboured to beat down the aspersion, and worse than neglect, with which he was at first greeted; and at last reaped its reward, not in spite of what was anti-popular in his books, but because the hard crust of his style inclosed so much of that which ever captivates the public. He generally deals with recognizable persons and facts, and very seldom launches into the vague field of speculation; he loves to tread on the firm earth, and feel his footing sure. On the persons and facts he has elected to illustrate, he moralizes and reflects after his own peculiar fashion; occasionally decking his theme with a certain kind of humour, which is too original not to tell. Thus he has turned the French revolution into a magnificent heroic romance, which, were its phraseology less singular, would contain little to obstruct, and much to compel popularity. But Emerson's thoughts and conceptions lack this sensual embodiment. They are the dawnings of a vast creation, not yet perfected—obscure revelations of beauty and truth, seen through a "glass darkly." The English are with difficulty induced to sympathize with the struggles of a man, to reach the height of contemplation and wisdom; the result of his toil, pictured in some system or logical dissertation, is their sole care. Emerson just gives us the materials of thought, and then leaves us to work out a further road by ourselves; but an English reader takes up a book to avoid the trouble of thinking; he expects to find in it some system to which he can refer as an authority for all his words and deeds. The desires of such a reader, Emerson could not gratify; in his page, splendid idealisms gloam through the dark mist of a pantheistic wilderness; and we are left to disperse the dreariness in the best manner we can. Nevertheless, Emerson himself is but a restless sojourner in these wilds of Pantheism, and is earnestly seeking to wing his flight from thence into purer ether, and clearer sunshine. As the editor of the present volume of Essays remarks, "he will not long endure to be classed under *isms*."

We have, in the pages of this magazine, many a time and oft expressed our high admiration and reverence of Emerson; and therefore we may be pardoned for aught that seems depreciatory in what we have above uttered. We accept him as a stout and stalworth defender of that high school of *à priori* philosophy, the prosperity of which we have so much at heart; but to many of his tenets, we cannot render our allegiance.

But it is not our intention to treat these Essays, written by Emerson and edited by Carlyle antagonistically. All that we intend, at present, is to give our readers a just idea of their contents, by means of long extracts, and a loving commentary. A more elaborate consideration we must postpone to a future opportunity.

The best of these essays is that on "Self-Reliance." In it Emerson attempts to inculcate the doctrine that each man should accept as his rule of conduct, not the custom of others, but what is right in his own eyes. "Good and bad," says he, "are but names very readily transferable to that or this; the only right is what is after my constitution, the only wrong what is against it." This doctrine (though true) is liable to much misinterpretation; especially in the vague and paradoxical manner in which it is stated by Emerson. It might be libelled as being a sophistical excuse for vice; or ridiculed as a lame apology for individual obliquity. But if taken in its true width and depth, it forms no justification for yielding to the force of inclination; nay, in reality, exclaims against any such procedure, as an unmanly debasement. Rely on thyself, it does say; but a man's Self, and his inclinations are twain. The doctrine merely asserts the supremacy of Conscience, and declares, that when she has pronounced aught good or evil, the man should bow to her decision, regardless of the world's approval or displeasure. Man's inclinations are ever in rebellion against the dictates of conscience;

and must be subdued, if not destroyed, before his true personality can be assumed. The stumbling-blocks which Emerson raises in the enunciation of this principle, wholly owe their origin to his peculiar phraseology. Thus he says, "No law can be sacred to me, but that of my nature." Now there has been such a vast clatter made concerning the light of nature, and natural reason, that pietistic prejudice holds its nose at the imagined savour of infidelity. Read, however, "No law can be sacred to me but that of my *conscience*," and every objection disappears.

Let us, however, give Emerson's bold statement in his own words:—

["Self-Reliance," 29.30–35.10]

Again:—

["Self-Reliance," 41.10–44.5]

Let the reader turn Ostrich, and digest these sentences, as best he may.

The essay on "Compensation" is exceedingly beautiful. It exhibits the perfect justice that prevails throughout the universe; and declares that every apparent defect is compensated by a correspondent excellence—that, in reality, though there be variety, there is no inequality. The exemplification of this gives Mr. Emerson opportunity for the introduction of much noble prose poetry: but mindful of our limited space, we shall launch at once into the consideration of "*Spiritual Laws.*"

Emerson's philosophy will not permit the world we live in to be libelled. It is in his estimation, what its Maker declared it to be—very good. It is good because fitted for man; if we think it deformed, our thought convicts us of deformity ourselves. But common speculatists argue as if men, instead of being the lords of the creation, were its slaves; and thus self-degraded from their rightful dignity, they believe themselves miserable; exaggerate their sorrows; and are wretches because they will be so.

But however cloudy we may make the present, the past revels in a sunshine of its own.

["Spiritual Laws," 77.3–82.5]

The world, in the opinion of Emerson, must be just. It never reputes a man wrongly; but whether as hero or driveller accepts your own measure of doing and being.

["Spiritual Laws," 91.20–96.11]

We are next treated with some exquisite thoughts on that most delightful of all words—Love! We will not describe or criticise, but quote.

["Love," 99.3–101.29, 103.11–110.8]

We have only left ourselves room for the following extract from the Essay on Friendship.

["Friendship," 118.34–120.23]

Our extracts have been somewhat erratic; for having at present no point of our own to sustain, we have been only solicitous to give the reader ample materials from whence to form a correct estimate of the book before us. It will be perceived that although there is much of beauty—nay, even of sublimity—in these Essays, that they altogether want prominence and just relief. Emerson brings no treasure to the storehouse of the memory; if his words do not instantly excite kindred thoughts in the reader,—if they do not provoke him to elaborate the subject further for himself,—however they may please at the moment, they quickly evaporate and leave no trace behind. Other authors leave a remembrance of a concatenation of reasoning, or of a gracefully woven continuation of sentiment; but Emerson has no argument to support, and demonstrates nothing. We see that he is rich in gems and precious stones; but he displays them so partially as to tantalize rather than satisfy our curiosity.

However, these Essays are valuable as being the products of a man of great and original genius, who has earnestly sought for truth with no ill success. If he has done no more, he has at least erected sign-posts which will faithfully direct the steps of all who consult them into the paths of true philosophy. Fallen on such evil days as these, honour be to him who does even thus much!

But perhaps, in complaining of vagueness, we complain unjustly. What if Emerson's ideas be too pure—too ethereal for adequate expression? Ideas, in themselves, are incommunicable. They are silent intentions of the soul; suggested without the help of language. And if we would preserve them uncontaminated—if we would retain them in their original truthfulness—we must not seek to reduce them to words. Ideas are never false, for the soul cannot lie; but we may and do falsify them when we seek to clothe their loveliness in the rags and tatters of phrase. Nor is this all. Having once spoken an idea, it departs from us, leaving in its stead only the pitiful remembrance of the terms we have used in expressing it. These terms may be such as to lead to error and contradiction; and at the very best, will be but feeble and inefficient representatives of the idea we have lost.

In conceiving an idea, a flash of brilliant light seems to burst upon our soul; we stay not to seek arguments, or weigh evidence; our conviction of its truth is instantaneous. Mere thoughts are suggested to us already decked in a form of words; and we place no confidence in them until we have bolstered them up with reasoning and testimony. But our ideas apparently spring from a source that cannot err. I say apparently, for we know not whence they come, nor whither they go. Indeed, we might almost conclude that they were heavenly monitions addressed exclusively to ourselves; and that to impart them was a breach of confidence.

Among ideas—the noblest and the highest—has Mr. Emerson his abiding place; and hence arises his obscurity. The celestial visitants refuse to be confined to the dull earth. Nevertheless, let us gratefully listen to the broken utterances vouchsafed to us; for they may perchance prove oracles.

Checklist of Additional Reviews

[Orestes A. Brownson?], *Boston Quarterly Review*, 4 (April 1841), 258.

"Emerson's Essays," *Knickerbocker*, 17 (April 1841), 355.

New World, 2 (3 April 1841), 223.

New-Yorker, 11 (3 April 1841), 45.

Boston *Daily Times*, 8 May 1841.

"Emerson's Essays," *Trumpet and Universalist Magazine*, 13 (8 May 1841), 182.

B.M.B., "Emerson's Essays," *Monthly Miscellany of Religion and Letters*, 5 (August 1841), 90–7.

Atlas, 18 September 1841, pp. 605–6.

Tablet, 18 September 1841, pp. 613–14.

Britannia, 25 September 1841, pp. 834–5.

[J. W. Alexander], "Pantheism," *Biblical Repertory and Princeton Review*, 13 (October 1841), 539–64.

London and Westminster Review, 36 (October 1841), 491–2.

"Emerson's Essays," *Tait's Edinburgh Magazine*, 8 (October 1841), 666–70.

London *Evening Chronicle*, 29 October 1841, p. 3.

L., "'Facts for the People,' or, Easy Lessons for Tyros in Authorship," *Yale Literary Magazine*, 7 (November 1841), 7–13.

Kentish Mercury, 23 April 1842, p. 3.

C.L., *Christian Teacher*, n.s. 4 (October 1842), 381–8.

Eclectic Review, 76 (December 1842), 667–87.

Pioneer, 1 (February 1843), 95–6.

Literary World, 2 (16 October, 6 November 1847), 260, 325–6.

Massachusetts Quarterly Review, 1 (December 1847), 137.

Godey's Lady's Book, 36 (January 1848), 70.

Literary Gazette, 1680 (31 March 1849), 234. Reviews *Twelve Essays* (London: George Slater, 1849).

Potter's American Monthly, 7 (October 1876), 315. Also reviews *Essays: Second Series* and *Representative Men*.

The Method of Nature

"The Method of Nature,"
Knickerbocker,
18 (December 1841), 559

We are bound to thank the author, Mr. Ralph Waldo Emerson, for a copy of his Oration delivered before the Adelphi Society of Waterville college, (Maine,) in August last. It is the production of one who thinks much, often deeply, but who writes muddily; and this latter quality, we are sorry to be compelled to add, is the evident result of an imitation of the German-English system of Thomas Carlyle, which whoso handleth, not being expert therewith, useth an edged tool, and will assuredly be wounded thereby. There is *thought* enough in this production to furnish forth half a dozen of your modern college orators; but there is nevertheless not a thought in it, which is worthy any thing, that would not have produced tenfold more effect had it been left open to the hearer or reader's mind, instead of being covered with a grotesque garb of motley language. Now and then in a striking simile or felicitous illustration Mr. Emerson approaches the visible and the natural; as in this passage, for example: 'The universal does not attract us until housed in an individual. Who heeds the waste abyss of possibility? The ocean is everywhere the same, but it has no character until seen with the shore or the ship. Who would value any number of miles of Atlantic brine bounded by lines of latitude and longitude? Confine it by granite rocks, let it wash a shore where wise men dwell, and it is filled with expression; and the point of greatest interest is where the land and water meet. So must we admire in man the form of the formless, the concentration of the vast, the house of reason, the cave of memory.' But he soon relapses into the vague and shadowy, and we lose sight of him in a Cimmerian fog. Mr. Emerson, as he should know, has also *his* imitators; and we beg him to pause and reflect how much crude third-rate American transcendentalism he will be compelled to stand sponsor for, should he continue to perpetuate his peculiar style. We have seen essays from one or two of his inferior followers or pupils which would defy even himself to understand; essays in fact which remind us of nothing so much as the exordium of Monsieur Baisecul's 'Speech before Pantagruel and the Parlement of Paris,' which we render *ad lib.* from Rabelais, and shall venture to quote 'in this connexion,' though it has little connexion of its own: 'Monsieur: I confess it is indisputably true, that as a woman of my family, a good old soul she is too, was carrying eggs to market to sell, she passed between the two topics, six

109

degrees toward the zenith and a trifle over; inasmuch as the Rhiphæan mountains in that year suffered from great scarcity of chances, notwithstanding a sedition of pastry diamonds excited among the toll-keepers and pedlers for the rebellion of the Swiss, who were assembled as numerous as the humming-birds that dress in skirts and bodices of calico; in the first season of the year that they slopped their cows with turtle-soup, and gave the girls the key of the coal-house to feed the dogs with oats, because all the night they did nothing but despatch messengers on foot and messengers on horseback to retain the syllogisms; but the physicians said that in his skim-milk they did not detect any evident signs of their having eaten crabs with mustard, if the gentry of the court had not issued a decree prohibiting the peripheries to molest the vestal virgins, because the green cheese had gracefully begun to dance the dead march with one foot in the fire and the head in the middle, as Cæsar says in his treatise on weasels in Lapland; but alas! Messieurs; God regulates every thing according to his will, and a carman lost his whip!'

Checklist of Additional Reviews

Monthly Miscellany of Religion and Letters, 5 (December 1841), 346–7.
"The Method of Nature," *New York Review*, 10 (January 1842), 219–32.

Essays:
Second Series

Review of *Essays: Second Series*, *Spectator* [England], 17 (24 November 1844), 1122–3

This forms part of a speculation called the "Catholic Series,"—a title singularly inapplicable to the writings of Mr. Emerson; whose genius, however considerable, is remarkably tinged with those peculiarities of manner and idea which, as much as any doctrinal opinion, essentially constitute the sectarian. Even when true, the thoughts of Emerson are rather distinguished for a quaint shrewdness, and a limitation to a part or section of his subject, than for that justness, breadth, and universality, which in criticism is the counterpart of catholicity in the church. Often, however, his ideas are questionable—their truth is limited, disputable, as much matter of question as the views of a confined body of *opinionists*. Still oftener they have that sounding vagueness which generally obtains, we think, more among coteries of men who are without any established standards of authority or of taste, and who, unchecked by the example or influence of superiors, acquire a swelling air both of manner and language, rather proportioned to their estimate of themselves than to their true position in relation to the world. We beg to be understood that we are speaking absolutely, not relatively. This mannerism—for to that it comes at last—may be better than the coldness, formality, or dulness of a more universal body; and as great ability may perhaps be displayed, except, of course, in the highest range of the catholic school. All we mean is, that such writers as Carlyle, Hazlitt, and Ralph Waldo Emerson, could not be better described than by reserving the title of the library in which he is now placed.

As regards the particular volume of Emerson before us, we think it an improvement upon the first series of Essays. The subjects are better chosen. They come more home to the experience of the mass of mankind, and are consequently more interesting. Their treatment also indicates an artistic improvement in the composition. There is still quite enough of the iterative outpouring, where one general thought is partitioned into a succession of phrases, as if matter could be better impressed by much speaking; or mere opinions are dressed up to look like oracular truths; or the writer aims at making the common or the particular great by puffing it up. But the sentences are shorter and

111

neater; and each, considered by itself, is more pithy in expression. The thoughts also appear more deep or general; but this may be owing to their subjects.

The desultory character of the essay, which by usage admits of almost any digression, and the peculiar nature of Emerson's mind, render the title, as we formerly observed, but a slender suggester of the matter that will be found in each paper. The same digressive habit of passing from one branch of a subject to another having no very direct connexion, renders it difficult to convey any general idea of the matter of his Essays. These, however, are their avowed titles, "The Poet," "Experience," "Character," "Manners,"—the two last subjects admirably handled at starting, and in a catholic style, but soon lost sight of in the author's mannerism; "Gifts" is short, and means *presents*, not natural gifts. "Nature," "Politics,"—deriving its chief value from some passage in American affairs; and "Nominalist and Realist" complete the Essays: but a Lecture, addressed to the Society called New England Reformers, though differing little from the Essays, is added, and may be said to form an eighth.

The following is part of the opening of the chapter on Character which we have alluded to. The problem it puts forth is, we think, one universally felt to be difficult: and Emerson's solution may be received till we get a better. But when a man's fame in the eyes of posterity surpasses his apparent acts, we suspect that he must have embodied some new principle. Thus, Lord Chatham, Emerson's leading ex-

ample, first addressed himself to the spirit and patriotism of the middle class in civil politics—he threw himself upon the constituencies. Before his time, politics, unless it came to civil war, had been managed by the aristocratic parties, with occasional aid from the rabble and constant assistance from the corporations.

["Character," 53.3–54.3]

This leading idea, instead of being pursued in a true and catholic spirit, is lost sight of in minute and individual cases,—as a trader sitting in his parlour and looking Character, or in a series of phrases strung together, like these.

["Character," 56.21–57.1]

The essay on Manners begins with a similar breadth, which is dissipated in a similar way; though its variety—a gentleman, fashion, manners—better preserves its force and interest. There is a good deal of truth and keenness in the following remarks.

["Manners," 81.27–82.20]

["Politics," 122.36–123.22]

This edition is published under the typographical superintendence of Mr. Carlyle; who has contributed a preface; but it contains nothing beyond some quaint and forcible remarks on the law of copyright, or rather the practice of literary piracy. It appears that the volume is published in conjunction with Mr. Emerson.

112

[Margaret Fuller], "Emerson's Essays," New York *Daily Tribune*, 7 December 1844, p. 1

At the distance of three years this volume follows the first series of Essays, which have already made to themselves a circle of readers, attentive, thoughtful, more and more intelligent, and this circle is a large one if we consider the circumstances of this country, and of England, also, at this time.

In England it would seem there are a larger number of persons waiting for an invitation to calm thought and sincere intercourse than among ourselves. Copies of Mr. Emerson's first published little volume called "Nature," have there been sold by thousands in a short time, while one edition has needed seven years to get circulated here. Several of his Orations and Essays from "The Dial" have also been republished there, and met with a reverent and earnest response.

We suppose that while in England the want of such a voice is as great as here, a larger number are at leisure to recognize that want; a far larger number have set foot in the speculative region and have ears refined to appreciate these melodious accents.

Our people, heated by a partisan spirit, necessarily occupied in these first stages by bringing out the material resources of the land, not generally prepared by early training for the enjoyment of books that require attention and reflection, are still more injured by a large majority of writers and speakers, who lend all their efforts to flatter corrupt tastes and mental indolence, instead of feeling it their prerogative and their duty to admonish the community of the danger and arouse it to nobler energy. The aim of the writer or lecturer is not to say the best he knows in as few and well-chosen words as he can, making it his first aim to do justice to the subject. Rather he seeks to beat out a thought as thin as possible, and to consider what the audience will be most willing to receive.

The result of such a course is inevitable. Literature and Art must become daily more degraded; Philosophy cannot exist. A man who feels within his mind some spark of genius, or a capacity for the exercises of talent, should consider himself as endowed with a sacred commission. He is the natural priest, the shepherd of the people. He must raise his mind as high as he can toward the heaven of truth, and try to draw up with him those less gifted by nature with ethereal lightness. If he does not so, but rather employs his powers to flatter them in their poverty, and to hinder aspiration by useless words, and a mere seeming of activity, his sin is great, he is false to God, and false to man.

Much of this sin indeed is done ignorantly. The idea that literature calls men to the genuine hierarchy is almost forgotten. One, who finds himself able, uses his pen, as he might a trowel, solely to procure himself bread, without having reflected on the position in which he thereby places himself.

Apart from the troop of mercenaries, there is one, still larger, of those who use their powers merely for local and temporary ends, aiming at no excellence other than may conduce to these. Among these, rank persons of honor and the best intentions, but they neglect the lasting for the transient, as a man neglects to furnish his mind that he may provide the better for the house in which his body is to dwell for a few years.

113

When these sins and errors are prevalent, and threaten to become more so, how can we sufficiently prize and honor a mind which is quite pure from such? When, as in the present case, we find a man whose only aim is the discernment and interpretation of the spiritual laws by which we live and move and have our being, all whose objects are permanent, and whose every word stands for a fact.

If only as a representative of the claims of individual culture in a nation which tends to lay such stress on artificial organization and external results, Mr. Emerson would be invaluable here. History will inscribe his name as a father of the country, for he is one who pleads her cause against herself.

If New-England may be regarded as a chief mental focus to the New World, and many symptoms seem to give her this place, as to other centres the characteristics of heart and lungs to the body politic; if we may believe, as the writer does believe, that what is to be acted out in the country at large is, most frequently, first indicated there, as all the phenomena of the nervous system in the fantasies of the brain, we may hail as an auspicious omen the influence Mr. Emerson has there obtained, which is deep-rooted, increasing, and, over the younger portion of the community, far greater than that of any other person.

His books are received there with a more ready intelligence than elsewhere, partly because his range of personal experience and illustration applies to that region, partly because he has prepared the way for his books to be read by his great powers as a speaker.

The audience that waited for years upon the lectures, a part of which is incorporated into these volumes of Essays, was never large, but it was select, and it was constant. Among the hearers were some, who though, attracted by the beauty of character and manner, they were willing to hear the speaker through, always went away discontented. They were accustomed to an artificial method, whose scaffolding could easily be retraced, and desired an obvious sequence of logical inferences. They insisted there was nothing in what they had heard, because they could not give a clear account of its course and purport. They did not see that Pindar's odes might be very well arranged for their own purpose, and yet not bear translating into the methods of Mr. Locke.

Others were content to be benefitted by a good influence without a strict analysis of its means. "My wife says it is about the elevation of human nature, and so it seems to me;" was a fit reply to some of the critics. Many were satisfied to find themselves excited to congenial thought and nobler life, without an exact catalogue of the thoughts of the speaker.

Those who believed no truth could exist, unless encased by the burrs of opinion, went away utterly baffled. Sometimes they thought he was on their side, then presently would come something on the other. He really seemed to believe there were two sides to every subject, and even to intimate higher ground from which each might be seen to have an infinite number of sides or bearings, an impertinence not to be endured! The partisan heard but once and returned no more.

But some there were, simple souls, whose life had been, perhaps, without clear light, yet still a search after truth for its own sake, who were able to receive what followed on the suggestion of a subject in a natural manner, as a stream of thought. These recognized, beneath the veil of words, the still small voice of conscience, the vestal fires of lone religious hours, and the mild teachings of the summer woods.

The charm of the elocution, too, was great. His general manner was that of the reader, occasionally rising into direct address or invocation in passages where tenderness or majesty demanded more energy. At such times both eye and voice called on a remote future to give a worthy reply. A future which shall manifest more largely the universal soul as it was then manifest to this soul. The tone of the voice was a grave body tone, full and sweet rather than sonorous, yet flexible and haunted by many modulations, as even instruments of wood and brass seem to become after they have been long played on with skill and taste; how much more so the human voice! In the more expressive passages it uttered notes of silvery clearness, winning, yet still more commanding. The words uttered in those tones, floated awhile above us, then took root in the memory like winged seed.

In the union of an even rustic plainness with lyric inspirations, religious dignity with philosophic calmness, keen sagacity in details with boldness of view, we saw what brought to mind the early poets and legislators of Greece—men who taught their fellows to plow and avoid moral evil, sing hymns to the gods and watch the metamorphoses of nature. Here in civic Boston was such a man—one who could see man in his original grandeur and his original childishness, rooted in simple nature, raising to the heavens the brow and eyes of a poet.

And these lectures seemed not so much lectures as grave didactic poems, theogonies, perhaps, adorned by odes when some Power was in question whom the poet had best learned to serve, and with eclogues wisely portraying in familiar tongue the duties of man to man and "harmless animals."

Such was the attitude in which the speaker appeared to that portion of the audience who have remained permanently attached to him.—They value his words as the signets of reality; receive his influence as a help and incentive to a nobler discipline than the age, in its general aspect, appears to require; and do not fear to anticipate the verdict of posterity in claiming for him the honors of greatness, and, in some respects, of a Master.

In New-England he thus formed for himself a class of readers, who rejoice to study in his books what they already know by heart. For, though the thought has become familiar, its beautiful garb is always fresh and bright in hue.

A similar circle of like-minded the books must and do form for themselves, though with a movement less directly powerful, as more distant from its source.

The Essays have also been obnoxious to many charges. To that of obscurity, or want of perfect articulation. Of 'Euphuism,' as an excess of fancy in proportion to imagination, and an inclination, at times, to subtlety at the expense of strength, has been styled. The human heart complains of inadequacy, either in the nature or experience of the writer, to represent its full vocation and its deeper needs. Sometimes it speaks of this want as "under-development" or a want of expansion which may yet be remedied; sometimes doubts whether "in this mansion there be either hall or portal to receive the loftier of the Passions." Sometimes the soul is deified at the expense of nature, then again nature at that of man, and we are not quite sure that we can make a true harmony by balance of the statements.—This writer has never written one good work, if such a work be one where the whole commands more attention than the parts. If such an one be produced only where, after an accumulation of materials, fire enough be applied to fuse the whole into one new substance. This second series is superior in this respect to the former, yet in no one essay is the main stress so obvious as to produce on the mind the harmonious effect of a noble river or a tree in full leaf. Single passages and sentences engage our attention too much in proportion. These essays, it has been justly said, tire like a string of mosaics or a house built of medals. We miss what we expect in the work of the great poet, or the great philosopher, the liberal air of all the zones: the glow, uniform yet various in tint, which is given to a body by free circulation of the heart's blood from the hour of birth. Here is, undoubtedly, the man of ideas, but we want the ideal man also; want the heart and genius of human life to interpret it, and here our satisfaction is not so perfect. We doubt this friend raised himself too early to the perpendicular and did not lie along the ground long enough to hear the secret whispers of our parent life. We could wish he might be thrown by conflicts on the lap of mother earth, to see if he would not rise again with added powers.

All this we may say, but it cannot excuse us from benefitting by the great gifts that have been given, and assigning them their due place.

Some painters paint on a red ground. And this color may be supposed to represent the ground work most immediately congenial to most men, as it is the color of blood and represents human vitality. The figures traced upon it are instinct with life in its fulness and depth.

But other painters paint on a gold ground. And a very different, but no less natural, because also a celestial beauty, is given to their works who choose for their foundation the color of the sunbeam, which nature has preferred for her most precious product, and that which will best bear the test of purification, gold.

If another simile may be allowed, another no less apt is at hand. Wine is the most brilliant and intense expression of the powers of earth.—It is her potable fire, her answer to the sun. It exhilarates, it inspires, but then it is liable to fever and intoxicate too the careless partaker.

Mead was the chosen drink of the Northern gods. And this essence of the honey of the mountain bee was not thought unworthy to revive the souls of the valiant who had left their bodies on the fields of strife below.

Nectar should combine the virtues of the ruby wine, the golden mead, without their defects or dangers.

Two high claims our writer can vindicate on the attention of his contemporaries. One from his sincerity. You have his thought just as it found place in the life of his own soul. Thus, however near or relatively distant its approximation to absolute truth, its action on you cannot fail to be healthful. It is a part of the free air.

He belongs to that band of whom there may be found a few in every age, and who now in known human history may be counted by hundreds, who worship the one God only, the God of Truth. They worship, not saints, nor creeds, nor churches, nor reliques, nor idols in any form. The mind is kept open to truth, and life only valued as a tendency toward it. This must be illustrated by acts and words of love, purity and intelligence. Such are the salt of the earth; let the minutest crystal of that salt be willingly by us held in solution.

The other is through that part of his life, which, if sometimes obstructed or chilled by the critical intellect, is yet the prevalent and the main source of his power. It is that by which he imprisons his hearer only to free him again as a "liberating God" (to use his own words). But indeed let us use them altogether, for none other, ancient or modern, can more worthily express how, making present to us the courses and destinies of nature, he invests himself with her serenity and animates us with her joy.

"Poetry was all written before time

was, and whenever we are so finely organized that we can penetrate into that region where the air is music, we hear those primal warblings, and attempt to write them down, but we lose ever and anon a word, or a verse, and substitute something of our own, and thus miswrite the poem. The men of more delicate ear write down these cadences more faithfully, and these transcripts, though imperfect, become the songs of the nations."

"As the eyes of Lyncæus were said to see through the earth, so the poet turns the world to glass, and shows us all things in their right series and procession. For, through that better perception, he stands one step nearer to things, and sees the flowing or metamorphosis; perceives that thought is multiform; that within the form of every creature is a force impelling it to ascend into a higher form; and following with his eyes the life, uses the forms which express that life, and so the speech flows with the flowing of nature.

Thus have we in a brief and unworthy manner indicated some views of these books. The only true criticism of these, or any good books, may be gained by making them the companions of our lives. Does every accession of knowledge or a juster sense of beauty make us prize them more? Then they are good, indeed, and more immortal than mortal. Let that test be applied to these; essays which will lead to great and complete poems—somewhere.

117

Review of *Essays: Second Series*, *Athenæum*, 896 (28 December 1844), 1197

F[rederic]. H[enry]. H[edge]., "Writings of R. W. Emerson," *Christian Examiner*, 38 (January 1845), 87–108

As a pupil in the transcendental school of continental logic, Mr. Emerson heretofore asquiesced in the declaration of philosophical ignorance which is the result of the system—and having shut out the material universe by an impenetrable veil, nothing was left to him but to wonder. There remained no power of analysis, but that of his own sensations; nothing to produce and combine but his individual emotions, feelings, and ideas; he was therefore content to deliver from time to time the "words of his own mind," and this without respect to opinion, whether his own or other people's, whether inconsistent with themselves or with general experience. Enough for him that he expressed the feeling of the moment. But in this new series, the flag of conciliation is displayed; much account is made of all manner of conventions; in a word, the tone is conservative, and manifests a tendency to become more so. Something of the old leaven however, as might have been expected, still clings about him; of the old dissatisfaction with whatever is, has been, or will be: that standard of mind which assumes a superiority over all that comes before it.

Another volume of Essays from R. W. Emerson is a literary benefaction which we acknowledge with unfeigned gratitude. We congratulate the lovers of sprightly and profound discourse on this fresh extract from the mental life of a most loving and sincere spirit; for such, in spite of his heresies, and sins against custom and tradition, all who know him well must acknowledge him to be. Were it only for the rarity of such spirits and such books, we could hardly desire a more valuable accession to the national literature, or the world's literature, than these pages.

It takes a good deal in these days to justify a book, and but very little to provoke one. Time was when a new book was the arrival of a new spirit, a birth out of the deeps. But, now, writers of books have given place to book-wrights. What was once a mission has become a craft. Modern books are mostly manufacturers originating in a paltry speculation, or that mental pruriency and general determination to the surface, which characterize the times. When shall we see applied to literature, the golden maxim of Pythagoras in reference to oral communication,—either to be silent or to say something better than silence? The authors of scientific works, naturalists, voyagers, realists of every description, are always welcome. We accept without questioning—so they prove themselves reliable witnesses—all who bring us tidings of the actual; it matters not, whether from the arctic regions or the antarctic, or the interior of the earth, or the interior of any living thing upon its surface; from the lichen on the wall, or the nearest pebble, or the farthest nebula;—all who present new facts or new classify old ones. These are the actual producers of the intellectual world, they deal in positive values. But he who brings us only his speculations and his fancies, is justly held to a more strict account. It behoves him to consider well his statement; that it be not only plausible, but new, and not only new, but sufficiently weighty to claim a hearing amid the general pressure of such demands. With regard to all this class of writers, we make no conscience of being critical, and hypercritical. They must show good cause for their intrusion. They must say something better than silence. A sweeping condition, as we estimate silence, and one which would eliminate nine out of ten of such productions. "There is a kind of men, so loose of soul," that they bestow their tediousness upon us from mere incapacity of reticence. Mr. Emerson is not one of this kind. We are rather disposed to tax him with undue reserve. His works come slowly, as if wrung from him, like the ancient mariner's tale;

> "at an uncertain hour,
> That agony returns."

And then, to be sure, we have something worth listening to, for its novelty;—the adventures of a curious and lonely wanderer into new regions of speculation; revelations from "that silent sea" which lies far away from the ordinary route of your literary navigators.

The author himself has furnished a high standard, by which to judge him, in the first series of these Essays published some four years since. On comparing this new volume with that, it seems to us to possess less interest on the whole. It wants the point and the heartiness of the other; the questionable tendencies of the author's mind are more decidedly marked in it, and the peculiar and nameless charm of his rhetoric is less apparent. We pronounce this judgment with some hesitation and with some reservations. The essay entitled "Experience," in this series, we are inclined to place next to that on "Spiritual Laws," which strikes us as pre-eminently the best in the two; and the "Lecture at Amory Hall," appended to the new volume, surpasses all the essays, technically so called, in the free and graceful flow of its thought, and the benign humanity of its sentiment.

The essay on Experience, or rather, the essay so headed, possesses a completeness not usual in Mr. Emerson's writings, and which does not properly belong to his turn of mind. He tells us, it is true, "I know better than to claim any completeness for my picture. I am a fragment, and this is a fragment of me." But this disclaimer respects the matter, not the form. The matter is fragmentary, as all experience must be, but the form is complete, and gives to this chapter an epic character which distinguishes it from all the rest. We particularize it, however, not for its artistical merit, but for the personal interest it possesses as illustrating the individuality of the author. It is the essay, of all others, in which, of right, we may look to trace the moral lineaments of the man. It is his statement of human life; a private valuation of "this pleasing, anxious being," compiled out of all the moods in which he has conversed with it; a summing up of its phases and its forces, its riches and its defects, its illusions and its realities, the negations and affirmations of the soul, as they lie in his consciousness. Minds of a certain complexion please themselves with these digests of the universal experience. They love to take account of life, at a distance from its *mêlée*, and to describe the universe in philosophical observations from their private observatory. The character of different philosophies and different tendencies of mind is represented in these valuations. Horace, in the most celebrated of his odes, gives us the Epicurean estimate, Seneca gives us the Stoic, Fichte the Transcendental. The most remarkable of all is the "Ecclesiastes" of the Jewish Scriptures. This, also, is a statement of life and a chapter of experience,—like the one before us, beginning with doubt and negation, and ending with the highest affirmation. "Vanity of vanities, saith the Preacher, all is vanity. One generation passeth away and another generation cometh. The sun ariseth and the sun goeth down. All things are full of labor." "Where do we find ourselves?" asks the Essayist: "in a series of which we do not know the extremes and believe that it has none. All things swim and glimmer. If any of us knew what we were doing and where we were going when we think we best know!" "Cast thy bread upon the waters and thou shalt find it after many days;" "fear God and keep his commandments,"—is the ancient exhortation, and conclusion of the whole matter. And the modern is not unlike it;— "Patience and patience, we shall win at last. There never yet was a right endeavor, but it succeeded. There is victory yet for all justice; and the true romance which the world exists to realize, is the transformation of genius into practical power."

Mr. Emerson enumerates seven factors which he considers to be the chief constituents of our being. "Illusion, Temperament, Succession, Surface, Surprise, Reality, Subjectiveness,—these are threads on the loom of time, these are the lords of life." We shall not stop to inquire how far this classification represents the author's own moods, and how far the general consciousness. It has a hap-hazard and arbitrary look at first, but the more we study it, the more comprehensive and the more definitive we find his analysis.

What pleases us best in this chapter, is the strong emphasis which it gives to the present momentary life. This is not an article peculiar to the Emersonian philosophy. It is one, perhaps the only one, in which all philosophies unite. The "carpe diem" of the Epicurean is, in one sense or another, the conclusion of each. Materialist and Idealist, Stoic and Epicurean, all preach to this effect. "Life is long and rich," says Seneca, "to those who know how to use it." "In this present that God hath made us," says Montaigne, "there is nothing unworthy our care. By how much the possession of life is more short, I must take deeper and fuller hold of it. It is absolute and as it were a divine perfection, for a man to know how to enjoy his being as he ought." But we have met with no statement of this doctrine so adequate to our conception of it, as Mr. Emerson's in this essay.

> "To finish the moment, to find the journey's end in every step of the road, to live the greatest number of good hours, is wisdom. Five minutes of to-day are worth as much to me as five minutes in the next millennium. Let us be poised and wise and our own to-day. I settle myself ever firmer in the creed that we should not postpone and refer and wish, but do broad justice where we are."

This is the top and sum of all ethics, of all religion. This is the "everlasting life" of the Christian Scriptures;—to possess and subject the present; to fill, with all the fulness of our being, the passing hour. It is too much the fashion with good people, and is thought to be the genuine language of piety, to flout and degrade the present life, to speak disparagingly of this world, to call it a vale of tears, a state of sin and sorrow, scarce worthy a single thought or care from a rational and immortal being. How large a portion the hymns employed in the religious worship, even of our own Connexion, are surcharged with this sentiment! The doctrine of a life to come has been so handled as to throw, not light, but a shadow on the life that now is. We doubt, more harm than good is done by such representations. Harm is done by every thing which tends to beget indifference to the present, and to disgust us with the actual conditions of our being. On this account, the frequent use of that metaphor, so beloved by the preachers of religion, which likens life to a pilgrimage, has seemed to us of doubtful expediency. Beautiful and appropriate as it was in its original, Scriptural application, the inordinate expansion of it in the popular theology has served to throw a sad and false coloring over the being of man, and to cherish a weakly, puling sentimentality, incompatible with a healthy and vigorous life. A heavy day's journey through a tedious, barren land, with a comfortable inn at the end of it;— is the translation of this metaphor, as it lies in the common apprehension. It is time the popular theology should reconsider this view of life. We need to set up the strong claims of the present against an hereafter, which would cheat us out of here and now. This life is no more a pilgrimage than every future state. The conditions of well-being are the same for man in all states. The way to heaven is heaven, and heaven is nothing but a way—a method of the soul. The true doctrine is, as Mr. Emerson states it, "to find the journey's end in every step of the road."

Of the remaining essays in this volume, the "Lecture at Amory Hall," and the two chapters—"Character" and "Manners," are those which have interested us most. They seem to us the most able, and consequently the most characteristic. The subject of the first is, "the New England Reformers;" its aim, a more expansive theory of reform than those which have hitherto been put forth by that class of persons. It is the answer of a sane looker-on—a very sufficient, but a very good-natured one—to the practical ultraisms of the day. The lecturer commences with a strain of graceful raillery, commenting on those memorable Conventions which have met in this city, from time to time, during the last five years, for the discussion of social and religious institutions and modes of life.

["New England Reformers,"
149.25–150.7]

He allows great significance to these movements as an indication of the growing trust in "the private, self-supplied powers of the individual," and the "gradual casting off of material aids," which he conceives to be the affirmative principle of the new philosophy. But,

["New England Reformers," 154.21–24, 28–31; 154.36–155.1; 155.19–22]

The charm of this performance, as hinted above, is its humanity,—the faith it discovers, in the preponderance of good over evil in human kind.

["New England Reformers," 163.29–34; 164.6–11]

This is explained, farther on, by the existence of something in man behind his own consciousness, which sometimes speaks another language than his lips.

["New England Reformers," 165.24–29]

We find we are multiplying our extracts, but the lecture is a favorite among its fellows, with us, and we give but the tithe of what we have marked in our copy. The conclusion is a lofty appeal, from the littleness of partial reformers, and the vain attempts to realize freedom by set modes of living on the principle—"magna pars libertatis est bene moratus venter," to the higher liberty, possible to man.

["New England Reformers," 167.3–25]

The two essays on "Character" and "Manners" are well placed side by side, for they are the complement each of the other. One treats of the essential and self-subsisting, the other of the phenomenal and extrinsic. They relate to each other as the fact to the sign, the latent soul to the atmosphere of society and fashion which it creates around it. On looking over the first of these once more, we are not sure but it claims even a higher relative position than we at first accorded to it, and should rank with the best in either of the two volumes—so rich is it in accurate observations and sharp intuitions of man and life, as it now strikes us. We dare not linger over it, for want of room to set down what we are tempted to transcribe.

With regard to the others, we confess a shade of disappointment in the degree of satisfaction we have derived from them. Mr. Emerson has taught us to be exacting where his own writings are concerned. We have fallen into a habit of expecting from him the very best, as a thing of course. We hold him to the proof which he has given of his extraordinary powers. The essay entitled "Nominalist and Realist," is full of good things; but they refuse to arrange themselves, to our apprehension, in any intelligible order, or to answer to the rubric into which they have been thrust. Either we are dull readers, or this parcel has been wrongly labelled. It is the most ill-arranged of the whole, and should be, of right, the most systematic and logical, with that title on its front. The question between the Nominalists and

the Realists is one of the most comprehensive and curious in the history of philosophy. An essay from Mr. Emerson, which should front it fairly, would be a special favor. The essay on "Politics" has nothing so good as the lines prefixed to it, which are fine. That on "Nature" and that on "The Poet" do not fulfil the promise of their titles, and the just expectation created by such subjects in such hands.

We have been led into more detailed criticism than we intended when we took up this book. We meant to make it the occasion of some remarks on the character and value of Mr. Emerson's writings, based on a somewhat different view of his merits from that which seems to have been entertained in the notices that have met our eye. If in our estimate of him, we are found to contradict opinions formerly expressed in the pages of this journal, let it be understood that we are not careful to preserve on all subjects an identity of judgment. The only identity we mean to maintain, is that of *Christian* examiners, and a Christian spirit of examination.

As Christian examiners, then, we are met at the outset by a difficulty which we may not omit to notice. We mean, our author's relation to the Christian Church. Our admiration of his genius and our deep conviction of the worth of his labors are brought into collision with our want of sympathy with him in this particular. It is generally understood, and has constituted the chief ground of complaint against him, that Mr. Emerson is not a Christian in the usual and distinctive sense of the term, that is, not a believer in a special and miraculous revelation. It would be easy to blink this fact, seeing it is not made prominent in his writings; but we think it more honest to meet it fairly. We are not disposed to underrate its importance. Though it may not destroy our interest in his writings, we feel that it must qualify essentially their general influence. Mr. Emerson, if we understand his views on this subject, regards Christ as a mere teacher of moral and religious truths,—a reformer, not distinguished from other teachers and reformers except by the greater number of followers that have *chanced* to rank under his name, and the longer continuance and wider spread of his doctrine and influence in the world;—a Jewish Socrates or Plato; a little more perfect, perhaps, in his character, and a little wiser in his precepts, than those Greek sages, and perhaps not; at any rate, sustaining essentially the same relation to the rest of mankind. The Christian Church is a school or sect, founded by Jesus, in the same sense in which any other school is founded by any other philosopher. On this point we are at issue with him, and the difference between us is heaven-wide. We utter the deepest conviction of our soul, when we pronounce this view to be utterly inadequate and radically false. We profess our inability to comprehend how a mind, with any pretensions to philosophic culture, can be satisfied with it; how so acute a thinker as the writer of these Essays can overlook the violence it does to that fundamental principle in philosophy, which requires an adequate cause for every effect, or can fail to perceive that, in its anxiety to avoid a miracle, it substitutes a greater wonder for a less. For what more wonderful, than an effect without a cause? The most philosophical view of Christianity is that which best satisfies the law of cause and effect, in other words, which best explains the facts in the case. What are the facts in the case? Here is this mighty power, the like of which has never, before or since, been exerted in human affairs;—a power which has wrought, for nearly two thousand years, with beneficent effect on the human condition, embracing and embraced by the most civilized nations of the earth, and constituting the chief source of their civilization;—a power which has ministered and still ministers comfort and peace and the means and motives of virtue to millions of human souls; which countless millions have clung to, and still cling to, as their chief dependence and highest good and everlasting hope;—a power which has done more than any other to beautify and gladden the earth, which has tamed the wild passions of men, brought rest to the heavy-laden, taken the poor and weak and the sinful by the hand, and filled the world with gentleness and peace. Whence came it, and by what means was it introduced into the world? Did the philosophers and potentates of the earth,—the collective wisdom and patronage of man, combine to produce it? They combined for centuries, with all the force that was in them, to oppose and put it down. It wanted patronage, it wanted the intellectual aids which are usually thought requisite for the diffusion of truth, it wanted all those conditions which give success to human efforts. It grew from nothing that human sagacity could point out as a probable cause of such a result; from nothing but that Divine Providence, which can make "the foolish things of this world to confound the wise, and the weak things of this world to confound the mighty."

We said Mr. Emerson's dissent from the common faith was not made prominent in these Essays. But we come here and there upon a passage, like the following, from which it is impossible not to infer it.

["Experience," 44.11–19]

We have no objection to the term "providential man." Strictly interpreted, it involves, perhaps, all that is essential in the idea of a special revelation. But when we are told that the value attached to the name of Christ is the result of an "agreement," we demand to know how this agreement came about. In what age of the world, in what Congress of nations, was it so settled? The agreement is not a voluntary, but a necessary one, and cannot be accounted for, but on the supposition of an adequate, that is, a Divine cause. Will Mr. Emerson explain to us how it has happened that *this* man, of all others, should have this position in the centre of the horizon? Why have we no churches in the name of Plato, or Seneca, or Plotinus? The case of Plato deserves special consideration. If ever a philosopher could have succeeded in establishing a divine authority in the world, it was he. Among them that are born of women, there has been no greater philosopher, seldom a more perfect man. Why have we no church, embracing half the earth, in the name of Plato? It is not for want of systematic efforts, on the part of his disciples, to secure the prevalence of his doctrine. As soon as the Christian sect began to look formidable, the attempt was made by the most cultivated and powerful of the earth, to run Platonism against Christianity and to secure to the Pagan religion, seconded and interpretated by that philosophy, the ascendancy over the new and growing faith. All the genius, all the wit, and no small part of the virtue and piety of that time were devoted to the cause. The Emperor Julian gave to it all his learning as a philosopher, all his patronage as Emperor, and all his influence as a man. A Christian by birth, and still, after his conversion to Paganism, a better Christian in his practice than the Christian Emperors who preceded and who came after him; a man of singular abstinence and sobriety, who lived as frugally and as industriously on the throne of the world as the poorest Christian in his dominions; he devoted himself, with all the weight which such a character and such a position could give, to the work of building up Platonic Paganism at the expense of Christianity. History has shown us with what result. All the power and wisdom of man availed not to reinstate the Olympian gods in their ancient seats, and of that philosophy which the sinking cause had summoned to its aid only so much survived, or ever came into general circulation, as had been engrafted on the Christian doctrine by the Fathers of Alexandria. The very books which contain it would have been lost forever, had they not been preserved by the Christian Church. Such is the difference between a Church and a School of philosophy; and such the difference between the founder of a sect and the Church's Christ!

But while we condemn this view of the Christian revelation, we are far from denying to Mr. Emerson all participation in the Christian faith. On the contrary, we affirm him to be a true Christian, in that sense in which one of the Fathers, we believe it was Jerome, declared Seneca to be a Christian,—as an asserter, that is, of Christian truth and Christian principles. Among the distinguishing features of Christianity,—we are ready to say *the* distinguishing feature—is its humanity— its deep sympathy with human kind and its strong advocacy of human wants and rights. In this particular, few have a better title to be ranked among the followers of Jesus, than the author of this book. Humanity is the distinguishing feature, also, of his writings. Not the humanity now in vogue, which views mankind in the lump and has respect only to the race; but a genuine regard for individual man. The *solidaire* view of the human race is not the doctrine of these Essays. It is not the Christian view of man. We do not call it anti-Christian, but we find no support for it in the Gospel. The words and actions of Jesus do not look that way. They point in a different direction; they emphasize the individual soul. It is not society in its collective capacity, but man in his personal and private capacity, that Christianity contemplates and addresses. So far, then, as this point is concerned, we affirm that our essayist has drunk more deeply of the Christian spirit, than some who in these days put forth peculiar pretensions to the Christian name.

Mr. Emerson is by no means a denier of the Christian faith. If he errs in rejecting the form of revelation, he is very far from rejecting its substance and its spirit; very far from being a general unbeliever. That name belongs properly to those who reject not only the idea of a revelation, but everything that revelation contains, everything connected with the spiritual world. Mephistophiles describes this class, when he designates himself as the spirit "that always denies." Mr. Emerson is not one of these spirits. We should rather characterize him as the spirit that always affirms. We lay great stress on this distinction. No prejudice, it seems to us, can fail to perceive the difference between such a writer and that class who deal wholly or mostly in negations, such as Byron, Rousseau, Voltaire. He is not a denier, but an affirmer; a sincere and consistent affirmer of moral and spiritual truth. It is of great consequence what a man believes, but of still greater consequence is it, that we do believe something with real and intense conviction. He who embraces a few great principles, with heart and soul, though he reject much that is worthy to be received, has a better title to be called believer, ay, and Christian too, than one who yields a feeble and politic assent to all that tradition prescribes without converting the smallest portion of it into spiritual life. In this view, we pronounce the writer of these Essays a believer. One shall not easily find so great faith, no, not in Israel, as some of them manifest. We particularize the chapter on "Spiritual Laws," and that on "Compensation." It is this that constitutes the chief value of his writings, and makes him, although not gener-

ally ranked in that category, a more efficient teacher of morals, than most of those who are. Without any system,—for system is, once for all, no feature of his intellect,—but with keen perceptions in his mind, and noble sentiments in his soul, he inculcates the great virtues of truth and justice, with a persuasiveness not parallelled in any modern writer known to us. What preaching can be finer than the following passages from the Essay on Compensation?

["Compensation," 66.12–15, 17–20; 67.25–30; 69.13–21]

Or this from the "Spiritual Laws."

["Spiritual Laws," 92.5–19]

We should say that moral philosophy was Mr. Emerson's peculiar province, were it not that the over-weight of the poetical over the practical, in his composition, disposes him to look at things too much in the order of the imagination, not in the order of the understanding; and to show virtue as a beautiful phenomenon, rather than to illustrate its practical application.

Mr. Emerson possesses all the intellectual qualifications of a great poet;—eye, imagination, language, "the vision and the faculty divine." The reason why he has not fulfilled the destination implied in these endowments is a defect of temperament— an excess of purely intellectual life. To constitute a poet, there must be a certain proportion between feeling and intellect, between the sentimental and the sciential. Excess of one makes the enthusiast; excess of the other, the philosopher. The poet occupies a middle stratum of humanity, combining the two. When the reign of ideas, or the sciential tendency prevails in an age or an individual, the poet becomes philosopher. Hence poetry declined in Greece with Plato and Aristotle; and hence so many poets of this age have turned from poetry to prose, in their riper years.

With a little more activity of feeling, and a little less activity of speculation, Mr. Emerson would have made a first-rate poet. As it is, the little poetry he has published possesses rare merit. In point of vividness, melody, and force of expression, it is unsurpassed; in these days, unrivalled. The following specimens may serve as illustrations of these qualities. They are not the best, perhaps, that might be found; but they are the only ones we have at hand. The first is from "The Problem."

["The Problem," 7.6–8.3]

Our next specimen is from "The Sphinx."

["The Sphinx," 21.19–26, 23.7–14, 23.23–24.4]

Mr. Emerson's poetry is a striking exception to the remark of Goethe, that "modern poets put too much water in their ink." He does not dilute his verse with the washy sentimentality which floods the pages of his contemporaries. He chants no lullabies for love-sick, life-sick souls, "sighing like a furnace;" but carols a lay that is tart and wholesome, and stirs the blood with a keen delight, like a draught of morning air. It was Dugald Stewart, if we mistake not, who explained the pleasure produced by rhyme, to consist in surprise. Coleridge rejects the explanation, and justly; but we are reminded of it in reading Mr. Emerson's poetry. A perpetual joy of surprise accompanies his strains. One has not the *ennui* of knowing, from long experience, what is to come next. As a poet, he seems not to belong to this age, but to mate with the singers of a former, more free-mouthed and great-hearted race. Not that there is any affectation of antiquity, any disposition to ape an obsolete style. On the contrary, it is his originality that gives him this character, distinguishing him from all his contemporaries. Nowhere does it appear more conspicu-

ous, than in the structure of his verses. He has an ear for melody, as every true poet, and every finely organized person has. But how different his rhythm from the monotonous, mechanical movement of modern versifiers which reminds one of a hand-organ. It is the free, gushing, careless, live melody of an elder age. It smacks of Milton and of Marvell.

Whether poetry or prose, force of statement is always a distinguishing trait in his writings. It constitutes their highest merit, rhetorically considered. The merit is not mechanical,—a trick of speech that can be copied. Many of the characteristics of his style have been imitated, but not this. It results from a vividness of conception peculiar to himself. To perceive a truth, with him, is to be on fire with it, is to blaze with it: it bursts from him in flashes of intense illumination. With most writers there is a certain distance between the thought and the word. The union is not complete. The thought is wedded, as well as may be, to a given vocabulary, or the vocabulary to the thought; but it is not always a perfect match. But Mr. Emerson's thoughts seem to make their own words. Thought and word hang together, like the lightning and the thunder in a summer cloud. It was said of Walter Scott, that no writer who has produced so much, is so little quoted or has so little that is "quotable." The reverse is true of Mr. Emerson. We know not the writer who offers so much quotable matter, within the same compass. No writer compresses more meaning in fewer words. His sentences are compact and portable, like proverbs and axioms. They often take that form. For example: "God loveth not size." "A fact is the end of spirit." "We can love nothing but nature." "Action is the perfection of thought." "The eye is the best of artists."

We concede, to a certain extent, the *euphuism* charged upon these volumes.

The prevailing style of them is, certainly, very far from being a model of good English. It could not be that and, at the same time, be what we have just said of it, and what we consider a greater merit. The excellences which constitute a model in style are negative. To serve this purpose, a style must not be distinguished by anything idiomatic or striking. The words must be colorless and suggest no associated thought or fancy. They must approach, as nearly as possible, the character of algebraic signs. Every violation of this rule is an approach to euphuism; and Mr. Emerson violates it to such an extent, as almost to make the rule the exception. The question is, does he compensate for these transgressions by high and higher excellences of his own? We could wish indeed, that he had not seen fit to adopt so frequently an unusual collocation of words, and had placed his parts of speech in the order in which nature and Murray designed that they should go; but we can pardon some conceits where there is so much force; and, if we must either have both or lose both, are willing to put up with his mannerism for the sake of his originality. The worst of that mannerism is not its awkwardness in the original, but the facility with which it is copied and the temptation to copy it. What is most peculiar in his writing, is also most excellent and cannot be transferred. His imitators may out-do the contortions of his syntax, but they will never be able to wriggle themselves into the secret of his inspiration.

Perhaps we ought to go deeper than the syntax, while speaking of the vices of his rhetoric, and attack the peculiarities of his logic and his philosophy, to which these vices are, in part, referrible. Much may be said, and has been said of the strange quirks and freaks of thought, the heresies and paradoxes, the love of the "novum, audax, indictum ore alio," with which these Essays abound. We grant it all and offer no justification of that, which, if there is any justice in it, will one day justify itself, and cannot be made to appear just if there is not. But neither are we disposed to hold it up for reprobation, and to add another vote to the full-voiced censure so distinctly pronounced. After all that has been said on this subject, we could offer nothing so superfluous as blame. The gravest charge has already been considered; the rest we leave to the arch-critic Time, whose long-pending and unpurchaseable verdict all books and philosophies must abide. To be frank, the beauties and merits of Mr. Emerson's writings—the much that is true and good in them—so preponderate, in our estimation, over their defects, that it seems to us a littleness and an ingratitude to lean with all the weight of exact criticism upon these latter, and to make light of the rest. We love a bold and original thinker too well, not to extend some indulgence to the vagaries and extravagances which we have come to regard as inseparable from this kind. Such intellects are gracious gifts of the Most High, to be received with due thankfulness by a world not over-rich in that line, and needing all the varied lights which the Fountain and Father of all intelligence may see fit to shed on the unsolved problems of its perplexed life.

'But this light is of too meteorous and flashy a nature to be trusted with safety.' Well, then, view it as a meteor and enjoy it as such. Do not regard the author as a teacher at all, nor the book as a doctrine. It does not claim to be that. Regard it as a book of confessions; as a piece of beautiful egotism, than which nothing is more charming when it is sincere and without vanity or littleness. Viewed in this light, too, the book possesses great merit. A more sincere one was never written. A true record of a true soul; the rarest of all literary phenomena! There occur to us, in

127

the whole history of literature, but two or three instances of the kind. Montaigne is one, and Jean Paul, perhaps, is another. Augustine and Rousseau are not in this category. The first was possessed, and viewed all things, himself among the rest, in the light of one master-thought which colored all his revelations. The other was not a true soul. Goethe's autobiography would belong here, were there not in it, as in all his writings, something incommensurable that defies classification. As a book of confessions then, these volumes offer, to those who can find nothing else in them, the peculiar interest of a marked individuality, which belongs to works of this kind.

It is folly to expect all things from all men. Moderation is good, and caution is good, and a correct syntax is good; we prize them all, and, if it lay with us, no book or discourse should lack these virtues. But the dulness and mediocrity, which often accompany them, are not good; they are sore trials. If it lay with us, they should altogether cease from the earth. Nevertheless, we are willing to bear with them for sweet charity's sake; knowing that all things are not to be expected of all men. So, when there appears among us a great and original writer, fresh from the Father of lights, with new and rare gifts,—an eye that looks creation through, a heart that clasps creation round, and a voice of melody that surprises us out of our long sleep, piercing through all the folds of custom and indifference that were wrapped about our spirits,—when such an one comes and spreads for us an entertainment like that which these Essays provide, we will take what he brings and give God thanks, "asking no questions for conscience' sake;" and not lose the good which we have, in fretting for that which we have not; knowing that all things are not to be expected of all men. Nor is it a mere transient entertainment, which these authors provide. They do great service to the cause of truth; were it only by the stimulus which they give to inquiry, and the opportunity which they furnish, of settling anew, on new and higher grounds, the ancient faith. Whether they fight against the truth or for it, every way the truth is preached; and we "therein do rejoice, yea, and will rejoice." We rejoice that this spirit has been sent among us to live and work in our midst. We rejoice in being his contemporaries. We rejoice in the indications we perceive, of a growing appreciation of his works abroad. We believe that they are destined to carry far into coming time their lofty cheer and spirit-stirring notes of courage and of hope. We dare to predict for them a duration coetaneous with the language in which they are composed. They are books, the world "will not willingly let die." We do not think they will ever have an extensive circulation. Popular books they can never be. They will number but few readers at any one period; but every period will renew that number, and so long as there are lovers of fine discourse and generous sentiment in the world, they will find their own.

"A Disciple"
"Emerson's Essays," *United States Magazine, and Democratic Review*, 16 (June 1845), 589–602

"The highest office of the intellects is the discovery of essential unity under the semblances of difference."—COLERIDGE.

"Surprising, indeed, on whatever side we look is the revival of the individual consciousness of a living relation with All Good. Our literature is every day more deeply tinged with a sense of the mysterious power which animates existence, and governs all events."—W.H. CHANNING.

It has been said that "the office of criticism is to bridge over the waters that separate the prophet from the people—to compass the distance that divides the understandings in the auditor from the intuition of the utterer,"—an office more easily indicated than fulfilled; and one which few persons have attempted to perform, for one of the most profound thinkers and inspired seers of our time: perhaps because the partition waters were too wide—the intervening gulf too deep.

Carlyle, who has lovingly unfolded to his countrymen the pure and cloistral genius of Novalis, the profound significance of Goethe and the intricate opulence of Jean Paul, has, in presenting them with the evangel of our western prophet, left them to solve the problem as they may.

His preface to the English edition of the Essays, imports that the name of Ralph Waldo Emerson is not entirely unknown in England. Distinguished travellers, he says "have carried thither tidings of such a man—fractions of his writings have found their way into the hands of the curious: fitful hints that there is, in New England, some spiritual notability, called Emerson, glide through Reviews and Magazines." For himself, he finds that "*the words of this man, such words as he finds it good to speak, are worth attending to,* and that by degrees, a small circle of living souls, eager to hear, are gathered." And in these few words, he has, perhaps, said all that the critic can effectually say in his office of Mediator between the prophet and the people. He cannot induct his readers with the "*aura*" of an author's genius, he can only point them to the source from which it emanates. He may say much that will be received with delight by those who are already the participators or recipients of the new revelation, but he cannot construct any bridge or thoroughfare by which "understanding of the populace shall pass to the intuition of the Seer." No mechanical aids can avail us here. The wings of love and faith can alone bear us to those serene heights whence the prophet overlooks the universe.

"Authority decides in the circle of the sciences, but intuition alone, a fine inner sense assumed by all, and possessed by few, judges of the true and the beautiful, or poetry and philosophy, the two foci in the intellectual ellipse." For the highest act of philosophy also, is a divination—an intuition and not an inference.

Bulwer, in his preface to the translations from Schiller, says that the chief aim of the poet, with that of the orator on the husting, should be to make himself intelligible to the multitude; but Bulwer has little insight of the subject on which he writes; else would he know that the poet never troubles himself with thoughts like these. He sings as the bird sings, because his soul is o'erburthened with love and beauty. He casts the fertilizing flower-dust of his heart to the winds of heaven, nor asks if they have borne it to a fitting receptacle.

The most profound thinker cannot defend his faith in the inner world, nor the poet his vision thereof from the vapid gainsaying of the scoffer. Not the Seer, but the Savant is honored of the world. Spinoza had not a single follower in the age in which he lived, and it has been said that there are not at any time ten men on earth who read Plato.

The great philosopher and poet is he, who understands the spirit of his age. To do this, he must transcend the existing order of things, overlooking it from a point of view above the level of his contemporaries, and attainable as a common standpoint, only to succeeding generations; and just in proportion as he transcends the popular level, is his speech an enigma or a reproach to the multitude, who, regarding their own minds as the normal measure of human intelligence, oppose themselves with sullen determination to the new revelation, and groan, like the mandrake, when a new idea threatens to uproot them from the soil in which they vegetate.

There is no paradox so absurd, no heresy so dangerous, that men will not sooner forgive it than a truth prematurely enunciated. And no man excites such pious horror, such unmitigated reprobation, as the promulgator of such truth. The effect of a resisting medium becomes perceptible only as the planet approaches its perihelion.

The world, unwillingly aroused from its slumbers, thinks, like the silly housemaids in sop, by wringing the neck of poor Chanticleer to retard the dawn!

"Beware," says Emerson, "when the great God lets loose a thinker on this planet, then all things are at risk—the very hopes of man, the religion of nations, the manners and morals of mankind are all at the mercy of a new generalization. Generalization is always a new influx of the Divinity into the mind." But to see things under this new law, they must be seen from the same level, and through the same medium. The results of the synthetic intellect cannot be reached through any critical or analytical process.

A man of Emerson's large faith and intuitive reason, who has drunk deep at the fontal truths of being, and sent his plummet to the ocean-depths of thought, cannot accommodate his free unchartered utterance to the limited apprehension of men who, engrossed by the narrow arts of detail, have no capacity for the wisdom of the complex. Yet, perhaps few persons could so command the rapt attention of a popular audience, to thoughts so abstruse, expressed in language so delphic and poetic. The charm of his presence is pervasive, like music. He commands the attention of his audience, and constrains their sympathy by a power which they cannot analyze, by a spell that transcends their knowledge.

Severe truthfulness characterizes every look, tone, and gesture. He speaks from the commanding and regal attitude of one who reposes firmly on his convictions. Those earnest eyes seem to hold commune with *soul*, and regardless of the world's penalties and rewards, make their direct appeal to the inner tribunal of the conscience. Their look of profound repose, or concentrate thought deepening at times beneath a frown (severe, yet beautiful in its passionless rebuke) which can hardly fail to remind one of the austere majesty in the countenance of the angel sent to expel Heliodorus from the temple, one of the finest of Raphael's inimitable heads. At such moments our prophet might, with Heraclitus, be compared to the Sybil, who "speaking with inspired mouth, inornate and severe, pierces thought centuries by the power of the God."

The spell of his immediate influence is felt and acknowledged by the most uncultivated audience, yet we hear a constant reference to his obscurity and vagueness. Men complain that no intelligible ideas have been gained, no definite notions acquired. They were charmed while they listened, but when they seek to explain and seize the charm, its secret escapes them. They cannot analyze it—they cannot appropriate it. It is a fairy gift that turns to dross in the handling. In return for their time and money, they have brought away nothing positive and available—nothing that can be weighed and measured and turned to useful account.

But what went ye forth for to see? A partizan? a polemic? an exponent of creeds and doctrines? a propounder of articles of faith, and theories of civil polity? Verily ye have sought in vain! Yet somewhat have ye heard that stirred your stagnant souls, but what, ye know not. A wild, mysterious music, as of the winds of paradise, murmuring afar off through the Tree of Life. An improvisation, as it were, of the central laws of being. The oracular enunciation of a mystic and sublime Theosophy. Ye hear the sound thereof, yet know not whence it cometh nor whither it goeth. It is as the heavenly manna which cannot be heaped or hoarded, but which refreshes the pilgrim on his weary life-path, and imparts new strength to bear the burthen of the way.

Emerson's speech is affirmative and oracular. We must be satisfied to receive from him the enunciation of the idea, we cannot hope to hear it demonstrated, or explained. We find no attempt at a formal, scientific statement of truth, but rather an oriental dogmatism, an apostolic yea and nay. His mind betrays a quick apprehension of logical sequence, yet he renders no account of the actual process by which he arrives at results. He attacks no creed, convinces no sceptic, but he gives adequate and beautiful expression to the most profound and cherished convictions—to the most earnest and devout aspirations of the age. To some of the loftiest minds and purest spirits of the nineteenth century, his voice is as "the voice of their own souls, heard in the calm of thought."

His novel statements of the most familiar phenomena of life, have often a strange force and directness, and startle us by their simple verity, like the naive cadences of a child's voice heard amid the falsetto tones of the conventicle or the theatre.

No man is better adapted than Emerson to comprehend the spirit of the age and to interpret its mission. His insight is marvellously clear, and though less conversant than many others with concrete, special instances, he yields to none in the synthetic grasp of his intellect, and in a comprehensive and generic classification of the facts of experience. He looks not so much at that aspect of things, often partial, trivial and grotesque, which they bear to time, as that solemn and serene, which faces eternity. The earth is to him not one of Gardiner's globes, mapped off into petty divisions of province and empire, state and territory, but one of the more recent planets of our system, moving on its destined path through space and harmoniously fulfilling its part in the grand diapason of the universe. He sees not so much the things in which man differs from man as those grand features common to humanity.

Life is viewed by him from no parish belfry, but from an "exceeding high mountain, from whence he can behold all the kingdoms of the world and the glories thereof." Seen from these serene altitudes, all conventional distinctions fade into insignificance, and Satan cannot tempt the soul even to a momentary deviation from its worship of essential truth and beauty.

With the same synthetic glance, he looks at inanimate nature; and, with Novalis, studies her not in her isolated phenomena, but in her essential unity. To him she is not the chance playmate of an hour, but the fair bride of the spirit, and its destined companion through eternity,—reflecting back from her loving and gentle eyes all that the soul hopes or fears, enjoys or suffers. He lives with her in sweet and intimate communion, as one who has won from her the "heart of her mystery," and divined the last word of her secret, or rather as one who has learned that she has no "last word," but like the fair *raconteur* of the Arabian tale, improvises from day to day, from year to year, from age to age, an interminable romance—a series of inventions, the last of which has still some mysterious connection with the first, elucidating and carrying forward but never ending her wondrous story. "To the intelligent Nature converts herself into an infinite promise."

Nor is this view of Nature, as the inseparable companion and counterpart of spirit, contradictory to the Berkeleyan idealism which frequently manifests itself in Emerson's writings, particularly in the earlier Essays. For in proportion as matter is divested of its rigid positiveness and substantial objectivity, do we the more readily conceive of it as a permanent mode of existence, capable of infinite adaptation to the wants of the spiritual intelligences that are associated with it. "The vast picture which God paints on the instant eternity of the soul." The inferences of modern science in relation to this subject are pregnant with results of the highest importance to spiritual and mental philosophy. But while science is slowly collecting facts, inducting theories and deducing results, the poet, with a surer instinct, suggests the true of nature, divines her mission and indicates her method. His sentient and mobile being faithfully transmits all her influences. In all her aspects and changes, he perceives a significant beauty and a mysterious sympathy with humanity. In her presence he feels not weariness, nor fears satiety: he knows that her resources are inexhaustible, and that, elastic, ductile, and permeable to spirit, she reforms herself for ever in conformity with the soul's infinitely expanding ideal.

Like Gray, Emerson delights to hear the gnarled and hoary forest-trees droning out their old stories to the storm. He listens to the song of the winds in the pine-tree and

"Hears within their cadent pauses
The charms of the ancient causes—
Heeds the old oracles,—ponders the
    spells
Song wakes in their pinnacles when the
    wind swells,"

and responds to these sylvan melodies in "wood-notes" not less wild and Orphic than their own.

We find in him always that uniform repose and serenity of mind that affects us somewhat like the aspect of nature itself,

"Calm pleasures there abide, majestic
    pains."

There is an absence of that vivid sense of personality—that intense individualism which so often manifests itself in the morbid and jealous sensitiveness, peculiar to what is called the "temperament of genius." Instead of this, we find a cheerful, inflexible courage, an Oriental quietude. We might fancy him dreaming away his life with the Sacontala, among the Lotus flowers that border the Ganges, or like the starry Magian evoking from night and silence their eternal mysteries. The words of Plotinus in relation to the supersensual portion of the triune soul, might aptly be applied to him—"Remaining free from all solicitude, not seeking to modify the world in accordance with the discursive reason, nor to transform anything in its own nature, but by the vision of that which is prior to itself informing the world with an infinite beauty."

This severity has been termed by critics, "a vice of temperament," "an undue preponderance of the intellectual faculty," "a want of harmonious development," of "generous sympathy with humanity." I do not so understand it, nor can I assent to the criticism of a rare contemporary genius when, in speaking of these essays, he says—"They are truly noble, reporting a wisdom akin to that which the great and good of all time have lived and spoken; yet the author neither warms nor inspires me: he writes always from the intellect to the intellect, and hence some abatement from the depth of his insight, purchased always at the cost of vital integrity. But this is the tax on all pure intellect."

Can we then so separate the functions and faculties of our nature, as to believe that an intellect whose product is "a wisdom akin to that which the great and good of all times have lived and spoken," is developed at the cost of vital integrity? A sufficiency of life—a true vital integrity—would enable us to transcend these pernicious distinctions, and to see that love and wisdom are inseparable. Can the contemplation of eternal verities leave the heart cold and void? Is not the holy energy of true love ever sagacious, far-sighted and prophetic? Truth is not isolated: it is not a part, but the whole. It is love, and beauty, and joy. The wise man does not believe and opine, but he knows and *is* the very truth which he utters. His thought is action: his knowledge is love.

It is very common to hear persons speak of the mind as if reason, imagination and sensibility constituted different and distinct portions of it, though the consciousness speaks, *ex cathedra*, of a living unity. This is in part attributable to the popular empirical psychology which bears the same relation to the true, as the Grecian Theology to the Mosaic. And as the Hellenic deities make war upon each other, so in the popular psychology the faculties are represented as antagonistic, as a profound intellect and a loving heart. Yet, all great philosophers and theosophists have been devout and good men—else were their theories as profitless as their lives. Do not the bard and the prophet offer sacrifice at the same altar? Must the laurel crown extinguish the pure flame of the saintly aureole? The greatest thinker of modern Europe, who united the poetic insight of Plato with the exact method of Aristotle, says, "*Voluntas et intellectus unum idemque sunt.*" Nay, more: *that we know the right through the very attraction which it possesses for us.* "Quod quisque ex legibus naturæ suæ (rationalis) necessario appetit et adversatur id bonum vel malum hujus naturæ est."—*Spinoza, Ethic., pars II.*

This doctrine, that the soul, in its entire, unperverted action, instinctively seeks its highest good—a doctrine which lies at the foundation of all pure ethics—is held by Emerson with a cheerful, invincible faith, based on his knowledge of an infinite and divine life instant in the finite.

Of the *soul* he would says what Dr. Pusey says of the *Church*—"Our duty is not to reform it, or take away from it, but to *obey* it."

"For to the soul, in her pure action, all the virtues are natural and not painfully acquired." We want, then, not so much self-denial as self-knowledge and self-trust.

And as that friendship only is sweet to us which is won without any concession or compromise of our own individuality, so those virtues only are gracious and beautiful in which the whole nature transpires.

133

"People," says Emerson, "represent virtue as a struggle, and take to themselves great airs on their attainments, and the question is everywhere vexed, when a noble nature is commended, whether the man is not better who strives with temptation?" And here the most acute casuists are often at fault, and are fain to confess with honest Geoffrey Chaucer—

"For me, I cannot bolt it to the bran
As can the holy Doctor Aúgustin."

Carlyle, who, with all the dazzling lights and electric splendors of his cometic genius, seldom sees a truth with that calm and steadfast glance with which Emerson transfixes and holds it, in his review of Diderot loses himself in what he calls the "eternal ravelment" of the subject; asks if virtue is indeed synonymous with pleasure?—if Paul the apostle was not virtuous, and if virtue was its own reward when *his* approving conscience told him that he was the chief of sinners?—gets warm at the self-complacent tone in which the poor encyclopedist speaks of the delights of "*vertu, honnêteté, grandeur de l'ame*," &c., and piously adjures him in the Devil and his grandmother's name, to *be* virtuous and say no more about it:— predicts, nevertheless, that the ascetic system will not soon recover its exclusive dominancy, and admits that the close observer may discern filaments of a nobler system, wherein this of self-denial and duty may be included as one harmonious element. Yet again relapsing into his doubts, asks how tolerance for the wrong can co-exist with an ever-present conviction that the right stands related to it as a God to a Devil?"

Here, then, lies the grand difficulty— the radical error of the popular creed—as of the Kantian ethics which closely approximate to it. Kant makes the highest morality to consist in the strength of a man's will—a power to conform his life to an idea of duty. Yet that which reason or conscience imposes as "the right" neither wins his credent love by its beauty, nor brings with it blessedness and joy. Its rewards are referred to a distant period and an exoteric source. Kant has been not unjustly charged with dislocating and subdividing the faculties of the human mind. He puts far apart knowledge and power, being and doing, wisdom and love. In like manner he divides the universe into antagonistic parts and principles, as matter and spirit, God and nature, good and evil &c. Yet, not until men saw this opposition projected in a strong light, did they feel its inadequacy, and seek to restore the great idea of essential unity in a system adapted to the wants and culture of the age. Jacobi was one of the first to call attention to the vital defects of the Kantian philosophy, which sees nothing in Christianity but a code of duties, and represents the Creator of the universe as a mere Supreme Being—"*Deus extramundanus*"—apart from the creation and from man. In referring all action to a sense of obligation, in defining duty, as an antagonistic principle, Kant leaves the subject involved in that "eternal ravelment" from which few men know how to disengage it.

But these difficulties lie not in Emerson's path. He dwells ever in that clear and serene region where neither Loke nor Ahriman, Typhon nor Devil, interfere to divide with God the empire of the universe. With the great thinkers of all time, he sees that no evil is pure; that the principle of good enters into all things. "There is no pure lie, no pure malignity in nature—the belief in depravity is the last profligacy and profanation—there is no scepticism, no atheism but that." The malevolent man is he who holds all things as evil; and hence his destructive propensity. Sir Thomas Browne, on the other hand, who was incapable of forming strong conceptions of evil, says, he could never bring himself heartily to hate the Devil. Emerson seems, with the Platonists, to regard evil as a defect, a privation, a deviation from subsistence. He sees that God imparts to all things good, and to each that quantity of good which it is qualified to obtain. This faith cannot subsist with any purely dualistic philosophy where wrong stands opposed to right, as a Devil to a God rather than as Negation to Being; but in proportion as we free ourselves more and more from a false, fragmentary and superficial life, the soul more distinctly articulates her gospel of peace and love; we then not only believe, but know, that all evil is relative, all being progressive, all life an emanation from the Divine.

It is this beautiful soul-trust, and not self-trust, as some would render it, that Emerson inculcates from a faith so sweet and inward, that the scoffer is silenced and the caviller rebuked.

I have dwelt longer on this subject, because it forms so intimate and essential a part of the entire view of life which I find in these volumes—a view so pregnant and suggestive, that an expansive and liberal theory of morals must necessarily grow out of it.

Although Emerson claims no consistency for the speculations here presented to us, I do not find in the whole range of modern literature a mind that overlooks life from a point of view so high and commanding—that arrives so surely, by an induction so rapid and unerring, at the last results from the speculative reason. And moreover, notwithstanding (or I might rather say in consequence of) the large and free scope of his intellect, I find everywhere a pervasive consistency, a living unity of thought, which is never violated.

He has in truth no affinity with that class of thinkers described by Novalis who construct a theory in order to free themselves from the weariness of thought, nor, on the other hand, with that barren Eclecticism, which, consisting only of a fortuitous collection of ideas and having no internal principle of growth, is, like fossil substances, capable of enlargement only by accretion. For whenever thought is genuine, proceeding from a true inner life, its most spontaneous and unpremeditated enunciation manifests something of that formative energy, that harmonious adaptation of parts which marks the development of organic structure.

We are told by one of Mr. Emerson's most discerning readers, that "it may be said of him that he has never written one good work if such a work be one where the whole commands more admiration than the parts—where, after an accumulation of materials, fire enough be applied to fuse the whole into one new substance." The Essays are said to resemble "a string of mosaics, or a house built of medals."

It may be so; yet will I say of them as Andrew Marvell of his flower garden—

"What Rome, Greece, Palestine e'er said,
I, in this light Mosaic, read."

They are in truth Sibylline leaves, whose price decreases not with their want of completeness in number or arrangement. They have the unity of nature, where the whole reappears in all its parts.

"Out of house scattered Sibyl leaves
Strange prophecies my spirit weaves."

A single aphorism often suggests the whole economy of being, and unlocks to us the secret passages of things. To me they breathe a harmony so pure and responsive that I recognize therein no jarring element.

They are faithful transcripts of thought, as it evolves itself in a mind of the ripest and most harmonious development, fragmentary only in so far as the view which every man takes of life must be fragmentary, and, as are the oldest and most costly scriptures, for life itself, as read or readable by man, is but a fragment—a "*Verden*," and not a "*Seyn*."

In addition to his alleged want of unity and explicitness, we are told of his contra statements on every great question. His report is so faithful, he gives us so impartially all the aspects of things, that his meaning escapes us—"We get now one idea and then another, but seldom such a permanent and final result." Men prefer to have the bolted wheat prepared and garnered for their use. Yet always these antitheses, these apparent contradictions, are coordinates of a single law, and spanned by a central principle. Through conscious dualism only do we pass to conclusions conscious unity.

The great truth to which all Emerson's affirmations point is Absolute Identity—the unity of all things in God. This is the "*mot d'enigme*" to his whole philosophy—it lies at the foundation of his entire theory of life, and is the secret alike of his singleness and his universality.

In giving such prominence to this idea he has shown himself an apt representative of the philosophical character of his age, a philosophy standing as yet far in advance of its popular and prosaic character, yet destined ultimately to determine, as it has already indicated, the point of view from which science, art, religion, law and social polity are to be contemplated.

The idea of Absolute Identity furnishes the type, in conformity with which thought develops itself in all the master spirits of the time. It suggested to Swedenborg his doctrine of correspondences—to Fourier his theory of "universal unity" and "universal analogy"—and to Schelling the parallelism that exists between the laws of nature and the laws of thought—or as Hegel has more intensively expressed it— *Die Absolute Einheit des Begriffs und der Objectivitat*—"the absolute oneness of thought and its object." It inspired St. Simon with his devout conception of the collective life of humanity, and revealed to him its harmonious and progressive development, thereby imparting to history an epic character which ennobles every phase of its progress. Under its influence science itself seems rapidly outgrowing its purely empirical limits, and approximating to a more large and poetic conception of the generic unity and dynamic power of nature. Perhaps, without falling back on the abhorrent theory of the materialists, we shall yet find that the mind has its physique and nature her Psyche. If the same law prevails in the natural as in the moral world—if the same primal energy informs them, then science becomes at once mystic and devout,—a portal through which we have access to the penetralia of that beautiful temple of nature, of which Heraclitus said, "*Enter, for here too are Gods.*"

The Pythagoreans taught that if the essence of all things admits of cognition, it is only in so far as the things of which the world consists, partake of it. With equal truth might we say, that if the things of which the world consists admit of cognition, it is only in so far as they partake of the essence of all things—"*Deus immundanus.*" Only through our oneness with actual being can we assume the possibility of actual knowledge.

An able writer in the Westminster Review, in analyzing this great doctrine of Spinoza, says, "No believer in Ontology, as a possible science, can resist the all-embracing dialectic of Spinoza, but it is our strength that we reject all metaphysics as frivolous. Men can never arrive at a knowledge of things as they are in themselves. Turn it which way you will there is nothing in the consciousness but the con-

136

sciousness itself—to know more would involve the necessity to be more." Aye, verily!—but this identical fact of *being more* is that on which the believer in absolute cognition grounds his faith. No philosophy can explain the relation of thought to its object, which conceives of man as an isolated and detached particle of the great *whole* (a belief which we cannot even state without a paradox). But a more profound observation shows us the manifold, living and essential union which inwardly and invisibly unites all individuals with each other and with nature. Only through "a mystical union of all things resting in God" can we explain the most familiar facts of experience—far less the subtle mysteries of those evanescent and abnormal states in which the soul, transcending the limits of time and space, holds commune with the invisible world, recalls the past and foresees the future—moods when

"We ebb into a former life, or seem
To lapse far back in a confused dream
To states of mystical similitude."

The new Platonists, who regarded this class of phenomena as a kind of natural magic of divination, based the possibility of such powers on the essential connection and dependence of all things.

The great idea then which has exercised so vast an influence on the literature of the age is the *unity of being*, or as a recent critic on the "Teutonic Metaphysics or American Transcendentalism," has satirically expressed it, "everything is everything, and everything else is everything, and everything is everything else." We cannot be surprised at the vagueness and folly which this writer finds in a Philosophy which he vainly attempts to grasp. The same plant will not grow in every soil. Yet is this "Each in all" philosophy no mere "Hall of Phantasy," no

"Blind man's Holiday" or "Fool's Paradise," but a sure ground of holiest love, of sternest courage, of serenest patience, and above all of unfailing charity. Old as thought itself, it is necessarily modified by the psychical and physical culture of the ages in which it manifests itself. Dimly foreshadowed in the vast and gloomy Pantheism of India, it has shed a shimmering glory on the vistas of all the Poets of antiquity from Orpheus to Virgil. On the secret shrine of the Cabirii, it cast a lurid and fitful gleam, flashed through the night of Egyptian darkness, and shot back a pale reflex ray from the pages of the Talmud. In the mediæval age it illumined the dream of the mystic and the theory of the naturalist, while in our own it animates and cheers with its full solar beam the whole hemisphere of thought. Receiving from the adamantine logic of Spinoza a scientific statement invulnerable to criticism, it remained for a long time without any perceptible influence on the literature and philosophy of the age. Spinoza gave to the theory of identity a complete anatomical structure, but it waited for Schelling to breathe into it the breath of life, to unfold the profound significance that was involved in it as a system that at once infused life into nature, while it recognized in humanity and the control of laws as beneficent and inevitable as those which obtain in the natural world.

At the period immediately preceding his enunciation of this philosophy, society was evidently in a subversive or transition state.

Empiricism had done its work well, and proved a vigilant vassal in the temple of science, but it knew not how to avail itself of the stores it had aggregated with such tireless industry. It was overwhelmed with its own wealth, and waited for the hand of a master to dispose of its treasures. Not until philosophy had learned, like Deucalion, to cast behind it these stones of the earth could they become living forms. The Tree of Knowledge was heavy with golden fruit, but a flaming sword still barred the way to the Tree of Life.

Kant was but the precursor and not (as is sometimes thought) the founder of the recent philosophy, for he left untouched the great idea of the essential union of God with Humanity, and regarding the reason as strictly subjective, he desired all knowledge of absolute truth, and analyzed the laws of mind only as subjective phenomena. His method was therefore purely experimental. Yet it must be confessed that he gave to empiricism the noblest character of which it is susceptible, and sought to arrange for it an honorable compromise with idealism. Nor can it be denied that he proved himself an able diplomatist; but he could not succeed in satisfying the large demands of the intellect, which asks nothing less than absolute cognition.

The Manichæan hypothesis which had been reaffirmed by Bayle, and against which Leibnitz composed his Théodicée, had still many advocates. The ghost of Gnostic heresy (the belief in two principles) still walked the earth. The time was full of discord, and waited for the atonement, or reunion. The age of indeterminate although of healthful and impulsive action had long since yielded to an era of blind, unquestioning faith. With the introduction of Printing, this blind faith of the middle ages was at an end, and the sceptical, critical, self-conscious life commenced. The development of new powers and the consciousness of new wants involved the age in moral and political conflicts. With inquiry came doubt and denial, speculation and negation. All the learning and intellect of the eighteenth century was unequal to the solution of the great controversial questions that had been transmitted to it. While it examined and tested all creeds and opinions, it regarded none as worthy of belief. The work of destruction was the only work to which it seemed appointed, and faithfully did it perform its mission.

Man had eaten to satiety of the fruit of the Tree of Knowledge, and had become familiar with change and death. All things seemed shadowy and unreal. Human life was a mere point in time compared to the vast periods of history—the endless æons of science. The researches of the historian had opened interminable vistas into the twilight realms of mythical and traditionary story. Every spot of earth was hallowed by the footsteps of the departed, every city was a mausoleum of the dead.

The literature of the period, enriched with countless accessions from the distance and the past, and presenting such varied modes of apprehending life and nature, was calculated to stimulate to their highest action the reflective faculties, and particularly the faculty of comparison, thereby tending to induce that critical, self-conscious character which then began to distinguish it, and which Carlyle denounces as the unpardonable sin. Man had now learned that he must find repose in clear and adequate ideas of being, or find it not at all. Not by any grace of manner, any play of fancy, or novelty of incident, could he be lapt into forgetfulness of himself,—of his own mysterious being. For him there was no self-oblivion. He cannot be amused—he will not be deceived.

Literature was no longer an heroic song or a devotional anthem. It was introspective, self-involved, and meditative.

"It's sweetest songs were those
That told of saddest thought."

The poet no longer dwelt with God in the garden of innocence, where the fruits and flowers of existence proffered their willing treasures, but was driven forth to delve wearily, and often ineffectually, for the "bread of life" in the thorny fields of the intellect.

In his eloquent lament we see only the fact that an ideal was unfolding to his awakened thought, to which he could as yet in no way conform the real—the soul meanwhile awaiting in bitter travail the birth of the new conceptions that had sprung to life within it.

In reviewing this period of the history of modern literature, we seem to stand with the immortal Florentine, looking down from the brink of an abyss "that receives the thunder of infinite lamentations."

"Vero e che in su la proda mi trovai
Della valle d'abisso dolorosa,
Che tuono accoglie d'infiniti quai."
Inferno, Canto IV.

The heart of man was riven asunder with fierce conflicts; perplexed with inexplicable contradictions. The Sphinx had fixed on him her evil eye, torturing him with questions which he must answer or die. The aggregated treasures of science and learning seemed to mock the imperious demands of the restless intellect with their unavailing hoards; while History unrolled her vast scroll but to threaten or to warn, "for within and without it was written with lamentations, and mourning, and wo[e]." From the wide Orient echoed the cry of desolation and despair—from Judea was the wail borne onward, "the wail of multitudinous Egypt"—Greece and Rome swelled with their choral voices the ancient burden, till all articulate sounds were lost in the sullen boom of a cathedral bell, heard solemnly tolling throughout the long and dismal night of the dark ages. No beneficent purpose was yet detected in the annals of the race—the development of no inherent law, either recognized or divined therein—far less that

plenary inspiration now claimed for the entire record of Humanity.

The old Gods had deserted the earth— Priests and lawgivers had lost their sanctity. Man listened in vain for the spheral harmonies—no voice, no tone from those eternal depths. The song of the stars was drowned in the Babel clamor of sophists and sciolists.

At the close of the eighteenth century there was no theory too visionary, no opinion too paradoxical, to find its advocates and disciples. Pyrrhonism and Materialism, Epicurianism and Stoicism had their successive culminations. The gay and mercurial, like Diderot and Voltaire, laughed and made merry with "the great humbug of the Universe," and sought only, like Aristippus, to win from the passing hours its full complement of pleasure. Amusement was their only aim—annihilation their only hope.

The severe and saturnine, affecting the masculine virtues and indomitable volitions of the Stoics, found a congenial system in the imperious ethics of Fichte, and in his pure and proud faith in the omnipotence of the will, a pretence and a paradigm for their self-complacent egotism. Both Sybarite and Stoic expressing, under opposite forms the extremes of sublimated self-seeking.

From this Chaos of partial and opposing systems, Schelling freed himself by a daring and sublime hypothesis, a bold affirmation of ontological truth, which affected not to justify itself by any laborious psychological analysis, but to the elucidation of which all recent discoveries in mental and physical science indubitably tend.

The fatal defect of the Kantian philosophy, the difficulty of imputing validity to our subjective conceptions, is here supplied by assuming the identity of that which knows, with that which is known; thus integrating all antagonisms, even the

139

great antagonism of matter and spirit, the insuperable problem in every dualistic system.

In the philosophy of Schelling, the real and the ideal are equally represented. God and nature no longer appear as two conceptions fundamentally and essentially distinct, but all things are living and instinct with a divine energy. The idea of progress as the gradual development in Humanity of this inherent energy was now for the first time intelligibly and distinctly stated. Only recently have men begun to know that the destiny of the race is onward, forever onward. The successive forms, laws, creeds and institutions of society are no longer regarded as ultimate, and it is seen that any attempt to perpetuate the same beyond the time when they represent the average intelligence of society, can only lead to stagnation and paralysis. We have learned the significance of the proverb that says the new wine cannot be kept in the old bottles.

Intimately associated with the belief in progress, is that recognition of the true value of the present, which is so prominent a feature of our time.

In this despised present, men begin doubtfully to acknowledge a divinity—the last messenger of God to man—in whose bosom lies treasured the hoarded wealth of the past, and the possibilities of the infinite future.

To live well and happily in the moment is our perfect wisdom. "Five minutes today," says Emerson, "are as much as five minutes in the next millennium."

An abandonment to this serene, instinctive and trustful life, is a virtue of our age, and a legitimate product of its philosophy. Jesus also taught men to live in the moment without anxiety or fear, but his disciples failed to imbibe his cheerful faith.

The Greek philosophers, almost without an exception, represented life under a gloomy aspect. Endurance and sub-mission, rather than love and joy, were the virtues of their age.

The Germans, who have been the enunciators of so many great truths, were the first to give emphasis to the idea that man's immediate duty and true mission is to conform the present to his ever expanding ideal. If God is the "Life of the world," if he is in the process as well as in the form, then is he in every phase of the process, and every moment has its message and its import.

"Surprising, indeed, on whatever side we look" (says one of the young, Heaven-taught seers of our day), "is that revival of the individual consciousness of a living relationship with the All-Good. Our literature is every day more deeply tinged with the sense of the mysterious power which animates existence and governs all events."

This philosophy of identity, under which are included all those views and opinions which are generally in New England classed under the name of Transcendentalism, perhaps we can nowhere find so pure and poetic an expression of these ideas, from which the intellect has derived at once inspiration and repose, as in the writings of Emerson. Yet, although the truths which inform his pages are essentially the same with those of the new German school, he seems to hold them rather after the manner of the Neo-Platonists than of the modern Germans. Plotinus and Proclus, Plutarch and Marcus Antoninus are evidently greater favorites with him than Schelling and Hegel. If I were inclined a look for a flaw in Emerson's crystalline intellect, I should probably find it in a want of that due appreciation of the real, the eternal and necessary correlative of the ideal, which constitutes one of the distinguishing merits of Schelling's system. Not the less true is it that the Essays contain the essential oil and expressed perfume of those truths which have infused a new spirit into the life and literature of the nineteenth century, while in their author we see a striking example of that serenity of soul which is a necessary result of his philosophy. "Beholding identity and eternal causation, the soul is raised above passion, and becomes a tranquillity out of the knowledge that all things go well."

Goethe also tells us that he derived from the theory of identity, as he obtained it from Spinoza, the serenity which pervaded his maturer life. "After seeking in vain for a means of interpreting my strange moral being, I found in the Ethics of Spinoza a calm to my passions, a wide free view over the sensuous and moral world."

By superficial observers, Emerson is often compared to Carlyle; but in Carlyle this all harmonizing sense of the unity of being (the distinguishing characteristic of Emerson's intellect), is manifestly wanting; and notwithstanding his frequent allusions to the new German philosophy, as containing the secret of a higher revelation for those who are capable of receiving it, yet it is evident that the struggle of man with destiny entirely possesses and absorbs him. The mountain of reality presses heavily on his giant heart, and its Titanic throes cannot shake off the superincumbent weight. A fierce unrest consumes him. His incessant calls to labor sound in our ears like the dismal knell of the "work-house clock" summoning a benighted race to their hopeless toil. "For, man's highest blessedness," he tells us, "is that he toil and knows not what to toil at." We recognize in him vast energies, impetuous volitions, a wit emanating from the consciousness of dissonance and disruption; a mirthfulness that makes us weep or shudder, but never do we see in him "the level glance, serene and steadfast, that marks the God."

Carlyle is still struggling with destiny, still overwhelmed and saddened by the contemplation of the "void and formless infinite," perplexed by the fearful antagonisms of good and evil, life and death, time and eternity.

The editor of the Boston Quarterly has been sometimes classed among the New England disciples or teachers of Transcendentalism, and he has, in fact, from time to time exhibited some predilections for its doctrines, as diluted by Cousin, but he has never found that point of view, from which alone these truths can be seen and comprehended as one harmonious system. He has by turns affirmed and denied the great truth of man's knowledge of the absolute, through the mystical union of God with humanity. Yesterday he believed in the impersonality of the reason; today to deny its *personality*, is to deny our own. In laboring to define human personality, and to demonstrate the exact nature and scope of its powers of cognition, will, &c., he involves himself in endless contradictions and inextricable difficulties, thus furnishing another evidence that nature abhors limitation, overflowing all our landmarks and annulling all our distinctions. In one of those aphorisms of Novalis, where a profound truth is often expressed under the form of a bold and startling paradox, he says, "men think it a vulgar error to represent God as a person, but we have yet to learn that man is not less impersonal than God." When we attempt to separate man from his life in God, we have nothing left but Mr. Brownson's "simple faculty of cognition," or the "*Tabula rasa*" or Locke. In his denial of the impersonal reason, in his review of Charles Elwood, April, 1842, Mr. Brownson seems already to have forgotten "that life which is the light of the world, and in which we live, and move, and have our being," a gospel, which in 1841, he quoted as containing the only intelligible solution of these problems.

Like a comet moving in a narrow

ellipse, he sweeps athwart our hemisphere "with fear of change perplexing nations"—darts towards the central orb of truth, and is off again ere we can say "*Ecce Venit*" to the regions of outer darkness.

Carlyle, too, is to many readers but one of those nebulous meteors that hide in their rapid and eccentric course the very stars of heaven from our bewildered gaze. But with Carlyle a sincere faith lies behind this apparent scepticism—and when a calm telescopic glance is turned upon this blazing glory—this mighty mass of phosphorescent splendor, through the very centre of its burning heart, these constant stars may be seen shining afar off in the serene depths of ether.

The fact that Schelling himself has apostatized from the large faith of his philosophical creed, which has exercised so vast an influence on his age, does not in any way affect the truth of his doctrines and need not excite our surprise. Few men, says Menzel, are able to maintain themselves in a position so central, of such perfect equipoise and impartiality— and a wiser than Menzel has said index or mercury of intellectual proficiency is the perception of identity.

Schelling's theory of a God immanent in Nature and in Humanity, on which rested the possibility of absolute cognition, was, as we have seen, but a sublime hypothesis, and the sceptic still proposes to the idealist, although in fainter tones, the eternal question respecting the validity of his intuitions. "How will you demonstrate, how legitimate the truth of these eternal truths?"

As well might we ask the seer to demonstrate his apocalyptic vision of the future—the poet his fine sense of beauty and of love! Can a soul not beautiful, asks Plotinus, attain to an intuition of beauty?

The error seems to lie in the assumption, that all true conceptions and adequate ideas are capable of being immediately demonstrated as such to all minds. Unquestionably all the possibilities of humanity are latent in every individual of the race, but the degrees of actual development differ more than men are disposed to admit. No man can construct or accept a philosophy which transcends the level of his actual life. "The spring cannot rise higher than its source." "*Alle philosophie muse geliebt und gelebt werden.*"

Although true being is everywhere present, it is, as Plotinus has said, more or less present in proportion to our ability of receiving it.

According to Sir James Mackintosh, who is indeed no other than an agreeable Philistine, the theories of Fichte, Schelling, and Hegel, are so many attempts to fix the absolute as a positive in knowledge, while the absolute, like the water in the sieve of the Danaides, has run through as a negative into the abyss of nothing—

If we could arrest and appropriate it, it would no longer be the absolute. The individual intellect is in truth a sieve through which it *passes*, but in which it can never be arrested or contained.

Plato, who was disposed to seek the essence of our knowledge in ideas alone, did not attempt to enumerate these ideas, as if he shrank from subjecting them to a profane analysis. Schelling, as we have said, took his stand with Plato in the region of supra-sensible truths, where no partial results of observation could either confirm or refute him in his reasoning; yet his sublime hypothesis, in so far as it rests on the assumption of absolute identity, strictly coincides with the rigid deductions of experimental science.

Every new discovery in physics teaches that all difference is phenomenal. The integrity of being is detected under manifold disguises. The farther we push our inquiries into the different departments of science, the more obvious are the analogies subsisting between them. In nature all the lines blend and converge towards a common centre. The moment we attempt to distinguish and define, to draw lines and affix boundaries, we are perplexed and baffled by her fluidity and sameness. In the crystal we already detect a paradigm of vegetable forms, in the vegetable an approach to the sentient instinct, while sensation and volition present strange and subtle analogies with electricity.

The discovery of the dependence of the chemical affinities of bodies on their electric states—the detection of electric forces in magnetic phenomena—the close analogies subsisting between light, heat, and sound, all point to one primal energy in nature, the agent in all natural phenomena, as in the mind that perceives them—for mind itself, in so far as we are acquainted with its mode of being, is but a subtle force vibrating to the impulsion of other forces external to itself.

And what then is the omnipresent energy which determines alike the regular form of a crystal, the symmetrical structure of a flower, and the cyclic motions of a planet;—perhaps even the mysterious concords and harmonies of a human soul?—What is this invisible power, itself intangible and imponderable, from which all this bright apocalypse of visible nature is evolved?—which under certain ascertained conditions originates life in inanimate matter (see Vestiges of Creation, page 141), which dissolves into airy nothing the substance of the most solid mountains, which makes and unmakes all things.

"Nature," says Emerson, "is the incarnation of a thought and turns to a thought again." Paradoxical as this may seem, it is the affirmation of a simple fact. Berkeley, after all, was perhaps nearer the truth than has been imagined. For the question between him and his opponents was not whether the objects of perception have a *real* existence out of the mind, but simply whether they have a solid substantial existence—whether the things which affect us from without be matter or spirit?

When Berkeley says that these objects and qualities are but the immediate effects of the ever present Deity, he assumes a sublime truth in strict accordance with the results to which all modern researches in the internal structure and equilibrium of matter evidently point.

All that we know of matter may be comprised in a statement of the laws by which certain forces emanating from certain centres act upon each other. None of our senses ever go behind these forces, and we are unable to determine whether they have a substantial basis or proceed simply from an ideal centre.

Since Leibnitz rejected the Newtonian theory of hard, impenetrable, insoluble atoms, and introduced his own hypothesis of monads, or simple, spiritual, inextended units, essentially possessed of attractive and repulsive forces, science has been slowly but surely approximating to a more spiritual apprehension of the material world and of the laws by which it is governed,—to a theory which should remove the great stumbling-block of matter which has proved so formidable an obstacle in the path of the cosmogonist, and which the Manicheans and their modern disciples have elevated into the rival and adversary of Deity.

This Theory of Leibnitz, when presented in a more finished state by Boscovitch, very generally superseded that of Newton. His idea that the properties of bodies depend on certain forces emanating from geometric points, or points bearing certain relations to each other in space, has subsequently received a striking confirmation from the discovery that the chemical affinities of bodies depend on their electric states; and the physical philosopher already confidently anticipates the time when the chemical problem shall be changed into a mechanical problem—a question of forces, distance and time.

"But what, then," asks the materialist, "are these ultimate atoms—these inextended points—or, as Exley has recently more correctly designated them, these 'spheres of force?'—in what do the powers and properties that pertain to them inhere?"

To this question science has returned no positive answer. All our inquiries into the laws of sensation and the phenomena which induce sensation have revealed to us only "an elastic fluid (?) vibrating to the impulsion of elastic media."

"The intellect ignores matter." "Solidity is an illusion of the senses." May we not then reasonably assume that the latent, yet immediate and inherent principle of the forces which represent matter is the great "caused entity" of Spinoza, which manifests itself under the two modes or attributes of "extension and thought." The life of "the world?" Thus are we again brought back to the great fact of unity in diversity—to the primal manifestation of that mysterious law of polarity which comprehends all phenomena—to that absolute identity which is the starting point and result of all philosophy. And thus is the mystic God-lore of an earlier age elucidated and justified by the scientific researchers of our own.

Let us not decry the age in which we live—it is rich in good gifts and instinct with an infinite hope. Though conversant in all prudential and practical arts, it is not deserted of the ancient wisdom. It is mystic and devout, yet patient and diligent in investigation and research. An age in which mighty secrets have been won from nature by the ceaseless questioning of her solitary votaries, in which science seems about to restore to us all that the imagination has from time to time surrendered to the narrow scepticism of the understanding. Already she has whispered to us the secret law of Nature's boldest miracles,—she has imparted to us a spell by which we may restore the oracles of the past, and has initiated us into the possible modes and conditions of a more spiritual and sublimated existence.

The limits of human knowledge, so accurately defined in the Augustan age of French literature, are now removed beyond even the range of conjecture.

But yesterday man pondered in blank over the origin of worlds; today we read the secrets of creation in the cavernous depths below and in the starry vaults above. We not only weigh the massive bulk of Jupiter or Saturn as in a balance with unerring precision, but by the sublime induction of La Place, we have ascended from investigations concerning the size, figure and motion of planets, to an intelligible theory of their birth. We see worlds in every stage of information slowly evolving from an imponderable ether, and by the aid of the subtle process of analysis, invented by Newton and Leibnitz, are enabled to map out the bright pathway of the stars on the vast blank of the unrecorded past and illimitable future! Science in these latter days has wonderfully enlarged our perspective.

Our range of observation both in space and time is infinitely expanded. The reflecting man is no longer in danger of mistaking his garden wall for the boundary line of the universe, nor the nineteenth century for the hour of doom.

The old fountains from which the great and good past ages drank wisdom and power are reopened, and their sacred and long sealed waters flow freely beside the dusty highways of life. Even the silent tombs of Etruria and the desolate temples of Egypt yield up their jealous secrets, and teach through their eloquent anaglyphs the universality of our own mythology. The torch of science gleams athwart fretted altars and graven obelisks, and the old stones become vocal beneath its ray, and pour forth a Memnonian music. Yet in the very presence of the mighty past, men aspire to a future that shall confirm the great idea of unlimited progress. Everywhere they recognize a progressive life, a beneficent law; and know that to place themselves in harmony with these laws, to "fall into the divine circuits," is to find both freedom and repose.

"Though baffled seers cannot impart
The secret of its laboring heart,
Throb thine with nature's throbbing
    breast
And all is clear from east to west."
Essays—2d Series.

In asserting that the fontal idea of Emerson's writings, as of the philosophy of the age, is absolute identity, I have not been careful to avert from them the imputation of Pantheism, Platonism, Spinozism, &c., &c. It matters little how we designate this manner of interpreting the phenomena of being, since it contains an inherent vitality which alike survives neglect and defies ridicule.

Superficial and timid men may decry these ideas as unintelligible or profane; but what rational ground of faith is left to him who doubts that God is over all and in all, that evil is but the absence and privation of good, and that all apparent evil must give way before a fuller development of the life that is within us? Only when the knowledge that the highest dwells ever with us becomes "a sweet enveloping thought," shall we be enabled to lead a single and trustful life, "to live in thoughts and act with energies that are immortal."

Review of *Essays: Second Series*, *Southern Quarterly Review*, 9 (April 1846), 538–9

There are many bright and bold thoughts in these essays, and not a few strange ones. We cannot go along with the authors of the European schools very cordially. They rely too much on man and too little on God. Their theatre of action is more in the future, than in the present, and, as prophets, we do not think they are to be depended on. If we were to take the work just as it is, and do our duty, we think we should be well occupied. Let the next age work out its own destiny. It is enough for us to keep up with our own times, to adorn them as we may, and to march on with a fearless spirit. If we must have human guides, we should prefer persons who can define their own position and views with a little more distinctness than the transcendentalists do. We do not know what they would be at, nor, we think, do they know themselves. They sometimes utter capital proverbs, but they seem to have a sad horror for mysteries of all sorts, and are startled where ideas are presented to them in a regular and orderly series.

Still, Mr. Emerson often thinks justly and beautifully. His genius sometimes fires, and sometimes cheers us, and if he would use his mother tongue without affectation and speak in pure Addisonian English, we might be well content to read his books and listen to his lectures. He may call himself an American, but the copyist of the copyist of a bad model belongs to no nation or tribe or kindred of scholars who deserve the name. Let the scholar, who wishes to be so regarded, employ the language of educated men of his own century. It is good enough for all the purposes of letters and philosophy. We cannot agree with Mr. Emerson, that "thought makes every thing fit for use." There must be an adaptation between thoughts and the words employed to express them, or they are not fit for use even in the ordinary intercourse of life. An affected dialect is just as bad as an outlandish dress, or a garb that is too large or too small for the wearer. If you have any thing really original and wonderful to say, use plain and wholesome English, gentlemen, and we shall like you all the better for it. The world may not be so wise as you wish it to be, but it has too much sense not to despise cant, even when it affects to utter the oracles of genius.

Checklist of Additional Reviews

Christian Register, 23 (26 October 1844), 170.

New York *Daily Tribune*, 31 October 1844, p. 1.

Spectator [England], 17 (24 November 1844), 1122–3.

Graham's Magazine, 25 (December 1844), 293.

Yale Literary Magazine, 10 (December 1844), 92.

Douglas Jerrold's Shilling Magazine, 1 (February 1845), 184–7.

Hunt's Merchants Magazine, 12 (April 1845), 398.

[Charles Wicksteed], *Prospective Review*, 1 (2nd Quarter 1845), 252–63.

"Emerson's Essays," *Biblical Review and Congregational Magazine*, 1 (April 1846), 148–52.

"***," "Essays by R. W. Emerson.— Second Series," *Christian World*, 4 (4 April 1846), 3.

"Daniel Stern" [Marie de Flavigny, Comtesse d'Agoult], "Etudes contemporaines: Emerson," *Revue Indépendante*, 2nd ser., 4 (July 1846), 445–56.

New York *Mirror*, 4 (18 July 1846), 234.

Literary Gazette, 1723 (26 January 1850), 61. Reviews *Eight Essays* (London: George Slater, 1850) and *Nature, An Essay; Lectures on the Times, and on War.*

Whittington Club and Metropolitan Athenæum Gazette, n.s. 5 (9 February 1850), 37. Reviews *Eight Essays* (London: George Slater, 1850).

Knickerbocker, 35 (March 1850), 254–63. Also reviews *Nature; Addresses, and Lectures.*

Poems

Review of *Poems*,
Critic [England], n.s. 5
(2 January 1847), 9–11

Philosophy and Poetry are nearer of kin than they are commonly accounted. The true Poet is the profoundest Philosopher; the sagest Philosopher breathes the sublimest Poetry. He may not be a master of the mechanism of verse; unskilled he may be in the rhymester's craft; these are not poetry, but only its outward vestments and decorations; the spirit that is the life of poetry lies in the thoughts, and exists and glows, however coarsely clothed, and whether expressed in the plain garb or prose, or in the musical accents of verse.

Emerson is undoubtedly a Philosopher, and, therefore, he is also a Poet. And they who have read his "Essays," so rich, not alone in poetical thought, but in him a volume of Poetry in proper lyrical form, nor to learn that, whereas in his previous publications he has scattered poetry throughout his philosophy, so here he has preached his philosophy in poetry.

But while cordially admitting Emerson's right to the title of a Philosopher, we must express regret that he has not answered the expectation excited by his first efforts. He began with distinct and definite views; he has plunged so far into the mystical that he has fairly lost his way; he is begirt with fog and mist; his mind is obfuscated; and having substituted vague, shapeless dreams for clear ideas, his language has come to reflect the confusion of his thoughts, and he fails to make himself intelligible to his readers simply because he does not clearly comprehend his own views. The second series of his Essays was vastly inferior to the first, both in thought and in composition, and it is with sorrow that we see in these poems a repetition of the vagueness mistaken for grandeur, and mysticism for profundity, which has unhappily clouded the brilliancy of a career that opened so hopefully.

There are in this volume unmistakeable evidences of genius; the soul of the poet flashes out continually; and the hand of the poet is seen often. Nevertheless, it is not a work that will become popular: these rhymes will never pass into the hearts of men, to mould their thoughts, and be a part of their language. They will be read as a curiosity, and for the name's sake of their author, but they will not linger in the memory, or be turned to again and again, or placed among the gems of song in the collections of "Beauties of the Poets," which everybody deems it a duty to possess, even if they never read them.

And the reason is, that the defects of his most recent lucubrations in philosophy are apparent in his poetry, and that the vagueness of the thoughts is not compensated by the mechanical excellence so often accepted for poetry. Perhaps the poet had a meaning in many of these lyrics, but certainly it is unintelligible to his readers. And it is no excuse that we might find it if we would search deep enough, and exercise sufficient patience. A poet has no right so to tax his reader's brain. A poem is not a problem to be solved like a thesis in the mathematics: it is not even an argument to be pursued with logical precautions. The business of the poet is not to *prove*, but to *preach*. By the help of his high intellect, he must master great truths, and that is his task as philosopher. But when he has found them, his business as poet is simply to proclaim them in worthy language, that shall write them for ever upon the hearts of men.

This glorious mission Emerson has performed but imperfectly. He is too dreamy in his thoughts and too imperfect in the art of verse-making. In all these two hundred pages we are unable to glean half-a-dozen extracts, worthy of his name and fame. Scraps there are, indeed, here and there—scattered images that mark the footsteps of a poet—but the result of the perusal of the whole volume is disappointment, that with such capacities so little has been accomplished.

He opens with a mystical rhyme, entitled "The Sphynx," a fragment of his philosophy, which, amid some better verses, contains such doggerel as this:

["The Sphinx," 22.25–24.4]

This shews him at his worst in matter and in manner. There are better things, or we should have thrown the book aside with a notice of half-a-dozen lines. Thus, for instance, is there some poetry in

["The Problem," 6.11–9.3]

Better still, because he has descended from his stilts, and condescends to utter the impulses of the natural man, in this address to

["The Humble Bee," 38.13–40.24]

Equally pretty and fanciful is

["The House," 128.10–129.12]

We reserve the best for the last; that the reader may rise with kindly impressions towards the labours of one who, with all his faults, has not only enlarged the boundaries of thought in himself, but has performed the still more important service of making others think. It is very much in the best manner of Coleridge. It is entitled

["Blight," 139.10–141.18]

A note at the beginning states, that this volume has been printed from the author's manuscript, and is therefore a copyright. It is very elegantly got up, as poetry always will be by a publisher of taste.

149

"Emerson's Poems," New York *Daily Tribune*, 9 January 1847, p. 1

There are those who say they can discern neither Poetry in the verse nor meaning in the prose of Emerson and his school—only a parti colored haze—misty straining after grand effects for which there are no adequate causes—a daring but vague aspiration, of which the impulse is a wish not to do but merely to aspire, or rather to seem to be soaring heavenward. Dissenting utterly from this estimate of the writings of those termed Transcendentalists, (we speak not here of their Philosophy, so far as they may be said to have any, but of their utterance regarded as contributions to Literature,) we have yet no argument to offer for our faith save the writings themselves. He who can read the volume before us, for instance, and not *feel* that its author is in a high and pure sense a Poet, is not likely to be persuaded by anything else we could offer.

But while we regard Ralph Waldo Emerson as one of America's greatest Poets if not absolutely her greatest Poet, we are aware that he can never be deemed such by those who do not share and rejoice in his defiance of prescription and formula.— To all martinets in metre his rhythm must frequently seem most defective—scarcely bearable. Nay, more: We confess that its Æolian wilfullness is often unpleasing to us, who love the man and admire his works, and that in the structure of his verse he is inferior to Bryant or even Longfellow. But, on the other hand, we feel that there is no living man whose writings could so illy be spared from our Literature as could those of Emerson.

Our reading public may be divided into two classes, the few who know our author as he is, and the many who know of him next to nothing. For the former, we could quote from the larger and profounder poems in this volume—— 'Woodnotes,' 'Initial, Demonic and Celestial Love,' 'Saadi,' 'Threnody,' &c. But those who would delight in these will not be satisfied with less than the entire volume, so that to quote from them would be a thankless labor. We choose, therefore, to quote instead for the mass of readers a number of the smaller and in the main less characteristic pieces, which we trust will yet indicate to many the richness of the mine whence they are drawn. But first a single quatrain from 'Woodnotes:'

["Woodnotes," 48.18–21]

With a brief citation from 'Monadnoc,' we pass to the simple copying without comment of a few of the minor Poems, which seem to us, not so much the finest as the least likely to be pronounced obscure by those unfamiliar with Emerson. And first of the mountain known to all who have visited South-western New Hampshire, as 'the grand Monadnoc:'

["Monadnoc," 61.15–62.6]

["Good-bye," 3.3–4.10]

["The Apology," 119.2–21]

["Musketaquid," 141.20–144.22]

["The Snow-Storm," 41.15–42.21]

["The Day's Ration," 138.2–139.8]

150

Review of *Poems, Athenæum*, 1006 (6 February 1847), 144–6

As a philosophical essayist, Mr. Emerson has won for himself an extended reputation;—partly due to the peculiarity (not ineloquent) of his prose style, and partly to a tone of independent thinking which, however much it may shock the reader's prejudices, begets respect for the author's courage. Hitherto, however, he has not been generally known as a poet. Some few verses under his name have, from time to time, appeared in the more transcendental periodicals of the United States; and been read with curiosity by his immediate disciples. These, with others, collected into the volume before us, now challenge public criticism in a more formal manner.—A strong mind expressing itself in a form under which we have not been accustomed to study it demands some share of our attention.

It has happened more than once in the history of literature, that the critic has been compelled to take a distinction between that which is Poetry and that which is a Poem. Keats's 'Endymion' is a case in point:—a production full of fine poetic material, but wanting the decision of outline and form necessary to a finished work. Mr. Emerson's volume presents the same deficiency. No one can have read his philosophical essays with care and not been struck with a certain poetic spirit pervading their conception and structure. That same spirit in this book of verses has sought metrical expression. But in seeking utterance, it has recognized no law—referred to no exemplars. Both rhythm and rhyme there are in these stanzas—many a

fine image, and sometimes a cluster of such—scattered symbols of deep significance—and the presence of sincere and earnest thinking everywhere: but there is no art prescribing the mould into which such materials would be best cast—no aim, in fine, at composition. Simple utterance, in verse more or less rude, is all that has been desired,—and that is but imperfectly achieved. A wild, low music, indeed, accompanies these artless strains; an indistinct, uncertain melody—such a tune as an untaught musical nature might choose to itself in solitary places: but those scientific harmonies which are among the mysteries of the poetic craft, and identify a member of the minstrels' guild, are not so much as emulated by Mr. Emerson. He even ignored—perhaps despised them. It may be, that he would have us recommence singing with those unaided impulses in which song began. There is an obvious error in this. But let him speak for himself on this score—as we think he means to do—in a piece, entitled—

["Merlin," 120.3–121.27]

We perceive, then, that Mr. Emerson has made a theory of his practice; which we would fain believe to have been spontaneous in the beginning, and only thus systematically justified in reply to subsequent objectors. Setting this consideration aside—having, once for all, pointed out the defect of these poems as *poems*—we will give such indication of the poetical material of which they are composed as will best dispose the reader to recognize their merits. The following lines exhibit a cluster of pleasing images:—

["The Sphinx" 20.18–21.26]

The verses that follow are from a piece entitled 'The Problem.' It is more of a whole than any other in the book; and might almost be called a poem:—

["The Problem," 6.11–9.3]

Notwithstanding their apparent completeness, upon investigation these verses prove to be a fragment. They treat only half the subject. The poet should have told us why he could not personally endure the assumption of a sacred character confessed by himself to be so attractive. He takes it for granted that the reader understands his feeling in this respect; yet this is the very point on which we need a revelation.

Many pieces headed with ideal titles—such as 'The World-Soul,' 'Fate,' 'Uriel,' 'Each and All,' &c.—consist merely of philosophical memoranda preserved in rhyme. Nevertheless, in these there are sometimes stanzas which are suggestive, not only in a poetical relation, but in one far higher—as touching those social reforms which now everywhere command the attention of society:—

["The World-Soul," 15.21–17.10]

Some portions of a series of poems, entitled 'Wood Notes,' are, in their peculiar way, yet finer; and the entire succession has been enthusiastically received on the other side of the Atlantic. They begin with a summary of the adverse conditions to which the modern poet is liable. Then, we have a description of the true bard; who in Mr. Emerson's idea seems to be identified with the mystic. A specimen of this series we will give—exhibiting the Poet in the wilder and more fantastic moods of his Protean enthusiasm:—

["Woodnotes," 48.18–50.20]

From this point we are plunged at once into mysticism,—through the mazes of which there is no finding our way. There are some things both lofty and strange in many others of the poems: and there are a few examples of a more familiar kind and subject—two or three fables, and descriptive blank verse poems, which lie level to the common understanding. But all are marked with the same characteristics—and are more properly to be termed effusions than compositions. As specimens of American poetry fresh from the author's mind and not indebted to imitation for their existence,—they are, nevertheless, welcome.

C[yrus]. A. B[artol]., "Poetry and Imagination," *Christian Examiner*, 42 (March 1847), 250–701

[. . .]

We come now to by far the most original and peculiar of these volumes,[1] the poems by Mr. Emerson. To his genius, considered in its peculiarity, we bow. We own the spell which, more powerfully perhaps than any other American writer, he has thrown over our fancy. We know of nothing in the whole range of modern writers superior in original merit to his productions. He is "of imagination all compact." To read his finer pieces is to our poetic feeling like receiving a succession of electric shocks; and each additional line in them, communicating subtilely with all the rest, multiplies the force of this ideal battery. He is so frugal of language, as to let no phrase stand which is not charged with meaning. His merit, however, is not uniform. He is sometimes trivial in his themes, but never weak or wordy in their treatment. He is occasionally vague and mystical, but the brilliant distinctness usual in his thoughts and illustrations we take for proof that all his sentences refer to something real in his own mind. His best strokes cut below the superficial impressions made upon us by ordinary writers, and chisel themselves in the memory; while the softest musical rhythm is often so connected with the sharply arranged parsimony of his words, that passages repeat themselves in our involuntary recollection, as in the mysteriously sounding chambers of the spirit we hear over and over again the tunes of some great master. We are always glad to confess our obligation for intellectual helps, and we have to thank Mr. Emerson for the strong flashes of wit and sense, clad in bright imagery, with which he has often waked our minds from slumber. His discernment is as keen as his invention is fruitful. No man has a finer eye than he to trace those secret lines of correspondence which run through and bind together all parts of this lower frame of things. And even when we have been in the very spot in the realms of thought where he pitches his tent, he will detect some hidden analogy, and surprise us with a new observation. We know of no compositions that surpass his in their characteristic excellence. Even his unshaped fragments are not bits of glass, but of diamond, and have always the true poetic lustre, an inward gleam like that playing amid the layers of a sea-shell. Some of his conceptions are turned into as admirable expression as we find in Milton's sonnets or Shakespeare's songs.

We have thus praised this writer, and, as some may think, overpraised him, in the sincerity of our hearts. Our reference has, we find, unconsciously included his prose as well as his poetry. But they are both of a piece, and bear alike the stamp of their author's intellectual unity. The same affluent and over-mastering imagination, the same grasp of all the powers of language, the same faithful report from sight and experience, prevail throughout all his productions. But our criticism must find fault with the same frankness with which it bestows eulogy, and will be for that but the more prized by our friend's magnanimous spirit. He has, we think, more height than breadth. He shoots up like the pinnacle of an *aiguille* mountain into the atmosphere of the great poets, but he lacks altogether their various richness and comprehensive proportions. He is dry and cold in the comparison. The productive fields do not so spread out below the frosty cone of inaccessible sublimity which towers above. There is more of a hard, steel-like glitter than of the hue of life in his landscape. He is, in fact, rather the poet of a class than of the race. The circle of his sympathies is narrow. His intense admiration of a few forms of life and character threatens to banish the broad spirit of humanity. With all his nobleness and purity of sentiment, in the ascendency of his fancy he can hardly restrain himself from pouring contempt on most of his kind. In view of vague possibilities of achievement, he unworthily disparages actual genius and character. The heart in his poetry is less than the head, and this causes a deficiency for which nothing else can fully atone. Only a transcendent splendor and wealth of intellect could redeem many of his pieces from condemnation and forgetfulness, as being frigid and unfeeling. These are sad flaws in such noble workmanship. Did a fellow-feeling for human nature in all its varieties equal and fill out his other traits, we might think the great poet of America had been born, to bring on our flourishing Augustan age. But, as yet, our hearts acknowledge a more genial and enlivening influence from several of our other native bards. Would that one whom we unfeignedly respect might not only show his power of soaring to the empyrean, but hover with a more wide and loving interest over the lot of his fellow-men! It may be for want of this all-embracing sympathy that his flights are so infrequent, and that he can but seldom continue long on the wing. If he could but kindle his soul with some great conception of human fortunes, and write a generous epic of this our human life, including its great trials and accomplishments, its sublimer aspirations and hopes, we hazard little in predicting that it would be a production to mark the age.

And yet we hardly know how he could have the kind of human sympathy which we most value for the inspiration of such an undertaking, with his present views of religion. There is no recognition in his pages of the Christian faith, according to any, however catholic, idea of it which we are able to form. He seems to have no preference of Jesus over any other great and good man. He either does not accept the evidences authenticating a divine revelation, or they press with but little interest upon his preoccupied mind. But what we must regard as his religious unsoundness strikes still deeper. He does not even appear to own any distinction between man and Deity. He talks of "the gods" as an old Roman would do. One personal Creator is not present to his thought. He does not go for the signs of such a Being into the broad circumference of his works, but confines himself within the little rim of his own individual consciousness. He puts aside Bible and ritual, and all human speech and outward light, for the "super-solar beam." In religion he fills the whole space of thought with that mystic element, which we must perhaps admit, but should confine in a corner. He does not, with a plain trust, examine the world which God has made, but curiously inspects the inverted image of it upon his own mental retina. He does not pay to the instincts of mankind or of society the respect he would render to the peculiar instincts of the animal, the bee or the beaver. And not taking cordially to his heart the Christian doctrines of a Father and a particular Providence, how can he strongly embrace the dependent doctrine of human brotherhood, or feel the unlimited sympathy which this doctrine inspires? We speak here, of course, of his system. We doubt not the kindness of his actual relations with men. We believe a hearty historical faith in Christianity would add greatly to the power of his genius. The views we have alluded to so underlie and run through his writings, as almost to amount to the proposal of a new religious faith,—a presumption which of course astounds us, simple believers in the New Testament on what we deem irrefragable grounds. His ideas carry him wide of the humility of the Gospel,—though they give rise in his own mind not so much to personal pride as to an immense self-respect and an enormous self-reliance. He is willing to trust to or lean upon nothing but himself;—a wonderful state of feeling, when we consider our real condition of dependence in all our powers,—our bodies resting on the attractions of material nature, every vital organ in us doing its part involuntarily, and only a single silvery thread branching into various filaments of the nerves of motion being held by our own will,—our intelligence but the shadowy reflex of Divine wisdom, like the light from distant worlds in the focus of the astronomer's telescope,—and even our moral nature roused not by an internal force of conscience alone, but quickened and kept alive so greatly by instruction and example. We are made to lean, and are stronger when we lean; and, if we do not lean, we fall. Our poet is dragged by his philosophy to a lower, or at least less commanding, height than, with a better understanding on this point, he might well attain.

We ought, however, to say, that the noblest principles of conduct are often asserted in his pages. We rejoice to find instances of a truly grand morality, and surpassing expressions of a pure and beautiful spirit; but are suddenly perplexed, as we proceed, by an optimism confounding all moral distinctions. He seems, in some places, to know no difference between light and darkness, sweet and bitter. Some revelations, hinted at in one of these poems, respecting a moral indifference in all things, are represented as made by "Uriel,"

and as causing the older deities, who had been in the secret, to blush. Alphonso of Castile, who is said to have thought he could improve upon the world as described in the Ptolemaic system, makes a bold figure, as the *protégé* of our author's pen, entering in heaven's court a general and unqualified complaint about all things under the sun.

There is an undertone of sadness running through these rhymes, sometimes harsh and scornful, and sometimes tender and refined, like angelic melancholy. We fancy this, too, may proceed from the peculiarity of the writer's belief. Seldom do we hear from him the truly cheerful strain which an earnest faith in Christianity would prompt. In that marvellously beautiful "Threnody," near the close of the book, the sorrow at the commencement is out of all proportion to the comfort at the end. It is the song of a stricken and struggling stoicism. The note falls irresistibly into the minor key. The very voice of consolation dies away in a wail. Alas! it is a poor application here made to the heart's wounds. They still bleed into the very ointment and balm. Every stroke of genius seems but to sharpen the regret. We remember in all our reading nothing more cheerless. It is a picture we would not hang in our heart's chambers. Every touch of the pencil draws a tear. As a painting of grief it is unrivalled,—but it is of grief alone. His hand proves false to him, when he undertakes to draw the form of the angel of peace. But that the soul of the poet might be deaf to our entreaty, we would implore him to turn his eye to those fountains of comfort which God has opened in the Gospel of his Son. For nothing can be more manly than an humble reliance on the means of revival and support, in our distress, which our Father has provided. Let him in lowliness receive these, and then, for the "Threnody," and the "Dirge" which precedes it, we should hope to receive lines as highly adorned with the lights of a creative fancy, but gilded from above also by the beams of heaven. There would at least be nothing in them of the "grief whose balsam never grew."

But we must pause. The analysis of Emerson's writings is no short or easy task. We would not pretend to oversee his summit, but only to note our impressions as we stand and contemplate it. His works, on account of their peculiarity, if nothing else, will probably be among the most enduring of the present time. There is much in them to admire and be improved by. And while we must think there is much also that is unsound and must be injurious to any mind imbibing it, we intend no personal commendation in expressing our conviction that he is a true-minded and righteous man, raised above every thing unworthy, and living a blameless life according to the monitions of his own conscience. Our calling is not to speak of the man, but of the author. We think the intellectual states and tendencies which we have noted chill and cripple his genius. He would make better poetry under the sway of views and opinions which he rejects or holds slightly. Were we writing with a different design, we might state other reasons for our regret at some of the sentiments which he expresses. We have now only to say, that they have injured his book, and must restrict the width and impair the quality of its influence. Would he fetch an echo from the universal heart, as it beats in the breasts of men from generation to generation, he must add to his style a faith and fervor as signal as its brilliancy and force.

We must retire from our survey of these fruits of Mr. Emerson's labors. And as we retire, the traits we have objected to fade away from our attention, and many a melodious note from "Each in All," "The Problem," "The Humble-Bee," "Monad-noc," and "The Forerunners," lingers and renews itself pleasantly in our ear.

But having been constrained in our criticism of Mr. Emerson's volume to suggest radical objections as well as to confess strong admiration, we feel it to be right that we should here try to characterize very briefly his mind. Poetry with him is no recreation or trial of skill, but the sincerity and very substance of his soul; it shows not the passing figures of a magic-lantern, but the convictions and views of life for which he would be a martyr. What, then, is the mind that we see on his page? It is a mind subtile, brilliant, rapid, and decisive. It is a mind in which intuition takes the place of logic, and an insatiable aspiration banishes every form of philosophy. The lightning of his genius reveals the landscape of his thought, and the darkness quickly swallows it up again, till another flash reveals more or less of it. It is a mind scorning forms, conventions, and institutions, and, if it could have its way, would substitute for all this stable platform of law and custom on which we live and work the extemporaneous impulses of the spirit. It is a mind that despises all that has been done, and regards the highest and most inspired utterances of men as but "syllables" dropping carelessly from the tongue; and holds in slight esteem achievements to which even itself is not equal, except in the dreamily anticipated efforts of some distant time and unknown world to come. It sees an ideal which makes it contemn all that is actual. It draws upon the well of its own conceptions, and deems that single draught will suffice though it pass by all other fountains. It aims at a lonely, insulated being, shut up to what may come to it from the general life of the universe, and prizes all foreign helps from its fellows only in proportion to their accordance with its independent results. It weighs and oversees, in its own notion, all characters of intellect and virtue that ever were, and Jesus Christ as confidently as the rest. As we might expect, the consequence of these tendencies is much narrowness, a very partial and unfair estimate of other and differing minds, great injustice in many respects to existing arrangements and instrumentalities, and a continual rising above the useful agencies of life into an atmosphere too rarefied to support any organization less singular than his. But let us more gladly observe, in addition to these things, moral courage, fearless candor, freedom from vanity and from many false leanings, if he has not reached all that are true.

The most important effect of the intellectual habits which he indulges is seen in the aspect of his religious faith. We have barely touched on this in remarking upon the quality of his poems. We feel, however, that perfect truth to our own persuasions requires us to take here distinct notice of the point. Of the primary religious sentiment of the soul, that of reverence, we perceive, especially in his last publication which we have reviewed, but the faintest traces. The personal God of the Gospel, as well as the supernatural manifestation of that God in Christ, is in exile from all his pages. We have already alluded in another connection to this singularity. We recur to it that we may do justice to his positive faith, by noticing the substitute for an Almighty Parent which he finds in an impersonal universal essence, identical with his own spirit and with the common life of nature and of man. There is no print of kneeling on any ground he traverses, save to this vague and undefinable power. We must think his idea a poor basis for any just or truly elevated worship. We know he may think

that he exalts the Deity by pantheistically making all things deity. But we affirm that he so degrades the Deity, and not only weakens the religious sentiment, but saps the foundations of good morals, though no devoted friend of his could appreciate more highly than we his personal integrity and purity of heart. So imaginative, so passionless, and so beautiful a frame of spirit as his could be left with moral safety under the influence of views which the virtue of the millions of men could not abide for an hour. If his mind were popular, we should fear that the tenor of his writings would lead multitudes away from God, and set them adrift upon the stream of their own undisciplined inclinations. We admire, nay, we will confess, in spite of all we have said, love the man, but all the more we feel it to be necessary to set up a bar against the operation of many of his sentiments upon our own minds. We wish him the largest success in all that he has done to refine and elevate the community, but we are obliged by a sense of duty to put in a protest against the soundness of much that is implied in his various publications. And may God, for him and us all, bless the truth and prosper the right! [. . .]

Note

1 Also reviewed are *The Estray: A Collection of Poems* by Henry Wadsworth Longfellow, *Schiller's Homage of the Arts* translated by Charles T. Brooks, *The Island Bride and Other Poems* by James F. Colman, *Poems* by Thomas Buchanan Read, *Poems of Many Moods* by C. G. Fenner, *Poems* by William Wetmore Story, *Poems* by William Ellery Channing, *Songs of the Sea, with Other Poems* by Epes Sargent, and *The New Timon. A Romance of London.*

[Orestes A. Brownson], "Emerson's Poems," *Brownson's Quarterly Review*, 4 (April 1847), 262–76

If we could forget that Almighty God has made us a revelation, and by faith solved for us the problem of man and the universe; and if we could persuade ourselves that we are here with darkness behind us, darkness before us, and darkness all around us, relieved only by the fitful gleam from the reversed torch of reason, at best serving only to confront us, turn we which way we will, with the dread unknown, we should greet these poems with a warm and cordial welcome, and saving the mere mechanism of verse-making, in which they are sometimes defective, assign them the highest rank among our American attempts at poetry. The author is no everyday man; indeed, he is one of the most gifted of our countrymen, and is largely endowed with the true poetic temperament and genius. He has a rich and fervid imagination, a refined taste, exquisite sensibility, a strong and acute intellect, and a warm and loving heart. He is earnest and solemn, and, taking his own point of view, a man of high and noble aims. If truth were no essential ingredient of poetry, if the earthly were the celestial, and man were God, and if the highest excellence of song consisted in its being a low and melodious wail, we know not where to look for any thing superior to some of the wonderful productions collected in the volume before us.

But the palm of excellence, even under the relation of art, belongs not to poetry which chants falsehood and evil. The poet is an artist, and the aim of the artist is to realize or embody the beautiful; but the beautiful is never separable from the true and the good. Truth, goodness, beauty, are only three phases of one and the same thing. God is the True, the Good, the Fair. As the object of the intellect, he is the True; as the object of the will, the Good; as the object of the imagination, the passions, and emotions, the Beautiful; but under whichever phase or aspect we may contemplate him, he is always one and the same infinite, eternal God, indivisible and indistinguishable. In his works it is always the same. In them, no more than in him, is the beautiful detached or separable from the true and the good; it is never any thing but one phase of what under another aspect is good, and under still another true. The artist must imitate nature, and he fails just in proportion as he fails to realize the true and the good in his productions. His productions must be fitted to satisfy man in his integrity. We have reason and will, as well as imagination; and when we contemplate a work of art, we do it as reasonable and moral as well as imaginative beings, and we are dissatisfied with it, if it fail to satisfy us under the relation of reason or will, as much as if it fail to satisfy us under that of the imagination.

Moreover, the beauty which the artist seeks to embody is objective, not subjective,—an emanation from God, not something in or projected from the human soul. Mr. Emerson and the Transcendentalists contend that beauty is something real, but they make it purely ideal. With them, it is not something which exists out of man and independent of him, and therefore something which he objectively beholds and contemplates, but something in man himself, dependent solely on his own internal state, and his manner of seeing himself and the world around him. But the ideal and the real are not identical; and if the beautiful were the projection or creation of the human soul, and dependent on our internal state and manner of seeing, it would be variable, one thing with one man and another thing with another, one thing this moment, another the next. We should have no criterion of taste, no standard of criticism; art would cease to have its laws; and the boated science of æesthetics, so highly prized by Transcendentalists, and on which they pride themselves, would be only a dream. Beauty is no more individual, subjective, than is truth or goodness. It neither proceeds from nor is addressed to what is individual, idiosyncratic; but it proceeds from the universal and permanent, and appeals to what, in a degree, is common to all men, and inseparable and indistinguishable from the essential nature of man.

Mr. Emerson's poems, therefore, fail in all the higher requisites of art. They embody a doctrine essentially false, a morality essentially unsound, and at best a beauty which is partial, individual. To be able to regard them as embodying the beautiful, in any worthy sense of the term, one must cease to be what he is, must divest himself of his own individuality, and that not to fall back on our common humanity, but to become Mr. Emerson, and to see only after his peculiar manner of seeing. They are addressed, not to all men, but to a school, a peculiar school, a very small school, composed of individuals who, by nature or education, have similar notions, tastes, and idiosyncrasies. As artistic productions, then, notwithstanding they indicate, on the part of their author, poetical genius of the highest order, they can claim no elevated rank. The author's genius is cramped, confined, and perverted by his false philosophy and morality, and the best thing we can say of his poems is, that they indicate the longing of his spirit for a truth, a morality, a freedom, a peace, a repose, which he feels and laments he has not.

We know Mr. Emerson; we have shared his generous hospitality, and enjoyed the charms of his conversation; as a friend and neighbour, in all the ordinary relations of social and domestic life, he is one it is not easy to help loving and admiring; and we confess we are loath to say aught severe against him or his works; but his volume of poems is the saddest book we ever read. The author tries to cheer up, tries to smile, but the smile is cold and transitory; it plays an instant round the mouth, but does not come from the heart, or lighten the eyes. He talks of music and flowers, and would fain persuade us that he is weaving garlands of joy; but beneath them is always to be seen the ghastly and grinning skeleton of death. There is an appearance of calm, of quiet, of repose, and at first sight one may half fancy his soul is as placid, as peaceful, as the unruffled lake sleeping sweetly beneath the summer moonbeams; but it is the calm, the quiet, the repose of despair. Down below are the troubled waters. The world is no joyous world for him. It is void and without form, and darkness broods over it. True, he bears up against it; but because he is too proud to complain, and because he believes his lot is that of all men and inevitable. Why break thy head against the massive walls of necessity? Call your darkness light, and it will be as light—to you. Look the fiend in the face, and he is your friend,—at least, as much of a friend as you can have. Why complain? Poor brother, thou art nothing, or thou art all. Crouch and whine, and thou art nothing; stand up erect on thy own two feet, and scorn to ask for aught beyond thyself, and thou art all. Yet this stoical pride and resolve require a violent effort, and bring no peace, no consolation, to the soul. In an evil hour, the author overheard what the serpent said to Eve, and believed it; and from that time, it would seem, he became unable to believe aught else. He loves and wooes nature, for he fancies her beauty and loveliness emanate from the divinity of his own being; and he affects to walk the fields and the woods, as a god surveying his own handiwork. It is he that gives the rose its fragrance, the rainbow its tints, the golden sunset its gorgeous hues. But the illusion does not last. He feels, after all, that he is a man, only a man; and the enigma of his own being,

"The fate of the man-child,
    The meaning of man,"

torments him, and from his inmost soul cries out, and in no lullaby tones, for a solution. But, alas! no solution comes; or, if one, it is a solution which solves nothing, which brings no light, no repose, to the spirit wearied with its questionings. As a proof of this, take the poem with which the volume opens, entitled *The Sphinx*. In this the author proposes and attempts to solve the problem of man. He begins by chanting the peace, harmony, and loveliness of external nature, and proceeds:—

["The Sphinx," 22.1–24.20]

The contrast between moral and physical is founded in fancy. The disorders of the external world are not less striking than those of man, and the strife of elements is as terrible as that of the passions. There are blight and mildew, earthquakes and volcanoes, floods and droughts, in nature, as well as wars and revolutions in states and empires. But let this pass. Whence comes the evil in man? "The fiend that man harries is love of the Best." That is, man is never satisfied with what he has; but imagines that he sees always something better just beyond and above him. Advance or ascend as he may, the Ideal floats ever before him, urging him

on, and bidding him climb higher up, ever higher up yet. There is no rest for him. What is good and what is evil in his condition spring alike from this aspiring disposition. In this originate his virtues, and in this his vices,—what is noblest in his being and character, and what is lowest and meanest; and his sorrow is at the distance there is ever between his aspirations and his realizations. But in this the author confounds the love of the Best, or aspiration to the Perfect, with pride. He teaches, and consciously, that Satan in aspiring to be God was actuated by love of the Best, and therefore holds,—what his disciples do not hesitate to preach,— that Satan has been greatly wronged, and that the sin for which he was cast out of heaven and down to hell, and bound in chains of darkness for ever, was only the pure aspiration of a noble nature after a higher perfection! "Pride ruined the angels, their shame them restores." Indeed, their ruin was no ruin, but a stage in their progress,—"And the joy that is sweetest lurks in the stings of remorse."

But pride and the love of the Best are not identical. Pride is the perversion of the love of the Best, and consists in believing one's self already perfect, not in seeking after a perfection not yet possessed. Lucifer did not rebel because he would be more perfect than he was, but because such was his lofty estimate of himself that he would acknowledge no being as his superior. This is the essential nature of pride. It believes itself to be the highest, and places all else below itself. The basis of love of the Best is humility, and humility springs from a consciousness of our own defects, and the reverent contemplation of the superior merits of others,—a deep and living conviction that there is a Being above us whom we are to love and obey, honor and exalt. Pride would usurp the perfect,—humility would love, reverence, and glorify it; pride would possess it

160

to exalt and glorify itself,—humility for the sake of glorifying Him who is perfect. Humility loves perfection itself with a pure, disinterested love; while pride loves it only for the sake of self, and therefore loves only self, and not perfection at all. The sorrow of pride flows from the mortification of being compelled to admit that there are others which occupy positions above it; the sorrow of humility is that it can never worthily love and reverence, honor and exalt, the good and perfect God as it feels he deserves; but, unlike that of pride, it is a sorrow which has its own consolations, and which is compatible with inexpressible internal peace and joy. The love of the Best, a love which is not the love of self, but really love of the Best, is no "fiend that man harries"; it breeds no disorder, occasions no fall, no vice, no strife, but bears man onward and upward to God, his true beginning and end.

But, mistaking pride for love of the Best, Mr. Emerson makes it the glory of our nature; and as pride knows no peace so long as it sees aught above it, he teaches that we must always be harried, that we must run ever, but never attain our goal. The Best dances ever before us, and above our reach. It is always farther on, and higher up, and as man ascends, he sees new

"Hills peep o'er hills, and Alps on Alps arise."

The West recedes the farther from the weary emigrant the farther he travels.

"To his aye-rolling orbit no goal will arrive,
The heavens that now draw him with sweetness untold,
Once found,—for new heavens he spurneth the old."

Each height is scorned as soon as gained, and man must be ever the child who, as soon as you give him one bawble, throws it away and cries for another.

"Couldst see thy proper eye,
Alway it asketh, asketh;
  And each answer is a lie.
So take thy quest through nature,
  It through thousand natures ply;
Ask on, thou clothed eternity;
  Time is the false reply."

There is no remedy, no hope. Each new solution, as soon as obtained, ceases to be true. The answer to the question from one height discloses a height which is higher yet, from which it becomes a lie. There is no truth for us. The truth in the valley is falsehood on the mountain; the history to-day is falsehood to-morrow. Thus are we, thus must we be, "ever learning, never able to come to the knowledge of the truth." Ever does the secret intense longing for an unseen something spur us onward, upward from height to height, and ever must continue the same evils, the same vices, the same crimes, the same misery and wretchedness,—endless motion, and yet no advance.

"Eterne alternation, now follows, now flies,
And under pain, pleasure,—under pleasure pain lies."

What more sad and gloomy? In our very virtues lie and germinate the seeds of our vices; and what is lowest, meanest in us springs from what is purest, noblest, best. And this is man's normal order, the glory of his being, the source of joy and gladness! No change, no deliverance, no day of pleasure without pain, of joy without sorrow, of virtue without vice, of love without hatred, of light without darkness, life without death, is ever to come, to be

161

hoped for, or even desired! And this is the gospel of the nineteenth century, preached in this good city of Boston, by one of the most gifted and loving of our countrymen, who has himself once worn the garb of a professed minister of Him who died that man might live! O my brother, how low hast thou fallen! The old heathens themselves might shame thee. Their Islands of the Blest, nay, their dark Tartarean gulf, were a relief to thy cold and desolating philosophy. Warble no more such music in our ears. We would rather hear the ravings of the wildest fanaticism, or the mutterings of the foulest superstition.

We have never read any thing more heart-rending than the poem entitled *Threnody*. It is, indeed, a lamentation, and the saddest part is the consolation it offers. It is no imaginary lament. The author speaks in his own character, his own grief over the early death of his own son,—a son of rare sweetness and promise. It was a lovely boy, one a father might well love, and be pardoned for weeping. The grief is natural. The stern pride of the father gives way to it, and the stoic becomes wild, all but frantic, and blasphemes nature, his only god after himself.

["Threnody," 151.15–154.10]

How different is this from the temper which the Christian father would have exhibited at the grave of his son cut down in early morning! He too might have wept, but he would not have been desolate; and a joy would have mingled with his grief, and turned it to gladness. He would not have felt that his child was lost to him or to nature; that a bright existence had been blotted out, a sun extinguished and gone to the wastes of nature; but he would have looked upon his boy's death-day as his birthday, and rejoiced that he was so soon removed from the evil, so soon permitted to return from his exile, to be re- ceived to his home, and permitted to behold the face of his Heavenly Father, and there in fulness of love and joy, by his prayers and intercessions, obtain new graces for the dear earthly parents whose term of exile had not yet expired. For nature, for the "flown Muses," for the mysteries to be unlocked for the race, for the glorious future the boy-sage was to usher in, he would have felt no uneasiness; because he would have known that the boy in heaven could effect more than the boy on earth; because there has been given to the world the Babe of Bethlehem; and because, as the German proverb says, "The old God still lives," and can take care of nature and of man.

But the author checks the wildness of his grief, and in his excessive charity directs us to the sources of his consolation. But here he is sadder to us than in his grief. Here all becomes sombre and dark, vague and misty, and—what is rarely the case with Mr. Emerson—words, words with no distinct meaning, with scarcely any meaning at all. The verse flows on, but the sense stands still. The father's heart recoils from the pit of annihilation; the proud, unbelieving philosopher scorns to yield to the sweet hope of immorality. The father shrinks with horror from the thought that his bright-eyed boy is lost for ever; the Transcendentalist disdains to believe in an uprising of the dead. What, then, shall he say? What hope can he indulge, what solace dare trust? The bright-eyed boy is not all extinguished. What was elemental in him could not die, and he lives absorbed in the Infinite, as the drop in the ocean!

["Threnody," 157.12–158.12]

"Heart's love will meet thee again." Yes, love without the loving heart, love without a lover! O my brother, is this all thy consolation? Is this

"What rainbows teach, and sunsets show?"

Nay, most desolate father, not rainbows or sunsets taught thee this; it was the moon, the moon, fickle goddess of the night; for no man not moonstruck would talk of hearts' loves remaining when hearts are no more. Thou consolest thyself with a vain shadow, nay, not so much as a shadow, but a very absurdity, a sheer impossibility; for whoever heard of heart's love without the loving heart, any more than of thought without a thinker, or act without an actor? Thou boastest thyself wise, thou makest the "great Heart" say to thee,

["Threnody," 155.3–16]

And yet thou here revivest the old Hindu dream, stripped of its self-coherence, reduced to an absurdity so palpable that the veriest child can detect it; and this thou claspest as a spiritual balsam to thy torn and bleeding heart, and wouldst gravely persuade us that it is a sovereign remedy, that it heals thy wound and makes thee whole, a man, a hale and joyous man again. "Hearts are dust, hearts' loves remain,"—remain when hearts are no more! O my brother, how true it is, that when we turn our back on God and his word, esteem ourselves wise, and boast that we have been taught

"Beyond the reach
Of ritual, Bible, or of speech,"

we become—fools! Thou art a man of rare gifts, and thou hast studied long and much, thou hast questioned the past and the present, the living and the dead, the stars and the flowers, the fields and the groves, the winds and the waves, the day and the night, and thou hast a keen, penetrating glance, and thou hast a warm, sympathetic soul, and yet thou art solitary in thick darkness; thou seest not the plainest things under thy very nose, thou seest not clearly even thy hand before thee. There is a bright and glorious universe around thee, full of light, love, and gladness, of which thou dreamest not; angels hover round thee and fan thee with their soft breath, and thou feelest them not; angel voices call to thee, in sweet music that trances the soul, but thou hearest them not; and because thou art blind, and deaf, and insensible, in thy foolish pride thou deniest what to every faith-illumined eye is as clear as the sun in the heavens, and to every faith-opened heart as distinct and dear as voice of lover or of friend.

Alas! we are not ignorant of the blindness and deafness of those who are without faith, or of the strange illusion which makes us obstinately persist that we both see and hear. There is something weird and mysterious in the thoughts and feelings which come to us, unbidden, when we leave faith behind, and fix our gaze intently upon ourselves as upon some magic mirror. The circle of our vision seems to be enlarged; darkness is transformed to light; worlds open upon worlds; we send keen, penetrating glances into the infinite abyss of being; the elements grow obedient to us, work with us and for us, and we seem to be strong with their strength, terrible with their might, and to approach and to become identical with the Source of all things. God becomes comprehensible and communicable, and we live an elemental life, and burn with elemental fire. The universe flows into us and from us. We control the winds, the waves, the rivers and the tides, the stars and the seasons. We teach the plant when to germinate, to blossom, or ripen, the reed when to bend before the blast, and the lightning when to rive the hoary oak. Alas! we think not then that this is all delusion, and that we are under the influence of the Fallen Angel, who would persuade us that darkness is light, that weakness is strength, that hell is heaven, and himself God. Under a similar influence and delusion labors the author of these poems. There are passages in them which recall all too vividly what we, in our blindness and unbelief, have dreamed, but rarely ventured to utter. We know these poems; we understand them. They are not sacred chants; they are hymns to the devil. Not God, but Satan, do they praise, and they can be relished only by devil-worshipers.

Yet we do not despair of our poet. He has a large share of *religiosity*, and his soul needs to prostrate itself before God and adore. There is a low, sad music in these poems, deep and melodious, which escapes the author unbidden, and which discloses a spirit ill at ease, a heart bewailing its bondage, and a secret, intense longing to burst its chains, and to soar aloft to the heaven of divine love and freedom. This music is the echo of the angel voices still pleading with him, and entreating him to return from his wanderings, to open his eyes to the heaven which lies around him, his ears to the sweet voices which everywhere are chanting the praises of God. We must hope that ere long he will, through grace, burst the Satanic cords which now bind him, open his eyes to the sweet vision of beauty that awaits him, and his ears to the harmony which floats on every breeze. Bear with me; nature never intended thee for an Indian Gymnosophist or a heartless Stoic. Thou art a man, with a warm, gushing human heart, and thou wast made to love and adore. Say, Get behind me, Satan! to the vain philosophizing you have indulged; have the courage to say you have been wrong, open your heart to the light of heaven as the sunflower opens her bosom to the genial rays of the sun, and thy spirit will be free, thy genius will no longer be imprisoned, and thy heart will find what it sighs after, and wail no more. One who was as proud as thyself, and who had wandered long in the paths thou art beating, and whose eye was hardly less keen than thy own, and who knew by heart all thy mystic lore, and had as well as thou pored over the past and the present, as well as thou had asked

"The fate of the man-child
The meaning of man,"—

and had asked the heavens and the earth, the living and the dead, and, in his madness, hell itself, to answer him, and whose soul was not less susceptible to sweet harmonies than thy own, though his tones were harsh and his speech rude,—nay, one who knows all thy delusions and illusions, assures thee that thou shalt not in this be deceived, and thy confidence will not be misplaced or betrayed.

[Francis Bowen], "Nine New Poets," *North American Review*, 64 (April 1847), 402–34

[...]

But it is time to look more particularly at the merits of this batch of poets.[1] At the head of the list stands Mr. Emerson, whose mystical effusions have been for some years the delight of a large and increasing circle of young people, and the despair of the critics. He is a chartered libertine, who has long exercised his prerogative of writing enigmas both in prose and verse, sometimes with meaning in them, and sometimes without,—more frequently without. Many of his fragments in verse—if *verse* it can be called, which puts at defiance all the laws of rhythm, metre, grammar, and common sense— were originally published in *The Dial*, *lucus a non lucendo*, a strange periodical work, which is now withdrawn from sunlight into the utter darkness that it always coveted. These fragments, with some new matter, are now first collected in a separate volume, and published, as we believe, with a sly purpose on the part of the author to quiz his own admirers. His prose essays, on their first appearance, were received with about equal admiration and amazement; always enigmatical and frequently absurd in doctrine and sentiment, they also contained flashes of better things. Quaint and pithy apothegms, dry and humorous satire, studied oddities of expression, which made an old thought appear almost as good as a new one, and frequent felicities of poetical and picturesque diction, were the redeeming qualities that compensated the reader for toiling through many pages filled with a mere hubbub and jumble of words. Startling and offensive opinions, drawn mostly from systems of metaphysics that were long ago exploded and forgotten, were either darkly hinted at, or baldly stated without a word of explanation or defence. Poet and mystic, humorist and heretic, the writer seemed, on the one side, to aim at a revival of Heraclitus and Plotinus, and on the other, to be an imitator of Rabelais and Sterne. A few touches of recondite learning, obviously more fantastic than profound, added to the singularity of the compound which he presented to the public. He probably accomplished his first purpose, when his essays simply made people stare,—

"While some pronounced him wondrous wise,
And some declared him mad."

But it is only in his prose that Mr. Emerson is a poet; this volume of professed poetry contains the most prosaic and unintelligible stuff that it has ever been our fortune to encounter. The book opens, very appropriately, with a piece called *The Sphinx*. We are no Ædipus, and cannot expound one of the riddles contained in it; but some of our readers may be more successful, and a specimen of it shall therefore be placed before them. It matters not what portion is extracted, for the poem may be read backwards quite as intelligibly as forwards, and no mortal can trace the slightest connection between the verses.

"The fiend that man harries
   Is love of the Best;
Yawns the pit of the Dragon
   Lit by rays from the Blest.
The Lethe of nature
   Can't trance him again,

Whose soul sees the perfect,
  Which his eyes seek in vain.
"Profounder, profounder,
  Man's spirit must dive;
To his aye-rolling orbit
  No goal will arrive;
The heavens that now draw him
  With sweetness untold,
Once found,—for new heavens
  He spurneth the old."

We pause here to ask if, in the Italicized lines, the epithet "aye-rolling" is not a misprint for *eye*-rolling. We never heard of an *ever-rolling* orbit, inasmuch as the orbit usually remains still, and the object, or body, rolls in it. "The eye rolling in its orbit" is a phrase intelligible enough by itself, though it has no imaginable relation here with the context. Then, again, it is not strange that "No goal will arrive"; goals do not usually arrive, but remain fixed; they are the points arrived at.

"Pride ruined the angels,
  Their shame them restores;
And the joy that is sweetest
  Lurks in stings of remorse.
Have I a lover
  Who is noble and free?—
I would he were nobler
  Than to love me.
"*Eterne alternation,*
  Now follows, now flies;
And under pain, pleasure,—
  Under pleasure, pain lies.
Love works at the centre,
  Heart-heaving alway;
Forth speed the strong pulses
  To the borders of day.
"Dull Sphinx, Jove keep thy five wits!"

Amen! We will quote no farther here, lest we should entirely lose ours. An "alternation," that "now follows, now flies," is an idea profound enough to puzzle the wits of most philosophers.

We cite one other stanza from a different page, as it shows what improvements the poem has undergone in the process of incubation.

"Uprose the merry Sphinx,
  And crouched no more in stone;
She melted into purple cloud,
  She silvered in the moon;
She spired into a yellow flame;
  She flowered in blossoms red;
She flowed into a foaming wave;
  She stood Monadnoc's head."

We have not *The Dial* at hand for reference; but if memory serves us aright, in the poem as first published, instead of the lines here printed in Italics, we had the following:—

"She jumped into a barberry bush,
She jumped into the moon."

This original reading seems to be preferable, as it is more simple and graphic; but the poet probably struck it out, lest he should appear indebted to the highly imaginative lines of Mother Goose,—

"Hey, diddle-diddle, the cat and the
    fiddle,
  The cow jumped over the moon."

The Sphinx concludes her oracles with this tempting declaration:—

"Thorough a thousand voices
  Spoke the universal dame:
'Who telleth one of my meanings,
  Is master of all I am.'"

We doubt whether the fulfilment of this promise will ever be claimed by any body; certainly, not by us, for we do not even know what is meant by a "universal" old lady.

As original in his choice of subjects as in his mode of treating them, Mr. Emerson has some dainty lines addressed to the humble bee. We can quote only the two concluding stanzas, which show the minuteness and delicacy of the poet's observation of nature.

["The Humble-Bee," 40.1–24]

Mr. Emerson delights to build a poem on some nearly forgotten anecdote, or myth, or recorded saying of the wise and great, either in ancient times or the Middle Ages. A sort of misty reference to this theme appears here and there in the verses, and if the reader is lucky enough to remember the anecdote, he may flatter himself that he can see a glimpse of meaning in them. But if unlearned or forgetful, no reference, no direct statement, no charitable foot-note, gives him the least hint of the writer's purpose; all is dark as Erebus. Sometimes, an uncouth Sanscrit, Greek, or German compound word stands as the title of a few verses, and answers the poet's object to puzzle his readers quite delightfully. The contrivance is ingenious, and shows how highly obscurity is prized, and that a book of poetry may almost attain the dignity of a child's book of riddles.

Thus, some lines headed *Alphonso of Castile* seem to be founded on the saying recorded of this king, ironically surnamed "The Wise," that if the Almighty had consulted him at the creation, he would have made a much better universe. A few lines may be quoted from this poem, as a specimen of Mr. Emerson's more familiar style. It begins in this original manner:—

["Alphonso of Castile," 25.8–13]

After enumerating many other evils and imperfections, equally important in character, the king proceeds to give his advice

to the gods in the following choice expressions:—

["Alphonso of Castile," 27.15–22]

The poet probably meant to be satirical, referring to the pragmatical and conceited tone of many foolish busybodies in the affairs of this world. The purpose was well enough; we can only call attention to the neatness and elegance of the machinery contrived for this object, and to the poignancy of his wit.

Another string of rhymes, entitled *Mithridates*, seems to be founded on the old myth respecting that monarch, that having discovered a sure antidote, he was able to subsist entirely on the most active poisons. After babbling for a time about dogwood, hemlock, "the prussic juice," and upas boughs, the poet breaks out into the following witty and coherent apostrophe:—

["Mithridates," 29.12–19]

We commend Mr. Emerson's intention not to be an owl, though when he utters such dismal screeches as these, one may doubt whether the transformation has not already been effected. We never before felt the whole force of Horace's exclamation, *aut insanit homo, aut versus facit.* Is the man sane who can deliberately commit to print this fantastic nonsense?

Another of these effusions is called *Hamatreya*. The word sounds like Sanscrit; we frankly confess our ignorance of its meaning, and have not time to hunt through lexicons and encyclopædias, from one of which it was probably fished up, for a solution of the enigma. The reader may discover Mr. Emerson's drift, if he can, in the following introductory lines.

["Hamatreya," 35.2–11]

We have not room to quote the whole

of this delectable stuff. After proceeding for a while, in a similar strain, the poet breaks out into what he calls the Earth-Song. "Hear what the earth says."

["Hamatreya," 36.6–37.4]

Those who think this Earth-Song is unparalleled are mistaken; we can produce a very similar passage in prose, which the poet possibly had in view, and endeavoured to imitate. That witty buffoon, Foote, happening to hear a person boast of the facility with which he could commit any passage to memory, undertook to write a few lines which the other would not be able to remember accurately, even after repeated perusal. The challenge was accepted, and Foote immediately produced the following, which we will match, for coherency of ideas, with any thing that Mr. Emerson has ever written.

> "And she went into the garden to cut a cabbage to make an apple pie; and a she-bear, walking up the street, pops his head into the shop,— What! No soap! and he died; and she very imprudently married the barber, and at the wedding were the Hoblillies and the Joblillies, and the great Panjandrum, with the little button at top, and they all danced till the gunpowder ran out of the heels of their boots."

We mean to be fair with the poet. Having read attentively—*horresco references!*—the whole book, we affirm that the specimens now laid before our readers fairly represent far the larger portion of it. Here and there, a gleam of light intrudes, and we find brief but striking indications of the talent and feeling which Mr. Emerson unquestionably possesses. But the effect is almost instantly marred by some mystical nonsense, some silly pedantry, an intolerable hitch in rhythm

or grammar, or an incredible flatness and meanness of expression. In one of the longer poems, *Monadnoc*, one may cull a few single lines, and occasionally a couplet, or a quatrain, of great poetic beauty. But these are like a few costly spices flung into a tub full of dirty and greasy water; they are polluted by the medium in which they float, and one cannot pick them out without soiling his fingers. Here is a couplet containing one of the best, and one of the worst, lines in the piece. The poet, addressing the mountain, exclaims with inimitable bathos,—

"Ages are thy days,
Thou grand expresser of the present tense!"

The greater part of the poem is made up of such senseless jingle as this:—

"For the world was built in order,
And the atoms march in tune;
Rhyme the pipe, and Time the warder,
Cannot forget the sun, the moon.
Orb and atom forth they prance,
When they hear from far the rune;
None so backward in the troop,
When the music and the dance
Reach his place and *circumstance*,
But knows the *sun-creating sound*,
And, though a *pyramid, will bound.*"

We can find no nominative to "cannot forget," there is no word to rhyme with "troop," and, in the last four lines, subject and object are mingled in inextricable confusion. Mr. Emerson is evidently one of those poets

"Who, free from rhyme or reason, rule or check,
Break Priscian's head and Pegasus's neck."

The following pretty and graceful lines

168

form the only tolerable entire piece in the book.

["To Eva," 95.10–21]

The publication of a volume of such poetry at the present day is a strange phenomenon; but a stranger, still, is the eagerness with which it is received by quite a large circle of neophytes, who look down with pitying contempt on all those who cannot share their admiration of its contents. It is stereotyped, and we hear that one or two thousand copies of it have been sold. How far the taste may be perverted by fashion, prejudice, or the influences of a *clique* or school, it is impossible to say; but there must be limits to all corruptions of it which come short of insanity. It is possible to profess admiration which one does not feel; or for the faculties to be so impaired by disease as to become insensible to their appropriate gratifications. The ear may lose its perception of the finest harmonies, the olfactory nerve may no longer be gratified by the most delicious perfumes; these would be mere defects, a loss of the sources of great enjoyment. But we cannot conceive of enjoyments being created of an opposite character. The ear cannot be trained to receive pleasure from discords, nor the sense of smell to enjoy a stench. As with the pleasures of sense, so is it with intellectual gratifications. We may never have acquired a relish for them, or we may lose it by neglect. But one cannot change the nature of things, and derive positive pleasure from that which is distasteful and odious by its original constitution. Incoherency of thought and studied obscurity of expression, an unmeaning jumble of words and a heap of vulgar and incongruous images, cannot, as such, be agreeable objects to contemplate. If praised by a sect, it must be because each one relies on the opinion of his fellows, so that there is not one independent judgment among them. If the hierophant of the sect be a shrewd humorist, it is most likely that he is mocking the weakness of his admirers. [. . .]

Note

1 Also reviewed are *Poems* by William Ellery Channing, *Schiller's Homage of the Arts* translated by Charles T. Brooks, *Poems* by William Wetmore Story, *Poems* by Thomas Buchanan Read, *The Island Bride, and Other Poems* by James F. Colman, *Poems* by Frances Elizabeth Browne, *Songs of the Sea, with Other Poems* by Epes Sargent, and *Shells from the Strand of the Sea of Genius* by Harriet Farley.

Review of *Poems*, *Literary World*, 1 (3 April 1847), 197–9

Elegant mediocrity has in the past literature of America clearly the advantage of native strength and beauty. To be free of faults has been a safer passport to the welcome of reviews and drawing rooms than to be fertile of excellence. The fingers and the comma have been more considered in our poetry than the music and spirit which give to poetry all its worth. The door has been closely held against all comers who failed to approach seeking admittance, measuring as they came along after the manner of Aguecheek, the fashionable cinq-pace or coranto. To the neglect of these forms and observances we attribute in a great degree the comparatively cold reception of Mr. Emerson among his countrymen. Although a New Englander in his origin, he has had to contend with a species of criticism which belongs more particularly to that portion of the country, and which has not, till very recently, relaxed in its judgments even in behalf of one of its most favored and gifted sons. That the publication of this collection should have brought him, as it certainly has, a greater harvest of praises than has attended any of his previous efforts, is an argument as well of his prevailing merit as of an approaching change in the spirit of criticism in that quarter. We think we discern in the somewhat eager and earnest laudation of this volume in quarters heretofore cold and distrustful toward the compositions of this and other writers of a kindred spirit, a consciousness that their past idols are not sufficient for them: that some whom they hastily worshipped have been found on a closer inspection to be little better than the dry sticks on the altar, whom their most fervent prayers and adorations could not prevail upon for a moment to kindle with fire from heaven. In Mr. Emerson they have, or seem to believe they have, suddenly discovered a poetical Elijah, and the eastern reviews and journals are accordingly in a blaze, in strange contrast with the frozen silence of the past. There is one spot of critical ground, however, where we believe will still remain inaccessible to the genius of the newly recognised bard; and which will gloomily refuse to take the fire. Our readers will at once understand by this the torpid and respectable North American Review. Charm he ever so wisely, we are afraid that calm old adder slumbering upon the lawn of Harvard will remain deaf to his incantations. The author of "Mithridates," however, whose oriental experiences have familiarized him with serpents, will, we are quite confident, outlive the encounter, and we should be by no means surprised if he should, in the long run, prove to be the better conjurer of the two.

Our interest in the present volume lies not in Mr. Emerson's speculations, in the consideration of any system of belief or philosophy, he may or may not have, in his sentiments as chief or as pupil in any school of thinkers—but simply in ascertaining what amount of genius for poetical writing belong to him, and how much he has, in this collection, contributed to the properly considered poetical literature of the country. For the rest, that which we find to condemn, and which is aside from the just and successful exercise of his poetical talents, we shall be quit of it in a few words from Dr. Johnson, who long ago, in his review of Cowley and metaphysical poets, with some differences, disposed of this whole class of cases. "The most heterogeneous ideas are yoked by violence together; nature and art are ransacked for illustrations, comparisons and allusions; their learning instructs, and their subtlety surprises; but the reader commonly thinks his improvement dearly bought, and though he sometimes admires, is seldom pleased. From this account of their compositions it will be readily inferred, that they were not successful in representing or moving the affections. As they were wholly employed on something unexpected or surprising, they had no regard to that uniformity of sentiment which enables us to conceive and to excite the pains and the pleasure of the mind; they never inquired what, on any occasion, they should have said or done; *but wrote rather as beholders than partakers of human nature; as beings looking upon good and evil impassive and at leisure; as epicurean deities, making remarks on the actions of men, and the vicissitudes of life, without interest and without emotion.* Their courtship was void of fondness and their lamentation of sorrow * * Their attempts were always analytic; they broke every image into fragments; and could no more represent, by their slender conceits and labored particularities, the chief prospects of nature, or the scenes of life, than he, who dissects a sun-beam with a prism, can exhibit the wide effulgence of a summer noon. What they wanted, however, of the sublime, they endeavored to supply by hyperbole; their amplification had its limits; they left not only reason, but fancy, behind them; and produced combinations of confused magnificence, that not only could not be credited, but could not be imagined."

To this we need add nothing. If we were disposed to dwell upon the character of Mr. Emerson's intellect in this respect, we should rather take the occasion of the publication of one of his volumes of "Essays," to which, with a few slight and inconsiderable changes, portions of this present collection might with the great-

est propriety be transferred. What, then, are Mr. Emerson's substantial and distinctive merits as a poetical writer? A brief poem published as "The Apology," and which might have been most appropriately employed as the motto of the book, furnishes at the same time an explanation and an example of his chief faculty as a poet.

["The Apology," 119.2–21]

Here, it will be noticed, there is more about the thing than of the thing itself. He regards objects more in reference to certain subtle trains of thought and fancy, than in their relations to the actual world of flesh and blood. Being thus freed of the necessity of actual truth and keeping in time and place, by the delineation of real life, and the beings and emotions of real life, it matters little whether his text be Hermione or Mary Brown, whether it be chosen from East or West; and accordingly his illustrations, neglecting what is immediate and present, take a distant range, although, for appearance sake, he sometimes introduces in the line Monadnoc, Concord, and New England—but these are not to be taken for the Monadnoc, Concord, and New England of that actual geographical position, but as Utopian places so named by the poet, figures of speech.

He outlines, therefore, all the necessary and concrete conditions under which humanity is ordinarily presented, and acknowledges only a mysterious something, a gentle and universal link which connects and underlies Asia and America, Africa and Europe as one.

His chief capital as a poetical writer consists in the profound belief of a mighty secret in nature, animating, connecting, irradiating, solving all things, which is worth all external things in a mass, which pervades and transcends them all, which it is worth the world and all the best effort

171

of the world to discover, and to discover which all other business, callings, avocations, should be laid aside; and he has an Ideal Man who is constantly on the search, and, whom to delineate so engaged, is the pleasure, and the chief success of our author. The Ideal Man, we have a shrewd suspicion, is no other than a first-rate man of genius, of the order poetical. Under all the titles, "Problem," "Fable," "Ode," "Blight," "Dirge," "Threnody," this is the substantial subject, and under the various names of "Alphonso," "Mithridates," "Bacchus," "Xenophanes," this the character that flourishes. In many passages this secret is most beautifully hinted at or shadowed forth: and the portraiture of the gifted seer often admirably drawn. This spirit is finely introduced in the poem, which is, perhaps, the best known in popular circulation, of all his collection.

["The Problem," 6.11–8.3]

In the verses darkly entitled "Each and All," we have it in some most melodious lines.

["Each and All," 4.22–5.5]

And again, in the guise of an immortal spirit conferring favors.

["To Rhea," 10.27–11.6]

Again he follows them as shining guides—

["Forerunners," 85.2–15]

Then as the spirit of Beauty—

["Ode to Beauty," 87.22–88.9]

In Hermione, we have it harmonizing the movement of the mind with the motion of the bird.

["Hermione," 100.9–15]

And for the Ideal Man, the Searcher of the Secret, we have many pictures of him, and often painted in most engaging col-

ors. he is the Hero of the Woodnotes.

["Woodnotes," 44.9–45.12]

In Merlin:

["Merlin," 120.11–121.3]

Merlin may be Ralph Waldo Emerson; for this seems to be quite as pointedly the system of versification adopted by the New England poet. The Ideal Man is presented again in the character of Bacchus, and at the very height of his revelling, seems to be satisfied with a draught from the same secret crypt—*The* (as Captain Cuttle significantly suggests to his friend, the mathematical instrument-maker).

["Bacchus," 125.2–126.2]

What is the wonderful, all-embracing, all-sufficient secret? Simply, we take it, the sympathy with nature which belongs to all the better and nobler spirits of the world, and by which her finer issues are caught and appreciated. In Mr. Emerson nature, all external objects are regarded merely in relation to the intellect, in its creative and constructive qualities, in reference to beauty and proportion and fitness, as in works of art. This is the aspect of nature remotest from the general interests of mankind. The English poet, Wordsworth, comes a step nearer to humanity by employing external objects in the illustration and enforcement of moral truth, of which a thousand examples will occur to our readers. His reception is, accordingly, *cæteris paribus*, a degree nearer popularity than Mr. Emerson's. In Lord Byron we have the external world identified with human passion, sweeping a still wider and more animated circle of readers. Take an example from the two of these writers most widely separated. Mr. Emerson laments the loss of a lovely boy:

"Returned this day, the south wind searches,

And finds young pines and budding
    birches;
But finds not the budding man;
Nature, who lost him, cannot remake
    him;
Fate let him fall, Fate can't retake him;
Nature, Fate, men, him seek in vain."

What tone does Lord Byron strike for a
similar occasion?

"There must have been tears and break-
    ing hearts for thee
And mine were nothing had I such to
    give;
But when I stood beneath the fresh
    green tree,
Which living waves where thou didst
    cease to live,
And saw around me the wide field re-
    vive,
With fruits and fertile promise, and the
    spring
Come forth her work of gladness to
    contrive,
With all her reckless birds upon the
    wing,
*I turned from all she brought to all she
    could not bring.*"

In one we have the voice of lamentation lost in a vague speculation on fate—
interesting only to the intellect: in the
other, piercing to the very well-springs of
the heart. There is a range, even beyond
Byron, in which but one writer in our
language, as yet, walks alone: the delineation in which all these elements are
grandly and nobly summoned to one
centre, and made, from a single personage, to utter the whole heaped-up force of
the intellectual, moral and passionate
nature. In the *King Lear* of Shakespeare
this is achieved with the highest success.
    In the quotations we have already made,
and in the strictures attending them, we
have, we believe, done justice to the spirit

of the portions of the volume which are
most peculiar and characteristic. For the
rest, such portions as do not, as we before
suggested, properly belong to his prose
essays, are occasional, incidental, and
fugitive. Some of these are respectable,
others rise to a degree of excellence often
before attained in this country, and many
are to be given over to utter condemnation, as obscurely conceived and badly
rhymed. Two or three only give us an
idea of a general poetical ability, which
would enable Mr. Emerson to contend in
the open field against the ordinary and
popular poets of the language, looking
for his inspiration to ordinary sympathies
and ordinary subjects. In this class we
have (with recollections of Sir Walter
Raleigh)

["Good-bye," 3.3–4.10]

The little plaintive sonnet—

["The Rhodora," 37.18–38.11]

Then is a dainty and delectable spirit—

["The Humble-Bee," 38.13–40.24]

We hope we have not failed now to
convey to the reader our conviction, that
we have in Mr. Emerson one of the finest,
as he is certainly one of the most singular,
poetical spirits of the time. By the constitution of his faculties and his peculiar training, he is restricted in his sphere,
and utters rather the voice of a class refined, delicate, and pregnant with rare
sympathies, than the common feelings and
passions of mankind at large. With this
limitation, however, he at times darts from
the inner shrine, where he loves to worship and commune, a long, keen, piercing
ray which reaches the general mass, and
commends him to them as a poet of a
charming fancy, and a heart open to the
delight inspired by the beauty of the
flowing brook, the waving tree, and the
bird that trills accents having in them, to

the humblest ear, something exquisitely responsive to the best affections of our nature. We are well aware that, in some of those compositions, he is indebted to Marvell, to Shelley, to Milton for a suggestion, to Butler for a rhyme; that there is a good deal of his seriously-intended verse Hudibrastically presented; many, many hitches in the measure, and many lamentable conclusions of no meaning to passages that promised much. But putting these behind, brushing them from off the page as blemishes and dusty spots, we have left enough of manly feeling, of delightful fancy, of pure and lucid expression, and melodious measure, to confer on the author a distinct and conspicuous position as a poet.

"Emerson's Poems," American Review: A Whig Journal, 6 (August 1847), 197–207

The aims of poetry being equally pleasure and instruction; but first pleasure, for if this condition is unfulfilled the form becomes rather an obstacle than a medium; we, (the reader, not the critic,) require that a certain propriety and regularity shall inspire the form and the measure of verses; that the line be full, sounding, and of a free construction, not feeble, harsh, or cramped. The accents and pauses must fall agreeably, and the sense follow easily along the line, rather helped than impeded by it. If these conditions are not fulfilled we lay the work aside with indifference, or with a feeling of dislike.

In prose, on the other hand, we seldom seek no pleasure in the form, but look to the substance; and if the writer, failing in his subject, seeks to deceive us with a monotonous, rhetorical, or false metrical movement, we are as quickly wearied or disgusted. As our perceptions are more universal and refined, these conditions become more essential, and the absence of them occasions a more lively dissatisfaction. If the matter is good, or merely extraordinary, we may easily neglect or overcome our repugnance, and read a bad writer to be possessed of good matter; but in such case we concede nothing to the writer but fair intentions, which are at best a weak substitute for good works. The design is well enough, but the work inferior; it serves a purpose of utility, but must presently give way to something better; and in making a choice we very readily prefer a present pleasure before a contingent good—a handsome lie to a homely truth.

But what shall be said of a writer who neglects to please his reader, at the same instant that he assaults his virtue?

We said that it was an absolute condition of poetry that it should give pleasure by its form; but if our own experience may be admitted as valid,—and whose shall guide us if not our own?—poetry, to give pleasure, must have a form, internally as well as externally beautiful, else we concede it no praise. It must discover the character of the poet as in itself excellent, or at least acquainted with excellence.

As the refinements of human society are but the exhibition of human honor and courtesy, presiding over all and turning all to their proper expression, so we are compelled to think of poetry, that the poet prefers it only as a more acceptable medium of generous and courteous sentiments.

He does not merely harmonize his loves and griefs, warbling tenderly or fiercely, like a bird, but rather, as in tragedy, endeavors to express the controlling principles, the laws and consolations of the passions, that he may secure himself a more perfect title to the name of man.

Supposing our conditions to be just, it were still unjust to abuse or vituperate any person who writes with honest intentions, for showing himself unable to fulfil his own design. What is weak or imperfect, the reader lays aside with an emotion perhaps of pity; but if he meets with a writing which offers a didactic front, puts itself in a position of authority, with a power of attraction, he reads with attention the expressions which seem to insult or to console him.

Whatever would be likely to insult him, in the personal bearing of the author, will have the same effect in an inferior degree

through his writings. Whatever sweetness, justness, or modesty delighted him in the man, will please him in the author; but here we suppose, first, that the author is so far skilled as to be at least able to put *himself* into words: he must be educated, and a master of words, to entitle himself to a trial by the moral test. He must be able to throw his own ideas of vice and virtue into the mind of the reader.

This will all doubtless be conceded by the intelligent reader and critic, who will only remark, that something is demanded also on the reader's part; if the author brings meanings, I must find brains to comprehend them. Thus, when the poet begins his poem with a declaration that

"The sense of the world is short,"

which is the first line of a piece of six lines, entitled "Eros," in this volume of Mr. Emerson's Poems, I simply regret my inability to understand him. The words are good English; the construction grammatical, and the meaning, doubtless profound: I, only, am to blame, for missing it. The first rule of interpretation, however, is to read on.

"The sense of the world is short:
Long and various the report,
   To love and be beloved:
Men and gods have not outlearned it,
And, how oft soe'er they've turned it,
   'Tis not to be improved."

It is as difficult to conceive of a "short sense," as of a *long* report—unless we think of short-sightedness or treasury report. Yet the author undoubtedly had a design in forcing the words into these connections. He wished to add new phrases to the language. Upon a rather tedious investigation, we seem to know his meaning; he informs us that love is an ultimate fact of nature, and has no explanation; which no man will deny,—but against this modern association of men and gods, as if they were persons of the same category, and against the comparison of their joint experience in love matters to the turning of a coat, which was not improved by the turning, having, indeed, been very frequently turned, it seems proper to enter a modest protest. "The gods" are just now quite extinct, and need not be respectfully alluded to in any poems that are not imitations of the classics, under which head the stanza just quoted does not fall. The title of this stanza also attracts our attention: Eros, is the Greek word for Love. Seeing the name of the passion in good Greek, we look for some delicate or powerful expression of it in the Greek manner; but this was not the object of our poet; he sought rather by this assemblage of obscurities and uncouth phrases, and, perhaps, even by the comparison of amatory experience, to the turning of a coat, to impress us in a mystical manner, with the difficulty and obscurity of Eros itself, the whole being to say, that we know nothing of that passion. On the whole, this very empty and creaking little stanza, though it give neither pleasure nor instruction, must be regarded as a masterpiece of art; and its faults, doubtless voluntarily exposed, like the rags of penitents, serve to symbolize the philosophical humility of the spirit which conceived it.

Looking farther, guided by the titles of the pieces of these poems, which are all of a very mystical sound, as for example, "The Visit," "The Problem," "Guy," "Woodnotes," "Monadnac," "Astrea," "Good Bye," "The Sphinx," "Uriel," we allow our fancy to be swayed by the last, as it is the prettiest, indeed, very pretty. "Uriel," is an octo-syllabic poem, of some sixty lines, containing mystical anecdote of that very impudent young angel:

"It fell in the ancient periods
  Which the brooding soul surveys,
Or ever the wild Time coined itself
  Into calendar months and days."

The reader will not fail to observe this pretty epitaph of "wild," applied to the venerable Saturn, the ancient time; or the near mechanical comparison of that gray-haired deity "minting" and stamping *himself,*

"Into the *calendar* months and days."

Which makes him also the inventor of the calendar, as distinguished from natural months and days; to which arrangement astronomers might pedantically object, claiming the calendar for their own invention; but the whole world, and Saturn himself, have agreed, that poets need not be astronomers, or have better notions of Time than they have of money.

"This," continues the poem, "was the lapse of Uriel," whom *Said*—that is the perfect participle of the verb to say—overheard talking among the younger deities, who in a treasonable manner,

  "discussed
Laws of form and metre just"—

a conversation at which it might have been profitable to be present;—when

"One, with low tones that decide,
And doubt and reverend use defied"—

that is to say, which do *now* decide and *at that time* defied—an instance of what may be termed breadth, or, in a more immediate sense, agility, of expression, which overleaps all obstacles of grammar, and pays a grand compliment to the reader's penetration,—this same Uriel,

176

"With a look that solved the sphere,"—
mark—he was a divine kind of geometer, who could square the circle,
with a look,

"And stirred the devils everywhere"

The devils appear simmering in hell,
and Uriel stirs them up with a beam of his
eye, as with a rod of bright glass,

"Gave his sentiment divine
Against the being of a line;"

that is to say, he denied that there were
any real lines or boundaries, but that all
lines or boundaries being negations, are
nought;—which being an excessively true
proposition, we enter fully into the merit
of this grand way of enunciating it. Observe the singularly ideal and mystical
character of this passage. Here we have
the perfect participle *Said*, walking by itself, or himself. The perfect participle
overhears the young gods in a metaphysical debate. Uriel, with an air of hauteur
not unworthy of a Kepler'd Israeli, if such
a creature were possible, pronounces
against the existence of mathematical
negations, all the while squaring the circle
with his eye; in such a fashion the very
devils, simmering in the pits of Tophet,
are stirred up by it.

"As Uriel spoke with piercing eye
A shudder ran through all the sky."

He, it must be observed, not only
squares the circle and stirs up Tophet with
'his eye,' (he seems to have but one,) but
actually *speaks* with it in a piercing manner.

"Line in nature is not found;
Unit and universe are round;
In vain produced, all rays return,
Evil will bless and ice will burn."

These astonishing propositions, which
might well stir up the pit of this world's
theater, he delivers with 'his piercing eye;'
by nods and winks doubtless of the most
complicated significance. He informs his
friends in a deep voice, like a general
officer's that '*line*,' that is to say, the abstract of all kinds of lines, is a substance
not to be found in nature,—he then adds
that *units* are round;—meaning of course
to except those which are square or of
other figures;—that all rays are produced
in vain, having to return whence they were
produced, like the money of the usurer,
lent in vain, since it must return to his
pocket;—and lastly, that evil, or that which
does not bless, does nevertheless bless, and
vice versa. When Master Uriel delivers
himself in this style, "a shudder runs
through all the sky," as it well might,
seeing that all things seemed, in danger of
being turned up, and set upon their heads.

"Strong Hades could not keep his own,
But slid all to confusion,"

just because of this speech of Uriel's, who
for his part profited little; for

"A sad self-knowledge withering fell
On the beauty of Uriel."

Which line requires to be read,

On the beautee of You-rye-ell,

It seemed that by his valuable mathematical discovery of the nonentity of lines,
and his chemical one of the hot character
of ice, he unfortunately calls upon himself
a withering self-knowledge; he retires from
society, and indulges his metaphysical
spleen apart. Meanwhile, the angels, who
are no great lovers of science on their

177

part, forget the propositions of Uriel, but are occasionally reminded of them, much to their own discontent on observing the

"Speeding change of water,"

or the fact,

"Of good from evil-born,"—

on which occasions, a blush

> "tinged the upper sky
> And the gods shook, they knew not
> why."

Of Perfect Participle's opinion of the treason, or of what action he took we are not informed, but only that he overheard it; which has its value as a piece of information at least.

In a spirit of profound reverence, inspired by the study of our poet's "Eros" and "Uriel," we again open the volume, and fall upon this lot—"Hermione"—beginning,

"On a mound an Arab lay,"—

which Arab, it seems affected this Hermione. The name being Greek, we conclude the lady to have been so; but this particular is left to the imagination of the reader. Of the Arab himself, who lay in this manner on a mound, the story runs thus, that having been a hermit in the schools of Bassora—

"In old Bassora's schools, I seemed
Hermit vowed to books and gloom—
Ill bestead for gay bridegroom"—

he sees this Hermione, and on a sudden

"was by her touch redeemed."

"When thy meteor glances came,
We talked at large of worldly fate,
And drew truly every trait."

The comparison of meteors, though forcible, will not perhaps satisfy the fastidious, nor the uncertainty hanging over the word "trait," with the question, trait of what?—but here, too, Wordsworth's admirable theory comes in aid of the poet, that if *he* finds words, the reader must find meanings to them, and the loftier the meanings, the better will the verses appear; which shows how absolutely the quality of verse depends upon the imagination and taste of the reader. At some future age, highly as we appreciate our poet, who knows but a prevailing ignorance and gross common sensicalness may sink his works into oblivion, their deep subtleties being all in vain.

Before quitting this part of the poem, we would recommend the reader to notice the artistical effect of the omission of *a*, indefinite article, before *hermit*, in the second line. It intensifies and generalizes the word. He seemed not only to be a hermit, but *hermit* in general—the very substance or notion of hermit so very eremitish was his look.

The poem opens very prettily—

"On a mound an Arab lay,
And sung his sweet regrets—
And told his amulets;
The summer bird
His sorrow heard,
And when he heaved a sigh profound,
The sympathetic swallow swept the
    ground."

Why on a mound? Was this mound a green or a dry, a low or a high one? What is the summer bird? and what kind is the sympathetic swallow?—are these two one? To one only on which we reply—that as the action of "sweeping the ground" in a swallow, is for the purpose of catching flies or grasshoppers, we must conclude that fly-catching instinct of the swallow, supposed also to be identical with "the

178

summer bird," to be in secret sympathy with the sighing or gaping propensities of our Arab; not that analogy leads, therefore, to conclude that both the parties in sympathy were at fly-catching—which would be to consider too curiously—but only that as one eased his desire by gaping or sighing, the other gratified it by swooping a grasshopper—an analogy which discovers, also, the deep philosophy hidden in the image of this sympathy.

The second verse is as harmonious as the first, and contains a depth of original remark really extraordinary—

"If it be, as they said, she was not fair,
Beauty's not beautiful to me,
But sceptred genius aye inorbed
Culminating in her sphere."

Here is a strong example of the use of the conditional:—*If* she was not beautiful, says the bard, rather doggedly, *then* beauty is not beautiful to me—an instance of the strongest kind of conditioning: as if one should say, If such an one's verses are not stiff and barren, then stiffness and barrenness are not stiff and barren; or, if he is not a poetaster, a poetaster is not a poetaster; or, in common-sense language, and to save logic, you and I have different names for the same thing, and what you call beauty, I call ugliness; what you call works of genius, I call barren *concetti*. Then continuing, he says: It is not beauty that I call beautiful, but genius always inorbed, complete and rounded, and culminating, or at her summit; that is what I call beautiful. Handsome is that handsome does, in the adage—or, in our poet's sense, that handsome thinks: from all of which we conclude that this same Hermione was no beauty, but a very great wit and genius, like Madame George Sand; and our hero, the Arab, thought proper to argue this point with himself, whether he had not a right to consider her handsome, on

behalf of her genius and wit, notwithstanding all that might be hinted by short-sighted persons of no wit or genius to the contrary. In the next verse he compares her to a kind of spiritual sponge, or the god Brem of the Hindoos.

"This Hermione *absorbed*
The lustre of the land and ocean,
Hills and islands, clouds and tree
In her form and motion."

This Hermoine is here plainly distinguished from *that other* Hermione, which is a very neat, and modern distinction. Wordsworth has the same thought in his "Lucy," that is expressed in regard to *this particular* Hermione, whom, once for all the reader is desired not to confuse with that other.

"The floating clouds their state shall lend
To her; for her the willow bend;
    Nor shall she fail to see,
Even in the motions of the storm,
Grace that shall mould the maiden's form
    By silent sympathy.
The stars of midnight shall be dear
To her; and she shall lean her ear
    In many a secret place,
Where rivulets dance their wayward round,
And beauty, born of murmuring sound,
    Shall pass into her face."

Here we do not find the image of a sponge, but merely a description of a natural effect of melody and visible beauty in softening the expression of the human features. Our author not only imitates Wordsworth and most other poets, but far excels them in their own peculiarities. Thus in the next verse who but Dr. Donne appears in exaggerated outline—Donne more Donneish than Donne, or as one might say, over-Donne.

179

"I ask no bauble miniature,
Nor ringlets dead,
Shorn from her comely head,
Now that morning not disdains
Mountains and the misty plains
Her colossal portraiture;
They her heralds be,
Steeped in her quality,
And singers of her fame
Who is their muse and dame."

Having a colossal picture of her depicted by the hills and plains, though in what fashion none but a Swedenborgian may conceive, he asks no miniature nor lock of hair. But the plains and mountains that were just now her picture, are suddenly become her heralds, and are also in some mysterious manner steeped or soaked in the quality, or in a kind of "essence of Hermione," which essence she has previously "absorbed" from land and ocean, and now squeezes out upon the hills and mountains at the instant of their transformation from a picture into a company of heralds, singing her praises. In some Asiatic poets, we have hills skipping and clapping their hands in honor of the Being who made them; but here they execute much more remarkable vagaries, in honor of a certain homely Greek woman, who seems to have eloped with a Syrian of bad reputation, and in their mountainous folly these deluded eminences mistake her for a tenth muse.

By these figures, it seems the very swallows were astounded; and our Arab pathetically solicits them 'not to mind him,' but to fly a little higher out of hearing—
"Higher, dear swallows, mind not what
    I say;
Ah! heedless how the weak are strong,
Say, was it just,
In thee to frame, in me to trust,
Thou to the Syrian, couldst belong?"

which being addressed entirely to Hermi-

one, and very properly made incomprehensible to us, it would be unfair in this connection to adduce Aristotle's rather illiberal remark, that the first virtue of a good style is perspicuity.

The sixth verse of this poem is in no particular inferior to the others.

"Once I dwelt apart,
Now I live with all;
As a shepherd's lamp on far hill-side
Seems, by the traveller espied,
A door into the mountain heart,
So didst thou quarry and unlock
Highways for me through the rock."

As a shepherd's lamp *seems* a door, so didst thou quarry a door; by which conjunction, *seems* is made a very active verb, and to *seem* a door means the same as to hew out a door. But *this* Hermione not only quarries doors through the rocks, but unlocks them after they are quarried—

"So didst thou quarry and unlock," &c.—

which shows her very worthy of his confidence. She not only made the doors for him expressly but also unlocked them.

Nevertheless, he adds:

"Now, deceived thou wanderest
In strange lands unblest;
And my kindred come to sooth me."

Now the kindred of ordinary mortals are his cousins, uncles, aunts, parents, children, &c.—but this mysterious Arab informs us that

"South wind is my next of blood,
He is come through the fragrant wood,"
    &c.
"And in every twinkling glade,

And twilight nook,
Unvails thy form," &c.

expressions which lead to a suspicion of the sanity of our Arab friend, who calls the south wind his next of kin, and personifies him as a kind of amiable Sir Pandarus in the same breath.

Then come all the genera of nature.

"River and rose and crag and bird,
Frost and sun and eldest night,"

bringing consolation to our disconsolate Arab. Their catalogue, though it be an enumeration of genera without their definite articles, is in no sense a classification; poets being exempted from the forms of science, by the same judgment that acquits them of logic and grammar; but none more than these same profound or mystical poets, who see no shame in comparing true love to the joint of a pair of compasses, and will easily straddle over the widest analogy, and compare a good to a goose, or the silence of eternity to the tenor of an idiot, with the greatest indifference; and without the least sense of the absurd.

The general of nature assemble about our Arab, and bid him console himself for the absence of his love; that he and she so closely resemble each other, they will be always doing the same things:

"Deed thou doest she must do;"

hinting that perhaps, after all was said, he might find her in himself, or in nature; that she in her turn should find him in waterfalls and woods; that he had better give up the intention of following her steps in distant regions, and be content with this ideal intercourse of souls in nature; to which, if Hermione herself acceded, and would as soon find her Arab in "wood and water, stubble and stone," we give her credit for more philosophy than affection.

And with this recommendation of the elements, our Arab seems to have been satisfied, for we hear no more of him. If the reader has not yet penetrated the meaning of this poem, we venture to suggest that it is intended for a kind of esthetic consolation to ideally disposed young men and women, unsuccessful in love; and as it happens for the most that such persons are well disposed to console themselves with the flatulent diet of metaphysics, this production is likely to be of eminent service; nor will any but the most ill-favored and utterly inhumane quote against it that saying of scripture, "If my son ask bread, shall I give him a stone?" or exclaim with Socrates, "Rocks and trees teach me nothing, therefore I keep the company of men?" For be it known to these hard-hearted persons, the best substitute for the passion of love itself, is the passion of self-love, and that is most successfully cultivated by a resort to rural solitudes, where the studious mind sees only its own image in the forms of nature, and is seldom offended by the insults of a laughing world.

In this truly precious and inexhaustible volume, written by the author, not in his sleep, I fancy, but in moods of wayward genius, casting off the fetters of rhyme, metre, logic, grammar, and science, and with a grand scorn trifling with very Deity itself, in its great fits, drunken with the wine of the spirit, and like some oracle, uttering verses more rude than Rhunic rhymes, and shriller and more incoherent than what he himself has elsewhere styled the screams of the prophets, but, like those screams, and oracular sentences, precious for depth of meaning.

There begins to be needed in anthropology a division of a class of spiritual epicures. We have epicures of all the inferior desires, but none recognized for the superior. Yet there are certainly epicures of praise, and epicures of pride, inventors and tasters of the most delicate flatteries, who make the pleasure and glow of these tastes the whole aim and purpose of their existence. We need not now enter into a psychological inquiry concerning the nature and causes of these kind of epicurism; but supposing them to be well known and distinguished, let us suppose a perfect analogy existing between their several degrees.

The epicure of foods and drinks is not glutttonous or indelicate in his meats and wines, on the contrary, nothing can be imagined more elegant and even philosophical. Your ideal epicure lives to eat, but he lives with an air. He exercises to eat, rides to eat, travels, sleeps, thinks, converses, philosophizes, is social, hospitable—nay, prays, and is religious—that he may live, and live to eat. Eating he lives, and eating he will die; but in a gentlemanly—if possible, in a Christian fashion. This is your sensuous epicure.

A step higher brings us to your epicures of intellect and passion, who live to fight, to argue, to dream, to make friendships, to ride hobbies:—their field is wide and well investigated. Come we now to the spiritual.

These are they who sip daily with an epicurean relish the pure wines of egotism. To quarrel with this species of epicurism, or abuse those who enjoy it, would be a proof of indiscretion which we shall not be the first to give; our desire is not to destroy, nor even to remove, the species, but simply to have its place assigned in the scientific museum of human nature, with the proper labels and descriptions.

Far from despising or affecting stoically to contemn this species of epicurism, may we not rather admit it among the more exalted recreations or relaxations of the soul, to be sometimes curious in its own felicities. Vanity is an intolerable fault, but no man breaks his own looking-glass. There is amusement, experience, and plea-sure even in vanity, and if the heart receives no evil taint from it why should we too bitterly despise it: Let us say the same of this metaphysical or mystical egotism, that in the young and enthusiastic it is at worst an epicurism, indulged like dandyism, for a year and a day, and thrown by with the accession of seriousness. Or, to be more liberal, if our neighbor fancies a fine horse or a bit of dress, frequents the opera or the camp-meeting, why quarrel with these harmless excitements? He will repent of them, if I let him alone; if I persecute, he will seriously adopt them.

We mean not, therefore, to persecute this species of epicurism, or to pelt it with the common-places of morality; nay, our intention is the reverse, namely, to show it up, and give it all praise possible. It is innocent;—it does not appear before the world, clad in logic or the facts of the past; it is unscientific; it is not satirical, bitter, devilish, or curiously insinuating and ingenious;—it comes with no dangerous array of maxims or precedents, the authority of the States, the church or the worthies;—it hurts no man, is able to hurt none;—he were a brute that would abuse it. Its defiances are even like the threatenings of two men seated upon opposite mountain-summits, a breath, and nothing more. It asks only to be let alone; it triumphs in solitude; it is in love itself; but to others, discovers, neither hatred nor love. Its maxims are passive, though it seems even to set all at defiance. It lies in wait for the kingdom of heaven; and what others get by strife, it will have by a stratagem of pride. "To him who waits long enough, all things come in their turn;" but above all things, this epicurism forbids tumult, and angling for bliss in troubled waters:

"Seek not the spirit of it hide,
Inexorable to thy zeal;

Baby, do not whine and chide,
Art thou not also real?"

Here the mood changes suddenly, and the oat proceeds thus:

"Why shouldst thou stoop to poor
    excuse
Turn on the accuser roundly; say,
Here am I, here will I remain
For ever to myself sooth fast;
Go thou, sweet Heaven, or at thy plea-
    sure stay;
Already Heaven with thee its lot has
    cast,
For only it can absolutely deal."

Which seems to be treating Heaven very nearly like a jilt, who follows most when least desired; and contrary to that saying of Christ, "knock and it shall be opened unto you," and other of the school of Christian humility. When Heaven accuses us, you are to turn upon it with a quiet scorn of excuse, and declare you have no need of it; upon which Heaven will immediately "come in," and be your friend. Now let the faithful cry out, if they please, "God deliver us from such a heaven!"— they can never understand this matter, they are the children of humility, but now we are conversing of spiritual epicurism, which is a very different matter.

Here, then, we have it, in this piece, entitled "Bacchus," an imitation of the Persian mystic, Hafiz.

"Bring me wine, but wine which never
    grew,
In the belly of the grape, * * *

            *   *

Wine which music is,—
Music and wine are one,
That, I drinking this,
Shall hear far Chaos talk with me;
Kings unborn shall walk with me,

And the poor grass shall plot and plan
What it will do when it is man.
Quickened so, will I unlock
Every crypt of every rock."

And in this poem headed,

THE DAY'S RATION:
        "When I was born,
From all the seas of strength fate filled a
    chalice,
Saying, 'This be thy portion, child; this
    chalice,
Less than a lily, thou shalt daily draw
From my great arteries, — nor less, nor
    more,'
All substances the cunning chemist Time
Melts down into that liquor of my
    life,—
Friends, foes, joys, fortunes, beauty and
    disgust."

He then complains, that this liquor of life-love, which is also the wine of the spirit, and the "music" quoted above, is too easily exhausted by excitement:

"If a new muse draw me with splendid
    ray,
And I uplift myself into its heaven,
The needs of the first sight absorb my
    blood,
And all the following hours of the day
Drag a ridiculous age," &c.

Then follows an argument for regarding this one sip from the epicurean chalice, as sufficient:—

"Why need I volumes, if one word
    suffice?
Why need I galleries, when a pupil's
    draught,
After the master's sketch, fills and
    o'erfills
My apprehension? why seek Italy,
Who cannot circumnavigate the sea

Of thoughts and things at home, but still
    adjourn
The nearest matter for a thousand
    days."

This admirable description of the spiritual epicure, shall suffice us for an instance. He begins with an estimate of the quantity of the spiritual liquor given for each day. If he drinks it all at once, he has bibbed his cup, and all is over for that twenty-four hours. But he cannot pip it and have it—a terrible dilemna! Observe—*first*, the end of all existence is taken to be a certain private tipple or morning dram at this little cup of liqueur. The whole theory and art of life is then, how to eke out the allowance. A more perfect exposition of the matter could hardly be conceived. The epicure counts his income, so much for the year, month, day;—if he lays out the whole in one day, he can taste no more, unhappy wretch!

That the end of life is happiness, all men seem to be agreed; but we have few who philosophize in this fashion; few who so skillfully, and deliberately defend epicurism; who so leave out of the account all the common considerations; or sit down upon their spiritual income with a more Apician resolution to spend it in the most delectable style.

The world is wide, and there is room in it for all philosophies, systems, creeds, and epicurism; and on a more liberal view of the matter, we have our doubts whether it is not best that there should be a great variety; surely 'tis all for the best. Whatever is for the best is good; therefore this new epicurism is good. It must be so, we are convinced. Evoe! Bacchus! bring us the cup; come, we will drink deep; we will do what the god instigates—laugh, fleere, flout—or applaud and wonder; it is all right: good: all one;—why not? I am a man as well as you, sir; come, sir, put up your sour looks. What! I put up my sour looks! I am a free man, sir, and will be as sour as I please. I concede it, friend; be sour, in Heaven's name! No, neighbor, you shall not concede any thing; I despise your concessions, &c. &c. &c.

Nevertheless, we like the doctrine; it leaves one at liberty. For example, we have the glorious privilege, and no man to gainsay it, of running over this same volume of poems, and pronouncing it a very idle collection of verses; a slovenly, unpoetical, conceited little volume, narrow in sentiment, and fulsome in style; teaching doctrines of rank pride; or we might cry it up, admire its splendors, be drowned in its depths; and in either course the doctrines of the author will sustain us, so perfectly liberal are they. But this is nothing to the point.

We regret our want of room to lay before the reader a kind of extract, or medulla of the philosophy of our author, from this collection of his poems. Each one of them expresses a sentiment peculiar to himself; the key-note of all is self-respect. The god of this world is self-respect, and this is his book of rules, or rhythmical creed. His creed is to have no creed; his rule, to have no rule; his law, to have no law. Young and old, he would have us obey the law inscribed upon our hearts by mother nature, and that law is impulse—Impulse. But, as we have said, our limits forbid a full exposition. At present let us pass over the *substance*, however elevated and instructive, and seek what pleasure may be found in the *form*.

Our poet is, we believe, the first of modern time who has imitated the manner of Donne, Cowley, Cleveland, and their contemporaries. Images in poetry, has been said, are either to exalt, to illustrate, or to debase and vilify the subject of the comparison. This is the ordinary opinion concerning the uses of imagery. But no critic that we have ever read, has let us completely into the secret of imagery, or the reason of its use. Poetry that is merely witty or rhetorical, may give delight by similitude, as by comparing a hero to a lion, a chattering fool to a magpie, a clown to a clod, &c. It is the art rhetorical which assists the fancy by comparisons. In these lines of Tasso,

"As from a furnace flew the smoke to
    the skies,
Such smoke as that when damned
    Sodom burnt,"

we have a splendid instance of simple rhetorical simile or comparison in the first line, and a figure of a different kind, (which we shall, for present convenience, name the complex rhetorical) in the second. The first, or simple rhetorical, merely enables us to imagine a thing which no man ever saw or can see, the wall of smoke and fire about the enchanted grove of Ismeno; but the second, or complex rhetorical, adds eminent power to the first, by infusing a living and human interest into this phenomenon of smoke: "it was such a smoke as that which rose from Sodom." This is said in the true spirit of oratory, or of the grandest rhetoric. It *exalts* the subject.

Let us now seek an example of the rhetorical comparison intended to debase or vilify the subject. This from the Dunciad is most convenient—

"So take the hindmost, h-ll!" he said,
    and ran,
Swift as a barb the bailiff leaves behind,
He left huge Lintot, and outstripped the
    wind,
As when a dabchick waddles through
    the copse,
On feet and wings, and flies, and wades,
    and hops,
So labouring on, with shoulders, hands,
    and head,
Wide as a wind-mill all his figure spread,

With arms expanded, Bernard rows his
    state," &c. &c.

Which does most perfectly debase and vilify the subject, but in a rhetorical manner merely, and not in a poetical.

To give now a perfect example of poetical imagery—of which the object is not either to illustrate, to exalt, or to vilify and debase, but only to delight and satisfy, in a profound and peculiar manner—take these lines of Shakespeare—

"From you I have been absent in the
    spring,
When proud pied April dress'd in all his
    trim,
Had put a spirit of youth in every thing,
    And heavy Saturn laughed and leaped
    with him."

The excellence here lies not, we think, merely in a certain subtle harmony of metres, but in the nature of the imagery. The lines are pregnant with life. Assuming, without fear of contradiction, that the great end of the art poetical, as distinguished from the art rhetorical, is to infuse life and sentiment in the dead matter and gross organisms of nature; to make stones and trees love and feel with us, and persuade us of an all-pervading humanity, existent even in brutes and vegetables; we shall find it easy in every instance, whether ancient or modern, to detect the true poet and distinguish him from the rhetorical rhymer. By this test the great contest in English literature, concerning the poetry of Pope and his school, and the similar dispute among Italian savans, in which Galileo took part, concerning the poetry of Tasso, is finally put at rest. Without diminishing the glory of our greatest wit and master rhetoric, or of the amiable and chivalrous Tasso, we are yet compelled to assign them a class by themselves, among the most eloquent and admirable, not among the most poetical of versifiers.

At the same time, it will be necessary to admit that all the great poets were also great rhetoricians, and most of them great wits; and that they always use a mixture of rhetorical imagery with that which vivifies. But in Pope's verses we find few of these (if I may so call them) life-giving forms of speech. In Tasso they are certainly much more frequent than in Pope; at least, they are so in Fairfax's admirable translation; and if the great controversy which raged on this topic in Galileo's time were to be decided by Fairfax's version, we are inclined to believe that Tasso would be admitted as holding only as secondary rank among the great poets.

To illustrate this controversy more perfectly, let us examine another verse of Shakespeare, who stands first (we think, beyond all question) on the poetical side, when judged by the test we have just offered—

"O hateful, vaporous, and foggy night,
Since thou art guilty of my cureless
    crime,
Muster thy mists to meet the eastern
    light,
Make war against proportioned course
    of time."

Into this imaginary night, the poet, by a wonderfully bold figure, has thrown all the worst qualities of humanity at a single effort: cruelty, dullness, obscurity of mind, evil intent, obduracy of soul, positive unrepentant guilt; authority, as of a commander, actual war against all the symbols of virtue; to crown all, she becomes the personal enemy of a noble spirit, the accessory of a base one.

Under this torrent of vivifying expression, the judgment cannot hold out an instant; imagination (or rather, that function of the soul by which *persons* are

conceived) is compelled to conceive and adopt the dreadful deity—the mistress of hell, and fell her poisonal reality.

The poet has invented the goddess, has shaped her with a few touches of his creative hand; she waits only an altar and a worship; and in another age, when poets were law-givers, she had one.

Or, take these three lines of a sonnet by the same hand—

"No longer mourn for me, when I dead,
Than you shall hear the surly, sullen
    bell,
Give warning to the world that I am
    fled."

The bell receives a human character, of hardness, dutifulness, and a public function; the soul is astonished with this beautiful art, which places even dead forms, and hard, heartless things in an amiable or unamiable relation with itself; and to be persuaded that this is natural and delightful, we need only remember our childhood, and the animosities and loves which we delighted to exercise toward inanimate objects. But in poetry it is more than mere animation, it is moral sympathy that is thus imparted. Thus, when Lear appeals to 'the gods'—

"You see me here, ye gods, a poor old
    man,
As full of grief as age, wretched in both
If it be you that stir these daughters'
    hearts," &c. &c.

We are not offended, and we can understand that Lear is addressing personifications of the divine attributes of justice, mercy and power; and it is this poetic faculty which gives them the rights of persons over us, and compels us to address them.

Again, in those dreadful lines which begin—

"Blow, winds, and crack your cheeks!
    rage! blow!
Ye cataracts!"

The imagination of the mad and anguished soul, cut off from all sympathy with things living, pours out its grief in talk with imagined creatures, with which it stands in natural sympathy.

We have said enough and instanced enough to explain our meaning, in making this distinction between rhetorical and poetical imagery. The grandest passages of the great poets contain a mixture of both kinds; but the poetical predominates. On the other hand, oratory demands an absolute exclusion of the poetical kind, or, to speak modestly, a very sparing use of genuine poetical imagery.

Our author, whom we return to with a peculiar satisfaction, furnishes beautiful examples of an imagery which neither illustrates, exalts, not intentionally vilifies. Thus in the following—

"And universal nature, through her vast
And crowded whole, an infinite parro-
    quet,
Repeats one note!"— (p. 220.)

Nature, a mere abstraction, is vivified by making her like a part of herself, to wit, a parroquet, and the simplicity and perpetual echo of her laws, is delicately symbolized in the monotonous "Pretty poll, poll, poll, pretty poll!" of a —what?—a parroquet! This is a slight error; it should be parrot, not parroquet. But, as we have often remarked before, great poets are the masters of all arts, and if they choose to call an eagle an owl, or a parrot a parroquet, we submit in silence; and even were we disposed to carp, the splendor and vivifying beauty of the image should prevent us.

Here, too, is another, more remarkable and more illustrative—Cupid's eyes are the subject. Of these the poet says, that with them

"He doth eat and drink, and fish, and
    shoot,"— (p. 157.)

Which, if it be very bad verse, is nevertheless very fine imagery. Indeed, we observe this of our author, that when he puts us off with a particularly bad line, it is sure to be supported by something rare and curious in imagery. Thus he never cheats his reader. This poem on Cupid proceeds in the following fashion. "He (with his eyes) doth eat and drink, and fish and shoot"—an order to which sportsmen will object; the eating and drinking should come after the fishing and shooting.

"And write, and reason, and compute,
And ride and run, and have, and hold,
And return, and flatter, and regret,
And kiss, and couple, and beget."

And this he does

"With those unfathomable orbs,"

hight mystically his eyes. Observe the singular beauty and vivification of the imagery. Of this Cupid, one may say, he has it all in his eye, as the Hindoo god Chrishna had the world in his mouth. The eye of Uriel was a wonderful eye, but Cupid's is still more wonderful. This species of poetry we find at once instructive and full of pleasure; it teaches one the vast difference between the mere mystical comparing of all the universe to a three-legged stool, and that true poetry which throws the life of humanity into the meanest things. The last three actions ascribed to the eye of Cupid, surpass anything we have ever met with for delicacy and power of conception; what a certain Roman emperor is said to have attempted, Cupid here appears actually accomplishing. But this is nothing to what follows. Of these same eyes it is said—

"Undaunted are their courages,
Right Cossacks in their forages;"

A language, be it observed, which out-Chaucer's Chaucer, and is more Saxon than the very Saxon itself.

"Fleeter they than any creature,
They are his steeds, and not his feature;"

Where the strength of the image is so intense, it obliges the poet to snap the comparison in two, and finally to deny that they are his eyes, after all:

"Inquisitive and fierce and fasting,
Restless, predatory, hasting," &c.
    "He lives in his eyes,"—

A new species of verse—

"There doth digest, and work and spin
And buy and sell, and lose and win,"
    &c.

In short, does everything in his eyes. They are, in fact, his all in all; and yet the prettiest part is to come;—

"Cupid is a casuist.
A mystic and cabalist"—

and,

"He is headstrong and alone."

Aloneness, is one of his qualities:

"He affects the wood and wild,
Like a flower-hunting child;
Buries himself in summer waves,
In trees, with beasts, in mines and caves;
Loves nature like a horned cow,
Bird or deer, or caribou."

Here are some important facts in the history of Cupid, and in the romantic instincts of the horned cow (is not that a mistake for horn*less*? or does the horned love nature more than the hornless?) and of the caribou, which is a species of reindeer, says Richardson, the naturalist. The poet too is generous with us: he doesn't stint us to one species of deer,—"bird, or deer, or caribou;" as if one should say, "bird or quadruped, or dog,"—first, he gives us the whole kind, "bird or *deer*," and then adds one species for earnest:

"or caribou;"

for which the reader is doubtless much obliged; as also for the other poetic favors and condescensions in general. A more mysterious poet than our author hath not arisen in this age. We are fain to place him at the head of his class, if class he have, before whose intellect all divisions and distinctions shrink up, are resolved into the primeval condition. If we have in any particular thrown light for the reader on his mysterious works, be it in a mere rush-light capacity, then is our soul content. We climb not to his altitudes.

But it is necessary to conclude. Our poet himself reminds us of our duty.

"But, critic, spare thy vanity,
    Nor show thy pompous parts,
To vex with odious subtlety,
    The cheerer of men's hearts."

To which we reply, again offering the crown, that we cannot allow the modesty of a poet, however delicate and heroical, to stand in the way of his poetical honors. Words are things. Ideas have the force of laws. Literature is the guard of the commonwealth. Looseness and affectation in language and philosophy, lead by but one step to looseness of manner and morals. Next to the expression of an untruth, is the expression of a truth in an affected and impertinent style. The mass of men are imitative, and readily adopt a bad fashion. What defence has the world of letters, then, but to seize upon the first bright example, and set it plainly before the eyes of men. We have done so with this little book of poems. We wish to see it appreciated.

Checklist of Additional Reviews

Boston *Courier*, 29 December 1846.

Christian Register, 26 (2 January 1847), 3.

J[ohn]. S[ullivan]. D[wight]., *Harbinger*, 4 (23, 30 January 1847), 91–4, 106–9.

Graham's Magazine, 30 (March 1847), 202.

Southern Quarterly Review, 11 (April 1847), 493–9

T.S.K., *Universalist Quarterly*, 4 (April 1847), 153–72.

Westminster Review [England], 47 (April 1847), 250.

"New Poetry in New England," *United States Magazine, and Democratic Review*, 20 (May 1847), 392–8; 21 (October 1847), 294–300.

"Our Library. Poems, by Ralph Waldo Emerson," *People's Journal*, 3 (1 May 1847), 249–50.

Examiner, 2049 (8 May 1847), 292.

Daguerreotype, 1 (4 September 1847), 142–3.

Christian Remembrancer, 15 (April 1848), 300–52.

Ladies' Repository, 25 (June 1865), 380.

"American Literature," *Saturday Review*, 42 (30 December 1876), 827.

Essays, Lectures, and Orations

Review of *Essays, Lectures, and Orations*, *Critic* [England], n.s. 6 (18 December 1847), 386–7

It is impossible to mistake the tendency of our times, and of our country especially. This is a period of intellectual decline. Mind, in our generation, has lost its daring, its power, and its grasp, its originality, its self-reliance, its lofty aspirations, its individuality; and enfeebled and timid, it finds occupation in false sentimentalism, or a material philosophy, of which selfishness is the principle, and £ s. d. the sum. As Wordsworth says, "The world *is* too much with us."

The proofs are patent where they would most readily be found—in our literature. Philosophy in its loftiest form is extinct among us. Poetry, which is philosophy revealing itself in language intelligible to the work-day world, can find no listeners. The periodical press, which faithfully reflects the popular taste, sedulously shuns either topic. Every day, more and more are they compelled to cater for the *amusement* of their readers, and to avoid anything that has the form, or even the substance, of *instruction*. The only writings that reward their authors, because the only works that find an extensive sale, are exciting romances, jest-books, and illustrated works—publications which either kindle the passions, or create a laugh, or please the eye, and impose no labour on the understanding; and stir not up the mind to the task of thought. Of the numerous periodicals published in Great Britain, *The Critic* alone devotes the slightest attention to the highest branches of human knowledge—the divinest efforts of the immortal spirit that our age is striving to bind and chain to earth—the Mental Philosophy which is really the most valuable of all knowledge, measured by the most grovelling calculations of utility, and the Philosophy of Being, which, if it do no more than lift us nigher to God, is entitled to some notice from those who profess to guide the age, though, in fact, they but reflect it. Our reading memory extends backward about five-and-twenty years, and comparing *then* and *now* this intellectual decline is painfully visible. Then there was Philosophy;—the quarterly reviews and the magazines never passed three numbers without an article belonging to that class. The *Edinburgh*, the *Quarterly*, and the *Westminster*, after their different creeds, did battle each for its own doctrines, and by the conflict was the public mind stimulated to thought, and out of the strife came truth. Poetry was then read by everybody, and all professed at least a regard for it. Now, even the quarterlies shun Philosophy in any shape; the literary journals, save this alone, pass it in silence, or treat it with ridicule; and few would have the hardihood in private society, still fewer in a public assembly, to own themselves lovers and cultivators of poetry. It would be far better for *The Critic*, commercially, to follow the fashion, eschew Philosophy, and sneer at Poetry; but we cannot find it in our conscience to do so. Although we do not pretend to disregard the question of profit or loss, and should be glad to be rewarded in substantial cash for our weekly toils, instead of labouring, as we have yet done and still do, with no other reward than the consciousness of diffusing honest, if mistaken, views of books, and art, and society, we cannot refuse such influence as The Critic has created in a circle, already by no means despicable, and daily extending, to the sustainment of that cultivation of the loftier powers of the intellect which are man's proudest distinction, and the neglect of which by any people is inevitably the forerunner of national decay.

Therefore do we welcome with heartiest congratulations to our shores, Ralph Waldo Emerson, the Philosopher of America. He has already begun his mission here. Our readers have doubtless read the abstracts of some of his lectures delivered at Manchester, which have appeared in these pages. Glad are we to learn that they were numerously attended and heard with reverence. If they stir up but a few minds to thought, Mr. Emerson will leave behind him the *nuclei* from which it will radiate in ever increasing circles, by the force of example no less than by the influence of teaching. We care not that Emerson is termed abstract and dreamy—that he is often crude, obscure, and visionary. We fix our eyes upon his excellences, not upon

his faults. He is a man with a great soul, nevertheless. A mightier man than a thousand of the pigmies who shoot their small arrows at him. If he be obscure, it is because he soars so high that he loses sight of his landmarks; but how can there be discovery without daring—how explore without sometimes erring? With Emerson, and such as he who lose themselves in *height*, there is, however, this great advantage, that their followers profit by their fault. The mind seeks to trace their path and soars too, and the effort to rise is a gain even though the attempt fail. It is something in this frivolous age to arrest the attention of the intellectual idler, to make him pause and listen; if it be but for the purpose of fault-finding and abuse, still to make him *think*. The very controversies occasioned by such a philosophy are beneficial, and therefore we forgive even the most eccentric dreams of Mr. Emerson for the sake of the agitation they make in the stagnant waters of our intellectual kingdom.

The volume before us is a collection of his Essays and Orations, which, at this time, when the author is among us, will doubtless be received with eager welcome by all who have heard, or intend to hear, his eloquent teachings from his own lips. The interest thus temporarily excited in him we shall make use of for the purpose of forwarding the object we have most at heart,—the revival in Great Britain of a taste for the cultivation of the loftier occupations of the intellect; and therefore we purpose to dwell upon these papers at some length, the more especially as Mr. Emerson is rather a discursive writer. He professes no measured system of Philosophy. He has an aim, of course;—principles, we may be sure;—definite aims, that is certain;—but his essays are rather written thoughts than formal compositions—thoughts about man, his destinies and duties, than arrays of arguments logically set forth, and advancing from axioms to conclusions.

Still there is a principle pervading all. He has a distinct, definite IDEA, which is the soul of every sentence. It is stated in the preface after this manner. Under all circumstances we should possess a grand self-reliance, coupled with a reverend attention and obedience to the voice of our moral nature—heedless of mere custom and courtesy, wealth or ease, we should strive to attain a noble simplicity and truthfulness of life and language,—while books and teachers, facts and systems, may aid us if they can, but in no case masters to mould our free and natural thoughts into their forms—and, above all, that we should keep our minds in a constant state of receptivity for that divine thought or idea which, underlying the sensuous appearances and mechanical uses of things, has for us manifold teachings that are the truest and highest ends of this "real workday world." Only in proportion to a man's reception of the voice of Deity, thus speaking, is he great, is he true, in impulse and action—does he stand in unison with the order of the universe.

The style of Emerson is inspired by study of the German philosophers; but it is not a servile imitation—his individuality is visible everywhere; as he thinks for himself, so he speaks after his own fashion. Sometimes he is obscure, when his ideas are not clear; but when he has a distinct perception in his mind, no man can express it more distinctly or transfer it more vividly to the minds of others. His language is always *tinged with poetry*, and occasionally it becomes poetry all over. He has been an extensive reader, and he gleans largely from the utterances of the loftiest intellects of all ages and countries. Careless and thoughtless must he be who could read a page of these essays and orations without being startled into reflection, and made to think. In this age of intellec-

tual laziness such a book is of incalculable worth.

But we are dwelling too long upon merely introductory matter. It is time to introduce the reader to the contents, and without further tracing a philosophy which it would demand the space of a quarterly review to do justice to, we will at once proceed to cull some of the more striking passages, accompanying them with such comments as may be suggested by them.

In the Essay on "History," he maintains the doctrine that all history is but, as it were, the development of the individual man. We see in it but an expansion of ourselves, and in ourselves may all history be read. Thus he finds

["History," 18.2–19.6]

In the Essay on "Self-Reliance," one of the finest in the volume, he breaks forth into the following eloquent and indignant denunciation of *the* vice of our times—the want of self-will, self-respect, and moral courage:—

["Self-Reliance," 43.7–44.9]

The essay on "Compensation" is designed to show the dispensation of strict justice by Providence, and that virtue is rewarded and vice punished in this world as certainly as they will be in the next. "In labour, as in life," he says, "there can be no cheating. The thief steals from himself; the swindler swindles himself. For the real price of labour is knowledge and virtue, whereof wealth and credit are signs." Thus was he induced to the consideration of the subject:—

["Compensation," 55.22–56.23]

All nature proclaims the great fact of

["Compensation," 64.25–66.9]

And again—

["Compensation," 67.25–36]

192

On the other hand—

> ["Compensation," 68.11–24]

We conclude with the picture of

> ["Compensation," 73.10–28]

Of course we shall return to this volume, and perhaps more than once.

Checklist of Additional Reviews

Literary Gazette [England], 1613 (18 December 1847), 879.

Massachusetts Quarterly Review, 1 (March 1848), 270.

People's Journal, 4 (21 April 1848), 210.

Leader, 2 (28 January 1851), 612.

Nature; Addresses, and Lectures

[George E. Ellis],
Review of *Nature;
Addresses, and Lectures,
Christian Examiner*, 49
(November 1849), 461

"Emerson's Addresses,"
Literary World, 5
(3 November 1849),
374–6

Doubtless there is nothing in this volume which the admirers of its distinguished author have not already in possession. But the contents of it have never appeared together before, nor in such an inviting form. The fair type and paper will even help to the better understanding of some of the oracles in these pages. We apprehend that the highest, the most enduring, and the most just encomium which Emerson will receive will not be from the coterie who regard him as an inspired seer, but from the larger, the more discriminating, and the really more intelligent body of his readers, who find on every page of his proofs of a most pure spirit and a loving heart, without one breathing of an unholy or rancorous feeling. Nine Addresses and Lectures, before various literary societies and lyceums, beside the Essay on Nature, compose the contents of this volume, which will be as original a century hence as it is now.

This volume is a republication of articles long since printed, but now first collected together. We have never read any of it before. We opened it with curiosity, knowing the power of the author as a thinker and writer; read it with mingled delight and disgust; and closed it in sadness. Let us remember, now what we have learned from a careful, thoughtful, (we will venture to say) *humble* perusal; for we are always content to sit down in patience at the feet of a thinking, honest man, no matter of what school, to hear how this great vision of nature and humanity looks to him, knowing we shall grow wiser for his truth, and for his error.

And here we do cheerfully acknowledge, that to us Mr. Emerson seems to regard Nature with a just, and not undue valuation. When he speaks of her, there is the freshness and the power of poetry about his words, so that we follow him involuntarily into the sunlight or the starlight, and feel imagination at its wonderful work. As in reading Wordsworth, we are continually reminded how rich is nature in meaning, in joy, and consolation. He shows us clearly, too, the value of a life with her as a discipline to mind and beast; as the ingathering of a language which we may convert to high uses in the world of man; and as a means whereby we may listen to the speaking of the "universal spirit." We have found, too, here, as elsewhere in Mr. Emerson's writings, sentiments, flashes of thought of a *scientific* value; many valuable hints for those who shall build Æsthetics into a science; things thrown out as transient intuitions, which will bear logical analysis.

We are content and glad, then, to sympathize with Mr. Emerson in his estimation of nature, and to hold, indeed, that her *noblest* function "is to stand as the apparition of God."

Nor can one read this book without feeling that the author has a deep and earnest abhorrence of evil, not only in its grosser, but in its more refined forms; the common, ignoble dishonesties of society in action and word; the deep injustice of much that yet lingers in existing institutions. But while he feels man's need of elevation to a higher ideal, he sees with a clear sight the vanity and folly of the existing schemes for reform, and exposes the fallacy upon which they are moving:—

["Lectures on the Times,"
178.28–179.1, 176.28–37, 178.4–27]

An estimation similar to this would be formed by any man of serene mind and heart, who should look around upon what is doing or attempted to be done now in the civilized world. Mr. Emerson, then, is not to be reckoned among the common tribe of Innovators. He acknowledges, as do thousands of those whom he calls Conservatives, the party of the Past; that the Reformers, the party of the Future, have a right ideal of justice, mixed up with, and to give life to their schemes, but

he prophesies a failure in their method of realizing it. His reform is of a deeper kind. He would reform the soul. He would strike at the root of the evil, and convert the individual soul to what he thinks its purpose. We have in his writings no *Utopia*, no ideal of society. It would be hard to find how extensively he thinks his ideal of the individual man could be realized. We are reluctant to believe him so shallow-sighted as to ignore the mournful fact for which humanity has been wailing, since its birth, of spiritual evil; that eternal mystery by which some, no matter how much enlightened, will, of their own deliberate choice, determine *not* to follow the law of right, call it revelation of reason, or the moral sentiment, or God's will externally pronounced or what you will. Still, we are not sure that Mr. Emerson is not liable to this charge. But let it pass. He would that some,—many men should be ennobled, and cast, a leaven into the world,—how *far* to work upon it is no matter. His ideal of virtue is high and lofty,—in common phrase, not unlike the ideal of the stoics; to understand it one must know something of his metaphysic and his religion. To gather his aphorisms and paradoxes into a connected system, that one may understand his philosophic and religious creed, is not so easy a matter. It seems to be the law of his mind to throw these out without order, and leave his readers to translate them into the language of logical sequence. He gives us a random defence of an idealism, not unlike that of Berkeley or Fichte, that will look rather lame to those who acknowledge the refutation of these systems by Reid and Stewart, or Cousin. But this idealism, which makes everything of the soul, and refuses to acknowledge an objective essence in matter, is a part of his moral theory. It makes the individual soul more valuable,—then, we find often appearing, the doctrine that God manifests himself in the individual soul, incarnates himself in every man. We are left without grounds for this assertion. We cannot find what is Mr. Emerson's starting point. But with the refutation of this we are not now concerned. We introduce it simply to show how it makes the soul precious in our author's estimation. To him the soul is complete in itself, with a possibility of perfection, nay of perfecting itself. That is the task for it. To set itself "perfect as a star" in the spiritual firmament. And this ideal is to realize by—*Self-Reliance*.

There is no doubt about this. It appears everywhere in the book. He "cannot find language of sufficient energy to convey his sense" that this is the secret of virtue and strength.

In one of his addresses Mr. Emerson lets us into his religious opinions—to him all history is alike, and it is a degradation to make much more use of the mind of Christ, than of Epaminondas or Washington. Miracles are profanations. Inspiration is a common or ever possible fact. Jesus was a man whose intuition of truth was clear and intense, who "saw the mystery of the soul" and "estimated the greatness of man," who saw in prophetic vision the great truth, the result of this modern philosophy, that God incarnates himself in man, and who, beside himself in a "jubilee of sublime emotion," said, "I am divine, through me God acts; through me, speaks; would you see God, see me, or see thee, when thou thinkest as I now think."

We cannot tell (we speak in no irony, but in deepest seriousness) whether Mr. Emerson thinks his own intuition of truth as clear and intense as that of Jesus. If he does, would he dare to assume the sentence above quoted, as his own words, and cast it forth into the world? If this be indeed the sense of Jesus' words, men have forgotten that sublime truth for centuries. Now it is re-uttered from one of authority equal to that of Jesus. Now we have it in clear terms, no longer in tropes as Jesus uttered it. Are we not to expect still grander results from the new Apostle than from the old? How far will man's hardihood carry itself, and his pride make a fool of him?

But if Mr. Emerson will acknowledge a purer and intenser intuition of truth in Jesus than his own, then from his own mouth is he condemned, for nothing can be more opposite than Mr. Emerson's plan for man's information, and that of Jesus. We have the one saying—"To aim to correct a man by miracles is a profanation of the soul"—and the other, "Woe unto thee, Chorazin, woe unto thee, Bethsaida, for if the mighty works which have been done in thee had been done in Tyre and Sidon, they had long ago repented in sackcloth and ashes," and "if I do not the works of my Father, believe me not." We hear the one say, "Rely on thyself"—and the other, "Believe in me." The one says the soul is complete in itself, and that the divine soul pervades humanity,—the other prays that his disciples, and they who shall believe through their word, and they only, "may be one," "as we are one." But enough of this. Our readers will see that the contrast might be extended indefinitely. We have adduced it simply to show into what an inconsistency our author has been betrayed. Indeed his ideal of virtue and the means to attain it, are the diametric opposite of the Christian; the one is, self-reliance—the other, self-renunciation. The culminating virtue of the one is pride, of the other humility: for who will say that this brooding over our own value, this imagination that God in us is incarnate, this self-reliance, self-isolation, will result in anything but pride; and who does not remember the words of the other, "When ye have done all that ye can do, say we are unprofitable servants!" And, "Whosoever exalteth himself shall be abased, and whosoever humbleth himself shall be exalted." We are not entering upon an argument from Scripture; but, if truth is one, and intuition of it differs in degree, and not in kind, how is it possible that in two claiming so much of it, such opposite conclusions should be reached?

But to meet our author on other grounds. He gives no proof for his maxim, that self-reliance is this unusual panacea. But try it by the test of experience. Throw it into the world. Let each man take to himself this new gospel—"Rely on thyself." Give it the benefit of the utmost explanation. Show that it means not, "Rely on thy whims and fancies, trust thy inclinations:" but, "believe thy intuition of right, believe in the treasures of thy reason, and ennoble thyself by thy self-trust in endeavoring to execute this law within thee." What will the countless thousands who now *choose* to violate their conscience, do with such a maxim as this? And those who are little minded, can they be trusted thus to confide in the resources of their own reason? Is not an education of humanity to a fitness for it impossible? And who shall decide between differing judgments in the matter? For our author needs to be reminded, that to determine between right and wrong is an intellectual act; and conscience, or the moral sentiment, but preserves the obligation. Have not good men arrived at different ethical theories, and lived not to deplore the practical consequences of their own deductions? Or is the world but just now fit for this maxim? To the common sense, to the instinct of humanity, we will trust its refutation. Take it to thyself in imagination, O Neophyte, and see if thou wilt not seem to crystalize into selfishness. Let each new disciple grow to regard himself as the ideal man, and worship his own perfection, God incarnate in him; say to others, "invade not my privacy, my integrity, touch me not, I am God,"—and what a world of love, and unity, and mutual self-sacrifice we should have! We have no fear of the spread of such philosophy, such religion as this. Nature will cry out against it, love and pity will melt down this icy pinnacle of pride for all but the high priests of this idolatry.

How different the Christian philosophy. Beware thy inclinations, trust not thy heart;—look into thy reason, if thou wilt, for intuitions, and judgments of truth and justice, but test its conclusions by this external law of God, which alone has taught man the riches of his own reason,—which alone has illuminated the dim chaos he found within himself.

Trust not thy own will and wisdom, but thy Maker's; remember thy weakness in following what thou knowest to be good, thy failures, and thy griefs;—trust no more thy strength, but receive the offer of His who died for thee. Here thou mayest find union with the divine nature; here thou mayest like thyself to God. Remember that evil is the world, and that external, formal, as well as internal, essential union is necessary to subdue it. Believe, then, in the necessity of organization, and if thou seest the excellence of unity in that organization, believe that God has not left his will unknown concerning it. Now thou hast found thy Saviour, now thou has found his Church.

But the vices, the deficiencies, the mournful unworthiness of the Christian lands? Alas, they are owing to these very principles that Mr. Emerson is now pushing upon the world,—dimly seen, but not less certainly acted upon. "My will, my wisdom," was in the heart and mind of those who have gone on in the sliding scale,—"not mine, but thine, O God," was the prayer of those who have been the salt of the earth. Self-reliance!—self-renunciation!—these have been on the banners of the opposing armies, and will be until the end of time—the one is, faith in self, the other faith in God. This goes out of itself for trust and reliance, and acknowledges that the same hand which upholds the heavens and the earth, upholds its own willing integrity,—that, in the deification of its own essence, has no security that it shall not deify its inclinations; and its natural result is slavery to its own corruption. Were the law of the one, self-renunciation, universal, all disorders of society would vanish,—were the law of the other, self-trust, universal, it would lead ultimately to that state of war, which, according to Hobbes, was the normal state of man. That isolation to which it leads, the cold grandeur of Goethe, the aloofness from all warm, kindly sympathy, something like which we see in Mr. Emerson;—contrast it with the self-forgetfulness of apostics and saints, the men who went about doing good, seeking only the welfare of others, and yet in the pursuit finding their own truest welfare. And yet to this freezing realm Mr. Emerson would have all men draw themselves.

We have dwelt the longer on this, because it is the one principle to which our author is ever guiding us. With it the worth of his writings, for all other than their poetic merit, must stand or fall. We think, then, they have too little of eternal truth to take their place in our permanent literature. But the fallacy which underlies them will for ever start up anew till the end of the world. In many shapes has it already appeared in the world's history; with pure-minded men generally for its heralds, the immorality of whose followers the world has grown ashamed of again and again.

We have sought to stand on Mr. Emerson's own ground, or we might have spoken of our horror at his irreverent blasphemy, his cool, patronizing way of speaking of Him "by whom all things are made." We cannot but think there is some affectation in this, and that even He must have done violence to his own heart to speak in this manner. And when he says— "the manner in which his name is surrounded by expressions—official titles— kills all generous sympathy and liking," how little he seems to know, that they who adore can *love* with their strongest heart!

Review of *Essays, Essays: Second Series,* and *Nature; Addresses, and Lectures,* Knickerbocker, 35 (March 1850), 254–63

A Yankee Mystic! a Platonic philosopher from the region of 'Boston notions!' The words sound incongruous: yet such is the fact. Yes; right there, in the heart of practical Yankee-land, in the shrewdest, keenest, most money-loving population, sits a circle as 'idealistic,' as spiritual, ay, as noble in thought, as any ever gathered around Plato or Alexandrian Philo. A school of mystic Brahmins, suddenly discovered in Liverpool, would hardly be more strange. And what a change from those simple, devout men, who, two centuries ago, reared their churches and governments there!—men whose whole life was 'practical,' who abhorred all 'self-exaltation,' and who would almost crush the individual man in bowing prostrate before God. Only imagine the horror of honest John Harvard, for instance, if told that in a few generations one of the Puritan descendants were to utter such sentiments as these, and find approval for them too:

> 'I am part or particle of God. I am God. It is the soul that degrades the past, turns all riches to poverty, confounds the saint with the rogue, shoves Jesus and Judas equally aside.'

And what is stranger still, these Yankee philosophers differ from any in history; their system is a copy from no other; no sect or school is like them. They are called 'Transcendentalists;' but it will be found, when compared with the German 'Transcendentalists;' that they differ exceedingly. Far less vague and mystic in thought, and more fitted to reach the common mind, they are immeasurably above them, as it seems to us, in sincere devotion to truth and in the love of beauty. Their ideas are generally less healthy, less solemn, than those of the Carlyle school in England, while in a simple poetry, and in hopefulness for mankind, they are superior. The same difference will be found with the ancient philosophers. They have neither the allegorising spirit of Philo, nor the hopelessness of the Stoics, nor the religious tendencies of Plato; nor are they imbued with the self-submissive love of the later Christian mystics. They form a school by themselves; their system, though resembling in many points those of other ages, is original. It is the result of singular circumstances; the product of states of thought which could have arisen in no other age or nation. Our country, with all her inventions, has nothing more truly 'American' than this philosophy. And let no one suppose that these thinkers are a set of 'harmless dreamers.' Their influence, whatever may be thought of it, is certainly not negative. The teacher and leader of the school is Mr. Emerson; and we claim for him, and shall attempt to prove, something higher than the character of a mere dreaming mystic. We are aware that, with American thinkers, we are attempting a somewhat thankless task in defending Emerson; the laugh and the sneer and the parody have sounded too long against him to give much hope of a calm hearing. But reviewers and scholars should remember that this process has already been tried on a certain 'Transcendentalist' of England; that for years no man was so mimicked and laughed at and slashed by reviews; and yet it is beginning to be felt now that no thinker these last ten years has moulded earnest minds as Thomas Carlyle. It may be so with Emerson. Our critics too must bear in mind, that beyond all other peoples of the world this of the United States is affected, even in every day life, by abstract principles; and before they are aware of it, these 'dreams' of Emerson may be becoming realities through the mind of the nation. Systems have been uprooted and principles planted, before this, by weaker philosophies than Emerson's. We would not imply by this that all who condemn this philosophy do it through ignorance or prejudice. We know that there is much of it which might easily be misunderstood; much which, without its connection, is absurdity; and we grant with regret that there is much which most of us must sincerely condemn. But let us no longer laugh it down; let fair and just criticism be given it; and if there be evil, let it be met and reasoned away, and where there is good let it not be rejected because dressed in unusual language, or coming from a suspicious source.

The motto of the whole Emersonian system is the words 'I AM.' The grandeur, the awfulness of the soul; the exaltation of self. This stands out on every page. The greatness, the independence of the human will, is the idea which meets us every where; it is self which paints the varied beauty around us; self which curses or blesses us, here or hereafter; self which creates circumstances and fortune. Yes; GOD himself sometimes seems only the ideal reflection of this existence, the Mind. 'We believe in ourselves,' he says, 'as we do not believe in others. It is an instance of our faith in ourselves that men never speak of crime as lightly as they think; or every man thinks a latitude safe for himself which is nowise to be indulged to another.' Again: 'All private sympathy is partial. . . . Marriage (in what is called the spiritual world) is impossible, because of the inequality between every subject and

every object. . . . There will be the same gulf between every me and thee as between the original and the picture. The universe is the bride of the soul. . . . As I am, so I see. . . . Instead of feeling a poverty when we encounter a great man let us treat the new-comer like a travelling geologist who passes through our estate and shows us good slate or anthracite or lime-stone in our brush pasture. . . . They think society wiser than their soul, and know not that one soul and their soul is wiser than the whole world. See how nations and races flit by on the sea of time, and leave no ripple to tell where they floated or sank; and one good soul shall make the name of Moses or of Zeno or of Zoroaster reverend forever.' Then again, we have the old Stoic over again in his contempt for outward evil, his elevation above annoyance or sorrow. No suffering in this life, no future of pain, need bend this proud will.

While we recognise in much of this the language only of the philosophy which would reduce all outward appearances to the mind's mode of conceiving them; while we honor his attempt to convince men of their native nobleness, we do dissent from very much of it. It seems to us a cold and unsympathizing philosophy; it is very grand, but it is also very repulsive. He would make each human being an isolated, independent demi-god, instead of a weeping, laughing man, with a heart clinging in countless sympathies to every heart around him. Man was not made for independence; for this solitary self-worship. He was made to trust, to love, to depend; and we do believe that his highest nobleness, his greatest freedom, is found in subjection; subjection to what is right and true; his truest independence is in perfect dependence on HIM, the only self-supported. And for ourselves, we do doubt this much-vaunted strength of the human will. A head-ache will break it; sorrow or

200

poverty may crush it; it needs but a slight change in the bodily organs to loosen utterly its grasp over the mind. It is true, the soul can inflict a terrible punishment on itself, even here, and sometimes the strong will can set itself firmly 'against a sea of troubles;' but who will say it shall be so *beyond?*—who will dare say, when the mind whirls out into that dim void, a feather in the ceaseless tempest, that it can in any way direct itself? It is there, a feeble existence in the hands of Infinite Power; the knowledge which contrived its beautiful harmonies can as easily jar them to discords. Who can say what it shall brave then? Who, in such an untried life, will boast of that wavering, yielding will? Is not our truest course, after all, humility of self?

However cold this view of man's nature may seem, it is almost lost sight of in a certain *magnanimity* of sentiment, which to us throws an indescribable charm about all Emerson's writings. In this he is most original; there is no moralizer like him. One cannot avoid the conviction that a sincere, noble man is speaking out plainly his thoughts; thoughts which do not sound over-strained, as if too perfect for any human being to realize, nor 'sentimental,' as though the author were too amiable to be manly; nor do they smack of the essayist or philosopher; but they are manly, whole-souled sentiments, such as common men have to one another, but such somehow as books have quite failed to notice. It is like the dignity and simplicity of an Indian chief, speaking out in the tongue of civilized life. We see the soul of a *true man* opened to us, vigorous, stern, yet swelling with generous impulse and gentle affection; a man true in himself, and who demands plain truth from others; one who can clasp a friend to himself with all the deep love of man's heart, but who wants no sentimental talk or girlish dependence. He speaks of friendship, and you see it is

no boy's romance or pretty subject for an essay, with him. He has felt it; he has known the almost solemn delight when, after years of trial, the thought has settled on the mind that we have a *friend*; a man who without affectation loves us, who will deal plainly with us as with himself, who will stand by us through our follies and our sorrows; not dependent, but linked with us in the highest of all unions, a struggle for the same noble and grand ends. Friendship with him is no light thing; it is stern; it is religious: 'Not made of wine and dreams, but of the *tough fibre of the human heart.*' And we believe that in these essays he strikes at one great fault of American society—a fault often noticed by foreigners: the want of friendships between men and men. In Europe men of maturity and deed can unite in generous friendship for a life-time; the separation of a Fox and Burke could draw tears from an assembly of legislators; but what union often exists here between men of years except a dinner-union or business-partnership? Shall it be always so? But to return to our author. The same greatness, manliness of sentiment, we find expressed in all his analyses of the usages of society. Hear him on so common a subject as 'Gifts:'

["Gifts," 94.13–96.3]

The Essay on 'Manners' gives us a similar train of thoughts as he analyzes in a quite ingenious mode the opinions prevalent in polite society. Hear his definition of a 'Gentleman:'

["Manners," 73.11–16; 74.16–20, 32–33; 78.17-24]

The conclusion of it all thus is, that 'Every thing called fashion and courtesy humbles itself before the cause and fountain of honor, creator of titles and dignities, namely, the *heart of love:*'

It is high praise of any author, almost the highest, to say that he is an honest searcher for truth. Men who are odd for the sake of being odd, or independent for the fame of originality, are not so uncommon. But the simple, sincere lover of truth for truth's sake, is rare. When he does appear, mankind should meet him with their heartiest welcome. For after all our easy moralizing, what more difficult thing is there for a man than to be *true?* To break over the associations, endeared to him by long and pleasant memories, to find loosening from his heart, the sympathies and esteem of those he has been taught from childhood to respect; to expose himself to the quiet sneer or the settled dislike of men around him at his oddity; and worse than all, to have the awful fear gathering darkly over his soul that he may be losing the love of his GOD; all this perhaps must a man meet for truth. He who has done this, is no weak man. He deserves our honor. Yet it is very easy to forget this; it is very easy to forget, as a man stands up in simple humble spirit for his particular truth, what a weary course of darkness and struggling it may have cost him to win it. We believe Mr. Emerson has thus sought for truth. And more than this, we believe him striving, with all his varied powers, to raise his fellow men to this higher life of truth and spirituality. We know we are treading here near topics from which custom and cant have worn all their freshness. But we do believe every man, if asked plainly, with no whine of religious phrase, would acknowledge there was an infinitely higher life possible for him; would confess the meanness of the life he lives, compared to what he might live. Every one of us have had our moments of reflection, when the grandeur and beauty of a higher life floated before us. We have had some faint conception what it would be to live for noble and generous ends; to be free from this meanness and selfishness, which so chain mankind; to have a mind at length above these ever-clamoring appetites and passions. At such time, we saw the beauty and divine majesty of truth. We felt what the exalted consciousness would be, that within us not the slightest falseness harbored. We asked not for future happiness; but simply and with a trust in a higher, we gave up ourselves to live for human freedom and human happiness. All men have some such thoughts, whether these words express them or not. There are better moments in every man's life, nobler impulses than his common. And it is to these, in these volumes, Emerson so often speaks. He would show us how every-day life may at length be, what we have so often dreamed it. That it can be true, earnest, generous, though spent in the din of the market or quiet of the college. He tells us of a noble, spiritual life, which but few, with whatever professions, have ever realized. These sentiments of his are not Utopian; they are not impractical; unless christianity is Utopian, and to forget an endless life, is to be practical. They express what we all acknowledge as truth, but which we all hesitate to act upon; and must this always be so? Shall not the day come when men can realize all that Emerson, and all that a higher than Emerson, has pictured? Can we not, even in this day, resolve with him, that for our part we will make society a true and earnest thing, and no more an exchange of hypocrisies; that we will do away with every vestige of falseness in life or dealings; that for us, our days shall no more be given to appetite and selfishness, but to a life of love, to unchecked, fearless service of truth. To the scholar, he says:

'It becomes him to feel all confidence in himself, and to defer never to the popular cry. Let him not quiet his belief that a pop gun is a pop gun, though the ancient and honorable of the earth affirm it to be the crack of doom. In silence, in steadiness, in severe abstraction, let him hold by himself; add observation to observation, patient of neglect, patient of reproach; and bide his own time.'. . . 'Free should the scholar be, free and brave.'. . . 'It is a shame to him, if his tranquillity amid dangerous times arise from the presumption that like children and women, his is a protected class; or if he seek a temporary peace by the diversion of his thoughts from politics or vexed questions, hiding his head like an ostrich in the flowering bushes, peeping into microscopes and turning rhymes, as a boy whistles to keep his courage up.'

We commend his views of the pilgrims to some even of the more orthodox of their descendants at the present day:

'What a debt is ours to that old religion, which, in the childhood of most of us, still dwelt like a Sabbath morning in the country of New-England, teaching privation, self-denial and sorrow! A man was born not for prosperity, but to suffer for the benefit of others like the noble rock-maple, which all around our villages bleeds for the service of man. Not praise, not men's acceptance of our doing, but the spirit's holy errand through us, absorbed the thought. How dignified was this! How all that is called talents and success in our noisy capitals, becomes buzz and din before this man-worthiness!'. . . 'And what is to replace for us the piety of that race? We cannot have theirs: it glides away from us day by day, but we also can bask in the great morning which rises forever out of the eastern sea, and be ourselves the children of the light.'

We have said it was no easy matter to seek for truth as freely as Emerson has done. But in scarcely any country is it more difficult than in this. Our very equality of rights gives tremendous force to public opinion, and but few dare rise against it. The hootings of the mob are always more fearful than chains and prisons. A man may brace himself against mere persecution of power; but when the man by his side, his brother and messmate and friend, turn against him, who can face it? As a consequence, how few in this country think independently of all party organization! How bound up are we within our sects and our schools and our parties! Emerson must have seen this great fault of our people; and in this volume he has struck at it boldly and manfully; we doubt not his success. Our people do at least, after a course of years, acknowledge truth; and the bold, independent thinker, though his name be blackened now, shall not even here miss his reward. We think too we notice a change in this matter; the old boundary marks of creeds are being swept off; thought is freer. Even the popular taste in literature seeks the more earnest authors. Men are growing earnest, and they want true, hearty thinkers, no matter how many conventionalisms and elegancies they violate. Carlyle has a hundred times the influence of Macaulay; and Miss Bremer, Ruskin, and Jane Eyre are read, where James and Bulwer are scarcely heard of. In newspapers, it is your odd, honest, independent Greeley that thrills the farthest corner of the land with his thoughts, while 'leading journals,' with stately editorials, are dozed over most quietly. That Mr. Emerson's writings are crowded with faults, no fair reader can be disposed to deny; and yet we are inclined to think these have been much exaggerated; especially, let any one compare the earlier Essays with this volume of Addresses, and he will be surprised at the change for the better in these later writings. That which would most repel an earnest mind in the 'Essays,' is a certain unhealthiness of sentiment, an epicurean, skeptic-like view of life. We find him regarding all actions, whether noble or selfish, as equally indifferent; religion and happiness as results of a good state of liver; life itself is superficial and sickening; temperament governs every thing; and man is only a machine. But as we go on in his writings, a deeper and more earnest tone sounds through them. The skeptic is gone; and we see a man, solemn as under the shadow of eternity, with every power intensely strained to show to others the truth which so ennobles him. These 'Addresses' are strong, practical, earnest speeches; such as can reach the common mind of our American people. They treat of every-day matters; common political and moral questions. They are sermons on Economy, on Manliness, on Honesty, on Religious living; and they strike to the heart of these things, as few sermons we have seen. We give as an instance his views of Economy:

'Is our house-keeping sacred and honorable? Does it raise and inspire us, or does it cripple us instead?

'Our expense is almost all for conformity. It is for cake we run in debt; 't is not the intellect, not the heart, not beauty, not worship, that costs so much. . . . We are first sensual, and then must be rich. We dare not trust our wit for making our house pleasant to our friend, and so we buy ice-creams. . . . As soon as there is faith, as soon as there is society, comfits and cushions will be left for slaves. Expense will be inventive and heroic. . . . Let us learn the meaning of economy. Economy is a high, humane office, or sacrament, when its aim is grand; when it is the prudence of simple tastes; when it is practised for freedom, or love, or devotion. Much of the economy we see in houses is of a base origin, and is best kept out of sight. Parched corn eaten to-day, that I may have roast fowl for my dinner on Sunday, is a baseness; but parched corn and a house with one apartment, that I may be free of all perturbations; that I may be serene and docile to what the mind shall speak, and girt and road-ready for the lowest mission of knowledge or good-will, is frugality for gods and heroes.'

It may not be out of place here, also, to transcribe a little picture he draws of public worship:

'I once heard a preacher who sorely tempted me to say I would go to church no more. Men go, thought I, where they are wont to go, else had no soul entered the temple in the afternoon. A snow-storm was falling around us. The snow-storm was real; the preacher merely spectral; and the eye felt the sad contrast in looking at him and then out of the window behind him, into the beautiful meteor of the snow. He had lived in vain. He had no one word intimating that he had laughed or wept; was married or in love; had been commended, or cheated, or chagrined. If he had ever lived and acted, we were none the wiser for it. The capital secret of his profession, namely, to convert life into truth, he had not learned.... It seemed strange that the people should come to church. It seemed as if their houses were very unentertaining, that they should prefer this thoughtless clamor. It shows that there is a commanding attraction in the moral sentiment that can lend a faint tint of light to dullness and ignorance coming in its name and place.'

He deplores the 'decaying of the church,' as he calls it, and concludes: 'What greater calamity can fall upon a nation than the loss of worship? Then all things go to decay. Genius leaves the temple to haunt the senate or the market; Literature becomes frivolous; Science is cold. The eye of youth is not lighted by the hope of other worlds, and age is without honor.'

Mr. Emerson is frequently charged with inconsistency, and we certainly shall not attempt to deny it. We believe it the same inconsistency a man shows in an excited conversation. He takes one view of a subject; he is deeply moved by it; his words come forth strong and glowing; and yet an hour after we may find him arguing on a different side, and with honesty too. It is the inconsistency of excitement; the one-sided view of truth. We excuse it in a talker, but require something more complete in a writer. Still we are disposed to think, if authors were more honest, there would be far more inconsistency. Every man who *thinks* must be conscious of exceedingly different states of mind in regard to the same subjects. There are times when his metaphysical systems will melt away before his affections and hopes. There are others when Logic fixes the cold limits, and he cannot pass beyond them. At one time his deity seems hardly anything but lofty and eternal principles; at

another, he feels his heart close to a heart like his own, only infinite in its love and pity. Perhaps this is Emerson's self-contradiction.

No man should ever undertake to defend isolated expressions of Emerson's. A skilful culler from his writings could convict him of blasphemy and nonsense and obscurity, without the smallest difficulty. They must be taken in their connexion to appreciate their meaning. And when thus taken we venture to say that, with but few exceptions, they will convey a deep and true idea. His obscurity is singular. It is not in the use of strange or new conjoined words, like much of Carlyle's. His words are plain, strong, living Saxon. It is not, as we think, generally in vague thought, like much in the mystic writers. It seems rather to consist in abrupt, apparently isolated sentences, when in fact there is a true connexion; in figures, where the analogy is not at once clear, except to those accustomed to his style; in common words, which with him are signs of many qualities conjoined, or are particular words expressing general principles. Such an obscurity may be an objection, but it certainly is not without example in our best writers. An obscurity, too, which, unlike that in some of our 'best writers,' rewards investigation.

We do not deny, however, that there is in his writings an obscurity sometimes deeper than this. The analogies so favorite with him between matter and spirit seem not seldom to lead him into misty paths. A neat antithesis, too, occasionally throws a veil over the thought. And there are passages, beautiful in appearance, which no charitable construction or close study can in any way explain. We must conclude they are those vague sentiments, with misty outlines of beauty, which float through almost every mind. Mr. Emerson has had the frankness or the folly to express them. But however incomprehensible he is at times, all must allow the frequency in his works of those condensed expressions which contain such a world of truth. Vivid statements of wide-reaching principles, such as startle us so often in Shakspeare, or Goethe, or Richter. It is these compact forms of truth which last the longest in a language. Genius alone can frame them. Emerson has enriched our language with many. This we have said of his prose. Of his poetry we do not profess to judge. What little we have seen, we should not for a moment suspect to be from Emerson. We would speak diffidently; but if nonsense and utter *opaqueness* show a want of poetic talent, his poems can claim little. And yet there is hardly a page of his prose but shows the true poet. His love of beauty, his pure appreciation of nature, are wonderful. Not the thread-bare, worn-out descriptions of Nature; of flowing meads and purling streams, and sun-sets, and what not, which fill most writers, even poets; but a close, pure, loving observation of the thousand beauties around him. Hear him on this:

'Go into the forest, you shall find all new and undescribed. The screaming of the wild-geese flying by night; the thin note of the companionable titmouse, in the winter day; the fall of swarms of flies in autumn from combats high in the air, pattering down on the leaves like rain; the angry hiss of the wood-birds; the pine throwing out its pollen for the next century; the turpentine exuding from the tree; and, indeed, any vegetation, any animation, any and all are alike unattempted.'... Or again: 'The noon-day darkness of the American forests, the deep, echoing, aboriginal woods, where the living columns of the oak and fir tower up from the ruins of the trees of the last millennium; where from year to year the eagle and crow see no intruder; the pines, bearded with savage moss, yet touched with grace by the violets at their feet; the broad, cold lowland, which forms its coat of vapor with the stillness of subterranean crystallization; and where the traveller, amid the repulsive plants that are native in the swamps, thinks with pleasing terror of the distant town; this beauty, haggard and desert beauty, which the sun and the moon, the snow and the rain, repaint and vary, has never been recorded by art.'

The religious world generally, we suppose, look with suspicion even on Emerson's moral essays. And yet it will be found his moralizing rests to a certain extent on the truly christian basis. It is no outward, merely moral self-culture; no mere correcting of habits. The *Heart of Love* is his great theme. The purifying, the great principle of a man's life, is what he is ever urging. His political philosophy, too, is such as agrees remarkably with the (so-called) religious philosophy of the country. He would re-make society by infusing the higher principles: 'These beneficiaries (the reformers,') he says, 'hope to raise man by improving his circumstances; by combination of that which is dead they hope to make something alive. In vain;' and then he quotes the expression of the 'sad Pestalozzi:' 'The amelioration of outward circumstances will be the effect, but can never be the means of mental and moral improvement.' Then in another place, in regard to every experiment failing that has not the 'moral principle' within it, he concludes: 'The pacific Fourier will be as inefficient as the pernicious Napoleon.'

As we consider the whole style and philosophy of these writings, we are more and more struck with their peculiar originality. We doubt whether our literature has produced anything more truly native to it. Hitherto our authors have, for the most part, held before them some foreign model. Their expression and mode of thought have not been the natural fruit of this new soil. It is not so with Emerson. That rugged, energetic style of his, softened occasionally by gleams of wonderful beauty, could have had no model. It seems almost the reflection of the scenery in which he has lived; those gray granite hills, as they are gilded by autumn light or chequered by summer shadows. We have sometimes wondered whether much of this philosophy might not be a type of the future development of the national mind. There is just now peeping up through the American people a 'transcendentalism' not unlike that seen in these writings. A tendency to carry abstract ideas out into practical efforts; a worship of principles, of theories, no matter how impracticable at present they may seem. The ceaseless speculation, the fearless research of that philosophy, the exalting of the individual mind, yes, even the heartiness and bluntness it would infuse into society, we believe will all be traits of our national character, when it has at length had full play.

Thus far certainly our people have shown little of the love of beauty, or the devotion to truth which appear on almost every page of the Emersonian philosophy. The last is a worship which but few in any age can have courage to offer. Perhaps it shall be so with us. But in regard to the love of the beautiful, we do expect wonderful results in the future. No climate or country can show such varied and changing beauty as ours. No nation has yet appeared with such intense activity of mind. And when at length a more complete cultivation reaches every class; when the close observing power of our people, with its remarkable inventive faculty, are turned to objects of beauty, what should hinder the highest results? For our part, we expect throughout our people then a love of nature, a taste for art, higher even than any Emerson has yet shown; inasmuch as it shall be more genial and more purified by love of Him, of whom beauty is only the reflection.

Of Mr. Emerson's religious character we own we feel reluctant to speak. Not that it is out of place; for it can never be out of place in a frank and friendly manner to speak of an author's religious views; but because in an author of his peculiar modes of expression it is very difficult to determine his meaning on such subjects. The language of any original mind in regard to Deity and its religious hopes must be strange. Emerson's words may express so much more to himself than to us; possibly, too, his own thoughts may be no clearer than the terms which convey them. Still with all this, and with no wish to sound a religious alarm against him, or cram our theology upon him, we must say and say it sadly, that the highest principles of religion he seems utterly without. A God, living and personal, he does not recognize and does not love. We own it possible for a heart-felt devotion like his, to the principles of Truth and Justice and Love, to be as real worship of the unseen One, as the vague affection which most of us suppose to fill our minds. Possibly he may accept it as such. Yet the highest life of the soul, the love-confiding, overflowing to a Being, one who combines all these 'principles,' and who with boundless affection, *loves us*, is not there. With Emerson, God is the beauty which looks down to him from the solemn sunset, or the law which whirls the planets, or the thought which exalts and inspirits him. At times he seems some strange essence filling material nature. Then, he is the soul, or the soul is but emanation from Him, the universal principle of life.

We may judge harshly; and there are expressions in which Emerson seems bowing his very soul with unspeakable awe before a mysterious Creator. 'Of that ineffable Essence,' he says, 'He that thinks most, will say least.' Still that want of geniality and hearty love through all his writings; the little solemnity which, if we consider his works throughout, life seems to him to have its relation to an unbounded future; the few allusions to the infinite hopes for each individual man; the sad, unhealthy views expressed in a part of his writings, all seem to declare a mind not bound in affection to an invisible Father, or living for an awful existence beyond. How sadly in this he contrasts even with Carlyle! Bred under the shadows of a creed, which almost absorbed the individual in the Infinite One, he has deified the soul. It is infinite, and 'God is but a projection of it.' Living with men who would force upon all their own narrow definings of the mysterious One, he has rejected all conception of Him, and has made Him a vague and changing imagining.

There is a belief; no, not a belief, a *truth*, the most supporting, the most heart-satisfying, man has ever grasped. We almost hesitate to profane it with our description. Its divine import men have too nearly lost sight of in the incessant wranglings over it. Yet there have been many in every age and under various creeds, to feel it as the life of their life. It has been to them a sweet comfort, as they shrunk back appalled from the aspect of offended Deity. Without it, they could bow in fear and awe before the dread Omnipotent, but they could not *love*. We mean the truth, that through a human life of suffering and shame the unexplainable Being has revealed Himself, revealed his love, His pity, His more than human sympathies.

Of this truth, Emerson knows not. Christ to him is only the reformer; sincere; lovely, but with the defects and limitations of weak human nature. Those deep teachings, which it seems to us humanity has but feebly penetrated; those lofty Ideals toward which the ages have been fruitlessly struggling, he considers 'imperfect attempts,' steps only in that boundless progress before the human race.

We have spoken thus freely of Mr. Emerson's religious character. Possibly we may be wrong. Perhaps we should take as the best expression of his religious belief the noble sentiments strown so thickly through his writings. Yet we cannot avoid our conviction; we only hope the good may overbalance the evil. For ourselves we have never met Mr. Emerson. We live in another section of the country; we profess a different creed; yet, if this notice should ever meet his eye, we do offer the sincere gratitude of many whom he has never known, for the aid he has given them. His vivid, earnest thoughts have kept before them a higher and truer life, which they might reach. He has shown them one man who could think freely, though all men looked coldly upon him; one who appreciated a nobler and more generous code than the rules of polished life; one who, in all his words, and as we hear in his intercourse, is laboring to make society *real* and life *true*; something worthy of an earnest, true-minded man. For this they do heartily thank him.

As we thus set forth our view of Emerson's writings, we cannot better, in concluding, commend them to the American people than in his own words: 'Amid the downward tendency and proneness of things, when every voice is raised for a new road or another statute, or a subscription of stock, for an improvement in dress or in dentistry, for a new house or a larger business, for a political party or the

208

division of an estate, will you not hear one or two solitary voices in the land, speaking for thoughts and principles, not marketable or perishable?'

Checklist of Additional Reviews

Christian Register, 28 (29 September 1849), 155.
Holden's Dollar Magazine, 4 (November 1849), 698–9.
Godey's Lady's Book, 39 (December 1849), 484.

Representative Men

"Emerson's Representative
Men,"
Spectator [England],
23 (12 January 1850), 42

The distinction between Thomas Carlyle and his few followers is that which mostly exists between originals and imitations. However peculiar or discursive Carlyle may be, his principal subject is coherent, forming a definite whole and driving at a distinct object. If all of his successive works do not exhibit an advance upon their predecessors, (which we think they generally do,) they at least display variety; they are not mere repetitions. His followers, among whom Mr. Emerson is the most conspicuous, do not possess this coherence, or show much substantial improvement; doing, in fact, little more than repeat themselves. The diction, which with Carlyle is merely a mode, reflective of a cast of thought, or rather of a peculiar conception of ideas, is with Emerson a thing of itself, a substantive being. Hence Carlyle has a style, odd as it may be; Emerson's is more a mannerism than a style. Not the mannerism of habit, taste, or too much work, but a cultivated mannerism; a something which the writer not only sees but pronounces good. He not only moves in a rut, but makes the rut to move in.

As far as regards close and pointed expression, the present book may occasionally exhibit an improvement upon Mr. Emerson's former writings. In other respects it makes no advance, if indeed it does not fall back. Paradox, which formerly was confined to particular ideas, now extends to whole sections of the book; the views, if not the arguments, are often vague or unsatisfactory; and, except in certain passages, the composition seems to us rather inferior—there is effort without effect.

The idea of *Representative Men* seems to be derived from Carlyle's *Hero Worship*. But in Carlyle's book the conceptions were consistent, whatever might be thought of the logic. It may be denied that hero-worship is the good thing Mr. Carlyle represents it, or that the contemporary disposition to scrutinize heroes is so bad as he intimates. There is no doubt that Knox and Luther are hero-priests; that if there be such a thing as a hero-poet, Dante and Shakspere are the men; that Johnson, Rousseau, and Burns, are good enough representatives of hero-men of letters; that Mahomet, if we throw aside the idea of imposter, was a hero-prophet; and in short, as we remarked when noticing the book some nine years ago, Carlyle's heroes were selected with profound judgment or intuitive sagacity. Little of either is exhibited by Mr. Emerson in his "representative men": indeed, he seems to mistake his men; Napoleon does not represent "the man of the world," or, as the writer explains the title in his text, "the popular external life and aims of the nineteenth century." Bonaparte had little in common with the man of the world, the business, or the practical man. He wanted the caution, the coolness, the measure and moderation or wariness, which distinguish the members of that "tria juncta in una." As little did he represent the life or aims of the nineteenth century, even the portion of it contemporary with himself. Much as he hated the Jacobins, he was really the "child and champion of Jacobinism," with its reckless energy, its indifference to rights or agreements, its defiance of custom or precedent, and its daring because its ignorant audacity, which often procured its success, but insured its defeat when resolutely opposed. To all which qualities Bonaparte added a personal selfishness, that Jacobins do not always exhibit, and a childish vanity, which the party would have despised. Again, Shakspere, though undoubtedly a poet, was much more than a mere poet: he was a moral and social philosopher, a man of the world, and if not a statesman, the reader of statesmen. Spenser was a better representative of the "very poet." Shakspere, so far as he was bounded, represented the English character in its zenith of thought, action, and speculation. Goethe only represents the writer by a forced definition to make him fit Mr. Emerson's notions; and "the fit" is not a very good one, although made to order. Montaigne also represents the sceptic, under a definition on purpose; which first means an Epicurean, and then the beau ideal of a man of thought and action. The two other "representative men" are Plato, the philosopher,—though his philosophy was of an imaginative kind; and Swedenborg, "or the mystic."

It may be said that the fault indicated is mere error of opinion. This practical result, however, is produced. The introductory preface on the general subject is of necessity paradoxical, where it has any bearing upon the representative man; and the "character" itself is in a measure made subordinate to the writer's preconceived opinion. It is true that this cause does not operate so extensively as it might with a more logical genius; because Mr. Emerson does not always stick to his text even in exhibiting his man, while sometimes in the introduction or essay to each person, he goes away from it almost altogether. *Representative Men*, therefore, may be described as a series of what are called "characters," generally prefaced by an essay on the idea which the character is assumed to represent, and containing plenty of singular or paradoxical opinions clearly expressed; some of which are not very remarkable in thought or diction, and others possess great force and justness.

The following is one of these. It is taken from the introductory remarks to "Goethe, or the Writer," and may be called natural reporting.

["Goethe," 151.9–20]

There is more truth here than Mr. Emerson wots of. Nature records as much as is needful to be known; but there she stops, and does not over-record. Every falling drop may make its sculpture in the sand, (when it falls *upon* sand,) but it is obliterated as quickly as footsteps in snow. Peculiar circumstances alone preserve the scratches of the rolling rock, or the bones in the stratum, or the fern in the coal. To be preserved, these things must occur at remarkable epochs, which in fact they record; all the rest pass away. Mementoes of litterateurs!

The following passage is worth notice; not so much for the remark on Montaigne, as for the explanation of the grossness of the old writers.

["Montaigne," 93.25–94.1]

The best or at least the most informing paper is that on Swedenborg; whose
writings Mr. Emerson has been reading in
the English edition of his works, published
by the zeal of a disciple. Mr. Emerson, indeed, grossly exaggerates, as is his wont,
the merits of the mystical philosopher; but
this is neutralized by the manner in which
he is compelled to depict his subject's faults
and which faults are quite inconsistent
with the panegyric. The paper, however,
gives a succinct summary of Swedenborg's
life and character, and some notion of his
works and system. The following passage
is from the opening.

["Swedenborg," 53.4–21]

Review of *Representative Men,* Athenæum, 1160 (19 January 1850), 68–9

We suppose it is necessary for the race of
prophets to speak in symbols. The modern oracles are at least equal to the ancient in obscurity. From those old sounds
which issued from the cave of Trophonius
down to the voice which floats to us from
the savannahs of the West the same mysteries have been pronounced in all ages in
the same mysterious language. If the book
before us contain prophecies, they have
the appropriate quality of being unintelligible. Can any of our readers interpret
the following.—

> "Each man seeks those of different
> quality from his own, and such as
> are good of their kind; this is, he
> seeks other men and the *otherest*
> [!]. The stronger the nature, the
> more it is reactive. Let us have the
> quality pure. A little genius let us
> leave alone. A main difference be-
> tween men is whether they attend
> their own affairs or not. Man is the
> noble endogenous plant which
> grows like the palm from within
> outward. His own affair, though im-
> possible to others, he can open with
> celerity and in sport. It is easy to
> sugar to be sweet and to nitre to be
> salt."

Is this inspiration or folly? If the reader
understand or delight in it, there is a pleasure in store for him,—for the first three
of Mr. Emerson's lectures contain a good
deal more to match. This unintelligibility
is a thing to be seriously lamented in a

writer who has a vein of pure and original thought underlying his verbal phantasies. The oracle might with advantage take to heart one of his own lessons. Every thought, Mr. Emerson says, which is clearly conceived can be clearly expressed. We think so too.

Of the last four lectures in this volume we can speak in terms of higher praise. The rhapsodies on "The Uses of Great Men," on "Plato," and on "Swedenborg," are for the most part out of our region. Even when we fancy we understand the oracle—and we are rarely certain of that —we can seldom accept its dogmas. With "Montaigne," with "Shakspeare," with "Napoleon," and with "Goethe" we are more at home:—our guide is also more at home, and all the better for it. What he sees clearly he expresses well, and with the freshness and energy of an unworn mind.

The idea of this series of lectures is a good one; though there are of necessity exceptions to be taken to the way in which it is realized. The idea is, to expose the course, the varieties, of human life, as exhibited in the world's great men. The subject is one of vast dimensions. Every great race which has contributed its quota to civilization—every great system of theology or philosophy—should send a representative to such a congress. All actions, all ideas should find exposition. The biographies, so to speak, of art, of morals, of legislation should be given. But as on a canvas necessarily limited only a few figures can be drawn,—then comes in the difficulty of selection. What are the greatest elements of man, of society, of civilization? Those chosen by Mr. Emerson for exposition are,—Philosophy, Mysticism, Doubt, Poetry, Action, Culture. Many will deny that these things adequately represent the living world. Faith is omitted, though "Doubt" has a place, in the category. Love is away. Mysticism is there,—

but no place is found for Religion. The category is at least defective. Countries are ill represented. Rome and Palestine ought surely to have had representatives. Nor are the men themselves free from objection. If the six "foremost men of all this world" are to be marked off, Plato and Shakspeare would of course be retained; but would Swedenborg, Montaigne, or Goethe? Many sound objections might be taken to Mr. Emerson's plan:— but let us rather pass on to consider what has been done.

Mr. Emerson has a cordial love for "old Montaigne;" a love which leads him to assign a greater importance to the "skeptic" than he stands for in history. We share this weakness too far ourselves not to feel an interest in the story of how the prophet became acquainted with the writings of the unbeliever.—

["Montaigne," 92.15–93.8]

Prefixed to the essay on Montaigne is a quaint account of what might be called the sceptical element in man's mind and in society; from which we will transcribe a passage.—

["Montaigne," 86.37–88.14]

And again.—

["Montaigne," 89.27–90.20]

In all these facts and inferences Mr. Emerson finds the historical basis for the sort of scepticism which he brings Montaigne forward to represent.

Of Shakspeare and Napoleon—poetry and action—Mr. Emerson has a number of pointed and epigrammatic things to say,—but little that is novel. The ground was pre-occupied. Coming after Coleridge and Channing, a writer, be he prophet or proser, will have no easy task if he undertake to fix attention by mere speculation and ingenious rhetoric. Yet these essays abound in picturesque passages;

and the "Shakspeare" contains more than one paragraph which might be advantageously added to the notes in a Variorum edition of the poet.—We add a character of Goethe, by way of conclusion.

["Goethe," 163.17–164.14, 165.14–23]

We have said and quoted enough to show that this is not an ordinary book. It is remarkable as a suggestion of what its author *may* do hereafter when he descends from his tripod and walks the common earth. The true ore is in this American:— its uses ought not to be lost to mankind through a fantastic and wayward fancy for wasting it in unsubstantial filagree work.

Review of *Representative Men*, *Critic* [England], n.s. 9 (1 February 1850), 59–61

There can be no question that Emerson is an imitator of Carlyle, but not more so than Carlyle is himself an imitator of certain of the German philosophers. Carlyle's style is a representation of his mode of thought: so is Emerson's; but it is impossible not to see a marked similarity of the one to the other, both in thought and style, and of both to the German school of metaphysicians. But as Carlyle is not merely an imitator of his German predecessors, but rather a pupil of their school, so is not Emerson a mere imitator of Carlyle but rather a disciple, who has caught his inspiration from his master, and gives utterance in his phraseology to his own ideas, the creations of his own brain. It has been asserted by a contemporary (*The Spectator*), that "Carlyle has a style, odd as it may be; Emerson's is more a mannerism than a style. Not the mannerism of habit, taste or too much work, but a cultivated mannerism; a something which the writer not only sees but pronounces good. He not only moves in a rut, but makes the rut to move in."

This does not justice to Emerson. He has a mannerism, it is true, but it is precisely the kind of mannerism seen in Carlyle. The difference between a style and a mannerism we take to be simply this, that a style is an original creation of a mind expressing itself in a peculiar form: a mannerism is a borrowed style, it is the mode of expression *adopted* by the writer, and not inborn with him. Carlyle's style is not his own invention, but taken from the German: Emerson's is not his own, but borrowed partly from the German and partly from Carlyle. We do not so much admire the manner of Emerson as we do that of Carlyle, for it is less picturesque, more abstract, more *affected*: but neither can lay claim to the honour of originality.

In this volume, however, Emerson has certainly done more than imitate Carlyle's manner: he has copied his theme and its general treatment. The idea of Emerson's *Representative Men* was borrowed from Carlyle's *Hero Worship*. Carlyle sought for heroes according to his notion of the heroic, and having found those whom he deemed the greatest of certain classes of mind, he depicted them with wonderful force of description:—they live and move upon his pages. Emerson in like fashion searches after types of mind—men, representatives of classes—impersonations of ideas. Thus, Napoleon as "the man of the world," represents or typifies "the popular external life, and aims of the nineteenth century." Shakspere represents the poet: Goethe, "the writer," Montaigne, "the sceptic;" Plato, "the philosopher;" and Swedenborg, "the mystic."

Mr. Emerson's plan is to sketch each of these characters, prefacing each with a short essay on the character so represented, and which affords him an opportunity for indulging in the strange sort of mysticism that he probably imagines to be philosophy, but which, to others, appears very much like nonsense—words substituted for thoughts, and the unintelligible mistaken for the profound. When, however, Emerson keeps within his depth, he scatters about him a great deal of true wisdom, mingled with much genuine poetry, which will rescue his works from oblivion, and which makes them more popular, even now, than philosophy is usually found to be, in this age of materialism. There is also a merit in him which it would be un-grateful not to acknowledge; he has made others think: he has directed the minds of thousands to loftier exercises than they had known before; he has stimulated the reflective faculties of multitudes, and thus led to inquiry and inquiry will certainly conduct to truth. The difficulty is, to set men a thinking; this once done, half the work of human progress is accomplished. It will be Emerson's boast that he has more powerfully contributed to this intellectual movement of his generation, than any man of his time, Carlyle excepted.

Representative Men is much less mystical than his later works. It must have been observed how steadily Emerson had been progressing in indistinctness of idea and of expression, since his first essays attracted the attention of the world. We had been almost inclined to hope no more from him. This volume, however, proves that he is not yet irrecoverable. There is more common sense and practical wisdom to be found in it, than in any of the books he has given to the world, since his first. It is in parts that it is interesting, and its worth can be best exhibited to the reader by selections of passages, having each an intrinsic excellence.

Emerson is not such a hero-worshipper as Carlyle. He rather wants faith in heroes. He would substitute faith in humanity for faith in persons; man for individuals. Thus he argues for

["Uses of Great Men," 3.4–4.4]

He traces the

["Uses of Great Men," 18.8–33]

Thus he introduces his sketch of Swedenborg, whose writings have evidently made an impression upon him, at which we are not surprised, for Emerson is already half a mystic.

["Swedenborg," 53.4–21]

He prefixes to his essay on Montaigne,

215

a sketch of the sceptical element in the human mind, which remarkably exhibits his peculiar manner of composition.

["Montaigne," 85.4–89.3]

This is a long extract, but it is full of truth, well spoken. In a still loftier strain is his illustration of the maxim, that partial evil is universal good. However despondingly we may view the events within our narrow ken, we find invariably that the whole result is for good. This should produce in us a more cheerful, hopeful, charitable spirit.

["Montaigne," 104.18–105.7]

We conclude with an assertion that startles us, because it is so different from our wonted belief. But we would not pronounce it unsound, without giving to it long and serious consideration; and we commend it to our reader's reflections—to pronounce, aye or nay, is Emerson right in his assertion that "great men are more distinguished by range and extent, than by originality."

Review of *Representative Men,* *Literary World,* 6 (9 February 1850), 123–4

We are inclined to think this Mr. Emerson's best work; and that because in it he is most *objective*. He distracts us less than usual with his visionary, metaphysical, ethical, religious theories, and consoles us with more common sense, with a kind of dramatic power. He seats himself at the centre of another man's intellect, and thence illuminates it for our vision. We think that he shows himself an adept at intellectual characterization; but we doubt, after all, his ability to determine the right ethical value of human characters, and that because his own ethical theory is something low, fallacious (notwithstanding the fine words), and ultimately subversive of itself. Its tendency exhibits itself by bits here and there in this work, quite openly. It is marching on to its inevitable conclusion. Else what means such a passage as this:—"the Divine effort is never relaxed: the carrion, in the sun, will convert itself to grass and flowers; and man, though in brothels or jails, or on gibbets, is on his way to all that is good and true."

Now without speaking of the ground for the seemingly lofty theory of Providence from which such a passage as this could spring, we beg our readers to think, for a moment, of the consequences, could mankind be brought to believe this corollary. A fine world we should have of it surely! plenty of remorse for crime! and noble efforts for self-amelioration! Yet these are but the logical consequences of the stoicism of the nineteenth century. Indeed, this theory of "self-reliance," with however fine principles it may start, must necessarily result, to be self-consistent, in moral indifference.

As far, then, as a man's judgment can be worthy with this "dead fly" in his heart, we are disposed to give all praise to these specimens of Mr. Emerson's ability, to give a right intellectual and aesthetical valuation.

The equilibrium of the Eastern and Western intellect, of the Infinite and finite element, of the tendencies to unity and to multiplicity, to religion and to culture, in *Plato*, and his mental strength and opulence, are clearly and poetically exhibited, and could hardly be reproduced in fewer words. Plato's defect is—first, that

["Plato," 42.29–37, 43.5–14]

The portrait of Socrates is admirable;—

["Plato," 40.9–18, 41.10–28]

And much more on the same topic quite as good. Mr. Emerson brings a deal of enthusiasm to the consideration of Swedenborg, but we think the following estimate not far from just:—

["Swedenborg," 70.4–13]

Mr. Emerson shows that Swedenborg's Revelations of the other world destroy their own credit, by their running into inconsistent details;—

["Swedenborg," 79.18, 29–32]

Swedenborg was no poet.

["Swedenborg," 80.21–26, 32–35]

The doctrine of "Correspondence," or that the material universe is one vast and perfect type of that which is spiritual, of which every thoughtful and at the same time poetic mind has now and then, suspected the truth, was, according to Mr. Emerson, made much of by Swedenborg,

and might have been made more but for the exclusive theologic direction which his inquiries took. This is true undoubtedly, but what was "the vice of his mind" was an honor to his heart. The gravest fault of his intellect, according to Mr. Emerson, was that he could not ignore the fact that God had indeed spoken revelations into the world; that he could not from some grand, lofty, catholic, stand-point, look down upon Judaism and Christianity as in the same level with the other religions of the earth. Happy elevation! which Voltaire, and Strauss, and other honored ones have attained! Indeed, how dull-eyed must that philosophy be which can overlook the most stupendous fact which the world has witnessed, which cannot but be scrutinized by him who would bring forth the soul from the world's entire history!

The character of the sceptic, of which Montaigne is the representative, emerges from the contrast of the mental dispositions, of which one looks to the sensation side of every fact to the Finite and Apparent, producing men of talent and action; and the other to the moral and spiritual side, to the Infinite and Real, producing men of faith and philosophy, men of genius. Contempt for the first species, and indifference to the last, with a wise determination to make the most of life, without troubling one's self with chimeras of any kind, is that species of scepticism to which is devoted the paper upon Montaigne.

The lecture upon Shakspeare is admirable as the rest, yet contains nothing very unlike what has already been written on that exhaustless topic. But in giving the great poet his ultimate valuation, our author is just and impartial, and

["Shakespeare," 124.1–4, 10–12, 14–27; 124.32–125.5]

Napoleon is painted as the representation of the Democratic element, whose

217

"tendency is material, pointing at a sensual success, and employing the richest and most various means to that end: conversant with mechanical powers, highly intellectual, widely and accurately learned and skilful, but subordinating all intellectual and spiritual forces into means to a material success."

Because, then, he had precisely the same aims with the mass, and possessed such talent and energy that he was able to succeed in the same, therefore was he the idol of this class of mankind. "Napoleon renounced, once for all, sentiments and affections, and would help himself with his hands and his head. . . . He is never weak and literary, but acts with the solidity and the precision of natural agents. . . . Men give way before such a man, as before natural events.

Add to all this his immense physical vigor, and we have the ideal of the Democracy. For ever will it throw itself into the arms of absolutism and be obsequious, and find its ideal thus realized, in a Napoleon. It was because the common obstacles to a purely selfish aim, moral or religious restraints, natural affection, were no obstacles to him, that his energy was so exhaustless and his success so certain. Of course, a success, without moral principle, could not be permanent, and the author justly concludes:—"Every experiment, by multitudes or by individuals, that has a sensual and selfish aim, will fail. The pacific Fourier will be as inefficient as the pernicious Napoleon."

Not unlike the character of Napoleon is that of Goethe; their objects only were unlike. One pursued physical dominion, the other knowledge for the sake of himself; and both were unscrupulous as to the means. Goethe was quite as little swayed by affection, or ruled by the usual sentiment, as Napoleon. Monarchs were they both, but in different realms.

["Goethe," 163.17–30]

A character more selfish and despicable could not be painted. Indeed, there is something demoniac about both Napoleon and Goethe as here represented, and Mr. Emerson's portraits are flattering enough.

218

C[yrus] A. B[artol]., "Representative Men," *Christian Examiner*, 48 (March 1850), 314–18

Mr. Emerson's writing has a bold beauty that wins or arrests attention. He is one of the most notable and brilliant of American authors. In a sublime discontent with what exists, he aspires beyond all mediocrity of achievement. He takes the most adventurous positions, maintaining them by force, not of logic, or any method of philosophy, but by a defying statement and a soaring imagination. It is hard to pass critical sentence on him, for the subtilty of his mind abjures all system, and gives no bond of consistency. He is not so much a seer steadily beholding the globe of truth with the clear intuition of a capacious mind, as a watcher, catching occasional bright glimpses of spiritual realities, and opening upon us lightning-flashes of startling conjecture, rather than the calm noonday of wisdom. There is no waxing power or widening stream in his progress through a subject, no vast gain from the combination of arguments, no Greek phalanx from closely ordered thoughts, but he is throughout aphoristic and oracular. His intellectual life seems interrupted in its circulation, his pulse of feeling intermits, and when we try to survey his whole drift, we are stopped, as in gazing at those crystals in which the shining laminæ run in cross and faulty directions. In the midst of his discussions, masterly and original in their single points, we look back, at a loss, like a man with a vague clew in the centre of a labyrinth. He is not self-forgetful and inspired, but intensely conscious in his mood, and, though a celestial current sets into his soul,

the tide never rises so as to carry away him and his reader on a common swell of excitement. He gathers no heat to kindle or speed to quicken us, but, with cold finish, jots down each separate perception, thus making a book, which is no organization, like a living body or a plant, but a cabinet of gems. He constrains our admiration, stings us with suggestions, shocks us with audacious assertions, fills our mouth with quotations, and confuses us among the multiplied threads of his tangled skein, but stirs not our hearts, moves us to no self-surrender of sympathy, never brings us upon the knees of prayer, nor draws from us a single tear. It is a delight to peruse him, but no gain to our own creative power. He sings a siren melody, which debilitates more than it strengthens our capacity for individual meditation. The soul is not strong and nimble for effort after a large draught of his nectar, but often stupefied or overwrought as with a narcotic. He furnishes a marvellous entertainment to our faculties, to be jealously and sparingly used. He has not the characteristic of the greatest genius, that he emancipates us from himself, and tempts forth our original ability. Yet it is not easy by any analysis to detect and tell the essence of his bewitching singularity. His composition is a riddle, which contradictory solutions equally fit. He defends no distinct ground, abides by no definable opinion, nor, like the great creators in the metaphysical sphere, courts any comparison, or holds himself amenable to any jurisdiction of human judgment. He swears by nothing but his right to say and gainsay any thing. He will be free of the universe, and from his bravest sally runs with Cossack-retreat into the wilderness, to appear from his abyss, perhaps, in an opposite direction. One of his most marked traits is generalization, to such excess as to call evil good, and bitter sweet. He breathes at altitudes where others cannot live, cultivating and subsisting on mountain shrubs and flowers, but rarely seen among the corn and wheat of the plain and valley. There is more loss than gain in this ascension above human life. Love grows cold and the moral sense dies in the insatiable generality of a speculation ambitious to take God's place at the centre, and look knowingly abroad through the universe of being. Individual objects and persons disappear in the haze of distance and doubt, and the greatest human achievements, the splendors of worth and faculty, vanish before this sublimated vision. Yet, from these excursions he so loves, Mr. Emerson is drawn back by the topic of the present work. There is in biography a disinterestedness counteractive of the egotism of knowledge and the conceit of discovery. We have wonderful force and felicity mixed with dubious dicta in some of these delineations, in which the pencil is courageously tried upon such men as Plato, Socrates, Swedenborg, Montaigne, Shakspeare, Napoleon, Goethe. Nothing, for instance, could be finer than the portrait, in the lecture on Plato, of Socrates,—but that we are tormented with the query, whether it is not partly mistaken and imaginary, and desirous to call in the sober narrator, with his desire for plain truth, to correct the idealism of the artist. The simplifying, generalizing, shaping faculty appears too much, to allow quite the look of accuracy, or leave place for the variety of nature. We miss the internal evidence of artless records, and the peculiar charm of a speaking likeness. Probably no lover of any one of these great men would be satisfied with the picture given, and those thoroughly acquainted with the persons might say, that the characters had been rather uncertainly touched and imperfectly sketched, than judicially weighed and fairly comprehended. There is no feebleness in the drawing: the limner has a decided

hand: but a man may be as hardy at a guess as in the unquestionable veracity of his facts. A fatal certainty of justice and instinct for truth, the rare gifts of some men, do not seem always to get the better of our author's talent for hypothesis, and to overrule the prepossessions of his fancy. Still, we are glad to acknowledge, nothing of the biographic sort lately published has so stimulated, if not fully satisfied us, or is so likely to interest the public mind. People like to gaze through blue and green lenses as well as through colorless glass, and yield their minds to "the tricks of strong imagination," as they would try their nerves with magnetism or a draught of exhilarating gas. Without precisely ascertaining, as with perfect surety of conviction we cannot, how far the present biographer *supposes*, and how far he rigidly *describes*, we will gladly, if only in gratitude for our enjoyment, confess the magic of the brush he dips in these finer hues of words, and the scarcely equalled magnificence of his gallery. Historic doubts will last as long as any other skepticism, and, while even prosaic annalists dispute what is in any case the correct account, we will thank even him who romances or puts high tone on his canvas for all his unfolding of our higher susceptibilities and perceptions.

Mr. Emerson's incidental allusions to Christianity betray the already mentioned defect of his mind,—its restless struggle to reach broader classifications and reduce all things to ever lower terms, till the life of all is destroyed, and the spirit evaporated in the process. When he says that the "moral sentiment carries innumerable Christianities, humanities, divinities, in its bosom," we know not whether to admire most the cool, brief handling with which he despatches mighty problems in a breath and a moment of time, or the disrespect he casts upon the greatest minds; all of which, of the first order, without an exception, throughout the Christian era, have come to a different conclusion. He might as well declare, that the sensation of his skin carries in it the sun, moon, stars, and all the host of heaven. Or, when he says, "We too must write Bibles," we must think the promise, notwithstanding all our literature, easier than the achievement, and are tempted to answer, "Let not him that girdeth on his harness boast himself as he that putteth it off." He must speak less to the speculative faculty and to a mere poetic taste, must attain to greater transparency and breadth of views, and go down deeper into the wants of the human heart, among the sources of emotions and springs of life, before he can even chord with the old Bible, much less produce a new. The pantheism which asserts that "man, though in brothels, or jails, or on gibbets, is on his way to all that is good and true," is not likely to regenerate the world so effectually as will the New Testament. Could some of Mr. Emerson's principles get into the heads of bad and passionate men, or their passions into his own, the principles would work mischief enough. But, clad in mystic folds, and guarded with electric light, they may be safe, locking up or neutralizing their own bane. He has surely, with all we should count unsound, great qualities, genuineness, sincerity, magnanimity, a lustrous robe for every thought, a diamond-glitter on every sentence. Yet the deductions we have to make from the matter must be also suffered by the form of his productions. His single words and phrases shine and dazzle with poetic fire. But his paragraphs and pages do not fill the soul with great and ever-enlarging conceptions. There are writers, perhaps without the advantage of gorgeous imagery or the continual gleam of metaphor, whose simple and obvious terms of speech at first neither delight nor astonish, but yet, as we read passage after passage as

though they were the little measuring-rods of the celestial city, introduce vast ideas into our mind, stretching our faculties for their accommodation, swelling our hearts, moistening our lids, inspiring our tongues, and nerving our hands for duty. As rows of lamps flaming upon each other and shedding blended illumination all around, so their words proceed. We cannot, in the present case, award this highest praise of authorship. But though we may not regard Mr. Emerson as a great teacher and prophet of the race, there is a height of manhood in himself and in his works which requires us to mingle reverence and affection even with the exceptions of our blame. Meanness of thought, word, or act is far from him. Simplicity and elevation of purpose distinguish him. Generosity of aim runs through his worst deviations, and few are more sincere in their spirituality, or so innocent in their untruth. Behind all the strokes of his pen, beneath the shifting of his opinion, and glitter of his illustration, and immovable as the rock under the phantasmagoria and dream-land of his speculations about society, life, government, and all human conventions, are the solid principles of practical integrity and of a purity shrinking from every stain. His spirit is the corrective of his intellectual aberrations, and should be drunk by his disciples as the antidote to what is ill in his doctrines. He will not be widely a mover of mankind, but will powerfully affect a small circle of peculiar mental constitution and tendency, which is always in the world, and may own him as a leader for ages. He has been an influence in the community, and has wrought great good by many of his appeals. We fear not even his errors, we love his nobleness, we honor his integrity, we would emulate his candor, we respect him equally in our agreement and our opposition, and, though our notice of him now has been only critical, we think that, writing as he

221

has in this book about Napoleon and Shakspeare, he must speak benedictions to the world spite of his mistakes.

Review of *Representative Men,* Graham's Magazine, 36 (March 1850), 221–2

The subjects of these lectures, originally delivered before New England Lyceums, are Uses of Great Men; Plato, or the Philosopher; Swedenborg, or the Mystic; Montaigne, or the Skeptic; Shakspeare, or the Poet; Napoleon, or the Man of the World; and Goethe, or the Writer; subjects calculated to test the most various powers of the greatest mind, and, as treated by Mr. Emerson, appearing always in an original and fascinating, if not always a true light. The volume we consider, on the whole, the best of Mr. Emerson's works. It is not, rhetorically speaking, so carefully written as his "Essays," but it has more human interest, deals more generously with facts, and indicates a broader and more stalwart individuality. It is certainly one of the most fascinating books ever written, whether we consider its subtle verbal felicities, its deep and shrewd observation, its keen criticism, its beautiful mischievousness, its wit or learning, its wisdom or beauty. The best passages may be found in the lectures on Plato, Shakspeare, and Swedenborg; but the best lecture is probably that on Montaigne, which must have been written *con amors*. Indeed, the author seems a kind of Montaigne-Plato, with his eyes wide open both to material and spiritual facts, without a hearty self-surrender to either. There are in the volumes some speculative audacities which, in common with the rest of the human race, we consider equally erroneous and hurtful. In matters of religious faith it may be confidently asserted that mankind is right and Mr. Emerson wrong. Our author puts objectionable doctrines in language which shocks the minds of his readers without conveying to them his real ideas—a blunder, equally as regards prudence and expression.

The excellence of the book is not so much in its representations of the representative men who form its subjects, as in the representation of Mr. Emerson himself; and we doubt if, in all literature, there are revealed many individualities so peculiar, and so powerful in its peculiarity, as the individuality stamped upon every page of the present volume. We would not presume, in our limits, to attempt an analysis of an intellect so curiously complex as Mr. Emerson's—with traits which strike us as a Parthian's arrows, shot while he is flying, and which both provoke and defy the pursuit of criticism; but we will extract instead, a few of the beautiful and brilliant sentences which are inserted, like gems, in almost every lecture, and in each of which some sparkle of the writer's quality appears. The lecture on Goethe is a perfect diamond necklace, shooting out light in every direction, with some flashes that illumine, for the instant, labyrinths of thought which darkness is considered to hold as exclusively her own.

In speaking of the acting of Shakspeare's plays, he translates into words an emotion which every one has felt, but which we never dreamed could be perfectly expressed. "The recitation," he says, "begins; one golden word leaps out immortal from all this painted pedantry, and *sweetly torments us with invitations to its own inaccessible homes.*" Again, he remarks that Shakspeare is inconceivably wise; all other writers conceivably. "A good reader," he says, "can, in a sort, *nestle into Plato's brain*, and think from thence; but not into Shakspeare's. *We are still out of doors.*" Speaking of Montaigne's use of language, he exclaims, "but these words, and they would bleed; they are vascular and alive." Of Mr. Emerson's peculiar wit the present volume is full of Examples. Thus he speaks of "the heaven of law, and the pismire of performance under it;" of Plato as having "clapped copyright on the world;" of the possibility, as regards marriage, of dividing the human race into two classes; "those who are out and want to get in, and those who are in and want to get out;" but quotation of small sentences is impertinent, where so many paragraphs are thoroughly pervaded with the quality.

In speaking of Plato's mind, Mr. Emerson gives us some of his keenest and most characteristic sentences—sentences in which the thought seems to go in straight lines right at the mark, but to lack a comprehension of relations. In Plato, he says, "the freest abandonment is united with the precision of a geometer. His daring imagination gives him the more solid grasp of facts; as the birds of the highest flight have the strongest alar bones. . . . His strength," he says, a few pages after, "is like the momentum of a falling planet; and his discretion, the return of its due and perfect curve." Perhaps the best passage, however, in the lecture on Plato, is that in which he describes the divine delirium, in which the philosopher rises into the seer. "He believes that poetry, prophecy, and the high insight, are from a wisdom of which man is not master; that the gods never philosophize; but, by a celestial mania, these miracles are accomplished. Horsed on these winged steeds, he sweeps the dim regions, visits worlds which flesh cannot enter; he saw the souls in pain; he hears the doom of the judge; he beholds the penal metempsychosis; the Fates, with the rock and shears; *and hears the intoxicating hum of their spindle.*"

Sentences, bright and beautiful as these,

might be extracted from this volume to such an extent as to bring upon us an action for violating the copyright. For fineness of wit, imagination, observation, satire and sentiment, the book hardly has its equal in American literature; with its positive opinions we have little to do. With respect to these, it may be generally said, that Mr. Emerson is always beneath the surface, and never at the centre.

[Theodore Parker], "The Writings of Ralph Waldo Emerson," *Massachusetts Quarterly Review*, 3 (March 1850), 200–55[1]

When a hen lays an egg in the farmer's mow, she cackles quite loud and long. "See," says the complacent bird, "see what an egg I have laid!" all the other hens cackle in sympathy, and seem to say, "what a nice egg has got laid! was there ever such a family of hens as our family?" But the cackling is heard only a short distance, in the neighboring barnyards; a few yards above, the blue sky is silent. By and by the rest will drop their daily burthen, and she will cackle with them in sympathy—but ere long the cackling is still; the egg has done its service, been addled, or eaten, or perhaps proved fertile of a chick, and it is forgotten, as well as the cackler who laid the ephemeral thing. But when an acorn in June first uncloses its shell, and the young oak puts out its earliest shoot, there is no noise; none attending its growth, yet it is destined to last some half a thousand years as a living tree, and serve as long after that for sound timber. Slowly and in silence, unseen in the dim recesses of the earth, the diamond gets formed by small accretions, age after age. There is no cackling in the caverns of the deep, as atom journeys to its fellow atom and the crystal is slowly getting made, to shine on the bosom of loveliness, or glitter in the diadem of an emperor, a thing of beauty and a joy forever.

As with eggs, so is it with little books, when one of them is laid in some bookseller's mow, the parent and the literary

224

barnyard are often full of the foolishest cackle, and seem as happy as the ambiguous offspring of frogs, in some shallow pool, in early summer. But by and by it is again with the books as with the eggs; the old noise is all hushed, and the little books all gone, while new authors are at the same work again.

Gentle reader, we will not find fault with such books, they are as useful as eggs; yea, they are indispensable; the cackle of authors, and that of hens—why should they not be allowed? Is it not written that all things shall work after their kind, and so produce; and does not this rule extend from the hen-roost to the American Academy and all the Royal Societies of Literature in the world? Most certainly. But when a great book gets written, it is published with no fine flourish of trumpets; the world does not speedily congratulate itself on the accession made to its riches; the book must wait awhile for its readers. Literary gentlemen of the tribe of Bavius and Mævius are popular in their time, and get more praise than bards afterwards famous. What audience did Athens and Florence give to their Socrates and their Dante? What price did Milton get for the Paradise Lost; how soon did men appreciate Shakspeare? Not many years ago, George Steevens, who "edited" the works of that bard, thought an "Act of Parliament was not strong enough" to make men read his sonnets, though they bore the author up to a great height of fame, and he sat where Steevens "durst not soar." In 1686, there had been four editions of Flatman's Poems; five of Waller's; eight of Cowley's; but in eleven years, of the Paradise Lost only three thousand copies were sold; yet the edition was cheap, and Norris of Bemerton went through eight or nine editions in a quite short time. For forty-one years, from 1623 to 1664, England was satisfied with two editions of Shakspeare, making, perhaps, one thousand copies in all. Says Mr. Wordsworth of these facts: "There were readers in multitudes; but their money went for other purposes, as their admiration was fixed elsewhere." Mr. Wordsworth himself, furnishes another example. Which found the readiest welcome, the Excursion and the Lyrical Poems of that writer, or Mr. Macaulay's Lays of Ancient Rome? How many a little philosophist in Germany went up in his rocket-like ascension, while the bookseller at Königsberg despaired over the unsaleable sheets of Immanuel Kant!

Says an Eastern proverb, "the sage is the instructor of a hundred ages," so he can afford to wait till one or two be past away, abiding with the few, waiting for the fit and the many. Says a writer:

"There is somewhat touching in the madness with which the passing age mischooses the object on which all candles shine, and all eyes are turned; the care with which it registers every trifle touching Queen Elizabeth, and King James, and the Essexes, Leicesters, Burleighs, and Buckinghams; and lets pass, without a single valuable note, the founder of another dynasty, which alone will cause the Tudor dynasty to be remembered,—the man who carries the Saxon race in him by the inspiration which feeds him, and on whose thoughts the foremost people of the world are now for some ages to be nourished, and minds to receive this and not another bias." A popular player,—nobody suspected he was the poet of the human race; and the secret was kept as faithfully from poets and intellectual men, as from courtiers and frivolous people. Bacon, who took the inventory of the human understanding for his times, never mentioned his name. Ben Jonson, had no suspicion of the elastic fame whose first vibrations he was attempting. He no doubt thought the praise he has conceded to him generous, and esteemed himself, out of all question, the better poet of the two.

"If it need wit to know wit, according to the proverb, Shakspeare's time should be capable of recognizing it. . . . Since, the constellation of great men who appeared in Greece in the time of Pericles, there was never any such society;—yet their genius failed them to find out the best head in the universe. Our poet's mask was impenetrable. You cannot see the mountain near. It took a century to make it suspected; and not until two centuries had passed, after his death, did any criticism which we think adequate begin to appear. It was not possible to write the history of Shakspeare till now."

It is now almost fourteen years since Mr. Emerson published his first book: Nature. A beautiful work it was and will be deemed for many a year to come. In this old world of literature, with more memory than wit, with much tradition and little invention, with more fear than love, and a great deal of criticism upon very little poetry, there came forward this young David, a shepherd, to be a king, "with his garlands and singing robes about him;" one note upon his new and fresh-strung lyre was "worth a thousand men." Men were looking for something original, they always are; when it came, some said it thundered, others that an angel had spoke. How men wondered at the little book! It took nearly twelve years to sell the five hundred copies of Nature. Since that time Mr. Emerson has said much, and if he has not printed many books, at least has printed much; some things far surpassing the first essay, in richness of

material, in perfection of form, in continuity of thought; but nothing which has the same youthful freshness, and the same tender beauty as this early violet, blooming out of Unitarian and Calvinistic sand or snow. Poems and essays of a later date; are there, which show that he has had more time and woven it into life; works which present us with thought deeper, wider, richer, and more complete, but not surpassing the simplicity and loveliness of that maiden flower of his poetic spring.

We know how true it is, that a man cannot criticize what he cannot comprehend, nor comprehend either a man or a work greater than himself. Let him get on a Quarterly never so high, it avails him nothing; "pyramids are pyramids in vales," and emmets are emmets even in a Review. Critics often afford an involuntary proof of this adage, yet grow no wiser by the experience. Few of our tribe can make the simple shrift of the old Hebrew poet, and say, "*we* have not exercised ourselves in great matters, nor in things too high for *us*." Sundry Icarian critics have we seen, wending their wearying way on waxen wing to overtake the eagle flight of Emerson; some of them have we known getting near enough to see a fault, to overtake a feather falling from his wing, and with that tumbling to give name to a sea, if one cared to notice to what depth they fell.

Some of the criticisms on Mr. Emerson, transatlantic and cisatlantic, have been very remarkable, not to speak more definitely. "What of this new book?" said Mr. Public to the reviewer, who was not "seized and tied down to judge," but of his own free will stood up and answered: "Oh! 't is out of all plumb, my lord—quite an irregular thing! not one of the angles at the four corners is a right angle. I had my rule and compasses, my lord, in my pocket. And for the poem, your lordship bid me look at it—upon taking the length, breadth, height, and depth of it,

226

and trying them at home, upon an exact scale of Bossu's—they are out, my lord, in every one of their dimensions."

Oh, gentle reader, we have looked on these efforts of our brother critics not without pity. There is an excellent bird, terrene, marine, and semi-aerial; a broad-footed bird, broad-beaked, broad-backed, broad-tailed; a notable bird she is, and a long lived; a useful bird, once indispensable to writers, as furnishing the pen, now fruitful in many a hint. But when she undertakes to criticize the music of the thrush, or the movement of the humming bird, why, she oversteps the modesty of her nature, and if she essays the flight of the eagle—she is fortunate if she falls only upon the water. "No man," says the law, "may stultify himself." Does not this canon apply to critics? No, the critic may do so. Suicide is a felony, but if a critic only slay himself critically, dooming himself to "hoist with his own petard," why 't is to be forgiven

"That in our aspirations to be great,
Our destinies o'erleap our mortal state."

In a place where there were no Quarterly Journals, the veracious historian Sir Walter Scott, relates that Claud Halcro, ambitious of fame, asked his fortune of an Orcadian soothsayer:

"Tell me, shall my lays be sung,
Like Hacon's of the golden tongue,
Long after Halcro's dead and gone?
Or shall Hialtland's minstrel own,
One note to rival glorious John?"

She answers, that as things work after their kind, the result is after the same kind:

"The eagle mounts the polar sky,
The Imber-goose unskilled to fly,
Must be content to glide along
When seal and sea-dog list his song."

We are warned by the fate of our predecessors, when their example does not guide us; we confess not only our inferiority to Mr. Emerson, but our consciousness of the fact, and believe that they should "judge others who themselves excel," and that authors, like others on trial, should be judged by their peers. So we will not call this a criticism, which we are about to write on Mr. Emerson, only an attempt at a contribution towards a criticism, hoping that in due time, some one will come and do faithfully and completely, what it is not yet time to accomplish, still less within our power to do.

All of Mr. Emerson's literary works, with the exception of the Poems, were published before they were printed; delivered by word of mouth to various audiences. In frequently reading his pieces, he had an opportunity to see any defect of form and amend it. Mr. Emerson has won by his writings a more desirable reputation, than any other man of letters in America has yet attained. It is not the reputation which brings him money or academic honors, or membership of learned societies; nor does it appear conspicuously in the literary Journals as yet. But he has a high place among thinking men, on both sides of the water; we think no man who writes the English tongue has now so much influence in forming the opinions and character of young men and women. His audience steadily increases, at home and abroad, more rapidly in England than America. It is now with him as it was, at first, with Dr. Channing; the fairest criticism has come from the other side of the water; the reason is that he, like his predecessor, offended the sectarian and party spirit, the personal prejudices of the men about him; his life was a reproach to them, his words an offence, or his doctrines alarmed their sectarian, their party or their personal pride, and they accordingly condemned the man. A writer who should bear the same relation to the English mind as Emerson to ours, for the same reason would be more acceptable here than at home. Emerson is neither a sectarian nor a partisan, no man less so; yet few men in America have been visited with more hatred,—private personal hatred, which the authors poorly endeavored to conceal, and perhaps did hide from themselves. The spite we have heard expressed against him, by men of the common morality, would strike a stranger with amazement, especially when it is remembered that his personal character and daily life are of such extraordinary loveliness. This hatred has not proceeded merely from ignorant men, in whom it could easily be excused; but more often from men who have had opportunities of obtaining as good a culture as men commonly get in this country. Yet while he has been the theme of vulgar abuse, of sneers and ridicule in public, and in private; while critics, more remarkable for the venom of their poison than the strength of their bow, have shot at him their little shafts, barbed more than pointed, he has also drawn about him some of what old Drayton called "the idle smoke of praise." Let us see what he has thrown into the public fire to cause this incense; what he has done to provoke the immedicable rage of certain other men; let us see what there is in his works, of old or new, true or false, what American and what cosmopolitan; let us weigh his works with such imperfect scales as we have, weigh them by the universal standard of Beauty, Truth and Love, and make an attempt to see what he is worth.

American literature may be distributed into two grand divisions: namely, the permanent literature, consisting of books not written for a special occasion, books which are bound between hard covers; and the transient literature, written for some special occasion and not designed to last beyond that. Our permanent literature is almost wholly an imitation of old models. The substance is old, and the form old. There is nothing American about it. But as our writers are commonly quite deficient in literary culture and scientific discipline, their productions seem poor when compared with the imitative portion of the permanent literature in older countries, where the writers start with a better discipline and a better acquaintance with letters and art. This inferiority of culture is one of the misfortunes incident to a new country, especially to one where practical talent is so much, and so justly preferred to merely literary accomplishment and skill. This lack of culture is yet more apparent, in general, in the transient literature, which is produced mainly by men who have had few advantages for intellectual discipline in early life, and few to make acquaintance with books at a later period. That portion of our literature is commonly stronger and more American, but it is often coarse and rude. The permanent literature is imitative; the other is rowdy. But we have now no time to dwell upon this theme, which demands a separate paper.

Mr. Emerson is the most American of our writers. The Idea of America, which lies at the bottom of our original institutions, appears in him with great prominence. We mean the idea of personal freedom, of the dignity and value of human nature, the superiority of a man to the accidents of a man. Emerson is the most republican of republicans, the most protestant of the dissenters. Serene as a July sun, he is equally fearless. He looks every thing in the face modestly, but with earnest scrutiny, and passes judgment upon its merits. Nothing is too high for his examination; nothing too sacred. On earth only one thing he finds which is thoroughly venerable, and that is the nature of man; not the accidents, which make a man rich or famous, but the substance, which makes him a man. The man is before the institutions of man; his nature superior to his history. All finite things are only appendages of man, useful, convenient, or beautiful. Man is master, and nature his slave, serving for many a varied use. The results of human experience—the state, the church, society, the family, business, literature, science, art—all of these are subordinate to man: if they serve the individual, he is to foster them, if not, to abandon them and seek better things. He looks at all things, the past and the present, the state and the church, Christianity and the market-house, in the daylight of the intellect. Nothing is allowed to stand between him and his manhood. Hence, there is an apparent irreverence; he does not bow to any hat which Gessler has set up for public adoration, but to every man, canonical or profane, who bears the mark of native manliness. He eats show-bread, if he is hungry. While he is the most American, he is almost the most cosmopolitan of our writers, the least restrained and belittled by the popular follies of the nation or the age.

In America, writers are commonly kept in awe and subdued by fear of the richer class, or that of the mass of men. Mr. Emerson has small respect for either; would bow as low to a lackey as a lord, to a clown as a scholar, to one man as a million. He spurns all constitutions but the law of his own nature, rejecting them with manly scorn. The traditions of the churches are no hindrances to his thought; Jesus or Judas were the same to him, if either stood in his way and hindered the proportionate development of his individual life. The forms of society and the ritual of scholarship are no more effectual restraints. His thought of today is no barrier to freedom of thought tomorrow, for his own nature is not to be subordi-nated, either to the history of man, or his own history. "Tomorrow to fresh fields and pastures new," is his motto.

Yet, with all this freedom, there is no wilful display of it. He is so confident of his freedom, so perfectly possessed of his rights, that he does not talk of them. They appear, but are not spoken of. With the hopefulness and buoyant liberty of America, he has none of our ill-mannered boasting. He criticizes America often; he always appreciates it; he seldom praises, and never brags of our country. The most democratic of democrats, no disciple of the old régime is better mannered, for it is only the vulgar democrat or aristocrat who flings his follies in your face. While it would be difficult to find a writer so uncompromising in his adhesion to just principles, there is not in all his works a single jeer or ill-natured sarcasm. None is less addicted to the common forms of reverence, but who is more truly reverential?

While his Idea is American, the form of his literature is not less so. It is a form which suits the substance, and is modified by the institutions and natural objects about him. You see that the author lives in a land with free institutions, with town-meetings and ballot-boxes; in the vicinity of a decaying church; amongst men whose terrible devils are Poverty and Social Neglect, the only devils whose damnation is much cared for. His geography is American. Katskill and the Alleghanies, Monadnock, Wachusett, and the uplands of New Hampshire, appear in poetry or prose; Contocook and Agiochook are better than the Ilyssus, or Pactolus, or "smooth-sliding Mincius, crowned with vocal reeds." New York, Fall River, and Lowell have a place in his writings, where a vulgar Yankee would put Thebes or Pæstum. His men and women are American—John and Jane, not Coriolanus and Persephone. He tells of the rhodora, the club-moss, the blooming clover, not of the hibiscus and

229

the asphodel. He knows the humblebee, the blackbird, the bat, and the wren, and is not ashamed to say or sing of the things under his own eyes. He illustrates his high thought by common things out of our plain New England life—the meeting in the church, the Sunday school, the dancing-school, a huckleberry party, the boys and girls hastening home from school, the youth in the shop, beginning an unconscious courtship with his unheeding customer, the farmers about their work in the fields, the bustling trader in the city, the cattle, the new hay, the voters at a town-meeting, the village brawler in a tavern full of tipsy riot, the conservative who thinks the nation is lost if his ticket chance to miscarry, the bigot worshipping the knot hole through which a dusty beam of light has looked in upon his darkness, the radical who declares that nothing is good if established, and the patent reformer who screams in your ears that he can finish the world with a single touch,—and out of all these he makes his poetry, or illustrates his philosophy. Now and then he wanders off to other lands, reports what he has seen, but it is always an American report of what an American eye saw. Even Mr. Emerson's recent exaggerated praise of England is such a panegyric as none but an American could bestow.

We know an American artist who is full of American scenery. He makes good drawings of Tivoli and Subiaco, but, to color them, he dips his pencil in the tints of the American heaven, and over his olive trees and sempervives, his asses and his priests, he sheds the light only of his native sky. So is it with Mr. Emerson. Give him the range of the globe, it is still an American who travels.

Yet with this indomitable nationality, he has a culture quite cosmopolitan and extraordinary in a young nation like our own. Here is man familiar with books, not with many, but the best books, which he knows intimately. He has kept good company. Two things impress you powerfully and continually—the man has seen nature, and been familiar with books. His literary culture is not a varnish on the surface; not a mere polish of the outside; it has penetrated deep into his consciousness. The salutary effect of literary culture, is more perceptible in Emerson than in any American that we know, save one, a far younger man, and of great promise, of whom we shall speak at some other time.

We just now mentioned that our writers were sorely deficient in literary culture. Most of them have only a smattering of learning, but some have read enough, read and remembered with ability to quote. Here is one who has evidently read much, his subject required it, or his disposition, or some accident in his history furnished the occasion; but his reading appears only in his quotations, or references in the margin. His literature has not penetrated his soul and got incorporated with his whole consciousness. You see that he has been on Parnassus, by the huge bouquet, pedantic in its complexity, that he affronts you with; not by the odor of the flowers he has trampled or gathered in his pilgrimage, not by Parnassian dust clinging to his shoes, or mountain vigor in his eye. The rose gatherer smells of his sweets, and needs not prick you with the thorn to apprize you of what he has dealt in.

Here is another writer who has studied much in the various literatures of the world, but has lost himself therein. Books supersede things, art stands between him and nature, his figures are from literature not from the green world. Nationality is gone. A traveller on the ocean of letters, he has a mistress in every port, and a lodging place where the night overtakes him; all flags are the same to him, all climes; he has no wife, no home, no country. He has dropped nationality, and in becoming a cosmopolitan, has lost his citizenship everywhere. So, with all Christendom and heathendom for his metropolis, he is an alien everywhere in the wide world. He has no literary inhabitiveness. Now he studies one author, and is the penumbra thereof for a time; now another, with the same result. Trojan or Tyrian is the same to him, and he is Trojan or Tyrian as occasion demands. A thin vapory comet, with small momentum of its own, he is continually deflected from his natural course by the attraction of other and more substantial bodies, till he has forgotten that he ever had any orbit of his own, and dangles in the literary sky, now this way drawn, now that, his only certain movement an oscillation. With a chameleon variability, he attaches himself to this or the other writer, and for the time, his own color disappears and he along with it.

With Emerson, all is very different; his literary culture is of him, and not merely on him. His learning appears not in his quotations, but in his talk. It is the wine itself, and not the vintner's brand on the cask, which shows its quality. In his reading and his study, he is still his own master. He has not purchased his education with the loss of his identity, not of his manhood; nay, he has not forgotten his kindred in getting his culture. He is still the master of himself; no man provokes him even into a momentary imitation. He keeps his individuality with maidenly asceticism, and with a conscience rarely found amongst literary men. Virgil homerizes, hesiodizes, and plays Theocritus now and then. Emerson plays Emerson, always Emerson. He honors Greece, and is not a stranger with her noblest sons; he pauses as a learner before the lovely muse of Germany; he bows low with exaggerating reverence before the practical skill of England, but no one, nor all of these have

power to subdue that serene and upright intellect. He rises from the oracle he stooped to consult just as erect as before. His reading gives a certain richness to his style, which is more literary than that of any American writer that we remember; as much so as that of Jeremy Taylor. He takes much for granted in his reader, as if he were addressing men who had read every thing, and wished to be reminded of what they had read. In classic times, there was no reading public, only a select audience of highly cultivated men. It was so in England once; the literature of that period indicates the fact. Only religious and dramatic works were designed for pit, box, and gallery. Nobody can speak more clearly and more plainly than Emerson, but take any one of his essays or orations, and you see that he does not write in the language of the mass of men, more than Thucydides or Tacitus. His style is allusive, as an ode of Horace or Pindar, and the allusions are to literature which is known to but few. Hence, while his thought is human in substance, and American in its modifications, and therefore easily grasped, comprehended, and welcomed by men of the commonest culture, it is but few who understand the entire meaning of the sentences which he writes. His style reflects American scenery, and is dimpled into rare beauty as it flows by, and so has a pleasing fascination, but it reflects also the literary scenery of his own mind, and so half of his thought is lost on half his readers. Accordingly no writer or lecturer finds a readier access for his thoughts to the mind of the people at large, but no American author is less intelligible to the people in all his manifold meaning and beauty of allusion. He has not completely learned to think with the sagest sages and then put his thoughts into the plain speech of plain men. Every word is intelligible in the massive speech of Mr. Webster, and has its effect, while

Emerson has still something of the imbecility of the scholar, as compared to the power of the man of action, whose words fall like the notes of the wood-thrush, each in its time and place, yet without picking and choosing. "Blacksmiths and teamsters do not trip in their speech," says he, "it is a shower of bullets. It is Cambridge men who correct themselves, and begin again at every half sentence; and moreover, will pun and refine too much, and swerve from the matter to the expression." But of the peculiarities of his style we shall speak again.

Emerson's works do not betray any exact scholarship which has a certain totality, as well as method about it. It is plain to see that his favorite authors have been Plutarch, especially that outpouring of his immense common-place book, his "Moral Writings," Montaigne, Shakspeare, George Herbert, Milton, Wordsworth, Coleridge, and Carlyle. Of late years, his works contain allusions to the ancient oriental literature, from which he has borrowed some hard names and some valuable thoughts, but is occasionally led astray by its influence, for it is plain that he does not understand that curious philosophy he quotes from. Hence his oriental allies are brought up to take a stand which no man dreamed of in their time, and made to defend ideas not known to men till long after these antediluvian sages were at rest in their graves.

In Emerson's writings, you do not see indications of exact mental discipline, so remarkable in Bacon, Milton, Taylor, and South, in Schiller, Lessing, and Schleiermacher; neither has he the wide range of mere literature noticeable in all other men. He works up scientific facts in his writings with great skill, often penetrating beyond the fact, and discussing the idea out of which it, and many other kindred facts seem to have proceeded: this indicates not only a nice eye for facts, but a mind singularly powerful to detect latent analogies, and see the one in the many. Yet there is nothing to show any regular and systematic discipline in science which appears so eminently in Schiller and Hegel. He seems to learn his science from occasional conversation with men of science, or from statements of remarkable discoveries in the common Journals, not from a careful and regular study of facts or treatises.

With all his literary culture he has an intense love of nature, a true sight and appreciation thereof; not the analytic eye of the naturalist, but the synthetic vision of the poet. A book never clouds his sky. His figures are drawn from nature, he sees the fact. No chart of nature hangs up in his windows to shut out nature herself. How well he says:

["Nature," *Nature*, 8.29–9.4, 9.24–10.22]

["Beauty," *Nature*, 13.16–34]

Most writers are demonized or possessed by some one truth, or perhaps some one whim. Look where they will, they see nothing but that. Mr. Emerson holds himself erect, and no one thing engrosses his attention, no one idea; no one intellectual faculty domineers over the rest. Sensation does not dim reflection, nor does his thought lend its sickly hue to the things about him. Even Goethe, with all his boasted equilibrium, held his intellectual faculties less perfectly in hand than Emerson. He has no hobbies to ride; even his fondness for the ideal and the beautiful, does not hinder him from obstinately looking real and ugly things in the face. He carries the American idea of freedom into his most intimate personality, and keeps his individuality safe and sacred. He cautions young men against stooping their minds to other men. He knows no master. Sometimes this is carried to an apparent excess, and he underrates the real value of literature, afraid lest the youth become a bookworm, and not a man thinking. But how well he says:

["American Scholar Address," 56.18–22, 27–36; 57.1–9; 63.7–27]

To us the effect of Emerson's writings is profoundly religious; they stimulate to piety, the love of God, to goodness as the love of man. We know no living writer, in any language, who exercises so powerful a religious influence as he. Most young persons, not ecclesiastical, will confess this. We know he is often called hard names on pretence that he is not religious. We remember once being present at a meeting of gentlemen, scholarly men some of them, after the New England standard of scholarship, who spent the evening in debating "Whether Ralph Waldo Emerson was a Christian." The opinion was quite generally entertained that he was not; for "discipleship was necessary to Christianity." "And the essence of Christian discipleship" was thought to consist in "sitting at the feet of our blessed Lord (pronounced Laawd!) and calling him Master, which Emerson certainly does not do." We value Christianity as much as most men, and the name Christian is to us very dear; but when we remembered the character, the general tone and conduct of the men who arrogate to themselves the name Christian, and seem to think they have a right to monopolize the Holy Spirit of Religion, and "shove away the worthy bidden guest," the whole thing reminded us of a funny story related by an old writer: "It was once proposed in the British House of Commons, that James Usher, afterward the celebrated Archbishop of Armagh, but then a young man, should be admitted to the assembly of the 'King's Divines.' The proposition, if we remember rightly, gave rise to some debate, upon which John Selden, a younger man than Usher, but highly distinguished and much respected, rose and said that it reminded him of a proposition which might be made, that Inigo Jones, the famous architect, should be admitted to the worshipful company of Mousetrap Makers!"

Mr. Emerson's writings are eminently religious; christian in the best sense of that word. This has often been denied for two reasons: because Mr. Emerson sets little value on the mythology of the Christian sects, no more perhaps than on the mythology of the Greeks and the Scandinavians, and also because his writings far transcend the mechanical morality and formal pietism, commonly recommended by gentlemen in pulpits. Highly religious, he is not at all ecclesiastical or bigoted. He has small reverence for forms and traditions; a manly life is the only form of religion which he recognizes, and hence we do not wonder at all that he also has been deemed an infidel. It would be very surprising if it were not so. Still it is not religion that is most conspicuous in these volumes; that is not to be looked for except in the special religious literature, yet we must confess that any one of Emerson's works seems far more religious than what are commonly called "good books," including the class of sermons.

To show what is in Mr. Emerson's books and what is not, let us make a little more detailed examination thereof. He is not a logical writer, not systematic; not what is commonly called philosophical; didactic to a great degree, but never demonstrative. So we are not to look for a scientific plan, or for a system, of which the author is himself conscious. Still, in all sane men, there must be a system, though the man does not know it. There are two ways of reporting upon an author: one is to represent him by specimens, the other to describe him by analysis; one to show off a finger or foot of the Venus de Medici, the other to give the dimensions thereof. We will attempt both and will speak of Mr. Emerson's starting point, his *terminus a quo*; then of his method of procedure, his *via in quâ*; then of the conclusion he arrives at, his *terminus ad quem*. In giving the dimensions of his statue, we shall exhibit also some of the parts described.

Most writers, knowingly or unconsciously, take as their point of departure some special and finite thing. This man starts from a tradition, the philosophical tradition of Aristotle, Plato, Leibnitz or Locke, this from the theological tradition of the Protestants or the Catholics and never will dare get out of sight of his authorities; he takes the bearing of every thing from his tradition. Such a man may sail the sea for ages, he arrives nowhere at the last. Our traditionist must not outgo his tradition; the Catholic must not get beyond his church, nor the Protestant outtravel his Bible. Others start from some fixed fact, a sacrament, a constitution, the public opinion, the public morality, or the popular religion. This they are to defend at all hazards; of course they will retain all falsehood and in justice which favor this institution, and reject all justice and truth which oppose the same. Others pretend to start from God, but in reality do take their departure from a limited conception of God, from the Hebrew notion of Him, or the Catholic notion, from the Calvinistic or the Unitarian notion of God. By and by they are hindered and stopped in their progress. The philosophy of these three classes of men, is always vitiated by the prejudice they start with:

Mr. Emerson takes Man for his point of departure, he means to take the whole of man; man with his history, man with his nature, his sensational, intellectual, moral, affectional and religious instincts and faculties. With him man is the measure of all things, of ideas and of facts; if they fit man they are accepted, if not,

thrown aside. This appears in his first book and in his last:

["Introduction," *Nature*, 7.10–21]

Again he speaks in a higher mood of the same theme:

["Divinity School Address," 82.34–83.3, 89.10–19, 90.1–16]

["The Over-Soul," 172.2–17]

And again in his latest publication:

["Uses of Great Men," 4.5–9, 31–33; 5.1–6; 19.23; 19.30–20.1; 20.10–16]

["Goethe," 166.29–35]

In this Emerson is more American than America herself—and is himself the highest exponent in literature of this Idea of human freedom and the value of man. Channing talks of the dignity of human nature, his great and brilliant theme; but he commonly, perhaps always subordinates the nature of man to some of the accidents of his history. This Emerson never does; no, not once in all his works, nor in all his life. Still we think it is not the whole of man from which he starts, that he undervalues the logical, demonstrative and historical Understanding, with the results thereof, and also undervalues the Affections. Hence his Man, who is the measure of all things, is not the complete man. This defect appears in his ethics, which are a little cold, the ethics of marble men; and in his religious teachings, the highest which this age has furnished, full of reverence, full of faith, but not proportionably rich in affection.

Mr. Emerson has a method of his own as plainly marked as that of Lord Bacon or Descartes, and as rigidly adhered to. It is not the inductive method by which you arrive at a general fact from many particular facts, but never reach a universal law; it is not the deductive method, whereby a minor law is derived from a major, a special from a general law; it is neither inductive nor deductive demonstration. But Emerson proceeds by the way of intuition, sensational or spiritual. Go to the fact and look for yourself, is his command: a material fact you cannot always verify and so for that must depend on evidence; a spiritual fact you can always legitimate for yourself. Thus he says:

["Prospects," *Nature*, 39.16–30, 41.25–31]

["History," 16.11–14]

["Self-Reliance," 37.12–31, 38.4–17]

["The Over-Soul," 166.3–8, 170.4–14, 174.36–175.13]

[*Method of Nature*, 134.21–23]

The same method in his last work is ascribed to Plato:

["Plato," 33.17–20]

Sometimes he exaggerates the value of this, and puts the unconscious before the self-conscious state:

[*Method of Nature*, 130.15–23]

He is sometimes extravagant in the claims made for his own method, and maintains that ecstasy is the natural and exclusive mode of arriving at new truths, while it is only one mode. Ecstasy is the state of intuition in which the man loses his individual self-consciousness. Moments of this character are few and rare even with men like the St. Victors, like Tauler, and Böhme and Swedenborg. The writings of all these men, especially of the two last, who most completely surrendered themselves to this mode of action, show how poor and insufficient it is. All that mankind has learned in this way is little, compared with the results of reflection, of meditation, and careful, conscientious looking after truth: all the great benefactors of the world have been patient and continuous in their work;

"Not from a *vain and shallow* thought
His awful Jove young Phidias brought."

Mr. Emerson says books are only for one's idle hours; he discourages hard and continuous thought, conscious modes of argument, of discipline. Here he exaggerates his idiosyncrasy into a universal law. The method of nature is not ecstasy but patient attention. Human nature avenges herself for the slight he puts on her, by the irregular and rambling character of his own productions. The vice appears more glaring in the Emersonidæ, who have all the agony without the inspiration; who affect the unconscious; write even more ridiculous nonsense than their "genius" requires; are sometimes so child-like as to become mere babies, and seem to forget that the unconscious state is oftener below the conscious than above it, and that there is an ecstasy of folly as well as of good sense.

Some of these imbeciles have been led astray by this extravagant and one sided statement. What if books have hurt Mr. Oldbuck, and many fine wits lie "sheathed to the hilt in ponderous tomes," sheathed and rusted in so that no Orson could draw the blade,—we need not deny the real value of books, still less the value of the serious and patient study of thoughts and things. Michael Angelo and Newton had some genius; Socrates is thought not destitute of philosophical power; but no dauber of canvas, no sportsman with marble ever worked like Angelo; the two philosophers wrought by their genius, but with an attention, an order, a diligence, and a terrible industry and method of thought, without which their genius would have ended in nothing but guess-work. Much comes by spontaneous intuition, which is to be got in no other way; but much is to precede that, and much to follow it. There are two things to be considered in the matter of inspiration, one is the Infinite God from whom it comes, the other the finite capacity which is to receive it. If Newton had never studied, it would be as easy for God to reveal the calculus to his dog Diamond as to Newton. We once heard of a man who thought every thing was in the soul, and so gave up all reading, all continuous thought. Said another, "if all is in the soul, it takes a man to find it."

Here are some of the most important conclusions Mr. Emerson has hitherto arrived at.

Man is above nature, the material world. Last winter, in his lectures, he was understood to affirm "the identity of man with nature;" a doctrine which seems to have come from his Oriental reading before named, a doctrine false as well as inconsistent with the first principles of his philosophy. But in his printed works he sees clearly the distinction between the two, a fact not seen by the Hindoo philosophers, but first by the Hebrew and Greek writers. Emerson puts man far before nature:

["Beauty," *Nature*, 15.6–12, 17.14–16]

["Discipline," 25.24–27]

Nature is "an appendix to the soul."

Then the man is superior to the accidents of his past history or present condition:

["Prospects," *Nature*, 44.5–6]

["Self-Reliance," 27.12–17, 36.23–32]

Hence a man must be true to his present condition, careless of consistency:

["Self-Reliance," 33.31–36]

The man must not be a slave to a single form of thought:

["Intellect," 200.35–201.1]

Man is inferior to the great law of God, which overrides the world; "His wealth and greatness consist in his being the channel through which heaven flows to earth;" "the word of a poet is only the mouth of divine wisdom;" "the man on whom the soul descends—alone can teach;" all nature "from the sponge up to Hercules is to hint or to thunder man the laws of right and wrong." This ethical character seems the end of nature: "the moral law lies at the centre of nature and radiates to the circumference. It is the pith and marrow of every substance, every relation, every process. All things with which we deal point to us. What is a farm but a mute Gospel?" Yet he sometimes tells us that man is identical with God under certain circumstances, an old Hindoo notion, a little favored by some passages in the New Testament, and revived by Hegel in modern times, in whom it seems less inconsistent than in Emerson.

This moral law continually gives men their compensation. "You cannot do wrong without suffering wrong."

["Compensation," 64.4–19, 67.28–36, 71.1–9]

By virtue of obedience to this law great men are great, and only so:

["Self-Reliance," 40.21–24, 35.22–31]

Through this any man has the power of all men:

["Self-Reliance," 47.26–36]

["The Over-Soul," 171.8–15]

Yet he once says there is no progress of mankind; "Society never advances."

["Self-Reliance," 48.18–31]

But this is an exaggeration, which he elsewhere corrects, and justly says that the great men of the nineteenth century will one day be quoted to prove the barbarism of their age.

He teaches an absolute trust in God:

["The Over-Soul," 172.37–173.3, 173.6–18]

["Divinity School Address," 85.10–27]

God continually communicates Himself to man in various forms:

["The Over-Soul," 166.30–167.5]

"The nature of these revelations is always the same: they are perceptions of the absolute law."

["The Over-Soul," 171.20–27, 171.37–172.6, 173.4–6]

He says the same thing in yet more rhythmic notes:

["The Problem," 6.19–7.11, 8.6–13]

If we put Emerson's conclusions into five great classes representing respectively his idea of Man, of God, and of Nature; his idea of self-rule, the relation of man's consciousness to his unconsciousness; his idea of religion, the relation of men to God; of ethics, the relation of man to man; and of economy; the relation of man to nature; we find him in the very first rank of modern science. No man in this age is before him. He demonstrates nothing, but assumes his position far in advance of mankind. This explains the treatment he has met with.

Then in his writings there appears a love of beauty in all its forms—in material nature, in art, literature, and above all in human life. He finds it everywhere:

["Ode to Beauty," 88.2–9, 89.13–16]

Few men have had a keener sense for this in common life, or so nice an eye for it in inanimate nature. His writings do not disclose a very clear perception of the beauty of animated nature; it is still life that he describes, in water, plants and the sky. He seldom refers to the great cosmic forces of the world, that are everywhere balanced into such systematic proportions, the perception of which makes the writings of Alexander Von Humboldt so attractive and delightful.

In all Emerson's works there appears a sublime confidence in man; a respect for human nature which we have never seen surpassed—never equalled. Man is only to be true to his nature, to plant himself on his instincts, and all will turn out well:

["Prospects," Nature, 45.6–21]

He has also an absolute confidence in God. He has been foolishly accused of pantheism which sinks God in nature; but no man is further from it. He never sinks God in man, he does not stop with the law, in matter or morals, but goes back to the Lawgiver; yet probably it would not be so easy for him to give his definition of God as it would be for most graduates at Andover or Cambridge. With this confidence in God he looks things fairly in the face, and never dodges, never fears. Toil, sorrow, pain, these are things which it is impious to fear. Boldly he faces every fact, never retreating behind an institution or a great man. In God his trust is complete; with the severest scrutiny he joins the highest reverence.

Hence come his calmness and serenity. He is evenly balanced and at repose. A more tranquil spirit cannot be found in literature. Nothing seems to fret or jar him, and all the tossings of the literary world never jostle him into anger or impatience. He goes on like the stars above the noise and dust of earth, as calm yet not so cold. No man says things more terribly severe than he on many occasions; few in America have encountered such abuse, but in all his writings there is not a line which can be referred to ill-will. Impudence and terror are wasted on him; "upstart wealth's averted eye," which blasts the hope of the politician, is powerless on him as on the piles of granite in New Hampshire hills. Misconceived and misreported, he does not wait to "unravel any man's blunders; he is again on his road, adding new powers and honors to his domain, and new claims on the heart." He takes no notice of the criticism from which nothing but warning is to be had, warning against bigotry and impudence, and goes on his way, his only answer a creative act. Many shafts has he shot, not an arrow in self-defence; not a line betrays that he has been treated ill. This is small praise but rare; even cool egotistic Goethe treated his "Philistine" critics with haughty scorn, comparing them to dogs who bark in the court-yard when the master mounts to ride:

"Es will der Spitz aus unserm Stall
    Mit Bellen uns begleiten;
Allein der Hundes lauter Schall
    Beweist nur dass wir reiten."

He lacks the power of orderly arrangement to a remarkable degree. Not only is there no obvious logical order, but there is no subtle psychological method by which the several parts of an essay are joined together; his deep sayings are jewels strung wholly at random. This often confuses the reader; this want appears the greatest defect of his mind. Of late years there has been a marked effort to correct it, and in regard to mere order there is certainly a great improvement in the first series of Essays on Nature, or rather formless book.

Then he is not creative like Shakspeare and Goethe, perhaps not inventive like many far inferior men; he seldom or never undertakes to prove any thing. He tells what he sees, seeing things by glimpses, not by steady and continuous looking, he often fails of seeing the whole object; he does not always see all of its relations with other things. Hence comes an occasional exaggeration. But this is commonly corrected by some subsequent statement. Thus he has seen books imprison many a youth, and speaking to men, desirous of warning them of their danger, he undervalues the worth of books themselves. But the use he makes of them in his own writings shows that this statement was an exaggeration which his practical judgment disapproves. Speaking to men whose chief danger was that they should be bookworms, or mechanical grinders at a logic-mill, he says that ecstasy is the method of Nature, but himself never utters anything "poor and extemporaneous;" what he gets in his ecstatic moments of inspiration, he examines carefully in his cool, reflective hours, and it is printed as reflection, never as the simple result of ecstatic inspiration, having not only the stamp of Divine truth, but the private mark of Emerson. He is never demonized by his enthusiasm; he possesses the spirit, it never possesses him; if "the God" comes into his rapt soul "without bell," it is only with due consideration that he communicates to the world the message that was brought. Still he must regret that his extravagant estimate of ecstasy, intuitive unconsciousness, has been made and has led some youths and maids astray.

This mode of looking at things, and this want of logical order make him appear inconsistent. There are actual and obvious contradictions in his works. "Two sons of Priam in one chariot ride." Now he is all generosity and nobleness, shining like the sun on things mean and low, and then he says, with a good deal of truth but some exaggeration:

["Self-Reliance," 30.36–31.9]

Thus a certain twofoldness appears in his writings here and there, but take them all together they form a whole of marvellous consistency; take them in connection with his private character and life—we may challenge the world to furnish an example of a fairer and more consistent whole.

With the exceptions above stated, there is a remarkable balance of intellectual faculties, of creative and conservative, of the spontaneous and intuitive, and the voluntary and reflective powers. He is a slave to neither; all are balanced into lovely proportions and intellectual harmony. In many things Goethe is superior to Emerson: in fertility of invention, in a wide acquaintance with men, in that intuitive perception of character which seems an instinct in some men, in regular discipline of the understanding, in literary and artistic culture; but in general harmony of the intellectual powers, and the steadiness of purpose which comes thereof, Emerson is incontestibly the superior even of the many-sided Goethe. He never wastes his time on trifles; he is too heavily fraught, and lies so deep in the sea that a little flaw of wind never drives him from his course. If we go a little further and inquire how the other qualities are blended with the intellectual, we find that the moral power a little outweighs the intellectual, and the religious is a little before the moral, as it should be, but the affections seem to be less developed than the intellect. There is no total balance of all the faculties to correspond with the harmony of his intellectual powers. This seems to us the greatest defect in his entire being, as lack of logical power is the chief defect in his intellect; there is love enough for almost any man—not enough to balance his intellect, his conscience, and his faith in God. Hence there appears a certain coldness in his ethics. He is a man running alone, and would lead others to isolation, not society. Notwithstanding his own intense individuality and his theoretic and practical respect for individuality, still persons seem of small value to him—of little value except as they represent or help develop an idea of the intellect. In this respect, in his writings he is one-sided, and while no one mental power has subdued another, yet his intellect and conscience seem to enslave and belittle the affections. Yet he never goes so far in this as Goethe, who used men, and women too, as cattle to ride, as food to eat. In Emerson's religious writings there appears a worship of the infinite God, far transcending all we find in Taylor or Edwards, in Fenelon or Channing; it is reverence, it is trust, the worship of the conscience, of the intellect; it is obedience, the worship of the will; it is not love, the worship of the affections.

No writer in our language is more rich in ideas, none more suggestive of noble thought and noble life. We will select the axioms which occur in a single essay, which we take at random, that on Self-reliance:

"It needs a divine man to exhibit anything divine."
"Nothing is at last sacred but the integrity of your own mind."
"The virtue most in request is conformity. Self-reliance is its aversion."
"No law can be sacred to me but that of my nature, the only wrong what is against it."
"Truth is handsomer than the affectation of love."
"Your goodness must have some edge to it."
"Do your work and you shall reinforce yourself."
"A foolish consistency is the hobgoblin of little minds."
"To be great is to be misunderstood."
"Character teaches above our wills."
"Greatness always appeals to the future."
"The centuries are conspirators against the sanity and majesty of the soul."

239

"If we live truly we shall see truly."

"It is as easy for the strong to be strong as it is for the weak to be weak."

"When a man lives with God, his voice shall be as sweet as the murmur of the brook and the rustle of the corn."

"Virtue is the governor."

"Welcome evermore to gods and men is the self-helping man."

"Duty is our place, and the merry men of circumstance should follow as they may."

"My giant goes with me wherever I go."

"It was in his own mind that the artist sought his model."

"That which each can do best none but his Maker can teach him."

"Every great man is an unique."

"Nothing can bring you peace but the triumph of principles."

His works abound also with the most genial wit; he clearly sees and sharply states the halfnesses of things and men, but his wit is never coarse, and wholly without that grain of malice so often the accompaniment thereof.

Let us now say a word of the artistic style and rhetorical form of these remarkable books. Mr. Emerson always gravitates towards first principles, but never sets them in a row, groups them into a system, or makes of them a whole. Hence the form of all his prose writings is very defective and much of his rare power is lost. He never fires by companies, nor even by platoons, only man by man; nay, his soldiers are never ranked into line, but stand scattered, sundered and individual, each serving on his own account, and "fighting on his own hook." Things are huddled and lumped together; diamonds, pearls, bits of chalk and cranberries, thrown pell-mell together. You can

"No joints and no contexture find,
Nor their loose parts to any method bring."

Here is a specimen of the Lucretian "fortuitous concourse of atoms," for things are joined by a casual connection, or else by mere caprice. This is so in the Orations, which were designed to be heard, not read, where order is the more needful. His separate thoughts are each a growth. Now and then it is so with a sentence, seldom with a paragraph; but his essay is always a piece of composition, carpentry, and not growth.

Take any one of his volumes, the first series of Essays, for example, the book does not make an organic whole, by itself, and so produce a certain totality of impression. The separate essays are not arranged with reference to any progress in the reader's mind, or any consecutive development of the author's ideas. Here are the title of the several papers in their present order:—History, Self-Reliance, Compensation, Spiritual Laws, Love, Friendship, Prudence, Heroism, The Over-Soul, Circles, Intellect, Art. In each essay there is the same want of organic completeness and orderly distribution of the parts. There is no logical arrangement of the separate thoughts, which are subordinate to the main idea of the piece. They are shot together into a curious and disorderly mass of beauty, like the colors in a kaleidoscope, not laid together like the gems in a collection; still less grown into a whole like the parts of a rose, where beauty of form, fragrance, and color make up one whole of loveliness. The lines he draws do not converge to one point; there is no progress in his drama. Towards the end the interest deepens, not from an artistic arrangement of accumulated thoughts, but only because the author finds his heart warmed by his efforts, and beating quicker. Some artists produce their effect almost wholly by form and outline; they sculpture with their pencil; the Parcæ of Michael Angelo is an example; so some writers discipline their pupils by the severity of their intellectual method and scientific forms of thought. Other artists have we known produce the effect almost wholly by their coloring; the drawing was bad, but the color of lip and eye, of neck and cheek, and hair, was perfect; the likeness all men saw, and felt the impression. But the perfect artist will be true to both, will keep the forms of things, and only clothe them with appropriate hues. We know some say that order belongs not to poetic minds, but the saying is false. In all Milton's high poetic works, the form is perfect as the coloring: this appears in the grouping of the grand divisions of the Paradise Lost, and in the arrangement of the smallest details in L'Allegro and Il Penseroso, and then the appropriate hue of morning, of mid-day, or of night is thrown upon the whole.

His love of individuality has unconsciously deprived him of the grace of order; his orations or essays are like a natural field: here is common grass, only with him not half so common as wild roses and violets, for his common grasses are flowers—and then rocks, then trees, brambles, thorns, now flowers, now weeds, here a decaying log with raspberry bushes on the one side and strawberry vines on the other, and potentillas creeping among them all. There are emmets and wood-worms, earth-worms, slugs, grasshoppers and, more obvious, sheep and oxen, and above and about them, the brown thrasher, the hen-hawk and the crow—making a scene of beautiful and intricate confusion which belongs to nature, not to human art.

His marked love of individuality appears in his style. His thoughts are seldom vague, all is distinct; the outlines sharply drawn, things are always discrete from one another. He loves to particularize. He talks not of flowers, but of the violet, the clover, the cowslip and anemone; not of birds, but the nut-hatch, and the wren; not of insects, but of the Volvex Globator; not of men and maids, but of Adam, John, and Jane. Things are kept from things, each surrounded by its own atmosphere. This gives great distinctness and animation to his works, though latterly he seems to imitate himself a little in this respect. It is remarkable to what an extent this individualization is carried. The essays in his books are separate and stand apart from one another, only mechanically bound by the lids of the volume; his paragraphs in each essay are distinct and disconnected, or but loosely bound to one another; it is so with sentences in the paragraph, and propositions in the sentence. Take for example his essay on Experience; it is distributed into seven parts, which treat respectively of Illusion, Temperament, Succession, Surface, Surprise, Reality and Subjectiveness. These seven brigadiers are put in one army with as little unity of action as any seven Mexican officers; not subject to one head, nor fighting on the same side. The subordinates under these generals are in no better order and discipline; sometimes the corporal commands the king. But this very lack of order gives variety of form. You can never anticipate him. One half the essay never suggests the rest. If he have no order, he never sets his method a going, and himself with his audience goes to sleep, trusting that he, they, and the logical conclusion will all come out alive and waking at the last. He trusts nothing to the discipline of his camp; all to the fidelity of the individual soldiers.

His style is one of the rarest beauty; there is no affectation, no conceit, no effort at effect. He alludes to everybody and imitates nobody. No writer that we remember, except Jean Paul Richter, is so

241

rich in beautiful imagery; there are no blank walls in his building. But Richter's temple of poesy is a Hindoo pagoda, rich, elaborate, of costly stone, adorned with costly work, but as a whole, rather grotesque than sublime, and more queer than beautiful; you wonder how any one could have brought such wealth together, and still more that any one could combine things so oddly together. Emerson builds a rambling Gothic Church, with an irregular outline, a chapel here, and a tower there, you do not see why; but all parts are beautiful and the whole constrains the soul to love and trust. His manifold images come from his own sight, not from the testimony of other men. His words are pictures of the things daguerreotyped from nature. Like Homer, Aristotle and Tacitus, he describes the thing, and not the effect of the thing. This quality he has in common with the great writers of classic antiquity, while his wealth of sentiment puts him with the classics of modern times. Like Burke he lays all literature under contribution, and presses the facts of every day life into his service. He seems to keep the sun and moon as his retainers and levy black-mail on the cricket and the tit-mouse, on the dawdling preacher and the snow storm which seemed to rebuke his unnatural whine. His works teem with beauty. Take for example this:

["Love," 100.34–101.31; 103.11–19, 26–30]

Emerson is a great master of language; therewith he sculptures, therewith he paints; he thunders and lightens in his speech, and in his speech also he sings. In Greece, Plato and Aristophanes were mighty masters of the pen, and have not left their equals in ancient literary art; so in Rome were Virgil and Tacitus; four men so marked in individuality, so unlike and withal so skilful in the use of speech, it were not easy to find; four mighty

masters of the art to write. In later times there have been in England, Shakspeare, Bacon, Milton, Taylor, Swift and Carlyle; on the Continent, Voltaire, Rousseau and Goethe; all masters in this art, skilful to work in human speech. Each of them possessed some qualities which Emerson has not. In Bacon, Milton and Carlyle, there is majesty, a dignity and giant strength, not to be claimed for him. Yet separating the beautiful from what men call sublime, no one of all that we have named, ancient or modern, has passages so beautiful as he. From what is called sublime if we separate what is simply vast, or merely grand, or only wide, it is in vain that we seek in all those men for anything to rival Emerson.

Take the following passage, and it is not possible, we think, to find its equal for the beautiful and the sublime in any tongue:

["Love," 108.3–110.8]

We can now only glance at the separate works named above. His Nature is more defective in form than any of his pieces, but rich in beauty; a rare prose poem is it, a book for one's bosom. The first series of Essays contains the fairest blossoms and fruits of his genius. Here his wondrous mind reveals itself in its purity, its simplicity, its strength, and its beauty too. The second series of Essays is inferior to the first; the style is perhaps clearer, but the water is not so deep. He seems to let himself down to the capacity of his hearers. Yet there is an attempt at order which is seldom successful, and reminds one of the order in which figures are tattooed upon the skin of a South Sea Islander, rather than of the organic symmetry of limbs or bones. He sets up a scaffold, not a living tree, a scaffold, too, on which none but himself can walk.

Some of his Orations and Addresses are noble efforts: old as the world is, and much and long as men are given to speak, it is but rare in human history that such Sermons on the Mount get spoken as the Address to the students of Theology, and that before the Phi Beta Kappa, at Cambridge. They are words of lofty cheer.

The last book on "Representative Men," does not come up to the first Essays, neither in matter nor in manner. Yet we know not a man, living and speaking English, that could have written one so good. The lecture on Plato contains exaggerations not usual with Emerson; it fails to describe the man by genus or species. He gives you neither the principles nor the method of Plato, not even his conclusions. Nay, he does not give you the specimens to judge by. The article in the last classical dictionary, or the History of Philosophy for the French Normal schools gives you a better account of the philosopher and the man. The lecture on Swedenborg is a masterly appreciation of that great man, and, to our way of thinking, the best criticism that has yet appeared. He appreciates but does not exaggerate him. The same may be said of that upon Montaigne; those on Shakspeare and Goethe are adequate and worthy of the theme. In the lecture on Napoleon, it is surprising that not a word is said of his greatest faculty, his legislative, organizing power, for we cannot but think with Carlyle, that he "will be better known for his laws than his battles." But the other talents of Napoleon are sketched with a faithful hand, and his faults justly dealt with, not enlarged but not hid—though, on the whole, it seems to us, no great admirers of Napoleon, that he is a little undervalued.

We must briefly notice Mr. Emerson's volume of Poems. He has himself given us the standard by which to try him, for he thus defines and describes the poet:

["The Poet," 6.11–7.4]

It is the office of the poet, he tells us, "by the beauty of things" to announce "a new and higher beauty. Nature offers all her creatures to him as a picture language." The poorest experience is rich enough for all the purposes of expressing thought;" "the world being put under the mind for verb and noun, the poet is he who can articulate it;" he "turns the world to glass, and shows us all things in their right series and proportions." For through that better perception he stands one step nearer things, and sees the flowing or metamorphosis, perceives that thought is multiform; that within the form of every creature is a force impelling it to ascend into a higher form, and, following with his eyes the life, uses the forms which express that life, and so his speech flows with the flowing of nature." "The poet alone knows astronomy, chemistry, vegetation and animation, for he does not stop at these facts, but employs them as signs."

["The Poet," 15.24–16.18]

In reading criticisms on Emerson's poetry, one is sometimes reminded of a passage in Pepys's Diary, where that worthy pronounced judgment on some of the works of Shakspeare. Perhaps it may be thought an appropriate introduction to some strictures of our own.

"Aug. 20, 1666. To Deptford by water, reading Othello, Moor of Venice, which I have heretofore esteemed a mighty good play, but having so lately read the Adventures of Five Hours, it seems a mean thing. Sept. 29th, 1662. To the King's Theatre, where we saw Midsummer Night's Dream, which I had never seen before, nor shall ever again, for it is the most insipid and ridiculous play, that ever I saw in my life."

Emerson is certainly one

"Quem tu, Melpomene, semel
  Nascentem placido lumine videris;
Spissæ nemorum comæ
  Fingent Æolio carmine nobilem."

Yet his best poetry is in his prose, and his poorest, thinnest and least musical prose is in his poems.

The "Ode to Beauty" contains some beautiful thoughts in a fair form:

["Ode to Beauty," 87.2–21]

The three pieces which seem the most perfect poems, both in matter and form, are the "Problem," from which we have already given liberal extracts above; "Each in all," which, however, is certainly not a great poem, but simple, natural and beautiful; and the "Sphinx," which has higher merits than the others, and is a poem of a good deal of beauty. The Sphinx is the creation of the old classic mythology. But her question is wholly modern, though she has been waiting so long for the seer to solve it, that she has become drowsy.

This is her problem:

"The fate of the man-child;
The meaning of man."

All the material and animal world is at peace:

["The Sphinx," 20.18–21.2, 21.11–18]

In his early age man shares the peace of the world:

["The Sphinx," 21.19–26]

But when the child becomes a man he is ill at ease:

["The Sphinx," 22.1–8]

Mother Nature complains of his condition:

["The Sphinx," 22.13–16]

The Sphinx wishes to know the meaning of all this. A poet answers that this is no mystery to him; man is superior to nature, and its unconscious and involuntary happiness is not enough for him; superior to the events of his own history, so the joy which he has attained is always unsatisfactory:

["The Sphinx," 22.25–23.14]

Even sad things turn out well:

["The Sphinx," 22.15–18]

Thus the riddle is solved; then the Sphinx turns into beautiful things:

["The Sphinx," 24.21–25.2]

We pass over the Threnody, where "well sung woes" might soothe a "pensive ghost." The Dirge contains some stanzas that are full of nature and well expressed:

["Dirge," 145.11–146.12,
146.21–147.20]

Here is a little piece that has seldom been equalled in depth and beauty of thought; yet it has sometimes been complained of as obscure, we see not why:

["The Rhea," 9.5–11.27]

Several of the other pieces are poor; some are stiff and rude, having no lofty thoughts to atone for their unlovely forms. Some have quaint names, which seem given to them out of mere caprice. Such are the following: Mithridates, Hamatreya, Hermione, Merlin, Merops, &c. These names are not more descriptive of the poems they are connected with, than are Jonathan and Eleazer of the men thus baptized. What have Astrea, Rhea and Etienne de la Boéce to do with the poems which bear their names?

We should think the following lines,

from Hermione, were written by some of the youngest Emersonidæ:

["Hermione," 102.1–21]

Such things are unworthy of such a master.

Here is a passage which we will not attempt to criticize. He is speaking of Love:

["The Initial Love," 108.16–19]

Good Homer sometimes nodded, they say; but when he went fast asleep he did not write lines or print them.

Here is another specimen. It is Monadnoc that speaks:

["Monadnoc," 70.16–19]

And yet another:

["Woodnotes," 43.16–18]

We have seen imitations of this sort of poetry, which even surpassed the original. It does not seem possible that Emerson can write such stuff simply from "lacking the accomplishment of verse." Is it that he has a false theory, and so wilfully writes innumerous verse, and plays his harp, all jangling and thus out of tune? Certainly it seems so. In his poems he uses the old mythology, and in bad taste; talks of Gods, and not God; of Pan, the Oreads, Titan, Jove and Mars, the Parcæ and the Dæmon.

There are three elaborate poems which demand a word of notice. The "Woodnotes" contains some good thoughts, and some pleasing lines, but on the whole a Pine tree which should talk like Mr. Emerson's pine ought to be plucked up by the roots and cast into the depths of the sea. "Monadnoc" is the title of another piece which appears forced and unnatural, as well as poor and weak. The third is called "initial, dæmonic and celestial Love." It is not without good thoughts, and here and there a good line, but in every attribute of poetry it is far inferior to his majestic essay on Love. In his poetry Mr. Emerson often loses his command of language, metaphors fail him, and the magnificent images which adorn and beautify all his prose works, are gone.

From what has been said, notwithstanding the faults we have found in Emerson, it is plain that we assign him a very high rank in the literature of mankind. He is a very extraordinary man. To no English writer since Milton can we assign so high a place; even Milton himself, great genius though he was, and great architect of beauty, has not added so many thoughts to the treasury of the race; no, nor been the author of so much loveliness. Emerson is a man of genius such as does not often appear, such as has never appeared before in America, and but seldom in the world. He learns from all sorts of men, but no English writer, we think, is so original. We sincerely lament the want of logic in his method, and his exaggeration of the intuitive powers, the unhappy consequences of which we see in some of his followers and admirers. They will be more faithful than he to the false principle which he lays down, and will think themselves wise because they do not study, learned because they are ignorant of books, and inspired because they say what outrages common sense. In Emerson's poetry there is often a ruggedness and want of finish which seems wilful in a man like him. This fault is very obvious in those pieces he has put before his several essays. Sometimes there is a seed-corn of thought in the piece, but the piece itself seems like a pile of rubbish shot out of a cart which hinders the seed from germinating. His admirers and imitators not unfrequently give us only the rubbish and probably justify themselves by the example of their master. Spite of these defects, Mr. Emerson, on the whole, speaks with a holy power which no other man possesses who now writes the English tongue. Others

245

have more readers, are never sneered at by respectable men, are oftener praised in the Journals, have greater weight in the pulpits, the cabinets and the councils of the nation; but there is none whose words so sink into the mind and heart of young men and maids; none who work so powerfully to fashion the character of the coming age. Seeing the power which he exercises, and the influence he is likely to have on generations to come, we are jealous of any fault in his matter, or its form, and have allowed no private and foolish friendship to hinder us from speaking of his faults.

This is his source of strength: his intellectual and moral sincerity. He looks after Truth, Justice, and Beauty. He has not uttered a word that is false to his own mind or conscience; has not suppressed a word because he thought it too high for men's comprehension, and therefore dangerous to the repose of men. He never compromises. He sees the chasm between the ideas which come of man's nature and the institutions which represent only his history; he does not seek to cover up the chasm, which daily grows wider between Truth and Public Opinion, between Justice and the State, between Christianity and the Church; he does not seek to fill it up, but he asks men to step over and build institutions commensurate with their ideas. He trusts himself, trusts man, and trusts God. He has confidence in all the attributes of infinity. Hence he is serene; nothing disturbs the even poise of his character, and he walks erect. Nothing impedes him in his search for the true, the lovely and the good; no private hope, no private fear, no love of wife or child, of gold, or ease, or fame. He never seeks his own reputation; he takes care of his Being, and leaves his seeming to take care of itself. Fame may seek him; he never goes out of his way a single inch for her.

He has not written a line which is not conceived in the interest of mankind. He never writes in the interest of a section, of a party, of a church, of a man, always in the interest of mankind. Hence comes the ennobling influence of his works. Most of the literary men of America, most of the men of superior education, represent the ideas and interests of some party; in all that concerns the welfare of the Human Race, they are proportionably behind the mass who have only the common culture; so while the thought of the people is democratic, putting man before the accidents of a man, the literature of the nation is aristocratic, and opposed to the welfare of mankind. Emerson belongs to the exceptional literature of the times— and while his culture joins him to the history of man, his ideas and his whole life enable him to represent also the nature of man, and so to write for the future. He is one of the rare exceptions amongst our educated men, and helps redeem American literature from the reproach of imitation, conformity, meanness of aim, and hostility to the progress of mankind. No faithful man is too low for his approval and encouragement; no faithless man too high and popular for his rebuke.

A good test of the comparative value of books, is the state they leave you in. Emerson leaves you tranquil, resolved on noble manhood, fearless of the consequences; he gives men to mankind; and mankind to the laws of God. His position is a striking one. Eminently a child of Christianity and of the American idea, he is out of the Church and out of the State. In the midst of Calvinistic and Unitarian superstition, he does not fear God, but loves and trusts Him. He does not worship the idols of our time—Wealth and Respectability, the two calves set up by our modern Jeroboam. He fears not the damnation these idols have the power to inflict—neither poverty nor social disgrace.

In busy and bustling New England comes out this man serene and beautiful as a star, and shining like "a good deed in a naughty world." Reproached as an idler, he is active as the sun, and pours out his radiant truth on Lyceums at Chelmsford, at Waltham, at Lowell, and all over the land. Out of a cold Unitarian Church rose this most lovely light. Here is Boston, perhaps the most humane city in America, with its few noble men and women, its beautiful charities, its material vigor, and its hardy enterprise; commercial Boston, where honor is weighed in the public scales, and justice reckoned by the dollars it brings; conservative Boston, the grave of the Revolution, wallowing in its wealth, yet grovelling for more, seeking only money, careless of justice, stuffed with cotton yet hungry for tariffs, sick with the greedy worm of avarice, loving money as the end of life, and bigots as the means of preserving it; Boston, with toryism in its parlors, toryism in its pulpits, toryism in its press, itself a tory town, preferring the accidents of man to man himself—and amidst it all there comes Emerson, graceful as Phæbus-Apollo, fearless and tranquil as the sun he was supposed to guide, and pours down the enchantment of his light, which falls where'er it may, on dust, on diamonds, on decaying heaps to hasten their rapid rot, on seeds new sown to quicken their ambitious germ, on virgin minds of youth and maids to waken the natural seed of nobleness therein, and make it grow to beauty and to manliness. Such is the beauty of his speech, such the majesty of his ideas, such the power of the moral sentiment in men, and such the impression which his whole character makes on them, that they lend him, everywhere, their ears, and thousands bless his manly thoughts.

Note

1 Reviewed are *Nature, Essays [First Series], Essays: Second Series, Poems, Nature; Addresses, and Lectures*, and *Representative Men*.

L.W.B.,
"Ralph Waldo Emerson,"
Yale Literary Magazine,
5 (March 1850), 203–6

The appearance of a new book from the pen of Mr. Emerson is an event of no little interest and importance in the literary world. We say this with confidence, nothwithstanding the sneers and deprecations of many excellent people who are ignorant of his productions, and of a few who are not. It is a matter of fact that Mr. Emerson has numerous readers and warm admirers, and with these the cry of Nonsense! Absurdity! Blasphemy! will be of little avail. Since it can not be denied that he possesses a singular power of attraction and fascination over some minds, would it not be more just and philosophical to search for the elements of this power, than to decry and ridicule its effects?

We can not believe, as some would fain have us, that his power is merely that of obscurity and mystery,—a sort of Masonic profundity, into the dark emptiness of which many spend time and toil to penetrate, and then care not to confess that they have laid out a fool's labor. We have too much faith in human nature to admit it; besides this our own reading has convinced us that the judgment of his admirers here, and the almost universal voice of foreign criticism is not false in awarding to him at least the merit of great brilliancy and attractiveness of style and abundant originality and richness of thought. The grace and fitness of his metaphors, the freshness of his expressions, the poetic and truthful originality of his descriptions, in which by the introduction of new items and new facts, unknown to the common-

place book of the poet, he re-creates old scenes of which the eye was tired, and restores to them more than their primitive interest.—all these rare qualities it would be an easy task to illustrate from the volume before us; but they are so evident to the eye of the reader that we need not specify them particularly. Another and more important element of Mr. Emerson's power is an earnest and genial manliness. With this his writings are quickened and flushed as with a heart-blood. His reverence for virtue, his love of man, his hopeful faith in progress, his religious care for the spiritual above the material, and his unrestrained freedom of thought and speculation, must and do make him many friends among a class whom mere genius and intellect fail to conciliate. We think it no arrogance, if, in this place, we assume to represent the class of young men; and we may not believe that any cry of blasphemy or impiety, or any frightful exhibition of consequences, will ever convince the consciences of young men of the sinfulness of free-thought. The sin of blasphemy lies as we think, not in opinion, but in language. In the present instance, however Mr. Emerson's carelessness of other people's opinions, or rather his desire of irritating their ideas, may have led him into startling expressions, we are not ready to believe him guilty of intentional impiety.

We come now to speak of the substance of intellectual opinions which underlies the qualities we have described above. And we say in the outset that we speak of these with no favorable feelings. Mr. Emerson, both in his manner of life and manner of writing, seems to hold himself in a sphere beyond the weaknesses and limitations of ordinary humanity. Secluded in his cottage at Concord, he spends his time in rapt communion with Nature and with "the Spirit" only interrupting his meditations to make his annual journey to Boston, where his Egerian revelations are communicated to wondering disciples in lectures whose spiritual contents are afterwards set forth to the less appreciating vulgar by means of the material types of Monroe & Co. Now an oracular and exclusive style like this does not commend Mr. Emerson to the favor of this puritanic and democratic community. We feel toward him as toward those fantastic itinerant prophets, hatless and bearded, who sometimes attempt to enlighten our incredulous ears with a new apocalypse,—that is, we take pleasure in seeing him contradicted and "*snubbed.*" But we have always noticed that the most effectual method to pursue toward these characters is not a course of dispute and argument, but one of concession and respect; to receive their disturbing novelties as if they were the most unquestioned, old-fashioned, matter-of-course orthodoxy; or (when this is impossible) as if they were at least nothing but very old and commonplace error. Then certainly, if not before, will the unentertained angels be persuaded to shake off the dust of their feet, and leave the light-haters in peace and darkness. Thus we wish to show that the sublimated Emerson is much such an one as ourselves, that his oddities and peculiarities rise from very human causes, and that his oracular sayings find their proper category in some of the various "isms" known to the dictionary.

Perhaps the characteristic by which Mr. Emerson is best known is his obscurity. This we do not ascribe to affectation, though if we did there would be few to deny it. Neither is it due entirely to the abstract nature of his subjects, and the ethereal and spiritual substance of his thoughts, as his friends would fain persuade us. There is another cause, quite sufficient to account for it, and which is very well known to exist—*his excessive horror of cant.* This he learned in his early training as an Unitarian minister, and soon bettered his instruction so that his teachers discarded him. His hatred of cant has now risen to such a pitch that it has become a moral principle with him never to call a thing twice by the same name: we verily believe he would deny the Diety of Reason or his own inspiration, if it were offered to him in a formula and mentioned as "the same" and "the aforesaid," we only wonder that he has not conscientious scruples against the use of the personal pronouns. The obscurity that must result from the want of a nomenclature is too obvious to need further words.

Mr. Emerson's ostentation of universal learning has become in his later works, and particularly in this his last, so striking as to be a marked characteristic of his style. It is difficult to charge a character of such beauty and nobleness with the attempt to impose upon his reader's admiration; still we can not but think that this feature in his writing is some little relic of human weakness. We do not allude so much to his quotations from unused and unknown authorities, and his display of Chinese and Hindoo lore, as to the long and strangely diversified lists of names with which he continually decorates his pages, and which, however they may illustrate his meaning, excite an inward suspicion that they have a second object—to display the author's reading. His writings in this respect remind us strongly of compositions for the Piano-Forte, "arranged for the left hand only," instead of carrying his theme plainly along, with an explanatory counterpoint, he flies off in a celestial rhapsody of spiritual analogies, occasionally fetching in his harmony by sweeping up an arpeggio of great names, in incongruous juxtaposition, from Adam to the Poughkeepsie prophet,—the object being "to show the skill of the performer."

To leave these mere externals: in speaking of Mr. Emerson's philosophical opinions it will be our chief end to assign him his proper place among philosophers. And first, he is *not* an Idealist,—at least in the sense in which the critics are pleased to consider him so.[1] That is, he believes in the reality of matter, in contradiction to the Ideal Theory of Berkeley. We are aware that in his essay on "Idealism" ("Nature," p. 59) he exhibits the nature and grounds of this theory in his most beautiful and eloquent manner, and it is from this, doubtless, that the critics have formed their opinion. Yet in the very next essay, he discards it expressly, in terms like the following. . . . "if it only deny the existence of matter, it does not satisfy the demands of the spirit. . . . The heart resists it, because it baulks the affections" p. 78. And again: "Let it stand then, in the present state of our knowledge, *merely as a useful introductory hypothesis*" p. 79. Will not this clear him from the charge of "Idealism," which most of the critics seem to take for granted?

Mr. Emerson *is* a mystic. His belief that the soul is a member of God, is perhaps the most prominent feature of his philosophy. We say "a *member* of God," for to say an *emanation* would not express the whole of his meaning. His ideas on this point he has so often and so variously expressed, that there can be no mistake about them. His first volume of Essays opens with the following proposition—an intuitive one, we suppose, or a special revelation, for he does not attempt to prove it. "There is one mind common to all individual minds. Every man is an inlet to the same, and to all of the same. He that is once admitted to the right of reason is made a freeman of the whole estate. . . . Who hath access to this universal mind is a party to all that is or can be done, for this is the *only and sovereign agent*." So elsewhere, "man is conscious of a universal soul within or behind his individual life. . . . This universal soul he

calls Reason. . . . That which intellectually considered, we call Reason, considered in relation to nature, we call spirit. Spirit is the Creator." (Nature, p. 34). Not only does he consider himself in direct communication and connection with God, but he would fain have us believe that he is "in some degree divine." We know not just what he would think to be his share of Omnipotence. We have not yet heard of his attempting to show or lighten. He claims indeed to be the author of "Nature," and Mr. Thoreau quite worships him: but Mr. Emerson defines his own position more exactly in the following precise and philosophical terms. "Standing on the bare ground,—my head bathed by the blithe air, and uplifted into infinite space,—all mean egotism vanishes. I become a transparent eyeball. I am nothing, I see all. The currents of the Universal Being circulate through me; I am part or particle of God."

Mr. Emerson would apparently be glad to be considered an eclectic. He displays great liberality and catholicity in examining the doctrines of all schools except the materialists; for these he has no mercy. His eclecticism, however, seems more like the easy yielding of an amiable reader to what is said last, than the candid discrimination of a careful inquirer. We imagine that he justifies this style of criticism from some peculiar views of Universal Truth; he doubtless supposes that, as "all evil is good in the making," so all error may be undeveloped Truth—a truly transcendental conclusion.

After all, it is a very difficult task to say with certainty of Mr. Emerson, what he is, except that he is a poet. His opinions are set forth not in a system, nor with the clear and exact expression of the philosopher, but in the unconstrained and brilliant diction of the poet. He mingles in a splendid medley, the spiritual deductions of philosophy, and the graceful analogies of poetry, with the effect, if not with the intention, of making it extremely difficult for the mind to discriminate between the two. His pages appear in the dangerous disguise of simple prose; half their harmfulness would be prevented by the introduction of those warning capital letters which stand uttering their continual *caveat* along the pages of Bailey's Festus, and Pollok's Course of Time. It is by the grandness of his imagination, the brilliancy and beauty of his language, and the genial enthusiasm of the manner, rather than by logical power and the force of argument, that he succeeds in impressing opinions, from the plain statement of which, however true they may appear to himself, the minds of most of his readers would shrink in horror.

It only remains for us to say a word on the character of the work whose title stands at the head of this article. It exhibits in a high degree the beauty and strength of Mr. Emerson's style, at the same time presenting a practical and earthy character very unusual in his writings. Even had we room, it would not be easy to give a satisfactory account of it, for its beauties lie more in the execution than in the plan. It is sufficient to commend it as a "book to be chewed," but not to be swallowed.

Note

1 "See, for example, Westminster Review, vol. xxxiii, Blackwood, for Jan. 1848."

[C. C. Felton],
"Emerson's
Representative Men,"
North American Review,
70 (April 1850), 520–4

No American, perhaps we may add no English, reader needs to be told who and what Mr. Emerson is. In poetry and in prose, by spoken discourse and by written books, he has stamped his personality too deeply to be effaced upon the literature and speculations of the age. Some things he has published will live as long as the language itself; but much of his verse, constructed upon whims rather than under the influence of the spirit of poetry, will die out among the short-lived oddities of the day. Much of his prose, too, the product of imitation, unconscious perhaps, of vicious foreign models, can scarcely be expected to survive the charm which hangs about his person and lingers in the magic tones of his voice.

Mr. Emerson is a great writer, and an honest and independent thinker, on the whole. He is not, however, what one of the idolaters has lately called him, a Phæbus Apollo, descended from Olympus with hurtling arrows and the silver twanging bow. He is neither the god of the lyre, nor will his shafts deal death among the host of those who fail to reverence *his priest*, though Emerson, too, Phæbus–like, has often "walked in darkness like the Night." This conversion of a modern Yankee into a Pagan god is a dangerous attempt to apply the *rationalistic* principle to persons and things of the present day. Some disciple of the school of historical skepticism has been trying his hand at turning Mr. Emerson into a *myth*. We object to the proceeding altogether, not knowing where it will end, and whose turn will come next. Homer, Lycurgus, Solon, and other nebulous spots in the sky of antiquity, have already been resolved, and now Mr. Emerson is undergoing the same process. That great *realist*, Mr. Weller, Senior, hit the nail on the head and struck out the true principle for such cases. "Wot I like in that 'ere style of writing," said he, after listening to his son Sam's *valentine*, "is that there 'aint no callin' names in it,—no Wenusses, nor nothin' o' that kind; wot's the good o' callin' a young 'ooman a Wenus or a angel, Sammy?"

The present volume is marked strongly both by the excellence and defects of Mr. Emerson's other writings. His style is often musical, clear, and brilliant; words are selected with so rare a felicity that they have the shine of diamonds, and they cut their meaning on the reader's mind as the diamond's edge leaves it trace deep and sharp on the surface of glass. But by and by, we fall upon a passage which either conveys no distinct sense, or in which some very common-place thought is made to sound with the clangor of a braying trumpet. Quaintness of thought and expression is his easily besetting sin; and here lies the secret of his sympathy with Carlyle, that highly gifted master of oddity and affectation. As a writer, Mr. Emerson is every way Carlyle's superior, would he but let the Carlylese dialect alone. He has more imagination, more refinement and subtlety of thought, more taste in style, more exquisite sense of rhythm. Perhaps his range of intellectual vision is not so broad. He has not the learning of Carlyle, nor the abundant humor, which sometimes reconciles us even to absurdity. But Mr. Emerson has a more delicate wit, a wit often quite irresistible by its unexpected turns, and the sudden introduction of effective contrasts.

Carlyle has an extraordinary abundance of words, a store of epithets, good, bad, and indifferent, by which the reader is often flooded; Emerson is more temperate and artistic. And yet we catch him, every now and then, mimicking the Scotchman, as if Carlyle were the master, and Emerson the pupil. He imitates Carlyle's affectation of odd and quaint expressions; he imitates him in the structure of his sentences; he imitates him in borrowing from the Germans a transcendental coloring, and in putting on an air of indifference to all positive opinions, an assumption of even-handed impartiality towards all religious systems. The trick of grotesque illustration by common or vulgar objects, he has caught from the Platonic Socrates. But setting aside these imitations and affectations, there hovers over much of his writing a peculiar and original charm, drawn from no source but the delicate and beautiful mind of the author himself.

The six men, who are here brought forward as representative characters, are Plato, Swedenborg, Montaigne, Shakespeare, Napoleon, and Goethe. At first sight, the choice appears a little whimsical, as to some, at least, of the members of this representative body. The number is certainly small, and the names are select enough—an oligarchy which we suspect the republic of letters would be slow to submit to. We see, with regard to two or three of them, the personal sympathies of the author, as in Montaigne and Swedenborg. In the delineation of the characters of these six representatives, we find much knowledge, frequent brilliancy of expression, followed by intense darkness, and flashes of thought that shoot up like streams of fire from volcanoes in the night. But on the whole, they are rather attempts to set forth qualities of character than to represent characters. The effect is, in every case, fragmentary. They are like the studies of an artist, who has painted

252

portions of his picture on separate bits of canvas, and then, instead of combining them into a great and harmonious whole by working them together under the inspiration of a general idea, stitches the sundered members as chance may arrange them. We do not, therefore, rise from the study of any one of them with an idea of it as an organic whole. There is no method, no unity of effect, though there are separate and inimitable felicities of execution. To borrow another figure, the ingredients are not poured together and moulded at a single casting.

There is also a tone of exaggeration in the exhibition of each man's peculiar qualities. The true position of these individual representatives in the intellectual history of the world is not correctly given; at least, so it seems to us. For instance, though one can hardly overstate the *genius* of Plato, understanding by that word the sum total of his natural and acquired gifts, yet the first sentence of the lecture on Plato is a monstrous piece of overdone assertion. "Among books," says Emerson, "Plato only is entitled to Omar's fanatical compliment to the Koran, when he said, 'Burn the libraries, for their value is in this book.'" And again, "Out of Plato come all things that are still written and debated among men of thought."

Part of this vivid rhetoric is perhaps due to the exigencies of the lecture form. One is always tempted, while addressing a popular audience, to heighten the truth for the sake of deepening the effect. But making all proper deductions from the statements on this ground, is the residue correct and sound? To say nothing of great modern thinkers, who have mastered regions of thought which Plato never dreamed of,—did Plato include his immediate successor, Aristotle? Surely not. With a genius more profound than Plato's, with a bright imagination though not so vivid, with a comprehensiveness of positive knowledge, compared with which Plato's was that of a school-boy, with a keenness of analysis never yet surpassed, with a vigorous common sense which understood itself amidst the circumstances of the actual world,—Aristotle divided the empire over the human mind with Plato, to say the least; he founded an influence, which controlled the schools through the Middle Ages, and has not yet been overthrown. Let us not undervalue Plato's calm and lofty spirit, the magic of his style, the dramatic and exquisite skill of his dialogues, the impressive grandeur of his moral views upon justice and injustice, sin, future retribution, and the Divine character. But when he endeavored to carry out these conceptions of the academic groves, conceptions so nobly uttered in the Phædo, the Crito, and the Gorgias, when he undertook to construct a theoretic republic, wherein the faculties of men should be most freely unfolded, and the destiny of man rise to the highest exaltation which his nature is capable of attaining when freed from the weights that the imperfections of existing institutions hang about him,—what was the result? We confess that we never read the Polity of Plato without a profound sadness. It has noble and magnificent passages, which are inspired "with an earnestness," as Mr. Emerson truly says, "which amounts to piety." But his justice sanctioned perpetual bondage, and his piety was not outraged by community of women, both of which were among the fundamental ordainments of his ideal state; while Homer, on account of the unbecoming stories he tells concerning the gods, is to be civilly turned out of doors.

In the course of this lecture, we are entertained with a portrait of Socrates. This also is an exaggeration; that is, the whole effect is wide of the true impression which that great martyr-philosopher ought to leave upon the mind. Socrates had the whimsical peculiarities which Mr. Emerson delineates; but they were far from being such prominent and essential parts of him, as they appear in this sketch. Plato used the name of Socrates, and the witty, arguing, questioning characteristics of his daily life, because precisely these were the most dramatic—precisely these answered the end of Plato's art. But a justly proportioned figure of Socrates can only be made by combining the three representations of Plato, Xenophon, and Aristophanes;—the first for the peculiarities of his talk, for his lofty and inflexible morality, for his religious earnestness; the second for a historical account of the man; and the third for a parody upon his personal peculiarities and his modes of dealing with the minds of others. The first must be employed with caution, and with considerable deductions on account of Plato's artistic mode of representing the persons of his dialogue; the third must be looked on with great distrust, as the work of an unscrupulous wit, who really knew but little of Socrates, but was tempted by the salient points of his ludicrous exterior, to bring him with all the ingenuity of the richest comic genius the world has ever seen, upon the Athenian stage for the entertainment of an audience, who, so that they were amused, cared for little else. With these preliminary "monitions to the reader," we commend the passage to which we refer, as a pleasant piece of whimsical exaggeration.

Compare either of the Gospels with the Life of Mahomet, as it is candidly set forth by Washington Irving, and good taste, if not religious sensibility, should prevent a writer from putting the two names together. There are some, however, who are foolish enough to think that such outrages are proof of independence, and who see nothing in the alliteration of "Jesus or Judas" but a fine illustration of superiority to the prejudices of the world around them.

We have merely touched upon a striking peculiarity of Mr. Emerson, in a religious point of view—his apparent indifference to positive religious belief, as shown by his manner of classing all beliefs together. When Christ and Socrates are spoken of in the same breath, we wonder that the military exploits, the exclusive love of Athens, the neglect of domestic duties, the humor, the drollery, and the drinking bouts of the latter do not rise in strange contrast with the universality that embraced Jew and Gentile alike in the arms of divine love, the sad and gentle earnestness to which a jest would be a profanation, and the awful authority that went with our Lord as from on high, compelling the hearers of his word to cry out that "never man spake like this man." And more still do we wonder, when Mahomet and the Saviour are classed together as religious geniuses and reformers, that those who so contemplate them do not feel the shocking incongruity of placing the serene, self-denying, and spotless life of the one—even if we regard him as but a man—his pure and peaceful teachings, which stopped not at outward acts, but pierced to the root of wickedness in the heart, side by side with the worldly ambition, the violence, the imposture, the shedding of blood, the fierce and exclusive bigotry, and the insatiable licentiousness of the other.

Checklist of Additional Reviews

Springfield *Daily Republican*, 10 January 1850, p. 2.

[N. P. Willis], "Literary Notices," New York *Home Journal*, 19 January 1850, p. 3.

New York *Daily Tribune*, 22 January 1850, p. 1.

American Whig Review, n.s. 5 (February 1850), 216.

Eclectic Review, 4th ser., 27 (February 1850), 261.

Holden's Dollar Magazine, 5 (February 1850), 126.

[George H. Gould], *Indicator: A Literary Periodical* [Amherst, Mass.], 1 (February 1850), 214–20.

United States Magazine, and Democratic Review, 25 (February 1850), 189.

Hunt's Merchants Magazine, 22 (March 1850), 364.

Peterson's Magazine, 17 (March 1850), 160.

Critic [England], n.s. 9 (1 March 1850), 119.

Examiner, 2199 (23 March 1850), 181.

Britannia, ca. April 1850.

Westminster and Foreign Quarterly Review, 53 (April 1850), 149.

British Quarterly Review, 11 (May 1850), 281–315.

Christian Observer, n.s. 149 (May 1850), 355–6.

Eclectic Magazine, 20 (May 1850), 143.

[Daniel March], "Popular Lectures," *New Englander*, 8 (May 1850), 186–202.

People's and Howitt's Journal, n.s. 2 (June 1850), 361.

"Emerson's Representative Men," *Sharpe's London Journal*, 11 (June 1850), 364–70.

[George Gilfillan], *Palladium*, 1 (July 1850), 44–55.

"Panthea" [Sophia Dobson Collet], "Emerson's Representative Men," *Reasoner*, 10 (25 December 1850), 229–32.

[James A. Froude], *Eclectic Review*, 5th ser., 3 (May 1852), 568–82.

English Traits

Review of *English Traits,
Anthenæum*, 1506
(6 September 1856),
1109–11

Mr. Emerson crossed the seas to lecture to us—he re-crossed them to lecture *at* us. The first man he talked to in England was Coleridge—the last Mr. Carlyle; and between the first word and the last—as here recorded—there is an interval of talk, some of it pleasant, more of it eccentric, and not a little of it dreary. On the whole, England has been happy enough to please her critic; yet, with all his politeness and rosy compliments, Mr. Emerson leaves us with an impression that America, not England, is the *true seat of the Saxon race*. The same imperial character has been claimed, by various writers, for the Isle of Thanet, and for Guernsey and Jersey. Mr. Emerson likes our people, with a few drawbacks and qualifications, which he must record and deplore,—such as our want of wit and fancy; but we suspect he likes us chiefly for those qualities of mind and character in which he finds some resemblances to qualities nearer home. In fact, Mr. Emerson, when painting the model Englishman to his friends in the United States, is evidently thinking of the Broadway rather than the Strand; and the faults which he finds with us we read of with perfect good humour, because we know they are not our faults, so much as they are our neighbours'. For example, when he writes:—"A strong common sense, which it is not easy to unseat or disturb, marks the English mind for a thousand years; a rude strength newly applied to thought, as of sailors and soldiers who had lately learned to read. They have no fancy, and never are surprised into a covert or witty word." Do we care to array names and fames in opposition to such a sentence? Not at all. We are content; we see that Mr. Emerson is brooding over a provincial—possibly a colonial—state of mind and culture; that his words, if they be true at all, may be true of Manchester, of Sydney, of Graham's Town, and of New York; but that they are not true, in any sense, of London. Our metropolis, however, on the whole, fares pretty well with the author:—it is a fine place, worth a visit to Europe; but then it is at its best, and is about to descend, in favour—we suppose—of New York or Philadelphia. "If we will visit London," says Mr. Emerson to his countrymen, "the present time is the best time, as some signs portend that it has reached its highest point. It is observed that the English interest us a little less within a few years; and hence the impression that the British power has culminated, is in solstice, or already declining." Is not this exquisite and generous? The English interest *us* a little less than they did—*ergo*, they are on the road to ruin! In another place Mr.

Emerson tells us that the English, counting forty millions, rule over 182 millions of souls; and that America, "exclusive of slaves," contains twenty millions of a kindred race. By his own showing, the forty millions in England and her Colonies rule over 182 millions of freemen, while the twenty millions in America rule over three millions of slaves. Is it not a pretty Yankee Doodle then who will stand up and tell us that we are going down in the world because *it* has withdrawn from us a ray or two of the light of its countenance? No one ever charged our dear Jonathan with modesty; but this little trait of sentiment puts him far above the line of fantastic Bobadils and Malvolios. We in London fancy our city in its youth; we see new cities clustering to it every year, rounding it off with beauty; cities, we may remind American readers, larger than Charleston, almost as large as Boston, rising every twelve months in its suburbs.

Contrary to the common thought in Europe, Mr. Emerson finds that London is England,—nay, that the real Englishman is not found on the earth's surface, except in London. "What we think of when we talk of English traits really narrows itself to a small district. It excludes Ireland, and Scotland, and Wales, and reduces itself at last to London,—that is, to those who come to and to thither." No, the Englishman is not found in Ireland or Wales. He is a stranger in Scotland. He is not known in Manchester.—"As you go north into the manufacturing and agricultural districts, and to the population that never travels, as you go into Yorkshire, as you enter Scotland, the world's Englishman is no longer found. In Scotland, there is a rapid loss of all grandeur of mien and manners; a provincial eagerness and acuteness appear; the poverty of the country makes itself remarked, and a coarseness of manners; and, among the intellectual, is the insanity of dialectics. In Ireland are the same climate and soil as in England, but less food, no right relation to the land, political dependence, small tenantry, and an inferior or misplaced race."

London, though in its decline, is the only seat of the Englishman: he is its glory and its charm; but it has one other feature,—its precious fog. "The night and day are too nearly of a colour. It strains the eyes to read and to write. Add the coal smoke. In the manufacturing towns, the fine soot or *blacks* darken the day, give white sheep the colour of black sheep, discolour the human saliva, contaminate the air, poison many plants, and corrode the monuments and buildings. The London fog aggravates the distempers of the sky, and sometimes justifies the epigram on the climate by an English wit, 'In a fine day, looking up a chimney; in a foul day, looking down one.'" Mr. Emerson has surely seen *his* picture of London through a pair of Paris spectacles. We fancy we have a little sunshine,—that our sky is sometimes blue,—that our fields are bright with gold, and our gardens gay with roses,—even close to London, and in London.

What follows, perhaps, is still more exquisite fooling:—

["Land," 42.11–42.24]

—Why a bigger Birmingham? Is Birmingham a combination of plain, forest, marsh, river, seashore? Has the iron town any one of these features? Mr. Emerson must sometimes descend to platitude and nonsense. The strongest eagle will weary on the wing, and must sometimes rest on mother-earth. Nonsense, however, is not Mr. Emerson's strong point. In spite of some weakness, he is generally fanciful and picturesque—even where least correct; so that we read him with a certain zest, as we tear our way through a copse that leads no-whither, but offers glimpses of light and shadow, sunny tree-tops, and sombre pools. Here is a pleasant paragraph:—

["Race," 45.11–48.12]

Mr. Emerson leans to the opinion that England is without genius—a melancholy leaning, we should think, to a man who sees that with or without genius England is to transform the world into its own likeness. Behold what pleasant things a writer may be forced to say when bent on the use of very strong language:—

["Land," 35.16–36.18]

But if England is a nation without genius—a point which it no way wounds us to concede, if Mr. Emerson will—what of America? The author charitably allows us talent.—

["Times," 262.13–263.6]

Our talent, however, is not much troubled with modesty. In fact, we are a nation of Jack Brags.—

["Cockayne," 145.24–146.7, 147.8–16, 149.7–150.12]

Here is a kindly appreciation of our Norman chivalry—and of our pride in it and reverence for what it brought us.—

["Race," 60.15–61.9]

Philosophers like Guizot and writers like Thierry would smile at this fury, doubtless; but as Englishmen it does not touch us, such is our obstinacy. Let us pass from Mr. Emerson *solus* to Mr. Emerson in dialogue, or better still to Mr. Emerson listening. One of his earliest acquaintances was Mr. Landor, of whom we have incidentally a character sketch:—

["First Visit," 6.27–8.9, 9.16–10.6]

Mr. Emerson understates—perhaps misunderstands—the estimate of Mr. Landor prevalent in London society. We are aware that he is sometimes attacked in reviews—which of us, worth powder and shot, is not attacked in reviews?—but we are not aware that the best prose writer of our time is *ignored*. Afterwards we get a peep at Coleridge:—

["First Visit," 10.7–14.21]

Coleridge monopolized the talk—an unpardonable sin to any seer,—and we forgive our American for the wrath which he very naturally felt on his return from Highgate.

With Wordsworth he fared little better.—

["Personal," 294.14–296.10]

After these representations and characters—and by way of a pairing chat with Mr. Emerson on matters personal and literary—let us hear what *he* thinks of some of our eminent writers.—

["Literature," 245.8–249.18]

Mr. Emerson runs on—and runs off—to his friend Mr. Carlyle, with whom he made a journey to Stonehenge and Wilton,—which he describes at tiresome length; the tow seers talking a stream of turbulent jargon, meant to be drowningly deep. The Chelsea sage, we fear, amused himself with his drastic humour and frolicsome make-believe; but Mr. Emerson seems to treat the thing seriously, and chronicles the smallest small-beer, the lightest of passing whimsies uttered by his friend, *not* in the eternal silences, without a pang of suspicion or remorse. The play closes very like a farce.

On the whole, we have read these 'English Traits' without emotion; and the book, as a book, will be remembered—if remembered at all—as a work wanting in substance and genuineness.

"Emerson's English Traits,"

Spectator [England], 29 (13 September 1856), 981

These essays on England and the English, for such the "Traits" really are, originated in two visits to this country: the first a passing call so long ago as 1833, at the end of a Continental tour; the second took place in consequence of an engagement to deliver a series of lectures in the North during 1847 and 1848. This last furnished Mr. Emerson with a wider range of general observation, and much better opportunities of studying the national characteristics as well as the external forms of things, than could be obtained by a flying tourist without any specific object beyond *doing* all the sights he could in a short space of time.

A few personal incidents and the particular remarks they suggest will be found; but the subjects of the essays are generalized into broad topics—as Land, involving a description of the climate, soil, cultivation, and the results of labour as affecting the appearance of the country. Wealth in England is handled not only in the effects of accumulation, but in the industry, enterprise, and character of the people that has produced so much, as well as the good and evil consequences. Aristocracy is considered shrewdly, fairly, and broadly—with perfect freedom from anything like democratic prejudice or undue admiration. In Universities and Literature, Mr. Emerson favourably contrasts the results in scholarship and writing which the severe training of England produces, compared with America, even in the case of men who are not remarkable for study. And so he goes on through

some fifteen chapters out of nineteen; four taking a narrative cast—as the Voyage, or being more limited to himself—as the one headed Personal.

With the author's wonted characteristics of penetrating observation, striking illustration, and copious accumulation of ideas, there is, we think, more of mellowness in style, and less imitation of the peculiarities of Carlyle, than appeared in Mr. Emerson's earlier productions. *English Traits* is the work of an original-minded man, looking favourably upon a country and a people with whom he has so much in common as to prevent the foreign element from interfering with his judgment, yet sufficiently removed, from customs, habits, and native character, to have everything come freshly to him. Even the reader accustomed to reflect on his countrymen will find many things presented which he has overlooked, and mostly in a complimentary, never in a carping way.

On the other hand, there are several matters that indicate a disposition to rely on popular errors, or conventional notions of English character, or that touch upon defects which seem passing away. He tells us "the *right* of the husband to sell the wife has been retained down to our times." No such right ever existed as derived from the character of husband; it is not an indictable offence. In his picture of the sturdy opinion-despising Englishman, bravely following his own "humours," or resisting being "put upon" by rank or wealth even to the risk of ruin, we fear he is painting a traditional class. The equally traditional idea as to the almost sullen reserve of Englishmen with strangers, is as a fact passing away, with the extended locomotion, and the more varied intercourse consequent upon travelling facilities. Englishmen may not talk so much as foreigners in promiscuous company, because it is not their custom to "ring the changes" on topics that are settled or exhausted; nor is fluency a national gift. There is certainly less stiffness or reserve than formerly: we question if there is any reserve in any class where immediately useful information can be given. Von Raumer, when in England, a good many years ago, noticed the ready civility with which even men of the lower class furnished him with directions, and took trouble in doing so. These essays have this English characteristic—they are wanting in the broad generalization of the Frenchman, who from a very slender observation and very few facts will oracularly settle anything.

The most attractive parts of Mr. Emerson's essays are those which refer to obvious things, yet require some freshness of vision to bring out in their full force, and suggest some under-current of comparison with matters in America. In this sense, "Wealth" is one of the best papers. These remarks well show the results of eight hundred years of security from foreign devastation, though not exactly from foreign invasion.

["Wealth," 163.4–164.27, 165.17–166.7]

The following observations on the real advantages possessed by nobility and on manners are good.

["Aristocracy," 185.9–186.25]

This volume is a cheap edition, published by Messrs. Routledge "by arrangement with the author"; though what he can get out of it seems difficult to imagine.

Review of *English Traits*, *Critic* [England], n.s. 15 (September 1856), 446–7

It is generally objected against the American travellers that they found big books upon very little observation; and, with the mass, it must be admitted that this criticism is perfectly just. How often do we receive a volume from the other side of the Atlantic—a smart enough volume in its way, so far as paper, print, and the bravery of gilding is concerned—professing to contain the impressions produced by "the Old World" upon the ingenuous mind of some denizen of the New. We open it, with a sad foreboding, induced by some experience of such works, and find—just what we expected. The mind in question having been almost unprepared by previous knowledge of the subject, and being dangerously inflated with an immense amount of national conceit, has not fructified usefully under the experiences of foreign travel; an air of vulgarity pervades the whole; ignorance is partly concealed behind prejudice; presumption takes the place of well grounded confidence; everything is dwarfed to suit a preconceived and not very lofty standard; and the general result tends only to inspire us with contempt for the author, and wonder at the laudatory notices of his production that come to us from the American press. Under these circumstances, but one course has been open to us; to speak out plainly and openly, without fear or favour what we think of such presumptuous judges of things European. This has brought down upon us the accusation of being unfairly prejudiced against American books; and we have even noticed pretty significant hints of what "the editor of The Critic" may expect if ever book of his shall come within the purview of the American press. Awaiting that fearful vengeance, and not doubting that it would be very terrible indeed, we ask, what are we to do? (Are we to sit quietly by whilst this grand old continent of Europe, with all its noble artistic and intellectual possessions, is defiled by a swarm of travellers who understand it as little as a snail would the Arundelian marbles if it were to crawl across them?) It was said of a Frenchman that, after spending half-an-hour in the Court of the Old Bailey, he went home and wrote a ponderous treatise upon the English Criminal Law. The American travellers are worse, for they write the treatise without spending so much as the half-hour in preparation. Shall we then let such book-makers pass scatheless, while we hold a pen that can transfix the criminals in the fact? A thousand times, no; and whether such books be few or many, whether their author be Member of Congress or Consul's wife, whatever be the luxury of printing or the prodigality of gilding, they are sure of one uniform reception here, the expression of a righteous contempt.

(But what really good American work was ever underrated in these columns? What author of real greatness or of sound merit ever received anything but an honest tribute of admiration from us? In proportion as we condemn bitterly, so do we praise heartily. Do we not hold Irving to be one of the tenderest and most genial of his species—a very Charles Lamb in the eloquence of his heart-speakings? and we known no higher praise. Are not the names of Cooper, of Hawthorne, of Elizabeth Wetherell, of Edgar Poe, of Lowell, of Longfellow, and of Prescott, dear to us?) Who ever knew us to indite one single detracting word against those bright glories of the great American nation? And how could we honestly love and admire these, while with the same breath we heaped fulsome praise upon Mr. N.P. Willis and the authors of such works as we have referred to above? Yet one more name there is that should have been incuded in the list of those whom we cherish and admire, and that stands upon the title-page of the little volume before us— it is that of Emerson, a man with a larger heart, and a far larger brain, than falls to the lot of most men.

As we take it up and turn it about, it seems to us that never was there a more unpretending little book than this. A little thin duodecimo, not two hundred pages long, bound in plainest of paper, and costing precisely one shilling; what a contrast it presents to the rich argosies of folly which generally come sailing to us in all the pomp of gilt-lettering and hot-press from the stores of New York, Philadelphia, and Boston. Yet in this little vessel we have found more real wisdom than in the works of all the American travellers put together who have attempted to write about this country from the beginning of the Union until now. Emerson has been twice to England: he has examined carefully and thoughtfully; and the results are here. He is not always right; but he is oftener so than most Englishmen would be upon the same subject. His errors (and they are not very numerous) arise always from the deficiency of information which it is no disgrace to him to be without. Facts which lie upon the surface he neglects never; those which lie within the reach of a clever man he passes over seldom. Altogether, we may say that, whether his estimate be flattering to our nationality, or whether it be the reverse, it is one of the best and most truthful that have hitherto been made. With this preface we shall subjoin a few extracts; assuming that the generality of our readers will not be satisfied without perusing the entire volume.

While in England Emerson, visited some of our celebrated men. Among the rest—

["First Visit," 14.2–16.3, 16.25–17.16, 18.3–19.2]

Also

["First Visit," 19.3–18, 22.2–23.14]

We now turn to some of his own opinions about what he saw here. First of all, about England itself:

["Land," 37.14–39.13, 42.11–43.16]

["Race," 67.15–68.4]

["Manners," 102.1–19, 103.26–106.8]

["Cockayne," 147.12–25; 148.12–15, 26–149.7; 149.16–19]

["Wealth," 153.1–154.1, 159.17–160.24]

["Aristocracy," 185.18–187.14]

["Religion," 220.23–221.25, 222.11–23]

The worst chapter in the book is that upon the *Times* newspaper; for it is full of exaggeration and contradiction. Mr. Emerson makes the common mistake of treating this publication as if it were possessed of great *original* power; while at the same time he admits that the secret of its great popularity consists in the versatility with which it *follows* public opinion. Now, the fact is that the *Times* originates nothing, and only appears to be powerful by always taking care to be on the dominant side. Mr. Emerson understands this—in fact, he says as much; yet we find him inditing such nonsense as— "What would the *Times* say? is a terror in Paris, in Berlin, in Vienna, in Copenhagen, and in Nepaul." Another assertion is not less curious; namely, that "a statement of fact in the *Times* is as reliable as a citation from Hansard." Whereas the truth is that the number of blunders which it commits in matters of fact is incomprehensible to those who know anything about its expensive and large organisation, and can only be accounted for upon the theory that its managers care much more for popularity than for accuracy.

Review of *English Traits*, *Harper's New Monthly Magazine*, 13 (October 1856), 694–6

The fame of Mr. Emerson as a poet and a transcendental philosopher, will naturally attract no small degree of attention to this volume. Readers who have known him only as a thinker of singular boldness and subtlety, if not of a wide and vigorous grasp, will be curious to discover the effect produced on his mind by the study of a people so positive, so practical, and so unimaginative as the English. In the description of their manners, he enters upon a new sphere of thought and illustration. The subject presents a remarkable contrast to his favorite themes of discussion. It brings him from the ideal regions, in which he delights to expatiate, into a world of the most solid realities. But he applies to its treatment the same qualities which characterize his previous compositions. His writings all show a rare power of observation, an unrelenting fidelity in the description of material facts, a sagacious insight into human motives and character, and innumerable felicities of expression, which often operate as a surprise, combined with a love of fanciful analogies, a tendency to rash generalizations, and a total absence of consecutive order and development. His thoughts stand to each other, not in the relation of genesis, but of juxtaposition. They betray no vital, mutual affinities, like the leaves, blossoms, and fruitage of a tree, but are placed side by side, like the brilliant specimens in a cabinet of gems. We are not led onward by a gradual ascent to the sight of new points of beauty in a harmonious landscape, but are transported, as by some strange power, into the midst of magic scenes, each of which has no connection with the preceding, and is often repeated with some slight change of feature, which gives an expression of novelty to the whole aspect.

Mr. Emerson's mind is more disposed to introspection than to the contemplation of external facts. To him, the material universe is merely a type of spiritual being. Events are without significance, except as the exponent of a universal law. His interest in material beauty is derived from the spiritual principle, which it represents. England, with her wonderful developments in the practical order, is an object of curious study, as illustrating the character of her people. His accurate observation of the surface never contents him with the superficial. He values the experience of life as it leads to the discovery of laws. Hence, in this work, the phases of English society are always held strictly subordinate to their illustration of the English mind. It should, therefore, be read less as a descriptive journal of incidents, than as a commentary on character. In this point of view, its value is singularly enhanced by the justice and impartiality which strongly mark the intellect of the author. No man ever wrote with a less degree of prejudices. With a temperament of habitual coldness, his love of truth amounts almost to a passion. We presume that every word in this volume has been weighed with a care and deliberation, as if the destiny of the age depended on its accuracy. One proof of this is the interval which has elapsed between the date of his travels and the publication of his volume. The first visit to England, on which it was founded, was made more than twenty years ago, while it is nearly ten years since his return from his latest tour in that country.

The general impression of England here

given by Mr. Emerson is favorable to her character for industrial advancement, the possession of solid material comforts, and integrity and honor in the private relations of life; but the picture which he has drawn is by no means flattering to the intellect of the nation, or her sense of probity or justice in public affairs. On the whole, he regards England as the best of actual nations. But it is poor and imperfect, with all her comparative superiority. It can make no pretensions to ideal harmony; it represents no divine or noble thought; it does not approach the integral symmetry of nature; but is a piece of motley patchwork—an old pile built in different ages, with repairs, additions, and makeshifts. The mind of the English is in a state of arrested development. They do not occupy themselves on matters of general and lasting import, but on the goods of a corporeal civilization, which perish in the using. Their temperament is offensive from its want of facility, and is not relieved by their external refinement. Their habit of thought is one of sleepy routine. They are cramped within narrow limits, and have no wish to break their fetters. They have the instinct of the tortoise, to hold hard to the ground with his claws lest he should be thrown on his back. As an animal, the Englishman is of the best breed—a wealthy, juicy, broad-chested creature, steeped in ale and good cheer, and a little overloaded by his flesh. He has, to a great degree, the qualities of mettle and bottom, which he most values in his horse. No fighting-cock shows more pluck.

In the field of literature and art the English of the present day occupy a lower plane than that which was held by the greatest names among their ancestors. For two centuries England was philosophical, religious, poetic. The national mind flowered in every faculty. But these heights of genius could not be maintained. They were followed by a meanness and a descent of the mind into lower levels. The later English have no insight of general laws. In the region of pure science they move with timid steps. They accumulate mountains of facts, without the inspiration to search for the pivotal law, around which they revolve, as a bad general demands myriads of men and miles of redoubts to compensate for his want of courage and conduct. Bacon is almost unique among the prose writers of his country in the faculty of generalization. Milton, who formed the table-land for the transition of English genius from the summits of Shakespeare, rarely used this privilege, especially in prose. For a long time afterward, it is not found in English literature. Burke was addicted to a certain mode of generalizing, but his thoughts have neither the depth nor the compass of the earlier school. Hume's abstractions are as little profound as wise. Doctor Johnson's oracular sentences have slight worth, except in their tone of feeling. Among recent writers, Mr. Emerson finds the type of English genius in Hallam. In his history of European literature, he steadily denies the expansive element by which literature is created. His eye does not reach to the ideal standards. His verdicts are all dated from London. He passes in silence the more profound masters, and shows that a lover of ideas is not only uncongenial to his taste, but perplexing to his intellect. The English mind lives out the past. Rich in its capital, it makes no account of future acquisitions. It can not discern the signs of the times. It does not hail the new forms that loom up on the horizon—the new and gigantic thoughts which can not find fit raiment in any old wardrobe.

The poetry and fiction of the day, according to Mr. Emerson, are circumscribed by the same municipal limits. Dickens writes London tracts. Like Hogarth, he is a painter of English details, local and temporary in his tints and style, as well as in his aims. Bulwer appeals to the worldly ambition of the student, and reverences intellect for its temporal uses. Thackeray finds that God has made no place in the universe for the heart, and that we must renounce ideals, and accept London. Macaulay explicitly teaches that good means material commodity—good to eat, good to wear—that the glory of modern philosophy is to yield economical inventions—that its merit is to avoid ideas, and to avoid morals. The triumph of the Baconian philosophy over the old Platonic, he thinks, is the disentangling the intellect from theories of the all-Fair and all-Good, and pinning it down to making a better sick-chair and a better wine-whey for an invalid. The eminent benefit of astronomy is its improvement of navigation, enabling the grocer to bring his wine and lemons to the London market at a cheaper rate. The civility and religion of England for a thousand years thus ends in reducing the intellect to a sauce-pan. The English cant of practical covers a world of skepticism. The doctrine of Macaulay makes reason and conscience a romantic pretension. The fine arts fall to the ground. Beauty, except as a luxurious commodity, does not exist.

Coleridge is one of those who save England from the reproach of no longer possessing the capacity to appreciate what rarest wit the island has produced. But even with his catholic mind and his hunger for ideas, the traditional Englishman in him was too strong for the philosopher—he fell into accommodations with the spirit of the age, and attempted to reconcile the Gothic rule of the Anglican Church with eternal ideas.

Doubtless there are exceptions to the limited tone of English thought, especially in the region of general culture, where there is no end to the graces and amenities, the wit, sensibility, and erudition of the learned class. But the artificial character of all English performance is also visible in letters. Much of their aesthetic production is antiquarian and manufactured. Literary reputations have been achieved by forcible men, whose relation to literature was purely accidental, but who were driven by the arbitrary tastes of the day into their several careers. The bias of Englishmen to practical skill has reacted on the national mind. They worship the five mechanic powers even in their song. The tone of the steam-whistle is heard in the voice of their modern muse. The poem is created as an ornament and finish of their monarchy, and not as the morning-star of a brighter day. Every literary production is mechanical in its structure, as if inspiration and wisdom had ceased among men. No poet dares murmur of beauty out of the precinct of his rhymes. No priest dares hint at a Providence which does not patronize English utility.

Still England is not hopelessly given over to material idolatry. Mr. Emerson recognizes the presence of a redeeming power, and offers some profound comments on the nature of its influence. There is a minority of perceptive minds in the nation that appreciate every soaring of intellect, every whisper of a divine idea. They present a strong counterbalance to the prevailing tendencies of the day. Studious, contemplative, experimenting, they are the teachers of their countrymen in spite of themselves. The two classes, which represent genius and animal force, interact on each other, and produce a salutary counterpoise. Though the first consists only of a dozen souls, and the second of twenty millions, their accord and discord forever yield the power of the English State.

We have given a rapid abstract of some of the chief points in Mr. Emerson's volume. But no one should fail to peruse the work for himself. It will not command universal assent, and its inconsecutive, aphoristic style, makes it liable to misconstruction. Still, where the positions of the author can not be accepted, they are rich in suggestion, and open a fruitful vein of wise reflection. The fresh vitality of the composition, though toned down below the standard of blood-heat, presents a constant attraction to the amateurs of marked idiosyncrasies, and with its seductive beauties of expression, will always insure a succession of charmed readers.

[Andrew P. Peabody], "Recent Books on England," *North American Review*, 83 (October 1856), 503–10

These books are of a description which always attracts and seldom wearies us.[1] Yet we enjoy them less as the records of what has been seen and heard, than as autobiographies. It has been well said, that we cannot thoroughly know even a kinsman or an intimate, till he has been our companion in travel. The attrition of new and strange objects, nationalities, and experiences brings out traits that may have been latent in familiar scenes,—powers that may have been only possibilities in the home-circle,—merits or defects that may have been merged in the routine-life of domestic, professional, or public duty. This same revelation, which the traveller inevitably makes to fellow-pilgrims, he who publishes his adventures imparts of necessity to his readers. We learn what he carries with him by what he finds. We ascertain what questions were in his mind by the answers he puts on record. We test his temper by his opinions of men and things. We probe his culture by the depth or shallowness of his observations. We trace his sinuosities by the track they leave on his path. Therefore it is that, even in England, where every place of interest and monument of note and man of mark is too well known for any added intimacy of acquaintance through the testimony of others, we still love to renew the round with each new tourist; and, if we gain nothing else, we have at least hung up in our repository another well-analyzed specimen of our own race.

Conversely, if the traveller is one whom we previously knew, or if his individuality is patent in his book, we learn much by his descriptions even of the most familiar persons and objects. He presents them from a new point of view, which we can compare with others. He gives us a fresh perspective, by which we may correct outlines previously in our own mind. He discloses to us bearings and relations, which have their counterpart in fact. For his impressions, preferences, or aversions, be they well or ill grounded, there are existing causes, which, if we know him, we can divine. Especially is all this true, if our tourist is a man of genius, taste, or large specific attainments in art or literature. Then, however strong may be his prejudices, however abnormal his standard, we can allow for his parallax, and even his one-sided representations may give us more accurate knowledge than his own senses gave him. Thus, while Ruskin's entire artistical creed may have hardly a disciple, who would not gratefully adopt him as a guide through the whole world of art, though often finding food for admiration in what he might denounce, and repudiating what he might praise?

Mr. Emerson's book, did it profess to describe all of England, would be justly open to the severest criticism. It ignores pauperism, ignorance, and crime, aristocratic pretension and plebeian sycophancy, sinecure laziness and under-paid labor,— in fine, all the inequalities of condition, realized right, and availing privilege, which assimilate the moral and social landscape of Great Britain much more nearly to the broken surface of Switzerland, than to the gentle alternations of hill and valley on its own soil. But all of the less pleasing "English traits" have been set forth with ample minuteness of detail by the greater portion of recent travellers, and we are glad to open one book that revives our early pride in our mother-land,

and makes us feel anew the unparalleled queenliness of her position and belongings. We by no means say that the tourist who beholds only the glory of England, and is blind to her shame, possesses our moral sympathy. This we must reserve for itinerants of the Heraclitus school; but while we read their writings with heightened emotion, they do not entertain or edify us.

With the intense *subjectivism* of Mr. Emerson's philosophy we are at swords' points. We hesitate not to say, that, pushed to its legitimate consequences, it neutralizes moral distinctions, eliminates duty and accountability, obliterates religion, and excludes the conception of a personal and self-conscious Diety. And even in the book before us, when religious or ethical subjects are touched upon, (which they are but seldom, and lightly,) we discern traces of the indifferentism which proceeds from the author's philosophy. But this very element is propitious to merely æsthetic observation and impression. Mr. Emerson threw open his own broad, rich, delicately organized, and generously cultured intellect, with an Argus-eyed passiveness, with a receptivity which no emotion or affection weakened or distorted, to take the exact impress of what he heard and saw.

The greatness of England is in fact the theme of all his chapters. And there are many aspects in which she is the greatest of the nations. She has enriched herself with the spoils of every zone and soil. Her language, a conglomerate from all the tongues of ancient and modern civilization, is the type of her national personality and genius. With hardly a tithe of the learning of Germany, she is the fountain of elegant scholarship. With often a paucity and never a redundance of creative talent, her literature embodies the wealth and beauty of all times and lands. Inferior to France in science, she immeasurably transcends her in its concrete forms and practical uses. Later than the Continental nations in almost every branch of lucrative industry, she has domesticated all their processes, and has made her manufactures the staple of the world's commerce. Limited in her natural resources, she supplements them by the empire of the sea, and the lordship of the tropics and the Orient. What her arms might fail of, her diplomacy secures. Her defeats bear the fruit of victory. Her one signal loss during these latter centuries, that of her rebel colonies in America, has but erected the best market for her products, opened the most humane asylum for her surplus population, and furnished the most genial seminary for her intellectual and moral influence. In her home economy, her greatest of national debts only consolidates her government, and insures the loyalty of her myriad creditors. Her enormous landed estates but strengthen the conservative and cripple the revolutionary elements of her population. Her monopolies and arbitrary prescriptions have worn deep niches in her constitution, and are clothed with all the semblance and prestige of sacred right. Every decaying timber in her political and social fabric is so buttressed, that it cannot fall till slow time disintegrates it; every weak member of the pile is so built around and over, that it bears no strain.

Mr. Emerson gives few details of his English sojourn. The titles of his chapters are such general heads of remark as "Land," "Race," "Manners," "Wealth," "Aristocracy," "Religion." Under each he gives rather the sum total of his observations, than the specific instances that served for his generalization. He delights in antithesis and contrast, and brings out with unequalled rhetorical force very many of the anomalies of the English commonwealth and society,—those balancings and co-workings of seemingly opposite and antagonistic forces, by which strength is born out of weakness, and the ever fresh and new from decadence and decline. Among the most striking specimens of this style of delineation, (and in felicity and point it can hardly be surpassed,) is the following, under the running-title "Factitious."

["Ability," 93.26–99.3]

Mr. Emerson has been twice in England. His second voyage thither was in 1847, at the invitation of several Mechanics' Institutes in Lancashire and Yorkshire, to deliver a series of lectures. The greater part of the work purports to give the impressions received during the tour made in pursuance of and in connection with that engagement. His first chapter, however, is devoted to an earlier visit, in 1833, and is chiefly filled with his interviews with persons well known in the literary world, such as Landor, Coleridge, Carlyle, and Wordsworth. He does not heighten our reverence for Coleridge, who overwhelmed him with a torrent of windy declamation, fraught with the intensest egotism and the stalest commonplaces. "The visit," says Mr. Emerson, "was rather a spectacle than a conversation, of no use beyond the satisfaction of my curiosity. He was old and preoccupied, and could not bend to a new companion and think with him." His visit to Wordsworth afforded him much greater edification, and presents the same amiable picture, so often given us, of the simple, true, kind, reverent old man, full of unconscious oddities, and, with virgin modesty, not one whit less egotistical than the pompous philosopher of Highgate.
[. . .]

Note

1 Also reviewed are *Impressions of England; or Sketches of English Scenery and Society* by A. Cleveland Coxe and *A Month in England* by Henry T. Tuckerman.

[Parke Godwin?], "Emerson on England," *Putnam's Monthly Magazine*, 8 (October 1856), 407–15

The position of Mr. Emerson in our literature is so well-defined and established, that it no longer excites to controversy. His characteristics, as a thinker or writer—his peculiar points of view—and his method of conveying them—his keen insight—his utter want of logic—his limpid, racy style—his occasional obscurities—in short, his merits and defects, whatever we may think of them, are known, and demand no further comment. We say that he is Emerson, and have described him. Now and then, a half-crazy dyspeptic, like Gilfillan, fires off a pop-gun at him, but no one hears the report nor cares for it, and the unconscious object of it still walks forward with his serene and lofty smile.

This position of Emerson, it is worthy of note, he won soon after his first appearance, and has steadily maintained, without material increase or diminution, up to the present time. His little book on "Nature" revealed to discerning minds all that he has since done. He is to them no greater now than he was then. His last and seventh volume is no better than his first. There is more richness and mellowness of style in it, perhaps, but otherwise it is the same. Nor does this seeming want of growth argue any defect of genius. Quite the reverse. Goethe used to say of Schiller that if you separated from him for a week you would be astonished, on meeting him again, by his prodigious strides in advance; but the reason was that Schiller did not begin as a master. He presented himself as a pupil, and you afterwards saw the steps of his progress. Mr. Emerson, on the other hand, slipped into the arena with a native control of his powers and resources. He did not have to learn the use of his tools by using them: he was born to their use. His intellect, from the outset, appeared so clear, so penetrating, so fresh and so capable, that it promised everything that it has since performed. It prepared us by its immediate qualities against future surprises. Of every new manifestation of it, we feel that it is just what we expected. Some minds suffer a kind of ebb and flow in their inspirations—are now dull and depressed, and then glowing with life; and there are others which possess a steady, permanent action, like crystals which are brilliant in every light, or like stars which shine forever. Our author's is of the latter sort.

In this work on England, we see Mr. Emerson in a new field and in a new atmosphere, but it is the same Emerson. His theme is a much larger one than he has before tried, but he treats it in the old vein. In the language of the arts, we may say, that what he has hitherto tried in kitcat and cabinet sizes, he now essays in the broader historical style. The old manner is, however, retained. The practical, concrete life of England is described, but it is described from the high region of philosophy. It is painted (for Mr. Emerson is an artist as well as a philosopher), but it is painted for the thought rather than the eye. We do not mean that there is any want of color or warmth in his picture, because there is an intense reality in it; but it is a reality for the intellect more than for the senses, which the brain touches more than the hand.

John Bull has often sat for his portrait, but never before to a limner so coldly clairvoyant as this. Puckler Muskau and Von Raumer, Philarete Chasles and Bulwer, to say nothing of innumerable lesser artists—Italian, French, German,

American and native—have attempted likenesses of him, have given us sketches, more or less exact, of his head, face, and looks; but here is one who dissects him after another fashion; who turns him inside out, exhibiting such bowels as he has, and more than that, trepans his brain for him to show what texture it is of, and thrusts his hand into his chest to measure the power of the life-pulses. His country, his origin, his achievements in enterprise, and literature—his character and religion—his greatnesses, which are many, and his littlenesses, which are no less, are daguerreotyped with a perfectly free hand, and yet with the utmost sincerity.

Few men in this country were better qualified, in many respects, to approach this subject than Mr. Emerson. As a scholar of wide and various reading, familiar with the results of all the older civilizations, he was already furnished with materials for a wise comparative judgment. Never having been engaged in actual life, whether political or mercantile, he was free from the prejudices which the details of affairs are apt to engender. By habit and training accustomed to the formation of general opinions, seeing things in their broader relations, by the pure light of the intellect, he was not liable to be warped by his immediate observation, nor to gaze through the discolored mediums of passion. At the same time, a man eminent in his sphere, he was eminently received among men. The most secluded circles of cultivation were open to him, in their friendliest aspects; he saw what he saw in its best guise, but he saw it undazzled by accessory splendors; while he was free to move, in lower everyday walks, himself unobserved, yet observant of all that it was pertinent to note. These were his advantages as an observer; but to opportunity; to sharpness and alacrity of vision, to susceptibility and insight, he joined the ability of utterance. A rare command of the subtler forces of language—a racy, idiomatic, sinewy, yet polished and graceful style, render his methods of expressing himself as charming as they are trenchant and impressive.

But, it should not be disguised, that, in other respects, Mr. Emerson was not precisely the man that the world would have chosen to take the gauge and measure of England's success. As an abstract philosopher, more profoundly moved by the deeper relations of thought and sentiment than by the practical everyday life of men, it was to be doubted whether he would seize the peculiar genius of the most practical of all the nations. It was to be feared that he would dwell more upon the inward springs and sources of their characters than upon their real achievements. The English people are not so much a people of thoughts and sentiments as of deeds. They are the most *institutional* people on earth, and, to be comprehended rightly, they must be studied, in their laws and governments as well as in themselves, and in their manner, literature, and religion. Whether Mr. Emerson has done this, we shall, perhaps, inquire in the sequel.

The problem, which our author proposes to himself, after a brief record of an early visit to England, in 1833—during which he saw Coleridge, Landor, Carlyle, Wordsworth, etc.—is, Why England is England? What are the elements of that power which the English hold over other nations? If there be one test of national genius, universally accepted, it is success; and if there be one successful country in the universe, for the last millennium, that country is England. What is the secret of it?

This is a broad question, and in proceeding to answer it, Mr. Emerson first glances at the land itself, in which there is a singular combination of favorable conditions. The climate, which is neither hot nor cold, enables you to work every hour in the year. The soil abounds in every material for work, except wood—with coal, salt, tin, iron, potter's clay, stone, and good arable earth. The perpetual rains keep the rivers full for floating productions everywhere. Game of every kind animates the immense heaths, and the waters spawn with fish. As an island, it occupies the best stand; for it is anchored just off the continent of Europe, and right in the heart of the modern world. A better commercial position is not on the planet, affording shelter for any number of ships, and opening with the markets of all the world. Yet as a nation, conveniently small, disjoined from others so as to breed a fierce nationality, and still communicating with others, so that the people cannot depress each other, as by glut, but flow out into colonies and distant trade. It is this insular smallness which has influenced the internal culture. For more than a thousand years, the Englishman has been improving his little comfortable farm. The fields have been combed and rolled till they appear to have been finished with a pencil instead of a plow. Every rood of land has been turned to its best use: It is covered with towns, cities, cathedrals, castles, and great and decorated estates. Every corner and crevice is stuffed full, like a museum; every structure is solid, with a look of age, every equipage is rich; the trades are innumerable—and the whole country is a grand phalanstery, where all that man wants is provided within the precinct. Only the skies are very dull, heavy with fog and coal smoke—contaminating the air and corroding the monuments and buildings.

Next to locality, Mr. Emerson refers to the question of race. He does not give in to the modern theory, so verbosely expounded by Knox, and Count de Gobineau, of the superior energies of the pure races, but inclines to think that the composite, or mixed races, are the best. The simplest organizations are the lowest—a mere mouth, or jelly, or straight worm; but as organizations become complex, the scale mounts. As water, lime, and sand make mortar, so certain temperaments marry well. The English, at any rate, derive their pedigree from a wide range of nationalities. They are of the oldest blood of the world—of the Celtic, which has an enduring productiveness, gave to their seas and mountains names which are poems;[1] of those Germans, whom the Romans found it impossible to conquer, strong of heart as of hand, and of the fighting predatory Norseman, who impart to them animal vigor, prompt action, steady sense, and wise speech, with a turn for homicide, the composite result being a hardy, strenuous, enduring, and manly tribe. Having all these antagonistic elements in its veins, it is full of blood and of brain; full of fight and of affection; of contemplation and practical skill; of aggressive freedom and fixed law; of enterprise and stolidity—with whom "nothing can be praised without damning exceptions, and nothing denounced without salvos of cordial praise."

The Englishman of the present day Mr. Emerson found a capital animal, well preserved, ruddy in complexion, with voracious appetite, and excellent digestion; handsome, when not bloated with over-feeding, combining decision and never in the expression of the face; devoted to bodily exercises; to boxing, running, shooting, riding, and rowing; living in the open air, yet putting a solid bar of sleep between day and day; possessed of vast constitutional energy, yet domestic, honest and humane. "The island was renowned in antiquity," he says, "for its breed of mastiffs; so fierce, that when their teeth were set, you must cut their heads off to part them. The man is like his dog. The people have that nervous bilious temperament which is known by medical

271

men to resist every means employed to make its possessor subservient to the will of others. The English game is main force to main force, the planting of foot to foot, fair play and open field; a rough tug, without trick or dodging, till one or both come to pieces."

From this brief study of their locality and origin, our author turns, by a sudden transition, to a description of the present characteristics of England. His principal chapters are so many essays on "Manners," "Truth" "Character," "Wealth," "Aristocracy," "Religion," "Literature," and the "Times"—added to which is one chapter of personal reminiscences. As essays, they run over with nice observation, sagacious remark; quaint yet pertinent quotation, the most telling truths condensed in a phrase or a metaphor, dry humor, and placid good-nature. Out of every page, we might extract, for the entertainment of our readers, some novel and striking passage, which should contain either a remarkable image, a pleasant fancy, a stroke of wit, or a profound principle. But we shall not follow Mr. Emerson through his kaleidoscopic gallery, where the same materials are ever presenting some new wonder of form, or some new brilliancy of color, contenting ourselves with a few phrases descriptive of his general results, which we gleaned in reading. Speaking of the hard manner of the English, he says: "A sea-shell should be the crest of England, not only because it represents a power built on the waves, but also the hard finish of the men. The Englishman is finished like the cowry or the murex. After the spire and the spines are formed, or, with the formation, a juice exudes, and a hard enamel varnishes every part. The keeping of the proprieties is as indispensable as clean linen. No merit quite countervails the want of this, whilst this sometimes stands in lieu of all. 'Tis in bad taste,' is the most formidable word that an Englishman can pronounce. But the japan costs them dear. There is a prose in certain of them, which exceeds in wooden deadness all rivalry with other countrymen. There is a knell in the conceit and externality of their voice, which seems to say, *leave all hope behind*. In this Gibraltar of propriety, mediocrity gets entrenched and consolidated, and founded in adamant. An Englishman of fashion is like those souvenirs bound in gold vellum, enriched with delicate engravings, fit for the hands of ladies and princes, but with nothing in it worth reading and remembering."

The great virtue of the Englishmen, in Mr. Emerson's estimation, is their veracity. They are blunt in saying what they think, sparing of promises, and require plain dealing of others. Of old time, Alfred, the typical Englishman of his day, was called by his friend Asser—*Alueredus Veridicus*—the truth-speaker. The mottoes of the ancient families are monitory proverbs, as *Fare fac*, say do, of the Fairfaxes; *say and seal*, of the house of Fiennes; *Vero nil verius*, of the De Veres. The phrase of the lowest people is "honor bright." Even Lord Chesterfield with his French breeding, declared that truth was the distinction of the gentlemen. They, consequently, love reality in wealth, power, and hospitality; they build of stone, and they have a horror of adventurers. Connected with this love of truth is a certain grave and heavy demeanor, which disinclines them to light recreations. "*Ils s'amusaient tristement*," said old Froissart, "*selon le coutume de leur pays*." They are very much steeped in their temperament, like men just awaked from deep sleep. They are of the earth, earthy; and of the sea, as the sea kinds; attached to it for what it yields them, and not from any sentiment. They are headstrong believers and defenders of their opinion, and not less resolute in maintaining their whim and perversity. Their looks bespeak an invincible stoutness. They stoutly carry into every nook and corner their turbulent sense, leaving no lie uncontradicted, no pretension unexamined. The Englishman is a churl, with a soft place, however, in his heart. He says no, and serves you, and your thanks disgust him. "Here was lately a cross-grained miser," adds Mr. Emerson, drawing an illustration from Turner, "old and ugly, resembling in countenance the portrait of Punch, with the length left out, rich by his own industry, skulking in a lonely house, who never gave a dinner to any man, and disdained all courtesies, yet as true a worshiper of beauty in form and color as ever existed, and profusely pouring over the cold minds of his countrymen, creations of grace and truth, removing the reproach of sterility from English art, catching from their savage climate every fine hint, and importing into their galleries every tint and trait of summer cities and skies, making an era in painting, and, when he saw that the splendor of one of his pictures in the Exhibition dimmed his rivals, that hung next to it, secretly took a brush and blackened his own."

It is this love of reality, joined to an intense confidence in the power and performance of his own nation, which makes him not only incurious about other nations, but repulsive to them. He dislikes foreigners, but he is no less disliked by them. An English lady on the Rhine, hearing a German speaking of her party as foreigners, exclaimed, "No, we are not foreigners; we are English; it is you that are foreigners!" The English have not only a high opinion of themselves and a poor one of everybody else, but they are given to brag, often unconsciously, of their own exploits. "The habit of brag runs through all classes, from the *Times* newspaper, through politicians and poets, through Wordsworth, Carlyle, Mill and Sydney Smith, down to the boys of Eton. In the

gravest treatise on political economy, in books of science, one is surprised by the innocent exhibition of unflinching nationality." In a tract on Corn, an amiable and accomplished gentleman (William Spence) writes thus: "Though Britain were surrounded by a wall ten thousand cubits in height, still she would as far excel the rest of the globe in riches as she now does, both in this secondary quality, and in the more important ones of freedom, virtue, and science." Bull is apt to make his heavy fun over the national vanity of Jonathan; but Jonathan is only a distant imitation of himself.

Meanwhile, one of the finer sides of their strong nationality is that love of the domestic circle, which has rendered the English home proverbial for its sanctity, its purity, its sweetness, and its comfort. "Born in a harsh and wet climate, which keeps man indoors whenever he is at rest, and being of an affectionate and loyal temper, he dearly loves his home. If he be rich, he buys a demesne and builds a hall; if he be in middle condition, he spares no expense on his house. Without, it is all planted, within, it is wainscoted, cared, painted, curtained, hung with pictures, and filled with good furniture. 'Tis a passion, which survives all others, to deck and improve it. Hither he brings all that is rare and costly, and with the national tendency to sit fast on the same spot for many generations, it comes to be, in course of time, a museum of heirlooms, gifts, and trophies of the adventures and exploits of the family. He is very fond of silver plate, and, though he have no gallery of portraits of his ancestors, he has of their punch-bowls and porringers." "England produces, under favorable conditions of ease and culture, the finest women in the world; and as the men are affectionate and true-hearted, the women inspire and refine them. Nothing can be more delicate without being fantastical—

nothing more firm and based in nature and sentiment, than the courtship and mutual carriage of the sexes. The sentiment of Imogen, in Cymbeline, is copied from English nature; and not less the Portia of Brutus, the Kate Percy, and the Desdemona. The romance does not exceed the height of noble passion in Mrs. Lucy Hutchinson, or in Lady Russell."

Among other qualities of the English on which Mr. Emerson dilates, is the absolute homage they pay to wealth, which they esteem a final certificate of all worth. In exact proportion is the reproach of poverty. Sydney Smith said poverty is infamous in England. The ground of this pride in wealth is the prodigious labor by which it has been accumulated. The Englishman sees in it whole centuries of invention, toil, and economy. He derives from it an ideal perfection of property—the vastest social uses—miracles of luxury and enjoyment. Yet there is, also, an increasing danger lest this servant should become his master. The wealth of England has led to an intolerable despotism of expense. Not the aims of a manly life, but the means of meeting a ponderous outlay, is the end placed before a youth, emerging from his minority. A large family is reckoned a misfortune. At the same time there is a preposterous worship of aristocracy in England, through the aristocracy, which has not been without its uses in disciplining manners and fostering the fine arts, is now decaying. The old Bohuns and De Veres are gone; but lawyers, farmers, and silkmercers lie *perdu* in their coronets, and wink to the antiquary to say nothing. As to the Established Church of England, Mr. Emerson considers it pretty much a sham; having nothing left but possession, where people attend as a matter of good-breeding, but with no vital interest in its proceedings. The literature of the nation, however, is stronger and truer, showing the solidest sense, the

most earnest labor, the roughest vigor, and the readiest mechanical skill. But, excepting the splendid age of Bacon and Shakespeare, England literature has not attained the loftiest heights. It is too direct, practical, hard, unromantic, and unpoetic. It has accurate perceptions, takes hold of things by the right ends, but it must stand on a fact. A kind of mental materialism runs through it. Plain strong speech it likes better than soaring into clouds. Even in its elevation, its poetry is common sense inspired, or iron raised to a white heat. "The bias of Englishmen to practical skill has reacted on the national mind. They are incapable of an inutility, and respect the five mechanic powers even in their song. The voice of their modern muse has a slight hint of the steam-whistle, and the poem is created as an ornament and finish of their monarchy, and by no means as the bird of a new morning, which forgets the past world in the full enjoyment of that which is forming. They are with difficulty ideal; they are the most conditioned men, as if, having the best conditions, they could not bring themselves to forfeit them. Every one of them is a thousand years old and lives by his memory; and when you say this they accept it as praise. Nothing comes to the bookshops but politics, travels, statistics, tabulation, and engineering, and even what is called philosophy and letters is mechanical in its structure, as if inspiration had ceased, as if no vast hope, no religion, no song of joy, no analogy existed any more." "Squalid contentment with conventions, satires at the names of philosophy and religion, parochial and shop-till politics, and idolatry of usage betray the ebb of life and spirit. As they trample on nationalities to reproduce London and Londoners in Europe and Asia, so they fear the hostility of ideas, of poetry, of religion—ghosts which they cannot lay; and having attempted to domesticate and dress the blessed soul itself in English broadcoth and gaiters, they are tormented with fear that herein lurks a force that will sweep their system away. The artists say 'nature puts them out; the scholars have become an ideal.' Poetry is degraded and made ornamental. Pope's verses were a kind of frosted cake; Sir Walter Scott wrote rhymed travelers' guides to Scotland; Tennyson is factitious, 'climbing no mount of vision.' Hallam is a learned and elegant scholar, rich and wise but retrospective; Dickens prepares London tracts, generous but local; Thackeray thinks we must renounce ideals and accept London; and the brilliant Macaulay explicitly teaches that good means good to eat or good to wear, material commodity. The exceptions to this limitary tone of thought are Coleridge, who was a catholic mind; Wordsworth, whose verse was a voice of sanity in a worldly and ambitious age, and Wilkinson, the editor of Swedeborg, in the action of whose mind is a long Atlantic roll, not known except in deepest waters."

We should like to go on thus calling fine and sharp things from Mr. Emerson's pages; but if we should, it would leave us no space for the few words that it is necessary to say, in the way of a general estimate of his performance. As a collection of a apothegms on England, of which each one has a species of diamond clearness, and value, his book is exquisitely rich. Never in history have so many discriminating sentences been uttered about any people. But, as a whole, it does not entirely satisfy us, for the want of a certain gradation, or proportion in the parts, which gives harmony. The author's mind, being essentially instinctive, and not discursive or logical, he sees things absolutely rather than relatively, and in their kinds and not in their degrees. This is evident in the very form of his book, which has no organic structure, but is a miscellany of remarks on one topic. Whether you begin at the last chapter or the first— at the bottom of the page or the top, it is almost equally intelligible and equally interesting. There is no progress or march of thought in it—no rising and falling of the flood—no grand or rapid modulations—in a word, no growth—but an incessant succession of discharges as in a *feu de joie*. Each paragraph has it own independent validity, and would be just as good elsewhere, and in another chapter. As in *staccato* passages of music, each note is pointed, distinct, and of equal value, and when long continued gives the ear a painful sense of a want of variety and contrast. Mr. Emerson tells us an infinity of truths about John Bull; but he does not furnish us what the Frenchmen call an impression *d'ensemble*. He has anatomized him, but forgotten to organize him afterwards. He is like a painter who should make a most careful study of the several parts of his subject on different pieces of canvas—a head here, a leg there, and a torso in another place—and then fail to bring them together into one. Each study may be perfect; but what we want to see is the complete man. We want to see him as he moves and breathes in his multiplied relations. Mr. Emerson writes memoirs to serve, and not a biography. He nowhere lays hold of the central idea of English life. It is too vast, he confesses— a myriad personality. In the absence of this organic unity, not a few of his representations seem to contradict each other, because they are not qualified one by the other. His Englishman is more than a compound of antagonistic elements—he is a bundle of confusions. He loves truth above all things, and yet willingly immerses himself in fictions. He is a pink of propriety and full of freaks. His individuality is intense, and he cringes to aristocracy. He detests humbug, while he gladly worships a humbug church, a humbug nobility, humbug laws, and humbug newspapers;

and his mind is an arrested development, though it sprouts in the greatest men that the world has seen for five hundred years. It is difficult, we admit, to penetrate the spirit of a nation, as if it were a single hero; but it is not impossible to a mind which is able to generalize as well as discern. There are in every nation, as in every race, some traits which are central, and others only circumferential; some which are leading and determinative, and others which are merely superficial, and these, we presume, may be easily separated and combined into a living whole. In this regard, we may say, that "English *Traits*" answers admirably to its name, but it does not so completely answer the question of the opening chapter—Why England is England? It hints innumerable answers, but leaves the reader undecided as to which one or which dozen of these is the master-key of the problem.

What strikes the casual visitor to England most deeply, is the prodigious and compact activity of the nation, and the wealth which it has thereby accumulated, taken in connection with the extreme brutality and degradation of the more numerous classes. We remember, for ourselves, that a great deal of the anticipated pleasure of a tour in the old country, was dashed, on the evening of our arrival at Liverpool, by the sight of the multitudes of stolid and hopeless poor, who seemed to crowd every alley. Nor was it otherwise in the manufacturing towns, or even in the agricultural towns, or even in the agricultural districts. We were charmed by the rural beauty, we were dazzled by the urban opulence—but behind those trim hedges we could not help seeing the pale and skulking forms of the wretched cotters, and from beneath those munificent piles of masonry we heard the groans of the toiling millions. We found afterwards plenty of misery and indigence, in the cities of France—plenty in Italy—and plenty

in Germany—but nowhere did it seem so utterly miserable, and so imbruted in its misery, as in England. In the nations of the continent it is relieved by a gay vivacity of temper and by a greater picturesqueness of costume and custom; but in England, it is a sombre, stolid filthy sub-animal debasement. But among these classes Mr. Emerson does not appear to have tarried. "Cushioned and comforted in every manner," he says, "the traveler rides as on a cannon ball, high and low, over rivers and towns, through mountains, in tunnels of three or four miles at near twice the speed of our trains—reading quietly the *Times* newspaper," and we can from his book, readily believe that such was his method of progression. We doubt whether he laid his ear anywhere to the great heart of the people, to hear what they might have to say of the greatness and glory that was round about them. In fact, society as such, the relation and conditions of its several components, did not occupy much of his attention—though the social organization of England is one of the most peculiar and profoundly interesting of human phenomena.

A larger experience of this society would have saved him from some very singular misjudgments. When he commends the personal independence and freedom of Englishmen, for instance, when he says that each man walks, eats, drinks, shaves, dresses, gesticulates, and in every manner acts and suffers in his own fashion, he must draw his inferences from a narrow circle of intellectual men, and not from the community at large. Next to the extreme squalor and stupidity of the lower classes in England, what impresses the stranger most painfully is a certain despotism of opinion, which produces the utmost conformity in manners and conduct. In Paris, Vienna, Rome, and even New York, one does feel that he can do pretty much as he pleases, except to talk against the *peculiar* despotisms of each; but in London—wilderness as it is—you must dress, walk, and talk by the card, or you are either nobody or a notoriety. A friend of ours, who in his continental and Egyptian campaigns had sedulously avoided the barber, arrived at Dover in his hirsute condition, and, from the moment that he landed until he stepped on board of the Pacific at Liverpool, was as conspicuous an object as a traveling menagerie. At the eating-houses he was stared out of countenance by the wonder-smitten insulars (and it takes a great deal to make John look up from his dinner), and in the streets he was run after by the little boys, who called to their companions to come and see the Frencher. This was before the Great Exhibition had made the beard somewhat familiar, and a long agitation of the subject, by the newspapers, had modified the prevailing prejudice. Another friend, a merchant who had long worn a mustache in New York, having some business to transact in "the city," was careful to remove every vestige of hair from his lips, lest it might damage his credit with the plutocrats of the great metropolis. These small incidents we use to show the utter intolerance of eccentricity in England. Rich men and the privileged classes who step beyond the prescribed limits of propriety, are endured, but anybody else who might do so, would become instantly an object of the most unpleasant remarks. There are no greater slaves to fashion in the world than the English. You must live in a certain style, and dress in a certain mode, and be acquainted with certain people (generally belonging to the aristocracy), or you are neglected, if not despised. It is this obsequious deference to a peculiar standard which has given rise to that peculiar order of apes, which the slang literature denominates, snob. It is an order so numerous and so powerful that much of the best

modern wit, from Thackeray and Jerrold down to Punch, finds its chief nutriment in the exposure of it. Of course there are snobs everywhere, but London is their warren and city of refuge. Elsewhere they are vagrant and exceptional instances; but in London they are quite the rule. They are bred in the highly artificial structure of society there, and feed upon it like grubs.

Whatever the defects of English character, however, there is one thing to be said of the nation—that it has acquired a more durable and substantial civilization than any other of the Old World. Composed essentially of the same races as the northern continental nations, and beginning in the middle ages with essentially the same institutions, it has developed itself into a nobler strength. We wish Mr. Emerson had gone more deeply into the historical causes of this difference. There is no more interesting speculation now attracting the study of philosophical genius. Any one who will recall the condition of Germany, France, and England, during the great transition period from ancient to modern society, from the twelfth to the fifteenth century, inclusive, will be struck by the remarkable similarity of their laws, customs, maxims, and morals. There was, of course, a vast diversity in details—but the general arrangement, the general spirit, the general tendency was the same. Government was managed on the same principles—society was divided by the same classes, and there were kings, nobles, clergy, commons, people, and slaves, everywhere—with identical distinctions, as to privileges, rights and oppressions. In other words, feudalism was the prevailing and organic law; and, as De Tocqueville has lately remarked, in the fifteenth century, the social, political, administrative, judicial, economical, and literary institutions, were more nearly akin to each other than at the present times, when civiliza-

277

tion is supposed to have opened all the channels of communication, and to have leveled every obstacle. Even as late as the beginning of the sixteenth century, when Henry VIII. was monarch of England, and Francis I. of France, and Charles II. of the German Empire, there was a marvelous analogy in the condition and prospects of these several powers. But from that time, how diverse the development? Germany, in which the great reformation of thought opened with such signal glory, has attained to no more than a feeble political life. France, after swaying hither and thither between the shocks of successive sanguinary revolutions, is still destitute of any genuine constitutional freedom, while England alone, with few revolutions, and these neither protracted nor bloody, has reached something like freedom and prosperity. What have been the causes of this?

It is not our intention to attempt the answer, merely suggesting it as the life-task of some as yet unknown Guizot, or Hallam; but we may remark, that none of the English speculators themselves, who ascribe so much influence to the mixed character of their government, seem to us to have adequately stated or treated the problem. The artificial equipoise, which it has maintained between the several estates or orders, has been a fact of prime importance; but they have not always recognized the real ground of its importance. Or, in other words, the importance of that fact rests upon another fact contained in it, which is the larger infusion of the democratic element in English institutions than in those of the continent. The popular life which has ever and anon forced itself into the government has kept the political atmosphere sweet and wholesome. It is owing to this that the absolutism of the monarch has been restrained,

the selfishness of the nobles withheld from an extremity of corruption, and the middle classes lifted into wealth and intelligence; but it cannot be concealed, at the same time, that the lowest classes in England are so debased and forlorn, because they have not yet been made partakers of the common political life. England has prospered more than other nations, because, more than they, she has recognized the humanity of her people; but in so far as she has failed to recognize it, she has been smitten, like others, with barrenness and evil. Her mixed constitution has proved itself a better device than despotism, not because balances and counterpoises are the ultimate or perfect form of government, as many Englishmen suppose, but because of the element of freedom in it, and the true inference is, that a larger measure of that element would prove itself better still. In the transition from feudalism to freedom, a mixed government affords an easier and safer passage than any absolute form; but a mixed government can never be anything more than a transition, while democracy alone is final.

Note

1 "Which is only true to a small extent. The Celts have had about as much to do with the destiny of England as our Indian tribes have had with that of America. A few of the names of the streams and mountains in England are Celtic, but the large majority of all the names are Saxon, at least nine hundred and ninety-nine out of a thousand. Of ancient and pure Celtic words retained in our vocabulary, only thirty are enumerated, and these relate principally to female and domestic uses."

Review of *English Traits*, *New Quarterly Review* [England], 4 (4th Quarter 1856), 449–55

Ralph Waldo Emerson is the Confucius of the west. He has surveyed mankind from Concord to Calcutta, and reigns absolute over mystical philosophy from the St. Lawrence to the Mississippi, from the Thames to the Ganges, where we are credibly informed that he has dispossessed the ancient records of wisdom, and that his sayings form the spiritual consolation of deposed Rajahs and dyspeptic Nawabs.

In this country, no long time ago, he was the prevalent epidemic, and afflicted the young imagination with a yearning after that obscurity and indefiniteness which flatter the conceit, and at any rate soothe the disappointments, of over-souled *litterateurs* fallen upon an ungrateful age and a practical time. Indefiniteness in the Emersonian philosophy being the uncivil sphinx that always suggests and seldom satisfies questions, and obscurity the unpleasing but unfailing medium for portraying the warts and the wrinkles of truth. Mr. Emerson's philosophy not only begins but ends in wonder. He conducts us through a series of cloud-scapes, and gratifies our fancy with every effect of poetical penumbra; now and then we seem on the brink of the actual, but we are straightway drifted into the realm of haze and twilight and vapour, where life, love, nature, the universe, divinity itself, are shadows, and Mr. Emerson is the only abiding reality. Carlyle rends the mountains and breaks in pieces for our actual gaze the rocks and barriers of truth; he bursts open the gates of the terrible, and plunges us in, no matter how much propriety is shocked, or syntax offended; we are not the better for the rough usage, but earn something for our pains in solid sterling knowledge, and understanding of social or natural phenomena. We have tracked by his lamp the unregarded incidents, whose strange aggregate simultaneously blazed out into inextinguishable revolutions, or have felt woe stricken at the sight of Cromwell, have kissed the hand of Schiller, or bent over the face of Burns, not to speak of our sympathy with the grotesqueness of Teufelsdröck, or our admiration of the gracefulness of Stirling. We know the author, not by his monopoly of the personal pronoun, but as we know Shakespeare, dramatically. Emerson never lets concealment feed upon his individuality. Every page of his writings contains a portrait of himself; we need no biography; it is given in every sentence. He lives at Concord, digs in his garden philosophically, loves the twilight, paddles in the little river along with his friend, thinks love an idea; and though he is married, and does not care to travel, this and much more we can glean from his essays, which are written as near as may be upon the model of Montaigne. Swedenborg and Montaigne are his *penates;* and all that lies between scepticism and mysticism, the long range of beauty and barrenness whoever cares to explore, will do well to take up and study the essays of Emerson. Originally a Unitarian minister in Boston, he relinquished that responsibility on account of too near an approach in some of his doctrines to Christianity, though in which we are at a loss to imagine. After that he was an editor in Boston, contributor to the *North American*, lecturer, orator, and rural philosopher in pleasant-retired Concord, which he made his Nevay, only issuing forth to lecture or to monologize.

Some of his letters have been published, wherein he describes himself well. Here is an extract:—

I have always been, by very incapacity of methodical writing, "a chartered libertine," free to worship and free to rail, lucky when I could make myself understood, but never esteemed near enough the institutions and view of society to deserve the notice of the Nestors of literature and religion. I have appreciated fully the advantage of my position; for well I know that there is no scholar less willing or less able to be a polemic. I could give an account of myself if challenged; I could not give you any of the arguments upon which any doctrine of mine depends. I do not know what arguments mean in reference to my expression of a thought. *I delight in telling what I think:* but, if you ask me how I dare say so, or why it is so, I am the most helpless of mortal men. I do not even see that either of these questions admits of an answer. I shall go on, just as before, seeing whatever I can, and telling whatever I see; and I suppose, with the same fortune that has hitherto attended me, the joy of finding that my older and better brothers, who work with the sympathy of society, loving and beloved, do now and then unexpectedly confirm my perceptions, and find my nonsense is only their own thought in motley.

This is the gentleman who, in 1837, came over to lecture to audiences in Liverpool, and Manchester, and London, on Montaigne, and Swedenborg, and Shakespeare, and Napoleon, and impressed them by the solemnity of his oracles, and the incongruity of his talk. "Flattery would lick the sun and moon out of the firmament," was one of his *dicta*; yet who more worthy of being quoted upon Shakespeare, or where is the eulogy that can compare with this?—

What point of morals, of manners, of economy, of philosophy, or religion, of taste, of the conduct of life, has he not settled? What mystery has he not signified his knowledge of? What office, or function, or district of man's work has he not remembered? What king has he not taught state? What maiden has not found him fairer than her delicacy? What lover has he not out-loved? What sage has he not out-seen? What gentleman has he not instructed in the manner of his behaviour?

To this last question certain English *coteries* might readily supply an answer. Mr. Emerson's volley, or "flingings out," as Mr. de Quincey terms them, against our laws, customs, manners, religion, police, and even our literature, being still memorable. This antagonism forms the staple of the work before us.

It consists of a series of diatribes upon England and Englishmen, seasoned and served up so as to pique national self-complacency, and swell local conceit in Boston, New York and the semi-American, sympathising coterie that is in Montreal. Mr. Emerson had no desire to take up his parable against England. He could indulge his *mis-Anglicanism* well enough as he mediated under his green gourd at Concord, or cultivated his Indian corn and tomatoes; but a committee in twenty or thirty English towns importuned him, and he was "a little spent by some unusual studies," yearning after the infinite, &c. He wanted a change to get rid of an unusual overflow of bile, "and England was proposed." The pay we will say nothing about. "It was equivalent to the fees at that time paid in the country, and covered travelling expenses; what did a philosopher want more? He was assured of every aid and comfort, rocking-chair, and tooth-pick, and all sorts of fixings."

So he consented. He had a little dread of the sea; but "a great mind," we are told, "is a good sailor," as a great beast is. And the sea is not slow in disclosing inestimable secrets.

Here is a Montaigne like bit of egotism—and a peep into the philosopher's state-room:—

["Voyage," 28.26–31.22]

After sixteen lack-lustre sea-days he lands at Liverpool, and is met by the committee which has been pre-instructed to be—

Very kind and courteous to this gentleman,
Hop in his walks, and gambol in his
  eyes,
Feed him with apricots and bilberries;

and, above all, listen to him. Still he is not pleased. Some signs portend that "London has reached its highest point. The English interest us a little less within a few years," and he had the impression that the British power has culminated, is in solstice, or already declining. It is foggy weather, Novembral we suppose. The blacks in the manufacturing towns discolour Mr. Emerson's saliva (p. 22); he can't read or write well—he is very cold, too. Here is what he thinks of our appearance:—

["Race," 65.5–71.7]

We wear well—

["Race," 69.6–71.7]

We are all like our bull-dogs:—

["Ability," 78.8–79.2]

Birmingham in some way or other displeased our philosopher, and the worst epithet he can fling against us is that we are Birminghamized.

This is severe enough upon our common language:—

["Ability," 100.8–101.26]

Yet our elocution is "stomachic, as the American's is labial," (or nasal?) and every one of us is—

["Manners," 105.15–106.8]

The most formidable word an Englishman can pronounce, is "Tis in bad taste," and the gospel preached in our churches is, "By taste *are* ye saved." (p. 126.)

That which chiefly differences us from the American is the presence of spleen!

Here is a genuine republican outburst:—

["Cockayne," 146.21–147.11]

Compare our two national name-saints:—

["Cockayne," 152.1–27]

This is what our steam-power can do:—

["Wealth," 160.27–164.6]

We have no space to discuss Mr. Emerson's opinions on our aristocracy, our parliament, our religion. It appears we have no public speakers, at least comparable to those in Congress. We fear Mr. Emerson is right in saying our church is the church of the gentry, and not of the poor; and that our universities are hostile to geniuses as monasteries to youthful saints—but his notions upon our literature we cannot omit. There is not a single English name worth recording.

Hallam is uniformly polite, but with deficient sympathy; Dickens is local and temporary; Macaulay brilliant, but no critic; Bulwer, simply an industrious writer—who is Southey! this American asks.

Landor pesters him; Coleridge is incomplete; Wordsworth conscientious, but commonplace; Tennyson factitious— even Doctor Johnson of little value, except for resembling Emerson in his tone of feeling. Sir Walter Scott—what did he write? A rhymed traveller's guide to Scotland. Carlyle does not please him; we have hardly any scientific men either. Robert Brown, the botanist, perhaps— Richard Owen, perhaps. Faraday is not even named. Here is an opinion upon Turner we commend to Mr. Pyne, who is an admirer of Emerson:—

["Character," 135.10–25]

A picture of Landor—the grand old heroic,—we subjoin, as it is not untrue:—

["First Visit," 7.2–10.6]

And here is the author of the Life of Cromwell:

["First Visit," 14.25–19.2]

We can only reiterate to Mr. Emerson, the advice given to him by one of his friends, an ex-governor of Illinois:—

["Cockayne," 148.22–25]

And this, which tersely conveys the national English feeling—"If you don't like the country—d——n you—you can leave it!

Checklist of Additional Reviews

Boston *Daily Evening Transcript*, 7 August 1856, p. 2.

Boston *Daily Journal*, 7 August 1856, p. 4.

Boston *Post*, 12 August 1856, p. 4.

"Emerson on English Character," New York *Daily Tribune*, 16 August 1856, p. 6.

Central Presbyterian Magazine, ca. September 1856.

Christian Examiner, 61 (September 1856), 309–10.

"English Traits," *Harvard Magazine*, 2 (September 1856), 297–302.

[Frederic Dan Huntington], *Monthly Religious Magazine and Independent Journal*, 16 (September 1856), 214–15.

J.C., "English Traits," *Western Literary Messenger* [Buffalo, N.Y.], 27 (September 1856), 40–1.

Literary Gazette, 28 (6 September 1856), 657–8.

Nation [Ireland], 6 September 1856.

Boston *Daily Evening Traveller*, 9 September 1856, p. 4.

"Emerson on England," *Leader*, 7 (13 September 1856), 880–2.

Press, 13 September 1856, pp. 879–80.

Examiner, 2538 (20 September 1856), 599.

Reasoner, 21 (28 September 1856), 98–9.

"W., X., Y., & Z.," "English Traits," *Amherst Collegiate Magazine*, 4 (October 1856), 32–5.

British Controversialist and Literary Magazine, n.s. 2 (October 1856), 192.

Christian Review, 21 (October 1856), 625.

Freewill Baptist Quarterly, 4 (October 1856), 476.

Graham's Magazine, 49 (October 1856), 374–6.

Hunt's Merchants Magazine, 35 (October 1856), 527.

National Magazine, 9 (October 1856), 380–1.

National Review, 3 (October 1856), 496.

Quarterly Journal of the American Unitarian Association, 4 (October 1856), 100.

Rambler, October 1856, pp. 317–19.

[John R. Thompson?], *Southern Literary Messenger*, 23 (October 1856), 314–16.

West of Scotland Magazine–Review, n.s. 1 (October 1856), 75–80.

"Emerson's English Traits," *Westminster Review*, n.s. 10 (October 1856), 494–514.

[Charles Kingsley], "English Traits," *Saturday Review*, 4 October 1856, pp. 509–10.

National Era, 10 (9 October 1856), 162.

"Mr. Emerson's English Traits," *Dublin University Magazine*, 40 (November 1856), 569–79.

Godey's Lady's Book and Magazine, 53 (November 1856), 467.

"Emerson on England," *National Magazine*, 1 (November 1856), 39–40.

[Noah Porter, Jr.], "Emerson's English Traits," *New Englander*, 14 (November 1856), 573–92.

Peterson's Magazine, 30 (November 1856), 341.

Emile Montégut, "Le Caractère anglais jugé par un Américain," *Revue des Deux Mondes*, 2nd ser., 6 (15 November 1856), 274–300.

Knickerbocker, 48 (December 1856), 630–1.

London Quarterly Review, 7 (January 1857), 381–4–6.

Evangelical Repository, 3 (March 1857), 233–4.

"L'Ouvrier," *British Controversialist and Literary Magazine*, n.s. 3 (June 1857), 275–9.

"English Traits," *Church Review and Ecclesiastical Register*, 10 (July 1857), 197–216.

London Quarterly Review, 11 (January 1859), 377–95.

[Gerald Massey], "New Englanders and the Old Home," *Quarterly Review*, 115 (January 1864), 42–68.

The Conduct of Life

Review of *The Conduct of Life*,
Athenæum, 1929
(15 December 1860),
824–6

Many "seeking souls" will be looking forward to this new book from Mr. Emerson, in the hope that therein they may find words of help and guidance for themselves in the conduct of their own life. We are very sorry to have to warn them that they will be disappointed—

The hungry sheep look up—and are
    not fed.

We are sorry; for to be disappointed by a man who has given them reason to hope that he can show them the solution of some of the dark enigmas and hard problems of life, converting these into instruction, makes men feel "poor indeed!"

Many persons have had a superstition about Mr. Emerson, and many owe him gratitude for what he has formerly said and written; but the present work on "the conduct of life" shows his limits. He has come to the end of all he had to say, and is repeating himself, but with a colder and more feeble utterance. He has been chewing his own cud until all savour and nu-triment have gone out of it. He is to become a scarecrow likeness of Mr. Carlyle, wearing his old clothes—with a difference. It would be difficult for the most ingenuous youth to find a work less adapted to help him in the "conduct of life." Not only is the work utterly unpractical, but it is utterly unsuggestive. We take all works of this class not for what they actually say, but for the sake of the proximate truths which the intelligent reader may draw from them and adjust for himself,— for the *spirit*, not for the letter. One disappointment in the present work is that no noble, or heroic, or generous frame of mind is induced by it; there is nothing either stimulating or fertilizing in its effect. The words fall like a cold, drizzling rain, and the thoughts and sentiments have as much shape and consistency as the driving wreaths of mist. Mr. Emerson himself appears to have reached a sublime centre of indifference, from which he contemplates life and human things as a spectacle, which he declares *"pleases at a sufficient perspective."* To him, human life, with its joys and sorrows, has become a dumb phantasmagoria. It may add considerably to his own comfort to be out of the hearing and beyond the influence, of the noise, the labour, and the hopes and fears of men; but it destroys his power to be a friend or teacher. He has lost the power to sympathize. What he has gained in height, he has lost in breadth. There is no rhythm in the style, nor any breath of eloquence; the sentences are mechanical in their hard, dry, dogmatic utterances upon all that is most vital in the life and experience of men. The effect is the calmness of self-complacency, not the repose of the wisdom that comprehends. The spirit of his book is shown by one small remark, that in works of charity the first thing that strikes him is—the small value of those whom you are asked to save. The man who feels thus, will never be a world-wide teacher. In the Essay on Fate, he says:—

["Fate," 16.23–17.2, 11.22–12.5]

The mass of human nature is not very beautiful, nor are all men what one would choose for bosom friends, but they are our fellow men; and how different in its utterance is the voice of that Apostle of the Gentiles, who declared that the "Lord of heaven and earth hath made of one blood all nations of men for to dwell on all the face of the earth, that they should seek the Lord, if haply they might feel after him, and find him, though he be not far from any one of us. For we are also his offspring." It was for his faith in these unhappy human beings with so much "guano in their destiny" that the Great Teacher of Mankind dared to die, and it was amongst such that he passed the days of his life, preaching to them and teaching them words of life. Love and pity are the first qualities a man needs who sets up for a teacher; and patience as of the Infinite.

To examine Mr. Emerson's book more in detail. There are nine essays in all:—Fate—Power—Wealth—Culture—Behaviour—Worship—Considerations by the Way—Beauty—Illusions. In Fate he undertakes to state the absolute conditions under which a man comes into the world, that which is put upon him from the first, about which he has had no choice, and from which he has no escape—such are his birth, parentage and personal endowments:—

["Fate," 10.26–11.7]

Human nature is not a pea to be put under thimble after this fashion; anyhow, it refuses to stay there. If there is one thing more than another that excites the indignation of men it is the attempt to fix FINALITY upon them in any shape whatever, whether it be a question of destiny or a measure of policy. Men resent it as an insolence. They are vaguely conscious of the immense unrealized possibilities of life;

We *feel* that we are greater than we know.

Mr. Emerson does not confine himself to the fixed circumstances of Fate. He proceeds to discourse on the freedom of the subject:—"But to see how Fate slides into Freedom and Freedom into Fate. Observe how far the roots of every creature run. Or find, if you can, a point where there is no connexion. Our life is consentaneous and far related. This knot of Nature is so cunningly tied that nobody was ever cunning enough to find the two ends." The following moralizing is for those who can use it:—

["Fate," 22.1–23.2, 38.17–20]

Those last words seem to be the text of the book.

["Fate," 40.2–9]

Again:—

["Fate," 44.22–45.2]

Then follows a dogma, which we commend to the personal consideration of all whose own looking-glass tells them it concerns:—

["Fate," 45.3–18]

Here, however, is the comfort Mr. Emerson gives such a man; let him be thankful and make the most of it:—

One remarkable point in this work is, that throughout Mr. Emerson treats an illustration as equivalent to an argument,—as quite equal to a proof; and an assertion as superior to both,—it contains them. How an unfortunate mortal, born under the condition of ugliness, is to get the good thought which is to give him the power to "rally on his relation to the universe," Mr. Emerson does not tell,—it is one of the secrets for the elect, which he keeps to himself, if he has discovered it.

Having delivered his oracle on Fate, Mr. Emerson goes on to discourse of Power—the antagonist of Fate. Second only to his horror of ugliness, or deformity, is his scorn of all sickness, ill-health, and bodily infirmity,—especially of those unhappy ones who dare to complain, who venture to recognize their own ailments in the most distant manner. As to asking or expecting sympathy, that is too contemptible. Let them rather slink out of human sight and die, and at least do their duty as—guano. Mr. Emerson worships bodily health and muscular force; it is his only basis of Power:—

["Power," 55.1–56.11, 60.22–26, 64.24–65.3]

Mr. Emerson considers those "legislators in shirt-sleeves," as he calls them,— "Hoosier, Sucker, Wolverine, Badger, or whatever hard heads, half-orator half-assassin, Oregon, Arkansas, Utah sends to represent its wrath or cupidity,"—are like the ancient barbarians to the effete Roman citizens. For ourselves, we doubt the goodness and the grace of men who have graduated in bar-rooms, and under the stimulus of strong drinks. Mr. Emerson pauses to eulogize a surly Boniface in a rural capital, though he owns "there was no crime which he did not, or could not, commit"; that he united in his own person the functions of bully, incendiary, swindler, bar-keeper and burglar. He girdled the trees, and cut off the tails of the horses of the temperance-people during the night,—he led the "rummies" and radicals in town-meetings with a speech,— with all which he had the sense to see the value of improvements, and set this brute force in their favour, and carried them. But the whole essay on Power is open to grievous misconstruction. The assertions are too sharp, too sweeping, too paradoxical for the ground they have to stand upon. Let the candid reader imagine the effect of such teaching as the following upon any Young Men's Christian Association. Does Mr. Emerson mean it for instruction in doctrine? or does he really mean it as a fact to be followed? He says:—

["Power," 65.25–66.7, 66.16–23]

Of course we do not suppose that Mr. Emerson inculcates swindling—he only means that all energy and aptitude is so much force and animal life; or, as he expresses it elsewhere, "all *plus* is *good, only put it in the right place.*" But Mr. Emerson's whole book is full of wild, startling assertions, which he is not at the pains to work out and elaborate into their just proportions, to balance, or to guard either in letter or in spirit from the misconstruction of half-educated, untrained readers, from the weak and confused in judgment. With these Mr. Emerson has no sympathy; and yet a very wise old law giver pronounced a judgment against those who "caused the Blind to go out of his way;" and this holds against those who cause the ignorant to err as well as the physically sightless. The whole book on "the conduct of life" deals hastily and superficially with the great problems and questions which lie at the root of the Tree of Life, and which may not rashly nor lightly be opened up, not, at any rate, by one who only flings about paradoxes as a fool flings firebrands, without taking the time or the trouble needful to work them out, to show whence they came and whither they tend. As one who has earned the reputations of a man of character and high personal morality, Mr. Emerson has no *right* to indulge in unguarded assertions, which, from him, come with a weight which they would not have from the pen of a more suspected author. Those who have the charge of children are bound to be careful of every word they utter; watchful over act and look;—relatively to Mr. Emerson, many of his readers are but children. But he has no love in his heart, no reverence for his fellow men; he has as little sympathy with their virtues as with their temptations and crimes. It is not to be supposed, however, that there are *no* valuable axioms in the book; here is one which may be written in letters of gold:—

["Power," 73.24–74.14]

Such teaching is not new,—but it is well said, and it is a lesson that cannot be too often told. Again, he says:—"Concentration is the secret of strength."—"The second substitute for temperament is drill, the power of use and routine." These may be truisms, but truisms uttered by a master have an emphasis added to them which impresses the disciple.

In the essay on "Wealth," Mr. Emerson is as inexorable in requiring a man to be in easy circumstances as he is in exacting beauty and health. He begins by announcing that "He is no whole man until he knows how to earn a blameless livelihood. ** He is by constitution expensive, and needs to be rich. He cannot do justice to his genius without making some larger demand on the world than bare subsistence." "Man was born to be rich, or inevitably grows rich by the use of his faculties." So thought and acted (*minus* the honesty) Pullinger, Redpath, and many others, whose "use of their faculties" brought them into collision with law and justice, which barbarously refused to recognize the extenuating circumstances of an "expensive constitution."

Mr. Emerson entirely ignores the competition in all trades—the difficulty of "getting work," and the difficulties that beset the art of "earning money." It is enough to put a practical man beside his patience to see the jaunty, complacent, and utterly unpractical manner in which Mr. Emerson handles this subject. The one dogma that will detach itself from all the rest, and impresses itself on the heart of the candid disciple is that he *must* get plenty of money—"more than he requires for a bare subsistence"—if he would "do justice to his genius";—not exactly the teaching adapted to make men of an heroic stamp.

There are some wise observations about debt, thrift, economy, and concentration, which—although they are written in the pages of Franklin and Poor Richard—sound like words of King Solomon, coming as they do in the midst of so much that is rash and unguarded.

All the observations as to the best use of wealth are good—not new, not very profound, but reasonable and well said, and with a wise spirit.

A man being handsome, healthy, strong, and wealthy, needs culture;—accordingly, "Culture" is the next essay—Culture which is to restore man to the balance of his powers, which concentration on his chief business has deranged. Culture is to bring him back to the symmetry which belongs to a well-balanced human being. It is, on the whole, a good chapter. The things said and inculcated are commonplace, and have been often and often taught before—so often that, except for the fact that men never learn their lesson of life perfectly, and never can transmit it to their children, there would have been no need to repeat it. But as things are, the need exists always, and this essay on Culture is good, though it is needless to remark that there are no practical directions in it. But the spirit is good and sound, and the student must supply the details for himself. In the essay on "Behavior" there are some good observations, but there is nothing that Mr. Emerson has not said in his earlier essays with more of force and originality. The essay on "Worship" will find so many objectors that we will not add to the number of hard words which it will be sure to provoke. Mr. Emerson is a sincere man, and piques himself on saying what he thinks. He says:—

["Worship," 201.16–25, 203.24–27]

There is a want of good manners in speaking and writing thus on a subject which involves the deepest, the most secret, as well as the most intense feelings of mankind,—no matter what their specific theology may be. There is a hard, supercilious irreverence, which no man, under any pretext whatever, has the right to indulge. Mr. Emerson says, "A man bears beliefs as a tree bears apples."—"We are born believing." This is fantastic cynicism; not love of truth, nor any expression of philosophical doubt. There are some good detached observations here and there throughout the essay; but the whole tone is below the mark, and unworthy of the subject. The essay is flippant, and excessively conceited,—two sins which we suspect Mr. Emerson would repudiate more earnestly than a breach in any of the Commandments. He has a habit of grouping incongruous names together in a way that dislocates one's ideas of the fitness of things, and suggests an ill-arranged *ménu* of a dinner. He speaks of "the fame of

Shakspeare, or of Voltaire, of Thomas à Kempis or Buonaparte." His lists of things, whenever they occur, have an abruptness, that is especially disagreeable. Mr. Emerson's scheme of the Religion of the Future does not commend itself to our understanding, nor induce us to wish to exchange our old lamps for his new one:—

["Worship," 241.19–242.8]

To us the above, which is the culminating passage of the book,—"the crown and glory of our sphere,"—reads like pure and simple nonsense: we do not even pretend that we guess at what it means. In the last three essays—Considerations by the Way, on Beauty, and on Illusions,—there is here and there a sentence that might be quoted, but nothing that Mr. Emerson has not already said, and said better. The book leaves the reader "with the gods still sitting around him on their thrones—they alone with him there." What gods, we are not told; but it looks very much as if Mr. Emerson had at last been fairly driven back into the Greek Mythology, "the old substantial gods of wood and stone," whom for our own use we should prefer to Mr. Emerson's metaphysical figments.

Mr. Emerson's book is dogmatic, paradoxical, high-minded, and deals with confident assertions rather than with well-considered truths. It is very inferior to the first series of Essays by which Mr. Emerson became known in England. What is new in it is not good; and what is good is repetition. We judge Mr. Emerson by the standard he himself taught us to form of what might be expected: he has fallen short of it. This work is not worthy of him, nor is it good in itself. No father would give it to his son as a guide for his "Conduct of life."

288

Review of *The Conduct of Life,* New York *Daily Tribune,* 15 December 1860, p. 4

The position assumed by Mr. Emerson in this volume is that of an expounder of certain fragmentary ethical principles. It lays no claim to the character of a complete philosophical system, propounds no code of action that may be nicely fitted to the adjustment of all human relations, and, in spite of any intimations on the title-page, is free from the presumption of attempting to regulate "the whole duty of man." Indeed, as we gather from these pages, as well as from the previous writings of the author, he has little faith in the pretensions of philosophy. A connected, systematic exhibition of truth in any department of knowledge, is, in his view, an impossibility. No one but a charlatan or an ignoramus would engage in such a desperate task. The wise man confines his vision to a limited sphere, and has only to report faithfully the glances and glimpses of reality that may be vouchsafed to him. The universe is too vast to be explored by the researches of man, and our faculties are too imperfect to inspire much confidence in their decisions. Although Mr. Emerson is sometimes spoken of as a philosopher, we think, that is the last character to which he would wish to assert in title. Some have even represented him as an exponent of German philosophy, or of French philosophy, or of the dim Oriental philosophy of an early age. Nothing could be more absurd. Mr. Emerson is the exponent of nobody but himself. Certain wiseacres have traced his inspiration to Fichte, or Schelling, or Carlyle, or some other famous master of speculation. There is not the slightest ground for this assumption. Mr. Emerson is utterly his own master, bows to no authority, respects no system, represents no theory, consults no oracle, proclaims no faith, but faith in one's self. Truth, according to him, is the fruit of intuition, not the reward of investigation. He makes no use of the slow processes of research and analysis, but looks out on the world with open eye, and takes what comes. His writings, accordingly, owe their chief value to their subjective sincerity; he makes a frank confession of his perceptions or fancies at the moment; consistency is not among his jewels; his pages teem with perpetual surprises; he loves to present an old thought in a new light; his illustrations are sought from all the realms of nature, as well as from every department of literature; a brave egotism is curiously blended with a natural modesty; and he is rich in fresh and piquant suggestions, no less from the unexposed relations in which he presents a familiar idea, than from the fine poetical rhetoric with which he embellishes a thought that has been the patrimony of ages.

The present volume consists of a series of lectures addressed to various popular audiences, and preserves throughout the character of didactic illustration. The topics of which it treats, Fate, Power, Wealth, Culture, Behavior, Worship, Beauty, and Illusion, afford ample scope for the genius of the lecturer, and exhibit a unity of taste and feeling, though no unity of thought. Hence it is not easy to give a just view of its merits as a whole, although numerous passages attract the felicity of Mr. Emerson's diction, and the incoherence of his method.

In the lecture on Fate, he shows that he is not one of the dreaming enthusiasts who expect a paradise of delights in the bosom of the world, but is fully alive to

289

the terrors which lie concealed beneath the smile of nature.

["Fate," 6.22–8.16]

No culture, he maintains, can do away the influence of temperament. A man becomes what he was born to be, and the vice of the race, as well as the features of the family, are inexorably impressed on successive generations.

["Fate," 9.23–11.7]

Plump of the other side comes free-will, and the share it exercises on human destiny is explicitly stated, without an attempt to reconcile contradiction.

["Fate," 22.1–23.2]

As an illustration of power, a favorite type of character with Mr. Emerson is described in the following graphic portraiture:

["Power," 66.27–67.27]

Here is one of the admirable pieces of practical instruction, simply and forcibly expressed, which often relieve the prevailing tone of startling thought and ambitious phraseology.

["Wealth," 91.20–92.26]

Mr. Emerson has some explicit remarks on the efficacy of traveling as a means of culture.

["Culture," 145.1–146.4]

Still, cities may do something for the improvement of manners.

["Culture," 150.14–151.17]

The lecture on behavior abounds in excellent suggestions, that are not to be found in Chesterfield:

["Behavior," 169.1–171.17]

Below is a description of animals which most writers on natural history have overlooked:

["Behavior," 172.25–173.21]

Of the power of the human features, especially the eye, Mr. Emerson discourses handsomely.

["Behavior," 176.27–181.19]

It is difficult to read this volume without yielding to the enticements of Mr. Emerson's rhetoric; it is brilliant with flashes of his peculiar genius; noble sentiments and stirring suggestions are not unfrequent on its pages; it shows a singular ingenuity in the application of literary history to the embellishment of his discourse; but the reader who expects any fresh accessions of knowledge, or more intelligent perceptions of truth, or a clearer insight into the "conduct of life" from its oracular "utterances" will doubtless rise from its perusal with a sense of disappointment.

"Atticus" [William Maccall], "The Conduct of Life," *Critic* [England], n.s. 21 (22 December 1860), 778–9

Slowly, laboriously, elegantly turning ivory balls; then ingeniously playing with them: herein behold the whole faculty of Mr. Emerson, and the whole employment thereof. Marvellous is the mechanical dexterity, still more marvellous the legerdemain. But Mr. Emerson has been so long turning ivory balls and playing with them, that we are tired of the trick; for trick it is, and knack and juggle. Mr. Emerson is a small Yankee Montaigne, but a Montaigne without spontaneousness, without genius, without profound sagacity. He makes books out of books; he is not merely a second-rate, he is a second-hand, writer. To his quaintness he owes his reputation; his quaintness, however, is entirely artificial. Of nature he talks incessantly, yet it is doubtful whether he ever either saw or felt nature. He is resolved to strike; and questionless he is often striking. But analyse his pithiest sentences, and you find that they have either no meaning, or are the clever disguises of the merest commonplaces. There is nothing rich, robust, suggestive, or even in the meagrest sense instructive. In his heart he is a worshipper of Franklin; his system, if system he has, is a species of utilitarianism: he would exchange the almighty dollar of which the Americans speak for a kind of transcendental dollar. Yet, with the instincts of the artist—these he has in a high degree—he sympathises with whatsoever can be turned to artistic purposes.

As specimens of art Emerson's productions are exceedingly finished; they are, in fact, far too finished. Their smoothness is intolerably wearisome; and their roughness is not an honest roughness—it is like the miniature rocks and thickets and glens ingeniously created by landscape gardening. There would not be so much to be said about this if Emerson did not affect to wear the mantle of the prophet. As with his countrymen in general, Emerson has boundless arrogance; we never heard of a modest American. We can allow, then, this writer to be as oracular as he pleases; we permit even the blockhead who cuts our hair to be oracular rather than contradict him. But the prophetic is a different thing altogether. From him who claims to be a great moral teacher we expect simplicity, directness, earnestness, a thorough contempt for fine phrases. Prophets have nothing to do with ivory balls, with hocus pocus.

This is the age of phrasemongers; and we have no quarrel with these as long as they are content to remain phrasemongers. The oddity, however, in these days is, that the more a man is a phrasemonger the more he has the ambition to be a prophet too. So with Kingsley, Ruskin, Tupper, and so many more. There are numerous persons in England who read Emerson, not because he is a sparkling epigrammatic writer, but because he is supposed to reveal sublime spiritual truths. They have a sort of notion that they need moral physic; but they do not want to take too much of it or to take it in a disagreeable shape. They are therefore delighted with Emerson's homæopathic globules. We are not sure that Emerson's globules do either good or harm; he may nevertheless be a quack in administering them. The Emerson philosophy is far too vague, and when it is for a moment practical it is far too prosaic. Theological dogmas having in nearly every country lost their moral power, it is moral principles themselves which must be enforced—principles lofty, principles most definite. Now here Emerson is at once condemned. He is either indefinite, or he teases us with paltry microscopic rules. We are either in a mist or have our legs tied with Lilliputian cords. In a book on the "Conduct of Life" we naturally expect some guidance. But guidance Emerson does not give us, or only counsel which is puerile. For the conduct of life rules, even the best, must always be ineffectual. What we want is a grand organic doctrine, to strengthen and to impel. But Emerson would force us to alternate between a dim and dilettante Pantheism and the Stock Exchange. According to him, you can be a Pantheistic dreamer and a Stock Exchange speculator too. Contradictions and inconsistencies abound in this, as in all Emerson's works. As the noblest natures are the most self-contradictory and inconsistent, we are not inclined to dwell on contradictions and inconsistencies, when natural utterances. But the contradictions and inconsistencies of Emerson are not natural utterances; they spring simply from his mode of composition. In his reading—discursive, curious, but by no means comprehensive—he has gathered together a huge quantity of odds and ends. These must, in some fashion or another, be used up—fitted in; but so that there may be as little trace as possible of the original owner. We do not accuse Emerson of barefaced plagiarism. An intentional plagiary he certainly is not. But the scraps from Cudworth, from Plotinus, from the Scandinavian mythology, from Oriental writers, from the most recent scientific journal, from a thousand sources, are all clamouring to be interwoven in the newest Emerson web. Hence the most

singular contrasts of colour and of material. A much more famous writer than Emerson—Richter—manufactured books in the same way. But in Richter there were bursts of divine inspiration which compel us to forget how often he was a manufacturer instead of a creator. Emerson has a stock of facts, and similes, and illustrations, all waiting for an idea. If Emerson cannot catch his idea, he contrives to dispense with it; the illustrations and similes and facts seem to do without it quite as well. In reading some of our older English writers, notably Barrow, we feel as if we could expand a single page into a dozen pages, and yet furnish sufficient sustenance, so opulent and massive was the thought, so majestic were the words of these demigods. In Emerson, on the contrary, we are at at a loss to discern the very presence of thought. Everything is thin, meagre, and unsubstantial. We might condense and condense, yet never arrive at aught resembling an idea; or if we did, a familiar face would at once be recognised. Not seldom, good Mr. Emerson, having nothing to say, simply twaddles. We could gather from this volume a tolerable anthology of sillinesses. Like all his countrymen, he is an interminable talker; and you cannot talk for ever without babbling a good deal of nonsense. Now, for Mr. Emerson, Stoicism is the best, and now again Epicureanism is the best; now you are to be a stalwart son of the woods, and now you are to be the most polished man of your times; now you are to make money and have every luxury that money can command, and now you are to live on water and a crust, like a hermit; now you are to concentrate all your being on one pursuit, and now you are to panoply yourself for excelling in all pursuits. This is perplexing. What are we to do, or what to believe? We miss in Emerson's writings critical acumen and impartiality; he has no sense of intellectual proportion. He

292

names in one sentence Goethe, Hegel, Metternich, Adams, Calhoun, Guizot, Peel, Cobden, Kossuth, Rothschild, Astor, and Brunel. What a comical jumble! Why did he not add William Walker, John Heenan, and General Tom Thumb? A few years ago Mr. Emerson raised Mr. Wilkinson—a gifted man, but no Bacon—to a place beside Bacon, as if Bacons and Shakespeares were rather plentiful nowadays.

What has helped Emerson's popularity will be fatal to his permanent reputation; literature has obviously been for him a luxury, never a discipline. We are not justified in demanding from an author with Emerson's pretensions profound erudition, but we are right in demanding sound scholarship—knowledge accurate, ample, and catholic. He is too much of a student, too little of a scholar. Once he counselled an audience—to be sure it was a Manchester audience—always to read the translations of ancient and foreign books when they could be procured, and thus be saved the bother of grammars and dictionaries. This is comfortable, but rather lazy. We doubt not that his own practice corresponds to the counsel given. The intellect has a conscience as well as the soul. With the slovenliness of the student as compared with the diligence, the solidity, the correctness, of the scholar, Mr. Emerson is somewhat deficient in intellectual conscience. Anything, however improbable, is made to do duty as a fact, provided it can be hammered into the composite structures he raises. Claverhouse—who was a gallant Scottish gentleman—dressed as well as the Scottish gentlemen of his period; let us grant that he dressed a little better: Emerson converts him into a fop. He declares, with a platitudinarian emphasis not uncommon in the book, that man known to us only as a celebrity in politics or in trade gains largely on our esteem if we discover that he has some intellectual taste or skill; and he speaks of him whom he calls the regicide Carnot, and his sublime genius in mathematics. Now from these blundering and ridiculous words we should conclude that the principal circumstance connected with Carnot was the part that he took in the death of Louis XVI., and that his mathematical talents and acquirements were things completely subordinate. It is, however, for his scientific ability, still more than for his political importance, that Carnot will always be illustrious; and of all the events of his political career, his vote for the condemnation of the King was one of the least memorable—a vote, besides, given with the declaration that the performance of no duty had ever weighed more on his heart. Great in the mathematics, Carnot was great in military engineering, and still greater in military administration. In the early and triumphant days of the French Republic how beautiful and mighty was the shout in honour of Carnot; that it was he who had organised victory! Yet to Emerson Carnot is only the regicide Carnot; from which we conclude that Emerson has never read the life of Carnot, and is most imperfectly acquainted with the events of the French Revolution.

If a man is an eccentricity in literature, his worst book is always sure to be most to the taste of his worshippers. This work, therefore, is likely enough to be Emerson's most popular production. What is good in it will be overlooked, and its frequent and flagrant faults will kindle into rapture thousands of men and women. No evil of our times more deplorable than this idiotic idolatry of the eccentricities of literature. The literary sects are now more numerous than the religious. Formerly literature was a pantheon where every god had his place, and where for every god the pious worshipper had grateful and gushing homage. Now every literary Little Bethel deals damnation at the literary Little

Bethel over the way. The chief literary Little Bethel is crowded by Macaulayites of the pure Whig stamp; but if Macaulay is the favourite fetiche De Quincey is denounced, and if De Quincey is the favourite fetiche then Macaulay is trampled in the mire. The believers in Carlyle turn with contempt from both Macaulay and De Quincey. There are those to whom Coleridge is the divinity of divinities. But the most exclusive and bigoted of superstitious disciples are those who enter the Emersonian Little Bethel. This is easily explained. An admirer of Mr. Tupper once said that there have been three great men since the beginning of the world—Solomon, Shakespeare, and Tupper. Here then you see that even in the most enthusiastic Tupperian there is a certain tolerance. But he who is convinced that Emerson is a great man can admit no one else to be great. Emerson fills all his followers with his own conceit and conceits. They are persuaded that, even if *he* were dead, earth would be tolerably well off, having *them* to illumine it. The creatures are bores, as every one is a bore who has not enough of hospitality in his nature to welcome the godlike and the beautiful, come from what region they may. We have noted in Emerson the want of idea. We equally deplore the want of heart. He repeatedly ridicules the persons who yearn for sympathy; but we yearn for sympathy just in the degree that we lavishly pour sympathy forth. Nelson, when dying, asked Hardy to kiss him. The large, loving heart which had squandered so much affection asked a tender, fiery affection to be its chariot to immortality. Yet, of course, Nelson should have expired grim in visage, and silent, or babbling some pedantic lie of defiance to pain and death. When Garibaldi went through the hospitals he pressed his lips on the brow of the wounded. This was the best medicine; or

if the grave was inevitable, it was the most sacred of seals that could be stamped on the most heroic of sacrifices for the fatherland. What contemptible weaklings were these sick men, to hunger for the most opulent and celestial consolation which their mighty chief could bestow! Without ideas, without heart, Emerson has no divine insight for the awful mysteries of human sorrow and of human pain. Glibly, briskly, pungently, he can discourse of the social evils which come to the surface through the newspapers; but before the woe and the wrong which torment humanity from generation to generation—which will torment it evermore—he is dumb: they are things too serious to be stuck on epigrams and help up to the wonderment and applause of the public. The few really earnest, truthful, salutary words in the book are in the essay on Worship. But here, as usual, falsehood, fallacy, and exaggeration abound, along with that perpetual effort to be brilliant which is Emerson's besetting and fatal weakness. If the essay on Worship is the best in the book that on Beauty is the worst; showing how completely Emerson is in a foreign element whenever he attempts to treat a subject requiring poetical wealth and delicacy, metaphysical depth and grasp, and symbolical interpretation. We are glad to see, from an announcement at the commencement of the volume, that Mr. Emerson derives a pecuniary benefit from this edition; we trust that this will be balm to him for whatever the critics may say that is disagreeable. Some of the critics may manifest lenity or politeness, or kindness for Auld Lang Syne's sake; cordial praise Mr. Emerson's work will get from no honest critic; and if we prove the harshest of his judges, let us believe that it is because we are the most conscientious, fearless, and uncompromising.

[James Russell Lowell], Review of *The Conduct of Life,* *Atlantic Monthly,* 7 (February 1861), 254–5

It is a singular fact, that Mr. Emerson is the most steadily attractive lecturer in America. Into that somewhat cold-water-ish region adventurers of the sensation kind come down now and then with a splash, to become disregarded King Logs before the next season. But Mr. Emerson always draws. A lecturer now for something like a quarter of a century, one of the pioneers of the lecturing system, the charm of his voice, his manner, and his matter has never lost its power over his earlier hearers, and continually winds new ones in its enchanting meshes. What they do not fully understand they take on trust, and listen, saying to themselves, as the old poet of Sir Philip Sidney,—

"A sweet, attractive, kind of grace,
  A full assurance given by looks,
Continual comfort in a face,
  The lineaments of gospel books."

We call it a singular fact, because we Yankees are thought to be fond of the spread-eagle style, and nothing can be more remote from that than his. We are reckoned a practical folk, who would rather hear about a new air-tight stove than about Plato; yet our favorite teacher's practicality is not in the least of the Poor Richard variety. If he have any Buncombe constituency, it is that unrealized commonwealth of philosophers which Plotinus proposed to establish; and if he were to make an almanac, his directions to farmers would be something like this:— "OCTOBER: *Indian Summer;* now is the time to get in your early Vedas." What, then, is his secret? Is it not that he out-Yankees us all? that his range includes us all? that he is equally at home with the potato-disease and original sin, with pegging shoes and the Over-soul? that, as we try all trades, so has he tried all cultures? and above all, that his mysticism gives us a counterpoise to our super-practicality?

There is no man living to whom, as a writer, so many of us feel and thankfully acknowledge so great an indebtedness for ennobling impulses,—none whom so many cannot abide. What does he mean? ask these last. Where is his system? What is the use of it all? What the deuce have we to do with Brahma? Well, we do not propose to write an essay on Emerson at the fag-end of a February "Atlantic," with Secession longing for somebody to hold it, and Chaos come again in the South Carolina teapot. We will only say that we have found grandeur and consolation in a starlit night without caring to ask what it meant, save grandeur and consolation; we have like Montaigne, as some ten generations before us have done, without thinking him so systematic as some more eminently tedious (or shall we say tediously eminent?) authors; we have thought roses as good in their way as cabbages, though the latter would have made a better show in the witness-box, if cross-examined as to their usefulness; and as for Brahma, why, he can take care of himself, and won't bite us at any rate.

The bother with Mr. Emerson is, that, though he writes in prose, he is essentially a poet. If you undertake to paraphrase what he says, and to reduce it to words of one syllable for infant minds, you will make as sad work of it as the good monk with his analysis of Homer in the "Epitolæ Obscurorum Virorum." We look upon him as one of the few men of genius

295

whom our age has produced, and there needs no better proof of it than his masculine faculty of fecundating other minds. Search for his eloquence in his books and you will perchance miss it, but meanwhile you will find that it has kindled all your thoughts. For choice and pith of language he belongs to a better age than ours, and might rub shoulders with Fuller and Browne,—though he does use that abominable word, *reliable*. His eye for a fine, telling phrase that will carry true is like that of a backwoodsman for a rifle; and he will dredge you up a choice word from the ooze of Cotton Mather himself. A diction at once so rich and so homely as his we know not where to match in these days of writing by the page; it is like homespun cloth-of-gold. The many cannot miss his meaning, and only the few can find it. It is the open secret of all true genius. What does he mean, quotha? He means inspiring hints, a divining-rod to your deeper nature, "plain living and high thinking."

We meant only to welcome this book, and not to review it. Doubtless we might pick our quarrel with it here and there; but all that our readers care to know is, that it contains essays on Fate, Power, Wealth, Culture, Behavior, Worship, Considerations by the Way, Beauty, and Illusions. They need no invitation to Emerson. "Would you know," says Goethe, "the ripest cherries? Ask the boys and blackbirds." He does not advise you to inquire of the crows.

Review of *The Conduct of Life*, *Knickerbocker*, 57 (February 1861), 217–8

'There is nothing new under the sun.' There is no advice to be given on any subject which has not already been proffered; no lesson of experience; no suggestions to the young; no warning to the old; no praise; no judgment; no condemnation; no acquittal. The Wise Man, thousands of years ago, cautioned the world against sloth, avarice, sensuality, pride, conceit and vain-glory. He advised against the very every-day errors which are still rife. He proclaimed the certain law of cause and effect in evil-doing. He declared for wisdom and integrity; he denounced madness and sin. There is not an element which enters into the composition of our present routine, not a practice nor habit which obtains in our present social state, which Solomon has not commented on, approved of or denounced. Verily, '*The thing which hath been it is that which shall be.*' To present old truths, old opinions, old judgments under such forms and in such combinations that they shall strike the mind as fresh and novel, is to be original. In fact it is all we can claim for the term originality. Various men have achieved this in various ways. Mr. Webster reached it by investing the most simple idea in such simple language that it gave to it a momentous importance. Carlyle arrived at the same by employing a style most extraordinary and vicious, which, while it was inexcusable in him, has done the world of letters irreparable injury by giving birth to hundreds of small imitators who reproduce nothing of the giant but his grotesque form. Mr. Emerson also is original. We have watched his career the past twenty-five years with much interest. And he has always received, we believe, ample justice in the pages of this Magazine. In the beginning his mind, grasping after the *rationale* of this world's conduct, and seeking to give utterance to thoughts as yet immature, Mr. Emerson employed a style which while it could not be called either hyperbolical or stilted, yet was unnatural—from the clouds: yet being from the clouds, was startling. We recollect years ago, *apropos* of some pending discussion, undertaking to translate one of Mr. Emerson's essays into ordinary English, and after the process how little was left that could be called original or striking? For all that, he started with the true plan, the plan which he recommends and dilates on in this work, to wit: finding out what you are apt for, and sticking to it. Mr. Emerson is an apt thinker, and has stuck to that. Not satisfied at first with simple language, wherein the idea is always most forcibly clothed, he sought grotesque forms and out-of-the-way expressions. Had he been less in earnest, this would have been clap-trap. Had he been less genuine, he would have gone from bad to worse instead of to better. Not that we object sometimes to being surprised into reflection. When in one of his works he tells us '*the Present is a King in disguise*,' we pause, profoundly impressed. We are struck as by a new idea, and we do not seem aware that really it is but the old story about the value of the present moment. In 'The Conduct of Life' we have, perhaps, the most practical of Mr. Emerson's works: that is, where we readily see most closely connected the idea and its application. The style too is comparatively clear and simple, (we congratulate the author for this emancipation from what was certainly a false though brilliant perversion of the well of English undefiled,) and if the reader takes up the book we

promise him he will scarcely lay it down till he has reached the last page. To us it has all the interest of a romance. One runs no hazard in predicting the same for whoever lays hold of it. There are nine chapters. The headings are: 'Fate,' 'Power,' 'Wealth,' 'Culture,' 'Behavior,' 'Worships,' 'Considerations by the Way,' 'Beauty,' 'Illusions.' We intended to give some extracts from these, but in the attempt we encountered a difficulty of selection from *l'embarrras des richesses*. Let the reader purchase the book.

We say that the style is clear, and so it is. Yet it is the style of a man who dwells too much in the region of thought. Mr. Emerson has still another 'plane' to reach; that of the living, breathing actual, about which he *writes* so well. He has yet to *become* a portion of it. Mr. Emerson is a close student of Schiller, and 'The Conduct of Life' is much after some of the essays of the great German: practical to be sure, but *theoretically* practical.

Will our Boston friends forgive us when we say their favorite author smacks occasionally of the *provinces?* When Mr. Emerson tells us: '*Society in large towns is babyish;*' he descends to mere puerility: he forgets that God made man to dwell in cities as well as on the plains; that strength comes from combination; that to our 'large towns' we owe our advance in all the arts and in all which requries wealth for its production and culture.

There pervades this work generally a healthy tone. But it has not, we confess, altogether the ring of the true metal. And sometimes we are ready to quote, by way of criticism, the response of the earnest and simple-hearted Margaret, who answers to a pantheistic rhapsody of her love, (in reply to her question if he were a believer:) 'What you say sounds very fine, and is very nearly what the priest tells me, only in different words. For all that, THOU HAST NO CHRISTIANITY!'

297

[Noah Porter, Jr.], "Ralph Waldo Emerson on the Conduct of Life," *New Englander*, 19 (April 1861), 496–508

Of writers on The Conduct of Life, there have been very many from Solomon to Ralph Waldo Emerson. The majority of such writers, however practical their aims, have also held some avowed or underlying theory concerning the chief end of man, the conditions of human perfection and progress, the relations of man to himself, to nature, to his fellow-men, and to God, from which they have derived their precepts and rules of living. To this universal practice, the author of this sprightly volume has conformed—only with this difference, that he does not bring his speculative system very prominently into notice. Certainly he does not define it in very precise statements, nor phrase it in the language of the schools. He seems rather to avoid his own theory, and to prefer to keep shy of it; either because he does not exactly know what it is, or because all utterances concerning a creed so sublime and recently discovered are befittingly made in Orphic intimations, or may-hap, if the creed were declared in simple phrase, it might offend his more uncultured and unsophisticated readers.

Whatever the reason may be, the fact is certain, that little prominence is formally given by the author to his theory of life, and the cursory reader might conclude that he has not revealed it all, but has offered us instead, a series of practical remarks concerning what he has seen in life,—notings sharp, shrewd, and searching,—such as his practical sense, his cool observation, and his imperturbable *sang froid* have qualified him to jot down from his pretty wide observation of men, books, and society. These remarks are enlivened by his well-known wit, running not unfrequently into grotesque conceits, that are only saved from down-right extravagance by the pithy sense and the genial humor that relaxes the screwing lips of the critic into an irresistible smile, or a shouting peal of laughter.

Recovering from his laughter, the critic will have it, that the sage of Concord is too conscious of the effect which he would secure, and aims at this too directly either to satisfy or to indicate an earnest mind—that he finishes his sentences too often with a turn that plainly bespeaks Mr. Emerson's special delight at Mr. Emerson's bright achievements; that he writes with the air of a man who is accustomed to be looked up to with admiring and unquestioning deference—and is always aware that he is surrounded by those who attach great weight even to his absurd deliverances. With all his genius, he is not saved from the unmistakable manner which cleaves to the writer who composes for a private coterie, or for an initiated set, and from which he only is free who is accustomed to converse as well as to discourse, to take the thoughts of others as well as to give his own, to commend and adjust his thinking to the minds of men who can think as well as himself, as well as to inundate the souls of meek and admiring recipients with a deluge of discoursing.

We have said that Mr. Emerson has not made his speculative system prominent, but has rather confined himself to remarks on actual and concrete life. It might seem that for this reason we are excused from noticing this system altogether. But we find that notwithstanding the apparent absence of such principles, they are really present in every line, giving shape and meaning to what would otherwise be unmeaning. Though the philosophy of man's existence and of the end of man's living be not stated in formal propositions, it is diffused by a subtle influence through the entire structure of his remarks, and is fitted to exert an influence which is a thousand fold more dangerous because it steals upon the reader—he knows not why, nor how, nor whence—being conscious only of the spell in which the enchanter holds him, not knowing that it is the work of an enchanter.

Shaking from ourselves as best we may, the magic influences which are diffused from the genius of the author, and looking dispassionately at the principles which he directly asserts and indirectly insinuates, we encounter the ominous word *Fate,* which stands forth as the title of the first discourse. The word, however, is not so appalling as the author's treatment of it. Of all the descriptions which we have ever read of the merciless and remorseless absolutism of a universe of impersonal law, this strikes us as the most horrible save one, and that is the dream of J. P. Richter, of a universe bereft of its God; and this is the most horrible of the two in that it is not given as a dream, but as the strongest side of a potent reality. It would seem that the author had tasked to the utmost, his powers of conceiving and describing, to give expression to the hideous aspects of over-mastering necessity—breaking out on us from the earth, stifling us in the air, pressing down upon us from the sky, paralyzing our flesh, decomposing our very bones, tugging at our heart-strings—nay, bringing an incubus upon our intellect, sucking out the life from our affections, and infusing poison into the springs of character.

It is true that recoiling with horror,

"he knew not why,
E'en at the sound himself had made,"

he seeks to show that necessity and fate are not all-powerful—that the thought which reflects and comprehends law, is stronger than necessity, because it analyses and decomposes it,—that the moral sentiment which bravely looks fate in the face, has an eye that will not blench before this head of Medusa, and that the human will is able, with moral strength, to cope even with this monster of brutal force. He also dwells on the beneficent workings of this very necessity, showing that the very aspects which at first repel and appall us, are its most essential elements for good. These views are all in the right direction. We complain that they are only in a direction and bring us to no end—that they put us on a way which leads to no goal. In other words, he does not overcome Fate by substituting in its place a Providence that cares for the best ends of the whole by means of wide-reaching and sternly working laws, while yet it loves, and pities, and comforts the humblest individual that suffers by their action. There is no suggestion "that the very hairs of the head are all numbered," and that the suffering spirit is "of more value than many sparrows."

The practical conclusion to which Mr. Emerson would lead us, we state in his own words:

["Fate," 49.5–26]

The suggestion of an altar to the Beautiful Necessity, and of the place where such an altar might probably be erected, brings to mind an old book with which Mr. Emerson cannot be unacquainted, in which it is written, "Ye men of Athens, I perceive that in all things ye are too superstitious. For as I passed by, and beheld your devotions, I found an altar with this inscription—To the unknown God. Whom therefore ye ignorantly worship, him declare I unto you." It also reminds us of the saying of one who was not deficient in his recognition of and in his respect for law. "I had rather believe all the fables in the legend, and the Talmud, and the Alcoran, than that this universal frame is without a mind."

Passing over for the present the Chapters on Power, Wealth, Culture, Behavior, we come to that on Worship. At the beginning he says, with charming naiveté or provoking audacity, just as we chance to construe him: "Some of my friends have complained, when the preceding papers were read, that we discussed Fate, Power, Wealth, on too low a platform," &c., &c., implying, of course, that he had left out of view the religious element. Whereupon he proceeds to observe, with that air of entire unconsciousness or of injured innocence which is wont to be assumed by certain grave looking people when touched by a policeman, that his friends are altogether mistaken, inasmuch as to this element he attaches the greatest importance. But, he adds, that really it is of very little consequence what he or any man may say; that he is sure "a certain truth will be said through him, though he should be dumb, or though he should try to say the reverse," an apology, by the way, which would be just as pertinent for bad grammar, or for downright nonsense, as it is for Pantheistic Theosophy or Libertine Ethics. He then adds, "dipping his pen in the blackest ink, without the fear of falling into his own ink-pot," that "We are born believing. A man bears beliefs, as a tree bears apples." "I and my neighbors have been bred in the notion, that unless we come soon to some good church-Calvinism, or Behmenism, or Romanism, or Mormonism—there would be a universal thaw and dissolution. No Isaiah or Jeremy has arrived. Nothing can exceed the anarchy that has followed in our skies. The stern old faiths have all pulverized." "'T is a whole population of gentlemen and ladies out in search of religions." "Yet we make shift to live." "The decline of the influence of Calvin, or Fenelon, or Wesley, or Channing, need give us no uneasiness." "God builds his temple in the heart, on the ruins of churches and religions."

Again, speaking of the present times, he says, "I do not find the religions of men, at this moment, very creditable to them, but either childish and insignificant, or unmanly and effeminating. The fatal trait is the divorce between religion and morality."

["Worship," 209.8–19]

We question whether Mr. Emerson knows enough of the point technically known as the "state of religion," to be qualified to speak upon it with much authority. There are certain species of fish, that, for purposes of concealment and defense, can exude from their own bowels a liquid that causes the waters in their immediate vicinity to take an inky or a purple hue. Doubtless all the objects which the fish beholds through this medium are invested with the blackness of ink, or the glory of the Tyrian purple. Perhaps Mr. Emerson might profitably consider that the atmosphere created by his gloomy or his glorious fancies, need not of necessity extend farther than "his study" in Concord, or his "club" in Boston,—even though it seems to him to invest the universe. So much audacious positiveness in assertion, might properly rest upon a more careful induction of facts. It may be true that the power of certain scholastic formulæ concerning the person and work of Christ may occupy a smaller part of the world's thinking than in other times, but it is not true that, as between the moral teachings of Christ and the power of his ummatched personality—the personality is of inferior interest. Rather is it true, that there was never a time when Christ, as a divine and incomparable person, was

300

so powerful and plastic in his sway over the world's thinking and the world's literature as it is at this moment—that there was never an hour when Christ, as an object of affection and trust, was consecrated in so many believing hearts, and in so many Christian homes—never a time, within two centuries, when it might be said that more of the men who guide and mold the thoughts of the world were themselves molded and guided by a faith in Christ's Divine Personality. We are not disposed to deny to Mr. Emerson and his sort of people a very considerable influence over the thinking of this country and of England. We freely confess that they are the Representative men of a class which is much larger than we wish it were; but we think it goes quite beyond the limits of a becoming modesty that they should take it upon them to speak for all of Christendom that lies beyond Boston and twenty miles around. They are fully competent to speak for themselves, and in so doing, to express their estimate of Christ, but not therefore, qualified to testify as to what the rest of the world think, or to draw the inference that if these do not agree with themselves, they are thereby excluded from all good society, and must forego all fellowship with the cultivated and enlightened classes.

We are confirmed in our opinion that Mr. Emerson is incompetent to judge of what the world thinks, by the utter shallowness and flippancy of the judgments which he expresses concerning Christianity itself. The power of this system, he would have us believe, lies in the excellence of its moral teachings, and not in the wondrous mystery and charm that pertain to the Divine Person whose name it bears. Is it possible that he is so pitifully ignorant of the force of the New Testament teachings, and of the uniform sentiment of hosts of believing Christian philosophers, as not to be aware that the chief importance which they attach to what he calls "the dogma of the mystic offices of Christ" is that there lies in it a power and potency for man's moral welfare that is unmatched by any other and all other systems of faith and duty. That much of the religionism of the present day that is called after Christ, is superficial and cheap, is true indeed, but it is no more true, than that much of the worship which is called after Emerson, is twaddle and cant. That the speculative and practical ethics of many zealous Christians are sadly incomplete and inconsistent, is no news to those who "retain the Christian traditions," and, we add, is so far from being an argument against, that it is rather an argument for the necessity of these very traditions. Mr. Emerson says some just and some flippant things about the defective ethics and the superficial religionism of the current Christianity, somewhat brighter, but no more severe than are frequently uttered in sermons by those who "still maintain the old emphasis of Christ's personality." But that this is possible and true, Mr. Emerson is either very sublimely or very willfully ignorant.

But in the midst of his querulous dissatisfaction with the church of the present, he is cheered with the bright anticipations of the church of the future. Concerning this church, this new John the Baptist, this "voice of one crying in the wilderness" thus expresses himself in the conclusion of his long disquisition on worship:

["Worship," 241.10–242.8]

It strikes us that in this would-be jubilant strain, there is an undertone of concession and apology which betrays the conscious weakness of the prophet. What if the babe is "cold and naked," is not this the perfection and the glory of the "new church founded on moral science"? "Let us have nothing new which is not its

301

own evidence. There is surely enough for the heart and imagination in the religion itself. Let us not be pestered with assertions and half-truths, with emotions and snuffle." What do we want of "the nameless Thought, the nameless Power, the superpersonal Heart"? Why tell us that here is somewhat on which we may "repose"? Why not repose on the Laws themselves? Surely, anything more is, according to Mr. Emerson's theory, "emotion and snuffle."

But the Laws who are to be consolers, "the good Laws themselves," though alive, do not satisfy even Mr. Emerson. His heart and his flesh cry out for a personal God, whom he shadows forth as the "nameless Power, the superpersonal Heart." Through all this confident triumph the cry comes up in an undertone, low and sad, like the wailing of a deserted infant, but of which the meaning cannot be mistaken, "my soul thirsteth for God, for the *living* God."

Mr. Emerson seems entirely to overlook that it is the great peculiarity of the Christian system, that it provides a personal "Power" for man to worship—which is, at the same time, a personal "Heart," on which he may repose. The power which Christ has had over this world, and is still likely to retain, is not explained by "his genius as a moral teacher," but in the fascination and force, the constraining, nay, the magnetic influence of his divine personality. It is this which has held to their allegiance the myriads of believing spirits who gladly give him faith and obedience; and it is this which asserts a fascination over Mr. Emerson himself from which he would gladly escape, and which yet he cannot account for. He cannot hide from himself the truth that the phenomenon of Christ, as described in the evangelists, is the most inflexible fact in human history, and that this fact of his original appearance, and the still more inexplicable phenomenon of the tremendous and trans-forming force which has ever since streamed from him into the history of man, defy all the solutions which he can find in the "impersonal Laws."

Not only does Mr. Emerson fail to understand the power of Christ as a person, but he fails equally in understanding his "genius as a moral teacher." Surely he ought to be adequate to this, especially since more than eighteen centuries have added their contributions of thought and of application to the teachings of the master. But does he understand the moral system of Christ? Does he inculcate the same ethical principles? Or has he discovered those which are better?

We assert that his morality is not the morality of Christ, and that his whole volume on the conduct of life, shows that he does not understand what the Christian system is—that he does not understand it well enough to know wherein lay the genius and peculiarity of Christ when considered solely as a moral teacher. The distinctive feature of the ethical system of Christ, is, that it inculcates self-abnegation, benevolence in the form of self-sacrifice, charity, self-denial, forgiveness—that it warms the self-seeking and self-centered human soul with the glow of the love that seeks not its own, and that its comprehensive rule and motto is, "it is more blessed to give than to receive."

Mr. Emerson knows no such rule, and his book breathes no such spirit as this. We do not overlook the fact that his book contains many wise observations concerning wealth, behavior, and culture, that these observations have been made by a sharp and discerning eye, and are uttered with the pith and genius for which the writer is so justly admired. They strongly and clearly depict the emptiness and folly of the aims of such as seek to cheat themselves or their fellows by vulgar estimates of wealth, manners, and cultivation. They expose with a quiet, yet genial satire, the shams that are ever shooting up in modern society, especially under its American phases. They impress us with an unfeigned conviction that honesty is the best policy, in our aims, our judgments, our manners, and our hopes. They recognize distinctly, they even emphasize terribly the resistless supremacy, the crushing absolutism of the Moral Laws that support and maintain the changeless order of the universe. From these views of man and the universe they leave us to derive all our principles of life, wisely sparing the infliction of formal precepts and long drawn exhortations. But among these rules and principles, we do not find that law of love which was *the* characteristic of the moral system of Christ. Mr. Emerson would have us be humane, but not with the loving tenderness which Christ enjoined; patient with our fellow-men, but rather because it is unmanly to be ruffled, than because we ourselves are ever trying the patience of a divine master; forgiving, not because we ourselves need to be forgiven, but because our personal dignity is too lofty and self-sustained to allow us to condescend to revenge; kind and gentle, not from the overflow of loving affection, but because it saves the friction and loss of dignity which resentment and anger involve. The Ideal man which Emerson proposes to himself and others, is, through the absence of this feature of Christlike love, entirely unlike the Ideal which Christ himself exemplified and enforced. We cannot, therefore, escape the conclusion that his morality is not Christ morality. However much he bepraises Christ, the moral teacher, he does not receive nor teach morality which Christ represents.

The Christian Examiner says of a passage, "Although his voice is no longer heard in Christian pulpits, yet what preaching can be more practical and Evangelical than this?" What ideas the critic can have of the meaning of "Christian" and "Evangelical," we do not care to inquire. We had supposed that these terms had a precise and universally accepted meaning; at least when applied to the ethics of the Gospel—that these ethics, at least in their practical import, were too marked and peculiar to be mistaken or miscalled even by the most liberal interpreter. Tried by this acknowledged standard, the ethics of Mr. Emerson can, in our opinion, with no propriety be termed either Evangelical or Christian.

But perhaps he teaches a better morality than the Christian, one that is better suited to a more enlightened age, and which is to be regarded as a higher and more perfect development of the ethics of Christ. Precisely the opposite is true. His ethics are not only below those of Christ, but are not equal to the best ethics to which Paganism has attained. Stripped of modern phraseology, divested of illustrations drawn from modern life, and viewed in their principles and spirit, they sink below the believing and loving precepts of the conscientious Socrates—and are not to be compared with the glowing fervor of the inspired Plato. In one aspect they are simple Stoicism without the dogged earnestness of the indomitable Zeno. In another they are pure Epicureanism, applied to the enlightenment of modern culture, but without the quiet geniality which the Athenian could alone exemplify. Mr. Emerson is a stoic in his proud defiance of a Personal Divinity, in his quiet acquiescence in all powerful Fate and in the sovereign self-reliance with which he confronts the movements of destiny. He is a stoic in his contempt of the unenlightened masses, in his deification of intelligence, and in the arrogance with which he claims to humanity the prerogatives that belong to God alone. He is epicurean in his intense absorption in the present life, in his dependance on its resources for all the good which he contemplates, in

303

neglecting to honor the blessed uses of sickness and suffering, and in the exclusive regard for intellectual and æsthetic enjoyment.

The best and noblest of the ancient teachers aspired after an immortal existence, and drew their most inspiring influences from the very imagination that such an existence was possible. Mr. Emerson thinks it beneath his dignity to be indebted to faith in immortality, for any excitement to virtue. The present is enough for him to think and care for. The purest of the ancient moralists had an unquestioning faith in the personal responsibility of man, if not in the personality of the divine nature. Mr. Emerson is shy of an earnest faith in either. For these reasons we prefer Socrates, Plato, Plutarch, and Cicero, one and all, to the Sage of Concord.

We are not insensible to the many charms which Mr. Emerson lends to any subject which he treats, nor, on the other hand, can we fail to notice the rhetorical trickeries of which he not unfrequently avails himself. But his manifest power as a thinker and writer, lend no real authority to his opinions, however great may be the fascination with which they invest his treatment of them. It is with the principles that run through this book with an ever present though unseen influence, and that now and then crop out in statements that cannot be mistaken—it is with these principles that we have to do, not with the many and varied gems of thought which drop from his sparkling pen, nor with the sayings, both witty and wise, with which he has strown so richly the course of his discussions.

We must confess, however, to a sense of humiliation for the reputation of our country's literature, that it should be so largely and conspicuously represented by a writer who deals so superciliously with the profoundest problems of philosophy, and so dogmatically with the most stubborn facts of history—who through strength or weakness—from knowledge or conceit, assumes that he is emancipated from the obligations ordinarily recognized by the profoundest thinkers to cite facts and adduce arguments, and by virtue of a special license is allowed to dogmatize concerning the gravest matters, or flippantly dismiss them with an Orphic saying. That such a writer should mold the opinions and form the creed of so many scores of thoughtful spirits, and be accepted as one of the profoundest philosophers of America, excites both grief and shame for our generation and our country. It argues either lack of knowledge, or lack of individual independence, deficiency in moral earnestness, or an excess of literary toadyism which is anything but honorable to our countrymen. We confess, also, a sort of shame for Mr. Emerson himself, that he should seem to be so insensible to the poverty and flimsiness of the principles which he so gravely propounds and studiously puts forth as profound utterances, but which are nothing better than the *exuviæ* of the thinking of darker ages and earlier generations. But it is strangest of all that he should bestow on a creed so poor, so starveling, and so comfortless, the wealth of genius with which he has been so richly endowed by nature, and which he has wrought into such forms of beauty by a generous culture. We entreat him to take a few lessons both in good sense and ethics from the true hearted Socrates, if he will not condescend to learn somewhat from Christ.

Review of *The Conduct of Life*, *Westminster Review*, [England], 75 (April 1861), 588–90

We are inclined to think that the publication of his "Essays on the Conduct of Life," by Emerson, will add but little to his reputation, and may, perhaps, lead to a reconsideration of the grounds on which that reputation rests, with results far from favourable to its maintenance. We cannot remember any author who has written so much on moral questions whose name is so completely unassociated with any definite doctrine; his name does not even suggest any great subject fully treated, but stands for a certain manner and rhetorical way of putting things in general, and even on the topics he treats of we meet in his books no independent and original thoughts, but mere desultory musings; he has been called suggestive, but this is only true in the sense that all incompleteness is suggestive; a suggestive writer must have something of his own; extravagant dressing up of other men's thoughts is not suggestive; the extravagance attracts notice, but the more attention you pay to such writings, the less satisfactory the result; the fair and attractive exterior is as delusive as Dead Sea apples. The sum of all his vehement exhortations is mostly some ordinary truism, or some string of antithetical opinions, without an attempt at solution; the vestiges of patient inquiry are rare indeed, the colours of good and evil are laid on with an equal hand, and seldom more than the colours. Extravagant imagery and out-of-the-way illustration keep the reader in a constant state of surprise, but on laying down the book after the perusal of each essay, it is difficult to say to what result the author has arrived at all proportionate to the fire and energy of the language.

The mode, too, in which he treats his topics is as characteristic as the language; the strange disjointed heaps of sentences might often be read backwards with as much effect as in the sequence in which they are offered to the reader; there is no progress of thought, but loose remarks are accumulated round some arbitrary point which cannot be called a centre. These features, which characterize all Emerson's works, are more marked and salient in this last one; the mannerism which attracted when a novelty becomes oppressive in proportion to our familiarity with it; it has been said of style that it is the man; but style pre-supposes labour and thought, and is a source of endless enjoyment. It is with authors as it is with painters, those who have a style are immortal, but a mannerist, however popular he may be for a season, is soon forgotten, and after a time it becomes a matter of wonder that he was ever an object of popular admiration.

Mr. Emerson has much in common with the mocking bird of his own woods; of old he used to echo Fichte and Jean Paul, in the present volume he is evidently dominated by that disreputable countryman of his, Walt Whitman; many a page might be transferred to the notorious "Leaves of Grass," of course to the cleanest and most decent of that strange production, which he christened the first-fruit of American poetry.

That a student should admire the thews and sinews of a vigorous lumberer is very natural, but that his studies should not have lifted him above all sympathy with the animal excesses of the healthy, physical organization he envies, is to be deplored. The new influence shows itself in such passages as the following:—

["Power," 62.27–65.11]

This is a melancholy confession of faith, or rather of the absence of it, and is only possible in the mouth of a moral dilettante, a sad *caput mortuum* of superficial inquiry. To this complexion has the high scaring Icarus Emerson come at last. Can any man of principle or earnest conviction thus stand aside and let the unruly powers of nature take this course?

America is nobler than this account of her, and has things far more excellent to rely upon than the untamed strength of her backwoods-men. If the world emerged from chaos by the agencies of volcanic fire and cataclysmal deluge, it was fitted for human life by much milder forces; to long for the first throes of nature, because of the mere magnitude of their effects, is to desire a sterile and uninhabitable earth that the whole progress of civilization may be commenced anew; to wish to cut the human mind adrift from every tradition, because some of them are evil and effete, is a sign of radical irreverence of mind for which no wordy homage to some great names of old can atone. The recognition and manly support of what is good among men, the uncritical allegiance to some conviction that can be made the basis of practical action is infinitely more worthy than such criticism as this. This ready appeal to the lowest depths of man's nature is a practical denial of all faith in his past culture, and a complete disruption of that gradual progress on which alone the hopes of mankind are securely based.

Checklist of Additional Reviews

Dial, 1 (December 1860), 778.

Boston *Daily Advertiser*, 12 December 1860, p. 2.

Boston *Daily Evening Transcript*, 14 December 1860, p. 1.

Boston *Daily Journal*, 14 December 1860, p. 4.

London Publishers' Circular, 15 December 1860.

"The Conduct of Life," *Saturday Review*, 10 (15 December 1860), 762–3.

Springfield [Massachusetts] *Daily Republican*, 15 December 1860, p. 4.

Chicago *Tribune*, 19 December 1860, p. 2.

"Emerson's Conduct of Life," *Spectator*, 33 (22 December 1860), 1217–18.

Christian Mirror [Portland, Maine], 39 (25 December 1860), 86.

Boston *Post*, 28 December 1860, p. 1.

Literary Gazette [England], n.s. 5 (29 December 1860), 562–3.

Ladies' Companion and Monthly Magazine, 2nd ser., 19 (1861), 105–8.

[Frederic Henry Hedge], *Christian Examiner*, 70 (January 1861), 149–50.

Freewill Baptist Quarterly, 9 (January 1861), 107–8.

Hunt's Merchants Magazine, 44 (January 1861), 144.

[Rufus] E[llis]., *Monthly Religious Magazine*, 25 (January 1861), 65–6.

National Review, 12 (January 1861), 272.

New Englander, 19 (January 1861), 241.

Universalist Quarterly, 18 (January 1861), 110.

Independent, 13 (3 January 1861), 1.

Reasoner, 26 (13 January 1861), 19.

New Quarterly Review [England], 10 (1st Quarter 1861), 157–8.

Peterson's Magazine, 39 (February 1861), 180.

Sharpe's London Journal, n.s. 19 (February 1861), 105–8.

Press, 9 (2 February 1861), 110.

DeBow's Review, 30 (March 1861), 383.

Godey's Lady's Book and Magazine, 62 (March 1861), 275.

B.V., *National Reformer*, 1 (9 March 1861), 7–8, and (16 March 1861), 8.

American Theological Review, 3 (April 1861), 412.

[George William Bagby?], *Southern Literary Messenger*, 32 (April 1861), 326–7.

British Quarterly Review, 33 (1 April 1861), 548–51.

"Ralph Waldo Emerson and His Writings," *Christian Review*, 26 (October 1861), 640–53.

Eclectic Review, 8th ser., 3 (November 1862), 365–409.

May-Day and Other Pieces

[Charles Eliot Norton],
"Mr. Emerson's Poems,"
Nation, 4 (30 May 1867),
430–1

In the course of the twenty-one years that have passed between the publication of Mr. Emerson's first volume of poems and the issue of the volume which has just come from the press, there has been a great change in the regard of the public for their author. Mr. Emerson has had the felicity of living long enough to be assured of the gratitude of his own generation for his services to them, and of the permanence in the future of his influence and of his fame. Of hardly any other living American author can it be so confidently assumed that he will hold a place among the universal classics. The class whom he addresses and whom he directly affects through his work are the best. An idealist himself, he is the sage friend and counsellor of those who hold to the ideal as to the only absolute reality, and who, through the power which they draw from the sources of life, have virtue to lift the world, from age to age, to higher levels of thought and action.

It is in the influence of his writing upon character far more than in any direct intellectual effect that the chief worth of Mr. Emerson's teaching consists. He adds but little to the store of thought. His appeal is not so much to the understanding as to the soul of man. He regards thought as the wise man regards money; not as good in itself, but good for its uses and as a means. He seeks for absolute values, for what underlies and gives meaning to thought, for the universal of which the individual is the imperfect symbol and representative. He looks through shows and masks and illusions to the substance beneath them. He has the clear, practical judgment of the nineteenth-century American man of business, but he applies his judgment with the insight of the prophet, and he regards all things as if they were merely ideas.

In this idealistic turn of mind his nature is that of a poet, and in comparing his first and his last volume one can hardly fail to be struck with the fact that in all their most characteristic qualities they seem like contemporaneous productions. There is little in his latest volume which, so far as tone and spirit are concerned, might not belong appropriately with the poems of twenty years ago; little in his earlier volume which might not equally well find place in that of this year. His genius was mature from the start, and

308

there is so little of the artist in his composition that time and experience and culture add no new capacity to his powers of expression. True to himself, as few men are capable of being, from the beginning, he remains true to himself today, and the spirit that moves him to poetry touches the same chords and works the same harmonies now as when he was a young man. The sound of the wind in the forest does not change with difference of years. Mr. Emerson's poetic genius seems as little modified by conscious will—as simply natural and inartistic—as the genius of the pine or the hemlock.

Mr. Emerson's inspiration comes from ideas rather than from actual life. There is nothing in it of a dramatical or lyrical quality. The emotions and interests of individuals do not appeal to him in such a manner as to lead him to seek to give expression to them in his poetry. None of his poems are, in a proper sense, studies of character; none of them are narrative or have to do with events and stories. They are, consequently, not poems of delight so much as poems of invigoration. It is not men but man with which they are concerned; not human nature but Nature, the mother of us all, whom the poet has studied, and whose aspects and influences he reproduces in his poems. A sentence from his own essay on Shakespeare describes his poetic sense; he knows "that a tree has another use than for apples, and corn another than for meal, and the ball of the earth than for tillage and roads; that these things bear a second and finer harvest to the mind, being emblems of its thoughts, and conveying in all their natural history a certain mute commentary on human life." Most of his finer and most characteristic poems are inspired with this feeling. Take, for example, in his first volume, the exquisite verses entitled "The Snow-Storm," or "The Humble Bee," one of the most perfect of his poems in expression, or the little piece called "Berrying;" or, from his new volume, the noble poem called "The Sea-shore." But perhaps he rises to his highest level where this sentiment of nature is most distinctly expressed in direct relation to man as in "The Problem"—one of those poems which will always be held among the best—or as in passages from the "Wood-Notes."

Our space is too limited to permit us to cite from poems which ought to be familiar to every lover of poetry, but we must make room for a few lines from this latter poem, "Wood-Notes," which is not so well known as some of the poet's briefer pieces. The pine-tree sings to the poet:

["Woodnotes," 53.18–54.5, 54.14–21]

It is perhaps, due in part to the absence from Mr. Emerson's genius of any controlling æsthetic element that he not infrequently indulges himself in mysticism, and makes his verses puzzles and enigmas not only to the common reader, but even to the trained student of poetry. "Brahma," which excited so much cheap amusement and wonder when it first appeared some years ago in *The Atlantic Monthly*, was not, indeed, one of these riddles, but is plain and intelligible as an expression of Hindu Pantheism. It is a sign of the change brought about by years that there is far less of this obscurity in the new volume than in the old. But Mr. Emerson is, however, still careless about the shape in which his thought embodies itself, and fails to guard his poetry against the attacks of time by casting his poems in perfect and imperishable forms. If there be much of the Greek philosopher in his composition, there is very little of the Greek artist. Many far inferior poets have a freer gift of melody and a keener sense of harmony, order, and proportion. The music of his verse is rarely long sustained, and he does injustice to his own culture by not infrequent neglect of rhythm and of rhyme. Thus, in "May-Day" he ventures to rhyme *abroad* with *Lord*, and, still worse, *poured* and *abroad*; so, too, we find him rhyming *coats* and *spots*, *zones* and *towns*, *cavaliers* and *travellers* (where the accent is wrong as well as the rhyme). There are quatrains in the "Boston Hymn" and in "My Garden" which cannot be read musically.

It is not to find spots on the sun that we speak of these defects; but because of our regret that poems which ought to be popular, and ought to outlast most of our contemporary poetry, are deprived by them of the chance of immortality which attends a work fashioned in perfect form. It is the form which is the seal of duration of all human works. Happily, there are some of Mr. Emerson's poems of which the form is the worthy embodiment of the thought.

Mr. Emerson's muse loves to dwell on "those clear-ethered heights" which are the resort of calm and noble thoughts, of pure fancies and generous sentiment. Of the youth to whom such poetry is dear all good may be prophesied. It will nerve him to high thinking and high living. It will make his ideals more precious and more beautiful to him. It will serve him as a test of the purposes and motives of his life. In the best sense, Mr. Emerson is a moral poet; he writes not to draw a moral, but because he is possessed with a moral sentiment which he can best express in poetry. He is the utterer of the moral ideas by which the hearts of his generation are moved. He is a poet of his times, essentially American in spirit; that is, devoted to universal ends and to the common welfare. His strength lies not in the power of his imagination and the vivacity of his fancy so much as in the dignity and breadth of his sentiment. His poetry comes from a large and pure nature, and it will always be prized most by the readers who are most in sympathy with the qualities which gain for its author the respect and the gratitude of those whose respect and gratitude are best worth having.

We must please ourselves by making two brief citations from the "May-Day" volume. The first is from "Voluntaries:"

["Voluntaries," 207.11–26]

["Days," 228.9–20]

[Charles Eliot Norton], Review of *May-Day and Other Pieces*, *North American Review*, 105 (July 1867), 325–7

In the exquisite poem in this volume called "Terminus" Mr. Emerson speaks of himself as one who

"Obeys the voice at eve obeyed at
    prime."

He has, indeed, unquestioned right thus to speak of himself, for he has been true, as few men ever were, to the voice of his own genius, and his obedience has been to him both inspiration and power. Many years ago he said of the poet: "He is isolated among his contemporaries, by truth and by his art, but with this consolation in his pursuits, that they will draw all men sooner or later." And in his own experience he has had proof of this assertion. He has had the happiness of living long enough to see his contemporaries, those at least of the younger generation, drawing to him, and acknowledging him as one of those

"Olympian bards who sung
    Divine ideas below,
Which always find us young,
    And always keep us so."

His first volume of poems and his last, with twenty-one years' interval between them, are in the same key of harmony, and are expressions of the same voice. The first has some tones of youth, some fervors of imagination which are not found in the last, but their place is supplied by the clearer accents and composed strength of mature life. They are both alike the sincere utterances of a strongly marked and individual genius, and both in striking contrast to the popular poetry of the day.

The character of Mr. Emerson's genius is such that its expressions are not, and are not likely to become, in a strict sense, popular. He addresses a select audience, composed of those who like himself hold to their ideals, and have faith in the worth and efficacy of ideas. He speaks to the few, but those few are the masters of the world. As a poet he belongs to the small band of moral poets, of those whose power lies not in imagination as applied to the affairs and interests of men, not in fertility of fancy or in range of conception, but in the perception of the moral and spiritual relations of man to the nature which encompasses him, of the moral and spiritual laws which are symbolized by that nature, and of the universal truths which underlie the forms of existence, and coordinate the varieties of human experience. There is little passion in his poetry; passion is in its nature selfish; the emotions which his verses express are seldom personal. The events of life are as nothing to the poet as compared to the ideas which possess his soul. Very few of his poems have a lyrical quality; not one of them is truly dramatic. Men are little to him; man and nature, everything.

Idealist as he is, it is not strange that at times he shows himself the mystic. It is by inspiration, and not by reason, that he is guided, and he has no test of the quality of his inspiration. It may be a revelation of light; it may be an apocalypse of darkness. But poetry and mysticism have nothing properly in common. True poetry is neither a riddle, nor an illusion, and true inspiration is always rational. The inconceivable is as much beyond the reach of intuition as of reason. The vein of

311

mysticism in Mr. Emerson's genius is doubtless the more conspicuous from the comparative subordination in his nature of the artistic to the speculative element. The essence of art lies in definiteness of conception. The artist is he who can perfectly exhibit his idea in form; and excellence of form—whether in line, color, rhythm, or harmony—gives universality and permanence to the work of art. Perfect form is abstract, imperishable, archetypal; and he is the greatest artist who clothes ideas in the most nearly perfect form. Mr. Emerson, idealist as he is, too often pays little regard to this ideal form, and puts his thought into inharmonious verse. His poems are for the most part more fitted to invigorate the moral sense, than to delight the artistic. At times, indeed, he is singularly felicitous in expression, and some of his verses both charm and elevate the soul. These rarer verses will live in the memories of men. No poet is surer of immortality than Mr. Emerson, but the greater part of his poetry will be read, not so much for its artistic as for its moral worth.

The poem which gives its title to the new volume, May-Day, is a poem of spring,—a collection of beautiful praises and descriptions of our New England May, written by a lover of Nature, to whom she has told many of her secrets, and whom she has cheered with her smile. It is full of the new wine of the year; of the gladness, the comfort, and the purity of the gay season of youth and love. The next poem, "The Adirondacks," is of a different sort, save in its familiarity with nature, and reads like an American episode out of the best part of Wordsworth's "Prelude." Among the Occasional and Miscellaneous Poems which make up the rest of the volume are many already known to the lovers of the best poetry, and which, now collected, will be among the choicest flowers of the most select anthology. We need but name "Voluntaries," "Days," "My Garden," "Sea-shore," "Two Rivers," "Terminus," "The Past," to show what rare treasures this little volume holds.

Mr. Emerson seldom reminds of other poets. Least of all should we expect him to remind us of Horace; but in "The Past" he repeats a thought which Horace has expressed in a noble passage in one of his finest odes. The comparison and contrast between the two poets are interesting. Speaking of the certainty of the Past, Mr. Emerson says:—

"All is now secure and fast;
Not the gods can shake the Past;
Flies to the adamantine door,
Bolted down forevermore.
None can re-enter there."

And Horace:—

"Cras vel atrâ
Nube polum pater occupato,
Vel sole puro; non tamen irritum
Quodcunque retro est efficiet; neque
Diffinget, infectumque reddet,
Quod fugiens semel hora vexit."

And another verse of the same ode is recalled by the lines in "The Adirondacks" in which the poet tells how

"Ten scholars, wonted to lie warm and
    soft
In well-hung chambers, daintily be-
    stowed,
Lie here on hemlock-boughs, like Sacs
    and Sioux,
And greet unanimous the joyful
    change."

Is not this little more than a free translation of

"Plerumque gratæ divitibus vices;
Mundæque parvo sub lare pauperum
    Cæn, sine aulæis et ostro,
        Solicitam explicuere frontem"?

But enough. To have given these poems to us is another added to the many claims of Mr. Emerson on the gratitude of this and of coming generations.

D[avid]. A. W[asson]., Review of *May-Day and Other Pieces*, *Radical*, 2 (August 1867), 760–2

Mr. Emerson's prose style and that of this poetry have been moving in opposite directions. In prose we find of late years less color, and a more determinate form, less imagination and more reason, less of gleaming suggestion, more of steady light. He has applied the telescope, and resolved star-dust and shining nebulæ into definite stars, and he has learned to make his expression at a telescope for the eye of the reader,—though the lens is so transparent, and the mechanism so withdrawn from view, that the beholder may think himself looking with the naked eye. Or to change the figure, and suggest better certain qualities in his later prose, he has acquired at once more precision of aim and more projectile force. It is a telescope *rifle* that he uses. In the "Conduct of Life" the sentences go off like minie bullets. We remember to have been exceedingly impressed in reading that work by an intensity of projectile power fitted to cause some shrinking in sensitive nerves. One was half inclined to desire a little more of lambent luminous play, and to spare here and there a jet of searching flame. "Speak softly," we could have said, "electricity, they tell us, is necessary to life, but lightning kills."

The first poem, particularly, in the present volume shows, on the contrary, a richness of color and a fine flow of movement which he has never elsewhere attained. There does indeed appear the art of a master, the precision and governed expression which his prose has acquired; but

313

it is shown rather by ease than by demonstrative force, and rather by the ability to reconcile high color with delicacy of tint than by the emphasis of form and content in distinction from color. It is Turneresque. There is a diffused auroral glow and blush throughout the poem; dews sparkle, birds sing, there is the joy of opening blossoms, the love-whisper of young leaves and silent hilarity of springing blades. It is a poem which could have come only from the New World,—such a song of the morning, such a gush of exuberant young life, with no graves under its feet, its possibilities as yet infinite, no blight nor cankerworm, with untimely falling of fruit, as yet thought of. If there is any meditation upon the past, this appears only as longing for that future which has now become present. This is signified in a passage wherein we know not whether to admire more the fine observation on which it is based or the freshness of spirit which converts it to such a use.

"See every *patriot* oak-leaf throws
His elfin length upon the snows,
Not idle, since the leaf all day
Draws to the spot the solar ray,
Ere sunset quarrying inches down,
And half-way to the mosses brown."

As if they fell, and with joy sacrificed themselves, only out of love and desire towards the grass, which beneath the snow

"Has hints of the propitious time."

In other poems, as in the "Boston Hymn" and "Terminus," there is a simplicity as of primitive men, innocent of literature, and sublime without knowing it. Has this man read any books? Does he know that there are books? He is as aboriginal as Walt Whitman; nay, more so, for Walt has only taken the fig leaves, and in somewhat marked manner, but the nakedness is here only that of a noble spirit, clothed upon with the grace of self-forgetfulness. Was there ever a purer pathos, more hidden in lofty cheer, than that of "Terminus"?

A critic in the *North American Review*, says of Mr. Emerson, "His poems are for the most part more fitted to invigorate the moral sense than to delight the artistic." There is truth in this, but it hardly seems discriminating enough. The fact, as it appears to us, is that in the moral sense, or as we prefer to say in the moral intelligence, he is whole, but in the artistic sense he is broken. His artistic whole is a paragraph, it may be only a sentence or a line, while his moral intelligence is true to the centre. This is so of his prose and poetry alike, but less so of the latter, for in some poems, as in the "Humble Bee," for example, there is the unity of a perfect crystal. But in the faculty of intellectual as of artistic construction he is more deficient than any other writer we know, whose thought keeps the axis so surely, and whose esthetic feeling and beauty of expression are so rare.

[William Dean Howells],
Review of *May-Day and
Other Pieces*,
Atlantic Monthly,
20 (September 1867),
376–8

We wonder whether those who take up Mr. Emerson's poem now, amid the glories of the fading summer, are not giving the poet a fairer audience than those who hurried to hear his song in the presence of the May he celebrates. As long as spring was here, he had a rival in every reader; for then we all felt ourselves finer poets than ever sang of the season, and did not know that our virtue was but an effect of Spring herself,—an impression, not an expression of her loveliness, which must pass with her. Now, when the early autumn is in every sense, and those days when the year first awoke to consciousness have grown so far away, we must perceive that no one has yet been allowed to speak so well for the spring of our New World as this poet. The very irregularity of Mr. Emerson's poem seems to be part of its verisimilitude, and it appears as if all the pauses and impulses and mysterious caprices of the season—which fill the trees with birds before blossoms, and create the soul of sweetness and beauty in the May-flowers under the dead leaves of the woodlands, while the meadows are still bare and brown—had so entered into this song, that it could not emulate the deliberation and consequence of art. The "May-Day" is to the critical faculty a succession of odes on Spring, celebrating now one aspect and now another, and united only by their title; yet since an entire idea of spring is evolved from them, and

they awaken the same emotions that the youth of the year stirs in us, we must accept the result as something undeniably great and good. Of course, we can complain of the way in which it is brought about, just as we can upbraid the New England climate, though its uncertain and desultory April and May give us at last the most beautiful June weather in the world.

The poem is not one that invites analysis, though it would be easy enough to instance striking merits and defects. Mr. Emerson, perhaps, more than any other modern poet, gives the notion of inspiration; so that one doubts, in reading him, how much to praise or blame. The most exquisite effects seem not to have been invited, but to have sought production from his unconsciousness; graces alike of thought and of touch seem the unsolicited gifts of the gods. Even the doubtful quality of occasional lines confirms this impression of unconsciousness. One cannot believe that the poet would wittingly write,

"Boils the world in tepid lakes,"

for this statement has, for all that the reader can see to the contrary, the same value with him as that preceding verse, telling how the waxing heat

"Lends the reed and lily length,"

wherein the very spirit of summer seems to sway and droop. Yet it is probable that no utterance is more considered than this poet's, and that no one is more immediately responsible than he. We must attribute to the most subtile and profound consciousness the power that can trace with such tenderness and beauty the alliance he has shown between earth and humanity in the exultation of spring, and which can make matter of intellectual perception the mute sympathies that seemed to perish with childhood:—

["May-Day," 165.13–22]

Throughout the poem these recognitions of our kindred with external nature occur, and a voice is given to the blindly rejoicing sense within us when the poet says,

"The feet that slid so long on sleet
Are glad to feel the ground";

and thus celebrates with one potent and satisfying touch the instinctive rapture of the escape from winter. Indeed, we find our greatest pleasure in some of these studies of pure feeling, while we are aware of the value of the didactic passages of the poem, and enjoy perfectly the high beauty of the pictorial parts of it. We do not know where we should match that strain beginning,

"Why chidest thou the tardy spring?"

Or that,

"Where shall we keep the holiday,
And duly greet the entering May?"

Or this most delicate and exquisite bit of description, which seems painted a *tempera*,—in colors mixed with the transparent blood of snowdrops and Alpine harebells:—

["May-Day," 167.7–18]

There is not great range of sentiment in "May-Day," and through all the incoherence of the poem there is a constant recurrence to the master-theme. This recurrence has at times something of a perfunctory air, and the close of the poem does not seal the whole with any strong impression. There is a rise—or a lapse, as the reader pleases to think—toward a moral at the close; but the motion is evidently willed of the poet rather than the subject. It seems to us that, if the work have any climax, it is in those lines near the end in which the poet draws his reader nearest his own personality, and of which the delicately guarded and peculiar pathos scarcely needs comment:—

["The Harp," 239.25–241.21]

Among the other poems in this volume, it appears to us that "The Romany Girl," "Voluntaries," and "The Boston Hymn" are in their widely different ways the best. The last expresses, with a sublime colloquiality in which the commonest words of every-day parlance seem cut anew, and are made to shine with a fresh and novel lustre the idea and destiny of America. In "Voluntaries" our former great peril and delusion—the mortal Union which lived by slavery—is at first the theme, with the strong pulse of prophecy, however, in the mournful music. Few motions of rhyme so win and touch as those opening lines,—

"Low and mournful be the strain,
Haughty thought be far from me;
Tones of penitence and pain,
Moanings of the tropic sea,"—

in which the poet, with a hardly articulate sorrow, regards the past; and Mr. Emerson's peculiarly exalted and hopeful genius has nowhere risen in clearer and loftier tones than in those stops which open full upon us after the pathetic pleasing of his regrets:—

["Voluntaries," 207.12–27, 209.7–23]

It is, of course, a somewhat Emersonian Gypsy that speaks in "The Romany Girl," but still she speaks with the passionate, sudden energy of a woman, and flashes upon the mind with intense vividness the conception of a wild nature's gleeful consciousness of freedom, and exultant scorn of restraint and convention. All sense of sylvan health and beauty is uttered when this Gypsy says,—

"The wild air bloweth in our lungs,
The keen stars twinkle in our eyes,
The birds gave us our wily tongues,
The panther in our dances flies."

"Terminus" has a wonderful didactic charm, and must be valued as one of the noblest introspective poems in the language. The poet touches his reader by his acceptance of fate and age, and his serene trust of the future, and yet is not moved by his own pathos.

We do not regard the poem "The Adirondacks" as of great absolute or relative value. It is one of the prosiest in the book, and for a professedly out-of-doors poem has too much of the study in it. Let us confess also that we have not yet found pleasure in "The Elements," and that we do not expect to live long enough to enjoy some of them. "Quatrains" have much the same forbidding qualities, and have chiefly interested us in the comparison they suggest with the translations from the Persian: it is curious to find cold Concord and warm Ispahan in the same latitude. Others of the briefer poems have delighted us. "Rubies," for instance, is full of exquisite lights and hues, thoughts and feelings; and "The Test" is from the heart of the severe wisdom without which art is not. Everywhere the poet's felicity of expression appears; a fortunate touch transfuses some dark enigma with color; the riddles are made to shine when most impenetrable; the puzzles are all constructed of gold and ivory and precious stones.

Mr. Emerson's intellectual characteristics and methods are so known that it is scarcely necessary to hint that this is not a book for instant absorption into any reader's mind. It shall happen with many, we fancy, that they find themselves ready for only two or three things in it, and that they must come to it in widely varying moods for all it has to give. No greater wrong could be done to the poet than to go through his book running, and he would be apt to revenge himself upon the impatient reader by leaving him all the labor involved in such a course, and no reward at the end for his pains.

But the case is not a probable one. People either read Mr. Emerson patiently and earnestly, or they do not read him at all. In this earnest nation he enjoys a far greater popularity than criticism would have augured for one so unflattering to the impulses that have heretofore and elsewhere made readers of poetry; and it is not hard to believe, if we believe in ourselves for the future, that he is destined to an ever-growing regard and fame. He makes appeal, however mystically, only to what is fine and deep and true and noble in men, and no doubt those who have always loved his poetry have reason to be proud of their pleasure in it. Let us of the present be wise enough to accept thankfully what genius gives us in its double character of bard and prophet, saying, when we enjoy the song, "Ah, this is the poet that now sings!" and when the meaning is dark, "Now we have the seer again!"

317

Checklist of Additional Reviews

[F. B. Sanborn], "Emerson's Latest Poems—*May-Day, and Other Pieces,*" Boston *Commonwealth*, 11 May 1867, p. 1.

American Literary Gazette and Publishers' Circular, 9 (15 May 1867), 45.

"Emerson's Poems," *London Review*, 14 (1 June 1867), 629–30.

New York *Leader*, 27 July 1861, p. 1.

[Rufus] E[llis]., *Monthly Religious Magazine*, 28 (August 1867), 79.

Saturday Review, 24 (24 August 1867), 268.

"Some Recent Pieces of English and American Poetry," *Eclectic Review*, 8th ser., 14 (March 1868), 227–53.

"A Shoal of Verse-Writers," *Athenæum*, 2114 (2 May 1868), 625–6.

Society and Solitude

G. A. Simcox,
Review of *Society and
Solitude,*
Academy [England],
1 (9 April 1870), 172

Makebelieve, in one form or another, seems inseparable from American literature: either a writer sinks his nationality like Irving and G. P. R. James, and tries to pass for an European man of letters, which is comparatively an innocent delusion which sometimes approaches a reality, or he tries to pass off the actual circumstances of America as a substitute for all the ideal stimulants of the historic past. Emerson can scarcely be accused of neglecting history, but he is certainly the hierophant of the second and more mischievous school of American makebelieve. In every one of his writings he has inculcated with unwavering energy the dogma, which is the one thing needed to make our generation utterly joyless, that our present life of every day is divine and ideal if we could but think so. At first this unreasoning optimism was associated with other and more interesting elements. There was something certainly fresh and stimulating in Mr. Emerson's combination of a dreamy transcendentalism and a hardy personality, cynicism and neoplatonism,

and though neither element was new, each had the effect of novelty on both sides of the Atlantic. But a man who is sure of his own life gets tired of asserting it, and Mr. Emerson seems to have little else to assert. He can still invest an obvious aphorism with a quaint stateliness which recalls Sir Thomas Browne; but he is in danger of leaving off where Mr. Tupper begins, in a sort of commonplace ecstasy at things as they are or rather as they might be, if everybody were as cheerful and energetic as Mr. Tupper and perhaps a trifle more practical than Mr. Emerson. The whole of the work ostensibly bears upon life, and we gather from it the following suggestions:—that it would be well if men, instead of collecting pretty things in their own houses, would go to look at them in local museums; if people would read the classics of all languages (in translations by choice); and if, perhaps, young men would associate themselves to read the secondary classics, such as the *Romance of the Rose,* by deputy, and get one to report of such works to the rest.

The staple of the work is made up of writing like this, which may commend itself to the appropriate reader:

> "The imagination infuses a certain
> volatility and intoxication. It is a
> flute which sets the atoms of our
> frame in a dance like planets, and
> one so liberated, the whole man
> reeling drunk to the music, they
> never quite subside to their old

steady state. But what is the imagination? Only an arm or weapon of the interior energy—only a precursor of the reason."

It ought to be added that the first essay which gives its title to the book is really a distinguished piece of writing. It opens with a very delicate anonymous portrait of the shyness of Hawthorne, and remains brilliant almost to the last, though the epigrams become emptier as they succeed each other. There are some grandiose views of the subtler aspects of Nature (the most dignified subject open to writers who share Mr. Emerson's prejudices) in the essay on Farming, and a very naïve and dignified description by a lady of a beautiful act of self-devotion is appended to the essay on Courage.

Review of *Society and Solitude*, *Putnam's Magazine*, n.s. 5 (May 1870), 617–18

There are writers who take such a hold upon us that we are unable to judge them correctly, either to praise or blame; for it does not follow that we like them because they have us in their power for the time being. Whether the last volume of Tennyson, for instance, is better, or worse, than the one which preceded it, we cannot say, our only impression being that it is Tennysonian from beginning to end. We are in the same predicament with regard to Mr. Emerson's last volume, *Society and Solitude*, of which Messrs. Fields, Osgood & Co. are the publishers. It is Emersonian throughout; but if you ask us whether it is above or below the average of this unique writer, we confess that we don't know. We have found it delightful reading, but it has not fixed itself in our memories, either because we demand more *purpose* in what we read than is apparent here, or because we have become so accustomed to Mr. Emerson's peculiarities, or excellences, if his admirers prefer, that we are no longer affected by them. There is a story of an old English country squire who was so assured of the orthodoxy of his parson, that he regularly went to sleep as soon as he began to preach. We are not quite so sure of Mr. Emerson's orthodoxy, nor do we sleep under his ministrations; but, all the same, we are willing to let him say whatever he will, being fully assured in our minds that nobody will be harmed by it. He never seeks to make proselytes—as, indeed, how should he, when he never seems to quite know what he believes, nor where he stands, except that it is somewhere in the region of abstract Thought. What he aims to do, if he has any definite aim, is to impart to other minds what is, or was, in his own mind, and what the meaning is of this incomprehensible Universe in which we find ourselves. The most suggestive of living writers, he is every thing to those who are prepared to receive him, and nothing to those who are not; it depends entirely upon the barrenness or the richness of the soil whether the seed of his thought falls dead, or blossoms into the ripe, consummate flower. For his present volume, which contains twelve brief papers in his usual vein, we advise our readers to discard the first of the three "practical rules" which Mr. Emerson recommends in these cases, viz., "Never read any book that is not a year old," and to read this one now, no matter under what circumstances; for, if we may trust our imperfect impressions, it is suited alike for "Society and Solitude."

[John Burroughs], "Emerson's New Volume," *Appleton's Journal,* 3 (28 May 1870), 609–11

After a lapse of ten years, Emerson has made another draft upon his portfolio, and given us twelve more chapters upon the old, old themes—twelve more of those terse, epigrammatic essays of sense, poetry, and philosophy, all compact.

Many of these papers the author has had in pickle a long time, and they are seasoned through and through with the Emersonian salt. Perhaps indeed, they savor a little more of the mere brine of Emerson's style, so to speak, than any former collection of his writings or speakings. They savor unmistakably of the lecture-room, and of the disciplining which they have undergone before hundreds of sharp, intellectual New-England audiences. They bristle all over with point and epigram. Every sentence has been trained down to its fighting-weight; not one superfluous word, not a particle of adipose tissue, anywhere. All is sinew and fibre, tense braided, sharply articulated, yet (if it be necessary to make the qualifications) nervous rather than muscular—the expression of soil, and not of mere logical strength—a lesson in moral and literary hygiene, rather than on any lower plane.

Each of these papers has a history, and few of Emerson's readers, we imagine, will believe the little fiction of the publishers, that most of them are now in print for the first time; for, do we not smell them out wherever they appear, and having read them once, is their flavor ever gone from the mind afterward?

The first one, which names the collection, was published in the *Atlantic Monthly*, some years ago. "Civilization," "Eloquence," "Books," and "Old Age," were also printed in the *Atlantic*, after doing duty for several years in the lecture-room. "Art" is an old *Dial* paper, and is the runt of the litter. It is perhaps contemporaneous in the mind of the author with the chapter on the same subject in the first series of the Essays, but is of much less value. "Domestic Life" is also from the pages of the *Dial*, and deserves a place alongside of "Friendship" and "Love," in the Essays. "Works and Days" is one of a series of lectures which Emerson delivered in Boston in 1859. Other subjects of the course were "Manners," "Morals," "Criticism," "Instinct and Inspiration," and "Mental Temperance." The first named is included in the "The Conduct of Life," but the remaining four, and we hope many others like them, are still held in reserve for some future volume. "Farming," "Clubs," "Courage," and "Success," of the present collection, are veterans of the lecture-season, but, we believe, have never before been in print.

As a whole, the series is perhaps not quite so valuable as the former one, "The Conduct of Life." As the cook says, it has more the air of a "picked-up" dinner. No one knows better than Emerson himself that he has long ago had his say, and that he has nothing essentially new to add. Like all eminent writers, his mind has its water-shed, so to speak, and his thoughts tend inevitably in certain directions or channels, and these channels and all the attendant topographical features are clearly defined in his former works. He returns perpetually to the old themes—nature, character, illusion, compensation, great men, self-reliance, the sufficiency of the moral law, etc.—and it is not so much new thought that he has now to offer on these subjects, as new and agreeable changes and variations. There are certain formulas of great names also that he never tires of repeating, as Plato, Bacon, Swedenborg, Shakespeare, or this bolder classification—Buddha, Confucius, Moses, Jesus. No author that ever lived was less a plausible, extemporaneous writer. What Emerson has said he was born to say, and it has the force and sanction of his entire nature. In other words, he is one of those writers, the rarest and most precious of all, who speak more from their character and constitution, than from any special literary knack or talent, and hence is in greater danger of repeating himself.

He said long ago that "man can paint, or make, or think, nothing but man." No single remark applies more fully to himself. He preaches incessantly, though it must be admitted that it is the best preaching this generation has listened to. And he follows his own doctrine. "Don't be a cynic and disconsolate preacher," he says, in one of these late papers; "don't bewail and bemoan, omit the negative propositions, nerve us with incessant affirmation." Again, "To awaken in man and to raise the sense of worth, to educate his feelings and judgment so that he shall scorn himself for a bad action, that is the only aim." That is his theory, and that is certainly the moral effect of his writings upon those who are eligible to their deepest meanings. It is not by the method of the prosy moralists, that is, by argument and precept, that he influences the reader, but by his impassioned, imaginative treatment of the moral law. His words are steeped in the very essence of noble acting and thinking, and they go beyond the mind into the conscience and character of the reader. Indeed, the essential vitality of his writings as a whole is wonderful. A page so concrete and intensely realistic, yet exhaling such a subtle, potent, and pervasive idealism!—so full of nouns, and verbs, and homely images, and figures, yet affording such a fine, delicious tonic to the moral and religious sense! One reason of this is, that, however compact his style, his thought never crystallizes, his epigram never glitters. There is no crystallic brilliancy and perfection, but the perfection of germs, of grain, of acorns, so that the spirit retains the sense after the memory has lost the words.

Nevertheless, when Emerson goes into print, we would gladly have him drop the style of the lecturer, and resume that of the essayist. If any thing, these lectures have too much point, and not enough drift. It seems as if verbal emphasis had been arrived at, at the expense of the total effect. An audience must be pleased every moment, but a good reader can afford to wait, and holds by the general result. In Emerson's earlier writings, and perhaps in all first-rate prose, there are many passages that are necessarily preliminary, that clear the ground and lay the foundation; or, to vary the image, that conduct the reader along an uneventful way, till of a sudden the prospect opens, and vast truths and principles lie before him. Nothing pleases a reader more than this—to be placed in a commanding position, with reference to an author's facts and statements. But it seems as if Emerson does this less than he used to. He does not conduct us to the heights, but brings the heights (and they are the heights) down to us. Hence, in the majority of these papers, there seem to be no primary truths or principles duly controlling, under-running and out-running the secondary, but for the most part every sentence begins and ends where it is made, and the key of the whole is never found.

We make this remark less as an objection or as a criticism than with a desire to point out a specific difference between our author's earlier and later writings—perhaps we should say, his early writings and his late speakings. The latter are brilliant and suggestive, full of idiom and nerve and force; but the former are this, and more. Our pleasure in the latter is momentary—on the instant, and every instant alike; the value of "Works and Days," we may say, is in its separate and individual passages, not in its effect as a whole. But in "Nature," or the "Addresses," or the Essays, or in "English Traits," the pleasure of the reader is cumulative, deepens and widens as he goes on, and he feels that he has not only been entertained and instructed on the way, but that he has been conducted to large and important results.

This distinction, however, does not apply to all the papers of this collection. The essays on "Eloquence," on "Domestic Life," and on "Books," have the old, steady, tranquil flow, and every page gives an added impetus to the reader's mind.

Aside from their manner or style, some persons think they see in Emerson's later writings a decided falling off from his high spiritual aims and atmosphere—in fact, that his horse of the sun has become a little jaded and earth-stained. But we do not think this is so. True, he sounds a different key in these conversations, as we may call them, is more practical and direct, has more to say about society, manners, politics, our material greatness, mechanical inventions, the conduct of life, etc.; but this becomes him also. His standard is as high as ever, his aim as unworldly. Must he always be celebrating genius? Shall he not say something for tact and talent, also? Having enlarged on the uses of great men, shall he not speak an encouraging word for common folk? Having discoursed on literary ethics, and pointed out the duties and the province of the scholar, may he not glorify farming, or talk about clubs, especially since these subjects acquire new dignity and importance in his handling of them?

But his eyes are always open to the two

323

sides of the question. It is impossible to corner him; he is on all sides of the field. You think, for instance, he is insisting too strongly upon the value of society to the scholar; but the next moment he is putting in just as strong a claim for solitude. You think you have caught him overrating our material advantages, modern comforts and appliances; but wait a moment, and you shall see how he punctures this bladder: "What have these arts done for the character, for the worth of mankind? Are men better? It is sometimes questioned whether morals have not declined, as the arts have ascended. Here are great arts, and little men. Now that the machine is so perfect, the engineer is nobody." In reading the essay on "Clubs," it is plain the author sets too high a value on conversation, on wit, on a talent for repartee: "To answer a question so as to admit of no reply, is the test of a man— to touch bottom every time." But, before he has done, he says we cannot afford to be superfine, and quotes approvingly the words of a traveller of excellent sense, who confessed he liked low company, and found the society of gypsies more attractive than that of bishops: "The black-coats are good company only for black-coats."

Yet it is, no doubt, in this direction that we touch bottom in Emerson. It would be an ungrateful task to criticise him in any case. In fact, there is no room for criticism. He has no specific faults. He is what he is—perfectly consistent throughout. But, of course, he has his limitations; and we often find ourselves asking if there is not a larger truth than is contained in his word-culture, at least a truth more vital to the race and to the country at the present time. With all his admiration for practical power and for strong personalities, his ideal is finally the scholar, the man of books, of wit, and conversation; and it is to these things that he responds most readily. A curious illustration of this is his placing Plato above Homer, the critical intellect absorbed in the contemplation of great truths above the fresh-bounding blood and mighty volition of man immersed in great events. There can be no question but Plato and his like are a later and in one sense a riper result than Homer and his like; but are they not also farther from the fountains of power, of empire, of health, of wholeness? In the reflective, speculative mind, do not the currents of being begin to set in the other way from action, from longevity, etc.? The flower of the race is not the philosopher, but the singer, the poet; the sum of all good is not knowledge, but motive, volition—in short, fulness of life. Especially is the want of the modern world not ideas, but personal qualities; and Emerson's glorification of the scholar, the thinker, the man of ideas, needs to be mildly antidoted by the statement that man, viewed as a living, moving, sensuous being, is at the "top of his condition" before the meditative philosopher has yet emerged, and while all creeds and systems are held in vital fusion, nerving the will, and not detaching themselves at the intellect.

[Thomas Wentworth Higginson],
Review of *Society and Solitude*,
Atlantic Monthly,
26 (July 1870), 119–20

Lord Clarendon said of Lord Falkland, Secretary of State to Charles I., that as his house was within ten miles of Oxford, "the most polite and accurate men of that university frequently resorted and dwelt with him as in a college situated in purer air; so that his house was a university in less volume, whither they came not so much for repose as study."

It is a comfort to think that fate still makes ample provision for the suburbs of university towns, and that Concord is but about ten miles from Cambridge. For many years the two were "half-shire-towns" of the same county, and Emerson, as Knight of the half-shire, fitly shared the intellectual jurisdiction of his compeer, the President of the College. Indeed, he made his house, like that of Falkland, "a college in purer air"; and so inseparable has been the influence of his life from that of his books, that the whole has supplied for us "a university in less volume." It is the enviable lot of those who were pupils in this benignant seminary, that they can never know how much of their instruction came from the text-books and how much from the teacher. Thus the literary work of Emerson eludes the criticism of contemporaries, and awaits a colder audience which shall award its meed.

It is now ten years since the "Conduct of Life" was published. Most of the present essays, though printed later, were written earlier than that volume, and some of them were read as lectures a quarter of a century ago. Is it, then, from early association that some of us find in them, or seem to find, a fresher inspiration than in the "Conduct of Life"? We fancy that they show more variety, and a more distinct organic life in each essay, while they are no less finished and scarcely less concentrated. There is a provoking trait about some of his later lectures, and they seem like stray sheets caught up at random; or to have what botanists call premorse roots, that seem as if bitten off arbitrarily at the end, and can stop anywhere. But these have each a beginning, a middle, and an end, so that they seem alive and graceful, as well as nutritious and good. Literary ease and flexibility do not always advance with an author's years; as his thoughts deepen they sometimes press harder and harder on the vehicle of expression, and though his sympathies may mellow, his style does not. He is then in danger of becoming like the giant in the Norse Edda, who was choked by his own wisdom and needed a siphon for his relief. Far from our beloved Emerson be such a peril! but meanwhile there is a charm in the easier flow of his earlier essays, even though they be burdened with less weighty thought.

We sigh at not finding in this volume that admirable lecture on "The Natural Method of Intellectual Philosophy," which many of us heard with such delight a dozen years ago, and which came nearer to a positive system than anything which Emerson has ever printed. Possibly it forms the basis for his present course on "The Natural History of Intellect," and if so it may well be withheld. There was in it material enough for twenty lectures, without doubt. But there is no such compensation for the loss of the essay on "War," first read as a lecture in 1838, and printed eleven years later, in Miss Peabody's "Æsthetic Papers." There are other omissions; but if, on the other hand, we looked through Emerson's whole works, we could find nothing to take precedure of the essays here printed on "Books," on "Eloquence," on "Works and Days," and on "Society and Solitude." They are not surpassed by the "Method of Nature," nor by "Man Thinking." It is not enough to say that such papers as these constitute the high-water mark of American literature; it is not too much to say that they are un-equalled in the literature of the age. Name, if you can, the Englishman or the Frenchman who, on themes like these, must not own himself second to Emerson. Bearing these in his hand, the resolute American traveller can fearlessly unfurl the stars and stripes in presence of the *Académie* itself, were it necessary, and yet not feel himself to be swerving from the traditional modesty of his race.

[Bret Harte], Review of *Society and Solitude*, *Overland Monthly*, 5 (October 1870), 386–7

Perhaps there is little in this volume that will strike Mr. Emerson's admirers as being new, although there is undoubtedly much that is fine, and nothing that is not characteristic. Yet to most of us who rejoice and believe in him, will recur the suspicion that we entertained long ago, that the wonderful essay on "Compensation" comprised the substance of his philosophy. At least we feel that, given the theories of "Compensation," we can readily forecast what Mr. Emerson would say on any other subject. How he would say it—with what felicity of epithet or illustration—is another matter. "The orator possesses no information which his hearers have not, yet he teaches them to see the thing with his own eyes," is what Mr. Emerson says of the Orator, and is very possibly what the Orator might say of Mr. Emerson. Our disappointment comes perhaps from the tendency of all belief to get into condensed and epigrammatic statement. After a man has told us he is a pessimist or an optimist, he has nothing novel to say. And knowing that Mr. Emerson believes in a kind of Infinite Adjustment, his results no longer astonish us, although we are always entertained with his process. We come to listen to the pleadings, without caring for the verdict.

Besides the titular essay, this volume contains, "Art," "Domestic Life," "Works and Days," "Eloquence," "Books," "Old Age," and others of less moment—but all characterized by the old aphoristic directness; by the old, familiar completeness of phrase, but incompleteness of sequence, and by the old audacity that would be French but that it is free of levity, and has an Anglo-Saxon dignity and reliance on fact, peculiar to Mr. Emerson's thought. There is perhaps more of the latter quality in "Works and Days"—which we confess to admire beyond the other essays; a quality which is quite American in its practical boldness, and yet calmer, finer, and more subdued by a sense of equity and breadth than is usual to American picturesque statement and prophetic extravagance. Mr. Emerson is one of the few Americans who can talk appreciatively and even picturesquely of such things as "manifest destiny," "progress," and "invention," and yet be willing to admit that the millennium is not to be brought about by "steam" or "electricity."

All this is, perhaps, the more praiseworthy from the fact that he has a tendency to an extravagant appreciation of the power of progress, and is often tempted to utter such absurdity as the following:

> "Tis wonderful how soon a piano gets into a log-hut on the frontier. You would think they found it under a pine stump. With it comes a Latin grammar—and one of those tow-headed boys has written a hymn on Sunday. Now let colleges, now let Senates take heed! for here is one who, opening these fine tastes as the basis of the pioneer's iron constitution, will gather all their laurels in his strong hands."

If Mr. Emerson had been an observer instead of a philosopher; if he had ever studied the frontier and not evolved it from his moral consciousness, he would know that the piano appears first in the saloon and gambling house; that the elegancies and refinements of civilization are brought into barbarism with the first civilized idlers, who are generally vicious; that the proprietor of the "log-hut" and the "tow-headed" boys will be found holding out against pianos and Latin grammars until he is obliged to emigrate. Romance like this would undoubtedly provoke the applause of lyceum halls in the wild fastnesses of Roxbury (Mass.), or on the savage frontiers of Brooklyn (N.Y.), but a philosopher ought to know that, usually, only civilization begets civilization, and that pioneer is apt to be always the pioneer. So, too, we think should he, in speaking of "books," study his subject a little less abstractly than he does when he speaks of the "novel" as a "juggle;" as only "confectionery, not the raising of new corn;" as containing "no new element, no power, no furtherance"—in brief, when he exhibits that complete ignorance of its functions which makes his abuse of it solemnly ludicrous even in its earnestness. It is surely no way to make us in love with Plotinus, Porphyry, Proclus, Synesius, or even the excellent Jamblichus—"of whom the Emperor Julian" spoke so enthusiastically—to allude to the "great poverty of invention" in Dickens and Thackeray, and to sum up their theses in the formula, "She was beautiful, and he fell in love." "The colleges," says Mr. Emerson, "furnish no Professor of Books; and, I think, no chair is so much wanted." If the professor should also be a philosopher—and that is undoubtedly the suggestion of the above—perhaps it is well for literature that there is none. But these are not functions of the philosopher, who accepts and finds the true office of even those things he can not understand; and we are constrained to find Mr. Emerson's teachings at variance here with his philosophy.

In the essay on "Old Age" we expected more than we have got. Not, indeed, that we did not look for quotations from Cicero—for who has written on this subject without borrowing from *De Senectute*—but that we looked for more from Mr. Emerson, and of a better quality. His twenty pages, we fear, do not compare with the playful wisdom and tender humor with which Oliver Wendell Holmes has in a few paragraphs in the *Autocrat* adorned this theme, and who, if we except Bacon, has said the best that has been said since Cicero wrote.

There is no philosophy that will suit all the occasions of taste, prejudice, and habit. There are some things we all know, or believe we know, better than our advisors. But there remains to Mr. Emerson, we think, the praise of doing more than any other American thinker to voice the best philosophic conclusions of American life and experience. And it would be well for those who affect to regard him as a harmless mystic, to know that no other man, for years, has left such an impress upon the young collegiate mind of America; that his style and thought go far to form the philosophic pothooks of many a Freshman's thesis; that from a secular pulpit he preaches better practical sermons on the conduct of life than is heard from two-thirds of the Christian pulpits of America; and that, what is rare on many a platform and pulpit, he believes what he says.

Checklist of Additional Reviews

Examiner and London Review, 3243 (26 March 1870), 199.

New Englander, 29 (April 1870), 364–5.

Universalist Quarterly, 27 (April 1870), 259.

Saturday Review, 23 April 1870, p. 558.

Public Opinion, 7 May 1870, p. 584.

George Willis Cooke, "Emerson's New Book," *New Covenant*, 14 May 1870, p. 1.

S[idney]. H. M[orse]., *Radical*, 7 (June 1870), 511–12.

[Moncure D. Conway], "Emerson's *Society and Solitude*," *Fraser's Magazine*, 82 (July 1870), 1–18.

Charles G. Cattell, "Emerson on Books," *National Reformer*, n.s. 26 (12 December 1875), 378–9.

Letters and Social Aims

Review of *Letters and
Social Aims*,
Athenæum, 2516
(15 January 1876), 81

In his latest production, Mr. Emerson is
as crabbed, as entertaining, and as "cock-
sure" as when he first startled the Phi-
Beta-Kappa Society with his paradoxes on
the relations of man to the universe, or
when with Margaret Fuller he laid the
foundations of what at one time seemed
likely to be a new school of metaphysical
speculation. One advantage, however, he
still possesses over most of the *pseudo*-
philosophers at whose head he stands. He
is slow in utterance, and patient in labour.
His method of work is that of great thinkers. Gradually he absorbs and assimilates
whatever science or history can furnish,
and slowly and reflectively he gives us the
result of his thoughts. So patiently does
he brood over his eggs, that if they are
sometimes addled the fault is scarcely his.
Already, however, his influence is on the
wane. He wants that last and most useful
gift of genius, the power to keep young in
society, and to advance with advancing
years. Modern work and modern speculation scarcely reach him. Science, with the
dazzling visions it has of late suggested,
has, of course, some attraction for him,
and history illustrates his views on the
future of man; but modern art finds him
cold, distrustful, and unsympathetic, and
ready to apply old canons and shibbo-
leths. He begins to stand, accordingly,
among the men of today, a figure of the
past, not yet remote enough to be venerable, but unserviceable for present needs,
hanging

Quite out of fashion, like a rusty mail
In monumental mockery.

There is curiosity still to hear what he has
to say, but it is soon exhausted, and his
old-world arts are powerless to retain men
born under new conditions and nurtured
in new creeds. For this growing neglect
Mr. Emerson's style is, in part, responsible. Quaintness and eccentricity of language may hold people for a while by
force of mere curiosity, but they end by
wearying. They are like an absurd costume upon a wise man. Those who enter
into conversation with the wearer will find
out his merit. Unless, however, he is constantly displaying it, the new comers will
take him for a mountebank. The first
sentence in the essays, now collected from
the serials in which most of them appear
to have seen the light before, is enough
to frighten away a man who regards

language as intended to convey thought, and not as a means of darkening counsel. It runs thus:—"The perception of matter is made the common sense, and for cause." Here it ends with a full stop. If we quote the second sentence, it is for the purpose of enabling the reader to judge how completely isolated stands this thought, observation, or whatever it is to be called. The second sentence is, "This was the cradle, this the go-cart, of the human child." Now, out of the hundreds of thousands of readers in England or America to whom Mr. Emerson might appeal, how many will have the slightest idea of what is his meaning? Those who are familiar with other languages besides English may obtain a glimpse of meaning, and may charge him with nothing beyond extreme inelegance of style. Mr. Emerson, however, writes for the general public, and he has no right to envelope purposely his thought in phrases that are beyond their comprehension.

The essay which opens thus uncomfortably is on 'Poetry and Imagination.' This is in Mr. Emerson's old style. We hear much about veracity, transcendency, morals, and other like matters, with which poetry is but remotely connected. We are told that poetry is faith—which may mean anything or nothing; that it is the piety of the intellect, that it is the gai science (sic), and that it is "the little chamber in the brain where is generated the explosive force which, by gentle shocks, sets in action the intellectual world," and so forth. In one place we are informed, "When people tell me they do not relish poetry, and bring me Shelley or Aikin's Poets" (strange conjunction), "or I know not what volume of rhymed English, to show that it has no charm, I am quite of their mind. But their dislike of the books only proves their liking for poetry." This theory would carry one far. It reminds us, indeed, of the logic of Joseph Surface in his interview with Lady Teazle, as stated by her, that she must sin in her own defence, and part with her virtue to secure her reputation. If inability to enjoy the writings of poets is a proof of a liking for poetry, what an enthusiast in its behalf must be the man who has never learned to read! Turning to the essay on the Comic, we find it asserted that man alone has a perception of the comic; that neither birds nor beasts, any more than rocks, have a perception of jest or absurdity. This is just a trifle dogmatic. Those who consort most closely with animals will be reluctant to believe that no enjoyment of humour is possible in their case. What the higher order of animals can perceive is beyond our judgment or ken. When an elephant, grievously injured by a man, was handed by him an apple, he crushed it into pulp with his foot, and threw it in the face of his persecutor. This story rests on excellent testimony, the incident having been seen by men of position, some of whom are probably still alive. It is hard to say what processes of mental action it does not open out. When Mr. Emerson says that "the essence of all jokes, of all comedy, seems to be an honest or well-intended halfness," he is not far from Whately's definition of a joke as a mock fallacy. In the essay on Immortality, Mr. Emerson misquotes a well-known epigram which he took from a tomb in Melrose Abbey. It is possible, of course, that the mistake is the mason's:—

The earth goes on the earth glittering with gold;
The earth goes to the earth sooner than it *should* (*would*);
The earth builds on the earth castles and towers;
The earth says to the earth, All this is ours.

This substitution of *should* for *would* is

the reverse of the ludicrous new reading of 'Macbeth' by Mr. Irving, who persists in saying, *apropos* of the death of Lady Macbeth,

She *would* have died hereafter—

a statement which has, at least, the merit of incontrovertibility.

It would be ungracious to go through the work of a writer like Mr. Emerson and hunt out defects. This, however, we have not done. Quite characteristic are the views and the misstatements advanced, the entire work being that of a man who looks through coloured spectacles, and sees nothing except in their light. To the admirers of mysticism and rhapsody the new book will be welcome. It is deficient, however, in the common sense which, on the principle, we suppose, of Tacitus, "omne ignotum pro magnifico," is everywhere lauded through its pages.

"Emerson's 'Letters and Social Aims,'"
Scribner's Monthly Magazine,
11 (April 1876), 896–7

It is a little amusing to find keen critics of Emerson philosophizing on the modifications of style and form visible in this, his last volume, when compared with its predecessors. One at least of the present essays has floated down unchanged from the times of "The Dial;" the essay on "The Comic" having first appeared in that periodical more than thirty years ago, namely, in October, 1843, and being here reprinted with scarcely a syllable of alteration, though with the omission of the opening paragraph. There is, however, thus much of truth in these critical surmises, that we can either see or fancy in the essays, as a whole, a slightly increased love of structure, and a dawning taste for a beginning, a middle, and an end. They are less *premorse*, as the botanists say of those roots which end abruptly, as if bitten off— a phrase so perfectly descriptive of Mr. Emerson's habitual terminations that he would doubtless have used it if duty had called him to pass upon his own style as a subject for criticism. At least half the present essays begin with a studied opening, and lead up to a marked and even cadenced close. This is the more impressive and agreeable to the reader, because Emerson's manner as a lecturer, owing to increasing dimness of sight, has grown more fragmentary year by year; and the more satisfactory aspect of the printed pages may, after all, be due to the aid covertly rendered by some skillful editor or secretary,—a daughter, perhaps, or friend.

Be this as it may, there is still enough left of the old method, or non-method, to bring back something of the old exasperation—both at the excess of choice quotation, confusing the main thread,—if thread there be,—and also at the fact that in rearranging the loose sheets, some of the best things have fallen out and disappeared. Thus, in the "Social Aims" and the "Inspiration," which we personally heard as lectures, the one in 1864, the other in 1874,—we have looked in vain for certain delicious phrases or sentences which we were then tempted to note eagerly down, with furtive lead-pencil, on the backs of letters. Worse yet, we look in vain for a whole lecture which we have been accustomed to think the best given by Emerson since the days of the "Divinity Hall Address,"—a lecture on "The Natural Method of Intellectual Philosophy," given in his courses of twenty years ago—a lecture brilliant beyond even his wont with wit, and insight, and quotation; but having also a degree of method and continuity which would, if it could be printed, disarm the most Philistine critic.

Emerson's place in our and the world's literature is well fixed. We knew long since what to expect and what not to expect; we have learned to class him among the poets, not among the makers of systems. This being the case, the matter of chief interest with each reader is to know whether this is still the same Emerson, whether he is true to the dreams of his youth, or is falling within that "untimely shadow" which he himself has described as the tragedy of advancing years. No fact or thought contained in these volumes is, after all, so interesting as to know that our foremost man of letters is still true to his early visions; and that years have only mellowed him, without bringing him to the period of apology and retraction. The high, hopeful, resonant tone of the writer is better than any detail of the book itself.

If our descendants are ever to inhabit a planet where scientific systems are held more important than poetic glimpses, how valueless will Emerson seem beside Herbert Spencer! But those of us who look forward with joy to completing our earthly career before that era, may rejoice with confidence in those myriad fine thoughts and statements sown throughout this volume, any one of which seems for a moment to render all existing scientific results subordinate, as a sunbeam abolishes gas-light. Let us not be ungrateful to the gas-pipes: what would our modern life be without them?—as is justly remarked, no doubt, in the last report of the Social Science Association; but, after all, there are hierarchies in illumination, and we prefer to hold by the loftier shrine.

In no one of these essays is the maturing or mellowing of thought so visible as in that which fitly ends the volume, on "Immortality." Those who have claimed that in his earlier writings Mr. Emerson evaded or blurred this subject, will find peculiar delight in seeing the nobler and clearer light thrown upon it by his advancing experience. Indeed, there is something touching in the thought, how many humble souls will here find their own private assurances and hopes restated in grand rhetoric by the poet. Whether the theme be the being of Deity, or the promise of permanent life, Mr. Emerson approaches it in a way on which his clerical ancestors could not frown. Thus he says:

["Immortality," 334.1–11, 16–19]

This is theism and personal immortality, pure and simple; and yet more impressively in the following:

["Immortality," 336.7–10, 14–19; 336.23–337.2]

With perhaps some secret sense of fitness, Mr. Emerson chose the occasion of an address before a literary society of

Harvard College to re-affirm his faith in the fundamental principles of American civilization, and in the reforms to which he long ago pledged himself. But more important than his opinion on any particular point is his unflinching courage in urging his convictions:

["Progress of Culture," 231.14.–21]

Who can measure the tonic influence of a literary career that has met opposition and surmounted obstacles in a spirit like this?

[George Parsons Lathrop], Review of *Letters and Social Aims*, *Atlantic Monthly*, 38 (August 1876), 240–1

Mr. Emerson's latest volume, in the short time since its publication here, has been translated into German, and issued at Stuttgart, with an introduction by Julian Schmidt. Herr Schmidt, after a slight comparison with Carlyle and Goethe, says, "Emerson is a poet and a philosopher, but little is gained by describing him as the one or the other, or as a combination of the two;" and he goes on to define him further as a kind of conversationist, whose essays stimulate us as intercourse with the best company stimulates, making us think better of ourselves, giving our thoughts a higher impulse, and leaving us without decisive settlement of a given question, but teaching a great deal, nevertheless. The charm and the profit, he says, are quite similar to those which result from the action of art upon us. Herr Schmidt's exposition of his subject, though full of respect and admiration, is very strictly temperate. His definition, as just given, seems to us an excellent one; and this moderation of tone is no less admirable. Indeed, if we are not mistaken, it will be apt to accord well with the impression left by Mr. Emerson's recent publication upon that part of the reading world which most looks up to him. It is inevitable that in a case like the present one should look back, and inquire the relation between this result given us by the thinker of seventy-three and the contributions of the same mind at thirty-five or at fifty. What is the ultimate issue of this long intellectual career? What the ratio of increase in the rewards of its activity, or what the degree of decadence? Making these inquiries, we are forced to admit that the last milestone, though measuring a long route, stands singularly close to the first, as if the traveling had been done in a circle. Strictly speaking, these essays should perhaps not be treated as representative of the latest years, for their structure seems to indicate that they originated at various times as lectures, and have been remodeled for publication. They are a little more loosely written than the early essays, or Nature, or The Conduct of Life, and include a noticeably large proportion of quotation, unknown in what we are inclined to call by comparison Emerson's finished works. In any case, it would not be wise or profitable to dwell long on the reflection, "This book is not so good as those we used to read." But the difference which is observable has a peculiar value; the comparative informality of these papers brings out the different traits of the author in exaggerated form. The similes frequently appear forced, the illustrations not accurately applicable, and the feeling factitious in passages, as if from too fixed a habit of forcing impressions by extreme statement. "In certain hours we can almost pass our hand through out own body" is not an agreeable nor generally truthful phrase to indicate the exalting power of imagination. And the following seems to us a startling misapprehension: "In dreams we are true poets; we create the persons of the drama; we give them appropriate figures, faces, costume; they are perfect in their organs, attitude, manners; moreover, they speak after their own characters, not ours; they speak to us, and we listen with surprise to what they say. Indeed, I doubt if the best poet has yet written any five-act play that can compare in thoroughness of invention with this unwritten play in fifty acts, composed by the dullest snorer on the floor of the watch-house." To say nothing of the degradation which the greatest poets are made to suffer by the closing comparison, we may at least question the correctness of the value assigned to dreams, which are most often entirely wanting in true invention, and illogical in characterization, as well as foolishly improbable, though they undoubtedly have a juggling completeness of their own. Elsewhere occurs the statement that "the fable of the Wandering Jew is agreeable to men, because they want more time and land in which to execute their thoughts." We doubt the *agreeableness* of the fable to any one; and its origin and use point distinctly to the misery of having more time and space than the human lot affords, while we remain in human life,—a moral quite opposed to the inference which Mr. Emerson attributes. "The artist has always the masters in his eye," we read in The Progress of Culture, "though he affects to flout them.... Tennyson would give his fame for a verdict in his favor from Wordsworth." Surely the first statement, here finds no answer in the minds of sincere artists, for they in no wise "affect to flout" the masters; and it is quite as profitless an overstatement to deny the self-reliance of a poet like Tennyson (or any other mature, sane, and substantial poet) by such an imputation of weak distrust as that of the second sentence. Points like these abound in the book, and make it extremely fatiguing reading, especially to those who wish for the elixir of Emerson's earlier volumes. On the other hand, there are many clear-ringing enunciations of the truth and many noble phrases to be found, from page to page. Some of them appear in the long discourse on Poetry and Imagination, which we have nevertheless felt to be a somewhat unnecessary production, a kind of painful tracing-paper exercise upon thoughts that are original in the minds of poets and creators, but find their best embodiment in imaginative works, and become tiresome when thus drawn out in explanation. The essay on Resources is especially good and stirring. Very pleasing, also, is that entitled Social Aims; Quotation and Originality is admirable; and Greatness has a reassuring depth and quietude. The Persian Poetry takes us a long distance for not very large benefits; and one of the most noticeable things about the Immortality is that among all the inducements to continued earthly life brought forward by the author, that of love of our kind and all the exquisite and inexhaustible relations of the affections is not once mentioned as of any value. It is a little strange that Mr. Emerson should write so well as he does here, concerning The Comic, when in another of the chapters he treats laughter with a lofty disdain. In The Comic he eulogizes wit and its effects without stint; in Social Aims he makes laughter synonymous with "savage nature," and says, "Beware of jokes; . . . inestimable for sauce, but corrupting for food." This, to be sure, is wisdom; but it is added, "True wit never made us laugh." Consistency, we believe, is regarded by Mr. Emerson as by no means a jewel, but rather a stumbling-block to true intuitions; and indeed this is the gravest objection to his method, the greatest drawback on his advice to other thinkers, that he insists too strongly on the mood of the hour. "Life is a train of moods" is a well-known dictum of his; and in the present volume he values highly the "minorities of one" that have made the great revolutions of history and of art. Perhaps he does not value them too highly, but he does not enough remember that minorities may be wrong as well as majorities; and, though life be a train of moods, these are not all equally good. "And what is Originality?" he asks. "It is being, being one's self and reporting accurately what we see and are." But there must be a choice of *what* we will report, out of the total that we see and are: some reports would be valueless, and are therefore never made. In like manner, there may be a choice between one impression and another, for the sake of getting nearer to the truth; and the choice or reconcilement of these impressions is consistency. In so far, then, as Mr. Emerson disregards this essential, it seems to us that he weakens his hold on the younger generation, which is getting a distinctly scientific habit of comparing and contrasting and approximating, and will not allow too large a place to the unsupported intuition, especially if it proceed from a mind which in its several utterances directly conflicts with itself. We dwell upon this, because Mr. Emerson's lessons are too valuable to merit the clog which is thus continually hung upon them. But, in short, these essays deserve much of the same sort of praise that their predecessors have gained, with something more of accusation for want of sequence in the arrangement of ideas; and one cannot but regret that the sentences should meet the eye so bolt upright, and with that curious air of sitting for their photographs, which makes us suspect the iron head-rest behind them.

335

Checklist of Additional Reviews

New York *Herald*, 28 December 1875, p. 5.

New York *Herald*, 6 January 1876, p. 5.

Appleton's Journal, 15 (8 January 1876), 57–8.

Edith Simcox, *Academy*, 9 (22 January 1876), 67–8.

J. A. Bellows, "Mr. Emerson's New Book," *Liberal Christian*, 31 (22 January 1876), 3–4.

"Emerson's Letters and Social Aims," *Saturday Review*, 41 (26 February 1876), 275–6.

"Letters and Social Aims," *International Review*, 3 (March 1876), 249–52.

Celia P. Woodley, "Texts from Emerson," *Liberal Christian*, 31 (4 March 1876), 3–4.

Dublin Review, n.s. 27 (July 1876), 253–5.

American Catholic Quarterly Review, 2 (January 1877), 175–8.

Checklist of Reviews of Other Emerson Books

A Historical Discourse, Delivered Before the Citizens of Concord, 12th Sept. 1835.
[B. B. Thatcher], *North American Review*, 42 (April 1836), 448–67.

An Address Delivered in the Court-House in Concord, Massachusetts, on 1st August, 1844, on the Anniversary of the Emancipation of Negroes in the British West Indies.
Christian World, 2 (14 September 1844), 3.
Anti-slavery Reporter, 16 October 1844, pp. 197–8.
Christian Examiner, 38 (January 1845), 134.

Nature; An Essay. And Lectures on the Times (1844).
Critic [England], n.s. 8 (15 December 1849), 573.

Nature: An Essay. To Which is Added Orations, Lectures, and Addresses (1845).
Literary Gazette [England], 1484 (28 June 1845), 423.
Critic [England], n.s. 8 (15 September 1849), 431.
Critic [England], n.s. 8 (15 November 1849), 526.

Nature, An Essay; and Lectures on the Times; and On War (1850).
Literary Gazette [England], 1723 (26 January 1850), 61. Also reviews *Eight Essays*.

The Complete Works of Ralph Waldo Emerson (1866).
Littell's Living Age, 91 (13 October 1866), 86.

The Prose Works of Ralph Waldo Emerson (1870).
Saturday Review, 28 (25 December 1869), 837.
Universalist Quarterly, 27 (January 1870), 124.
[Orestes A. Brownson], "Emerson's Prose Works," *Catholic World*, 11 (May 1870), 202–11.

Parnassus (1874).
[F. B. Sanborn], "Emerson's *Parnassus*— A Review," Springfield *Daily Republican*, 26 December 1874, p. 4.
New York *Herald*, 28 December 1874, p. 3.
Appleton's Journal, 12 (9 January 1875), 53.
Harper's New Monthly Magazine, 50 (March 1875), 601.
J. D., *Penn Monthly*, 7 (April 1876), 328–33.
Westminster Review [England], 107 (January 1877), 292–3.

HENRY DAVID THOREAU

A Week on the Concord and Merrimack Rivers

[Horace Greeley],[1]
"H. D. Thoreau's Book,"
New York *Daily Tribune*,
13 June 1849, p. 1

A really new book—a fresh, original, thoughtful work—is sadly rare in this age of omniferous publication. Mr. Thoreau's, if not entirely this, is very near it. Its observations of Nature are as genial as Nature herself, and the tones of his harp have an Æolian sweetness. His reflections are always striking, often profoundly truthful, and his scholastic treasures, though a little too ostentatiously displayed, are such as the best instructed reader will enjoy and thank him for. His philosophy, which is the Pantheistic egotism vaguely characterised as Transcendental, does *not* delight us. It seems second-hand, imitative, often exaggerated—a bad specimen of a dubious and dangerous school. But we will speak first of the staple of the work.

Mr. Thoreau is a native and resident of Concord, Mass.—a scholar, a laborer, and in some sort a hermit. He traveled somewhat in his earlier years (he is still young), generally trusting to his own thoughts for company and his walking-cane for motive power. It would seem a main purpose of his life to demonstrate how slender an impediment is poverty to a man who pampers no superfluous wants, and how truly independent and self-sufficing is he who is in no manner the slave of his own appetites. Of his fitful hermit life and its results we have already given some account: Now for his 'Week on the Concord and Merrimac.'

The Concord is a dull, dark, sluggish creek or petty river which runs through the Massachusetts town of that name and is lost in the Merrimac at Lowell. On this stream, Mr. Thoreau and his friend embarked one Autumn afternoon in a small rowboat, and rowed or sailed down to the dam near its mouth, thence across by the old Middlesex Canal to the Merrimac above Lowell, thence up the latter to Hookset, N. H. where they left their boat and varied their experience by a pedestrian tour through the wild and rugged heart of the Granite State, returning to their boat after a week's absence and retracing their course homeward. They had a tent which, while boating, they pitched

341

in the most inviting and secluded spot—generally a wood, when night overtook them—they cooked and served for themselves, only approaching the dwellings rarely to purchase milk or fruit or bread. Such is the thread of the narrative: let us give a single specimen of its observations of Nature. It is a description of the commencement of their aquatic journey:

["Saturday," 19.35–21.25]

Here is another in a similar vein:

["Saturday," 25.10–26.14]

Our next extract is a specimen of his more didactic mood:

["Friday," 391.19–392.30]

Half the book is like and as good as this.—Nearly every page is instinct, with genuine Poetry except those wherein verse is haltingly attempted, which are for the most part sorry prose. Then there is a misplaced Pantheistic attack on the Christian Faith. Mr. Thoreau—we must presume soberly—says:

["Sunday," 65.11–17, 66.30–68.1, 71.31–72.2]

We have quoted a fair proportion of our author's smartest Pantheistic sentences, but there is another in which he directly asserts that he considers the Sacred Books of the Brahmins in nothing inferior to the Christian Bible. It was hardly necessary to say in addition that he is not well acquainted with the latter—the point worth considering is rather—*ought not* an author to *make himself* thoroughly acquainted with a book, which, if true, is of such transcendent importance, before uttering opinions concerning it calculated to shock and pain many readers, not to speak of those who will be utterly repelled by them? Can that which Milton and Newton so profoundly reverenced (and they *had* studied it thoroughly) be

wisely turned off by a youth as unworthy of even consideration? Mr. Thoreau's treatment of this subject seems revolting alike to good sense and good taste. We ask him to weigh all he has offered with regard to the merits of the Christian as compared with other Scriptures against the following brief extract from the last Edinburgh Review:

"The Bible, supposing it other than it pretends to be, presents us with a singular phenomenon in the space which it occupies throughout the continued history of literature. We see nothing like it; and it may well perplex the infidel to account for it. Nor need his sagacity disdain to enter a little more deeply into its possible *causes* than he is usually inclined to do. It has not been given to any other book of religion thus to triumph over national prejudices, and lodge itself securely in the heart of great communities,—varying by every conceivable diversity of language, race, manners, customs, and indeed agreeing in nothing but a veneration for itself. It adapts itself with facility to the revolutions of thought and feeling which shake to pieces all things else; and flexibly accommodates itself to the progress of society and the changes of civilization.—Even conquests—the disorganization of old nations—the formation of new—do not affect the continuity of its empire. It lays hold of the new as of the old, and transmigrates with the spirit of humanity; attracting to itself, by its own moral power, in all the communities it enters, a ceaseless intensity of effort for its propagation, illustration, and defense. Other systems of religion are usually delicate exotics, and will not bear transplanting. The gods of the nations are local deities, and reluctantly quit their native soil; at all events they patronize only their favorite races, and perish at once when the tribe or nation of their worshipers becomes extinct, often long before. Nothing, indeed, is more difficult than to make foreigners feel anything but the utmost indifference (except as an object of philosophic curiosity) about the religion of other nations: and no portion of their national literature is regarded as more tedious or unattractive than that which treats of their theology. The elegant mythologies of Greece and Rome made no proselytes among other nations, and fell hopelessly the moment *they* fell. The Koran of Mahomet has, it is true, been propagated by the sword; but it has been propagated by nothing else; and its dominion has been limited to those nations who could not reply to that logic. If the Bible be false, the facility with which it overleaps the otherwise impassable boundaries of race and clime, and domiciliates itself among so many different nations, is assuredly a far more striking and wonderful proof of human ignorance, perverseness and stupidity, than is afforded in the limited prevalence of even the most abject superstitions; or, if it really has merits which, *though* a fable, have enabled it to impose so comprehensively and variously on mankind, wonderful indeed must have been the skill in its composition; so wonderful that even the infidel himself ought never to regard it but with the profoundest

reverence, as far too successful and sublime a fabrication to admit a thought of scoff or ridicule. In his last illness, a few days before his death, Sir W. Scott asked Mr. Lockhart to read to him. Mr. Lockhart inquired what book he would like. 'Can you ask?' said Sir Walter,— 'there is but ONE;' and requested him to read a chapter of the gospel of John. When will an *equal* genius, to whom all the realms of fiction are as familiar as to him, say the like of some professed revelation, originating among a race and associated with a history and a clime as foreign as those connected with the birthplace of the Bible from those of the ancestry of Sir Walter Scott? Can we, by any stretch of imagination, suppose some Walter Scott of a new race in Australia or South Africa, saying the same of the Vedas or the Koran?"

Albeit we love not theologic controversy, we proffer our columns to Mr. Thoreau, should he see fit to answer these questions. We would have preferred to pass the theme in silence, but our admiration of his book and our reprehension of its Pantheism forbade that course. May we not hope that he will reconsider his too rashly expressed notions on this head?

Note

1 For a discussion of the attribution of this review to Greeley, see Michael Meyer, "The Case for Greeley's *Tribune* Review of *A Week*," ESQ: *A Journal of the American Renaissance*, 25 (2nd Quarter 1979), 92–4.

Review of *A Week on the Concord and Merrimack Rivers,* Liberator, 19 (15 June 1849), 96

We have not yet been able to give this volume such an examination as would justify us in pronouncing absolute judgment upon it. For its amiable author, we have much respect. His mode of life is *sui generis*—all alone by himself in the woods of Concord, an enthusiastic child and lover of Nature, in spirit an occupant of an ideal world, and with the eye of genius 'in a fine phrenzy rolling'—and this production of his is equally peculiar. We have spent many years 'on the Merrimack river,' our dear, native stream; but this was 'long, long ago.' We shall accept this invitation of Mr. Thoreau to pass 'a week' with him on the same river, and, making that the starting-point from which to ascend to 'cloud-land,' we shall accompany him on the wings of imagination as far as we can sustain such a flight. Of our entertainment and success, we may report hereafter.

The numerous admirers of Carlyle and Emerson will read this book with a relish; for Mr. T. writes in their vein, and to some extent in their dialect, and is a match for them in felicitous conceits and amusing quaintnesses; yet he is not a servile imitator—only an admirer, by affinity and kindred one of a trinity, having his own sphere in which to move, and his own mission to consummate. As a specimen of his thinking and speaking, take the following suggested by a grave-yard:

["Monday," 169.16–170.8]

Review of *A Week on the Concord and Merrimack Rivers,* New Hampshire Patriot and State Gazette, 26 July 1849, p. 2

This is a remarkable volume and its author is a remarkable man. The title is very unpretending and gives but a faint idea of the contents of the work. Few men think as much as they should. All is action; and if one is only busy about something, it is enough; no one can say contemptuously that he is idle—Now to us it seems that this fidgeting, itching, hustling turn of mind might frequently with profit be exchanged for a more meditative and thoughtful habit, which should enlarge the understanding and open the heart, develop the reason and chasten the passions. The author of the work before us, is a man of thought—retired from the busy scenes of life, he turns the mental eye inward and endeavors to read the mysterious page of his own soul. Again looking upon objects around which meet his senses, he reads lessons of wisdom. To him the very stones preach sermons and the reeds become eloquent. The thread of his narrative is very simple, but upon it he has strung pearls. With a single companion in his little boat, he courses leisurely down the Concord and up the Merrimack Rivers, some sixty miles or more and gives us the reflections and observations of each day. He discourses to us about the old inhabitants—describes the genius of fishes,—hears the "church-going bell" and talks about modern religion and its inconsistencies—seems strangely inclined to sympathise with the Ancient Greeks and

Romans, with their myths and many Gods—utters deep-felt thoughts about conscience, its office and uses—touches his lyre and gives us a sweet poem—discourses of the old Poets and with them glories over our relics and antiquities, and cares more for them than for those of Egypt—moralizes on Friendship, and in fine, gives utterance to a thousand beautiful thoughts upon the material and immaterial earth, air and heaven, until on closing the book we find ourselves in love with the author, satisfied with ourselves and at peace with the world. We do not by any means endorse the author's Pantheism, but will let it stand or fall for itself.

"Thoreau's Travels," *Literary World*, 5 (22 September 1849), 245–7

It is a singular thing—a fact which goes to maintain the universal average of human motives and actions, that a man no sooner sets up for a reformer, and begins to refute old heresies, but he contrives to involve himself in some new absurdity, charitably, perhaps, to hand over his trade of revolutionist, with materials, to his successors. Thus we see many men of subtlety, acuteness, reading, and reflection, to work at the present day; tinkering society, proposing new laws, new aids to morals, new theories of government, and involving in every one of their alterations some practical error. They make more holes than they fill up. In one point their argument is conclusive, and it is strengthened by their practice. They maintain the existence of much positive evil in the world, and their means for its removal assure us at a glance of its continuance. Now, we neither reverence the past as absolutely holy in itself, nor despair of something better in the future; but we have that respect for the government of the world, to think that the good to come must be built up out of the good already attained, by growth, not by revolution, and that there are certain facts established which cannot be controverted. Christianity, based upon the records of the Old and New Testaments, we hold to be of permanent authority, and there are lessons of experience for daily conduct which have never yet been superseded. What would experience or history be worth if they gave no laws?

We were struck with a reflection or

two of this nature on looking over Mr. Thoreau's book. The author is a man of humors, in Ben Jonson's good old sense, who uses his faculties in his own way, and cultivates more of them than most people, being, as we understand, quite independent of much of the slavery which people submit to under the word civilization. He can build his own house, raise his own food, cook it, and clothe himself: he can retire at any moment from a daintily furnished parlor and Robinson Crusoe it on any acre of land, of ordinary productive powers, on the Continent. He loves nature, of which he is a careful observer, relishes good books, estimates at their worth the manly qualities of work and endurance. We have read his book backwards, if he is not kind and humane. He has stored his mind with the fruits of much reading and reflection. He is patient of the most minute investigations of insects and fishes; can be reverent over an arrow head turned up from an old Indian field, or respect a voracious pickerel newly taken from the river which runs through it. Yet, when this writer, so just, observant, and considerate, approaches what civilized men are accustomed to hold the most sacred of all, he can express himself in a flippant style which he would disdain to employ towards a muscle [mussel] or a tadpole. Lest we should be thought to be doing an injustice to a writer whose merits we are very ready to admit, and who is somewhat known to the public by his painstaking and pleasing sketches of natural scenery, we justify our remarks by the following quotations:—

["Sunday," 64.32–65.17, 67.25–68.1]

In other passages we have a protest against the most generally received usages of Christianity—for example—"When one enters a village, the church, not only really, but from association, is the ugliest looking building in it, because it is the one in which human nature stoops the lowest and is most disgraced. If I should ask the minister of Middlesex to let me speak in his pulpit on a Sunday, he would object, because I do not pray as he does, or because I am not ordained. What under the sun are these things?" Now these things *are* something, for they have been well cemented together by the wisdom of ages. They are much stronger than Thoreau's whims.

A man may hold different language with regard to Christianity, as he looks upon it from either of two points of view, as it is taught, or as it is practised; and the best Christians will feel most deeply the truth of the loudest scoff of infidelity, as it points to the weaknesses and corruptions of those whose conduct is nearest, still how remote from, the sacred lesson. Lay on the lash upon the back of hypocrisy, insincerity, unworthiness, but respect the creed. The humblest church in any village of our country is *not* "the ugliest looking building in it."

Mr. Thoreau is a linguist and scholar, and tells us that he has scarcely yet reached the Hebrew Scriptures, having begun with the Chinese and Hindoo. It may serve with some of our readers as a test of his powers of mind, that he professes to prefer the former.

In other walks and in a lighter vein, Mr. Thoreau has some pleasant sketching and essay writing. His observation of nature, as we have suggested, is minute and laborious; and if we may judge from his success in a narrow field of investigation, in a few days' boating on the Concord and Merrimac Rivers, he might be associated profitably in those Geological and other surveys which are now frequently undertaken by the State Governments.

Apart from the pertness and flippancy against which we would warn our readers, Mr. Thoreau's is a readable and agreeable book. It is divided into seven heads, of the days of the week. Each day occupies a section of the journey, which is performed by the author in company with his brother, in a boat of their own construction, which is variously rowed, pulled, dragged, or propelled by the wind along the flats or through the canal; the travellers resting on the banks at night under a tent which they carry with them. The journey is down the Concord river, from Concord, Mass., to the Merrimack, an ascent of the latter river to its source, and from thence backward to the starting point. The record is of the small boating adventures, and largely of the reflections, real or supposed, suggested by the moods or incidents of the way. Thus we get a variety of illustrations of physical geography, the history of the settlements along the route (much of interest there), botanical excursions, philosophical speculations, and literary studies. In any of these departments, the reader will find a great deal that is ingenious and entertaining. According to our practice, we present a passage or two of these agreeable portions of the volume.

Referring our readers to Nathaniel Hawthorne's delightful sketch of the immediate scenery at Concord, in his introduction to the "Mosses from an Old Manse," we pass over our author's sketch of the river, to his account of the Merrimac, which we give at length.

["Sunday," 83.10–87.23]

For an example of the author's book reflections we could not probably find a passage which is a better instance of his mode of thinking and expression than the following:

["Sunday," 96.31–99.21]

There is good writing in this, and there is more in the volume. The author, we perceive, announces another book, "Walden, or Life in the Woods." We are not so rash or uninformed in the ways of the world as to presume to give counsel to a transcendentalist, so we offer no advice; but we may remark as a curious matter of speculation to be solved in the future— the probability or improbability of Mr. Thoreau's ever approaching nearer to the common sense or common wisdom of mankind. He deprecates churches and preachers. Will he allow us to uphold them? or does he belong to the family of Malvolios, whose conceit was so engrossing that it threatened to deprive the world of cakes and ale. "Dost thou think that because thou readest Confucius and art a Confusion there shall be no more steeples and towers? Aye, and bells shall ring too and Bishops shall dine!"

A——R. [William Rounseville Alger], Review of *A Week on the Concord and Merrimack Rivers,* Universalist Quarterly, 6 (October 1849), 422–3

Few books need expurgation more than this one, and few deserve it better. All sorts of subjects, foreign to the general drift of purpose implied in the title and running through the work, are treated in it,—the Christian religion, the church and its usages, poetry, history, great names of the past, philosophy, character, friendship, and many other topics connected with the various experiences of life. These portions of the volume should be separated from the rest, and, if it be thought that the world needs them, published by themselves. They would form a book, full alike of merits and of faults; interesting from its freshness and variety; worthy of perusal for being unusually packed with the fruits of observation, reading and meditation; composed in a rich, oracular style, showing, too evidently, both in substance of idea and in form of statement, imitative traces of the author's great neighbor; abounding in beautiful images happily caught at first hand from nature, in striking aphorisms, in really valuable original thoughts, and in suggestive hints; but, on the other side, interspersed with inexcusable crudities, with proofs of carelessness and lack of healthy moral discrimination, with contempt for things commonly esteemed holy, with reflections that must shock every pious Christian, with the transcendental doctrines of the new-light school, with obscurities of incomprehensible mysticism, with ridiculous speculations, moon-struck reveries and flat nonsense,—without moral purpose in the writing, and without practical results in the reading.

Of that part of the work which would remain after this selection was made from it, which would constitute about one half of the original bulk, we find it difficult to speak in terms of sufficient praise. In wondrous beauty the minute facts of that memorable voyage glide along a stream transparent as crystal before our mind's eye, as we read; and they cling to our thoughts with a tenacity singularly close and pleasant. The boat by day, the tent by night, the toiling or reposing twain, the shifting hues of the clouds and the air as the circling hours roll on, every flower, fish, frog, tree, lowland, hill, nightly bay of watch-dog and distant tone of Sabbath-bell, pass before us, distinctly defined, in a clear, objective existence. The unexaggerated simplicity of description, the uncolored fidelity to fact, the perfect freedom from cant, the childlike earnestness of sympathy for outward things, the poetic eye for interior meaning, pathetic analogy and external beauty, the felicitous phraseology which calmly paints the exact objects themselves,—these traits are beyond commendation. They have combined to make a modern week on two New England rivers, as romantic and new as ever a week in by-gone ages on the Simöis and Xanthus and antique climes could have been.

We have read this history with unmingled delight. We wish the book contained nothing else. Then to travel by its means from the meadows of Concord to the summit of Agiocochook would be a great joy to any man. It is invested with a strange, long-lingering charm, an indescribable fascination for which we can hardly account, except by saying that it springs from its pure, naked truth. For with that the soul of all nature is in unison; to that the core of every heart is loyal, and responds, even when unconscious of it, with an instinctive pleasure.

We are glad to learn that the author intends soon to publish another volume, called,—Walden, or Life in the Woods. On such a theme, owing to his singular familiarity with nature and love for her, he is able to write a work that will not die. For the satisfaction and advantage of his readers, for his own fame, and for the wide distribution and long existence of his book, we beg him to let it be, simply, what its title imports, and not crowd it with heterogeneous thoughts upon a thousand other subjects. That is not his forte. If he persists in thinking that it is, then let him pursue it, by itself, with a set purpose. Great works are not achieved accidentally, by the wayside, our author's authority to the contrary notwithstanding.

Review of *A Week on the Concord and Merrimack Rivers,*
Spectator [England], 22 (13 October 1849), 975

This volume is an American importation. The Concord and Merrimack are two rivers of New Hampshire and Massachusetts. The title of the book would have led one to expect an agreeable series of excursioning incidents and descriptions of landscape in a half-reclaimed state. There is something though not much of these two subjects, but neither of them done in a very lively or attractive way. The bulk of the book consists of Mr. Thoreau's reveries, that might have been written anywhere: they are rather flat and not of a kind to interest.

Review of *A Week on the Concord and Merrimack Rivers*, *Athenæum*, 1148 (27 October 1849), 1086

Review of *A Week on the Concord and Merrimack Rivers*, unidentified newspaper[1]

One of Mr. Chapman's importations from the United States. The Concord and Merrimak are not rivers which would be likely to yield much matter of interest to the traveller—even if he sought for it,—which Mr. Thoreau does not. His pages are the record of a week of picnicking, and boating—and the vagrant thoughts and fancies to which a man of education and reading habits may give himself up in "hours of idleness." The book would therefore be better described as a series of essays on love, poetry, religion—and so on. The matter is for the most part poor enough; but there are a few things in the volume, scattered here and there, which suggest that the writer is a man with a habit of original thinking, which with more careful culture may produce a richer harvest in some future season. The manner is that of the worst offshoots of Carlyle and Emerson: all Mr. Thoreau's best things are spoilt in the utterance. If he would trust in his own genius, he has that to say which might command a larger audience. But imitations of an imitation! The world is too old and the prophets are too many for such things to have a chance of a public hearing in these days.

We are glad to see a book that may be safely recommended as a *prophylactic* of the California fever. It is moreover a healthy and harmless stimulant to those who are removed from the circle of infection. The boy who is wild with the idea of sleeping in a tent and cooking his own dinner, will here find pointed out a readier and cheaper outlet for his enthusiasm than the "overland route"—with the added merit of increased facilities for repentance during a rain storm. To the sick heart and fevered brain, parched up by the thirst for the "golden streams," this book, if read aright, should be as cool and pure as the fall of dew in summer nights. It is a revelation to such, of the absolute non-essentialness of wealth to a man's happy life. It is the old Greek legend of Diogenes and his tub—honorably and gracefully realized in New England. Its author is a scholar and a naturalist, neither dissipated nor misanthropic, with abilities of hand and head, which, tried by the severest standard of ledger and day book, would be found pecuniarily available—one who has not been pushed inside nor left behind in the race of life, but who has calmly stepped apart from the tyrannous control of circumstances, to live after the fashion most congenial to him.

The seemingly slight material that the title page of this book promises, is worked up with a prodigal ingenuity. It is worth while to read it, if only to see how rich the lives of some men may be. The grain of gold has been drawn out into its miles of shining wire, and yet has not been attenuated.

From the author's door in Concord, up to the head of *Canoe Navigation* on the Merrimack, we float along with the voyagers—the whole scene almost as distinct to us as to them. With more fidelity and artistic skill than Champney or Banvard, Mr. Thoreau paints his river panorama, and in the pauses of his unrolling scrolls, he will tell you tales of his former wanderings, and unfold the pages of his genius and graceful criticisms—the free thoughts of one who has not learned of reviews or newspapers, but has lived alone with nature and the best books of the olden time. You shall have the secret history of the fishes in the stream and the flowers on the banks—you shall look into the pleasant New England farm houses and see the faces of the dwellers on the soil, quiet and unfevered, and unlike the nomadic, transitory townsman. If you have ever taken up the knapsack and "wonder-staff," for a week or two of summer weather, you will find this volume the echo of your still pleasantly remembered experiences. You will have for a guide here, one to whom the manifold mysteries of nature are open as the signs of the sky and the ocean to the pilot.

"It seemed that Nature could not raise
A plant in any secret place.
In quaking bog, on snowy hill,
Beneath the grass that shades the rill;
Render the snow beneath the rocks,
In damp fields, known to bird and fox,
But he would come the very hour
It opened in its virgin bower,
As if a sunbeam showed the place,
And tell its long-descended race."

If you would learn more of Thoreau, read the whole description of him (from which the above is quoted) in the first part of Emerson's "wood notes." Since Gilbert White wrote his 'Natural History of Selborne' there has appeared no such book.

We wish we could stop here, but there remains a word to be said. The poetry of the book is all confined to its prose; the hard ungrateful prose is measured off into lines and disguised by lyrical sembiances. With one or two exceptions Mr. Thoreau's rhymes might be spared.

There is something too, objectionable in the religious philosophy of the book, but luckily the objection goes only to the philosophy. In some books the good and evil are inextricably mingled—the error is implied rather than professed, is insinuated like the poison of the Borgias in sweet wine, is the logical consequence of seemingly innocent premises too hastily granted. But in this book, the peculiar speculations of the author stand by themselves. They may be absolutely skipped. They will be easily and naturally overlooked. The eye glances at them and then on to more attractive matter as if they were pages of another book carelessly bound up in this. Moreover, if read never so carefully, we cannot conceive of their doing harm. Neither by argument nor ridicule, or by anything more than mere profession does Mr. Thoreau present his philosophy. We should no more fear the "dangerous tendencies of this book" to propagate Pantheism than that the image of the Goddess of Liberty on our coin, would tend to revive her Pagan worship.

We would gladly make extracts from this volume did we know where to turn. But at every page something so fresh and sparkling catches the eye, that we must either give or leave the whole rather than settle the question of precedence. We read at school, moreover, the story of the simpleton—the Greek 'Till Eulenspiegel'—who brought a brick as a sample of his house—and have always interpreted it into a prophetic sarcasm on reviewers.

But let the reader see for himself. Such books—like the night-blooming Cereus, unfold but seldom—they pass unnoticed unless their coming be watched for, and they fade quickly from before the public eye. Their evanescence is one condition of their rare and peculiar beauty, and he who lets the hour of their effervescence go by will hardly know the pleasure he has missed.

Note

1 Reprinted from [Walter Harding], "An Early Review of Thoreau's Week," *Thoreau Society Bulletin*, 130 (Winter 1975), 8.

[James Russell Lowell], "A Week on the Concord and Merrimack Rivers," Massachusetts Quarterly Review, 3 (December 1849), 40–51

We stick to the sea-serpent. Not that he is found in Concord or Merrimack, but like the old Scandinavian snake, he binds together for us the two hemispheres of Past and Present, of Belief and Science. He is the link which knits us seaboard Yankees with our Norse progenitors, interpreting between the age of the dragon and that of the railroad-train. We have made ducks and drakes of that large estate of wonder and delight bequeathed to us by ancestral irkings, and this alone remains to us unthrift heirs of Linn. We give up the Kraken, more reluctantly the mermaid, for we once saw one, no *mulier formosa, supernè*, no greenhaired maid with looking-glass and comb, but an adroit compound of monkey and codfish, sufficiently attractive for purposes of exhibition till the suture where the *desinit in piscem* began, grew too obtrusively visible.

We feel an undefined respect for a man who has seen the sea-serpent. He is to his brother-fishers what the poet is to his fellow-men. Where they have seen nothing better than a school of horsemackerel, or the idle coils of ocean around Halfway Rock, he has caught authentic glimpses of the withdrawing mantlehem of the Edda-age. We are not for the monster himself. It is not the thing, but the belief in the thing, that is dear to us. May it be long before Professor Owen is comforted with the sight of his unfleshed vertebræ, long before they stretch many a rood behind Kimball's or Barnum's glass, reflected in the shallow orbs of Mr. and Mrs. Public, which stare but see not! When we read that Captain Spalding of the pink-stern *Three Pollies* has beheld him rushing through the brine like an infinite series of bewitched mackerel-casks, we feel that the mystery of old Ocean, at least, has not yet been sounded, that Faith and Awe survive there unevaporate. We once ventured the horsemackerel theory to an old fisherman, browner than a tomcod. "Hosmackril!" he exclaimed indignantly, "hosmackril be—" (here he used a phrase commonly indicated in laical literature by the same sign which serves for Doctorate in Divinity,) "don't yer spose *I* know a hosmackril?" The intonation of that "*I*" would have silenced professor Monkbairns Owen with his provoking *phoca* forever. What if one should ask *him* if he knew a trilobite?

The fault of modern travellers is that they see nothing out of sight. They talk of eocene periods and tertiary formations, and tell us how the world looked to the plesiosaur. They take science (or nescience) with them, instead of that soul of generous trust their elders had. All their senses are skeptics and doubters, materialists reporting things for other skeptics to doubt still further upon. Nature becomes a reluctant witness upon the stand, badgered with geologist hammers and phials of acid. There have been no travellers since those included in Hakluyt and Purchas, except Martin, perhaps, who saw an inch or two into the invisible at the Orkneys. We have peripatetic lecturers, but no more travellers. Travellers' stories are no longer proverbial. We have picked nearly every apple (wormy or otherwise), from the world's tree of Knowledge, and that without an Eve to tempt us. Two or three have hitherto hung luckily beyond reach on a lofty

bough shadowing the interior of Africa, but there is a Doctor Bialloblotzky at this very moment pelting at them with sticks and stones. It may be only next week, and these, too, bitten by geographers and geologists, will be thrown away. We wish no harm to this worthy Sclavonian, but his name is irresistibly suggestive of boiled lobster, and some of the natives are not so choice in their animal food.

Analysis is carried into everything. Even Deity is subjected to chemic tests. We must have exact knowledge, a cabinet stuck full of facts pressed, dried, or preserved in spirits, instead of a large, vague world our fathers had. Our modern Eden is a *hortus siccus*. Tourists defraud rather than enrich us. They have not that sense of æsthetic proportion which characterized the elder traveller. Earth is no longer the fine work of art it was, for nothing is left to the imagination. Job Hortop, arrived at the height of the Bermudas, thinks it full time to throw us in a merman,—"we discovered a monster in the sea who showed himself three times unto us from the middle upwards, in which parts he was proportioned like a man, of the complection of a mulatto or tawny Indian." Sir John Hawkins is not satisfied with telling us about the merely sensual Canaries, but is generous enough to throw us in a handful over: "About these islands are certain flitting islands, which have been oftentimes seen, and when men approached near them they vanished, ... and therefore it should seem he is not yet born to whom God hath appointed the finding of them." Henry Hawkes describes the visible Mexican cities, and then is not so frugal but that he can give us a few invisible ones. "The Spaniards have notice of seven cities which the old men of the Indians show them should lie toward the N.W. from Mexico. They have used, and use daily, much diligence in seeking of them, but they cannot find any one of them.

They say that the witchcraft of the Indians is such that when they come by these towns they cast a mist upon them so that they cannot see them." Thus do these generous ancient mariners make children of us again. Their successors show us an earth effete and past bearing, tracing out with the eyes of industrious fleas every wrinkle and crowfoot.

The journals of the elder navigators are prose Odyssees. The geographies of our ancestors were works of fancy and imagination. They read poems where we yawn over items. Their world was a huge wonder-horn, exhaustless as that which Thor strove to drain. Ours would scarce quench the small thirst of a bee. No modern voyager brings back the magical foundation stones of a Tempest. No Marco Polo, traversing the desert beyond the city of Lok, would tell of things able to inspire the mind of Milton with

"Calling shapes and beckoning shadows dire
And airy tongues that syllable men's names
On sands and shores and desert wildernesses."

It was easy enough to believe the story of Dante, when two thirds of even the upper-world were yet untraversed and unmapped. With every step of the recent traveller our inheritance of the wonderful is diminished. Those beautifully pictured notes of the Possible are redeemed at a ruinous discount in the hard and cumbrous coin of the actual. How are we not defrauded and impoverished? Does California vie with El Dorado, or are Bruce's Abyssinian Kings a set-off for Prester John? A bird in the bush is worth two in the hand. And if the philosophers have not even yet been able to agree whether the world has any existence independent of ourselves, how do we not gain a loss in

every addition to the catalogue of Vulgar Errors? Where are the fishes which nidificated in trees? Where the monopodes sheltering themselves from the sun beneath their single umbrella-like foot, umbrella-like in every thing but the fatal necessity of being borrowed? Where the Acephali, with whom Herodotus, in a kind of ecstasy, wound up his climax of men with abnormal top-pieces? Where the Roe whose eggs are possibly boulders, needing no far-fetched theory of glacier or iceberg to account for them? Where the tails of the Britons? Where the no legs of the bird of Paradise? Where the Unicorn with that single horn of his, sovereign against all manner of poisons? Where the fountain of Youth? Where that Thessalian spring which, without cost to the county, convicted and punished perjurers? Where the Amazons of Orellana? All these, and a thousand other varieties we have lost, and have got nothing instead of them. And those who have robbed us of them have stolen that which not enriches themselves. It is so much wealth cast into the sea beyond all approach of diving bells. We owe no thanks to Mr. J. E. Worcester, whose Geography we studied enforcedly at school. Yet even he had his relentings, and in some softer moment vouchsafed us a fine, inspiring print of the Maelstrom, answerable to the twenty-four mile diameter of its suction. Year by year, more and more of the world gets disenchanted. Even the icy privacy of the arctic and antartic circles is invaded. Our youth are no longer ingenious, as indeed no ingenuity is demanded of them. Every thing is accounted for, every thing cut and dried, and the world may be put together as easily as the fragments of a dissected map. The Mysterious bounds nothing now on the North, South, East, or West. We have played Jack Horner with our earth, till there is never a plum left in it.

Since we cannot have back the old class

of voyagers, the next best thing we can do is to send poets out a-travelling. These will at least see all that remains to be seen, and in the way it ought to be seen. These will disentangle nature for us from the various snarls of man, and show us the mighty mother without paint or padding, still fresh and young, full-breasted, strong-backed, fit to suckle and carry her children. The poet is he who bears the charm of freshness in his eyes. He may safely visit Niagara, or those adopted children of nature the Pyramids, sure to find them and to leave them as if no eye had vulgarized them before. For the ordinary tourist all wells have been muddied by the caravans that have passed that way, and his eye, crawling over the monuments of nature and art, adds only its quota of staleness.

Walton quotes an "ingenious Spaniard" as saying, that "rivers and the inhabitants of the watery element were made for wise men to contemplate and fools to pass by without consideration," and Blount, in one of the notes to his translation of Philostratus, asserts that "as travelling does much advantage wise men, so does it no less prejudice fools." Mr. Thoreau is clearly the man we want. He is both wise man and poet. A graduate of Cambridge—the fields and woods, the axe, the hoe, and the rake have since admitted him *ad eundem*. Mark how his imaginative sympathy goes beneath the crust, deeper down than that of Burns, and needs no plough to turn up the object of its muse. "It is pleasant to think in winter, as we walk over the snowy pastures, of those happy dreamers that lie under the sod, of dormice and all that race of dormant creatures which have such a superfluity of life enveloped in thick folds of fur, impervious to the cold."—p. 103. "For every oak and birch, too, growing on the hilltop, as well as for these elms and willows, we knew that there was a graceful ethereal

and ideal tree making down from the roots, and sometimes nature in high tides brings her mirror to its foot and makes it visible."—p. 49. Only some word were better here than *mirror*, (which is true to the fact, but not to the fancy,) since we could not see *through* that. Leigh Hunt represents a colloquy between man and fish, in which both maintain their orthodoxy so rigidly that neither is able to comprehend or tolerate the other. Mr. Thoreau flounders in no such shallows. He is wiser, or his memory is better, and can recreate the sensations of that part of his embryonic life which he passed as a fish. We know nothing more thoroughly charming than his description of twilight at the river's bottom.

["Sunday," 114.35–115.15]

One would say this was the work of some bream Homer. Melville's pictures of life in Typee have no attraction beside it. Truly we could don scales, pectorals, dorsals, and anals, (critics are already cold-blooded,) to stroll with our dumb love, fin in fin, through the Rialto of this subfluvial Venice. The Complete Angler, indeed! Walton had but an extraqueous and coquine intimacy with the fishes compared with this. His tench and dace are but the poor transported convicts of the frying-pan.

There was a time when Musketaquid and Merrimack flowed down from the Unknown. The adventurer wist not what fair reaches stretched before him, or what new dusky peoples the next bend would discover. Surveyor and map have done what they could to rob them of their charm of unexpectedness. The urns of the old river-gods have been twitched from under their arms and set up on the museum-shelf, or, worse yet, they serve to boil the manufacturer's plum-porridge. But Mr. Thoreau with the touch of his oar conjures back as much as may be of the old enchantment. His map extends to the bed of the river, and he makes excursions into Finland, penetrating among the scaly tribes without an angle. He is thoroughly impartial—*Tros, Tyriusve*—a lichen or a man, it is all one, he looks on both with equal eyes. We are at a loss where to class him. He might be Mr. Bird, Mr. Fish, Mr. Rivers, Mr. Brook, Mr. Wood, Mr. Stone, or Mr. Flower, as well as Mr. Thoreau. His work has this additional argument for freshness, the birds, beasts, fishes, trees, and plants having this advantage, that none has hitherto gone among them in the missionary line. They are trapped for their furs, shot and speared for their flesh, hewn for their timber, and grubbed for Indian Vegetable Pills, but they remain yet happily unconverted in primitive heathendom. They take neither rum nor gunpowder in the natural way, and pay tithes without being Judaized. Mr. Thoreau goes among them neither as hunter nor propagandist. He makes a few advances to them in the way of Booddhism, but gives no list of catechumens, though flowers would seem to be the natural followers of that prophet.

In truth, Mr. Thoreau himself might absorb the forces of the entire alphabetic sanctity of the A. B. C. F. M., persisting as he does in a fine, intelligent paganism. We need no more go to the underworld to converse with shadows of old philosophers. Here we have the Academy brought to our doors, and our modern world criticized from beneath the shelter of the Portico. Were we writing commendatory verses after the old style, to be prefixed to this volume, we should begin somewhat thus:—

If the ancient, mystique, antifabian
As (so he claimed) of them that Troy
    town wan
Before he was born; even so his soul we
    see

(Time's ocean underpast) revive in thee,
As, diving nigh to Elis, Arethuse
Comes up to loose her zone by Syracuse.

The great charm of Mr. Thoreau's book seems to be, that its being a book at all is a happy fortuity. The door of the portfolio-cage has been left open, and the thoughts have flown out of themselves. The paper and types are only accidents. The page is confidential like a diary. Pepys is not more minute, more pleasantly unconscious. It is like a book dug up, that has no date to assign it a special contemporaneousness, and no name of author. It has been written with no uncomfortable sense of a public looking over the shoulder. And the author is the least ingredient in it, too. All which I saw and part of which I was, would be an apt motto for the better portions of the volume: a part, moreover, just as the river, the trees, and the fishes are. Generally he holds a very smooth mirror up to nature, and if, now and then, he shows us his own features in the glass, when he had rather look at something else, it is a piece of nature, and we must forgive him if he allow it a too usurping position in the landscape. He looks at the country sometimes (as painters advise) through the triumphal arch of his own legs, and, though the upside-downness of the prospect has its own charm of unassuetude, the arch itself is not the most graceful.

So far of the manner of the book, now of the book itself. It professes to be the journal of a week on Concord and Merrimack Rivers. We must have our libraries enlarged, if Mr. Thoreau intend to complete his autobiography on this scale—four hundred and thirteen pages to a sennight! He begins honestly enough as the Boswell of Musketaquid and Merrimack. It as a fine subject and a new one. We are curious to know somewhat of the private and interior life of two such prominent and oldest inhabitants. Musketaquid saw the tremulous match half-doubtingly touched to the revolutionary train. The blood of Captain Lincoln and his drummer must have dribbled through the loose planks of the bridge for Musketaquid to carry down to Merrimack, that he in turn might mingle it with the sea. Merrimack is a drudge now, grinding for the Philistines, who takes repeated dammings without resentment, and walks in no procession for higher wages. But its waters remember the Redman, and before the Redman. They knew the first mammoth as a calf, and him a mere *parvenu* and modern. Even to the saurians they could say—we remember your grandfather.

Much information and entertainment were to be pumped into of individuals like these, and the pump does not *suck* in Mr. Thoreau's hands. As long as he continued an honest Boswell, his book is delightful, but sometimes he serves his two rivers as Hazlitt did Northcote, and makes them run Thoreau or Emerson, or, indeed, anything but their own transparent element. What, for instance, have Concord and Merrimack to do with Boodh, themselves professors of an elder and to them wholly sufficient religion, namely, the willing subjects of watery laws, to seek their ocean? We have digressions on Boodh, on Anacreon, (with translations hardly so good as Cowley,) on Persius, on Friendship, and we know not what. We come upon them like snags, jolting us headforemost out of our places as we are rowing placidly up stream or drifting down. Mr. Thoreau becomes so absorbed in these discussions, that he seems, as it were, to *catch a crab*, and disappears uncomfortably from his seat at the bow-oar. We could forgive them all, especially that on Books, and that on Friendship, (which is worthy of one who has so long commerced with Nature and with Emerson,) we could welcome them all, were

they put by themselves at the end of the book. But as it is, they are out of proportion and out of place, and mar our Merrimacking dreadfully. We were bid to a river-party, not to be preached at. They thrust themselves obtrusively out of the narrative, like those quarries of red glass which the Bowery dandies (emulous of Sisyphus) push laboriously before them as breastpins.

Before we get through the book, we begin to feel as if the author had used the term week, as the Jews did the number *forty*, for an indefinite measure of time. It is quite evident that we have something more than a transcript of his fluviatile experiences. The leaves of his portfolio and river-journal seem to have been shuffled together with a trustful dependence on some overruling printer-providence. We trace the lines of successive deposits as plainly as on the sides of a deep cut, or rather on those of a trench carried through made-land in the city, where choiceness of material has been of less import than suitableness to fill up, and where plaster and broken bricks from old buildings, oyster-shells, and dock mud have been shot pellmell together. Yet we must allow that Mr. Thoreau's materials are precious, too. His plaster has bits of ancient symbols painted on it, his bricks are stamped with mystic sentences, his shells are of pearl-oysters and mud from the Sacramento.

"Give me a sentence," prays Mr. Thoreau bravely, "which no intelligence can understand!"—and we think that the kind gods have nodded. There are some of his utterances which have foiled us, and we belong to that class of beings which he thus reproachfully stigmatizes as intelligences. We think it must be this taste that makes him so fond of the Hindoo philosophy, which would seem admirably suited to men, if men were only oysters. Or is it merely because, as he naïvely confesses in another place, "his soul is of a bright invisible *green*"? We would recommend to Mr. Thoreau some of the Welsh sacred poetry. Many of the Triads hold an infinite deal of nothing, especially after the bottoms have been knocked out of them by translation. But it seems ungrateful to find fault with a book which has given us so much pleasure. We have eaten salt (Attic, too,) with Mr. Thoreau. It is the hospitality and not the fare which carries a benedicto with it, and it is a sort of ill breeding to report any oddity in the viands. His feast is here and there a little savage, (indeed, he professes himself a kind of volunteer Redman,) and we must make out with the fruits, merely giving a sidelong glance at the baked dog and pickled missionary, and leaving them in grateful silence.

We wish the General Court had been wise enough to have appointed our author to make the report on the Ichthyology of Massachusetts. Then, indeed, would the people of the state have known something of their aquicolal fellow-citizens. Mr. Thoreau handles them as if he loved them, as old Izaak recommends us to do with a worm in impaling it. He is the very Asmodeus of their private life. He unroofs their dwellings and makes us familiar with their loves and sorrows. He seems to suffer a sea-change, like the Scotch peasant who was carried down among the seals in the capacity of family physician. He balances himself with them under the domestic lily-pad, takes a family-bite with them, is made the confidant of their courtships, and is an honored guest at the wedding-feast. He has doubtless seen a pickerel crossed in love, a perch Othello, a bream the victim of an unappreciated idiosyncrasy, or a minnow with a mission. He goes far to convince us of what we have before suspected, that fishes are the highest of organizations. The natives of that more solid atmosphere, they are not sub-

ject to wind or rain, they have been guilty of no Promethean rape, they have bitten no apple. They build no fences, holding their watery inheritance undivided. Beyond all other living things they mind their own business. They have not degenerated to the necessity of reform, swallowing no social pills, but living quietly on each other in a true primitive community. They are vexed with no theories of the currency which go deeper than the Newfoundland Banks. *Nimium fortunati*! We wish Mr. Thoreau would undertake a report upon them as a private enterprise. It would be the most delightful book of natural history extant.

Mr. Thoreau's volume is the more pleasant that with all its fresh smell of the woods, it is yet the work of a bookish man. We not only hear the laugh of the flicker, and the watchman's rattle of the red squirrel, but the voices of poets and philosophers, old and new. There is no more reason why an author should reflect trees and mountains than books, which, if they are in any sense real, are as good parts of nature as any other kind of growth. We confess that there is a certain charm for us even about a fool who has read myriads of books. There is an indefinable atmosphere around him, as of distant lands around a great traveller, and of distant years around very old men. But we think that Mr. Thoreau sometimes makes a bad use of his books. Better things can be got out of Herbert and Vaughan and Donne than the art of making bad verses. There is no harm in good writing, nor do wisdom and philosophy prefer crambo. Mr. Thoreau never learned bad rhyming of the river and the sky. He is the more culpable as he has shown that he can write poetry at once melodious and distinct, with rare delicacy of thought and feeling.

["Wednesday," 241.5–20]

358

If Mr. Emerson choose to leave some hard nuts for posterity to crack, he can perhaps afford it as well as any. We counsel Mr. Thoreau, in his own words, to take his hat and come out of that. If he prefer to put peas in his shoes when he makes private poetical excursions, it is nobody's affair. But if the public are to go along with him, they will find some way to boil theirs.

We think that Mr. Thoreau, like most solitary men, exaggerates the importance of his own thoughts. The "I" occasionally stretches up tall as Pompey's pillar over a somewhat flat and sandy expanse. But this has its counterbalancing advantage, that it leads him to secure many a fancy and feeling which would flit by most men unnoticed. The little confidences of nature which pass his neighbours as the news slip through the grasp of birds perched upon the telegraphic wires, he received as they were personal messages from a mistress. Yet the book is not solely excellent as a Talbotype of natural scenery. It abounds in fine thoughts, and there is many a critical *obiter dictum* which is good law, as what he says of Raleigh's style.

["Sunday," 104.7–16]

Since we have found fault with some of what we may be allowed to call the worsification, we should say that the prose work is done conscientiously and neatly. The style is compact and the language has an antique purity like wine grown colorless with age. There are passages of a genial humor interspersed at fit intervals, and we close our article with one of them by way of grace. It is a sketch which would have delighted Lamb.

["Saturday," 24.11–25.9]

[Sophia Dobson Collet], "Literature of American Individuality," *People's Journal*, 7 (April 1850), 121–5

Sincere autobiographies are always interesting, especially when they are rich in experiences that are important to many. But there is a species of literature which may be regarded as the flower of autobiography, in which the author takes some passage of his life or studies as a text, and illustrates it with all the varied life-lore that is suggested by the incidents; breathing to the ear of his fellows, not a circumstantial narrative of his every deed, but the essence of wisdom which they bequeathed in departing. While maintaining a quiet reserve upon his own inward conflicts, the author may here give free utterance to all the deep spiritual beauty which these have developed in him, and thereby communicate to those of kindred experience, all the chiefest realities of his life, without the aid of a picture alphabet.

Of this Literature of Individuality, New England has recently produced several remarkable specimens. Besides the writings of Emerson, so widely known as the very Prophet of Individuality, there are the musical and literary criticisms of John S. Dwight, which appeared in the *Dial*, the *Harbinger*, &c., but whose unusual merit ought to procure, for the chief of them, a separate re-publication; the 'Letters from New York' of Mrs. Child, the Poems and the 'Conversations on the Old Poets' of J. R. Lowell, and the 'Woman in the Nineteenth Century,' and 'Summer on the Lakes,' of Margaret Fuller. These writers belong to the Literature of

Individuality in a double sense. Not only do they reveal to us some of the highest secrets of individual being, but they vindicate the rights of individual being; they elevate the idea of Individuality from the rank of a sentiment or a whim to the dignity of a principle. Perhaps it is incumbent on us to explain *what* principle: the definition may be thus attempted. All human problems can only be tried by human consciousness and human experience; and the heights or depths to which these may extend, can only be known to each human being through his own individual capabilities of entering into them. He need not necessarily deny the truth of others' beliefs because they are not also his; but he considers that from his own beliefs alone is he bound to act. He brings to the light of an intelligent conscience and a conscientious intelligence, all the problems of life, Infallible Authority among the rest, and while he thankfully accepts the testimonies of others' minds and distant ages as invaluable aids, he does not allow any of them to usurp the sovereignty of his own spirit. That, he regards as a trust too sacred to be parted with to any one, even the most revered, living or dead.

We do not, of course, mean to assert that any one fulfils this ideal unfailingly. Any attempt at fulfilling it at all could only be made by men and women of unusual moral vigour. It will, therefore, not appear surprising that several shortcomings are noticeable in our above-named authors. Mr. Dwight, for instance, occasionally bends too low in his admiration of Fourier, in whom he tolerates defects which his otherwise pure moral taste would probably lead him to censure if he found them elsewhere. But his contributions to the Literature of Individuality are very valuable, especially his unfoldings of the grand ethical and social truths which speak to the inmost heart of the reformer in the sounds of true Music, particularly in that of Beethoven. Mrs. Child bears witness to spiritual and moral beauty, both in nature's free grandeur and amid humanity's downtrodden frailties, in a spirit of elastic hopefulness which will take no refusal from fate, when the demand is just. J. R. Lowell's Poems and 'Conversations' contain inspired glances into the Eleusinia of Art, and exquisite revealings of spiritual beauty, combined with a good, healthy, earnest interest in the politics of the day as *our* portion of the lessons of the ages. Miss Fuller has written much, but perhaps her best work is her 'Woman in the Nineteenth Century,' which is one of the most valuable revelations ever made of the Individuality of Woman. She takes the highest ground at once, and thus avoids much unnecessary trouble. She considers the *rights* of woman as simply co-ordinate with the *mights* of woman, and wishes these mights to be tested by experience. Her book lacks systematic order, and is, therefore, less useful as a manual of reference than it might have been; but it is invaluable as one of the most remarkable 'among the throng of symptoms which denote the present tendency to a crisis in the life of woman, which resembles the change from girlhood, with its beautiful instincts but unharmonised thoughts, its blind pupilage and restless seeking, to self-possessed, wise, and graceful womanhood.' It may be added that all these writers belong to different schools of thought and action; but they are all similar in one respect—that while they discard, more or less, the usual formulas of belief and society, there do not revere the less, but rather the more, all that is worthy of reverence. Their estimation of the revelations of the past is a grateful one; but their faith in the revelations of the present is no less earnest. And this strong, vital faith in the Present, united with unusual power of thought and integrity of character, gives their writings a deep charm for all those who would study the problems of to-day in their deepest significance and freest aspect.

Among this class of individuals (if the paradox may be employed), a high rank is due to the author of the works placed at the head of this article. Readers of Emerson's quondam Quarterly, the *Dial*, will recognise in Mr. Thoreau the H. D. T. who contributed so many valuable articles to that periodical, and who is introduced by Emerson (in No. 9) as 'a near neighbour and friend of ours, dear also to the Muses—a native and an inhabitant of the town of Concord.' The 'Week on the Concord and Merrimack Rivers,' is the record of an excursion made by Mr. Thoreau and his brother in 1839. The writer describes the scenery of his voyage with the vividness of a painter, and the scrutiny of a naturalist. He seems quite at home among birds, beasts, fishes, and plants, whose forms and movements he follows with the eye of a friend; and he possesses the art of conveying the peculiar spirit of a landscape, which he frequently does with much grace and power—an art which a mere observer of details often lacks. But Mr. Thoreau has a gift beyond this. Every object seen is, with him, an element in a higher vision. The infinity of meaning that dwells in everything existent, is visible to him. In the forest he beholds 'the uprightness of the pines and maples asserting the ancient rectitude and vigour of nature' (p. 177). The clear morning atmosphere, beautifying the landscape, suggests to him the inquiry, 'Why should not our whole life and its scenery be thus fair and distinct?' (p. 50.) And these thoughts fall from him not as moral lessons, tacked on, fringe-like, but as the natural hints which ever arise in those souls to whom nothing is profane, but to whom the whole universe perpetually chants sublime utterances of the divinest

ethics. To such souls, Life and Thought continually inter-act. Their thoughts are ever giving birth to free deeds, and their deeds are ever receiving impulse and sustainment from matured thought. To them, joy and sorrow, life and death, are equally welcome and sacred: they are, in truth, our 'representative men,' the elect of human kind.

An additional element of interest, in this work, is afforded by the occasional digressions, which are, in fact, essays, not unworthy to stand beside those of Emerson himself. Those on Eastern Literature, on Christianity, on Poetry, and especially the exquisite Essay on Friendship, would of themselves make the book valuable. Among these essays, and also among the poems scattered profusely through the volume, will be found some reprints from Mr. Thoreau's writings in the *Dial*.

It should be mentioned that our author's ideas on theology are ultra-heretical. The essay on Christianity is an expression of the freest Pantheism. It is very original, sacrastic, pathetic, and reverential. If any one marvel how these qualities may be combined, let him read the essay. Mr. Thoreau's language on this and other topics is sometimes rather random, a defect unworthy of one who usually displays such keen justness of thought. This random manner is especially visible in some expressions which show our author to be tinged with that contempt of politics which Emerson describes, in his Lectures on the Times, as characterising the Transcendentalists. These persons forget that if honest men will persist in abandoning political action to knaves and fools, they may not be held wholly guiltless of the bravery and folly perpetrated in consequence. Philosophers and artists, *may*, doubtless, be worthily occupied to a degree which precludes them from political action; but it is not therefore necessary that they should despise such action.

Indifference to that which so largely influences the fates of so many of our fellow-beings, always bears a tinge of selfishness. We are, therefore especially, pleased to see Mr. Thoreau's Lecture on 'Resistance to Civil Government,' delivered in 1847, and published in Miss Peabody's interesting volume of 'Æsthetic Papers.' The manly tone of this lecture rings on the ear. As it is not likely to be much known in England, we give the following extracts, premising that it ought to be read as a whole to be thoroughly appreciated.

["Resistance to Civil Government,"
67.3–31, 71.9–18, 74.32–75.24,
76.4–77.9]

It should be added that Mr. Thoreau carries out his own principle in action. He says he 'has paid no poll-tax for six years;' and he gives a graceful and genial account (appended to the lecture) of the imprisonment which once followed his non-payment.

Now let us follow our hero to his home, and dismiss him in the calm light of a Concord sunset.

["Friday," 389.32–391.4]

[Lydia Maria Child?], Review of *A Week on the Concord* and *Merrimack Rivers* and *Walden, National Anti-slavery Standard,* 16 December 1854, p. 3

These books spring from a depth of thought which will not suffer them to be put by, and are written in a spirit in striking contrast with that which is uppermost in our time and country. Out of the heart of practical, hard-working, progressive New England comes these Oriental utterances. The life exhibited in them teaches us, much more impressively than any number of sermons could, that this Western activity of which we are so proud, these material improvements, this commercial enterprise, this rapid accumulation of wealth, even our external associated philanthropic action, are very easily overrated. The true glory of the human soul is not to be reached by the most rapid travelling in car or steamboat, by the instant transmission of intelligence however far, by the most speedy accumulation of a fortune, and however efficient measures we may adopt for the reform of the intemperate, the emancipation of the enslaved, &c., it will avail little unless we are ourselves essentially noble enough to inspire those whom we would so benefit with nobleness. External bondage is trifling compared with the bondage of an ignoble soul. Such things are often said, doubtless, in pulpits and elsewhere, but the men who say them are too apt to live just with the crowd, and so their words come more and more to ring with a hollow sound.

It is refreshing to find in these books the sentiments of one man whose aim manifestly is to *live* and not to waste his time upon the externals of living. Educated · at Cambridge, in the way called liberal, he seems determined to make a liberal life of it, and not to become the slave of any calling, for the sake of earning a reputable livelihood or of being regarded as a useful member of society. He evidently considers it his first business to become more and more a living, advancing soul, knowing that thus alone (though he desires to think as little as possible about that) can he be, in any proper sense, useful to others. Mr. Thoreau's view of life has been called selfish. His own words, under the head of "Philanthropy" in Walden, are the amplest defence against this charge, to those who can appreciate them. In a deeper sense than we commonly think, charity begins at home. The man who, with any fidelity, obeys his own genius, serves men infinitely more by so doing, becoming an encouragement, a strengthener, a fountain of inspiration to them, than if he were to turn aside from his path and exhaust his energies in striving to meet their superficial needs. As a thing by the way, aside from our proper work, we may seek to remove external obstacles from the path of our neighbours, but no man can help them much who makes that his main business, instead of seeking evermore, with all his energies, to reach the loftiest point which his imagination sets before him, thus adding to the stock of true nobleness in the world.

But suppose all men should pursue Mr. Thoreau's course, it is asked triumphantly, as though, then, we should be sure to go back to barbarism. Let it be considered, in the first place, that no man could pursue his course who was a mere superficial imitator, any more than it would be a real imitation of Christ if all men were to make it their main business to go about preaching the Gospel to each other. Is it progress toward barbarism to simplify one's outward life for the sake of coming closer to Nature and London the realm of ideas? Is it civilization and refinement to be occupied evermore with adding to our material conveniences, comforts and luxuries, to make ourselves nor so much living members as dead tools of society, in some bank, shop, office, pulpit or kitchen? If men were to follow in Mr. Thoreau's steps, by being more obedient to their loftiest instincts, there would, indeed, be a falling off in the splendour of our houses, in the richness of our furniture and dress, in the luxury of our tables, but how poor are these things in comparison with the new grandeur and beauty which would appear in the souls of men. What fresh and inspiring conversation should we have, instead of the wearisome gossip which now meets us at every turn. Men toil on, wearing out body or soul, or both, that they may accumulate a needless amount of the externals of living; that they may win the regard of those no wiser than themselves; their natures become warped and hardened to their pursuits; they get fainter and fainter glimpses of the glory of the world, and, by and by, comes into their richly-adorned parlours some wise and beautiful soul, like the writer of these books, who, speaking from the fullness of his inward life, makes their luxuries appear vulgar, showing that, in a direct way, he has obtained the essence of that which his entertainers have been vainly seeking for at such a terrible expense.

It seems remarkable, that these books have received no more adequate notice in our Literary Journals. But the class of scholars are often as blind as others to any new elevation of soul. In Putnam's Magazine, Mr. Thoreau is spoken of as an oddity, as the Yankee Diogenes, as though the really ridiculous oddity were not in us of the "starched shirt-collar" rather than in this devotee of Nature and Thought. Some have praised the originality and profound sympathy with which he views natural objects. We might as well stop with praising Jesus for the happy use he has made of the lilies of the field. The fact of surpassing interest for us is the simple grandeur of Mr. Thoreau's position—a position open to us all, and of which this sympathy with Nature is but a single result. This is seen in the less descriptive, more purely thoughtful passages, such as that upon Friendship in the "Wednesday" of the "Week," and in those upon "Solitude," "What I lived for," and "Higher Laws," in "Walden," as well as in many others in both books. We do not believe that, in the whole course of literature, ancient and modern, so noble a discourse upon Friendship can be produced as that which Mr. Thoreau has given us. It points to a relation, to be sure, which, from the ordinary level of our lives, may seem remote and dreamy. But it is our thirst for, and glimpses of, such things which indicate the greatness of our nature, which give the purest charm and colouring to our lives. The striking peculiarity of Mr. Thoreau's attitude is, that while he is no religionist, and while he is eminently practical in regard to the material economies of life, he yet manifestly feels, through and through, that the loftiest dreams of the imagination are the solidest realities, and so the only foundation for us to build upon, while the affairs in which men are everywhere busying themselves so intensely are comparatively the merest froth and foam.

"Another Book by Thoreau," [Oneida Community] *Circular*, 25 April 1864

There is much about Thoreau that we like. When he speaks from his own experience and observation, there is a great deal that is fresh and original about his utterances. His eye is keen for what is beautiful and true in nature, and a quaint, subtile humor seems irrepressible in him. He has, moreover, a certain appreciation of the interior and spiritual in man. He has looked into the soul and seen depths there, though not the deepest depths. He has found the inner shores of his life, and in the light of early dawn has wandered there, and found many a gem among the golden sands, and gathered many a flower from the verdurous declivities. Yet, apparently, he never saw the clear sun rise there; his inner day was cloudy. He says truly, "Day would not dawn if it were not for the inward morning." Yet we feel that there is a full sunlight from the eternal world in which he has not bathed. The best thing that can be said about him is, perhaps, that he turns the attention in a fresh genial and original way to nature, and that he recognizes honestly the soul and the spiritual side of man.

There are however, some serious drawbacks to Thoreau. We cannot sympathize with his glorification of Hindoo philosophy; we cannot agree with his estimate of Christ. We would not quarrel with his objections to much of the common and popular theology. Only we think that the largest, truest, most liberal spirit, rising above the superstition of the past, or the superficiality of the present, will find in Christ, and the Spirit which wrote the

Bible, that knowledge of God and of the highest life, which Brahmin or Buddhist never knew. The purest and most truly catholic life; the wisest, most progressive spirit of science; the richest, and profoundest views of nature, have flowed into the world through channels that were opened far back in the Hebrew race. We believe that Abraham, the Friend of God, the father of the faithful, was the father of the world's best civilization of to-day. We know that, so far as our own experience is concerned, the New Testament has been our guide to more radical thought, to more complete freedom of life, than any other book. Yet we are no Bible-worshiper. We accept and value it as the text-book of the Spirit of truth—not designed to supersede the present and direct teaching and inspiration of that Spirit, but to lead us to such teaching and inspiration, and to the reception of new truth which the Bible does not utter. It seems to us unfortunate that any mind, glowing with enthusiasm for truth and nature, in freeing itself from the shackles of custom and religious and spiritual conventionalism, should lose its appreciation of the Bible. We do not apologize for such, for we think there is some profound heart-earnestness wanting in them, or they would not reject so noble a guide because the foolishness or bigotry of unwise friends has surrounded it with so much that is repulsive. To justly understand and appreciate the Bible, and reach its pure elements of power and wisdom, one must *rise above,* not merely reject, the Bibliolatry and false theology of the past.

In "Walden" there is comparatively little to offend a just and enlightened reverence. In "A Week on the Concord and Merrimack," written some years before, there are some pages about Christ and the New Testament which only a novice in the study of them would have produced. But neither Christ nor the New Testament need a defender or lawyers, any more than the granite of our New England hills. There they are, imbedded in the world's history. Any one who will, can sink a shaft down through the strata of the past eighteen hundred years, and touch and know their component elements. No one, we are persuaded, will estimate them irreverently who has thus explored and known them. We will not mis-estimate their power and influence today, by supposing that the failure of this or that man to understand and appreciate them, will hinder for a moment their triumphant advance to the conquest of the world. When so thoughtful and clear-eyed a man as Thoreau, misses a just conception of Christ, we feel how great is his loss, not how much will be the truth's loss; and we trust that in other years he found truer insight, or that the future will bring a better knowledge. When he exalts the Hindoo Vedas, we have no quarrel with him.—Many wise and moral precepts may there be recorded; yet the life that moves the world to-day and is conducting mankind to its final resurrection birth, does not flow from beyond the Euphrates. The Bhagvat-Geeta, and the Laws of Menu may be wonderful books, but we know that Christ has the words of eternal life; we know that Peter and John and Paul have touched the heart of the universe.

With all Thoreau's admiration of Hindoo philosophy, it does not fit harmoniously his New England nature, and we fancy he must have outgrown much of it. When he escapes from it and turns to his own woods, and streams, and sky, he becomes original and suggestive. That old-world philosophy does not suit the new, western nature. Europe and America, with their spirit of science, must overflow upon the east, and judge its spirit, its institutions, its darkness and idolatry. To acknowledge the supremacy of the wisdom of the old stagnant cast, is to turn from all that is progressive and regenerating in the present. There may be much there that is fascinating, but it is rather the fascination of asceticism and death, than of life and joyous conquest of matter. The *heavens* are our true Orient. Fresh inspiration from the external world, is our privilege to-day. The Spirit that led Abraham out from the borders of his fatherland, which spake through prophet and patriarch words which still vibrate with the magnetism of truth, which through Christ and the apostles opened the way to the throne of life, is ready to flow into men to-day and conduct them to the new birth. No day has surpassed our day. Never was the demand for sincerity more urgent. Never was there a better chance for obedience and an inspired life.

In "A Week on the Concord and Merrimack," there is much that one can profitably read. Like all the books of the day it should be read with discrimination, not accepted as a teacher. There are gems of original poetry in it, paragraphs of suggestive thought; together with pages that are hardly relieved from tediousness. It is not so original and clear as "Walden." It purports to be a record of the observations and reflections of the author while on a boat voyage, in company with his brother, on the Concord and Merrimack rivers. Here are a few extracts:

[Omitted is a long quotation from *A Week on the Concord and Merrimack Rivers* not in the source for this present reprinting: Geoffrey Noyes's "Thoreau at the Oneida Community," *Thoreau Society Bulletin*, 115 (Spring 1971), 4–5.]

"A Week on the Concord," *Saturday Review*, 68 (17 August 1889), 195–6

Those who like to record times and seasons may amuse themselves now, if they will, by keeping the jubilee of an elegant, but unexciting adventure, the voyage of John and Henry Thoreau on the Concord and Merrimac Rivers. There must be a distinct literary vitality about the style of a book which has kept alive for half a century the memory of a summer week spent by two New England brothers in a fisherman's dory on some local streams. The self-consciousness of Henry Thoreau was strenuous and effectual. When he weighed anchor in the port of Concord in August 1839 he set forth with an expressed intent of helping to immortalize the holy ground of the transcendentalists. He opens his little volume with a challenge to Xanthus and Seamander, and in some sort the proud boast has been justified. In 1834 Emerson had become a citizen of Concord, a little village-town scattered among secular elms, which was henceforth destined to form a centre of New England intelligence. When the Thoreaus made their voyage in 1839 the Delphi of Massachusetts was still but faintly illustrious intellectually, although it preserved a proud recollection of "the embattled farmers" and how their first fatal volley was "heard round the world." But between the fact of the voyage and the record—for Thoreau's book did not appear until 1849—much occurred to bring the name of Concord before the world of letters and to flatter the vanity or excite the parochial patriotism of the recluse of

Walden. By the later date Emerson had come before the world as a poet and as an essayist; the Brook Farm experiment at Roxbury had sprung from the recesses of Concord, and had been withdrawn into its bosom; Hawthorne had arrived in 1842, and had settled in that ancient Manse from which he was to pull so many picturesque *Mosses*. The very boat, if we mistake not, in which the voyage was made had been, by 1849, transferred by Thoreau to Hawthorne's possession. The voyager is ever conscious, as he records his adventures, of the classic nature of the spots around him, and in his queer verse he celebrates the New Reformers together with the bitterns and the pickerels:—

["Saturday," 19.14–25]

This mixture of the student and the wild Indian, of the lamp and the morning star, this perpetual confusion between nature in its unconsciousness and Yankee transcendentalism in its conscious pomp, gives a peculiar flavour to all the writing of Henry Thoreau, but perhaps to no book so strongly as to *A Week on the Concord and Merrimac Rivers*.

It is strange that Thoreau, with his love for the native names of streams and places, should have accepted the conventional form of Concord River, instead of the Indian one which Emerson and Hawthorne use, Musketaquid. Unless we recognize that these two are the names of the same stream, we lose the pleasure of comparing Thoreau's prose with Emerson's verse. It is to the Musketaquid, and therefore to the Concord River, that the latter has addressed one of the finest of his lyrics, that which opens

Thy summer voice, Musketaquid,
Repeats the music of the rain;

and the exceptionally graceful study in blank verse in which the poet attributes

the favour of the wood-gods to his own modesty in being contented with the "low, open meads" which surround this slender and sluggish stream. This famous river, the Concord or Musketaquid, after entering the town of the Philosophers, receives the tributary waters of the Assabeth, and then flows down until it empties itself into the Merrimac at Lowell. The Musketaquid is sacred to Emerson; the Merrimac is Thoreau's by right of conquest; while the Assabeth, which Thoreau passes without a single word of appreciation, was specially favoured by the shy and recluse genius of Hawthorne. Those who have the *Week* before them may turn aside from it for a moment to hear Hawthorne's description of the voyages which he and Thoreau were wont to make over the confluent waters:—

Strange and happy times were those, when we cast aside all irksome forms and strait-laced habitudes, and delivered ourselves up to the free air, to live like the Indians or any less conventional race, during one bright semicircle of the sun. Rowing our boat against the current, between wide meadows, we turned aside into the Assabeth. A more lovely stream than this, for a mile above its junction with the Concord, has never flowed on earth—nowhere, indeed, except to lave the interior regions of a poet's imagination. It comes flowing softly through the midmost privacy and deepest heart of a wood which whispers to it to be quiet; while the stream whispers back again from its sedgy borders, as if river and wood were hushing one another to sleep. Yes; the river sleeps along its course, and dreams of the sky and the clustering foliage.

367

In none of his later volumes did Henry Thoreau express his peculiar philosophy with so much geniality and so little straining after exaggerated effect as in the *Week*. He was a closer observer later on, perhaps; he was certainly a quainter forger of *concetti*, but never more himself than here. The traveller by the railway from Boston to Concord, to whom is pointed out on his right-hand side the very tame and mild pond which is Walden, is apt to think that Thoreau, after all, knew but little of the wilder parts of nature. But his acquaintance with his native country was really extensive, and was formed before he had fallen under the influence of Emerson, had learned to commune with the Over-soul, or had lapsed into literature. On the present voyage, when he reached the Merrimac, it was not to greet it as a stranger. He was familiar with all the windings of its romantic waters. He had patiently traced it from its source in the White Mountains "to where it is lost amid the salt billow of the ocean on Plum Island beach." He had been a real nomad of the mountains before Emerson tamed him; he was personally friendly with those Titanic monsters of the back of New Hampshire, Agiochook and Contochook and the rest, of whose acquaintance Emerson rather ineffectually and unreally boasted in early and most indifferent odes and canticles. This is perhaps the reason why the Indian names, which sound pathetically exotic on the lips of Hawthorne, and downright barbarous on those of Emerson, seem genuine and inevitable when Thoreau uses them. Rivers are as pleasant company to meet Thoreau in as ever we find. His fault is to be stationary, to keep us poring over some little natural object long after we have extracted the mental nourishment from it. "A day passed in the society of the Greek sages who are described in the *Banquet* of Xenophon would not," he says in one of his most characteristic utterances, "be comparable with the dry wit of decayed cranberry-vines and the fresh Attic salt of moss-beds." But this is quite a matter of opinion, and there are those who love moss-beds and cranberry-vines and who yet cannot patiently endure a whole day on their knees in front of them. For such readers it is a great consolation to get Thoreau on board his boat. The inevitable current carries him along. Talk as he will, the burdock passes, the yarrow is left behind, and we come in the process of time to fresh promontories with juniper on them and no longer catnip.

It cannot be said that Thoreau travels very fast, even when the Concord or the Merrimac is hurrying him along. He clings to the shore, he is the victim of every variety of eddy, he slips into backwaters and hums there, like a lost fragment of timber, for hours on hours. Take Friday, for instance, in this adventurous chronicle. We start fairly well, though in a fog; but we are soon caught in the Corybantes and "the whole paraphernalia of the Panathenæa." Here we hang for two or three pages, and when at last we start again we are caught almost instantly in a disquisition on genius and inspiration. Five pages are dedicated to a criticism of Ossian, and we are losing all hope, when suddenly "we sail fleetly before the wind, with the river gurgling under our stern, and glide past the mouth of the Nashua." We pause to indite a lyric to "Salmon Brook, Panichook," and so this delightful Friday wears itself out. Why should we proceed any faster? We are not travelling any whither. We have no duties, no engagements. Why not listen patiently to this pleasant and fantastic garrulity? Certainly it is agreeable to do so, but, nevertheless, we are glad to be on board, to have the moving water under us, for Thoreau's intellectual self-absorption is apt to resemble, in its wearying capacity, the faculty of a bore. This is a hard saying to the Thoreau fanatics, of whom we have a few among us. But it does not preclude the admission that the work of this writer is often enjoyable, and still more often valuable. We must not take Thoreau too seriously. We must not forget Dr. Holmes's really splendid definition of him as "the nullifier of civilization, who insisted on nibbling his asparagus at the wrong end." But we who know how to handle our asparagus may nevertheless take an acute intellectual pleasure in this curious Rousseau of Massachusetts, who had certainly mastered the art of favourably interesting those who can never agree with him.

The present reprint belongs to a series in which *Walden* has already appeared. A few years ago, in order to study Thoreau, it was necessary to procure from America editions, and in some cases even the original issues, of his works. While we do not think that he can ever, or should ever, be very widely read, we are glad that the most characteristic of his publications should be freely circulated. His books, and in particular the book now before us, started a kind of new thing in literature, much less simple and unaffected than Gilbert White or Gilpin, more fantastic than Cobbett, who, moreover, was as sociable as Thoreau was solitary, full of oddity and mistiness, but, at all events in their early manifestations, neither cynical nor empty. Thoreau was a true lover of books as well as of woodchucks. His knowledge of literature was perhaps more curious than profound, and he emulated Emerson a little over-boldly in his Oriental illustrations. But he could write English prose, although he could not manage good verse, and in the former section of literary labour he has accomplished some of the most satisfactory work of his time. Setting aside his great friends Hawthorne and Emerson, who was there in America in 1839 capable of the Praise of Friendship in the Wednesday chapter of *A Week on the Concord and Merrimac Rivers*? Perhaps not one, certainly none of the Ripleys and Alcotts and Channings who passed for prose writers at that dim and distant epoch.

Checklist of Additional Reviews

Boston *Semi-weekly Journal*, 1 June 1849, p. 1.

New York *Evening Post*, 8 June 1849, p. 2.

[William Ellery Channing?], "A Week on the Concord and Merrimack Rivers," New Bedford *Mercury*, 20 June 1849, p. 2.

[Charles Frederick Briggs], "Deferred Books," *Holden's Dollar Magazine*, 4 (July 1849), 448.

Pictorial National Library, 3 (July 1849), 60–1.

Knickerbocker, 34 (August 1849), 177.

[Sarah Josepha Hale], *Godey's Lady's Book and Magazine*, 39 (September 1849), 223.

Westminster Review [England], 52 (January 1850), 309–10.

Edwin Morton, "Thoreau and His Books," *Harvard Magazine*, 1 (January 1855), 87–99.

[Samuel Storrow Higginson], "Henry David Thoreau," *Harvard Magazine*, 8 (May 1862), 313–18.

Universalist Quarterly, 22 (October 1865), 530–1.

[Franklin Benjamin Sanborn], Boston *Commonwealth*, 21 December 1867, p. 16.

Walden

"A Massachusetts Philosopher,"
[Oneida Community]
Circular,
1 August 1854,
pp. 410–11

A very curious book is in press, entitled 'Life in the Woods,' by H. D. Thoreau; from which the *Tribune* prints a few extracts in advance. It is a narrative of the author's experience and mode of life during a two years' solitary hermitage in the woods, by the shore of Walden Pond, in Concord, Mass. The writer, being of a philosophical turn, and much given to Homer, and similar antique models, seems to have proposed to himself to reduce his mode of life to the standard nearest to primitive nature. So he took an axe, and went into the woods, to a pleasant hillside overlooking the pond, and built himself a cabin. Of his furniture, and his views on the subject of furniture in general, he gives the following account:

["Economy," 65.14–67.10]

There is an evident spice of truth in this. We like *Communism* particularly for its effect in relieving folks from the great mass of furniture—useless *exuviæ* as Thoreau says,—that accumulates about them and seems necessary, in isolation. The Communist moves freely without being tied to any such trap. He goes from one home to another, without care for what he leaves or carrying anything with him and finds all needed furnishing in the Commune where he sits down. This is better we think than our hermit's method of getting rid of incumbrance. Here follows his agricultural experience:

["Economy," 54.16–56.13]

Bating the solitude, we think Thoreau's plan of agriculture is worth consideration. There is a simplicity and independence about it, that is rather fascinating, and if practicable in single solitude it would be certainly no less so in Association. In fact our method at Oneida and the other agricultural Associations in confining ourselves mostly to thorough garden-tillage, is substantially carrying things out to a similar result.

371

Review of *Walden*, Boston *Daily Bee*, 9 August 1854, p. 2

An original book, this, and from an original man—from a very eccentric man. It is a record of the author's life and thoughts while he lived in the woods—two years and two months. It is a volume of interest and value—of interest because it concerns a very rare individual, and of value because it contains considerable wisdom, after a fashion. It is a volume to read once, twice, thrice—and then think over.— There is a charm in its style, a philosophy in its thought. Mr. Moreau [sic] tells us of common things we know, but in an uncommon manner.

There is much to be learned from this volume. Stern and good lessons in economy; contentment with a simple but noble life, and all that, and much more. The author "lived like a king" on "hoe cakes," and drank water; at the same time outworking the lustiest farmers who were pitted against him.

Get the book. You will like it. It is original and refreshing; and from the brain of a *live* man.

Review of *Walden*, Boston *Daily Evening Traveller*, 9 August 1854, p. 1

This is a sort of autobiography of a hermit, who lived two years alone in the woods of Concord, Mass., a mile from any neighbor. Mr. Thoreau's object in thus turning hermit, appears to have been—so far as he had any particular end in view— to ascertain by experiment, what are the absolute necessities of man, to illustrate in his own person the truth of Watt's line: "Man wants but little here below." And his return to civilized life again, confirmed that companion line of Watts—"Nor wants that little long;" though it must be confessed Mr. Thoreau held out on little or nothing, longer than most men could have done. It is a curious and amusing book, written in the Emersonian style, but containing ·many shrewd and sensible suggestions, with a fair share of nonsense.

Review of *Walden*, Boston *Daily Journal*, 10 August 1854, p. 1

This is a remarkable book. The thread of the work is a narrative of the personal experience of the eccentric author as a hermit on the shores of Walden Pond. The body consists of his reflections on life and its pursuits. Mr. Thoreau carried out his ideas of "communism" by building with his own hands an humble hut, cultivating his own garden patch, earning with the sweat of his brow enough of coarse food to sustain life, and living independent of the world and of its circumstances. He continued this selfish existence for two years, and then returned to society, but why, he does not inform his readers. Whether satisfied that he had mistaken the "pleasures of solitude," or whether the self-improvement which the world has charitably supposed was the object of his retirement had been accomplished, it is certain that he was relieved of none of his selfish opinions—that he left behind in the woods of Concord none of his misanthropy, and that he brought back habits of thought which, though profound, are erratic, and often border on the transcendental.

The narrative of the two years hermit life of such a man can hardly fail to be attractive, and the study of the workings of a mind so constituted must possess a peculiar interest. But the attraction is without sympathy—the interest is devoid of admiration. The outré opinions of a mind like that of Mr. Thoreau, while they will attract attention as the eccentric outbursts of real genius, so far from finding a response in the bosom of the reader, will excite a smile, from their very extravagance, and we can easily imagine that if Mr. Thoreau would banish from his mind the idea that man is an oyster, he might become a passable philosopher.

Mr. Thoreau has made an attractive book—more attractive than his "Week on the Concord and Merrimack." But while many will be fascinated by its contents, few will be improved. As the pantheistic doctrines of the author marred the beauty of his former work, so does his selfish philosophy darkly tinge the pages of "Walden," and the best that can be said of the work in its probable effects is, that while many will be charmed by the descriptive powers of the author, and will smile at his extravagant ideas, few will be influenced by his opinions. This is a negative virtue in a book which is likely to be widely circulated, and which might do much mischief if the author could establish a bond of sympathy with the reader.

[John Sullivan Dwight],
"Editorial
Correspondence,"
*Dwight's Journal of
Music,* 5
(12 August 1854), 149–50

. . . For indoor reading, in the interims of physical fatigue and the lull of social excitement, say, for a few minutes after the evening company have dispersed and left us to our thoughts which will not sleep without some soothing efficacy of thoughts printed and impersonal, we have another book:—kindly placed in our hands upon the eve of starting on our journey, and with a delicate instinct of what was fitting, by our friend Fields, the poet partner in the firm of Ticknor and Co., the publishers,—a copy in advance of publication. In such hours one retires from Nature only to live her over in dreams and by whatever rush-light of his own reflections; and for such hours no truer friend and text book have we ever found than this wonderful new book called *Walden, or Life in the Woods,* by Henry D. Thoreau, the young Concord hermit, as he has sometimes been called. Thoreau is one of those men who has put such a determined trust in the simple dictates of common sense, as to earn the vulgar title of "transcendentalist" from his sophisticated neighbors. He is one of the few who really thinks and acts and tries life for himself, honestly weighing and reporting thereof, and in his own way (which he cares not should be others' ways) enjoying. Of course, they find him strange, fantastical, a humorist, a theorist, a dreamer. It may be or may not. One thing is certain, that his humor has led him into a life experi-

ment, and that into a literary report or book, that is full of information, full of wisdom, full of wholesome, bracing moral atmosphere, full of beauty, poetry and entertainment for all who have the power to relish a good book. He built himself a house in the woods by Walden pond, in Concord, where he lived alone for more than two years, thinking it false economy to eat so that life must be spent in procuring what to eat, but cultivating sober, simple, philosophic habits, and daily studying the lesson which nature and the soul of nature are perpetually teaching to the individual soul, would that but listen. Every chapter of the book is redolent of pine and hemlock. With a keen eye and love for nature, many are the rare and curious facts which he reports for us. He has become the confidant of all plants and animals, and writes the poem of their lives for us. Read that chapter upon sounds, that of the owl, the bull-frog, &c.; or that in which he commemorates the battle of the red and black ants, "red-republicans and black imperialists," which "took place in the Presidency of Polk, five years before the passage of Webster's Fugitive Slave Bill." Truer touches of humor and quaint, genuine, first-hand observation you will seldom find. And then his vegetable planting—read how he was "determined to know beans!" And his shrewd criticisms, from his woodland seclusion, upon his village neighbors and upon civilized life generally, in which men are slaves to their own thrift, are worthy of a philosophic, though by no means a "melancholy, Jacques." It is the most thoroughly original book that has been produced these many days. Its literary style is admirably clear and terse and elegant; the pictures wonderfully graphic; for the writer is a poet and a scholar as well as a tough wrestler with the first economical problems of nature, and a winner of good cheer and of free glorious leisure out of what men call the "hard realities" of life. Walden pond, a half mile in diameter, in Concord town, becomes henceforth as classical as any lake of Windermere. And we doubt not, men are beginning to look to transcendentalists for the soberest reports of good hard common-sense, as well as for the models of the clearest writing. . . .

Review of *Walden*, New Bedford *Mercury*, 12 August 1854, p. 2

This is a remarkable history of remarkable experiences. Mr. Thoreau is an eccentric genius, and affects the philosopher, despising all the ordinary aims and petty ambitions of the world, looking in a half cynical, half amused mood upon men and things, and meanwhile retiring into a semi barbarous state builds with his own hands a hut on Walden Pond in Connecticut, where for twenty-six months he lives like a hermit on the labor of his hands, looking to nature, 'kindest mother still,' for the supply of his physical wants, and as a perpetual fountain of delight to his eye and soul. This volume is in some measure a record of his external and internal being during his retiracy, and is perfectly unique in experience and expression. A simple, pure heart, high cultivation and a luxuriant fancy, give to Mr. Thoreau a vigorous intellectual life, and impart a freshness and charm to his style which leads one on quite enchanted. For its fine descriptions of nature, it will bear more than one reading, while its stern and true lessons on the value of existence, its manly simplicity, its sage reflections, will drop many a good seed for content and true living, to spring up and flourish and beautify new homes, albeit in civilized life, for we do not think any will be so enamored of Mr. Thoreau's experience, as to seek it in his way.

Review of *Walden,* Worcester *Palladium,* 16 August 1854, p. 3

We do not suppose any of our readers need be informed who Thoreau is; but if any are ignorant of his name or existence, this book will be their best introduction. Looked upon as one of the Concord oddities, as a wayward genius, many have smiled and turned away their heads as they would at a clown who for a moment might make them stare and laugh, but leave them no wiser in the end. A few interested themselves in the Walden philosopher, amused with his quaintness, struck with the sense of some of his philosophy, and pleased with his originality. Almost the only opportunity he has given the public to become acquainted with him, has been through the medium of lectures. These will be eclipsed in popularity by the book which has many decided advantages over the lectures. A man can write about himself with better effect than he can talk about himself. The pen is a more modest communicator than the tongue, and is not so easily charged with egotism.

Walden is a prose poem. It has classical elegance, and New England homeliness, with a sprinkle of Oriental magnificence in it. It is a book to be read and re-read, and read again, until another is written like it; so great is the popular tendency towards artificialities. It can not be complained against the book that it is not practical in its theories. Does not its author tell us of every board that built his house? Also the cost of the laths, the windows, the chimney, and the food he eats? He shows us that life is too hard work now-a-days; that it grows harder and more perplexing the farther it advances from primitive simplicity. With portions of the volume the public are familiar, but the whole of it is well worth being acquainted with. Our readers will find extracts from it on our first page. Elegantly published in a neat and convenient form, it is for sale at Livermore's.

Review of *Walden*, Newark [New Jersey] *Daily Advertiser*, 21 August 1854, p. 2

We have read this volume while lying upon a sick bed, and never before better appreciated the convenience of the light octavo form, so generally adopted by this house for its publications. There were other works which more urgently demanded attention, but the convenience of this gave it the preference. Light as it was, even this was very fatiguing to hold—the others impossible. Thoreau is an original. Although of Harvard education, colleges have not formed him. He has lived according to his whims, and here is his justification. Perhaps there is nothing new in the idea, but his application and incidents are fresh. He lived alone for two years in the Walden woods near Concord, Mass., some miles from the village, away from all society, in a house (shanty) built by himself, raising his own food, principally preparing it himself, and at an actual cost of about $100 per year, all told—and that earned by himself. This life is a novel one, but his account of it is full as curious. He writes almost as many thoughts as words. Indeed, his pages are more fully peppered with ideas than commas.—The reader cannot fail to be entertained with a book, which took two years of almost entire solitude to write, and will take as many more to think out. We would urge those tired with every day issues of the press, to seek for this, as a fresh bouquet from the wilds, fragrant and inspiring.

Review of *Walden*, New York *Morning Express*, 24 August 1854, p. 2

Mr. Thoreau is a young but promising writer.—He is a manly thinker; his opinions betray a clear judgment, careful intellectual cultivation, and a great deal of talent. But the tendencies of his mind are at times too speculative. He is too impractical, and although many of the social habits against which he declaims, are susceptible of improvement; yet, he takes the privilege of most men with a "mission," as the strong-minded philosophers and philosoperesses say, and condemns what cannot well be remedied, or what is so trivial as hardly to be worth the trouble of a chapter of Carlylean rhapsody, or epigrammatic abuse. Yet he is indubitably sound in much of what he says, and right in the main. His style is crude but forcible. Its harshness appears to be in a measure the result either of carelessness or of affectation; for some of the more elaborate passages a reader meets with in turning over the work, display a great mastery of language, much facility in expression that is at once easy and strong, and a happy fancy. When Mr. Thoreau wrote the book, he lived, he says, a mile from any neighbor and alone in the woods in a house which he had built himself on the shore of Walden Pond in Concord, Massachusetts. There he lived for two years and two months and supported himself by the labor of his hands, only. During the whole of this time he appears to have been a sort of anchorite; the eccentricity of his mode of life, as he relates it, is laughable. Yet it has a moral.

Here are the statistics of the first year's outlay.

["Economy," 60.10–15, 17–29]—The philosophy of such a Pythagoras could not be else than odd, of course, and will repay perusal.

[Thomas Starr King], Review of *Walden*, *Christian Register*, 26 August 1854, p. 135

A young man, eight years out of college, of fine scholarship and original genius, revives, in the midst of our bustling times, the life of an anchorite. By the side of a secluded pond in Concord, he builds with his own hands a hut which cost him twenty-eight dollars and twelve and a half cents; and there he lived two and a half years, "cultivating poverty," because he "wanted to drive life into a corner, and reduce it to its lowest terms, and suck out all its marrow." Here he found that the labor of six weeks would support him through the year; and so he had long quiet days for reading, observation, and reflection, learning to free himself from all the hollow customs and false shows of the world, and to pity those who by slavery to inherited property seemed to be doing incredible and astonishing penance. In the account he gives us of his clothes, house, food, and furniture, we find mingled many acute and wise criticisms upon modern life; while in his descriptions of all living things around him, birds, fishes, squirrels, mice, insects, trees, flowers, weeds, it is evident that he had the sharpest eye and the quickest sympathy. One remarkable chapter is given to the sounds that came to his ear, with suggestions, full of poetry and beauty, of the feelings which these sounds awakened. But nothing interested him so much as the Pond, whose name gives the title to his book. He describes it as a clear sheet of water, about a mile in circumference; he bathed in it every morning; its cool crystal depths were his well, ready dug; he sailed upon its bosom in summer, he noted many curious facts pertaining to its ice in winter; in short, it became to him a living thing, and he almost worshipped it. But we must not describe the contents of this book any farther. Its opening pages may seem a little caustic and cynical; but it mellows apace, and playful humor and sparkling thought appear on almost every page. We suppose its author does not reverence many things which we reverence; but this fact has not prevented our seeing that he has a reverential, tender, and devout spirit at bottom. Rarely have we enjoyed a book more, or been more grateful for many and rich suggestions. Who would have looked to Walden Pond for a *Robinson Crusoe*, or for an observer like the author of the *Natural History of Selbourne*, or for a moralist like the writer of *Religio Medici*? Yet paragraphs in this book have reminded us of each of these. And as we shut the book up, we ask ourselves, will the great lesson it teaches of the freedom and beauty of a simple life be heeded? Shall this struggle for wealth, and this bondage to the *impedimenta* of life, continue forever? Will the time ever come when it will be fashionable to be poor, that is, when men will be so smitten with a purpose to seek the true ends of life that they will not care about laying up riches on the earth? Such times we know there have been, and thousands listened reverently to the reply, given in the last of these two lines, to the inquiry contained in the first;

"O where is peace, for thou its path hast
      trod?"
"In poverty, retirement, and with God."

Who can say that it is impossible that such a time may come round, although the fashion of this world now runs with such a resistless current in the opposite direction.

Review of *Walden*, *Graham's*, 45 (September 1854), 298–300

Whatever may be thought or said of this curious volume, nobody can deny its claims to individuality of opinion, sentiment, and expression. Sometimes strikingly original, sometimes merely eccentric and odd, it is always racy and stimulating. The author, an educated gentleman, disgusted with the compliances and compromises which society enjoins on those to whom it gives "a living," goes off alone into Concord woods, builds his own house, cooks his own victuals, makes and mends his own clothes, works, reads, thinks as he pleases, and writes this book to chronicle his success in the experiment. Mr. Thoreau, it is well known, belongs to the class of transcendentalists who lay the greatest stress on the "I," and knows no limitation on the exercise of the rights of that important pronoun. The customs, manners, occupations, religion, of society, he "goes out" from, and brings them before his own inward tribunal for judgment. He differs from all mankind with wonderful composure; and, without any of the fuss of the come-outers, goes beyond them in asserting the autocracy of the individual. Making himself the measure of truth, he is apt to think that "difference from me is the measure of absurdity"; and occasionally he obtains a startling paradox, by the simple inversion of a stagnant truism. He likes to say that four and four make nine, in order to assert his independence of the contemptible trammels of the world's arithmetic. He has a philosophical fleer and gibe for most axioms, and snaps his fingers in the face of the most accredited proprieties and "do-me-*goodisms*" of conventional life. But if he has the wildness of the woods about him, he has their sweetness also. Through all the audacities of his eccentric protests, a careful eye can easily discern the movement of a powerful and accomplished mind. He has evidently read the best books, and talked with the best people. His love for nature, and his eye for nature, are altogether beyond the ordinary love and insight of nature's priests; and his descriptions have a kind of De Foe-like accuracy and reality in their eloquence, peculiar to himself among all American writers. We feel, in reading him, that such a man has earned the right to speak of nature, for he has taken her in all moods, and given the same "frolic welcome" to her "thunder and her sunshine."

But we doubt if anybody can speak so well of Mr. Thoreau as Mr. Thoreau himself. He has devoted so much of his life to the perusal of his own consciousness, that we feel it would be a kind of impertinence to substitute our impressions for his knowledge. We will first extract his account of his expenses for eight months in his woodland home:—

["Economy," 60.10–16]

As the article of food, put down at $8.74, is unaccompanied by the items thereof, we subjoin them in order that our readers may see on how little a philosopher can live:—

["Economy," 59.7–21]

One of the great trials of authors and sages has its source in the necessity of being clothed. Mr. Thoreau has discussed this matter with unusual sagacity, and what thinker, after reading the following, can mourn over the fact of being out at the elbows:—

["Economy," 21.16–22.21, 23.21–24.11]

In a description of his visitors, occurs the following testimonial to a Concord philosopher, who occasionally penetrated to his residence. Although the name is not given, we suppose Mr. Thoreau refers to A. Bronson Alcott:—

["Former Inhabitants; and Winter Visitors," 268.17–270.12]

Here is a defense of individualism, in its large sense of following one's genius, the sense in which Mr. Thoreau uses it:

["Higher Laws," 216.13–217.2]

The volume is so thickly studded with striking descriptions that it is difficult to select an average specimen of Mr. Thoreau's power and felicity. We take the following as one of the best:—

["Baker Farm," 201.1–203.2]

We fear that our extracts have not done justice to the attractiveness of this curious and original volume. We might easily fill a page with short, sharp, quotable sentences, embodying some flash of wit or humor, some scrap of quaint or elevated wisdom, or some odd or beautiful image. Every chapter in the book is stamped with sincerity. It is genuine and genial throughout. Even its freaks of thought are full of suggestions. When the author turns his eye seriously on an object, no matter how remote from the sphere of ordinary observation, he commonly sees into it and through it. He has a good deal of Mr. Emerson's piercing quality of mind, which he exercises on the more elusive and fitting phenomena of consciousness, with a metaphysician's subtilty, and a poet's expressiveness. And as regards the somewhat presumptuous manner in which he dogmatizes, the reader will soon learn to pardon it for the real wealth of individual thinking by which it is accompanied, always remembering that Mr. Thoreau, in the words of his own motto, does not

380

intend to write an "ode to dejection, but to brag as lustily as chanticleer in the morning, standing on his roost, if only to wake his neighbors up."

Review of *Walden,* New York *Churchman,* 2 September 1854, p. 4

The book of a humourist—a man of humours rather than of humour—and a lover of nature. Mr. Thoreau, living at Concord, is known among literary circles by his association with the good company of Emerson and Hawthorne, and by his production of a book a few years since, *A Week on the Concord and Merrimack Rivers*, which, with some unpleasant peculiarities of its school, savouring greatly of a species of irreverent egotism, contained many close and faithful observations of nature, and many shrewd reflections on life. Every man has his humour, though from the present pressure and overlaying of society it is not always easy to discover it. Mr. Thoreau brings his out into prominent relief. It is the stoic affectation of a lover of personal freedom, with a grudge against civilization for its restrictions. He looks upon all the trappings of society, of Church and State, of conventional usages, cities and towns, even clothes and houses, as so many impediments to the free growth of the unfettered man. The only concession he seems disposed to make to the social state is to work for it a sufficiently long time,—in his case it is a very short time,—to secure honestly a portion of the spoils adequate to keep body and soul in company, that the former, strengthened by toil, may enjoy a vigourous sense of existence, and the latter be free to watch its own motions and imbibe the simple thoughts of primitive poetry and philosophy. In all our modern reading, unlike as the situation and circumstances are, and different as Mr. Thoreau is from Diogenes in many respects, we have not met with so complete a suggestion of what used to be considered, by the vulgar at least, a philosopher. He realizes the popular notion of an impracticable, a man who rails at society and is disposed to submit to as few of its trammels as possible, and who has the credit of resources within himself which the majority of people do not possess, and, in fact, do not much care for. The world is very ready to give the title, for it is of very little mercantile value, and the world can afford to part with it. On his part, the philosopher can return the compliment. He says to the hard workers about him, my friends, you are all wrong, shortening your lives in toil and vanities, working for that which does not profit, and reaping an endless harvest of failure and dismay. Ninety-seven out of every hundred merchants, he continues, according to an old calculation, fail in business, and it is pretty safe to put down the other three as rogues. As in merchandize, so in farming. People are toiling with real pain after imaginary pleasure. The true secret of life is to ask for little; to live on the minimum. Mr. Thoreau has made the experiment. Entering manhood with a good education and a vigorous frame, he has, after various attempts, come to the conclusion, recorded in his book, that, after all, "the occupation of a day labourer was the most independent of any, especially as it required only thirty or forty days in a year to support one." School-keeping he had tried; but that, as a trade, was a failure. There was no love in it, and it did not gratify the mind; beside, it was expensive:—he was "obliged to dress and train, not to say think and believe accordingly, and time was lost in the bargain." Trade was still worse. It was tried, but the experimentalist for freedom found "it would take ten years to get underway in that, and that then he should probably be on his way to the devil." He was "actu-ally afraid that he might by that time be doing what is called a good business." At one time, when he was looking about to see what he could do for a living, some sad experience in conforming to the wishes of friends being fresh in his mind to tax his ingenuity, "*he thought often and seriously of picking huckleberries*"; which indeed would not be a very self-sacrificing occupation, and certainly has its agreeable features. The difficulty is, the season of huckleberries is short, the demand limited, and it requires so little capital of head or pocket that,—if it would pay,—it would soon be overstocked. We fear it would not be adequate to the support of a family in respectability, and that if it could be generally adopted, much of what is valuable in the present system of society, school-houses, churches, lyceums, architecture, opera, and generally all costly things, would go by the board. However this may be, for more than five years Mr. Thoreau supported himself by about six weeks' labor of his hands *per annum*; and the conclusion to which he came was "a conviction both by faith and experience, that to maintain one's self on this earth is not a hardship, but a pastime, if we will live simply and wisely, *as the pursuits of the simpler nations are still the sports of the more artificial*," which is a point in illustration exceedingly well made, and is really a poetical defence of the author's theory. He adds, "It is not necessary that a man should earn his living by the sweat of his brow, unless he sweats easier than I do."

Mr. Thoreau is thus at war with the political economy of the age. It is his doctrine that the fewer wants man has the better; while in reality civilization is the spur of many wants. To give a man a new want is to give him a new pleasure and conquer his habitual rust and idleness. The greater his needs and acquisitions, the greater his safety; since he may fall back from one advance post to another, as he is pressed by misfortune, and still keep the main citadel untouched. He may give up his couch and still keep his gig; resign his Madeira and retain at least his small beer; if he fails as an orator he may be eloquent in the parlor or the school-room; a condemned poet may cut down into a profitable prose-writer; the bankrupt citizen may become a proud villager. He has, by his devotion to luxury, the fostering of his spiritual and bodily appetites, his deference to the standards set up about him, interposed a long series of steps, which he may gradually descend, before he touches the bottom one, of starvation. As a general thing in the world, the people who aim at most get most. The philosophical negation keeps no account in the bank and starves. Nay, it keeps robbing itself till from him that hath not is taken away even that which he hath. In the woods, on the edge of a fine pond, aloof from markets and amusements, our author begins to doubt even of his favourite and ultimate resource of fishing. Life and reality seem oozing out of his feeble grasp, and he holds to the world only by the slender filament of a metaphysical whim. Says he in his chapter on the "higher laws":

["Higher Laws," 213.33–214.35]

With the preparation in his experiences which we have alluded to, Mr. Thoreau, in the spring of 1845, borrowed an axe, and set forth to level a few trees, for the site of a house, on the edge of Walden pond, in a wood near Concord. He did not own the land, but was permitted to enjoy it. He dropped a few pines and hewed timbers, and for boards bought out the shanty of James Collins, an Irishman who worked on the Fitchburg railroad, for the sum of four dollars, twenty-five cents. From his allusion, he was assisted, we presume, in the raising, by Emerson and other friendly literary celebrities of the region. Starting early in the spring, long before winter he had secured, with the labour of his hands, "a tight shingled and plastered house, ten feet wide by fifteen long, and eight feet posts, with a garret and a closet, a large window on each side, two trap doors, one door at the end and a brick fire-place opposite." The exact cost of the house is given:

["Economy," 49.3–26]

The rest of the account is curious, and will show "upon what meats this same Cæesar fed," that he has interested the world so greatly in his housekeeping:

["Economy," 58.33–60.32]

He had nothing further to do after his "family baking," which, the family consisting of a unit, could not have been large or have come round very often, than to read, think and observe. Homer was his favourite book; the thinking was unlimited, and the observation that of a man with an instinctive tact for the wonders of natural history. On this last point we cannot give the author too high praise. He has a rare felicity of sight and description, which Izaak Walton would have approved of and Alexander Wilson envied. To many of his moral speculations we could take exceptions. He carries his opposition to society too far. A self-pleasing man should have a more liberal indulgence for the necessities of others, and something more cheerful to tell the world than of its miseries. We should be sorry to think this a true picture of the "industrial classes":

["Economy," 6.25–7.35]

And again:

["Economy," 37.17–38.11, 38.27–32]

We are all wrong, it seems, and had better go back to savage life. The "lendings" of society and civilization are all impediments. The railroad is a humbug, the post-office an absurdity, for there are really no letters worth reading, it is "a penny for your thoughts": all "mud and slush of opinion and prejudice and tradition and delusion and appearance,—alluvion which covers the globe, through Paris and London, through New York and Boston and Concord, through Church and State, through poetry, philosophy, and religion." Rising to transcendental emotion, our author exclaims, ["Where I Lived, and What I Lived For," 98.19–30]

This excessive love of individuality and these constant Fourth-of-July declarations of independence, look very well on paper, but they will not bear the test of a practical examination. We say excessive, for there is no doubt there is such a thing as a neglect of a proper cultivation of a man's isolated, individual self. In many things "the world is too much with us"; the soul needs retirement, sequestration, repose. We are slaves to idle expenses, and "walk in a vain show." "Poor Richard" might come among us with profit and tell us how dearly we are paying for the whistle, and show us how much richer we might become, not by acquiring more but by wanting less. But let us look at Mr. Thoreau's contempt for the labour of the harassed farmer. We may admit that the yoke is on his shoulder, as well as on the neck of his patient ox; but where is the condition of life which has not its yoke of some fashion or other? We cannot all be philosophers, or affect the pleasures of a hermit life in the wilderness. Even "the mean and sneaking fellows," whom Thoreau, in the kindness of his sublimated philanthropy, so tenderly describes, have their little compensations of pleasure and satisfaction, and no doubt frequently pitied the recluse of Walden at his lone habitation in the wood. *His* pleasure, stretched out on a piece of damp turf, displacing with his frame huge shoals of insect life,

and gazing intently on space in an arduous endeavour to think that he is thinking; this sort of enjoyment would be simple misery to the "swinkt hedger," the poor unthinking clown, who

> like a lackey, from the rise to set,
> Sweats in the eye of Phobus, and all
>   night
> Sleeps in Elysium; next day, after dawn,
> Doth rise and help Hyperion to his
>   horse;
> And follows so the ever-running year,
> With profitable labour, to his grave.

The man of toil, with all his woes, has probably the common permanent consolation of humanity, he does not toil always, and with the sterile harvest of his fields he reaps, too, some bounties of friendly countenances in his little sphere of society, the treasures, perhaps, of wife and children; and though he is sublimely unconscious of Eddas and Zendavestas, he can read his Bible—the best book which any sage has in his library—and learn from it that there is a felicity in labouring patiently and cheerfully in one's vocation, and doing one's duty in that state of life in which it has pleased God to call us. Retiring from civilized life, in a vain attempt to escape its ills, must be the casual chance experiment of the few, and those few will hardly prosecute the work with any great degree of consistency. Even Mr. Thoreau, who loves the society of lizards and mosquitos, and can eat an acorn with as much zest as any man, cuts the pleasing connection after awhile, and hastens back to civilization, to secure the admiration of the very vicious public whose unprofitable heart-aches and barren pursuits he had, for the moment, abandoned. Why was not Mr. Thoreau satisfied with carving his elegies on the bark of trees, mingling his philosophic ejaculations with the wild laugh of the loon, or swelling the brimming flood of Walden Pond with his sympathetic tears? We hold that in publishing he has given up the whole argument. Seriously, he cannot expect many people to follow his example; comically, his experience is published as a curiosity, a piece of quaintness, an affectation for the simple amusement of a wicked world.

Look where the author's principles would carry him were we to listen to his suggestions, and follow this instinct of our nature for idleness and the wilderness. This day, if any, would be a favourable one for putting this experiment in operation. It is sleepy, heavily laden mid August, with a sultry temperature, and we are writing, surrounded by bricks and mortar, in a city which strangers are just now avoiding on suspicion of the lugubrious pestilence lurking in its atmosphere. We should certainly, on his showing, neither stay here to earn money to buy his book, or earn money by reviewing it: yet these are duties which he challenges us to perform, and one or other of which some considerable number of people must execute; or there will be no sale of "Walden," and the philosophic soul of Thoreau will be shaken at Concord, and the face of Fields, most beneficent of publishers, will lengthen, and when the author presents himself in Washington street to receive his six months' profits, the results will be small, and, instead of cash, he will be entertained with that most bitter of all receptions for an author, when his publishers take to analyzing his book—a critical proceeding which they never think of attempting unless the book is a failure; when one partner will say it was the too much Zoroaster, and infidelity in it which killed it; another will doubt whether the public cares very much about the infinitesimals of insect life, or is disposed to be imaginative on mosquitos, and a third, taking up the "Barclays of Boston," will venture the

suggestion that Mr. Thoreau had better, after all, emigrate to Beacon street and write a book that will sell like that. From this fearful fate, we say, may this author be preserved! Yet he will owe it to the tender mercies and degraded toil of the civilization he despises, if he is.

We are not disposed to throw any unnecessary obstacles in the way of this author, but *The Churchman* would be reckless of its duty if it were not to ask the question why Mr. Thoreau so frequently throws doubt over and suggests a spirit of disaffection to the sacred Scriptures. There is not so much of this as in his previous book, *A Week on the Concord and Merrimack Rivers*, but a little of this nonsense is quite too much: for example, "Our manners have been corrupted by communication with the saints. Our hymn-books resound with a melodious cursing of God and enduring Him forever. One would say that even the prophets and redeemers had rather consoled the fears than confirmed the hopes of man. There is nowhere recorded a simple and irrepressible satisfaction with the gift of life, any memorable praise of God." If we may credit the quotations of the writer of this unhappy passage, he enjoys a privileged literary intimacy with Confucius; if it would not be taken as an impertinence, we should like to ask if he has ever perused the Psalms of David. The fact is, that the great discoveries and revelations of Mr. Thoreau's solitude turn out to be very familiar affairs after all. Wriggle as he may among his scraps of Sheik Sadi and the Vishnu Purana, he will find it difficult to bring forward anything of a sacred character, or illustrating human life, which is not included with tenfold more effect in the Bible. His aphorisms from these old oriental sources are frequently very happy; but it is the most pitiful affectation to use them as he occasionally does. Humour is not the author's highest faculty, but we may suspect the exercise at least of an ingenious pleasantry, when he treats us to this significant quotation. "Says the poet Mîr Camar Uddîn Mast, 'Being seated to run through the region of the spiritual world, I have had this advantage in books. *To be intoxicated by a single glass of wine; I have experienced this pleasure when I have drunk the liquor of the esoteric doctrines.*'"

We may, after all, be looking at this matter too seriously. The author, in spite of his sarcasm and denunciations, is only playing the part of an individual humourist. He knows as much as any one how much he is indebted to civilization; and is only taking a view of life dramatically, as a looker-on for the moment. In this view he carries out the humour admirably. A book was published some years since, entitled "The Hermit in London," which, though it was quite successful, had not half the humour or philosophical amusement of this volume. Who but a man who had projected himself as it were into another state of being could see so clearly the humours of the village life.

["The Village," 167.22–168.33]

There is some geniality in this, as there is in the sketch of the Homeric or Paphlagonian man who came along from Canada, who is thus introduced.

["Visitors," 144.13–145.36]

We could add to these pleasant extracts many of the natural history observations, which, as we have said, are the writer's *forte*. The agriculture, the woods, the life of the pond, are all eminently well described. He was fortunate one day to witness that remarkable sight, a battle between two forces of red and black ants, of which a rather poetical account, rivalling the combats of Turks and Russians, was once given by a M. Hanhart, an improvement upon Huber which Leigh Hunt has pleasantly commented upon and the original of which may be found in the *Edinburgh Journal of Science* for 1828.

386

Review of *Walden,* *Albion* [England], n.s. 13 (9 September 1854), 429

One of those rare books that stand apart from the herd of new publications under which the press absolutely groans; moderate in compass but eminently suggestive, being a compound of thought, feeling, and observation. Its author, it seems, during 1845, 6, and 7, played the philosophic hermit in a wood that overlooks Walden Pond, in the neighbourhood of Concord, Massachusetts. Here he tested at how cheap a rate physical existence may healthfully be maintained, and how, apart from the factitious excitement of society and the communion of mind with mind, he could cultivate a tranquil and contemplative spirit, yet resolute withal. This experiment was undeniably successful; and he has here set forth the record of his sylvan life and the musings of his happy solitude. He probably errs in believing, that life is an isolated shanty, and the strict vegetarian system, could be made profitable or pleasant to the men and women of this age. But we shall not discuss the question with this voluntary and most practical hermit. We can admire, without wishing to imitate him; and we can thank him cordially for hints on many topics that interest humanity at large, as well as for page upon page of research and anecdote, showing how lovingly he studied the instincts and the habits of the dumb associates by whom he was surrounded. The choicest and most popular works on natural history contain no descriptions more charming than those that abound in this volume. A little humour and a little satire are the pepper and salt to this part of the entertainment that Mr. Thoreau serves up. Into it we advise the reader—of unvitiated taste and unpalled appetite—to dip deeply. We at least do not come across a Walden, every day.

Possibly our strong commendation may be borne out by the two lengthened and characteristic extracts that we quote. The first may well be called the "The Battle of the Ants."

["Brute Neighbors," 228.25–232.11]

We might have found something writ in gentler strain; but there is a point and a quaintness in the above warlike episode, that catches our fancy. Our second borrowing from this clever book—a sketch of character and a striking one—may be found on another page.[1]

Note

1 In the same issue (p. 424), the *Albion* quoted from "Visitors," 114.13–150.22.

Review of *Walden*, *Morning Courier and New-York Enquirer*, 9 September 1854, p. 2

Half mad, but never silly; and the half that is not mad, full of truths which if they are not entirely new, have at least lain hidden under the crust of fashion, folly, and listlessness so long as to seem new on being dug out and placed boldly before us. Mr. Thoreau built himself with his own hands a hut, shanty, or cottage on the shores of Walden pond, near Concord, Mass., and lived there two years and two months doing all his own working and thinking. In this volume we have such of the results of his work and thought as can be put on paper; and to a reflecting, well trained mind it is a book full of matter for careful consideration. It is at times repulsively selfish in its tone, and might easily help a bad man to be worse; but to readers of an opposite character who peruse it, not with the intent of imitating the author in his mental or physical habits, but for its suggestiveness, it cannot prove other than an occasion for healthy mental exercise. In style it partakes of the characteristics of Thomas Carlyle and Sir Thomas Browne: indeed had not the *Clothes-Philosophy* and the *Pseudo-doxia Epidemica* and the *Urn Burial* been written, *Walden* would probably never have seen the light. The author has Carlyle's hatred of shams and Carlyle's way of showing it: he has Sir Thomas Browne's love of pregnant paradox and stupendous joke, and utters his paradoxes and his jokes with a mysterious phlegm quite akin to that of the Medical Knight who "existed only at the periphery of his being." *Walden* is a book which should have many readers, if readers were always sound thinkers.

Review of *Walden,* New York *Times,* 22 September 1854, p. 3

The author of this book—Mr. Henry D. Thoreau—is undoubtedly a man of genius. It is not possible to open twenty pages without finding plentiful indications of that fact. Unfortunately, however, he is an erratic genius, thoroughly impracticable, and apt to confuse rather than arrange the order of things, mental and physical.

Mr. Thoreau, it will be remembered, was one of the earliest contributors to Emerson's remarkable transcendental publication, the *Dial.* His eccentricities constituted one of the features of that very eccentric journal, and were well suited to it. Subsequently he published a volume called *Week on the Concord and Merrimack Rivers.* A great deal of observation and quaintness were incorporated in the latter work, and obtained for it some popularity here and in Europe. Influenced by a peculiar philosophy of his own, Mr. Thoreau abandoned literature in 1845. He was probably disgusted with social life, and thought an experience of its savage phase might be agreeable. With this idea he "borrowed an axe" and went down to Walden Pond, in the vicinity of Concord, with the intention of building a house and living in it. The Cabin was constructed, and Mr. Thoreau occupied it for two years. Why he returned to society after that period he does not inform us. The present book was written in solitude, and occupied those spare moments when the author was not more profitably engaged in the labors of the field.

As a contribution to the Comic Literature of America, *Walden* is worthy of some attention, but in no other respect. The author evidently imagines himself to be a Philosopher, but he is not. He talks constantly of "vast cosmogonal themes," but narrows them all down to the nearest line of self. The mere fact of existence seems to satisfy Mr. Thoreau. He wonders why men aspire to anything higher than the cultivation of a patch of beans, when by that they may live—perhaps grow fat. Mr. Thoreau has been accused of communistic principles. This is his idea of communism: "I would rather sit on a pumpkin, and have it all to myself, than be crowded on a velvet cushion. I would rather ride on earth, in an ox cart, with a free circulation, than go to Heaven in the fancy car of an excursion train, and breathe a *malaria* all the way."

This is one of Mr. Thoreau's "vast cosmogonal themes": "While civilization has been improving our houses, it has not equally improved the men who are to inhabit them. It has created palaces, but it was not so easy to create noblemen and kings. And *if the civilized man's pursuits are no worthier than the savage's—if he employed the greater part of his life in obtaining gross necessaries and comforts merely—why should he have a better dwelling than the former?*" In other words, why should he not live like a savage, to save the trouble of living like a Christian?

Mr. Thoreau denounces everything that indicates progress. Railroads, telegraphs, steam engines, newspapers, and everything else which the world values, offend him. There is nothing estimable in his eyes but a log hut and a patch of beans. On the latter he dwells with infinite delight. It is one of the few things that does not disgust his philosophical mind. Ascetics who have a taste for beans will find comfort in this volume.

Mr. Thoreau is a good writer, possessed of great comic powers, and able to describe accurately many peculiar phases of nature. But the present work will fail to satisfy any class of readers. The literary man may be pleased with the style, but he will surely lament the selfish *animus* of the book.

[Gamaliel Bailey?], Review of *Walden*, *National Era*, 8 (28 September 1854), 155

In its narrative, this book is unique, in its philosophy quite Emersonian. It is marked by genius of a certain order, but just as strongly, by pride of intellect. It contains many acute observations on the follies of mankind, but enough of such follies to show that its author has his full share of the infirmities of human nature, without being conscious of it. By precept and example he clearly shows how very little is absolutely necessary to the subsistence of a man, what a Robinson Crusoe life he may lead in Massachusetts, how little labor he need perform, if he will but reduce his wants to the philosophical standard, and how much time he may then have for meditation and study. To go out and squat, all alone, by a pretty pond in the woods, dig, lay the foundation of a little cabin, and put it up, with borrowed tools, furnish it, raise corn, beans, and potatoes, and do one's own cooking, hermit like, so that the total cost of the whole building, furnishing, purchasing necessaries, and living for eight months, shall not exceed forty or fifty dollars, may do for an experiment, by a highly civilized man, with Yankee versatility, who has had the full benefit of the best civilization of the age. All men are not "up to" everything. But, if they were, if they all had the universal genius of the "Yankee nation," how long would they remain civilized, by squatting upon solitary duck-ponds, eschewing matrimony, casting off all ties of family, each one setting his wits to work to see how little he could do with, and how much of that little he could himself accomplish?

At the end of eight months, Mr. Thoreau might remain a ruminating philosopher, but he would have few but ruminating animals to write books for.

But, with all its extravagances, its sophisms, and its intellectual pride, the book is acute and suggestive, and contains passages of great beauty.

[Charles Frederick Briggs],
"A Yankee Diogenes,"
Putnam's Monthly Magazine,
4 (October 1854), 443–8

The New England character is essentially anti-Diogenic; the Yankee is too shrewd not to comprehend the advantages of living in what we call the world; there are no bargains to be made in the desert, nobody to be taken advantage of in the woods, while the dwellers in tubs and shanties have slender opportunities of bettering their condition by barter. When the New Englander leaves his home, it is not for the pleasure of living by himself; if he is migratory in his habits, it is not from his fondness for solitude, nor from any impatience he feels at living in a crowd. Where there are most men, there is, generally, most money, and there is where the strongest attractions exist for the genuine New Englander. A Yankee Diogenes is a *lusus*, and we feel a peculiar interest in reading the account which an oddity of that kind gives of himself. The name of Thoreau has not a New England sound; but we believe that the author of Walden is a genuine New Englander, and of New England antecedents and education. Although he plainly gives the reasons for publishing his book, at the outset, he does not clearly state the causes that led him to live the life of a hermit on the shore of Walden Pond. But we infer from his volume that his aim was the very remarkable one of trying to be something, while he lived upon nothing; in opposition to the general rule of striving to live upon something, while doing nothing. Mr. Thoreau probably tried the experiment long enough to test its success, and then fell back again into his normal condition. But he does not tell us that such was the case. He was happy enough to get back among the good people of Concord, we have no doubt; for although he paints his shanty-life in rose-colored tints, we do not believe he liked it, else why not stick to it? We have a mistrust of the sincerity of the St. Simon Sylites', and suspect that they come down from their pillars in the night-time, when nobody is looking at them. Diogenes placed his tub where Alexander would be sure of seeing it, and Mr. Thoreau ingenuously confesses that he occasionally went out to dine, and when the society of woodchucks and chipping-squirrels were insufficient for his amusement, he liked to go into Concord and listen to the village gossips in the stores and taverns. Mr. Thoreau informs us that he lived alone in the woods, by the shore of Walden Pond, in a shanty built by his own hands, a mile from any neighbor, two years and half. What he did there besides writing the book before us, cultivating beans, sounding Walden Pond, reading Homer, baking johnny-cakes, studying Brahminical theology, listening to chipping-squirrels, receiving visits, and having high imaginations, we do not know. He gives us the results of his bean cultivation with great particularity, and the cost of his shanty; but the actual results of his two years and a half of hermit life he does not give. But there have been a good many lives spent and a good deal of noise made about them, too, from the sum total of whose results not half so much good could be extracted as may be found in this little volume. Many a man will find pleasure in reading it, and many a one, we hope, will be profited by its counsels. A tour in Europe would have cost a good deal more, and not have produced half as much. As a matter of curiosity, to show how cheaply

a gentleman of refined tastes, lofty aspirations and cultivated intellect may live, even in these days of high prices, we copy Mr. Thoreau's account of his first year's operations; he did better, he informs us, the second year. The entire cost of his house, which answered all his purposes, and was as comfortable and showy as he desired, was $28 12 1/2. But one cannot live on a house unless he rents it to somebody else, even though he be a philosopher and a believer in Vishnu. Mr. Thoreau felt the need of a little ready money, one of the most convenient things in the world to have by one, even before his house was finished.

"Wishing to earn ten or twelve dollars by some agreeable and honest method," he observes, "I planted about two acres and a half of light and sandy soil, chiefly with beans, but also a small part with potatoes and corn, peas and turnips." As he was a squatter, he paid nothing for rent, and as he was making no calculation for future crops, he expended nothing for manure, so that the results of his farming will not be highly instructive to young agriculturists, nor be likely to be held up as excitements to farming pursuits by agricultural periodicals.

["Economy," 55.3–24]

We will not extract the other items which Mr. Thoreau favors us with in the accounts of his *ménage*; according to his figures it cost him twenty-seven cents a week to live, clothes included; and for this sum he lived healthily and happily, received a good many distinguished visitors, who, to humor his style, used to leave their names on a leaf or a chip, when they did not happen to find him at home. But, it strikes us that all the knowledge which the "Hermit of Walden" gained by his singular experiment in living might have been done just as well, and as satisfactorily, without any experiment at all. We know what it costs to feed prisoners, paupers and soldiers; we know what the cheapest and most nutritious food costs, and how little it requires to keep up the bodily health of a full-grown man. A very simple calculation will enable any one to satisfy himself in regard to such points, and those who wish to live upon twenty-seven cents a week, may indulge in that pleasure. The great Abernethy's prescription for the attainment of perfect bodily health was, "live on sixpence a day and earn it." But that would be Sybaritic indulgence compared with Mr. Thoreau's experience, whose daily expenditure hardly amounted to a quarter of that sum. And he lived happily, too, though it don't exactly speak volumes in favor of his system to announce that he only continued his economical mode of life two years. If it was "the thing," why did he not continue it? But, if he did not always live like a hermit, squatting on other people's property, and depending upon chance perch and pickerel for his dinner, he lived long enough by his own labor, and carried his system of economy to such a degree of perfection,

["Economy," 69.7–71.3]

There is nothing of the mean or sordid in the economy of Mr. Thoreau, though to some his simplicity and abstemiousness may appear trivial and affected; he does not live cheaply for the sake of saving, nor idly to avoid labor; but, that he may live independently and enjoy his great thoughts; that he may read the Hindoo scriptures and commune with the visible forms of nature. We must do him the credit to admit that there is no mock sentiment, nor simulation of piety or philanthropy in his volume. He is not much of a cynic, and though we have called him a Yankee Diogenes, the only personage to whom he bears a decided resemblance is that good humored creation of Dickens, Mark Tap-

ley, whose delight was in being jolly under difficulties. The following passage might have been written by Mr. Tapley if that person had ever turned author, for the sake of testing the provocatives to jollity, which may be found in the literary profession:

["Solitude," 131.22–134.2]

There is a true vagabondish disposition manifested now and then by Mr. Thoreau, which, we imagine, was more powerful in leading him to his eremite way of life, than his love of eastern poetry, and his fondness for observing the ways of snakes and shiners. If there had been a camp of gipsies in the neighborhood of Concord, he would have become a king among them, like Lavengro. It breaks out here with unmistakable distinctness:

["Higher Laws," 210.1–211.24]

There is much excellent good sense delivered in a very comprehensive and by no means unpleasant style in Mr. Thoreau's book, and let people think as they may of the wisdom or propriety of living after his fashion, denying oneself all the luxuries which the earth can afford, for the sake of leading a life of lawless vagabondage, and freedom from starched collars, there are but few readers who will fail to find profit and refreshment in his pages. Perhaps some practical people will think that a philosopher like Mr. Thoreau might have done the world a better service by purchasing a piece of land, and showing how much it might be made to produce, instead of squatting on another man's premises, and proving how little will suffice to keep body and soul together. But we must allow philosophers, and all other men, to fulfill their missions in their own way. If Mr. Thoreau had been a practical farmer, we should not have been favored with his volume; his corn and cabbage would have done but little towards profiting us, and we might never have been the better for his labors. As it is, we see how much more valuable to mankind is our philosophical vagabond than a hundred sturdy agriculturists; any plodder may raise beans, but it is only one in a million who can write a readable volume. With the following extract from his volume, and heartily recommending him to the class of readers who exact thoughts as well as words from an author, we must take leave, for the present, of the philosopher of Walden Pond.

["Economy," 35.30–37.16]

[Elizabeth Barstow Stoddard], "Letter from a Lady Correspondent," *Daily Alta California*, 5 (8 October 1854), 279

... If my limits would allow, the Book I would most like to expatiate upon, would be Thoreau's *Walden, or Life in the Woods*, published by Ticknor and Fields, Boston. It is the result of a two or three years' sojourn in the woods, and it is a most minute history of Thoreau's external life, and internal speculation. It is the latest effervescence of the peculiar school, at the head of which stands Ralph Waldo Emerson. Of *Walden*, Emerson says, that Thoreau has cornered nature in it. Several years ago Thoreau sought the freedom of the woods, and built him a little house with his two hands, on the margin of Walden Pond, near Concord, Massachusetts. There he contemplated, on "cornered" nature, and hoed beans, determined, as he said, to know them. Notwithstanding an apparent contempt for utility, he seems a sharp accountant, and not a little interest is attached to his bills of expense, they are so ludicrously small. Coarse bread, occasional molasses and rice, now and then a fish taken from Walden Pond, and philosophically matured vegetables, (he sold his beans) were his fare. His ideas of beauty are positive, but limited. The world of art is beyond his wisdom. Individualism is the altar at which he worships. Philanthropy is an opposite term, and he does not scruple to affirm that Philanthropy and he are two. The book is full of talent, curious and interesting. I recommend it as a study to all fops, male and female. . . .

Review of *Walden*, Boston *Transcript*, 19 October 1854, p. 1

To the Editor of the Transcript: The volume with the above title, recently issued by Messrs. Ticknor & Fields, is a very remarkable book; one which appeals to the loftiest instincts of men, and which, we are sure, is already making a deep impression upon some souls. Few books have sprung from a genius so clear of extraneous influences, whether from Church, State, Society or Literature. Here is one person, at least, who is not swallowed up by the whirlpool of civilization, who though feeling no respect for any special form of religion, so that he would be shouted at by many as an infidel, yet has such a sense of the greatness of our nature, such an appreciation of intellectual and spiritual satisfactions, that it is no sacrifice, but rather a pleasure for him to resign many of the so-called advantages of society, as being obstacles in the way of his true life.

There can be no question that even in the best *class* of society, however it may be with here and there an individual, intellectual culture does not hold the first place, but is made secondary to worldly ends; to the attainment of wealth, social position, and honors. Even most of our poets and priests, whatever they may say professionally or in their better moments, yet, in the general tenor of their lives, accept the popular standard. The peculiarity of Mr. Thoreau's position is, as indicated both by this book and the other which he has published, "A Week on the Concord and Merrimac Rivers," that he finds another kind of wealth so attractive that he cannot devote his life to the ends which society has in view. However we may speculate about spirit and intellect, it is obvious that our civilization is too exclusively material. In these books we are made acquainted with a life which rests soberly and substantially upon a spiritual basis.

The influence which Mr. Thoreau exerts will not at once spread over a large surface, but it will reach far out into the tide of time, and it will make up in depth for what it wants in extent. He appeals, with all the truly wise, to elements in our nature, which lie far deeper than the sources of a noisy popularity. There are doubtless already many thoughtful persons here and there, to whom his words are exceedingly precious. This, of course, is the truest outward success, and however convenient, though dangerous, a more abundant pecuniary return for his work might be, none can know better than this writer, that the capacity for entertaining and uttering such thoughts as he gives us is its own and the only adequate reward.

"D'A," Review of *Walden*, Boston *Atlas*, 21 October 1854, p. 1

It is an old and well established doctrine, that any man's expression of opinion should be viewed and examined from his own point of vision; that we must judge of his idiosyncrasy of thought, by the light which illumined the mind that recorded it; and not by any greater or lesser brilliancy available to us. Under this rule Mr. Thoreau's volume will fall into the hands of few who can fully appreciate him or assimilate to him; for he has thought and lived and wrought under the sparkle of a moral phosphorescence which illuminates but a small portion of mankind. Not that his speculations and moralizations are in themselves novel in character; not that he has more deeply explored the varied expanse of human nature, its longings and yearnings and dreamings, than many other travellers, some of whom have recorded their explorations, and many more of whom have been silent upon the sights they have beheld. Philosophers of all ages and lands and tongues, have indulged in the same reveries; have been also weighers and gaugers of human pursuits and aspirations. In many a silent, taper lighted chamber in the heart of populous cities, as well as in the depths of the wilderness, have the same sad verdicts been passed upon the busy avocations of our race. It is not necessary to become a hermit, an exile from the companionship of our fellows, to form just such a valuation of their hopes and fears, their efforts and aims, their thoughts and deeds, as the philosopher of Walden Pond. He differs from his brother moralizers simply in this:—they think and speak of mankind as being themselves units of the many, participators in the heritage over which they mourn:—he fondly deems himself emancipated from this thraldom, and looks down upon them as an inferior tribe. He shakes the dust from his shoes as he leaves their thresholds, and goes forth to the green woods, as a temple wherein his greater holiness may dwell uncontaminated. His love for Nature, his sympathy for her wild beauty and contentedness with her society, make him forget that it is only one of her many phases which he views in his sylvan solitude. That the simplicity he adores exists nowhere in the range of human vision. The huckleberries, which he picked for his food, are more complicated in their structure than any human viands. The shadowy trees, over his lonely hut, are more intricate than any human dwelling. The laws of this wonderful world have more articles than any human code, and rule in the midst of densely aggregated human beings as surely, as beneficently and as ruthlessly as in that little patch of woodland where his philosophy, in its self glorification, sought a temporary sleeping and eating and dreaming place. By leaving the homes of men, he did not merely isolate himself from their meannesses, their sins and life long mistakes; but from their virtues, self-denials, and heroism. He did not understand that man's passions, impulses and turbulent desires are one part of the great scheme, of which his woodland abiding place was only another. He left men preying on each other, to watch ants do the same. He left the fond loves which do sometimes bless with their purity the hearts of our misguided race, to note the couplings of brutes. He left the noblest animals in the scale of being, which with all its follies and errors and degradation is still the noblest, to watch the habits of owls and woodchucks, and

imagine that he was in the society most blessed of the great Author, and occupied in pursuits most worthy of our destiny. Our destiny! what is it? Can any one corner of this little sphere, itself minute in the vast universe, afford peculiar light to our groping souls?

In speaking of "Walden," it is impossible not to identify the author with his work. It is a series of observations upon the pursuits of mankind, mingled with descriptions of natural objects. It is the author's autobiography for a year, recording his doings, his thinkings and his human measurements. His doings, as recorded, are the erection of his own dwelling, mostly by himself, partly his acquaintances; and subsequent culture of a little pulse, on which he mainly subsisted, varied by a little fishing and much rambling. His thinking is the indulging of those inexpressible mental sensations which visit all poetic, sensitive natures in the midst of woodland solitudes. The rest, except the descriptive portion, is devoted to moralizations upon the emptiness of human aims and employments. The descriptive portion is terse and graphic. He has a keenly observant relish for all natural scenery, and has painted minutely the changing face of nature in her summer and winter garb. There is a simple, expressive truthfulness in these descriptions, which renders them both interesting and instructive in the highest degree. In spite of his depreciation of human attainments, they exhibit a familiarity with studies which are the legitimate offspring of civilization, and are none the less creditable to him as a student or as a man. No savage, be he ever so much a poet by nature or a savant by practice, could achieve the results which his play-savage, but still civilized intellect has recorded. The lore of bygone ages, written in languages long dead, has furnished this word-warrior with weapons, to use against the very foe which fed and nourished him into his present strength.

The natural enquiry why a young man should leave kindred, and friends, and comfort, to dwell for two years in Concord woods, in a board shanty, and cultivate beans for his sustenance, is answered by the man himself.

"I went to the woods because I wished to live deliberately, to front only the essential facts of life, and see if I could not learn what it had to teach, and not when I came to die, discover that I had not lived . . . . I wanted to live deep and suck out all the marrow of life; to live so sturdily and Spartan-like as to put to rout all that was not life."

Whether he lived as deeply as he desired, or whether he learned out what life has to teach, he does not state, but he quitted his Spartan-life after two years indulgence therein. He relates minutely the story of his house-raising and bean-hoeing, and discloses one great, fatal error, which completely vitiates the experiment. He was no true hermit. He did not bid farewell to human kind and "front only the essential facts of life." He borrowed the cunning tools and manufactured products of civilization, to enable him to endure the wilderness. He did not go unaided and unprovided into the untamed woods, to see life and spend life in its primitive state. He only played savage on the borders of civilization; going back to the quiet town whenever he was unable to supply his civilized wants by his own powers. The war-whoop of a Comanche Indian would have made his heart knock at his ribs in that lonely spot, for all his attempts to exalt and glorify the savage life. Were he indeed in those distant wilds where he sometimes imagined himself, instead of a patch of woodland as safe as his mother's fireside, his romance and self-satisfaction might have fled before the stern unrelenting reality. No, he went back to the village to chat with the people he af-fects to despise, and spend cosy winter evenings with those who enjoyed the same natural beauties that he did without resigning those unostentatious comforts, which not only had no connexion, but did not in the least conflict with such enjoyments. One glaring mistake throughout the volume, is an apparent conviction that to really and fully relish the sights and sounds of Nature, to adore its spirit through all these noble revelations, it is necessary to shun human kind, and to eat, drink and sleep in the forest depths. As though there is not many and many a dwelling more comfortable than his own erected in the bosom of the woods, and peopled by happy, intelligent men and women, who value their dwelling for its very seclusion, enjoying its charms together.

His descriptions, admirable as they are, are bald in comparison with the glowing word-painting of many lovers of Nature, as devout, and more genial than himself. The sensations he describes are such as have thrilled the hearts of thousands before him. His yearnings to discover that mysterious secret, the end and use of life, have gushed in the bosoms of multitudes who never fancied that the key was hidden in a hermitage. Did he find it there? Did he find that life was truest away from all those dear affections which are given to man for indulgence, as freely as these very longings themselves? Did he fancy that life was only life when shorn of all its attributes? When he had taken the warm, breathing creature, had lopped away its limbs, and cut away, remorselessly, the quivering flesh, and at last reached the throbbing heart; when he had split open that palpitating centre, had he at last found out *what* that life was which animated it? No! he had only thrown from him the very parts for which that heart was made to beat; without which it were worthless.

It is a sorrowful surprise that a constant communion with so much beauty and beneficence was not able to kindle one spark of genial warmth in this would-be savage. Pithy sarcasm, stern judgment, cold condemnation—all these abound in the pages of this volume. The follies and emptiness of men are uncovered with a sweeping hand. There is truth in it; strong vigorous, nervous truth. But there is not a page, a paragraph giving one sign of liberality, charitableness, kind feeling, generosity, in a word—HEART. The noble deeds, the silent fortitude, the hidden sorrow of mankind, are nowhere recognized. It is difficult to understand that a mother had ever clasped this hermit to her bosom; that a sister had ever imprinted on his lips a tender kiss. The occasional ridiculousness of some of his propositions is only exceeded by the total absence of human affection which they evince. It is scarcely to be credited that any man can have lived thirty years in New England and written a volume treating expressly of human life, which exhibits such an utter dearth of all the kindly, generous feelings of our nature. Could not the warm, budding spring arouse one genial throb in his cynic soul? Could not the instinctive loves of birds and beasts have awakened within him one thought of the purer, loftier, nobler passion accorded to his own race? Did he never people that bare hovel, in imagination, with a loving and beloved wife and blooming children, or did he imagine that to know what life is he must ignore its origin? Did he utterly forget that pain and sickness might have quenched the light of his reason, and drawn a dreadful night over his unsolaced soul? A night in which the meanest of human kind would have beamed at his side like an angel from Heaven! He has much to say to men, and tells them bitter truths; but there is not one recognition of the presence on this earth of woman. There is not a word of that pure, constant, suffering woman's love, beside which his philosophic judgments shrink and shiver in their frigidity. Back to the town, the crowded city, oh, forest philosophers, if the sweet smiles of nature cannot warm within you more than this, the hearts that are better worth your culture than your intellects or your bean fields! No soul is truly expanded by confinement to solitary reverie. It is an old truth that natural scenery does not, of itself, improve the heart to nature. The finest countries in the wood are peopled by sanguinary savages. The laborers upon the soil are last to appreciate the glories around them. The loftiest praises ever sung to the majesty and magnificence of nature, have come from the lips of poets whose minds and perceptions were cultivated in the haunts of men.

The Spirit who placed us on this little planet, for his own good purpose, gave us the desire to live in company. Civilization, as it now exists, is merely the culminating point to which this desire, working through the varied channels of human idiosyncrasies, have now attained. We do not all go to the woods and live on pulse, simply because we were not inspired with the desire to do so; and human history does not date back to the time when such was the case. The errors of mankind are simply the creatures of those passions, more or less developed, which are part of our nature. If it were better that we should be entirely without them, they would never have been given to us. Strong thinkers, skilful anatomists of human impulse, would be better occupied in seeking to assuage the troubles of the body corporate, than in crossing on the other side and railing at it.

Mr. Thoreau's book will be admired by some for its truthful and graphic delineations of natural objects; by others for its just valuations of human pursuits. It is marked by vigorous expression and quaint illustration, though this last sometimes verges into nonsense and puerility. He argues at times with apparent gravity upon topics scarcely worth the consideration of a man seeking to solve the problem of human life. His propositions with regard to dress are certainly unworthy of him. The question may simply be asked, if a man be "fit to worship God" in "patched pantaloons," is he not equally so in whole ones? The preference for clean, well made clothes over dirty, ragged ones, scarcely argues any moral degradation or idle folly in any one. Still, even on this as other topics, he has much truth and sense on his side, so long as he attacks abuse and not use. There is much freshness and vigor in the thoughts strewn through the volume; but it is marred by an affected mannerism belonging to the school which he copies, and by the absence of a genial, truly philosophical, broad-hearted, pervading spirit.

Review of *Walden*, *Yankee Blade*, 28 October 1854, p. 3

This is a charming volume by a writer who reminds us of Emerson by his philosophy—of the Elizabethan writers by his quaintness and originality—and by his minuteness and acuteness of observation, of Gilbert White, the author of the Natural History of Selborne. Mr. Thoreau lived alone in the woods for two years, a mile from any neighbor, in a house which he had built himself in Concord, Mass., on the shore of Walden Pond. In the present volume he relates in a lively and sparkling, yet pithy style, his experiences during that period—describing the various natural phenomena, the sights and sounds, as well as the different phases of humanity, that fell under his observation and favoring us with exact statistics of the cost of supporting his hermit life. It is rarely that one finds so much originality and freshness in a modern book—such an entire absence of conventionality and cant—or so much suggestive observation on the philosophy of life. Almost every page abounds in brilliant, and piquant things, which, in spite of the intellectual pride of the author—the intense and occasionally unpleasant egotism with which every line is steeped—lure the reader on with bewitched attention from title-page to finis. Mr. Thoreau has an odd twist in his brains, but, as Hazlitt says of Sir Thomas Browne, they are "all the better for the twist." The best parts of the book, to our mind, are those which treat of Sounds, Solitude, Brute Neighbors, Winter Animals, The Pond in Winter, and Reading; the poorest, the Conclusion, in which he tries to Emersonize, and often "attains" triumphantly to the obscurity which he seems to court.

"Town and Rural Humbugs," *Knickerbocker*, 45 (March 1855), 235–41

When Philip, King of Macedon, had made preparations to march against the Corinthians, the latter, though utterly incapable of coping with that sagacious and powerful monarch, affected to make great efforts at defence with a view to resist him. Diogenes, who took great delight in ridiculing such follies as he was too proud to indulge in himself, or did not happen to have a taste for, began to roll about his tub in a bustling and excited manner, thus deriding the idle hurry and silly show of opposition by which the feeble Corinthians were trying to deceive themselves or Philip into a belief that he had something to fear from them.

It is a wonder to a certain Yankee Diogenes, that there are not more tubs rolled about now-a-days; for the world, in his estimation, never contained more bustling, shadow-pursuing Corinthians, than at the present time.

A Concord philosopher, or modern Diogenes, who has an eye of acute penetration in looking out upon the world, discovered so much aimless and foolish bustle, such a disproportion of shams to realities, that his inclination or self-respect would not permit him to participate in them; so he built himself in the woods, on the banks of a pond of pure water—deep enough for drowning purposes if the bean-crop failed—a tub of unambitious proportions, into which he crawled. In this retreat, where he supported animals and intellectual life for more than two years, at a cost of about thirteen (!) dollars per annum, he wrote a book full of interest, containing the most pithy, sharp, and original remarks.

It is a fortunate circumstance for Mr. Thoreau, the name of this eccentric person, that his low estimate of the value of the objects, compared with their cost, for which the world is so assiduously and painfully laboring, should have received, so soon after the publication of his book, such an important, substantial, and practical confirmation in the auto-biography of Barnum. If any thing is calculated to induce a man to see how few beans will support animal life, we think it is a contemplation of the life and career of the great show-man. If there is any thing calculated to reconcile us, not to the career of Barnum, but to whatever laborious drudgery may be necessary to procure good beefsteaks and oysters, with their necessary accompaniments, it is the thought of those inevitable beans, that constituted so large a part of the *crop* of Mr. Thoreau, and that extraordinary compound of corn-meal and water, which he facetiously called bread.

Beyond all question, the two most remarkable books that have been published the last year are the "Auto-biography of Barnum," and "Life in the Woods," by Thoreau. The authors of the two books, in tastes, habits, disposition, and culture are perfect antipodes to each other; and the lessons they inculcate are consequently diametrically opposite. If ever a book required an antidote, it is the auto-biography of Barnum, and we know of no other so well calculated to furnish this antidote as the book of Thoreau's.

If any of the readers of the *Knickerbocker* have so long denied themselves the pleasure of reading "Walden, or Life in the Woods," we will give them a slight account of the book and its author; but we presume the information will be necessary to only very few. Mr. Thoreau is a graduate of Harvard University. He is a bold and original thinker; "he reads much, is a great observer, and looks quite through the deeds of men." "Beware," says Emerson, "when the great God lets loose a thinker on this planet. Then all things are at risk." Are thinkers so rare that all the moral, social, and political elements of society may be disturbed by the advent of one? The sale Barnum's book has already met with is not, to be sure, suggestive of an overwhelming number of thinkers in the country. Thinkers always have been considered dangerous. Even Cæsar, if he could have feared any thing, would have been afraid of that lean Cassius, because

He thinks too much: such men are dangerous.

And why are thinkers dangerous? Because the world is full of "time-honored and venerable" shams, which the words of thinkers are apt to endanger.

After leaving college, Mr. Thoreau doffed the harness which society enjoins that all its members shall wear, in order for them "to get along well," but it galled and chafed in so many places that he threw it off, and took to the woods in Concord. He built a hut there, a mile from any neighbors, that cost him twenty-eight dollars, twelve and a-half cents, and lived there more than two years—eight months of the time at an expense of nearly nine shillings a-month. Before adopting this mode of life, he first tried school-keeping, reporting for a newspaper, and then trading for a livelihood; but after a short trial at each, became persuaded that it was impossible for his genius to lie in either of those channels.

After hesitating for some time as to the advisability of seeking a living by picking huckle-berries, he at last concluded that "the occupation of a day-laborer was the most independent of any, as it required only thirty or forty days in a year,

to support one. The laborer's day ends with the going down of the sun, and he is then free to devote himself to his chosen pursuit, independent of his labor; but his employer, who speculates from month to month, has no respite from one end of the year to the other. In short, I am convinced, both by faith and experience, that to maintain one's self on this earth, is not a hardship, but a pastime, if we will live simply and wisely, as the pursuits of the simpler nations are still the sports of the more artificial. It is not necessary that a man should earn his living by the sweat of his brow, unless he sweats easier than I do."

The establishment in the woods, kept up by the extravagant expenditures we have mentioned before, was the result of these reflections.

If there is any reader of the Knickerbocker—native-born and a Know-Nothing—who needs to be told who P. T. Barnum is, such a person might, without doubt, "hear something to his advantage," by inquiring out and presenting himself before that illustrious individual; for the great showman has made a good deal of money by exhibiting less extraordinary animals than such a man would be.

It was pretty well understood by physiologists, before the recent experiment of Mr. Thoreau, how little farinaceous food would suffice for the human stomach; and Chatham-street clothiers have a tolerably accurate knowledge of how little poor and cheap raiment will suffice to cover the back, so that his "life in the woods" adds but little to the stock of information scientific men already possessed. But it was not clearly known to what extent the public was gullible until the auto-biography of Barnum fully demonstrated the fact. This renowned individual has shown to a dignified and appreciative public the vulgar machinery used to humbug them, and they (the public) are convulsed with laughter and delight at the exposition. Cuteness is held in such great esteem that the fact of being egregiously cajoled and fooled out of our money is lost sight of in admiration for the shrewdness of the man who can do it. And then there is such an idolatrous worship of the almighty dollar, that the man who accumulates 'a pile' is pretty sure to have the laugh on his side. 'Let him laugh who wins,' says Barnum, and the whole country says amen. It is very evident that shams sometimes 'pay better' pecuniarily than realities, but we doubt if they do in all respects. Although Thoreau 'realized' from his bean-crop one season— a summer's labor—but eight dollars seventy-one and a-half cents, yet it is painful to think what Barnum must have 'realized' from 'Joice Heth' and the 'Woolly Horse.'

If we were obliged to choose between being shut up in 'conventionalism's airtight stove,' (even if the said stove had all the surroundings of elegance and comforts that wealth could buy,) and a twenty-eight dollar tub in the woods, with a boundless range of freedom in the daily *walk* of life, we should not hesitate a moment in taking the tub, if it were not for a recollection of those horrid beans, and that melancholy mixture of meal and water. Aye, there's the rub, for from that vegetable diet what dreams might come, when we had shuffled off the wherewith to purchase other food, must give us pause. There's the consideration that makes the sorry conventionalisms of society of so long life. We rather bear those ills we have, than fly to others that we know not of. A very reasonable dread of something unpleasant resulting to us from eating beans in great quantities, would be likely to be a consequence of our experience alone, if we happened to be deficient in physiological knowledge. Whatever effects,

however, different kinds of diet may have upon different persons, mentally or physically, nothing is more clear than the fact that the diet of Mr. Thoreau did not make him mentally windy. We think, however, between Iranistan, with Joice Heth and the Mermaid for associates, and the tub at Walden, with only Shakespeare for a companion, few probably would be long puzzled in making a choice, though we are constrained to say that the great majority would undoubtedly be on the side of the natural phenomena—we mean on the side of Barnum and the other mentioned curiosities. Still, in contemplating a good many of the situations in which Barnum was placed, it is impossible to conceive that any person of a comparatively sensitive nature would not gladly have exchanged places with the man of the woods. (We refer of course to the author of "Walden," and not to the animal known as "the man of the woods." Some perhaps would not have taken pains to make this explanation.)

There is a good deal more virtue in beans than we supposed there was, if they are sufficient to sustain a man in such cheerful spirits as Thoreau appears to have been in when he wrote that book. The spirit oftentimes may be strong when the flesh is weak; but there does not appear to be any evidence of weakness of the flesh in the author of "Walden." We cannot help feeling admiration for the man

That fortune's buffets and rewards
Has ta'en with equal thanks:

and since Sylla so coolly massacred so many Roman citizens, there has not been a man who apparently has contemplated his fellow-men with a more cheerful, lofty, and philosophical scorn than the occupant of this Walden tub. If a man can do this upon beans, or in *spite* of them, we shall endeavor to cultivate a respect for that vegetable, which we never could endure.

It was a philosopher, as ancient as Aristotle, we believe, who affirmed that "they most resemble the gods whose wants were fewest." Whether the sentiment is a true one or not, we have no hesitation in saying that the gods we worship will bear a good deal more resemblance to H. D. Thoreau than to P. T. Barnum. We believe it requires a much higher order of intellect to live alone in the woods, than to dance attendance in the museum of a great metropolis upon dead hyenas and boa constrictors, living monkeys and rattle-snakes, giants and dwarfs, artificial mermaids, and natural zanies. There is, however, a good deal of society worse than this.

Of the many good things said by Colton, one of the best, we think, is the following:

"Expense of thought is the rarest prodigality, and to dare to live alone the rarest courage; since there are many who had rather meet their bitterest enemy in the field, than their own hearts in their closet. He that has no resources of mind is more to be pitied than he who is in want of necessaries for the body; and to be obliged to beg our daily happiness from others, bespeaks a more lamentable poverty than that of him who begs his daily bread."

We do not believe there is any danger of proselytes to Mr. Thoreau's mode of life becoming too numerous. We wish we could say the same in regard to Barnum's. We ask the reader to look around among his acquaintances, and see if the number of those whose resources of mind are sufficient to enable them to dispense with much intercourse with others, is not exceedingly small. We know of some such, though they are very few; but their fondness for solitude unfortunately is not associated with any particular admiration for a vegetable diet. It is a melancholy circumstance, and one that has been very bitterly deplored, ever since that indefinite period when "the memory of man runneth not to the contrary," that the accompaniments of poverty should go hand-in-hand with a taste for a solitary life. A hearty appreciation of and love for humble fare, plain clothes, and poor surroundings generally, are what men of genius need to cultivate. "Walden" tends to encourage this cultivation.

The part of Mr. Barnum's life, during which he has become a millionaire, has been spent almost wholly in a crowd. It would be no paradox to say that if the time he has spent as a show-man had been spent in the woods, neither the brilliancy of his imagination nor the vigor and originality of his thoughts would have enabled him to have produced a book that would have created any very great excitement, notwithstanding the extraordinary attributes of that intellect which could conceive the idea of combining nature and art to produce "natural curiosities," and which was shrewd enough to contrive ways and means for drawing quarters and shillings, and for the smallest value received, indiscriminately from residents in the Fifth Avenue and the Five-Points, from the statesman and "the Bowery-boy," from savans, theologians, lawyers, doctors, merchants, and "the rest of mankind," to say nothing about Queen Victoria, the Duke of Wellington, and a large portion of the Eastern continent beside.

Unlike as Barnum and Thoreau are in most every other respect, in one point there is a striking resemblance. Both of them had no idea of laboring very hard with their hands for a living; they were determined to support themselves principally by their wits. The genius of Barnum led him to obtain the meat he fed upon by a skillful combination of nature with art— by eking out the short-comings in the animal creation with ingenious and elaborate manufacturers, and then adroitly bringing the singular compounds thus formed to bear upon the credulity of the public. And thus, while he taxed the animal, vegetable, and mineral kingdoms, either separately or combined, to gratify the curiosity of the public, the most valued products of the last-mentioned kingdom flowed in a large and perpetual stream into his pocket. But his expenditures of "brass" in these labors were enormous. Thoreau had no talent for "great combinations." The meat he fed upon evidently would not be that of extraordinary calves or over-grown buffaloes, baked in the paragon cooking-stove of public curiosity; or rather, as he ate no meat, the vegetables he lived upon would not come from the exhibition of India-rubber mermaids, gutta-percha fish, or mammoth squashes. His genius did not lie at all in that direction. On the contrary, he preferred to diminish his wants, instead of resorting to extraordinary schemes to gratify them.

Mr. Thoreau gives a description of a battle fought upon his wood-pile between two armies of ants, that is exceedingly graphic and spirited. We think it surpasses in interest the description of battles fought about Sebastopol, written by the famous correspondent of the London Times. Perhaps, however, we are somewhat prejudiced in the matter. The truth is, we have read so much about the war in Europe, that the whole subject has become somewhat tiresome; and this account of the battle of the ants in Concord had so much freshness about it—so much novelty, dignity, and importance, which the battles in Europe cease to possess for us—that we have read it over three or four times with increased interest each time. We regret that the whole account is too long to copy here, but we will give the closing part:

["Brute Neighbors," 229.21–230.29]

The more you think of it the less the difference between this fight and those battles about Sebastopol. There appears, however, to have been this advantage in favor of the battle of the ants, there was no "mistake" made in the orders, (that the chronicler could discover), by which many valuable lives were lost, as in the charge of cavalry at Sebastopol. All the operations of the ants appeared to be systematic and well-timed. This rather goes to show that the commanders of ants are more cautious than the commanders of men, for the reason probably that they hold the lives of their combatants in greater estimation.

The machinery that is used to bring about battles between different nations by "the powers that be," is very much like that Barnum used to divert the public—to divert money from their pockets into his. By adding to the age of his remarkable "nurse"—the vivacious and interesting Joice—in about the same proportion that he increased the age of his juvenile phenomenon, General Thumb, he was guilty of a departure from truth not a whit more extraordinary than the discrepancy between the conversation of the Emperor of all the Russias with the English ambassadors in regard to the health of Turkey, and his actions at the same time. Barnum unquestionably possesses superior diplomatic talents. Talleyrand would have approved them.

We said some little way back that there was one point of resemblance between Barnum and Thoreau. There are half-a-dozen. Both are good-natured, genial, pleasant men. One sneers at and ridicules the pursuits of his contemporaries with the same cheerfulness and good-will that the other cajoles and fleeces them. The rural philosopher measured the length, breadth, and depth of Walden Pond, with the same jovial contentedness that the metropolitan show-man measured the

405

length, breadth, and depth of the public gullibility. Both too are compassionate men. Flashes of pity are occasionally met with in the book of Barnum's, at the extent of the credulity of that public he seemingly so remorselessly wheedled; and Thoreau evinced a good deal of compassion for some of his well-to-do townsmen. His sympathy was a good deal moved in behalf of the farmer that owned "a handsome property," who was driving his oxen in the night to Brighton, through the mud and darkness. Both were artists. He of the wood constructed himself the unpretending edifice he occupied—a representation of which graces the title-page of his book. Barnum's artistic skill was more evinced in constructing such "curiosities" as we have alluded to. And finally, both were humbugs—one a town and the other a rural humbug.

But both of them have nevertheless made large contributions to the science of human nature. Malherbe, once upon hearing a prose work of great merit extolled, dryly asked if it would *reduce the price of bread*! If "Walden" should be extensively read, we think it would have the effect to reduce somewhat the price of meat, if it did not of bread. At all events it encourages the belief, which in this utilitarian age enough needs encouragement, that there is some other object to live to except "to make money."

In the New England philosophy of life, which so extensively prevails where the moral or intellectual character of a man is more or less determined by his habits of *thrift*, such a book as "Walden" was needed. Extravagant as it is in the notions it promulgates, we think it is nevertheless calculated to do a good deal of good, and we hope it will be widely read. Where it exerts a bad influence upon one person, Barnum's autobiography will upon a hundred.

[George Eliot], Review of *Walden, Westminster Review* [England], 65 (January 1856), 302–3

. . . in a volume called "Walden; or, Life in the Works"—published last year, but quite interesting enough to make it worth while for us to break our rule by a retrospective notice—we have a bit of pure American life (not the "go a-head" species, but its opposite pole), animated by that energetic, yet calm spirit of innovation, that practical as well as theoretic independence of formulæ, which is peculiar to some of the finer American minds. The writer tell us how he chose, for some years, to be stoic of the woods; how he built his house; how he earned the necessaries of his simple life by cultivating a bit of ground. He tells his system of diet, his studies, his reflections, and his observations of natural phenomena. These last are not only made by a keen eye, but have their interest enhanced by passing through the medium of a deep poetic sensibility; and, indeed, we feel throughout the book the presence of a refined as well as a hardy mind. People—very wise in their own eyes—who would have every man's life ordered according to a particular pattern, and who are intolerant of every existence the utility of which is not palpable to them, may pooh-pooh Mr. Thoreau and his episode in his story, as unpractical and dreamy. Instead of contesting their opinion ourselves, we will let Mr. Thoreau speak for himself. There is plenty of sturdy sense mingled with his unworldliness.

["Where I Lived, and What I Lived For," 90.32–91.15; "Economy," 72.18–73.16, 76.15–32, 77.6–16]

We can only afford one more extract, which, to our minds, has great beauty.

["Sounds," 111.18–33, 112.11–24]

"America,"
Critic [England],
1 May 1856, pp. 223–4

Originality is the chief virtue of a book. It includes veracity for the truly original man is the truly veracious; he is not a mere soundpipe or echo, but alive in the world, and tells us how he finds it. Thousands of books are published ever year, most of them the pouring of one vessel into another, books about books, old nations, old phrases turned once again. Professional critics, too, living in the thick of this noisy manufacture, are usually the last, among men who read, to distinguish a real from a pseudo excellence, or to greet the truly original book which has nature's pure juices in its veins. Their great poet is never the true dawning star, their supreme philosopher is likely to prove an ignisfatuus; but the heavens move on, and at last they too acknowledge the genuine ray, they loudest of all, when it is lifted high from the horizon. So much for a general remark. Mr. Thoreau, author of "Walden" and "A Week on the Concord and Merrimack Rivers," is not a literary artist or professional teacher; but he has given us two volumes of homegrown experiences—mark! *homegrown experiences*—things he has seen and known—thoughts and feelings actually born in the mind of an honest intelligent man among the trees and streams of Massachusetts. Books he has studied, new and old, and the society of cultivated persons, but still better the language of birds, fishes, herbs, clouds, fogs, snow, sunbeams, nor failed in sympathy and collaboration with the farmer, squatter, hunter, woodman and villager. In short, he has lived heartily where he was put, has tried, observed, and reflected on all that came near him, and out of his store given us some pages of record very delightful to read, and comprising a suggestion for the amelioration of human life not the least practical in the crowd of such suggestions. His Walden text is this, *simplify your wants*, and, in accordance with it, he himself went out to the banks of a clear pool, about a mile and a half from the village of Concord, in Massachusetts, and there built and lived for two years in a hut of wood, growing most of his own victuals with easy labour. The example could seldom be followed in its particulars, and, perhaps, should not if it could; but *the principle* is well worth the consideration of thoughtful men— Nature *versus* Fashion, Substance *versus* Appearance, Real Education *versus* Luxury, Life *versus* Cash. Henry Thoreau has written down some things from his life at Walden Pond; and the volume is worth reading and re-reading. We do not get such a book every day, or often in a century.

["Economy," 3.21–4.7]

We shall present some extracts, requiring little or no comment to explain or recommend them. Here are pregnant sentences.

["Economy," 31.9–16; 38.11–13, 27–30]

["Where I Lived, and What I Lived For," 90.18–28, 92.4–18, 95.30–96.9]

["Sounds," 112.30–35]

["Solitude," 134.6–8]

["Baker Farm," 208.1–3]

["Higher Laws," 218.28–30]

His sketches of natural history and the landscape are most fresh and charming. Here is a glimpse of

["Where I Lived, and What I Lived For," 86.3–32]

["The Ponds," 199.21–32]

["Baker Farm," 201.1–202.15]

["Winter Animals," 272.9–32]

How graphic and interesting is this

BATTLE OF THE ANTS

["Brute Neighbors," 228.25–231.26]

In conclusion, Mr. Thoreau tells us merely that he "left the woods for as good a reason as he went there," adding—

["Conclusion," 323.29–324.8]

This volume has its faults, no doubt, and the realising and rhetorical jar together sometimes on our ear. The letter is not for general application, but the spirit is—*Walden* being a brave book, one in a million, an honour to America, a gift to men. A grateful reader of it wrote these lines on the fly-leaf of his copy:

Walden's a placid woodland pool
    Across the wild waves hoary,
In whose fountain clear and cool
    I intend to swim.
British lakes, Italian, Swiss,
Prouder, lovelier than this,
    Echo song and story;
Wide are the Indian waters; but
By Walden one man built a hut—
    I often think of him.

"An American Diogenes," *Chambers's Journal* [England], 21 November 1857, pp. 330–2

When Philip of Macedon announced his intention to invade Corinth, the inhabitants of that city, overlooking, or feigning not to perceive, their utter incapacity of resistance, affected to make great preparations for defence; while Diogenes, who, like many of us even at the present time, delighted to ridicule the follies he did not himself commit, rolled about his tub in an excited, bustling manner, by way of deriding the fussy, fruitless show of opposition made by the feeble Corinthians. The transatlantic Diogenes, however, when he observed the foolish, aimless bustle made by the modern Corinthians of the world, in pursuit of the sacred dollar and its glittering accessories, instead of rolling about his tub, quietly sat down in it, and wrote an interesting book, replete with pithy, original observations, but strongly tinctured with the inevitable dogmatism that ever attends the one *soi-disant* wise man who assumed to be the teacher of all the rest of his race. Henry D. Thoreau, the American Diogenes, if we may presume to term him so—assuredly we mean no offence—is a graduate of Harvard university, a ripe scholar, and a transcendentalist of the Emersonian school, though he goes much further than his master; his object, apparently, being the exaltation of mankind by the utter extinction of civilisation. When Nat Lee was confined in Bedlam, the unfortunate dramatist roundly asserted his perfect sanitary, exclaiming: 'All the world say that I am mad, but I say that all the world are mad; so being in the minority, I am placed here.' Now, the truth, as it generally does, may have lain between the two extremes; and in like manner, Mr. Thoreau, when he lazily lived in a hut, in a lonely wood, subsisting on beans, was not half so mad as his neighbours, the 'cute New Englanders, supposed him to be; nor, on the other hand, were they so mad as he considered them, though they lived in comfortable houses, in towns, and ate beef and mutton, which they consequently worked hard to pay for.

Mr. Thoreau had 'tried school-keeping,' but without success, because he 'did not teach for the good of his fellow-men, but simply for a livelihood.' He had tried commerce, but found 'that trade curses everything it handles; and though you trade in messages from heaven, the whole curse of trade attaches to business.' He had tried 'doing good,' but felt satisfied that it did not agree with his constitution. Indeed he says: 'The greater part of what my neighbours call good, I believe in my soul to be bad; and if I repent of anything, it is very likely to be my good-behaviour.' At last, as he could fare hard, and did not wish to spend his life in earning rich carpets or other fine furniture, or a house in the Grecian or Gothic style, he concluded that 'the occupation of a day-labourer was the most independent of any, especially as it required only thirty or forty days' work to support a man for the whole year. Besides, the labourer's day ends with the going down of the sun, and he is then free to devote himself to his chosen pursuit; but his employer, who speculates from month to month, has no respite from one end of the year to the other.' So, borrowing an axe, he boldly marched into the woods of Concord, where, on the pleasant bank of Walden Pond, he built himself a hut, in which he lived alone for more than two years, subsisting chiefly on beans planted and gathered by his own hands. In the book, already adverted to, his thoughts and actions during this period are pleasantly and interestingly related; though, like all solitary men, the author exaggerates the importance of his own thoughts, his *I* standing up like an obelisk in the midst of a level, though by no means barren expanse.

The building of his hut gave rise to many reflections. He wondered that in all his walks he never came across a man engaged in so simple and natural an occupation as building his own house. 'There is,' he says, 'some of the same fitness in a man's building his own house, as there is in a bird's building its own nest. Who knows but if men constructed their dwellings with their own hands, and provided food for themselves and families, simply and honestly enough, the poetic faculty would be universally developed, as birds universally sing when they are thus engaged.' So, as he hewed his studs and rafters, he sang—if not as musically, at least quite as unintelligibly as any bird—

'Men say they know many things;
But lo! they have taken wings—
The arts and sciences,
And a thousand appliances;
The wind that blows
Is all that nobody knows.'

As Mr. Thoreau squatted, he paid no rent; but the glass, ironwork, and other materials of his hut, which he could not make himself, cost twenty-eight dollars. The first year he lived in the woods, he earned, by day-labour, thirteen dollars, and the surplus produce of his beans he sold for twenty-three dollars; and as his food and clothing during that period cost him thirteen dollars only, he thus secured health, and independence, besides a comfortable house, as long as he chose to occupy it. Rice, Indian meals, beans, and molasses, were his principal articles of food. He sometimes caught a mess of fish; and the wood gratuitously supplied him with fuel for warmth and cooking. Work agreed with his constitution as little as 'doing good.' He tells us:

["Sounds," 111.22–112.2, 112.19–22]

As he walked in the woods to see the birds and squirrels, so he sometimes walked in the village to see the men and boys. The village appeared to him as a great newsroom: its vitals were the grocery, the bar-room, the post-office, and the bank; and as a necessary part of the machinery, it had a bell, a big gun, and a fire-engine. The houses were arranged to make the most of mankind, in lanes and fronting one another, so that every traveller had to run the gantlet, and every man, woman, and child might get a lick at him. But to one of his village visits there hangs a tale, which he shall tell himself:

["The Village," 171.20–36]

Mr. Thoreau failed in making any converts to his system; one person only, an idiotic pauper, from the village poor-house, expressed a wish to live as he did. An honest, hardworking, shiftless Irishman, however, seemed a more promising subject for conversion. This man worked for a farmer, turning up meadow, with a spade, for ten dollars an acre, with the use of the land and manure for one year, while a little broad-faced son worked cheerfully at his side. So as Mr. Thoreau relates:

["Baker Farm," 205.2–21, 206.1–5, 206.7–12]

Puzzled, but not convinced, the Irishman and his 'greasy-faced wife' stared and scratched their heads. Such teaching must have sounded strangely to them, who had crossed the Atlantic to do their share of work in the world, and enjoy its reward

410

in the form of tea, coffee, butter, and beef. Patrick, however, was silly enough to leave his work for that afternoon, and go a-fishing with the philosopher; but this 'derivative old-country mode of fishing disturbed only two fins.' So he wisely went back to his work the next morning, probably studying the proverb of his country which teaches, that 'hunger and ease is a dog's life;' and our author thus rather uncourteously dismisses him: 'With his horizon all his own, yet he is a poor man, born to be poor, with his inherited Irish poverty, or poor life, his Adam's grandmother and boggy ways, not to rise in this world, he nor his posterity, till their wading, webbed, bog-trotting feet get *talaria* to their heels.'

Another Irishman, of a very different stamp, a squatter of the woods of Walden, might have proved a more facile subject for conversion; but he died just after making Mr. Thoreau's acquaintance. This man's name was Quoil; and when he did work, which was very seldom—for he liked work as little as Mr. Thoreau himself did—followed the occupation of a pitcher. Having, however, been a soldier in the British army, his American neighbours gave him the brevet rank of colonel. Colonel Quoil, Mr. Thoreau tells us,

["Former Inhabitants; and Winter Visitors," 262.6–30]

The natural sights and sounds of the woods, as described by Mr. Thoreau, form much pleasanter reading than his vague and scarcely comprehensible social theories. He says:

["Sounds," 112.25–30, 114.22–34, 124.17–125.6, 126.7–36]

Those were the summer sounds; in winter nights he heard the forlorn but melodious note of the hooting-owl, such a tone as the frozen earth would yield if struck with a suitable plectrum.

[Reprints "Winter Animals," 272.5–32, 273.6–18]

Mr. Thoreau went to the woods, because he wished to live deliberately, to front only the essential facts of life, and see whether he could learn what it had to teach; so that when he came to die, he might not discover that he had not lived. After supporting animal and intellectual life for two years, at the cost of thirteen dollars per annum, he 'left the woods for as good a reason as he went there.' It seemed to him that he had several more lives to live, so he could not spare any more time for that particular one. He learned, however, by his experiment, 'that it is not necessary a man should earn his living by the sweat of his brow; and to maintain one's self on this earth is not a hardship but a pastime, if we will live simply and wisely. Moreover, if a man advances confidently in the direction of his dreams, and endeavours to live the life which he has imagined, he will meet with a success unexpected in common hours. In proportion as he simplifies his life, the laws of the universe will appear less complex, and solitude will not be solitude, nor poverty poverty, nor weakness weakness.'

Who is it, we have more than once mentally inquired, when penning the preceding sketch, that Mr. Thoreau reminds us of? Surely it cannot be—yes, it is—no other than his renowned compatriot Barnum. As homespun, beans, and water differ from fine linen, turtle, and champagne, so do the two men differ in tastes, habits, disposition, and culture; yet we cannot think of the one without an ideal association of the other. In one respect only do they seem to agree—both have an antipathy to hard work; but while one prefers diminishing his wants, the other, increasing them, invents extraordinary schemes for their gratification. If Barnum's

411

autobiography be a bane, Thoreau's woodland experiences may be received as its antidote; but, unfortunately, the former musters its readers by tens of thousands, the latter probably in hundreds only. It is to be hoped, however—though all of us have a reasonable predilection for beef, pudding, and the society of our fellow-creatures—that there are few readers of this Journal who would not prefer eating beans in the woods with Thoreau to living on the fat of the earth, in the best show in all Vanity Fair, with Barnum.

Review of *Walden,* Concord [Massachusetts] *Monitor,* 7 June 1862, p. 53

Once in a great while come down like manna new words of wisdom and truth. As the blessing falls around us in the evening, we do not distinguish it from the ordinary dew of summer. After the dark hours of night, comes the morning with its sunlight, and we spring from our slothful couch and go out into the fields, and find them covered with elysian food. Walden is crammed full with delicious morsels: rare philosophy, sweet poetry, invaluable facts, suggestive imaginations, strangely charming beauties, gems from the diadem of Queen Nature herself. From this recluse the man of the world may learn experience. Walden is the book to take by one's hand for a companion for your whole summer rambling. When you are snugly ensumed in the shade of a tree at the mountains, or a rock at the seashore, open at the chapter on Sounds or Solitude, and read until the delight of the *dolce far niente* has carried you into dreamland too far for any earthly sympathy. Doze awhile, then read again. Walden is the book for the business man to study, for, strange to say, this man who never saw the inside of a counting room, knew more of Economy than the owner of "sails that whiten every sea."

Walden is a book for boys and girls, for men and women, for it is written by a man of heart, mind, and soul. Perhaps you may not break the shell at once with your teeth, but persevere, read it again and again, as the writer has done, and you will surely find the sweet kernal of beauty, knowledge, and truth.

412

Review of *Walden*, [Oneida Community] *Circular*, 28 March 1864

Ten years ago "Walden" came before the public, but owing to unappreciative, if not thoroughly hostile reviews, together with a strong suspicion on our part, of its egotism and eccentricity, it failed to get our attention. It is with some humiliation that we make this confession. But some years later, we chanced to read a portion of an agricultural address by our author on the "Succession of Forest Trees." Here is a man, thought we, who interrogates the squirrels and the trees to some purpose, and who does not deal in hearsay and old clothes; a man who stands wonderfully close to nature; one, in fact, who has a habit of looking into the very atoms of a matter.

Here, at the foot of Mt. Tom, amidst orchards, healthfully remote from the gossip, the bad odors, and the slums of large towns and cities, we have set up our press. Here we take our stand to act as reporters for God and nature, and it is with a good degree of pleasure we call attention to so noteworthy phenomena as "Walden" and its author.

A true life may justly be called a compound notion—a diagonal resulting from two forces, neither of which can be implicitly obeyed nor wholly disobeyed. Do the best we can to express the truth, it often happens that for every *yea* we make, there must be a corresponding *nay*. And so we go on between yea and nay. In all criticism, either of character or of performance, one finds it necessary to bear in mind this dimly outlined philosophy. It is truly wonderful how much of the modern literature, full of Hindooism, pantheism and other paganism, as it is, unconsciously goes to prove the New Testament the best statement and solution of the central life questions. We do not wish to make this writing a substitute for "Walden" itself; on the contrary, we intend to induce people and read it; and later, we intend to make our author speak for himself. Therefore, we will speak in general terms. "Walden" is a picturesque and unique continuation of the old battle between the flesh and the spirit. It is a powerful *yea* in favor of the spirit, it is a novel and emphatic *no* to the flesh and fashion. It is the bold and sincere attempt of a young and educated man, who is not a technical Christian, to find the minimum due to his body, and the maximum due to his soul. We hail it as a helper. We do not feel called upon to follow its example, nor to invite others to do so. We may differ from its theology and sociology, but we cannot too heartily commend its philosophy, working so sincerely toward a high, spiritual life, its close and loving adhesion to nature, and its hatred of the conventional and trivial. We shall never hesitate to "speak the praises" of a man, however fractional he may be—in this case our man is a wonderfully perfected fraction—if in behalf of his deep spiritual wants he dares to boldly contradict society and his own body.

Undoubtedly "Walden" is the most original, sincere and unaffected book that has recently issued from the press. Easy and nonchalant in style, still it is densely packed with new thought. It comes to us warm with magnetism and vitality. A strong influence goes with it, which is perhaps hardly equaled by that of Carlyle. We stand in need of such formative books when we are under so much temptation to go to libraries to tell us what to find on the earth and under the water. On a first view one is struck by an apparent simplicity and homeliness of style, but soon

413

all this is transfused into a wonderful beauty. It is a book not only full of nature, but it is nature itself. It is woody, resinous, and strong with ground smells; there are none of the conventional scents of rose, pinks and violets about it, but rather odors of birch, ginseng, and skunk-cabbage. With all its familiarity with nature, it is untainted by the pedantry and literalness of your mere technical men of science.

We shall now let the book speak for itself, and our readers judge for themselves.

[Omitted is a long quotation from *Walden* not in the source for this present reprinting: Geoffrey Noyes's "Thoreau at the Oneida Community," *Thoreau Society Bulletin*, no. 115 (Spring 1971), 3–4.]

Checklist of Additional Reviews

Boston *Transcript*, 21 July 1854, p. 1.
"Thoreau's *Life in the Woods*," New York *Evening Post*, 24 July 1854, p. 1.
[Horace Greeley], "A Massachusetts Hermit," New York *Daily Tribune*, 29 July 1854, p. 3.
"A New Book by Henry Thoreau," *Norfolk Democrat* [Dedham, Mass.], 4 August 1854, p. 2.
"Life in the Woods," *Bunker-Hill Aurora and Boston Mirror*, 5 August 1854, p. 1.
"Algoma" [Charles C. Hazewell], "Our Boston Correspondence," New York *Herald*, 7 August 1854, p. 6.
Boston *Daily Bee*, 8 August 1854, p. 2.
Boston *Atlas*, 10 August 1854, p. 2.
Lowell *Journal and Courier*, 10 August 1854, p. 2.
Salem *Register*, 10 August 1854, p. 2.
Providence *Daily Journal*, 11 August 1854, p. 1.
Salem *Gazette*, 11 August 1854, p. 2.
Boston *Commonwealth*, 12 August 1854, p. 2.
Boston *Olive Branch*, 12 August 1854, p. 3.
W., Albany *Argus*, 15 August 1854, p. 2.
Worcester *Daily Transcript*, 17 August 1854, p. 2.
Boston *Saturday Evening Gazette*, 19 August 1854, p. 2.
Cincinnati *Daily Gazette*, 19 August 1854, p. 1.
Cummings' Evening Bulletin [Philadelphia], 19 August 1854, p. 2.
Daily Ohio State Journal, 19 August 1854, p. 3.

Portland (Maine) *Transcript*, 19 August 1854, p. 151.

Portsmouth *Journal of Literature and Politics*, 19 August 1854, p. 2.

Philadelphia *Sunday Dispatch*, 20 August 1854, p. 1.

Philadelphia *Dollar Magazine*, 23 August 1854, p. 3.

Springfield *Daily Republican*, 23 August 1854, p. 2.

Boston *Puritan Recorder*, 24 August 1854, p. 133.

New Orleans *Daily Picayune*, 24 August 1854, p. 2.

Philadelphia *Saturday Evening Post*, 26 August 1854, p. 2.

Philadelphia *Register*, before 29 August 1854.

Boston *Herald*, 29 August 1854, p. 2.

New York *Commercial Advertiser*, 29 August 1854, p. 2.

Richmond *Enquirer*, 29 August 1854, p. 2.

National Magazine, 5 (September 1854), 284–5.

Southern Literary Messenger, 20 (September 1854), 575.

[Jesse Clements?], *Western Literary Messenger*, 23 (September 1854), 44–6.

"Walden, or Life in the Woods," New York *Home Journal*, 2 September 1854, p. 2.

Portland (Maine) *Transcript*, 16 September 1854, p. 179.

Rochester *Daily American*, 16 September 1854, p. 2.

Daily Alta California, 5 (23 September 1854), 264.

Harrisburg (Penn.) *Morning Herald*, 30 September 1854, p. 2.

New York *Christian Inquirer*, 30 September 1854, p. 2.

Godey's Lady's Book and Magazine, 49 (October 1854), 370.

[Andrew P. Peabody?], *North American Review*, 79 (October 1854), 536.

Peterson's Magazine, 26 (October 1854), 254.

Louisville *Daily Courier*, 4 October 1854, p. 2.

Watchman and Reflector, 5 October 1854, p. 158.

New York *Home Journal*, 7 October 1854, p. 3.

Harvard Magazine, 1 (December 1854), 45.

RETROSPECTIVE ESSAYS BY CONTEMPORARIES

Ralph Waldo Emerson, "Thoreau," *Atlantic Monthly*, 10 (August 1862), 239–49[1]

Henry D. Thoreau was the last male descendant of a French ancestor who came to this country from the isle of Guernsey. His character exhibited occasional traits drawn from this blood in singular combination with a very strong Saxon genius.

He was born in Concord, Massachusetts, on the 12th of July, 1817. He was graduated at Harvard College, in 1837, but without any literary distinction. An iconoclast in literature, he seldom thanked colleges for their service to him, holding them in small esteem, whilst yet his debt to them was important. After leaving the University, he joined his brother in teaching a private school, which he soon renounced. His father was a manufacturer of lead pencils, and Henry applied himself for a time to this craft, believing he could make a better pencil than was then in use. After completing his experiments, he exhibited his work to chemists and artists in Boston, and having obtained their certificates to its excellence and to its equality with the best London manufacture, he returned home contented. His friends congratulated him that he had now opened his way to fortune. But he replied, that he should never make another pencil. "Why should I? I would not do again what I have done once." He resumed his endless walks, and miscellaneous studies, making every day some new acquaintance with Nature, though as yet never speaking of zoology or botany, since, though very studious of natural facts, he was incurious of technical and textual science.

At this time, a strong, healthy youth fresh from college, whilst all his companions were choosing their profession, or eager to begin some lucrative employment, it was inevitable that his thoughts should be exercised on the same question, and it required rare decision to refuse all the accustomed paths, and keep his solitary freedom at the cost of disappointing the natural expectations of his family and friends. All the more difficult that he had a perfect probity, was exact in securing his own independence, and in holding every man to the like duty. But Thoreau never faltered. He was a born protestant. He declined to give up his large ambition of knowledge and action for any narrow craft or profession, aiming at a much more comprehensive calling, the art of living well. If he slighted and defied the opinions of others, it was only that he was more intent to reconcile his practice with his own belief. Never idle or self-indulgent, he preferred when he wanted money, earning it by some piece of manual labor agreeable to him, as building a boat or a fence, planting, grafting, surveying, or other short work, to any long engagements. With his hardy habits and few wants, his skill in wood-craft, and his powerful arithmetic, he was very competent to live in any part of the world. It would cost him less time to supply his wants than another. He was therefore secure of his leisure.

A natural skill for mensuration, growing out of his mathematical knowledge, and his habit of ascertaining the measures and distances of objects which interested him, the size of trees, the depth and extent of ponds and rivers, the height of mountains and the air-line distance of his favorite summits,—this, and his intimate knowledge of the territory about Concord, made him drift into the professions of land-surveyor. It had the advantage for him that it led him continually into new and secluded grounds, and helped his studies of nature. His accuracy and skill in this work were readily appreciated, and he found all the employment he wanted.

He could easily solve the problems of the surveyor, but he was daily beset with graver questions which he manfully confronted. He interrogated every custom, and wished to settle all his practice on an ideal foundation. He was a protestant à l'outrance and few lives contain so many renunciations. He was bred to no profession; he never married; he lived alone; he never went to church; he never voted; he refused to pay a tax to the state; he ate no flesh, he drank no wine, he never knew the use of tobacco; and, though a naturalist, he used neither trap nor gun. He chose wisely, no doubt, for himself to be the bachelor of thought and nature. He had no talent for wealth, and knew how to be poor without the least hint of squalor or inelegance. Perhaps he fell into his way of living, without forecasting it much, but approved it with later wisdom. "I am often reminded," he wrote in his journal, "that, if I had bestowed on me the wealth of Cræsus, my aims must be still the same, and my means essentially the same." He had no temptations to fight against; no appetites, no passions, no taste for elegant trifles. A fine house, dress, the manners and talk of highly cultivated people were all thrown away on him. He much preferred a good Indian, and considered these refinements as impediments to conversation, wishing to meet his companion on the simplest terms. He declined invitations to dinner-parties, because there each was in every one's way, and he could not meet the individuals to any purpose. "They make their pride," he said, "in making their dinner cost much: I make my pride in making my dinner cost little." When asked at table, what dish he preferred, he answered, "the nearest." He did not like the taste of wine, and never had a vice in his life. He said, "I have a faint recollec-

tion of pleasure derived from smoking dried lily stems, before I was a man. I had commonly a supply of these. I have never smoked any thing more noxious."

He chose to be rich by making his wants few, and supplying them himself. In his travels, he used the railroad only to get over so much country as was unimportant to the present purpose, walking hundreds of miles, avoiding taverns, buying a lodging in farmers' and fishermen's houses, as cheaper, and more agreeable to him, and because there he could better find the men and the information he wanted.

There was somewhat military in his nature not to be subdued, always manly and able, but rarely tender, as if he did not feel himself except in opposition. He wanted a fallacy to expose, a blunder to pillory, I may say, required a little sense of victory, a roll of the drum, to call his powers into full exercise. It cost him nothing to say No; indeed he found it much easier than to say Yes. It seemed as if his first instinct on hearing a proposition was to controvert it, so impatient was he of the limitations of our daily thought. This habit of course is a little chilling to the social affections; and though the companion would in the end acquit him of any malice or untruth, yet it mars conversation. Hence no equal companion stood in affectionate relations with one so pure and guileless. "I love Henry," said one of his friends, "but I cannot like him: and as for taking his arm, I should as soon think of taking the arm of an elm-tree."

Yet hermit and stoic as he was, he was really fond of sympathy, and threw himself heartily and childlike into the company of young people whom he loved, and whom he delighted to entertain, as he only could, with the varied and endless anecdotes of his experiences by field and river. And he was always ready to lead a huckleberry party or a search for chestnuts or grapes. Talking one day of a public

420

discourse, Henry remarked, that whatever succeeded with the audience, was bad. I said, "Who would not like to write something which all can read, like 'Robinson Crusoe'; and who does not see with regret that his page is not solid with a right materialistic treatment, which delights everybody." Henry objected, of course, and vaunted the better lectures which reached only a few persons. But, at supper, a young girl, understanding that he was to lecture at the Lyceum, sharply asked him, "whether his lecture would be a nice, interesting story such as she wished to hear, or whether it was one of those old philosophical things that she did not care about?" Henry turned to her, and bethought himself, and, I saw, was trying to believe that he had matter that might fit her and her brother, who were to sit up and go to the lecture, if it was a good one for them.

He was a speaker and actor of the truth,—born such,—and was ever running into dramatic situations from this cause. In any circumstance, it interested all bystanders to know what part Henry would take, and what he would say: and he did not disappoint expectation, but used an original judgment on each emergency. In 1845, he built himself a small framed house on the shores of Walden Pond, and lived there two years alone, a life of labor and study. This action was quite native and fit for him. No one who knew him would tax him with affectation. He was more unlike his neighbors in his thought, than in his action. As soon as he had exhausted the advantages of that solitude, he abandoned it. In 1847, not approving some uses to which the public expenditure was applied, he refused to pay his town-tax, and was put in jail. A friend paid the tax for him, and he was released. The like annoyance was threatened the next year. But, as his friends paid the tax, notwithstanding his protest, I believe he

ceased to resist. No opposition or ridicule had any weight with him. He coldly and fully stated his opinion without affecting to believe that it was the opinion of the company. It was of no consequence if every one present held the opposite opinion. On one occasion he went to the University Library to produce some books. The Librarian refused to lend them. Mr. Thoreau repaired to the President, who stated to him the rules and usages which permitted the loan of books to resident graduates, to clergymen who were alumni, and to some others resident within a circle of ten miles' radius from the College. Mr. Thoreau explained to the President that the railroad had destroyed the old scale of distances,—that the library was useless, yes, and President and College useless, on the terms of his rules,—that the one benefit he owed to the College was its library,— that at this moment, not only his want of books was imperative, but he wanted a large number of books, and assured him that he Thoreau, and not the Librarian, was the proper custodian of these. In short, the President found the petitioner so formidable and the rules getting to look so ridiculous, that he ended by giving him a privilege which in his hands proved unlimited thereafter.

No truer American existed than Thoreau. His preference of his country and condition was genuine, and his aversation from English and European manners and tastes almost reached contempt. He listened impatiently to news or bon mots gleaned from London circles; and, though he tried to be civil, these anecdotes fatigued him. The men were all imitating each other, and on a small mould. Why can they not live as far apart as possible, and each be a man by himself? What he sought was the most energetic nature, and he wished to go to Oregon, not to London. "In every part of Great Britain," he wrote in his diary, "are discovered traces of the

421

Romans, their funereal urns, their camps, their roads, their dwellings. But New England, at least, is not based on any Roman ruins. We have not to lay the foundations of our houses on the ashes of a former civilization."

But idealist as he was, standing for abolition of slavery, abolition of tariffs, almost for abolition of government, it is needless to say he found himself not only unrepresented in actual politics, but almost equally opposed to every class of reformers. Yet he paid the tribute of his uniform respect to the anti-slavery party. One man, whose personal acquaintance he had formed, he honored with exceptional regard. Before the first friendly word had been spoken for Captain John Brown, after the arrest, he sent notices to most houses in Concord, that he would speak in a public hall on the condition and character of John Brown, on Sunday Evening, and invited all people to come. The Republican committee, the abolitionist committee, sent him word that it was premature and not advisable. He replied, "I did not send to you for advice but to announce that I am to speak." The hall was filled at any early hour by people of all parties, and his earnest eulogy of the hero was heard by all respectfully, by many with a sympathy that surprised themselves.

It was said of Plotinus, that he was ashamed of his body, and 'tis very likely he had good reason for it; that his body was a bad servant, and he had not skill in dealing with the material world, as happens often to men of abstract intellect. But Mr. Thoreau was equipped with a most adapted and serviceable body. He was of short stature, firmly built, of light complexion, with strong, serious blue eyes, and a grave aspect; his face covered in the late years with a becoming beard. His senses were acute, his frame well-knit and hardy, his hands strong and skilful in the use of tools. And there was a wonderful fitness of body and mind. He could pace sixteen rods more accurately than another man could measure them with rod and chain. He could find his path in the woods at night, he said, better by his feet than his eyes. He could estimate the measure of a tree very well by his eye; he could estimate the weight of a calf or a pig, like a dealer. From a box containing, a bushel or more of loose pencils, he could take up with his hands fast enough just a dozen pencils at every grasp. He was a good swimmer, runner, skater, boatman, and would probably out-walk most countrymen in a day's journey. And the relation of body to mind was still finer than we have indicated. He said, he wanted every stride his legs made. The length of his walk uniformly made the length of his writing. If shut up in the house, he did not write at all.

He had a strong common sense, like that which Rose Flammock, the weaver's daughter, in Scott's romance, commends in her father, as resembling a yardstick, which, whilst it measures dowlas and diaper, can equally well measure tapestry and cloth of gold. He had always a new resource. When I was planting forest trees, and had procured half a peck of acorns, he said, that only a small portion of them would be sound, and proceeded to examine them, and select the sound ones. But finding this took time, he said, "I think, if you put them all into water, the good ones will sink," which experiment we tried with success. He could plan a garden, or a house, or a barn; would have been competent to lead a "Pacific Exploring Expedition"; could give judicious counsel in the gravest private or public affairs. He lived for the day, not cumbered and mortified by his memory. If he brought you yesterday a new proposition, he would bring you today another not less revolutionary. A very industrious man, and setting, like all highly organized men, a high value on his time, he seemed the only man of leisure in town, always ready for any excursion that promised well, or for conversation prolonged into late hours. His trenchant sense was never stopped by his rules of daily prudence, but was always up to the new occasion. He liked and used the simplest food, yet, when some one urged a vegetable diet, Thoreau thought all diets a very small matter; saying, that "the man who shoots the buffalo lives better than the man who boards at the Graham house." He said, "You can sleep near the railroad, and never be disturbed. Nature knows very well what sounds are worth attending to, and has made up her mind not to hear the railroad-whistle. But things respect the devout mind, and a mental ecstasy was never interrupted."

He noted what repeatedly befel him, that, after receiving from a distance a rare plant, he would presently find the same in his own haunts. And those pieces of luck which happen only to good players happened to him. One day walking with a stranger who inquired, where Indian arrowheads could be found, he replied, "Every where," and stooping forward, picked one on the instant from the ground. At Mount Washington, in Tuckerman's Ravine, Thoreau had a bad fall, and sprained his foot. As he was in the act of getting up from his fall, he saw for the first time, the leaves of the *Arnica mollis*.

His robust common sense, armed with stout hands, keen perceptions and strong will, cannot yet account for the superiority which shone in his simple and hidden life. I must add the cardinal fact that there was an excellent wisdom in him, proper to a rare class of men, which showed him the material world as a means and symbol. This discovery, which sometimes yields to poets a certain casual and interrupted light serving for the ornament of their writing, was in him an unsleeping insight; and, whatever faults or obstructions of temperament might cloud it, he was not disobedient to the heavenly vision. In his youth, he said, one day, "The other world is all my art: my pencils will draw no other; my jack-knife will cut nothing else; I do not use it as a means." This was the muse and genius that ruled his opinions, conversation, studies, work, and course of life. This made him a searching judge of men. At first glance, he measured his companion, and, though insensible to some fine traits of culture, could very well report his weight and calibre. And this made the impression of genius which his conversation often gave.

He understood the matter in hand at a glance, and saw the limitations and poverty of those he talked with, so that nothing seemed concealed from such terrible eyes. I have repeatedly known young men of sensibility converted in a moment to the belief that this was the man they were in search of, the man of men, who could tell them all they should do. His own dealing with them was never affectionate, but superior, didactic; scorning their petty ways; very slowly conceding or not conceding at all the promise of his society at their houses or even at his own. "Would he not walk with them?"—He did not know. There was nothing so important to him as his walk; he had no walks to throw away on company. Visits were offered him from respectful parties, but he declined them. Admiring friends offered to carry him at their own cost to the Yellow Stone River; to the West Indies; to South America. But though nothing could be more grave or considered than his refusals, they remind one in quite new relations of that fop Brummel's reply to the gentleman who offered him his carriage in a shower, "But where will *you* ride then?" And what accusing silences, and what searching and irresistible speeches battering down all defences, his companions can remember!

Mr. Thoreau dedicated his genius with such entire love to the fields, hills, and waters of his native town, that he made them known and interesting to all reading Americans, and to people over the sea. The river on whose banks he was born and died, he knew from its springs to its confluence with the Merrimack. He had made summer and winter observations on it for many years, and at every hour of the day and the night. The result of the recent survey of the Water Commissioners appointed by the State of Massachusetts, he had reached by his private experiments, several years earlier. Every fact which occurs in the bed, on the banks, or in the air over it; the fishes, and their spawning and nests, their manners, their food; the shad-flies which fill the air on a certain evening once a year, and which are snapped at by the fishes so ravenously, that many of these die of repletion; the conical heaps of small stones on the river shallows, one of which heaps will sometimes overfill a cart,—these heaps the huge nests of small fishes; the birds which frequent the stream, heron, duck, sheldrake, loon, osprey; the snake, muskrat, otter, woodchuck, and fox, on the blanks; the turtle, frog, hyla, and cricket, which make the banks vocal,—were all known to him, and, as it were, townsmen and fellow-creatures: so that he felt an absurdity or violence in any narrative of one of these by itself apart, and still more of its dimensions on an inch-rule, or in the exhibition of its skeleton, or the specimen of a squirrel or a bird in brandy. He liked to speak of the manners of the river, as itself a lawful creature, yet with exactness, and always to an observed fact. As he knew the river, so the ponds in this region.

One of the weapons he used, more important than microscope or alcohol receiver, to other investigators, was a whim which grew on him by indulgence, yet appeared in gravest statement, namely, of extolling his own town and neighborhood as the most favored centre for natural observation. He remarked that the Flora of Massachusetts embraced almost all the important plants of America,—most of the oaks, most of the willows, the best pines, the ash, the maple, the beech, the nuts. He returned Kane's "Arctic Voyage" to a friend of whom he had borrowed it with the remark, that "most of the phenomena noted might be observed in Concord." He seemed a little envious of the Pole, for the coincident sunrise and sunset, or five minutes' day after six months. A splendid fact which Annursnuc had never afforded him. He found red snow in one of his walks; and told me that he expected to find yet the *Victoria regia* in Concord. He was the attorney of the indigenous plants, and owned to a preference of the weeds to the imported plants, as of the Indian to the civilized man: and noticed with pleasure that the willow bean-poles of his neighbor had grown more than his beans. "See these weeds," he said, "which have been hoed at by a million farmers all spring and summer, and yet have prevailed, and just now come out triumphant over all lanes, pastures, fields, and gardens, such is their vigor. We have insulted them with low names too, as pigweed, wormwood, chickweed, shad blossom." He says they have brave names too, ambrosia, stellaria, amelanchier, amaranth, etc.

I think this fancy for referring every thing to the meridian of Concord, did not grow out of any ignorance or depreciation of other longitudes or latitudes, but was rather a playful expression of his conviction of the indifference of all places, and that the best place for each is where he stands. He expressed it once in this wise: "I think nothing is to be hoped from you, if this bit of mould under your feet is not sweeter to you to eat, than any other in this world, or in any world."

The other weapon with which he conquered all obstacles in science was patience. He knew how to sit immoveable, a part of the rock he rested on, until the bird, the reptile, the fish, which had retired from him, should come back, and resume its habits, nay, moved by curiosity should come to him and watch him.

It was a pleasure and a privilege to walk with him. He knew the country like a fox or a bird, and passed through it as freely by paths of his own. He knew every track in the snow, or on the ground, and what creature had taken this path before him. One must submit abjectly to such a guide, and the reward was great. Under his arm he carried an old music book to press plants; in his pocket, his diary and pencil, a spy-glass for birds, microscope, jack-knife, and twine. He wore straw hat, stout shoes, strong gray trowsers, to brave shrub-oaks and smilax, and to climb a tree for a hawk's or a squirrel's nest. He waded into the pool for the water-plants, and his strong legs were no insignificant part of his armour. On the day I speak of he looked for the menyanthes, detected it across the wide pool, and, on examination of the florets, decided that it had been in flower five days. He drew out of his breast-pocket his diary, and read the names of all the plants that should bloom on this day, whereof he kept account as a banker when his notes fall due. The cypripedium not due till tomorrow. He thought, that, if waked up from a trance, in this swamp, he could tell by the plants what time of the year it was within two days. The redstart was flying about and presently the fine grosbeaks, whose brilliant scarlet makes the rash gazer wipe his eye, and whose fine clear note Thoreau compared to that of a tanager which has got rid of the night-warbler, a bird he had never identified, had been in search of twelve years, which always, when he saw it, was in the act of diving down into a tree or bush, and which it was vain to seek; the only bird that sings indifferently by night and by day. I told him he must beware of finding and booking it, lest life should have nothing more to show him. He said, "What you seek in vain for, half your life, one day you come full upon all the family at dinner. You seek it like a dream, and, as soon as you find it, you become its prey."

His interest in the flower or the bird lay very deep in his mind, was connected with Nature,—and the meaning of Nature was never attempted to be defined by him. He would not offer a memoir of his observations to the Natural History Society. "Why should I? To detach the description from its connections in my mind, would make it no longer true or valuable to me: and they do not wish what belong to it." His power of observation seemed to indicate additional senses. He saw as with microscope, heard as with ear-trumpet, and his memory was a photographic register of all he saw and heard. And yet none knew better than he that it is not the fact that imports, but the impression or effect of the fact on your mind. Every fact lay in glory in his mind, a type of the order and beauty of the whole.

His determination on Natural History was organic. He confessed that he sometimes felt like a hound or a panther, and, if born among Indians, would have been a fell hunter. But, restrained by his Massachusetts culture, he played out the game in this mild form of botany and ichthyology. His intimacy with animals suggested what Thomas Fuller records of Butler the apiologist, that "either he had told the bees things or the bees had told him." Snakes coiled round his leg; the fishes swam into his hand, and he took them out of the water; he pulled the wood chuck out of its hole by the tail, and took the foxes under his protection from the hunters. Our naturalist had perfect magnanimity; he had no secrets: he would carry you to the heron's haunt, or, even to his most prized botanical swamp;—possibly knowing that you could never find it again,—yet willing to take his risks.

No college ever offered him a diploma, or a professor's chair; no academy made him its corresponding secretary, its discoverer, or even its members. Whether these learned bodies feared the satire of his presence [sic]. Yet so much knowledge of nature's secret and genius few others possessed, none in a more large and religious synthesis. For not a particle of respect had he to the opinions of any man or body of men, but homage solely to the truth itself. And as he discovered everywhere among doctors some leaning of courtesy, it discredited them. He grew to be revered and admired by his townsmen, who had at first known him only as an oddity. The farmers who employed him as a surveyor soon discovered his rare accuracy and skill, his knowledge of their lands, of trees, of birds, of Indian remains, and the like, which enabled him to tell every farmer more than he knew before of his own farm. So that he began to feel as if Mr. Thoreau had better rights in his land than he. They felt, too, the superiority of character which addressed all men with a native authority.

Indian relics abound in Concord, arrowheads, stone chisels, pestles, and fragments of pottery; and, on the river bank large heaps of clam-shells and ashes mark spots which the savages frequented. These, and every circumstance touching the Indian, were important in his eyes. His visits to Maine were chiefly for love of the Indian. He had the satisfaction of seeing the manufacture of the bark-canoe, as well as of trying his hand in its management on the rapids. He was inquisitive about the making of the stone arrowhead, and, in his last days, charged a youth setting out for the Rocky Mountains, to find an Indian who could tell him that: "It was well worth a visit to California, to learn it." Occasionally, a small party of Penobscot Indians would visit Concord, and pitch their tents for a few weeks in summer on the river bank. He failed not to make acquaintance with the best of them, though he well knew that asking questions of Indians is like catechizing beavers and rabbits. In his last visit to Maine, he had great satisfaction from Joseph Polis, an intelligent Indian of Oldtown, who was his guide for some weeks.

He was equally interested in every natural fact. The depth of his perception found likeness of law throughout nature, and, I know not any genius who so swiftly inferred universal law from the single fact. He was no pedant of a department. His eye was open to beauty, and his ear to music. He found these, not in rare conditions, but wheresoever he went. He thought the best of music was in single strains; and he found poetic suggestion in the humming of the telegraph wire.

His poetry might be bad or good; he no doubt wanted a lyric facility, and technical skill; but he had the source of poetry in his spiritual perception. He was a good reader and critic, and his judgment on poetry was to the ground of it. He could not be deceived as to the presence or absence of the poetic element in any composition, and his thirst for this made him negligent and perhaps scornful of superficial graces. He would pass by many delicate rhythms, but he would have detected every live stanza or line in a volume, and knew very well where to find an equal poetic charm in prose. He was so enamoured of the spiritual beauty, that he held all actual written poems in every light esteem in the comparison. He admired Æschylus and Pindar, but when some one was commending them, he said, that, "Æschylus and the Greeks, in describing Apollo and Orpheus, had given no song, or no good one. They ought not to have moved trees, but to have chaunted to the gods such a hymn as would have sung all their old ideas out of their heads, and new ones in." His own verses are often rude and defective. The gold does not yet run pure, is drossy and crude. The thyme and marjoram are not yet honey. But if he want lyric fineness, and technical merits, if he have not the poetic temperament, he never lacks the causal thought, showing that his genius was better than his talent. He knew the worth of the Imagination for the uplifting and consolation of human life, and liked to throw every thought into a symbol. The fact you tell is of no value, but only the impression. For this reason his presence was poetic, always piqued the curiosity to know more deeply the secrets of his mind. He had many reserves,—an unwillingness to exhibit to profane eyes what was still sacred in his own, and knew well how to throw a poetic veil over his experience. All readers of "Walden" will remember his mythical record of his disappointments:—

> "I long ago lost a hound, a bay horse, and a turtle-dove, and am still on their trail. Many are the travellers I have spoken concerning them, describing their tracks, and what calls they answered to. I have met one or two who had heard the hound, and the tramp of the horse, and even seen the dove disappear behind a cloud, and they seemed as anxious to recover them as if they had lost them themselves."[2]

His riddles were worth the reading, and I confide that, if at any time I do not understand the expression, it is yet just. Such was the wealth of his truth, that it was not worth his while to use words in vain.

His poem entitled "Sympathy" reveals the tenderness under that triple steel of stoicism, and the intellectual subtlety it

could animate. His classic poem on "Smoke" suggests Simonides, but is better than any poem of Simonides. His biography is in his verses. His habitual thought makes all his poetry a hymn to the Cause of causes, the spirit which vivifies and controls his own.

> "I hearing get, who had but ears,
> And sight, who had but eyes before;
> I moments live, who lived but years,
> And truth discern, who knew but
>   learning's lore."

And still more in these religious lines:—

> "Now chiefly is my natal hour,
> And only now my prime of life,
> I will not doubt the love untold,
> Which not my worth or want hath
>   bought,
> Which wooed me young, and wooes me
>   old,
> And to this evening hath me brought."

Whilst he used in his writings a certain petulance of remark in reference to churches or churchmen, he was a person of a rare, tender and absolute religion, a person incapable of any profanation, by act or by thought. Of course, the same isolation which belonged to his original thinking and living detached him from the social religious forms. This is neither to be censured nor regretted. Aristotle long ago explained it, when he said, "One who surpasses his fellow citizens in virtue, is no longer a part of the city. Their law is not for him, since he is a law to himself."

Thoreau was sincerity itself, and might fortify the convictions of prophets in the ethical laws, by his holy living. It was an affirmative experience which refused to be set aside. A truth-speaker he, capable of the most deep and strict conversation; a physician to the wounds of any soul; a friend knowing not only the secret of

427

friendship, but almost worshipped by those few persons who resorted to him as their confessor and prophet, and knew the deep value of his mind and great heart. He thought that without religion or devotion of some kind, nothing great was ever accomplished: and he thought that the bigoted sectarian had better bear this in mind.

His virtues of course sometimes ran into extremes. It was easy to trace to the inexorable demand on all for exact truth that austerity which made this willing hermit more solitary even than he wished. Himself of a perfect probity, he required not less of others. He had a disgust at crime, and no worldly success could cover it. He detected paltering as readily in dignified and prosperous persons as in beggars, and with equal scorn. Such dangerous frankness was in his dealing, that his admirers called him "that terrible Thoreau," as if he spoke, when silent, and was still present when he had departed. I think the severity of his ideal interfered to deprive him of a healthy sufficiency of human society.

The habit of a realist to find things the reverse of their appearance inclined him to put every statement in a paradox. A certain habit of antagonism defaced his earlier writings, a trick of rhetoric not quite outgrown in his later, of substituting for the obvious word and thought its diametrical opposite. He praised wild mountains and winter forests for their domestic air; in snow and ice, he would find sultriness; and commended the wilderness for resembling Rome and Paris. "It was so dry, that you might call it wet."

The tendency to magnify the moment, to read all the laws of nature in the one object or one combination under your eye, is of course comic to those who do not share the philosopher's perception of identity. To him there was no such thing as size. The pond was a small ocean; the Atlantic, a large Walden Pond. He referred every minute fact to cosmical laws. Though he meant to be just, he seemed haunted by a certain chronic assumption that the science of the day pretended completeness and he had just found out that the savans had neglected to discriminate a particular botanical variety, had failed to describe the seeds, or count the sepals. "That is to say," we replied, "the blockheads were not born in Concord, but who said they were? It was their unspeakable misfortune to be born in London, or Paris, or Rome; but, poor fellows, they did what they could, considering that they never saw Bateman Pond, or Nine-Acre-Corner, or Becky Stow's Swamp. Besides, what were you sent into the world for, but to add this observation?"

Had his genius been only contemplative, he had been fitted to his life, but with his energy and practical ability he seemed born for great enterprise and for command: and I so much regret the loss of his rare powers of action, that I cannot help counting it a fault in him that he had no ambition. Wanting this, instead of engineering for all America, he was the captain of a huckleberry party. Pounding beans is good to the end of pounding empires one of these days, but if, at the end of years, it is still only beans!—

But these foibles, real or apparent, were fast vanishing in the incessant growth of a spirit so robust and wise, and which effaced its defects with new triumphs. His study of nature was a perpetual ornament to him, and inspired his friends with curiosity to see the world through his eyes, and to hear his adventures. They possessed every kind of interest. He had many elegances of his own, whilst he scoffed at conventional elegance. Thus he could not bear to hear the sound of his own steps, the grit of gravel; and therefore never willingly walked in the road, but in the grass, on mountains, and in woods. His senses were acute, and he remarked that by night every dwelling-house gives out bad air, like a slaughter-house. He liked the pure fragrance of melilot. He honored certain plants with special regard and over all the pond-lily,—then, the gentian, and the *Mikania scandens* and "Life Everlasting," and a bass which he visited every year when it bloomed in the middle of July. He thought the scent a more oracular inquisition than the sight,—more oracular and trustworthy. The scent, of course, reveals what is concealed from the other senses. By it he detected earthiness. He delighted in echoes, and said, they were almost the only kind of kindred voices that he heard. He loved nature so well, was so happy in her solitude, that he became very jealous of cities, and the sad work which their refinements and artifices made with man and his dwelling. The axe was always destroying his forest—"Thank God," he said, "they cannot cut down the clouds. All kinds of figures are drawn on the blue ground, with this fibrous white paint."

I subjoin a few sentences taken from his unpublished manuscripts not only as records of his thought and feeling, but for their power of description and literary excellence.

"Some circumstantial evidence is very strong, as when you find a trout in the milk."

"The chub is a soft fish, and tastes like boiled brown paper salted."

"The youth gets together his materials to build a bridge to the moon, or, perchance, a palace or temple on the earth, and, at length, the middle-aged man concludes to build a woodshed with them."

"The locust z———ing."

"Devil's-needles zig-zagging along the Nut-Meadow brook."

"Sugar is not so sweet to the palate, as sound to the healthy ear."

"I put on some hemlock boughs, and the rich salt crackling of their leaves was like mustard to the ear, the crackling of uncountable regiments. Dead trees love the fire."

"The blue-bird carries the sky on his back."

"The tanager flies through the green foliage, as if it would ignite the leaves."

"If I wish for a horse-hair for my compass-sight, I must go to the stable; but the hair-bird with her sharp eyes goes to the road."

"Immortal water, alive even to the superficies."

"Fire is the most tolerable third party."

"Nature made ferns for pure leaves, to show what she could do in that line."

"No tree has so fair a bole, and so handsome an instep as the beech."

"How did these beautiful rainbow tints get into the shell of the fresh-water clam, buried in the mud at the bottom of our dark river?"

"Hard are the times when the infant's shoes are second-foot."

"We are strictly confined to our men to whom we give liberty."

"Nothing is so much to be feared as fear. Atheism may comparatively be popular with God himself."

"Of what significance the things you can forget? A little thought is sexton to all the world."

"How can we expect a harvest of thought, who have not had a seed-time of character?"

"Only he can be trusted with gifts, who can present a face of bronze to expectations."

"I ask to be melted. You can only ask of the metals that they be tender to the fire that melts them. To nought else can they be tender."

There is a flower known to botanists, one of the same genus with our summer plant called "Life Everlasting," a *Gnaphalium* like that, which grows on the most inaccessible cliffs of the Tyrolese mountains, where the chamois dare hardly venture, and which the hunter, tempted by its beauty, and by his love, (for it is immensely valued by the Swiss maidens,) climbs the cliffs to gather, and is sometimes found dead at the foot, with the flower in his hand. It is called by botanists the *Gnaphalium leontopodium*, but by the Swiss, *Edelweisse*, which signifies, *Noble Purity*. Thoreau seemed to me living in the hope to gather this plant, which belongs to him of right. The scale on which his studies proceeded was so large as to require longevity, and we were the less prepared for his sudden disappearance. The country knows not yet, or in the least part, how great a son it has lost. It seems an injury that he should leave in the midst his broken task, which none else can finish,—a kind of indignity to so noble a soul, that it should depart out of nature before yet he has been really shown to his peers for what he is. But he, at least, is content. His soul was made for the noblest society; he had in short life exhausted the capabilities of this world; wherever there is knowledge, wherever there is virtue, wherever there is beauty, he will find a home.

Notes

1 The text reprinted here is from Joel Myerson, "Emerson's 'Thoreau': A New Edition from Manuscript," *Studies in the American Renaissance 1979*, ed. Myerson (Boston: G. K. Hall, 1979), pp. 17–92.

2 "*Walden*," p. 20.

"A Parish Priest," "Henry D. Thoreau," *Church Monthly*, 7 (October 1864), 228–37

Thoreau, the Concord stoic, is one of those writers who, indebted to civilization and the university for much culture, used that culture in fresh explorations of Nature. His books, peculiar in their structure, are the freshest and the best in their own department.[1] He was, first of all, a naturalist. He outgrew society. He became a citizen of the forest. His books, in their very titles, show the spirit of the man. They are: "A Week on the Concord and Merrimack Rivers," "Walden, or Life in the Woods," "Excursions," and "The Maine Woods." Their contents are what their titles indicate. His "Week" is the record of an actual week's voyage upon those rivers; but its leisurely flow shows that the book was by no means written in a week or a month, but was the slow outcome of a thoughtful manhood. It is filled with the settled principles, facts, convictions of a man who is in his prime. The thoughts arise from his subject and range through religion, morals, society, literature, and the facts of humble life. His "Walden" shows how the retiring and determinate scholar may bury himself in the woods, and with a celibate life, may simplify his wants and divide his time equally between the exercise of muscle and of mind. It is a biography wholly unique, not so attractive nor surprising as Robinson Crusoe's, but to the inquiring few having a winning interest, which will always make it a classic in its kind. His "Excursions" is a volume of miscellaneous papers, collected since his death, and perhaps his most valuable contribution to natural history. The papers on the "Natural History of Massachusetts," "Wild Apples," "The Succession of Forest Trees," "Walking," "Autumnal Tints," and "A Winter Walk," are each fresh with new facts, and have permanent value not only to science, but to the literature or poetry of outward nature. Thoreau always distinguished between the uses of science and of literature, and while ignoring neither exactness nor truthfulness, he preferred to give the literary expression to scientific truth; and hence has increased his audience without lessening the value of his writings. His "Maine Woods" is the freshest of all. Reading it in these very days when such adventures are possible, and when so many parish priests, if they have healthy bodies and sound heads, and full purses (which last is the chief difficulty) are away in similar wild sporting-places of Nature, rekindling their love of the eternal and unchanging works of God, I have myself, while sitting by my library window, ascended the rugged rocks of Mount Katahdin by the single mountain-torrent, and walked over the matted tops of aged cedars; I have camped in the trackless wilderness, and killed the moose at Lake Chesuncook; I have wandered miles and miles with the Penobscot Indian in the birch canoe; I have lost myself in those unnamed wilds where only the Indian, and the moose, and the deer are at home, and where the busy hum of civilized life may never come. No one can rest easy after reading this book, till he has seen the forests of Maine, and any one who has even set his eyes on them from a distance cannot but be entranced by their solemn spectral grandeur. I expect that scholars and thoughtful men not a few have been drawn thither this season by the inspiration of the "Maine Woods." To the worth of the volume this is the highest tribute which can be given. No one before Thoreau has explored their secrets and written the story of his adventures; and perhaps none had gone to them before with the true instincts of the naturalists, equally interested in the flower, the mountain, the forest, the lake, the animals, and the Indians. Our Concord hermit was prepared by the studies of his life to carry much away from them, and his instinct is so true for noteworthy things, that no one is disappointed. There remain materials for yet another volume from Thoreau. There are his papers in "The Dial" of transcendental fame; there are poems and essays scattered through the magazines; there are some yet unpublished. He was such a rare and singular man, that whatever he wrote is worth preservation. Even when you altogether dissent from his views, you recognize the unmistakable stamp of a *man*.

Coming now to a more minute examination of his writings, you are struck by their oneness of sentiment. The key-note of them all is sympathy with Nature. He sees all things from this point of view. It is said of Wordsworth, that his library was in his house, but his study was all out-doors. So it was with Thoreau. The more he was in the open air, in strange and beautiful scenery, among those whose ways were primitive and conformed to Nature, the better he enjoyed himself. His habits were regulated according to the single purpose which animated his life. Emerson, whom he was like in some respects, says of him: "He chose wisely, no doubt, for himself, to be the bachelor of thought and of Nature." "He knew how to sit immovable, a part of the rock he rested on, until the bird, the reptile, the fish, which had retired from him, should come back, and resume its habits, nay, moved by curiosity, should come to him and watch him." "He knew the country like a fox or a bird, and passed through it as freely by paths of his own. He knew every track in the snow or on the ground,

and what creature had taken this path before him." "Under his arm he carried an old music-book to press plants; in his pocket, his diary and pencil, a spy-glass for birds, microscope, jack-knife, and twine. He wore straw hat, stout shoes, strong gray trousers, to brave shrub-oaks and smilax, and to climb a tree for a hawk's or a squirrel's nest. He waded into the pool for water-plants, and his strong legs were no insignificant part of his armor." "Snakes coiled round his leg; the fishes swam into his hand, and he took them out of the water; he pulled the woodchuck out of its hole by the tail, and took the foxes under his protection from the hunters. Our naturalist had perfect magnanimity: he had no secrets; he would carry you to the heron's haunt or even to his most prized botanical swamp,—possibly knowing that you could never find it again, yet willing to take his risks." "So much knowledge of Nature's secret and genius few others possessed, none in a more large or religious synthesis." "He chose to be rich by making his wants few and supplying them himself." Such is a glimpse of his habits from one who knew him best.

He also says: "he was equally interested in every natural fact. The depth of his perception found likeness of law throughout Nature, and I know not any genius who so swiftly inferred universal law from the single fact. He was no pedant of a department." "He loved Nature so well, was so happy in her solitude, that he became very jealous of cities, and the sad work which their refinements and artifices made with man and his dwelling." These quotations give us the pith of his life. They tell us the kind of naturalist he was. They stamp his writings beforehand with a certain thoroughness and authority. But it will not be possible for me here to give more than the briefest hint of the wealth there is in his pages. I shall quote him rather to show the spirit and purpose of the author than to enlarge the reader's knowledge. Every thinker will demand the whole of Thoreau and for himself; only the full detail and all of it will satisfy the naturalist. Here are a few of those select paragraphs which are characteristic. In describing Mount Katahdin, he says: "The mountain seemed a vast aggregate of loose rocks, as if sometime it had rained rocks, and they lay as they fell on the mountain sides, nowhere fairly at rest, but leaning on each other, all rocking-stones, with cavities between, but scarcely any soil or smoother shelf. They were the raw materials a planet dropped from an unseen quarry, which the vast chemistry of Nature would anon work up, or work down, into the smiling and verdant plains and valleys of earth. This was *an undone extremity of the globe.*" "The tops of mountains are among the unfinished parts of the globe, whither it is a slight insult to the gods to climb and pry into their secrets, and try their effect on our humanity. Only daring and insolent men, perchance, go there. Simple races, as savages, do not climb mountains,—their tops are sacred and mysterious tracts never visited by them." "Here was no man's garden but the unhandselled globe. It was not lawn, nor pasture, nor mead, nor woodland, nor lea, nor arable, nor waste land. It was the fresh and natural surface of the planet earth, as it was made forever and ever—to be the dwelling of man, we say—so Nature made it, and man may use it if he can. Man was not to be associated with it. It was matter, vast, terrific,—not his mother-earth that we have heard of, not for him to tread on, or be buried in,—*no, it were being too familiar even to let his bones lie there,*—the home this of necessity and fate. There was felt there the presence of a force not bound to be kind to man."

He thus enters into the feeling of mountain power with a sympathy which bends the very language to his purpose. His words are reverent; his thoughts, expressed with such point, are yet common to all minds. You see him in another mood in the following:—

"Who shall describe the inexpressible tenderness and immortal life of the grim forest, where Nature, though it be midwinter, is ever in her spring; where the moss-grown and decaying trees are not old, but seem to enjoy a perpetual youth; and blissful, innocent Nature, like a serene infant, is too happy to make a noise, except by a few tinkling, lisping birds and trickling rills?

"What a place to live, what a place to die and be buried in! There certainly men would live forever and laugh at death and the grave."

Here again the naturalist gives one of his finest touches:—

"When I detect a beauty in any of the recesses of Nature, I am reminded by the serene and retired spirit in which it requires to be contemplated, of the inexpressible privacy of a life,—how silent and unambitious it is. *The beauty there is in mosses must be considered from the holiest, quietest nook.*"

He says beautifully of the fox's step: "He treads so softly, that you would hardly hear it from any nearness, and yet with such expression, that it would *not be quite inaudible at any distance.*" And this, too, shows such an observant eye: "I am struck with the pleasing friendships and unanimities of Nature, as when the lichen on the trees takes the form of their leaves."

Each of these quotations has a beauty of its own. The naturalist becomes the thinker or the poet, and invests Nature with the charm of new fancies. Notice how he strikes the very marrow of our own unexpressed thoughts concerning Nature in most fitting language. The description is cut out, clear and bold,—not a word to spare. But there is one paper in the "Excursions," the one on "Autumnal Tints," which I should like to quote entire. He says there: "October is the month for painted leaves. Their rich glow now flashes round the world. As fruits and leaves, and the day itself, acquire a bright tint just before they fall, so the year near its setting. October is its sunset sky; November the later twilight." And he goes on to paint in his own matchless way all the glories of the ripened leaves. Who of us will not enjoy this glorious October as we enjoy no other month in the year? Who of us will not feast the eye and soul, too, with the inexhaustible variety of plumage? Who does not like to tread upon the dry leaves, or toss them back with a stick while searching for the brown chestnuts? Ah! reader, there is such joyous life in this October month as fills every true lover of Nature with ecstasy. You cannot be too thankful that your life is spared each year to witness anew the glory of the forest colors. To go up a high hill, not too high, and with the glass or naked eye, to tell the different trees by the scarlet of their leaves, or even without analysis, to drink in the full glory of this beautiful world, and then not to forget that a Divine Hand has made the eye to see, and the landscape to be seen, and to feel the gushing thankfulness moistening the eye and quickening the pulse—such moments are worth a lifetime to one who tries to enjoy the world which God has made for us to dwell in. Let every one read this paper in this month and learn to enjoy Nature through Thoreau's eyes, if he does not know how through his own. And let me assure every one, that such warm sympathy with Nature, such close discrimination of the features of our American landscape, such minute knowledge of our natural history, such inspiring thoughtfulness, such unerring instinct, have seldom been found in any one writer as they are in Thoreau. Emer-

son truly describes him as "the bachelor of thought and of Nature." His life found its natural outlet through this channel. Hence his writings are personal, autobiographic. He reveals *himself* in his books. He throws the charm of a passion around his favorite subjects. The day will come when his writings will be held as one of our most original contributions to literature.

A sort of pendant to Thoreau lies upon my table, a pendant, too, to his labors as a naturalist, "A Summer Cruise on the Coast of New England," by Robert Carter. The only way in which Thoreau destroyed animal life was by fishing. His accounts of the fish in our rivers, scattered through all his books, are helped out by this short account of those which may be caught off shore. The two men differ widely. One could fish contentedly all his days; the other became a naturalist as a relief from editorial duties; yet the one is as accurate as the other, so far as he goes. I know not where you can find better descriptions of our common seacoast fish than in this book; and the story of the cruise, though smacking a little too much of whisky to suit my fancy, and in some parts carelessly written, has abundant force and vivacity. It has the seabreeze, the sea-spray, the sea-fish; and it is just long enough to make you wish it were longer. I shall put it on the same shelf with my Thoreau.

As an essayist, Thoreau takes a high rank. His writings may all be classed under this head. He never wrote mere rhetoric, sacrificing truth to words. He says very truly, that "steady labor with the hands, which engrosses the attention also, is unquestionably the best method of removing palaver and sentimentality out of one's style, both of speaking and writing." It is true of his own. The intense truthfulness of his nature makes his every sentence and word crisp and honest. In few writers do you find sentences so short and pointed, and which are not epigrammatic. He is never sententious, but you linger over his sayings, because they touch some secret spring in your humanity. In short, call it what you will, there is a pervasive charm about Thoreau's page which draws you on, and when you come to know him well, you see that there is great truth in his views of things. He is just enough removed from the common current of life to be original, and the ideal look which he always puts on, and by which he judges of all things, leads him aside just far enough to give a mild, scholarly fascination to his style and thoughts. His "Week" has many pages which are charming specimens of the literary essay. His thoughts upon Literature, upon Friendship, upon Life, much as I must dissent from most of them, tell very truthfully for the side of life on which he looked too exclusively. Whenever he treads the common highway, he sees so much more than we do, that we gladly listen. His style was his own; not pedantic; but having just the touch of the wildness of the forest about it, just the freshness which makes the woods inviting in June.

But liking Thoreau so well, willing to commend the rare qualities of his head and heart, his genius, like the pearl, was the fruit of disease. Or is it that some men (I have known two or three) are so made constitutionally that they turn off from the common life of man, and rebel, like Satan, from the appointments of God? Thoreau was drawn aside into companionship with Nature from the first. He was made with certain strong tendencies; it was not education, but the original bent of genius; but his education followed his genius; his intellectual associations were all in one way. His biography is given in what Emerson says of his habits. It has been a study with me to trace out how much his peculiarities of religious belief were the fruit of his genius, and how much came from his antagonisms from the social circumstances of his life. The plain fact is, that he had no religion, in our sense of the word. What he says of Christianity in his "Week" shows an indifference which shocks an honest mind. He believes in it no more than he does in any mythology. He sneers continually at the Puritan forms; their doctrines and creeds seem to him outworn and vain and useless. Yet in his most secret intercourse with Nature, when he pours out his soul in meditation, his thoughts wander painfully after an object of faith. There is a soul there hungering after God.

I discover in Thoreau no lack of religious instincts. In his heart he is not irreverent; the problems of life were ever pressing upon him, and making him serious; he turns from religion, because, as he sees it, it has lost its truthfulness, and seems only a mixture of prejudice and bigotry. Growing up amid a religious system, which presents the terrors without the amenities of the law, his instincts turned him from it, and meeting none of its more lovable forms, he made his religion for himself. It was a sort of pantheism; that he was safe in Nature; that the spirit of the universe was the same as his own; that somehow at death his own spirit would be absorbed in the general life. Vague, misty as was this faith, when once embraced, it held him always. It was meat and drink to him. The same alternative has been accepted by hundreds of the best minds in New England. You, my reader, may be one of those who has sometime in his life turned to Nature for a God, and believed only in the reflected image of himself.

Yet the deepest love of Nature exists when we see God in Nature. Wordsworth had as deep an inspiration as Thoreau, and he raises you at times almost to infinity itself, by the sublimity of his communings with the outward world. Says Thoreau,

"The deepest thinker is the farthest travelled;" but the deepest thinker in Nature is he who goes beyond the form, and penetrates to the great face of a Maker. The Scriptures have the most ravishing conceptions of outward Nature, but they always join them with the deeper truth of Nature's God. It is this truth which the devout and thoughtful Christian carries upon the hillside and the mountain, and into the great solitudes of the forests. It inspires and consecrates this earth as God's handiwork. So that those who do not blindly worship Nature, but enjoy Nature and worship God, are the truest interpreters of Nature.

I charge, then, much of Thoreau's prejudice and perversion of religious truth upon the religious system under whose shadow he grew up. That system was a degenerated Puritanism. Thoreau is the logical fruit of New England Unitarianism. His principle of making his reason his sole guide, selecting for himself, is a prime thing in their creed. Using their principle with a generous liberty, he rejected their whole faith as untrue to his own instincts. Using the same principle, Theodore Parker and Ralph Waldo Emerson rejected revealed religion altogether.

Thoreau's writings will always be instructive; they will endure; they are full of beauty; they are honest and sincere; but while I shall always prize his green-bound volumes in my companionship with Nature, I shall ever point to him as a most signal instance of one whose religious instincts were perverted, in part by the prejudice of a gloomy faith, in part by adopting for his guidance the faulty principles which are at the bottom of that faith.

Note

1 Reviewed are *A Week on the Concord and Merrimack Rivers*, *Walden*, *Excursions*, *The Maine Woods*, and *A Summer Cruise on the Coast of New England* by Robert Carter.

[James Russell Lowell],
"Thoreau's Letters,"
North American Review,
101 (October 1865),
597–608

What contemporary, if he was in the fighting period of his life, (since Nature sets limits about her conscription for spiritual fields, as the state does in physical warfare,) will ever forget what was somewhat vaguely called the "Transcendental Movement" of thirty years ago? Apparently set astirring by Carlyle's essays on the "Signs of the Times," and on "History," the final and more immediate impulse seemed to be given by "Sartor Resartus." At least the republication in Boston of that wonderful Abraham à Sancta Clara sermon on Lear's text of the miserable forked radish gave the signal for a sudden mental and moral mutiny. *Ecce nunc tempus acceptabile!* was shouted on all hands with every variety of emphasis, and by voices of every conceivable pitch, representing the three sexes of men, women, and Lady Mary Wortley Montagues. The nameless eagle of the tree Ygdrasil was about to sit at last, and wild-eyed enthusiasts rushed from all sides, each eager to thrust under the mystic bird that chalk egg from which the new and fairer Creation was to be hatched in due time. *Redeunt Saturnia regna,*—so far was certain, though in what shape, or by what methods, was still a matter of debate. Every possible form of intellectual and physical dyspepsia brought forth its gospel. Bran had its prophets, and the pre-sartorial simplicity of Adam its martyrs, tailored impromptu from the tar-pot by incensed neighbors, and sent forth to illustrate the "feathered Mercury," as defined by Webster and Worcester. Plainness of speech was carried to a pitch that would have taken away the breath of George Fox; and even swearing had its evangelists, who answered a simple inquiry after their health with an elaborate ingenuity of imprecation that might have been honorably mentioned by Marlborough in general orders. Everybody had a mission (with a capital M) to attend to everybody-else's business. No brain but had its private maggot, which must have found pitiably short commons sometimes. Not a few impecunious zealots abjured the use of money (unless earned by other people), professing to live on the internal revenues of the spirit. Some had an assurance of instant millennium so soon as hooks and eyes should be substituted for buttons. Communities were established where everything was to be common but common sense. Men renounced their old gods, and hesitated only whether to bestow their furloughed allegiance on Thor or Budh. Conventions were held for every hitherto inconceivable purpose. The belated gift of tongues, as among the Fifth Monarchy men, spread like a contagion, rendering its victims incomprehensible to all Christian men; whether equally so to the most distant possible heathen or not, was unexperimented, though many would have subscribed liberally that a fair trial might be made. It was the pentecost of Shinar. The day of utterances reproduced the day of rebuses and anagrams, and there was nothing so simple that uncial letters and the style of Diphilus the Labyrinth could not make into a riddle. Many foreign revolutionists out of work added to the general misunderstanding their contribution of broken English in every most ingenious form of fracture. All stood ready at a moment's notice to reform everything but themselves. The general motto was:

"And we'll *talk* with them, too,
And take upon's the mystery of things
As if we were God's spies."

Nature is always kind enough to give even her clouds a humorous lining. We have barely hinted at the comic side of the affair, for the material was endless. This was the whistle and trailing fuse of the shell, but there was a very solid and serious kernel, full of the most deadly explosiveness. Thoughtful men divined it, but the generality suspected nothing. The word "transcendental" then was the maid of all work for those who could not think, as "pre-Raphaelite" has been more recently for people of the same limited housekeeping. The truth is, that there was a much nearer metaphysical relation and a much more distant æsthetic and literary relation between Carlyle and the Apostles of the Newness, as they were called in New England, than has commonly been supposed. Both represented the reaction and revolt against *Philisterei*, a renewal of the old battle begun in modern times by Erasmus and Reuchlin, and continued by Lessing, Goethe, and, in a far narrower sense, by Heine in Germany, and of which Fielding, Sterne, and Wordsworth in different ways have been the leaders in England. It was simply a struggle for fresh air, in which, if the windows could not be opened, there was danger that panes would be broken, though painted with images of saints and martyrs. Light colored by these reverend effigies was none the more respirable for being picturesque. There is only one thing better than tradition, and that is the original and eternal life out of which all tradition takes its rise. It was this life which the reformers demanded, with more or less clearness of consciousness and expression, life in politics, life in literature, life in religion. Of what use to import a gospel from Judæa, if we leave behind the soul that made it possible, the God who keeps it forever real and present? Surely Abana and Pharpar *are* better than Jordan, if a living faith be mixed with those waters and none with these.

Scotch Presbyterianism as a motive of spiritual progress was dead; New England Puritanism was in like manner dead; in other words, Protestantism had made its fortune and no longer protested; but till Carlyle spoke out in the Old World and Emerson in the New, no one had dared to proclaim, *Le roi est mort: vive le roi!* The meaning of which proclamation was essentially this: the vital spirit has long since departed out of this form once so kingly, and the great seal has been in commission long enough; but meanwhile the soul of man, from which all power emanates and to which it reverts, still survives in undiminished royalty; God still survives, little as you gentlemen of the Commission seem to be aware of it,—nay, may possibly outlive the whole of you, incredible as it may appear. The truth is, that both Scotch Presbyterianism and New England Puritanism made their new avatar in Carlyle and Emerson, the heralds of their formal decease, and the tendency of the one toward Authority and of the other toward Independency might have been prophesied by whoever had studied history. The necessity was not so much in the men as in the principles they represented and the traditions which overruled them. The Puritanism of the past found its unwilling poet in Hawthorne, the rarest creative imagination of the century, the rarest in some ideal respects since Shakespeare; but the Puritanism that cannot die, the Puritanism that made New England what it is, and is destined to make America what it should be, found its voice in Emerson. Though holding himself aloof from all active partnership in movements of reform, he has been the sleeping partner who has supplied a great part of their capital.

The artistic range of Emerson is narrow, as every well-read critic must feel at once; and so is that of Æschylus, so is that of Dante, so is that of Montaigne, so is that of Schiller, so is that of nearly every one except Shakespeare; but there is a gauge of height no less than of breadth, of individuality as well as of comprehensiveness, and, above all, there is the standard of genetic power, the test of the masculine as distinguished from the receptive minds. There are staminate plants in literature, that make no fine show of fruit, but without whose pollen, the quintessence of fructifying gold, the garden had been barren. Emerson's mind is emphatically one of these, and there is no man to whom our æsthetic culture owes so much. The Puritan revolt had made us ecclesiastically, and the Revolution politically independent, but we were still socially and intellectually moored to English thought, till Emerson cut the cable and gave us a chance at the dangers and the glories of blue water. No man young enough to have felt it can forget, or cease to be grateful for, the mental and moral *nudge* which he received from the writings of his high-minded and brave-spirited countryman. That we agree with him, or that he always agrees with himself, is aside from the question; but that he arouses in us something that we are the better for having awakened, whether that something be of opposition or assent, that he speaks always to what is highest and least selfish in us, few Americans of the generation younger than his own would be disposed to deny. His oration before the Phi Beta Kappa Society at Cambridge, some thirty years ago, was an event without any former parallel in our literary annals, a scene to be always treasured in the memory for its picturesqueness and its inspiration. What crowded and breathless aisles, what windows clustering with eager heads, what enthusiasm of approval, what grim silence of foregone dissent! It was our Yankee version of a lecture by Abelard, our Harvard parallel to the last public appearances of Fichte.

We said that the "Transcendental Movement" was the protestant spirit of Puritanism seeking a new outlet and an escape from forms and creeds which compressed rather than expressed it. In its motives, its preaching, and its results, it differed radically from the doctrine of Carlyle. The Scotchman, with all his genius, and his humor gigantesque as that of Rabelais, has grown shriller and shriller with years, degenerating sometimes into a common scold, and emptying very unsavory vials of wrath on the head of the sturdy British Socrates of worldly common sense. The teaching of Emerson tended much more exclusively to self-culture and the independent development of the individual man. It seemed to many almost Pythagorean in its voluntary seclusion from commonwealth affairs. Both Carlyle and Emerson were disciples of Goethe, but Emerson in a far truer sense; and while the one, from his bias toward the eccentric, has degenerated more and more into mannerism, the other has clarified steadily toward perfection of style,—exquisite fineness of material, unobtrusive lowness of tone and simplicity of fashion, the most high-bred garb of expression. Whatever may be said of his thought, nothing can be finer than the delicious limpidness of his phrase. If it was ever questionable whether democracy could develop a gentleman, the problem has been affirmatively solved at last. Carlyle, in his cynicism and his admiration of force as such, has become at last positively inhuman; Emerson, reverencing strength, seeking the highest outcome of the individual, has found that society and politics are also main elements in the attainment of the desired end, and has drawn steadily manward and worldward. The two men represent respectively those grand personifications in the drama of Æschylus, *Bía* and *Kpáros.*

Among the pistillate plants kindled to fruitage by the Emersonian pollen, Thoreau is thus far the most remarkable; and it is something eminently fitting that his posthumous works should be offered us by Emerson, for they are strawberries from his own garden. A singular mixture of varieties, indeed, there is;—alpine, some of them, with the flavor of rare mountain air; others wood, tasting of sunny roadside banks or shy openings in the forest; and not a few seedlings swollen hugely by culture, but lacking the fine natural aroma of the more modest kinds. Strange books these are of his, and interesting in many ways,—instructive chiefly as showing how considerable a crop may be raised on a comparatively narrow close of mind, and how much a man may make of his life if he will assiduously follow it, though perhaps never truly finding it at last.

We have just been renewing our recollection of Mr. Thoreau's writings, and have read through his six volumes in the order of their production. We shall try to give an adequate report of their impression upon us both as critic and as mere reader. He seems to us to have been a man with so high a conceit of himself that he accepted without questioning, and insisted on our accepting, his defects and weaknesses of character as virtues and powers peculiar to himself. Was he indolent, he finds none of the activities which attract or employ the rest of mankind worthy of him. Was he wanting in the qualities that make success, it is success that is contemptible, and not himself that lacks persistency and purpose. Was he poor, money was an unmixed evil. Did his life seem a selfish one, he condemns doing good as one of the weakest of superstitions. To be of use was with him the most killing bait of the wily tempter Uselessness. He had no faculty of generalization from outside of himself, or at least no experience which would supply the material of such, and he makes his own whim the law, his own range the horizon of the universe. He condemns a world, the hollowness of whose satisfactions he had never had the means of testing, and we recognize Apemantus behind the mask of Timon. He had little active imagination; of the receptive he had much. His appreciation is of the highest quality; his critical power, from want of continuity of mind, very limited and inadequate. He somewhere cites a simile from Ossian, as an example of the superiority of the old poetry to the new, though, even were the historic evidence less convincing, the sentimental melancholy of those poems should be conclusive of their modernness. He had no artistic power such as controls a great work to the serene balance of completeness, but exquisite mechanical skill in the shaping of sentences and paragraphs, or (more rarely) short bits of verse for the expression of a detached thought, sentiment, or image. His works give one the feeling of a sky full of stars,—something impressive and exhilarating certainly, something high overhead and freckled thickly with spots of isolated brightness; but whether these have any mutual relation with each other, or have any concern with our mundane matters, is for the most part matter of conjecture,—astrology as yet, and not astronomy.

It is curious, considering what Thoreau afterwards became, that he was not by nature an observer. He only saw the things he looked for, and was less poet than naturalist. Till he built his Walden shanty, he did not know that the hickory grew in Concord. Till he went to Maine, he had never seen phosphorescent wood, a phenomenon early familiar to most country boys. At forty he speaks of the seeding of the pine as a new discovery, though one

440

should have thought that its gold-dust of blowing pollen might have earlier drawn his eye. Neither his attention nor his genius was of the spontaneous kind. He discovered nothing. He thought everything a discovery of his own, from moonlight to the planting of acorns and nuts by squirrels. This is a defect in his character, but one of his chief charms as a writer. Everything grows fresh under his hand. He delved in his mind and nature; he planted them with all manner of native and foreign seeds, and reaped assiduously. He was not merely solitary, he would be isolated, and succeeded at last in almost persuading himself that he was autochthonous. He valued everything in proportion as he fancied it to be exclusively his own. He complains in "Walden," that there is no one in Concord with whom he could talk of Oriental literature, though the man was living within two miles of his hut who had introduced him to it. This intellectual selfishness becomes sometimes almost painful in reading him. He lacked that generosity of "communication" which Johnson admired in Burke. De Quincey tells us that Wordsworth was impatient when any one else spoke of mountains, as if he had a peculiar property in them. And we can readily understand why it should be so: no one is satisfied with another's appreciation of his mistress. But Thoreau seems to have prized a lofty way of thinking (often we should be inclined to call it a remote one) not so much because it was good in itself as because he wished few to share it with him. It seems now and then as if he did not seek to lure others up "above our lower region of turmoil," but to leave his own name cut on the mountain peak as the first climber. This itch of originality infects his thought and style. To be misty is not to be mystic. He turns commonplaces end for end, and fancies it makes something new of them. As we walk down Park Street, our eye is caught by Dr. Windship's dumb-bells, one of which bears an inscription testifying that it is the heaviest ever put up at arm's length by any athlete; and in reading Mr. Thoreau's books we cannot help feeling as if he sometimes invited our attention to a particular sophism or paradox as the biggest yet maintained by any single writer. He seeks, at all risks, for perversity of thought, and revives the age of *concetti* while he fancies himself going back to a pre-classical nature. "A day," he says, "passed in the society of those Greek sages, such as described in the Banquet of Xenophon, would not be comparable with the dry wit of decayed cranberry-vines and the fresh Attic salt of the moss-beds." It is not so much the True that he loves as the Out-of-the-Way. As the Brazen Age shows itself in other men by exaggeration of phrase, so in him by extravagance of statement. He wishes always to trump your suit and to *ruff* when you least expect it. Do you love Nature because she is beautiful? He will find a better argument in her ugliness. Are you tired of the artificial man? He instantly dresses you up an ideal in a Penobscot Indian, and attributes to this creature of his otherwise-mindedness as peculiarities things that are common to all woodsmen, white or red, and this simply because he has not studied the pale-faced variety.

This notion of an absolute originality, as if one could have a patent-right in it, is an absurdity. A man cannot escape in thought, any more than he can in language, from the past and the present. As no one ever invents a word, and yet language somehow grows by general contribution and necessity, so it is with thought. Mr. Thoreau seems to us to insist in public on going back to flint and steel, when there is a match-box in his pocket which he knows very well how to use at a pinch. Originality consists in power of digesting and assimilating thought, so that they become part of our life and substance. Montaigne, for example, is one of the most original of authors, though he helped himself to ideas in every direction. But they turn to blood and coloring in his style, and give a freshness of complexion that is forever charming. In Thoreau much seems yet to be foreign and unassimilated, showing itself in symptoms of indigestion. A preacher up of Nature, we now and then detect under the surly and stoic garb something of the sophist and the sentimentalizer. We are far from implying that this was conscious on his part. But it is much easier for a man to impose on himself when he measures only with himself. A greater familiarity with ordinary men would have done Thoreau good, by showing him how many fine qualities are common to the race. The radical vice of his theory of life was, that he confounded physical with spiritual remoteness from men. One is far enough withdrawn from his fellows if he keep himself clear of their weaknesses. He is not so truly withdrawn as exiled, if he refuse to share in their strength. It is a morbid self-consciousness that pronounced the world of men empty and worthless before trying it, the instinctive evasion of one who is sensible of some innate weakness, and retorts the accusation of it before any has made it but himself. To a healthy mind, the world is a constant challenge of opportunity. Mr. Thoreau had not a healthy mind, or he would not have been so fond of prescribing. His whole life was a search for the doctor. The old mystics had a wiser sense of what the world was worth. They ordained a severe apprenticeship to law and even ceremonial, in order to the gaining of freedom and mastery over these. Seven years of service for Rachel were to be rewarded at last with Leah. Seven other years of faithfulness with her were to win them at last the true bride of their souls.

Active Life was with them the only path to the Contemplative.

Thoreau had no humor, and this implies that he was a sorry logician. Himself an artist in rhetoric, he confounds thoughts with style when he undertakes to speak of the latter. He was forever talking of getting away from the world, but he must be always near enough to it, nay, to the Concord corner of it, to feel the impression he makes there. He verifies the shrewd remark of Sainte-Beuve, "On touche encore à son temps et très-fort, même quand on le repousse." This egotism of his is a Stylites pillar after all, a seclusion which keeps him in the public eye. The dignity of man is an excellent thing, but therefore to hold one's self too sacred and precious is the reverse of excellent. There is something delightfully absurd in six volumes addressed to a world of such "vulgar fellows" as Thoreau affirmed his fellow-men to be. We once had a glimpse of a genuine solitary who spent his winters one hundred and fifty miles beyond all human communication, and there dwelt with his rifle as his only confidant. Compared with this, the shanty on Walden Pond has something the air, it must be confessed, of the Hermitage of La Chevrette. We do not believe that the way to a true cosmopolitanism carries one into the woods or the society of musquashes. Perhaps the narrowest provincialism is that of Self; that of Kleinwinkel is nothing to it. The natural man, like the singing birds, comes out of the forest as inevitably as the natural bear and the wild-cat stick there. To seek to be natural implies a consciousness that forbids all naturalness forever. It is as easy—and no easier—to be natural in a *salon* as in a swamp, if one do not aim at it, for what we call unnaturalness always has its spring in a man's thinking too much about himself. "It is impossible," said Turgot, "for a vulgar man to be simple."

We look upon a great deal of the modern sentimentalism about Nature as a mark of disease. It is one more symptom of the general liver-complaint. In a man of wholesome constitution the wilderness is well enough for a mood or a vacation, but not for a habit of life. Those who have most loudly advertised their passion for seclusion and their intimacy with nature, from Petrarch down, have been mostly sentimentalists, unreal men, misanthropes on the spindle side, solacing an uneasy suspicion of themselves by professing contempt for their kind. They make demands on the world in advance proportioned to their inward measure of their own merit, and are angry that the world pays only by the visible measure of performance. It is true of Rousseau, the modern founder of the sect, true of St. Pierre, his intellectual child, and of Chateaubriand, his grandchild, the inventor of what we may call the primitive forest cure, and who first was touched by the solemn falling of a tree from natural decay in the windless silence of the woods. It is a very shallow view that affirms trees and rocks to be healthy, and cannot see that men in communities are just as true to the laws of their organization and destiny; that can tolerate the puffin and the fox, but not the fool and the knave; that would shun politics because of its demagogues, and snuff up the stench of the obscene fungus. The divine life of Nature is more wonderful, more various, more sublime in man than in any other of her works, and the wisdom that is gained by commerce with men, as Montaigne and Shakespeare gained it, or with one's own soul among men, as Dante, is the most delightful, as it is the most precious, of all. In outward Nature it is still man that interests us, and we care far less for the things seen than the way in which poetic eyes like Wordsworth's or Thoreau's see them, and the reflections they cast there. To hear the to-do that is often made over the simple fact that man sees the image of himself in the outward world, one is reminded of a savage when he for the first time catches a glimpse of himself in a looking-glass. "Venerable child of Nature," we are tempted to say, "to whose science in the invention of the tobacco-pipe, to whose art in the tattooing of thine undegenerate hide not yet enslaved by tailors, we are slowly striving to climb back, the miracle thou beholdest is sold in my unhappy country for a shilling!" If matters go on as they have done and everybody must needs blab of all the favors that have been done him by roadside and river-brink and woodland walk, as if to kiss and tell were no longer treachery, it will be a positive refreshment to meet a man who is as superbly indifferent to Nature as she is to him. By and by we shall have John Smith, of No.—12,—12th Street, advertising that he is not the J. S. who saw a cow-lily on Thursday last, as he never saw one in his life, would not see one if he could, and is prepared to prove an alibi on the day in question.

Solitary communion with Nature does not seem to have been sanitary or sweetening in its influence on Thoreau's character. On the contrary, his letters show him more cynical as he grew older. While he studied with respectful attention the minks and woodchucks, his neighbors, he looked with utter contempt on the august drama of destiny of which his country was the scene, and on which the curtain had already risen. He was converting us back to a state of nature "so eloquently," as Voltaire said of Rousseau, "that he almost persuaded us to go on all fours," while the wiser fates were making it possible for us to walk erect for the first time. Had he conversed more with his fellows, his sympathies would have widened with the assurance that his peculiar genius had more appreciation, and his writings a larger circle of readers, or at least a warmer one, than he dreamed of. We have the highest testimony[1] to the natural sweetness, sincerity, and nobleness of his temper, and in his books an equally irrefragable one to the rare quality of his mind. He was not a strong thinker, but a sensitive feeler. Yet his mind strikes us as cold and wintry in its purity. A light snow has fallen everywhere where he seems to come on the track of the shier sensations that would elsewhere leave no trace. We think greater compression would have done more for his fame. A feeling of sameness comes over us as we read so much. Trifles are recorded with an over-minute punctuality and conscientiousness of detail. We cannot help thinking sometimes of the man who

> "watches, starves, freezes, and
> sweats
> To learn but catechisms and alphabets
> Of unconcerning things, matters of
> fact,"

and sometimes of the saying of the Persian poet, that "when the owl would boast, he boasts of catching mice at the edge of a hole." We could readily part with some of his affectations. It was well enough for Pythagoras to say, once for all, "When I was Euphorbus at the siege of Troy"; not so well for Thoreau to travesty it into "When I was a shepherd on the plains of Assyria." A naive thing said over again is anything but naive. But with every exception, there is no writing comparable with Thoreau's in kind, that is comparable with it in degree where it is best; where it disengages itself, that is, from the tangled roots and dead leaves of a second-hand Orientalism, and runs limpid and smooth and broadening as it runs, a mirror for whatever is grand and lovely in both worlds.

George Sand says neatly, that "Art is not a study of positive reality," (*actuality* were the fitter word,) "but a seeking after ideal truth." It would be doing very inadequate justice to Thoreau if we left it to be inferred that this ideal element did not exist in him, and that too in larger proportion, if less obtrusive, than his nature-worship. He took nature as the mountain-path to an ideal world. If the path wind a good deal, if he record too faithfully every trip over a root, if he botanize somewhat wearisomely, he gives us now and then superb outlooks from some jutting crag, and brings us out at last into an illimitable ether, where the breathing is not difficult for those who have any true touch of the climbing spirit. His shanty-life was a mere impossibility, so far as his own conception of it goes, as an entire independency of mankind. The tub of Diogenes had a sounder bottom. Thoreau's experiment actually presupposed all that complicated civilization which it theoretically abjured. He squatted on another man's land; he borrows an axe; his boards, his nails, his bricks, his mortar, his books, his lamp, his fish-hooks, his plough, his hoe, all turn state's evidence against him as an accomplice in the sin of that artificial civilization which rendered it possible that such a person as Henry D. Thoreau should exist at all. *Magnis tamen excidit ausis.* His aim was a noble and a useful one, in the direction of "plain living and high thinking." It was a practical sermon on Emerson's text that "things are in the saddle and ride mankind," an attempt to solve Carlyle's problem of "lessening your denominator." His whole life was a rebuke of the waste and aimlessness of our American luxury, which is an abject enslavement to tawdry upholstery. He had "fine translunary things" in him. His better style as a writer is in keeping with the simplicity and purity of his life. We have said that his range was narrow, but to be a master is to be master. He had caught his English at its living source, among the poets and prose-writers of its best days; his literature was extensive and recondite; his quotations are always nuggets of the purest ore; there are sentences of his as perfect as anything in the language, and thoughts as clearly crystallized; his metaphors and images are always fresh from the soil; he had watched Nature like a detective who is to go upon the stand; as we read him, it seems as if all-out-doors had kept a diary and become its own Montaigne; we look at the landscape as in a Claude Lorraine glass; compared with his, all other books of similar aim, even White's Selborne, seem dry as a country clergyman's meteorological journal in an old almanac. He belongs with Donne and Browne and Novalis; if not with the originally creative men, with the scarcely smaller class who are peculiar, and whose leaves shed their invisible thought-seed like ferns.

Note

1 "Mr. Emerson, in the Biographical Sketch prefixed to the 'Excursions.'"

Index

447

448